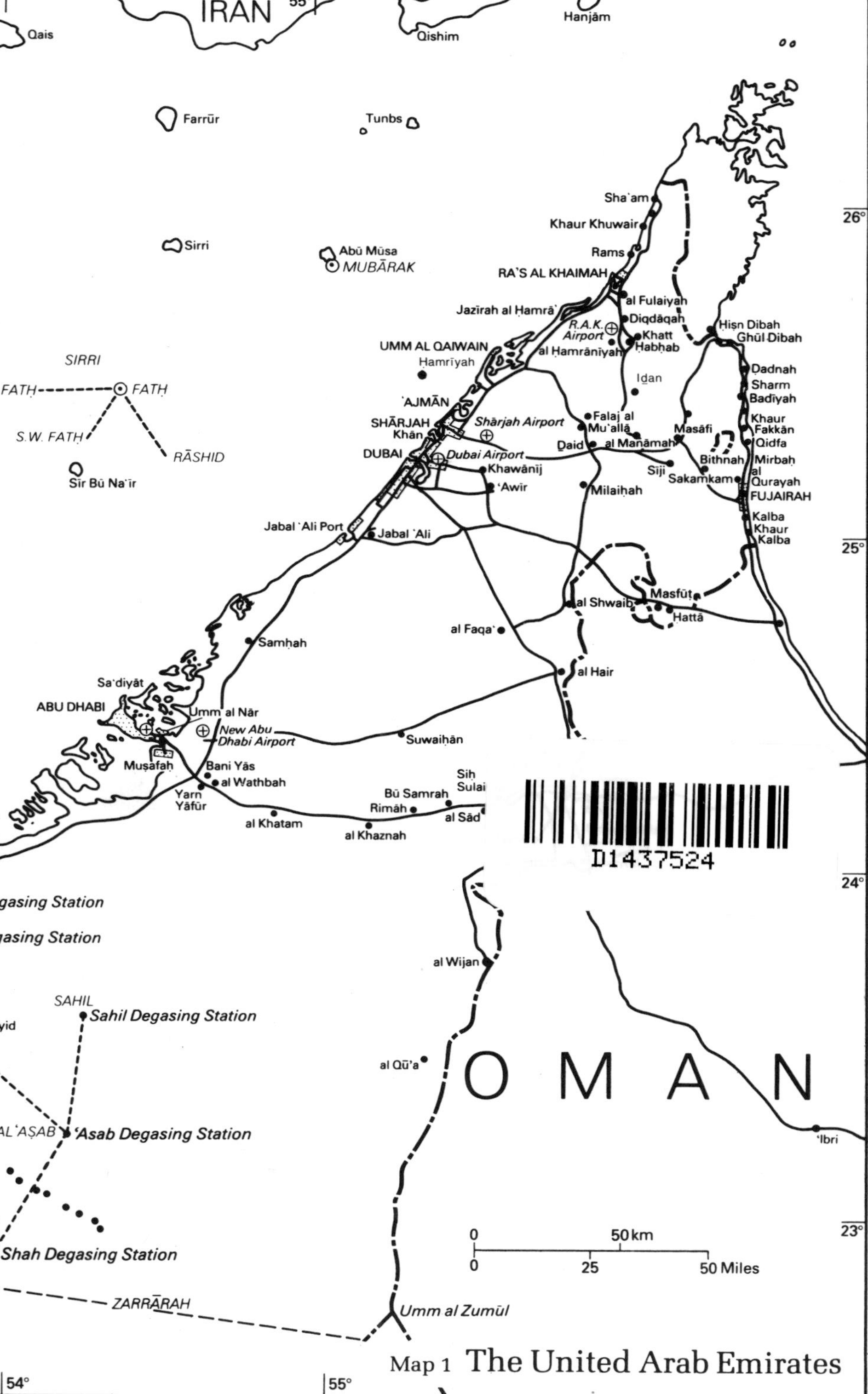

Map 1 The United Arab Emirates

From Trucial States to United Arab Emirates

From Trucial States to United Arab Emirates

A Society in Transition

Frauke Heard-Bey

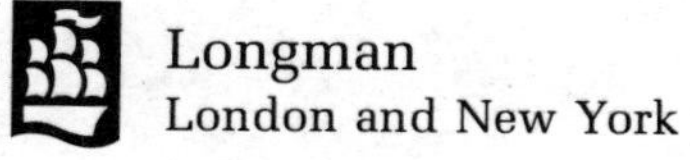

Addison Wesley Longman Limited
Edinburgh Gate, Harlow,
Essex CM20 2JE, England

First published 1982
Reprinted 1984
Second enlarged edition 1996

ISBN 0 582 27728 0

Set in 10/12pt Monophoto 2000 Melior

Produced by Longman Singapore Publishers Pte Ltd
Printed in Singapore

British Library Cataloguing in Publication Data

Heard – Bey, Frauke
From Trucial States to United Arab Emirates.
1. United Arab Emirates – Social conditions
I. Title
953'.5 HN781.T7

Contents

List of Maps

Abbreviations

AD — Christian Era (Anno Domini)
ADDF — Abu Dhabi Defence Force
ADFAED — Abu Dhabi Fund for Arab Economic Development (name changed in 1994 to Abu Dhabi Fund for Development ADFD)
ADIA — Abu Dhabi Investment Authority
ADMA — Abu Dhabi Marine Areas
ADNOC — Abu Dhabi Nation Oil Company
ADPC — Abu Dhabi Petroleum Company
AH — Muslim Era (*Anno Hegirae*)
ARAMCO — Arabian American Oil Company
ARR — *Arab Report and Record*
BAPCO — Bahrain Petroleum Company
BC — Before Christ
BCCI — Bank of Credit and Commerce International
BD — Bahrain Dinars
BOAC — British Overseas Airways Corporation
BP — British Petroleum
bpd — barrels per day
CFP — Companie Française des Pétroles
DDF — Dubai Defence Force
DUBAL — Dubai Aluminium Company
FAO — Food and Agriculture Organisation of the United Nations
FNC — Federal National Council
GCC — Gulf Cooperation Council
HMSO — Her Majesty's Stationery Office
IOR — India Office Records
IPC — Iraq Petroleum Company
KUML — *Årbog for Jysk Arkæologisk* Selskab
JRAI — *Journal of the Royal Anthropological Institute*
JRAS — *Journal of the Royal Asiatic Society*

JRCAS	*Journal of the Royal Central Asian Society*. (1914–30 *Journal of the Central Asian Society*; 1931–69 *Journal of the Royal Central Asian Society*; from 1970 *Asian Affairs*)
MEED	*Middle East Economic Digest*
MEES	*Middle East Economic Survey*
MEJ	*Middle East Journal*
MT Dollars	Maria Theresa Dollars
OAPEC	Organisation of Arab Petroleum Exporting Countries
OPEC	Organisation of Petroleum Exporting Countries
PCL	Petroleum Concessions Limited
PDO	Petroleum Development Oman
PD (TC)	Petroleum Development (Trucial Coast)
PLO	Palestine Liberation Organisation
RAF	Royal Air Force
TESG	*Tjidschrift voor economische en sociale geografie*
TOL	Trucial Oman Levies
TOS	Trucial Oman Scouts
UAE	United Arab Emirates
UDF	Union Defence Force
ZDMG	*Zeitschrift der Deutschen Morgenländischen Gesellschaft*

Note on Transliteration

The author and the publisher had hoped to be able to spare the reader the inconvenience of diacritical marks over and under Arabic words and names. But it is even more important to render, in particular the less well-known tribal names, into English in such a way that the Arabic-speaking reader can reproduce the original version. Because for an English d, t, th, s and h there is more than one Arabic letter and sound, one has to resort to dashes and dots or a combination of two letters in order to accommodate the full range of the 28 letters of the Arabic alphabet.

The system employed throughout this book makes use of the familiar two-letter combination for rendering the letters Thā ث , Khā خ , Shīn ش , Dhā ظ and Ghain غ . They are th, kh, sh, dh and gh, thus reducing the occurrence of diacritical marks. All other letters and the sign Hamza are transliterated as in the *Dictionary of Modern Written Arabic* by Hans Wehr. The reader is referred to the complete list of the Arabic and English letters on page xxi.

With hesitation the author decided not to use vowels other than a, i, and u, even if the pronunciation is in some instances much nearer to o or e. The choice of these three most distinctive vowels is a common compromise, also used in Wehr's Dictionary, to reproduce the three signs Fatḥa, Kasra and Damma which are part of the Arabic script although they are hardly ever written. However, if and when these signs are added in their places above and below consonants of an Arabic text, this process has to follow the rules of Arabic grammar. But colloquial Arabic, regionally coined words, local adaptations of foreign languages (particularly Farsi, Urdu and Hindi) and local place names and tribal names are not always governed by these rules. In some instances there may be some difference of opinion as to the correct Arabic version of such words and names. In a number of cases the author was given two or more different pronunciations or ways of spelling a name by different informants, and in the end there was nothing to do but toss the coin and settle for one version, while pointing out to the reader the existence of such pitfalls. The same applies to the use of long vowels where ai, aw or other diphthongs might also be in order (e.g. bīdār or baidār).

A long emphatic vowel, expressed in Arabic by the use of Fatḥa, followed by 'Alifى, Kasra followed by Yāي and Damma followed by Wāwو, is rendered into English with lengthening signs over the vowels ā, ī and ū.

Having opted for a letter-for-letter approach to the transliteration, the final Hā, with two dots over it (*Tā marbūtah*) and without dots is always represented by h, even if it has to be pronounced as t because of elision (e.g. *dawlah al* not *dawlat al*).

Furthermore, the definite article is always written as al, even when the pronunciation of it is governed by the initial consonant being a "sun-letter". (e.g. Umm al Nār not Umm an Nār).

The word Āl in conjunction with certain tribal names means approximately "the people of" (rather like Bani); it should not be confused with the definite article al.

Exceptions to the system of transliteration as used in this book are well-known names and place names such as Koran, Muscat or Doha which are written in their most common form.

English	Arabic
a	أ
b	ب
t	ت
th	ث

English	Arabic
j	ج
ḥ	ح
kh	خ
d	د
d̲	ذ
r	ر
z	ز
s	س
sh	ش
ṣ	ص
ḍ	ض
ṭ	ط
dh	ظ
ʿ (ʿain)	ع
gh	غ
f	ف
q	ق
k	ك
l	ل
m	م
n	ن
h	هـ
w	و
y	ي
ʾ (hamza)	ء

Acknowledgements

My thanks go first to my husband David. This book would never have been completed without his constant encouragement, support and constructive criticism.

While the book slowly took shape, our two children Nicolas and Miriam were born. They are still too small to realise that work on this book occasionally deprived them of my undivided attention. But I hope that when they grow up they will agree that we usually came to a very happy compromise before the day was out.

The Centre for Documentation and Research in Abu Dhabi has been my place of work since 1969. It is there that most of the final version was completed. I heartily thank the Director Dr Muḥammad Morsy ʿAbdullah and all my colleagues, in particular Mr ʿAli Tājir and Mr Saʿīd Salmān Abū Adarah, for their practical help and their sympathy with difficult queries in the anxious moments when time was running out.

During the past twelve years, my work at the Centre and in the preparation of studies for various publications has been encouraged consistently and very patiently by HE Aḥmad Khalifah Suwaidi, Foreign Minister of the UAE for many years. To him, to the Government of the UAE and officials in the Abu Dhabi Administration, I express my deep gratitude. I should also like to acknowledge my gratitude to Mr Alan Gilchrist, a former editor of Longman, who read and edited the manuscript and gave valuable advice. His untimely death is a great loss.

It is impossible to mention by name all the kind people without whose help this book would not have attained its present form—whether they granted lengthy interviews or they willingly answered questions as and when I posed them. There are those who assisted with locating archival material and books and with typing. The maps of Dubai were prepared with the assistance of Sir William Halcrow and Partners in Dubai.

Last but not least I would like to thank Mrs Joan Savona for her reliable assistance with typing much of the final manuscript and with the sorting, identifying and listing that had to be done, and Mr David Spedding OBE for his time spent on proof-reading.

Acknowledgements for the second edition

The UAE's expatriate population is constantly fluctuating; the new people coming are as keen as those leaving to understand their host country. Therefore, for some time many people have expressed their disappointment at finding that this book is out of print. Their urgent requests and Longman's agreement to publish a second edition made me attempt the near impossible to give an outline of the developments from the inception of the federation to the mid-1990s in the limited space of an additional tenth chapter.

The task of updating the book could not have been accomplished without my husband David's constant assistance in shaping the wealth of material to fit the limited space available. I cannot thank him enough.

I am indebted to Mrs Hermine Mahr and Mrs Jackie Schwarz for their assistance in material searches and in the best possible use of the computer for this project.

My three children deserve special thanks for their understanding, when during the gestation of this new version, they often had to wait longer for my weekly letters to reach them at their respective boarding schools.

The Publishers are grateful to ADCO and the Abu Dhabi Petroleum Company Ltd. for supplying the photographs for the text and cover, and to Mr. Ronald Codrai for the photograph of the Liwa oasis.

Foreword

By Sir Geoffrey Arthur, K.C.M.G., formerly Political Resident

When the United Arab Emirates was established as a state at the end of 1971 it had few admirers in the West: it was incomplete, it looked loose and ramshackle, and it was born—so said the facile commentators of the day—under the ill star of British patronage. It has since acquired a host of fair-weather friends, but I do not recollect that a single special correspondent of a major Western newspaper—let alone a politician or a statesman—took the trouble to attend the ceremony of its formation.

Those who were present on that December day were perhaps more optimistic than their distant critics, who could not forget the collapse, a few years earlier, of the South Arabian Federation, and who noticed the superficial similarities, but not the deeper differences, between the Aden Protectorates and the Shaikhdoms of the Trucial Coast. It was not the British who created the United Arab Emirates: it was the Rulers themselves, and in particular the Rulers of Abu Dhabi and Dubai, supported by a few trusted advisers of unusual ability. The new state thus attracted the support, and not the hostility, of the other Arab countries. It had no important internal enemies.

As Dr Heard-Bey points out, it had two further advantages: it was blessed with well-established natural leaders and endowed with great wealth. It is perhaps fortunate that at the time of the formation of the Federation, that wealth was not spread evenly among the Emirates. It was concentrated, but the hands that held it were exceptionally generous. The attractions of the Federation were manifest to all.

Despite these advantages the birth was not an easy one, and the Federation's first steps were unco-ordinated and erratic. Its critics saw the impending fulfilment of their prophecies of doom, and its friends wondered whether it would stay on course. Here again, Dr Heard-Bey has hit the mark. "The Federation", she writes, "would have had less chance to survive the first ten years if even the present stage of constitutional evolution had been imposed in 1971." In counselling caution, we used to put the same thing less elegantly—you can't destroy unity where there is not much unity to destroy. I have the impression that many people, both foreigners and citizens, blame us for pusillanimity and are disappointed that the progress towards greater unification during the first ten years of the Federation has been so slow. Their irritation is understandable, for it is not easy to conduct business in a society where power is dispersed and authority hard to identify. But I hope they will forgive me for reminding them—at any rate the foreigners—that ten years ago they were more prone to expect disintegration than coalescence.

It is to these people—and I include myself with them—that the value of Dr Heard-Bey's book will be most evident. She has not simply written a political and constitutional history of the United Arab Emirates. She has examined the social structures of its constituent states, explained the differences between village, town and tribal life, and set forth in detail the various functions and occupations of the inhabitants of the Trucial Coast before oil transformed their lives. The tribal bedu, small traders, date farmers, camel-drivers and pearl-fishers whose lives she describes are still alive and comparatively young: many of them are now very wealthy, hold positions of state, and have sons who were educated in the universities of the West and speak English as well as I do. Their history, their origins and their traditions are important to them and to any westerner who wishes to understand them.

From a distance the cities and the people of the United Arab Emirates may look alike; but the most superficial observer who resides there and travels between Abu Dhabi, Dubai and the Northern Emirates soon discovers startling differences in ethos. Dr Heard-Bey shows us why this is so. Her approach is encyclopaedic. Every westerner who sets out to do business in the Emirates should read this book and retain a copy for regular consultation. To those who live in the Emirates it will bring new insights. Even those who know the area well will find in it much that they did not know and much that will help them in understanding the strengths, weaknesses and paradoxes of the Federation. I wish I had had a book like this when I first started dealing with the Trucial States.

I venture to hope also that those readers who are citizens of the United Arab Emirates will themselves find pleasure and advantage in reading this book. Some of it they will think is wrong and perhaps even unfair. But the author is their friend; her readers will become their friends; and it is always useful to be able to see ourselves as our friends see us.

Pembroke College
Oxford, May 1982

Sir Geoffrey Arthur died in May 1984.

Introduction

Within the span of a few years the new State of the United Arab Emirates, before it was a decade old, had become a focal point of interest for oil-consuming countries of both the industrialised and the Third World. In the UAE's capital, Abu Dhabi, decisions have to be made on oil supplies and prices which affect companies, governments and people world wide. While its oil is being pumped out to sea to tankers which sail from the UAE to distant destinations on the globe, goods, technology, people and ideas streaming into this country are contributing to a rapid transformation of society, the urban environment and the desert.

Until the time of the 1973 oil crisis, historical studies of the shaikhdoms which joined together in the federation in December 1971 were of interest only to a limited number of specialists and people who lived and worked in the area; even more so because information about the domestic and external affairs of the Trucial States does not fill vast archives but has to be gleaned from the accumulated documentary material concerning the entire Gulf. Now that so many foreign people, governments and institutions are interested in the UAE, it is more than just an academic exercise to analyse its society today by tracing its roots in the Islamic, tribal and historical context, as well as by gauging the process of institution-building and by examining the positions of the decision-makers in relation to society.

At the turn of the century the population of the shaikhdoms, then collectively called the Trucial States, numbered some 80,000 souls. During the rapid expansion of the pearling industry leading up to its collapse at the end of the 1920s, the population structure was affected by a concentration of people on the coast and an influx of foreigners. The first census of the Trucial States, in the spring of 1968, counted 180,000 people a few years after oil exports began. A modern State has since emerged where an urbanised population of well over two million people live a life which at first sight differs only in climate from life in the shadow of multi-storey buildings in most other parts of the world. The material transformation and modernization even produced some unprecedented and superlative manifestations of the sudden wealth of the State, as well as of some individuals. The beholder may be equally astounded to see the traditional Arabian vista of palms against a background of sand or sea dwarfed by apartment blocks, as to be confronted with the particularly complex political structure of the UAE, comprising the federal and the seven very unequal local governments.

If one compares the environment, both material and socio-political, of the Trucial States in earlier decades of this century with that of the United Arab Emirates during the middle years of the 1990s, it may seem as though one is comparing two entirely different worlds. Yet the most important strand in the fabric of the UAE, the society of the native population, has itself changed remarkably little. Attitudes, values, behaviour and customs which were formed under quite different circumstances continue to be essential to the family's life; they are equally essential ingredients in the interaction of today's multinational society and the newly created State.

In the following chapters, the various factors which influenced and shaped the society are studied to prepare the ground for an analysis of the current internal structural transformation of this society.

When the first major development projects brought hundreds, later thousands, of foreigners to the coast from about 1965 onwards, society ceased to function as one homogeneous body of basically the same ethnic origins, bound together by one common religion providing a common understanding of morals, behaviour and law. The present day society is heterogeneous, multinational, multireligious and anonymous; it needs institutions to compensate for the disappearance of traditional direct rule and response to that rule. How the various groups of the new society live, and to what extent the required institution-building has been tailored to each phase in the structural transformation from the tribal to the multinational era, will be the subject of further chapters.

The country under observation falls into a number of familiar categories and presents a good object for related case studies. It may be called a "developing" country; it is a "Third World" country, an "Arab" country, an oil-producing country; and it is a Muslim State. The characteristics of each category are features of the UAE, but there are no more similarities between the UAE and other countries in these categories than there are vital differences, making the UAE a special case within most of these categories. While it shares many of the problems which developing countries face, the most ubiquitous of them all, poverty, is no longer a problem for the UAE. Most other Third-World countries have vestiges of some form of colonial administration; the UAE was strongly but only indirectly influenced by the British interests in the region.

This study is meant to serve the dual purpose of helping the interested outsider to understand the historical perspective of the UAE's present social and institutional complexity and also of offering the preoccupied local administrator in the Emirates a systematic interpretation of events leading up to the present situation.

Last but not least, this study will probably provoke controversy leading to further specialised social studies for the benefit of all who care for the well-being of the people in the UAE.

Chapter One

Geographical Conditions

1 The changing importance of immutable geographical factors

The geographical factors which determine a country's position in relation to the rest of the world—its access to communication lines such as rivers or the sea, its climate, the fertility of the land or its natural resources—are fundamentally responsible for the quality of life led by the inhabitants. These factors have to be considered as immutable natural conditions. Some of them might have undergone noticeable changes within historical times but this is hardly ever realised within the span of one generation. What might change even in the space of one decade, however, is the importance for the population of one particular feature or another of the country's geography. The way in which certain geographical factors influence and condition the life of the inhabitants can differ a great deal from one century to another. Their impact either varies in intensity, vanishes altogether or is reversed, depending on the socio-political and economic situation of the area at a given point in time. The geographical factors, for instance, which were at one time responsible for the country's isolation from the mainstream of history, become its vital strategic protection in another age. Similarly, climatic factors which may enhance certain economic assets such as the growth of pearl oysters may, a generation later, prove detrimental to finding an economic alternative when the commodity ceases to be in demand. Geographical proximity to an influential political, religious or cultural power, too, can be beneficial to a region's society in a certain age, but become a burden when constellations change.

Statements about the bare scientific facts concerning the geography of the country under consideration become meaningful when looked at in the context of the conditions of the area in economic, political, strategic or sociological terms. To show for the United Arab Emirates the mutual influence of the geographical and the historical factors, and to evaluate how they condition each other's relevance at this very point in time, provide the frame in which the present-day society in the UAE is to be seen.[1] The historical factors which are largely responsible for the way in which this present-day society functions are in themselves results of a varying relevance of the geographical factors to society in the past.

This chapter is concerned with the physical geography of the UAE. The order of priority reflects to some extent the effect of this geography on the country's economy and, as a result of this, on its present social and political structure. However, the more detailed discussions of this effect have to be deferred to later chapters in order to trace the changing importance of geographical conditions and to assess their role with regard to the various facets of present-day society in the UAE.

2 Ecology: Some implications of the UAE's geographical setting

Oil

In an enumeration of geographical factors according to their importance to the new State of the UAE, the occurrence of oil in certain geological formations under its territory occupies the first place. The known oilfields are located chiefly in the territory and the territorial waters of Abu Dhabi. Dubai also exports oil, Shārjah exports a small amount, and hydrocarbons have been found in small quantities in Ra's al Khaimah and Umm al Qaiwan. In 1995 a total of 90 million tons was exported from the UAE, (in 1979 it was 90 million), which constituted 10 per cent of the oil lifted from terminals situated on the Gulf. Oil put this State, together with some of its oil-producing neighbours, on the international map. It serves as a bridge for contacts with the rest of the world, in particular with the countries where the oil is consumed and with those countries which have provided the experts for its production. In the late 1980s and early 1990s about 8 per cent of the Abu Dhabi and Dubai oil went to Europe, barely 1 per cent to the USA, and the rest to the Far East. Of the companies which hold concessions to explore for and produce oil in the UAE, the majority of the shareholders used to be major American and European oil companies in various groupings. During the early 1970s Japanese companies found a footing in the area. Soon afterwards the governments of the oil-producing countries took an equity share in the oil companies operating on their land, and they have sought markets for their share of the crude oil, thereby broadening and diversifying their economic links with the rest of the world.

A country of the "Middle East"

Although the UAE is separated by hundreds of miles of desert from the traditional centres of the Middle East, it forms a part of this greater geographical unit. The very wording of the term "Middle East" indicates that the region is viewed from the direction of Western Europe. Much of the region's historical importance in recent centuries stemmed from the fact that it was in the middle, that is between Europe and the European interests in India and the Far East. Besides this crucial function as a gateway, the Middle East was by necessity of its geographical position influenced by the strategic importance of the Mediterranean to the whole of Europe. Thus, the Levant and Egypt have been for centuries focal points within the geographical unit of the Middle East.

As the constellations of the worldwide balance of power shift away from a predominantly European context, the Pacific and Indian Oceans gain in importance. For strategic reasons, the eastern extremities of the Middle East are of increasing worldwide interest. The rising demand for oil gives the producing countries of the Gulf greater economic strength and political weight both within the Middle East and throughout the whole world. One third of the Western World's oil consumption passed through the Straits of Hormuz in 1978, before the oil-production of Iran was reduced in the wake of political changes there.

Geographical features of the country

General

The UAE forms part of the geographical subdivision of south-eastern Arabia, together with its western neighbour, Qatar, and its eastern neighbour, the Sultanate of Oman.[2] It has some 750 kilometres of

Map 2 The Middle East

shoreline along the so-called Lower Gulf, constituting more than a third of the Arabian Coast of the Gulf. This shore is reached from the Indian Ocean after navigating the length of the Gulf of Oman and rounding the tip of the long and narrow Musandam Peninsula through the 46 kilometre-wide entry to the Gulf, the Straits of Hormuz, and past the southern shore of the Iranian province of Balūchistān. The UAE has also direct access to the Indian Ocean on the 75 kilometres of its eastern shoreline which border on the Gulf of Oman. Overland communications across the rugged peninsula were, however, problematic, since the two coasts, forming two sides of the triangular Musandam Peninsula, are separated by the Ḥajar Mountain Range. The eastern coast has only recently been made more easy of access from the major part of the State by the construction of asphalted roads.

The mountains

The Ḥajar range rises in nearly vertical cliffs from the fjord-like inlets of the Straits of Hormuz, and reaches within the triangle of the Peninsula a height of over 2,000 metres in the Ru'ūs al Jibāl. The range extends to the south-east as far as Ra's al Ḥadd in Oman, where the Gulf of Oman merges with the Indian Ocean at the most easterly point of the Arabian Peninsula. The barren igneous and limestone peaks, tumbling cliffs and steep intersecting valleys give to this range the character of a natural fortress towering astride the entrance to the Gulf. With the exception of the over 3,000 metre-high extensive plateau of the Jabal al Akhḍar in Inner Oman, the mountains are almost devoid of topsoil. There are no perennial rivers which reach the sea from the interior of the range. Since South-East Arabia is affected by the fringes of the winter monsoon, a limited rainfall can be expected throughout the whole area; during the summer occasional torrential storms break over the mountains. The average rainfall in the areas away from the mountains is, however, a scanty 107 millimetres a year.[3] Agricultural activities are possible in some of the valleys and in certain narrow tracts of land on either side of the mountains where the annually replenished water table is high and where flash floods have deposited fertile sediments.

This mountain range has been a major factor in determining the quality of life in South-eastern Arabia throughout the ages. It is responsible for some of the regional climatic conditions, since it bars the rainclouds forming over the Indian Ocean from travelling freely deep into the airspace over the Peninsula; on the other hand, it causes some of those clouds to rise and deliver the rain over its peaks. The run-off water from the range is the only source for the replenishment of the underground water table almost as far west as Dubai. The local economy has nearly always been totally reliant on the availability of this water.

The very rugged nature of the mountain range made it a perfect refuge throughout the ages, and was at one time a particularly important factor in preserving the independence of the Ibāḍi State in neighbouring Oman from the time when it broke away from the mainstream of the Ummayyad Caliphate at the end of the 7th century. The inaccessibility of its peaks and valleys is a factor that plays an important part even in modern strategic deliberations, while it is also responsible for the isolation in which some remote communities have lived until very recently.[4]

Although only a stretch of about one tenth of the Ḥajar actually forms part of the UAE territory, this mountain system, which as a whole covers some 35,000 square kilometres of south-eastern Arabian territory, has been the economic backbone and the political nerve-centre throughout much of the history of these States, which used to be called locally Sāḥil Oman (Coast of Oman) and were later generally known as the Trucial Coast.

The desert

Another geographical feature which exerts an equally vital influence on the day-to-day life in the UAE is the desert. More than two thirds of the territory of the seven States is taken up by tracts of mostly sandy desert with varying amounts of sparse seasonal vegetation. What contributes to the formidable nature of this desert is the fact that it forms part of the 800,000 square kilometres of desert called the Rubʿ al Khāli.[5] This sea of sand and gravel plains has always separated the Gulf Coast from the nearest areas of settled habitation such as Hadhramaut, Yemen, or Najd, more effectively than an ordinary sea. Communications along the fringes of this desert were maintained throughout the history of population movements in the Peninsula. Some migratory tribes customarily cross the desert to the south of the border of the UAE. Inhospitable as these particular waterless tracts of desert are, they afforded refuge for tribal beduin groups who, although mostly roaming the borderlands between the desert and the settled areas, were able to survive in the Rubʿ al Khāli proper for months with not much more than their camels and a few dates to live off. This desert was crossed for the first time by a European when Bertram Thomas rode by camel in 1930–31 from Ṣalālah in Dhufār on the Indian Ocean to Doha, the capital of Qatar.[6] Only in the last few years have the routes of commercial airlines begun to cross the length and breadth of this desert.

The fringes of the desert are ill-defined, because a period of several years without any rain can convert areas which were abundant in thorn-bushes and seasonal vegetation into utterly lifeless terrain for decades until rain falls again and the dormant plant life is revived. In times of drought or as a result of the ravages of sandstorms the desert encroaches on the fertile oases in the settled areas. On the other hand, a year or two of exceptionally heavy rains can open to grazing regions of the desert which have not been frequented for many years.

The desert within the borders of the UAE may be divided into two main sections. A desert foreland extends from the west of the mountains between Ra's al Khaimah and the al ʿAin oases towards the coast; in this area the gentle red dunes support extensive verdure in the form of perennial thorn-bushes, tamarisks and some annual vegetation. The more westerly tracts of the desert in the country support less vegetation, and eventually towards the southern border of Abu Dhabi the rolling dunes become distinctive crescent-shaped barren sand mountains encircling equally lifeless gravel plains.

The sea

The surrounding desert to the south and west accounts for the isolation of the country, whose contact with the outside world has mostly been by way of the sea which it faces in the north. The whole of the Gulf is very shallow, the maximum depth being only 50 fathoms (90 metres).[7] The southern waters of the Gulf are characterised by a great number of coral reefs and sandbanks, which together with the numerous low-lying islands make navigation extremely difficult and hazardous. Most of the southern coast is utterly flat, marshy or sandy; it is indented by a number of creeks along much of the Lower Gulf shoreline of the UAE, except for the short stretch north of Ra's al Khaimah, where the mountains rise steeply from the sea. Due to the extreme difficulty of approach and the lack of any sizeable natural harbours there was comparatively little long-distance shipping undertaken during the last few centuries from the ports of this coast, and overseas trade – at times almost an Arab monopoly – has consequently not been a very important feature of its economy until recently.

The shallowness of the Gulf accounts for conditions of water temperature and light which are favourable to the growth of the pearl oysters. Throughout the centuries pearl-fishing has been one of the most important economic activities of the population on the southern coast, although the intensity varied, depending on the changing factors such as regional security or international demand for the pearls. Just as in previous times the common interest in issues concerned with pearling encouraged contacts and co-operation between the various States around the Gulf, today matters concerning "Gulf oil" interest the same countries increasingly. Their sharing of the waters of the Gulf as an economic lifeline to the rest of the world requires that they should become more closely involved with one another.

In the past, even immediate neighbours found it easier to communicate by sea rather than by land. This same highway of local communication is, however, also a divide between two distinctly different worlds. The way of life on the southern coast has in many aspects retained features of early Islamic times and of its traditional Arab heritage, while the way of life across the water in Iran is influenced by a completely different heritage from ancient times and by the fact that the population belongs ethnically to another group. Islam has been the unifying factor that bridges the gap between different political developments on the two sides of the Gulf. But even within this common realm of Islam, the waters of the Gulf and the mountains of Iran divide the predominantly Sunni Arab coast from the traditionally Shīʿah Persians, as many of the inhabitants of the Persian coast are Sunni and of Arab tribal origin.

3 The main geographical features of the individual Emirates

Abu Dhabi

Abu Dhabi, by far the largest State, occupying approximately 87 per cent of the total UAE territory, owes its character to the desert.[8] However, there are some two dozen islands of significance in the coastal waters and some half dozen sizeable islands belonging to Abu Dhabi further out in the Gulf. Several of the latter are frequently described in geological terms as eruptive salt-plugs. Dalmā Island, 45 kilometres north of the western coast of Abu Dhabi, has fresh-water wells on it which used to provide water for the seasonal pearling fleet and support a small resident population. Facilities for producing, storing and exporting off-shore oil from Abu Dhabi are located on Dās Island, 170 kilometres from the capital; on al Mubarrāz Island, 100 kilometres away; on Arzanah Island, 190 kilometres away; and further facilities have been constructed on Zirkū Island, 140 kilometres from Abu Dhabi. One of the largest of Abu Dhabi's islands, Ṣīr Bani Yās, is situated to the west of one of the few deep-water channels which reach the coast. The rocky hills of Jabal al Dhannah on the mainland opposite Ṣīr Bani Yās provided a suitable site for the establishment of a tanker terminal for the oil produced in the desert.

The capital of Abu Dhabi, bearing the same name as the State, is also located on an island, which is connected to the mainland by two road bridges. The triangular island has about 10 kilometres of waterfront and extends for 16 kilometres towards the mainland between lagoons and other islands. It accommodates at present most of the capital's administrative and residential buildings, excluding the international airport, industrial and military establishments.

Sabkhah is the local name for the salty mud-flats, formed in geologically recent times from dried-up lagoons, which extend along the full length of this coast.[9] They are saturated with salt and cannot support any vegetation. Tidal movement or rain turn even those parts which might be passable at other times into a treacherous swamp unsafe for camel or car. The Sabkhah Maṭṭi, near the north-western border of the State with Qatar and Saudi Arabia, extends over 100 kilometres inland from the coast and provides an added hindrance to communications with neighbouring regions. The *sabkhah* belt stretches almost uninterrupted the whole length of the coast from the western border with Qatar near Khaur al 'Udaid to beyond Dubai in the north-east. Some rock outcrops and sand-spits relieve the utter monotony of this *sabkhah* landscape and afford access to the mostly sandy shoreline and its maze of tidal lagoons, sandbanks and islands.

The sands generally begin between 5 and 15 kilometres from the shore and rise gently towards the east and south, the oasis of al 'Ain being situated in the east at the foot of the mountains and about 200 metres above sea level. The extent to which the desert is habitable varies throughout Abu Dhabi's territory, depending on the availability of fresh or brackish water. The eastern reaches benefit from the run-off water from the mountains. Further west, dew and occasional rain accumulated over centuries in the sand-dunes provide in certain areas enough water to supply hand-dug wells.[10] In one area in the south called Līwā, a string of about four dozen small oases nestle in many of the hollows formed by a multitude of interlinking sand dunes, the highest of which rise up to nearly 200 metres above the floor of the plains.[11] The territory to the south and west of the Līwā forms the edge of the Rub' al Khāli, and water wells are few and far between. The wells in the Līwā oases support date palms but are usually not prolific and the water is not sweet enough to permit much additional agriculture. As a result of this, the Līwā has been the centre for a migratory population. The inhabitants had to seek additional means of livelihood by tending large camel herds migrating over an extensive area in the adjacent desert during the winter months, or by pursuing other economic activities on the coast. Situated about 100 kilometres south of the Gulf and isolated from the nearest coastal settlements by the desert, the exact location of this string of oases was not known to European geographers until the year 1906, when it came by accident to the attention of the author of the *Gazetteer of the Persian Gulf, Oman and Central Arabia*, who was compiling the information obtained by generations of officials in the British Government of India.[12] As a result of this, many villages and seasonal settlements in the hitherto unknown desert regions of Dhafrah,[13] Bainūnah, Qufā and Khatam in Abu Dhabi territory could also be located on the map.

Due east of the capital the second largest population centre, al 'Ain, is about 160 kilometres away. The recently built-up town of al 'Ain and its five neighbouring villages constitute Abu Dhabi's share of the whole oasis which, in European literature of the last few decades, has been called after Buraimi, one of the three neighbouring villages in the territory of the Sultanate of Oman. The oasis is situated some 20 kilometres from the last of the main ranges of the Ḥajar mountains. One solitary mountain, Jabal Ḥafīt, reaching the height of 1160 metres, extends from al 'Ain in a south-easterly direction for about 20 kilometres, straddling the border between Abu Dhabi and the Sultanate. The oasis owes its existence to the availability of underground fresh water at the foot of the mountains. Some of the water is brought to the oasis by underground channels, called *aflāj*, (sing. *falaj*) which were dug by hand at a still-disputed point in history. The seven *aflāj* in use at present yield some 10 million cubic metres of water a year. Additional water is obtained from wells sunk to the water table at between 5 and 30 metres' depth.

This brief description indicates two predominant features of Abu Dhabi's geography: firstly its vast areas of desert reaching towards the uninhabited interior of the Peninsula, and secondly its coastline, which is difficult of approach both from the land and by sea. These two features limited the population's choice for establishing settlements. Thus the territory of about 67,000 square kilometres is not evenly populated but has three sizeable population centres, where the majority of the State's now nearly 928,000 people live: the capital on the island of Abu Dhabi and its suburbs, with an estimated 470,000 inhabitants; the al ʿAin area near the Oman mountains, with an estimated population of 300,000; and the villages of the Līwā oases, which were home to beduin families, but whose permanent inhabitants include many immigrant labourers.[14]

The nature of the coastal *sabkhah* and of the desert is such that communication between these centres has been extremely difficult until recently. Abu Dhabi and al ʿAin are now connected by a dual-carriageway road 160 kilometres long. A tarred road was recently built along the coast to link up Abu Dhabi with the Qatar and Saudi Arabian road network and to complete the coastal road system between Abu Dhabi, Dubai and Ra's al Khaimah in the north-east of the UAE. There is now an asphalted road to the Līwā, and more roads are being constructed both across the State and around the periphery. In addition to the old international airport on Abu Dhabi Island there are landing-strips for small aircraft in the Līwā and at several other locations in the country which are used by the military or the operating oil companies. The new airport for Abu Dhabi was built 35 kilometres from the centre of town in the direction of Dubai. Another international airport at al ʿAin was opened on 31 March 1994. Now the population travels by four-wheel-drive car to the remote regions in preference to the traditional means of transport through the desert: the camel.

Dubai

The geographical conditions of neighbouring Dubai give this member State of the UAE a distinctly different character, although it, too, has the desert and the sea as its predominant features. The territory of

Dubai is only some 3,900 square kilometres of desert, but it includes the small mountainous enclave of Ḥattā at the border with Oman, and the relatively green desert surrounding the twin city of Dubai and Dairah, which extends inland along the border with Abu Dhabi. Dubai, however, straddles both sides of a creek which affords one of the few natural harbours on the shallow coast. Like the neighbouring creeks at Shārjah, Umm al Qaiwain, and several other coastal villages, the access route to this harbour is in jeopardy because the prevailing south-north current along the coast causes sandbars to build up across the mouth of the creek. In Dubai steps have been taken to counteract this natural process by dredging the approaches and stabilising the shores of the creek. These measures have proved beneficial to the fast-expanding maritime trade of this port. Further efforts were made to encourage this growing trade by building nearby a deep-water harbour which, with a dredged depth of 30 feet (10 metres) at low water, can take ocean-going vessels. By April 1980, 35 berths were in operation and more may be built. A new harbour with 67 berths and the 'Jebel Ali Free Zone' were built 22 miles west of the town to introduce new industries. The population of the State of Dubai has grown rapidly, as trade through its harbour expanded and more recently since the start of oil exports. It had reached 420,000 at the 1985 census and is 674,000 according to the national census of December 1995. It is only 14 kilometres by road from the town-centre of Dubai to that of the neighbouring Emirate of Shārjah. Dubai enjoys a pre-eminent position in the Northern States. There is a convenient road-link with the three other Emirates to the north, 'Ajmān, Umm al Qaiwain, and Ra's al Khaimah, and across the mountains to Fujairah on the east coast. This position is further underlined by the fact that its commercial connections and skills make it a convenient centre for the supply of goods and services to all these States.

Shārjah

Shārjah, which enjoys a similar geographical situation, might have grown into this same function but for the fact that its creek has been silting up faster, and a remedy came later to meet the challenge of the already advanced neighbour. In the late 1930s, at a time when the other Emirates were looking to the sea for a livelihood, Shārjah's population benefited from the establishment of a staging-post for Imperial Airways' flying boats en route to India. The 2,600 square kilometres of Shārjah territory are not confined to the western coast but include several enclaves in the mountainous hinterland and on the east coast of the UAE. These are in particular the newly-improved fishing port of Khaur Fakkān, the once independent territory of Kalba on the border with Oman, and a share of the seaside oasis of Dibah in the extreme north of the UAE's eastern coast. The island of Abū Mūsa in the Gulf, about 70 kilometres from Shārjah, has deposits of red oxide and there is a mature off-shore oilfield (Mubārak) nearby. In December 1985 the population of Shārjah was 269,000; in December 1995 it was 400,000.

The northern States and the east coast

The small Emirates of Umm al Qaiwain, of 770 square kilometres, and 'Ajmān, of 260 square kilometres, are very alike in their natural conditions, both having their main population centres with 35,000 and 70,600 respectively, on sand-spits formed parallel to the coast. The lagoons on the landward side afforded safe anchorage for local fishing vessels. 'Ajmān possesses a number of enclaves in the hinterland; the most important is Masfūṭ in the mountains. Umm al Qaiwain is confined to its coastal possessions, extending about 30 kilometres inland to a small oasis at Falaj al Mu'allā.

The most northerly member State of the UAE, Ra's al Khaimah, borders on an enclave of the Sultanate of Oman which occupies the tip of the Musandam Peninsula. The town of Ra's al Khaimah is also situated on an inlet which forms a natural port; it has about 100,000 inhabitants (the total population of the State is now 144,000). The Emirate's territory extends over the most inaccessible parts of the Hajar Range in UAE territory, and a number of settlements are tucked away in steep-sided valleys. Other villages occupy the narrowing coastal strip between the mountains and the sea where the run-off water from the mountains provides ample scoop for agricultural activities. Other natural resources of the Emirate are stone, which is quarried for building, and the very rich fisheries of the Gulf.

The only Emirate which is confined entirely to the east coast of the UAE is Fujairah. Its territory, with a total population of 76,000 extends from the town of Dibah in the north, which is shared with Shārjah and the Omani enclave, to Kalba in the south-east. The main population centre is the town of Fujairah itself, which, as well as its other dozen settlements, benefits from rain-water seeping underground from the mountains along *wādi* beds and through the gently sloping gravel coastal plain, which is an average of 7 kilometres wide. Wells have been dug and *aflāj* constructed to enable the water to be brought to the surface for use in the extensive gardens, which are mostly planted with date palms. Several of the small coastal villages were almost inaccessible by land until recently, when communications along the whole length of the eastern coast were revolutionised by the construction of a fine road which cuts across several rock-spurs projecting from the Ḥajar range into the sea. Previously these rocks isolated the settlements enclosed in the sandy bays. Fujairah's lifeline to the rest of the UAE is a good road across the mountains to Ḏaid and Dubai following a route which was opened up to vehicles in 1967 and asphalted in 1974. Communications with neighbouring Oman are along a dual carriage road to Ṣuḥār and thence along the length of the Bāṭinah proper to Muscat. Though no oil has been found yet in Fujairah, good use has been made of its geographical location. From 1983 onwards the new port with container terminal was widely used by shipping lines eager to avoid entering the Gulf. In 1989 a free trade and industrial zone was added. Fujairah International Airport was opened in 1987; in 1993 some 16,300 scheduled, charter, cargo and military flights were handled there.

A geographical feature common to the member States of the UAE is that they all have access to the sea. The development of the economic benefits that may be derived from the sea can be expected to exert some unifying influence. The predominance of mountainous country in some member States and desert in the others has in the past brought about different social structures within the States. The population in the primarily desert parts of the region included more nomadic or semi-nomadic groups than the mostly sedentary population of agriculturalists in the mountainous areas. It will be discussed in greater detail how these differences in geographical characteristics have influenced social groups in the region in different ways. As for the territorial extent of each of the Emirates, this is in no case dictated by geographical factors which might have provided natural boundaries; the borders of the individual political units were determined merely by historical developments.

Chapter Two

The Tribal Structure of Society

1 The basis of the tribal organisation of the population in Eastern Arabia

Ageless characteristics and changing conditions

"By and large, Arabia south of the Fertile Crescent has kept its political as well as its social independence. The reason, simple enough, is that the hard facts of Arabian climate and scene are not only changeless but their inhospitable rigour have [sic] always constituted its defence. No one has long or keenly envied the Arabians their country; they have on the whole been little molested, by reason merely of the very aridity and heat, dust and desert, of which so much of the peninsula is formed, and by which its various provinces are divided. They have enjoyed the safety of the undesired, and have lived lives to which a hundred generations have specialised them, in conditions barely tolerable to others."[1] As this sums up the position of most of the Arabian Peninsula through the centuries of worldwide conquest and colonisation, so its south-eastern corner was indeed by-passed by the main stream of history altogether. This cannot be said of the same region today, while its oil helps to keep the industries of the world running.

When the new age opened for this area, the local population had had only a distant glimpse of the industrialised world, its ways of life, its endeavours and its values. Adapting to some features of this other world would be difficult enough for a conglomerate group of people who had no particular clearly-defined concept of life nor of their position in their own environment. How much harder it must be to make a success of the necessary adaptation in the case of the population under study. Here change is superimposed on a very clearly structured society and on concepts of life which are meticulously defined in every detail and as such are upheld by most of the inhabitants.

There are three factors which are woven into the fabric of local society like three strands of fast colour: firstly the traditional tribal structures, secondly the lack of choice of economic opportunities, and thirdly the Islamic order of life. Besides these the contemporary society was influenced and moulded by the vicissitudes of history. Some such events which may have seemed decisive at the time have, however, not left much of a mark. Other events have had so strong an impact on the society living on this coast at the time that the transformation set in motion then can still be seen to be responsible for characteristics of the social structure of today. Some such historical events were caused by forces outside the area such as the two World Wars, others were just swirling motions in these "backwaters of history" while the main stream flooded past.

On the surface it may seem today as though most of the historically formed characteristics and habits have almost vanished since the new oil-age first gathered momentum in the shaikhdoms in the late 1950s. But the society which was contemporary with this event bore certain unmistakable features which stem from the age-old struggle of adapting to forbidding surroundings and from the equally formative influence of faith—the profound comfort under such harsh conditions of life. These features are too distinctive to be easily effaced or even very much altered by alien influences.

The following chapters attempt to spell out some of the importance of those three "fast colour" factors, and then, in Chapters Eight, Nine and Ten to point to those historical developments and events which conditioned the society of the present day in the UAE.

The major migrations

Very few facts are yet available about when and how people first came to live on the southern coast of the Gulf. So far, archaeologists are only sure about the fact that a society which seemed to live well above the mere subsistence level had settlements in the 3rd millennium BC on the island of Umm al Nār near the bridge to Abu Dhabi Island near al ʿAin and at several sites in or near the mountains. Similarities have been observed between this culture and the finds made in Bahrain, on the Kuwait island of Failaka and recently

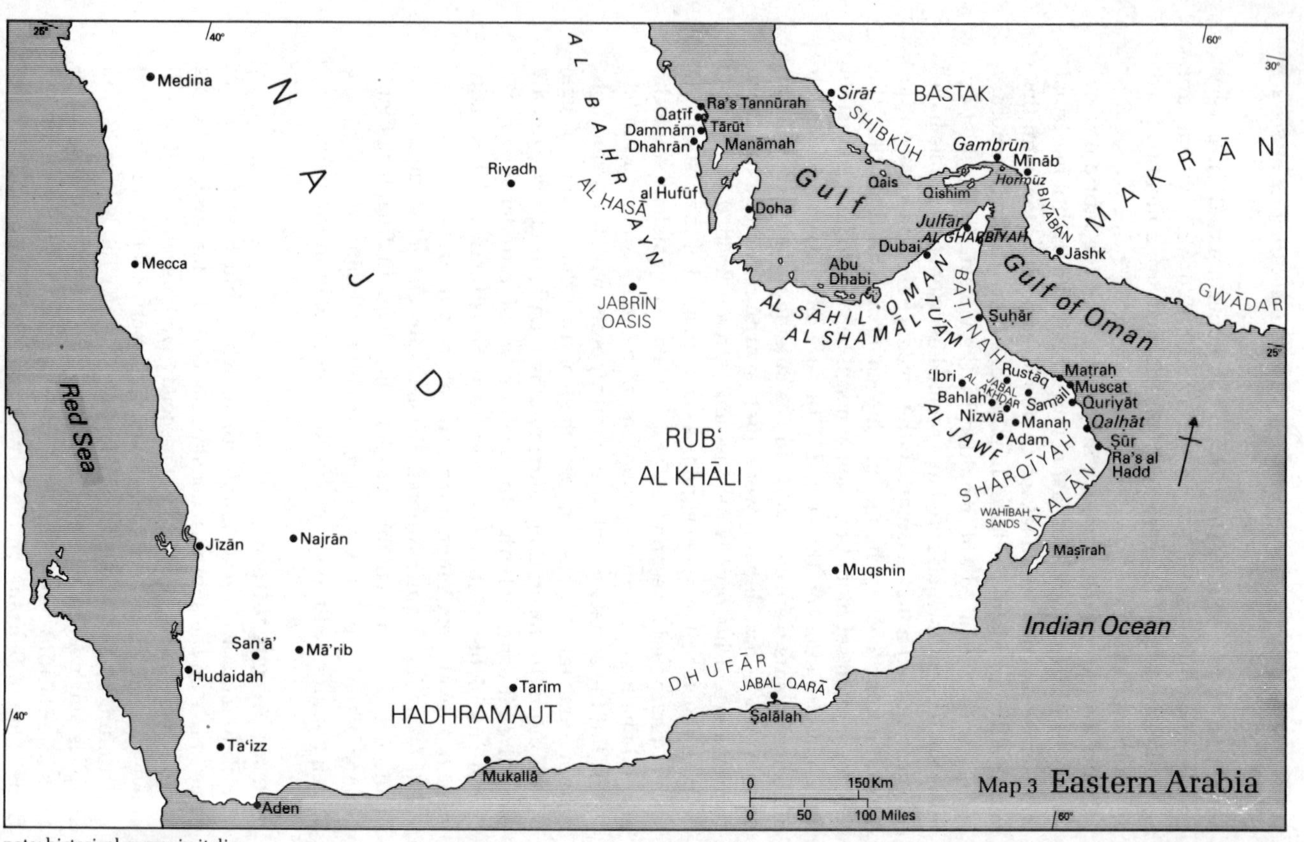

Map 3 Eastern Arabia

note: historical names in italics

in Oman.[2] It is still an open question whether these early inhabitants vanished from the area, whether they were overcome by subsequent invaders, or whether a part of the present population can be traced back to them. This is not very relevant to a study of the contemporary inhabitants, simply because it is of no importance whatsoever for their own concept of the society to which they belong.

Reports of dried-up river beds in the interior,[3] traces of ancient now unusable caravan routes as well as remains of settlements in waterless areas,[4] and some geological evidence have given weight to the theory that there might have been a gradual climatic change within historical times.[5]

The account of successive waves of population migrations and of smaller groups of invaders suggest that it might not have been quite so forbidding an adventure to move large numbers of people and their animals across some of the now almost waterless tracts. Thus the geographical setting of south-eastern Arabia might not have always afforded the same splendid isolation from the rest of the Arabian Peninsula as it has done for the last few centuries. With the question of the extent and impact of a possible climatic change still very much open, the fact remains that south-eastern Arabia witnessed several migrations from the West and North, as a result of which the population of the whole area is predominantly of Arab stock.

Semitic peoples may have moved to this region as early as two thousand years before Christ. The biblical sources, together with early South Arabian written material and with archaeological and anthropological evidence, do not seem to be enough to unite the differing views of the experts on the question of the population distribution in the Arabian Peninsula at that time.[6] In general such informed speculations do point to close links between various south-west Arabian kingdoms and Greater Oman.[7] The names of tribes and places in the south-east are traced by some scholars to the names of legendary tribes, ancestors and princes of the south-western corner of the Peninsula,[8] inspiring the search for Ūrbār of the Koran.

The population of neighbouring inner Oman was already sedentary during the periods of Persian domination of the area. In Achaemenid (700–330 BC) and Sassanid (226–651 AD) times the land under cultivation reached a maximum extent due to the construction of irrigation channels on the pattern of the Persian *qanāt*.[9] Where such irrigation was possible, settlements developed. These were easily ruled and administered even from a distance. The desert and the coasts beyond the mountains were under nobody's rule but that of transient nomadic communities.

From the second century AD, groups belonging to an Azdite subdivision of the Qaḥṭāni (or Yamāni) half of the Arab genealogy moved together with Quḍā'ah groups north-eastwards along the southern coast of Arabia. They first occupied the area south-west of the settled part of the Ḥajar range. These Azdite groups claimed as common ancestor the legendary Mālik bin Fahm. They spread his name far and wide in south-eastern Arabia while they took possession of many of the pastures and much of the irrigated land. By the middle of the 6th century the new arrivals from South Arabia dominated the south-western and western slopes of the Ḥajar range, leaving the eastern slopes of the Jabal al Akhḍar and the Bāṭinah to the Sassanid maritime interests for the time being.[10] The oases of the al 'Ain area, then called Tu'ām or Taw'ām, were well within this Azdite territory,[11] and Tu'ām was at times even the main Arab centre of the interior, while Dibah was the main Arab port.[12]

Thus, a connection was established with another main Arab migration route which also brought people through central Arabia to the countries bordering the Gulf. From then on the major population influx into south-east Arabia came from the North. The first such northern waves brought people who either claimed to be of direct Azdite ancestry or were distantly related to these groups. Most of them passed through the coastal region of the UAE which is called by Arab geographers al Baḥrayn.[13] Using the Tu'ām area as a gateway to the mountain passes to the east and south, they seemed to have been made welcome by those Azdites who were already in control of the greater portion of the well-watered *wādis*. Some tribes of other origin, notably the 'Abd al Qais, who had very amicable relations with the Azdites, came to dominate al Baḥrayn itself. Other new arrivals from the north were seen as unwanted intruders. They were of 'Adnāni (Nizāri) extraction, which is the second of the two branches of Arab genealogy. In south-eastern Arabia, as elsewhere in Arabia, this rather legendary, but to the tribesmen themselves very significant division between Qaḥṭāni (Yamāni) and 'Adnāni (Nizāri) groups resulted time and again in some very real political conflicts.[14] The Nizāri new arrivals thus seem to have been tolerated rather than made welcome by the Azdites and their befriended tribes in the area.

The secondary dispersal

After the major population migration which brought these tribes to south-eastern Arabia over a period of about three to four hundred years had subsided, the process of secondary dispersal took place. The coherence which the big tribal group had enforced during prolonged movement, and the occupation of an area as its exclusive *dār*, gradually broke up. The tribal components moved in small units into other areas, either settling in the neighbourhood of other tribes, or encroaching forcefully on to the *dār* of other groups, or even seeking a livelihood on hitherto unoccupied and unused land. However, the kinship links which had held the original tribe together for generations throughout its movement across Arabia remained strong, and the tribe could rally most of its units at a time of crisis even many centuries after this dispersal had taken place. In addition to these links the dispersed individual units began to develop new affinities when they identified themselves with groups which were geographically near to them or which had adopted the same primary source of livelihood.

The tribal groups were likely to give preference to any of these different loyalties and affiliations, be they genealogical, geographical, occupational or religious. Mention of this inclination of the population units to group and regroup along these very different lines is important in order to understand how and why some originally local conflicts set the whole area alight and why the inhabitants let themselves so often in history be affected by incidents which happened to their distant kinsmen in another part of south-eastern Arabia.

Before the advent of Islam, with the exception of the long-standing influence of the ʿAbd al Qais in Dhāhirah, the territory of the UAE was divided up among a number of groups who had obtained possession of the areas mostly through the above-mentioned process of secondary dispersal. One of these groups, the Mālik bin Fahm (the Ḥārith and Khamām sections) lived in the northern mountains.

Another part of the Mālik bin Fahm, together with the Quḍāʿah, who included or were related to the Mahrā of Dhufār and the Bani Riyām of inner Oman, spread westwards from the mountains into northern Dhāhirah and to the coast. The ʿAbd al Qais were a powerful, widespread nomadic group and maintained their dominance throughout the Dhāhirah. In the southern part of the Dhāhirah and the area around al ʿAin, the old Tu'ām, the latter shared the settlements and grazing with a number of other groups.[15]

The link between the tribal structure and the limited economic opportunities: the "versatile tribesman"

Throughout the major immigration movements and the secondary dispersal and dissemination of the tribal units, a fundamental issue became increasingly important: could the economic resources of the region support the increasing population? The problem facing each individual group in turn was how it could itself best utilise that share of the resources which it possessed or to which it had gained access.

There seems no way of assessing with any degree of certainty how large the population of South East Arabia was at the time of the advent of Islam. If, however, the many names of tribal groups and of places mentioned in the Arab and Persian texts mean anything comparable to what such names mean today, one can assume that the population density in south-eastern Arabia was similar to what it was in the 1930s. One can also assume that, even if climatic conditions had been more favourable, the need for economic diversification was an urgent one for the population of the area contemporary with the rise of Islam, and that this pattern did not change significantly over the centuries.[16]

It could be argued that this need for economic diversification was, more than any other factor, responsible for the fact that the tribal structure of society did not give way over the centuries to patterns typical of societies organised predominantly along the lines of village neighbourhoods or of occupational communities, as happened in other originally tribally-organised societies of the Arabian Peninsula and even to some extent in the settled areas of neighbouring Oman proper. There seems to be a close link between this unbroken preponderance for centuries of the tribal structure as the basis of society in the area now covered by the UAE, and the type of economies which the local conditions afforded and the way in which these limited economic opportunities were exploited. A more detailed description of the various aspects of the traditional economic activities and of the extent and mechanics of economic diversification is therefore a necessary step in order to arrive at a satisfactory analysis of the state of this essentially tribal structure of society in the UAE at the time of the economic and social changes due to the discovery of oil.

The economic activities to which the geography and climate of the country lent themselves were: camel-breeding, goat, sheep and cattle breeding, agriculture—mostly dependent on artificial irrigation—

fishing, pearling, trade by camel and ship, and crafts which were associated with the requirements of the other economic activities and were limited by the nature of the raw materials available.

The questions which arise out of the above are: which group did what? How did they come to do it—by choice and inclination or by force of circumstances?

It is not too sweeping a statement to say that most of the history of south-east Arabia has consisted of solving these very questions. They presented themselves time and again. Because of the shortage of arable land not everyone could lead a settled existence, nor could many people engage in a profitable trade. Throughout the history of the last two millennia in this area most tribes have for a period partaken of the beduin existence and at other times of the sedentary life in villages and towns. Fortunes have changed frequently, and so have the inclinations and desires of the tribes. Villagers have lived in fear of the incursions of the beduin raiding parties. Generations of nomadic tribes have scorned the sedentary life and preferred to live in fear of drought and persecution from the settled tribes on the fringes of the desert to which they had to resort when the rains failed. Time and again beduin tribes have taken possession of irrigated areas and eventually come to work the soil themselves. On the other hand, settlers of drought-stricken areas are known to have resorted to nomadism and eventually themselves become desert beduin. Thus, very few groups remained in the same economic circumstances for countless generations.

The above remarks on dispersal and dissemination of tribal groups have to be taken up again to point out another characteristic of the economic history. Conscious maintenance of strong kinship ties allowed quite often a sharing of economic activities between related or friendly groups. One tribal section would for instance take care of its own domestic animals as well as of those belonging to a related or friendly group, while the latter looked after its date gardens or went off for the pearling season.

Scarcity of resources and, in relation to these resources, relative density of population have formed the most characteristic phenomenon of the region's age-old economic pattern: the versatile tribesman. He is to be found throughout the area and throughout the ages. He spends the winter with his livestock in the desert and comes to the coast to fish in the summer in order to supplement his own and his animals' diet. He plants or harvests his dates and takes part in the pearling, or he sows and harvests his millet high up in the mountains and spends the hot months of the summer fishing at the coast, or he leads a caravan or steers a ship and then returns to engage in some quite different activity. In short, there have been at all times in this area not a few tribesmen, every one of whom knew all there was to know about camel-breeding, pearling, farming, fishing or sailmaking. A more detailed account of these economic activities will be given below in Chapters Five and Six.

The remarkable phenomenon that every group or even every individual usually participated in several economic activities points to the extreme scarcity of resources. Nature limited the expansion of every one of the economic options which the inhabitants of the area had. Agriculture and husbandry were limited by the lack of soil, water and verdure; trade and maritime carrying services were limited by the competition from ports with easier access such as Bahrain and Muscat or from more efficient vessels such as steam ships; pearling depended on a receptive foreign market; only fishing has always been consistent, but it was never a source of great wealth.

Until the advent of completely new economic opportunities with the discovery of oil, the limited resources also discouraged immigration. The obvious need for diversification of economic activities rendered the tribal basis of society indispensable. Before the advent of oil, the population could generally not afford to segregate as settled inhabitants, into merchants, fishermen and pearlers on the coast, agriculturists in the fertile oases and *wādis*, and other groups exclusively tending their animals. Because such specialisation was for most families throughout the ages impracticable, social separation into occupational groups did not take place either.

The society remained tribal throughout the country, until the time when changed economic circumstances made it possible for an ever-increasing number of families to find a livelihood entirely from one economic activity. This was the case even in the shaikhdoms which were strongly orientated towards maritime trade, such as Ra's al Khaimah, or Shārjah.

For an investigation of the changes in society after that crucial moment, it is relevant to give a picture of the distribution and respective weight of the various tribal groups living in the area at about the time of the Second World War. The tribal basis of the whole society is illustrated in the following enumeration of the tribes, their share in the various economic activities, and their general distribution at the time before the discovery of oil changed all these patterns.

2 The Bani Yās, their associates, and the development of Abu Dhabi into a "territorial state"

The tribes of Abu Dhabi

Bani Yās

The Emirate of Abu Dhabi is now, as it was in the days of the author of the Gazetteer,[17] co-extensive with the habitat of the Bani Yās. Among the originally tribal population of the UAE the Bani Yās are still the most numerous single tribe, although their numbers have decreased steadily since the beginning of the century. Lorimer estimated their numbers at 12,000 people, 2,000 of whom were nomadic but usually spent all the year in Abu Dhabi territory. Of the 10,000 settled Bani Yās about half lived in the Līwā, 2,800 lived in Abu Dhabi town, about 2,000 lived in Dubai, and the remainder lived in the Abu Dhabi villages of the Buraimi oasis, on the islands, and in small scattered settlements on the coast and in the hinterland.[18] In the early 1950s, the total number of Bani Yās on the Trucial Coast had decreased to 8,000 of whom some 1,700 were beduin.[19] In the first population census carried out in Abu Dhabi in spring 1968 only 5,884 Bani Yās were counted in the shaikhdom of Abu Dhabi.[20]

Since they are a confederated tribe, the numbers of genuine subsections and of allied tribes of the Bani Yās have been stated differently by different observers. Lorimer counted 15 sections in 1907; J.B. Kelly lists 14 major and 6 minor sections. The changing attitudes of the associated tribes to the Ruler of Abu Dhabi at times led them to want to integrate completely into the Bani Yās, while other political constellations in the area induced them to declare some sort of independence. At present the leading members of the Bani Yās in Abu Dhabi name over 20 sections as being considered part and parcel of the Bani Yās.[21]

The *Āl Bū Falāḥ* have always been a small subsection numbering, according to Lorimer, only 15 to 20 houses. The section is also known as the Āl Nahyān and traditionally provided the paramount shaikh of the Bani Yās, who was the Ruler of Abu Dhabi. The Āl Bū Falāḥ had date gardens and houses in seven villages of the Līwā but most of them did not live there permanently. They spent the winter with their camels in the desert, and many of them went pearling during the summer in the boats of other Bani Yās. The Āl Bū Falāḥ were the first of the Bani Yās to acquire property in the Buraimi oasis, and the members of the ruling family have systematically continued this policy until now.[22]

The most numerous section of the Bani Yās is the *Āl Bū Mahair*, listed by Lorimer as a separate tribe.[23] In the 1950s they had only about 35 houses in Abu Dhabi and another 20 in the Buraimi oasis, while the majority of the Āl Bū Mahair belonged to Dubai (300 to 400 houses), Shārjah (60 houses) and the other ports of the coast. Their main occupation was pearling and fishing.

The *Āl Bū Falāsah* section became well known as the one which seceded in 1833 to the fishing village of Dubai, which had been until then under the authority of the Āl Bū Falāḥ Rulers of Abu Dhabi.[24] The tribal leader of that section became the ancestor of all subsequent rulers of Dubai. The Āl Bū Falāsah were among those Bani Yās who took very readily to the water and engaged in pearling in Abu Dhabi as well as later in Dubai. Most of the families who remained with the Ruler of Abu Dhabi had either fishing rights and lived on the islands or lived in Abu Dhabi town. A few families had connections with the Buraimi oasis and went there for the summer.

The *Rumaithāt* are a section which lived mostly from pearling and had no date gardens in the Līwā. At the turn of the century they had about 100 houses in Abu Dhabi town and on the adjoining coast. With the decline of the pearling industry, several of the Rumaithāt families moved out to live on the islands north east of Abu Dhabi town (Saʿdiyāt and beyond), where they obtained fishing rights. A few families visited the Buraimi oasis but, having no possessions in the Līwā, they usually did not go with their camels into the desert during the winter but entrusted them to other Bani Yās tribesmen for a fee. They were thus less mobile than most other Bani Yās sections. A similar life was led by the much smaller section of the *Qumzān*,[25] whose strength in Abu Dhabi was further reduced when, after the recession in the pearling industry, more than half the Qumzān families moved to Dubai.

The *Qubaisāt* are in some ways the most representative of the Bani Yās in that their members were very mobile and participated in all the occupations which were traditionally pursued by the Bani Yās. The Qubaisāt used to be prominent participants in the pearling industry, and owned about 40 boats. They were also one of the most numerous tribes in many Līwā settlements; during the 1950s they had still between 40 and 50 houses there, of which about one-third were permanently inhabited. The Qubaisāt founded a settlement at the coastal inlet of Khaur al ʿUdaid, east of the base of the Qatar promontory. The whole section hived off from Abu Dhabi several times during the 19th century and declared their independence in order to avoid paying to the Ruler their share of the taxes and the special fines which had been imposed on Abu Dhabi for violating certain treaties.[26] In later generations some Qubaisāt became related to the ruling family when Shaikh Sulṭān bin Zāyid married a Qubaisi girl from Muzairaʿah in the Līwā. Her name was Salāmah bint Buṭi; she became the mother of the former Ruler, Shaikh Shakhbūṭ bin Sulṭān, the present Ruler Shaikh Zāyid and their brothers Khālid and Hazzāʿ.[27]

The principal beduin section of the Bani Yās were the *Mazārīʿ* (singular: *Mazrūʿi*). According to Lorimer they had about 315 houses in various villages in the Līwā and, in the *U.K. Memorial*, the Mazārīʿ still head the list of those six Bani Yās tribes who own property in the Līwā, with 142 families counted in 1951 and 151 families in 1954. But most Mazārīʿ accompanied their camels themselves during the winter to the grazing areas in Dhafrah or Khatam. They owned pearling boats which they launched from Bandar Rudaim and similar coves on the coast nearest to their settlements in the Līwā. In later years the Mazārīʿ bought more date gardens in Līwā villages where no Mazrūʿi was previously recorded. This may indicate that the Mazārīʿ became more settled during the first half of this century due to the decline in the value of camels, which had been the only means of desert transport. Many Mazārīʿ sold the larger part of their herd to obtain cash to purchase gardens and thereby to augment the supply of their staple food, dates. In the first two decades of the century this move by the Mazārīʿ coincided with the move by other Bani Yās, who could afford it, to obtain property in the Buraimi villages. Later, many Mazārīʿ sought temporary employment in the oil industries of neighbouring countries, and found it more convenient to leave date gardens behind (as a fall-back security in life) which could be tended by a few female or aged members of the family, rather than to leave a large herd of camels inadequately protected from raiders. Some Mazārīʿ settled in Dubai as a result of disagreements with previous Abu Dhabi Rulers.

The *Hawāmil* (singular *Hāmili*) have always formed a very

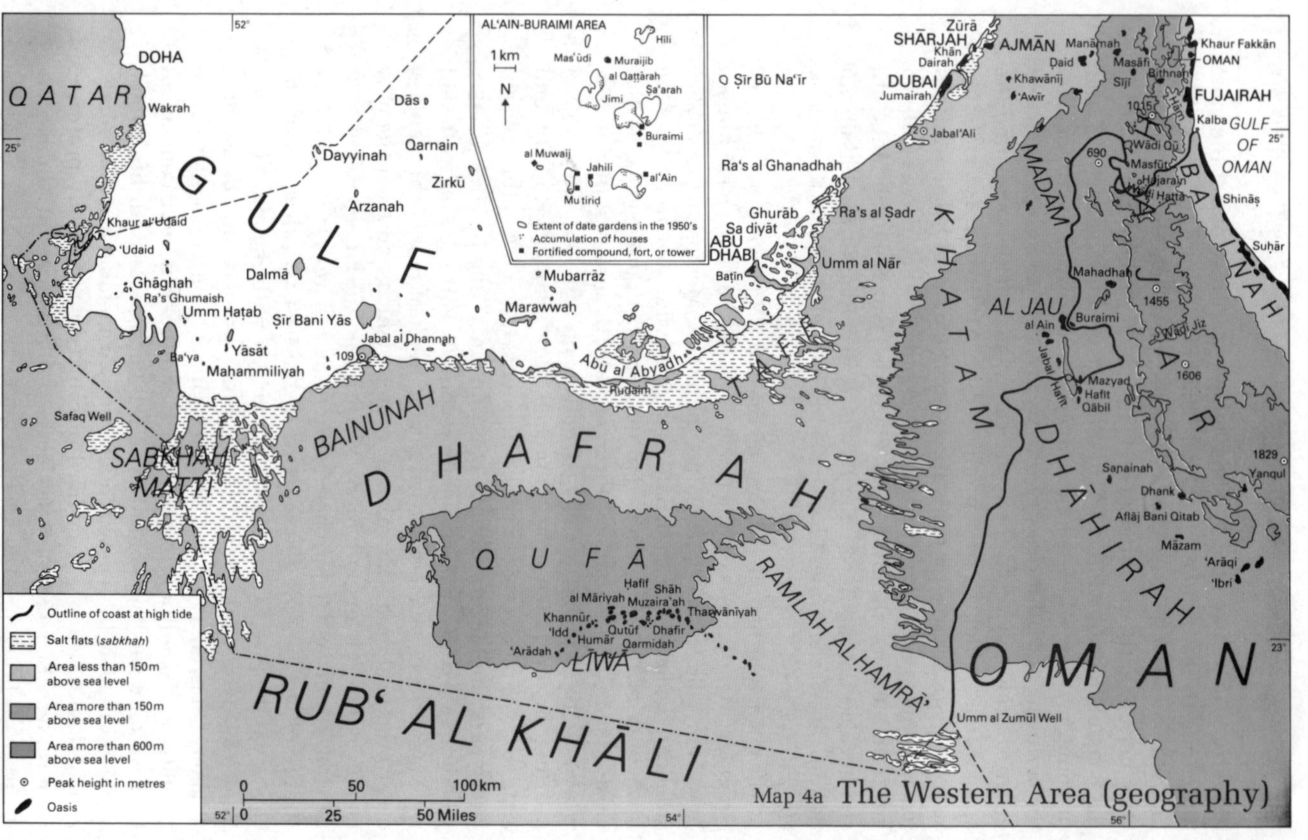

Map 4a The Western Area (geography)

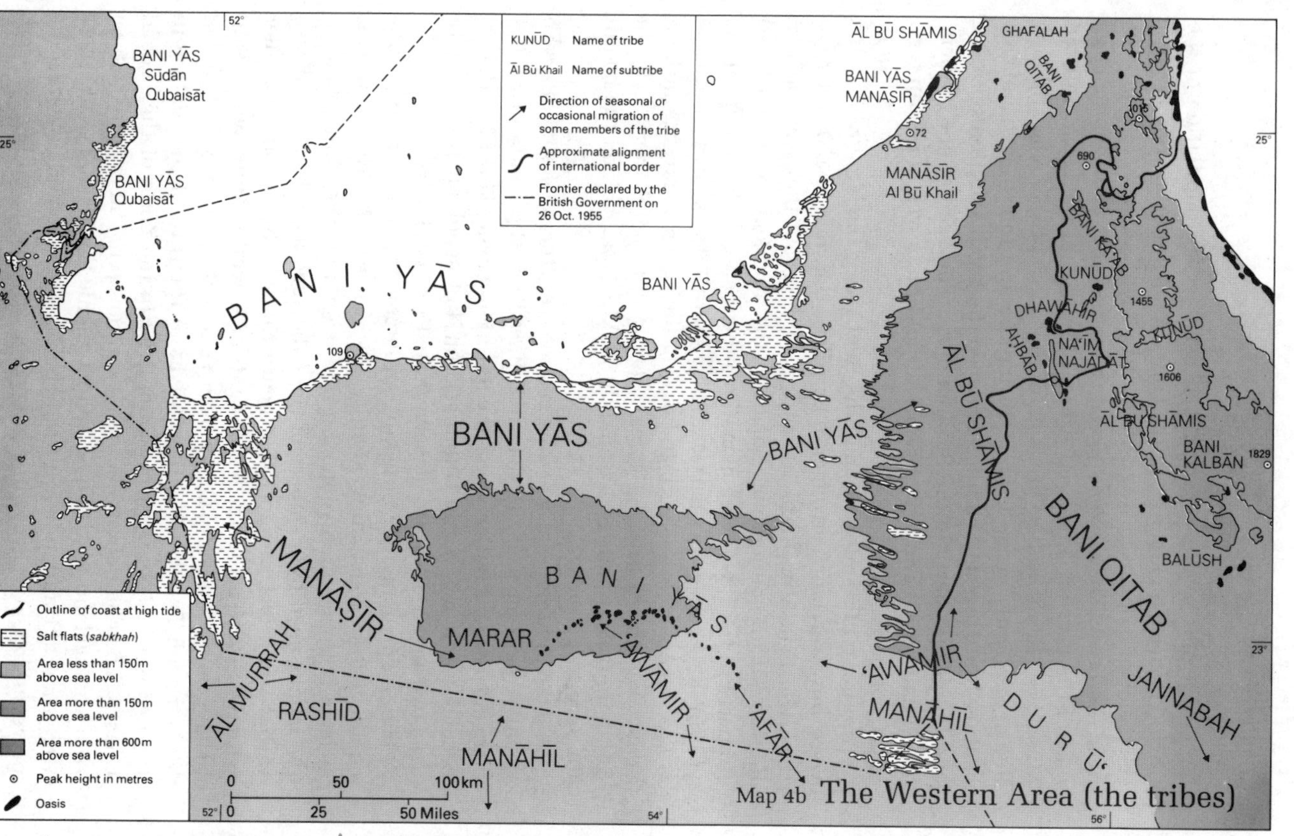

Map 4b The Western Area (the tribes)

For distribution of Bani Yās subtribes see appendix p. 501

important part of the permanent or semi-settled population of the Līwā. The settled existence of the Hawāmil is underlined by the fact that some of them also owned goats and sheep, which were kept in or near the Līwā. They owned pearling boats and some spent a large part of the year on Dalmā. At present the *wāli* of the Līwā, Saif bin Mūsa, is a Ḥāmili, and so are most of those few people who still now live permanently in the Līwā.[28] During the first four decades of this century four Hawāmil families achieved the much sought-after move and bought property in the Buraimi oasis. The head of one of them, ʿAbdullah bin Ghanūm, was Shaikh Shakhbūṭ's *wāli* of al ʿAin for a short period.[29]

Another typical subsection of the Bani Yās is the *Maḥāribah*, who were, however, much stronger in Lorimer's time (about 150 houses in the Līwā, 60 in Abu Dhabi, 50 nearby). In the 1950s they were only 75 houses strong altogether. Some of the Maḥāribah who owned property in the Līwā were nomadic; others spent a large part of the year in their houses in the Līwā. Their share in the pearling industry was also considerable, with 40 boats of their own. A few Maḥāribah spent even the winter on Dalmā island, and one of them, ʿAli bin Shaibān, was appointed by Shaikh Shakhbūṭ as *wāli* on the island for several periods.[30]

A small predominantly beduin section were the *Āl Mishāghīn*, who usually spent most of the year at Ṭaff, east of Abu Dhabi town, but also moved to Khatam near the Buraimi oasis. The *Marar* have become a predominantly Dubai section, but some have property in the Līwā where they are closely related to the Mazārīʿ.

The *Sūdān*, (singular *Suwāidi*), an important and numerous tribe on the whole coast, now identify themselves with the Bani Yās, especially those who live in Abu Dhabi. On the other hand, some of the names used by members of the tribe such as al Kindi, and also verbal traditions, support the theory that the Sūdān are, together with the Kunūd of Oman, descendants of Aswad al Kindi, who is said to have immigrated into Oman from Yemen at the time of the Prophet Muḥammad. The tribe's strength was at the turn of the century in the region of 5,500, most of whom lived in the ports of the Trucial Coast.[31] They had about 300 houses in Shārjah, 250 in Dubai, 20 on Abū Mūsa island and 12 in ʿAjmān. Outside the Trucial Coast there were some at Ḥadd in Bahrain, and before 1867 the Sūdān were quite powerful in Qatar, according to Lorimer still maintaining a strength of about 80 houses in Doha.

In Abu Dhabi at the turn of the century there were some 375

houses of the Sūdān in the town itself and about 30 in Baṭīn, both on the main island. None of the tribe ever owned date gardens in Līwā nor did they own a significant number of camels. Wherever they lived in the Gulf they engaged in pearling, fishing, trading in pearls and seafaring. The Sūdān of Abu Dhabi have usually been steadfast supporters of the policies of the Āl Bū Falāḥ, with whom they became connected in marriage throughout several generations. Shaikh Zāyid bin Khalīfah's mother, for instance, was a Suwaidi, and one of his wives was the daughter of the paramount shaikh of the Sūdān, Sulṭān bin Nāṣir.

At one point in time Shaikh Zāyid bin Khalīfah's overall political aim, to become the leader of all the beduin of the Trucial Coast and thus also to safeguard the possessions he had already added to the realm of the Āl Bū Falāḥ, relied on co-operation with the Sūdān. Both had their eyes on the sandbank of Zūrā opposite the beach extending from ʿAjmān to Ḥamrīyah. Shaikh Zāyid obtained from the British Resident in Bushire permission to send supplies for the use of some beduin, which he had assembled on Zūrā. In 1897 a section of the Sūdān led by Sulṭān bin Nāṣir started to colonise Zūrā, and the Shaikh of Abu Dhabi offered to protect the new settlement. This was, however, immediately opposed by all the Ghāfiri shaikhs, especially by the Ruler of ʿAjmān and by the Qāsimi Ruler of Shārjah, who was the overlord of Ḥamrīyah. They appealed to the Political Resident, invoking the terms of the treaties which forbade the use of boats to transport warlike material even to an island close by. Thus the joint plan of Shaikh Zāyid and the Sūdān to gain a foothold within reach of the traditionally Qāsimi territory and a potential base for maritime activities in the north came to nothing in the end.[32]

The Sūdān continued to play an important part in the politics of Abu Dhabi, and it was for instance one of their leaders in Abu Dhabi, Aḥmad bin Khalīfah, who spoke in front of members of the ruling family and some notables of the shaikhdom against the choice of Shaikh Shakhbūṭ bin Sulṭān as Ruler. He favoured the brother Hazzāʿ bin Sulṭān, and said so. In the 1950s the Sūdān were leaders in the exodus of scores of families from Abu Dhabi to Qatar. Having tribal relatives there and also good relations with the ruling family of Qatar, the Sūdān obtained work, housing and schooling fairly promptly there. They were then followed by many families of the Rumaithāt, Qubaisāt, and some families of most of the other Bani Yās sections.

This enumeration of the sections of the Bani Yās shows that there is within this tribal confederation considerable difference in the way of life between those sections which rely on the sea for their livelihood and those who were predominantly nomadic. And yet this tribal confederation was the basis for the creation of a nation-state within a large and geographically very varied territory.[33] The coherence of the confederation was due to certain characteristics of the Bani Yās. First of all, the subsections and allied groups did not live separate existences; they shared, mingled and intermarried in the villages of the Līwā, they had arrangements by which the nomads of one section cared for the camels of another section, and those who had no pearling boats of their own went on the boats of others. Secondly, most families of the Bani Yās had some members living permanently in Abu Dhabi town, so that all the sections mixed there easily at all times. During the summer the Līwā and Dalmā Island were further meeting points where the common bonds were yearly renewed by close contact and common concern for the few sources of livelihood. The interchange between Abu Dhabi, the Līwā, Dalmā and Buraimi, although it meant time-consuming journeys by camel or sailing boat, was by necessity very frequent, with daily new arrivals and departures in all these places particularly before and after the date harvest and the pearling season. It is therefore not surprising that it became a characteristic of the Shaikhdom of Abu Dhabi that their ruler could almost without fail rely on the loyalty of all Bani Yās sections in times of war.[34] This in turn meant that he was invariably made responsible for and had to stand by any Bani Yās group which had created or got into trouble. Last but not least the policy of the Bani Yās not to claim exclusive possession of any of their traditional *dār*, of the wells therein or of the pearling banks near Abu Dhabi's coast, resulted in their winning for themselves a number of strong allies, who in the course of time became undisputably subjects of the Āl Bū Falāḥ Rulers and eventually citizens of the modern State of Abu Dhabi and the UAE.

Manāṣīr

The Manāṣīr are, after the Bani Yās, the most important of the tribes which constitute the local population of the Shaikhdom of Abu Dhabi. This numerous tribe contributed many fighting men and the Rulers of Abu Dhabi could usually count on their support; also the Manāṣīr co-operated closely with some of the Bani Yās in the use of the scant economic resources.[35]

There are more than half a dozen Arab tribes which have the same name, but the Manāṣīr of the Arab coast of the Gulf and its hinterland do not maintain special connections with any of them. Until very recently the majority of the Manāṣīr were nomadic; most sections lived in Dhafrah but in some years many roamed as far away as Qatar, al Ḥasā and the Omani-held territory in the vicinity of the Buraimi oasis. Many of the Manāṣīr, both settled and beduin, have always been scattered throughout all the shaikhdoms of the Trucial Coast.

The leaders of the five distinct sections of the Manāṣīr were each recognised as the authorities in all matters concerning internal tribal affairs, while in many other matters the settled and even the nomadic groups accepted the authority of the Ruler of the Trucial shaikhdom in which they lived. This arrangement may be the reason why the Manāṣīr have not had within living memory one paramount shaikh. The five sections are of unequal strength: the larger ones are the Āl Bū Raḥmah, the Āl Bū Mun͟dir and the Āl Bū al Sha'ar; the Āl Bū Khail and the Āl Bū Ḥamīr are very much smaller.[36] In the *Gazetteer*, the total number of Manāṣīr in the area was estimated at 1,400, while the various authorities who investigated tribal matters in Abu Dhabi during the 1950s estimated that over 4,000 members of that tribe lived in the Emirates including Qatar, many of them frequently changing their habitat. At that time some 2,800 Manāṣīr usually lived in the Shaikhdom of Abu Dhabi; 1,200 led a settled or nomadic life in the towns and hinterland of the other Trucial States.[37]

In the census of spring 1968, 3,224 Manāṣīr were counted in the State of Abu Dhabi. Even taking into account the tendency to emigrate from Abu Dhabi during the 1950s, this latter figure indicates that the *Gazetteer's* estimate was probably too low. The way of life of the settled Manāṣīr usually blended in with the way of life of the rest of the population of the shaikhdom where they lived. In Abu Dhabi territory, beduin and settled Manāṣīr and the Bani Yās have for at least 150 years lived in harmony, sharing the few resources that were there to share, in much the same way as different sections of one tribe would live together. In both tribes some sections were more settled than others, and some preferred camels and the desert to pearling and fishing.

The three major sections of the Manāṣīr all owned property in the Līwā. Recently, of 42 settlements, some Manāṣīr were found in 36 of them.[38] Nine neighbouring villages in the eastern half of the Līwā were exclusively Manāṣīr; however, the gardens there did not yield enough dates to include the owners in the small group of Līwā date-growers who had to pay tax.[39] There were nine other exclusively Manāṣīr villages in the Līwā, but most other villages have been shared between the Bani Yās and the Manāṣīr since the first half of this century, because more Manāṣīr became at least semi-settled and wanted to own date gardens. They bought some established gardens, planted others or obtained them by inter-tribal marriage. The Manāṣīr also owned many of the scattered and usually fairly unproductive date gardens south of the Līwā and in various other desert locations. Some 30 families, most of whom lived as nomads in the Khatam, owned date gardens in the Buraimi oasis although very few of them have actually settled there. Like the Bani Yās, the Manāṣīr usually built palm-frond huts near their date gardens, especially in and around the Līwā oases. But the majority of the Manāṣīr used these houses only during the date harvest and very few remained in the Līwā throughout the year. After the date harvest the Manāṣīr families closed these houses, covered up the wells nearby and concentrated exclusively on the problem of where to find sufficient of the right kind of grazing for their large herds of camels. They preferred Dhafrah, Khatam and Ramlah al Ḥamrā', but some families also frequented other parts of the desert. Thus the Manāṣīr were particularly closely associated with the Mazārīʿ, who are the largely nomadic section of the Bani Yās. Some Manāṣīr went to Dalmā for the pearling season, but compared to the Bani Yās they owned fewer boats and usually participated on boats owned and partly manned by the Bani Yās.

The Manāṣīr owned camels but only about half of them owned date gardens in the Līwā, Khatam and the Buraimi oasis. An important occupation, according to the *Memorial*, was the transport of goods and persons when the Bani Yās moved in large numbers between Abu Dhabi and Buraimi at the beginning of the hot humid weather in Abu Dhabi, and for the return journey in autumn. Already during the 1920s when profits from pearling showed signs of stagnation, if not actual decline, and the carrying trade suffered from the general recession, the animals of predominantly camel-breeding Manāṣīr fell in value. As a result, there was a marked increase in raids by small groups of nomadic Manāṣīr on the settled population of the shaikhdoms in the north. On most occasions the families and villages who suffered losses from such raids turned to the Ruler of

Abu Dhabi, who was considered to be responsible for the beduin Manāṣīr.

In the decades following the rapid decline of the pearling industry the Manāṣīr beduin turned to seeking at least temporary employment with the oil companies in the region. Those who had often taken their camels to al Ḥasā for winter grazing found themselves work with the Arabian American Oil Company (ARAMCO); others worked in Doha or with the Qatar Petroleum Company, while their animals were left in the desert of Abu Dhabi in the charge of relatives. Petroleum Development (Trucial Coast), Ltd, had some 40 Manāṣīr on its payroll in Abu Dhabi at any one time during the early 1950s. But like the Bani Yās tribesmen, the Manāsīr considered such employment as a temporary arrangement to earn enough for a particular purpose: to buy a date garden, some camels, a new wife or in later years a Landrover. During the first few years they hardly ever worked for more than a couple of years at a time, and then they returned to their previous way of life.

As has been described earlier in this chapter, the Manāṣīr have shared the area and its resources for many generations with the Bani Yās in such a way that, when circumstances made it necessary to replace the system dependent on tribal loyalties and customary economic usages with a system requiring citizenship and State boundaries, the majority of the Manāṣīr could only be called Abu Dhabians. The fact that throughout the 19th and 20th centuries the Manāṣīr have joined forces with the Rulers of Abu Dhabi, who have equally consistently acted on behalf of the Manāṣīr,[40] and the occasional marriage between members of the Manāṣīr families and the Āl Bū Falāḥ had the effect that the Manāṣīr could demand some say in the choice of a Ruler. This became particularly obvious when some of the successors of Zāyid bin Khalīfah neglected the custom of paying subsidies to the leaders of the Manāṣīr. Shaikh Shakhbūṭ and his brother Shaikh Zāyid, who became his governor in the Buraimi area in 1948 were very aware of the necessity to recognise the somewhat special relationship with the Manāṣīr. One way of doing this was to employ a large number of them as retainers. During the war between Abu Dhabi and Dubai in 1945–7, the Manāṣīr fought on the side of Abu Dhabi and sustained heavy losses.

When the community which had so eagerly seized the jobs, which became available once the search for oil had begun, was transformed into a State with a multitude of opportunities for nationals to have their share in the wealth, the chiefly desert-bound families could not at first integrate very easily into the new multinational society. Even now, few of the Manāṣīr have settled in Abu Dhabi town, few aim at a "middle-class" type of existence by becoming civil servants. However, some have started transport companies as a direct follow-up to their previous employment as drivers for companies operating in the desert. The Manāṣīr in Abu Dhabi form a substantial part of those groups, who were settled in the last two decades.

Dhawāhir

After a large part of the Buraimi oasis had come under Āl Bū Falāḥ authority[41] during the rule of Shaikh Zāyid bin Khalīfah, the original Dhawāhir inhabitants of most of the villages became subjects of the Ruler of Abu Dhabi, thus also considerably increasing the number of men who were ready to fight for him. It was, however, even more significant that the Dhawāhir as the principal date cultivators of the oasis then formed the bulk of the settled population of the thus enlarged shaikhdom.

Estimates of the strength of the entire tribe vary between 2,000 and 4,500;[42] in the 1968 census 2,844 Dhawāhir were counted in the State of Abu Dhabi. Almost all the many sections and subsections of the tribe ceased to be nomadic a long time ago, and had established gardens. The once exclusively Dhawāhir villages, al ʿAin, Jīmi, Hīli, al Qaṭṭārah and Muʿtiriḍ were partly bought out by the Āl Bū Falāḥ during the last decades of the 19th century.[43] But the Dhawāhir continued to be the cultivators, some of them in the capacity of gardeners who were rewarded by the Bani Yās owners. The Dhawāhir were able to keep large flocks of sheep and some goats because there was plenty of grazing in the immediate neighbourhood of the villages. According to Lorimer the entire tribe became beduin during the winter, but they did not need to go very far to find grazing for their camels either. In the last century the Dhawāhir still owned large herds of camels. During the last few decades most Dhawāhir stayed in the oasis while only a few looked after the rather diminished camel herds in Khatam. In all of al Jau and particularly in the many *wādis*, shrubs and acacia trees grow in sufficient numbers to have made a charcoal industry worthwhile. The Dhawāhir who gathered the wood and produced the charcoal also carried it to the coastal towns on their own camels, along with the products of their gardens such as limes, mangoes, dates and some wheat.

In the *Gazetteer* only three sections of the Dhawāhir are mentioned, but the members of the tribe themselves distinguish many more sections and subsections.[44] They all recognise one paramount shaikh, who in turn delivered the tribe's loyalty to the Āl Bū Falāh Ruler. After the death of Aḥmad bin Muḥammad bin Hilāl in 1936 the *tamīmah* became Surūr bin Sulṭān, who was succeeded after his death later in that year by his son Shaikh Sulṭān bin Surūr;[45] and for some time Māni' bin Muḥammad of the Āl 'Ali bin Sa'īd section assisted him.

The Dhawāhir had to pay taxes on the date crop and also paid water fees, as did all the other subjects of the Āl Bū Falāḥ who owned gardens in the oasis.[46] According to Lorimer they also paid a subsidy,[47] which later must have become symbolic or lapsed, since there seems to be now no recollection of this among leading members of the tribe.

Nomadic tribes who frequent Abu Dhabi territory

The three Abu Dhabi tribes described above lived in general within the jurisdiction of the Ruler of Abu Dhabi. Other tribes, or sections thereof, could be counted as subjects of the Ruler of Abu Dhabi because they accepted his jurisdiction while sharing the desert areas with the Bani Yās and the Manāṣīr. At other times they disappeared almost completely from the area. The largest and politically most important of these tribes is the 'Awāmir.

'Awāmir The 'Awāmir is a large tribe which originally inhabited the steppe to the north-east and north of the Hadhramaut,[48] and spread many centuries ago into central Oman, where some sections are now settled in many of the major villages and *wādis* including Muscat town.[49] Beduin sections in due course moved even further through Dhāhirah and into Khatam, and into other areas which were the *dār* of the Bani Yās. The presence of some 'Awāmir in the areas which now form part of the territory of the State of Abu Dhabi was well known throughout the 18th century, and Captain Taylor even identified them in 1818 as a branch of the Bani Yās.[50] Those 'Awāmir who lived in this area for long periods became loyal to the Āl Bū Falāḥ Ruler, frequently supported the Bani Yās in time of war, and expected the shaikh of the Bani Yās to mediate between them and other tribes. In 1889 for example they helped in a counter-attack launched from the Līwā on the Ruler of Qatar during the prolonged dispute between the latter and the Manāṣīr.

In recent decades about 2,000 to 3,000 'Awāmir of the two beduin groups have lived in Abu Dhabi territory. By the 1950s about 50 families had acquired date gardens in the Buraimi oasis, but very few owned gardens in the Līwā. The rest were nomadic and rather less rigid in their migration pattern during the winter than other tribes of the area, the most regular feature of their movements being that many families would converge on the Buraimi oasis during the summer.

During the 1940s the *tamīmah* of the beduin ʿAwāmir was Sālim bin Ḥamaḍ bin Rakkāḍ. Because of the constant feuds he was forced to fight with the neighbouring Omani tribe, the Durūʿ, bin Rakkāḍ left the area with some of his followers for al Ḥasā in about 1943. Although he came back in 1948 he returned to al Ḥasā several times during the following years.

In the meantime, the bulk of the tribe contacted the Āl Bū Falāḥ Ruler, and, as one of his first actions as the newly-appointed *wāli*, Shaikh Zāyid bin Sulṭān sent for Sālim bin Musallam bin Ḥamm and helped him to assume the position of *tamīmah* of the beduin ʿAwāmir. Some members of the tribe, however, followed bin Rakkāḍ's move and became subjects of the King of Saudi Arabia, but the majority remained with Sālim bin Ḥamm. The temporary allegiance of some ʿAwāmir to Saudi Arabia played a part in the arguments of both parties in the "Buraimi Dispute".[51] A considerable number of the beduin ʿAwāmir remained in Abu Dhabi state as may be seen from the 1968 census figures, when a total of 1,721 was counted. The actual figure was probably even higher, since only 716 women were enumerated due to the fact that many of the men were counted as employees of the oil companies and were very vague about the whereabouts and number of their family members, who were most probably encamped somewhere in Khatam, Ramlah al Ḥamrā' or Bainūnah.

ʿAfār, Manāhīl and Rashīd The ʿAfār, who are a small and entirely beduin tribe, are often considered to be a section of the ʿAwāmir, but they consider themselves to be separate.[52] They are an important tribe in the Hadhramaut, but in earlier times a few came into Abu Dhabi territory using the same routes and wells on the way as the ʿAwāmir. Groups of both tribes used to join together for beduin raids. After the Āl Wahībah, an Omani tribe, had extended their *dār* north-westwards into traditionally Durūʿ country during the 1950s, the ʿAfār tended to be more closely allied with the Āl Wahībah than with the ʿAwāmir. Quite a number of the Manāhīl, another

Hadhramauti beduin tribe, entered Abu Dhabi territory, and some have settled there in recent years. Some came to Līwā and the Buraimi oasis in the summer, probably to buy dates as well as to graze their camels in the vicinity. After his first secret crossing of the Rubʿ al Khāli from Muqhshin, Thesiger did not enter the Dhafrah proper, but heard that during that winter (1946) some Manāhīl had been there. When he did travel the length of the Līwā in November 1948 he met some of them on their way south coming from the Līwā.[53]

Some members of the Rashīd also visited Abu Dhabi; they are described by Thesiger as "among the most authentic of the Bedu, the least affected by the outside world".[54] The migration range of this small tribe (only about 300 strong), whose homeland is between the Dhufār mountains and the Empty Quarter, extends from the Hadhramaut to the Gulf and includes at least all the eastern half of the Rubʿ al Khāli.

Individuals and groups of the beduin tribes visiting the area often referred their disputes to the Āl Bū Falāḥ as the nearest authority deemed to be neutral in their settling of cases arising from raids and desert warfare. Since Shaikh Zāyid bin Sulṭān became the *wāli* in the Buraimi area, most beduin who came to the district went to visit him because he commanded an unusual degree of respect. They were hospitably received and in keeping with beduin custom often obtained gifts. Not infrequently his beduin visitors got into trouble with the tribes in the vicinity of the oasis and the Āl Bū Falāḥ had to intervene on behalf of the former. One such example was Thesiger's guide, Sālim bin Ghabaishah (a Rashīdi) who went raiding in 1950 together with some ʿAwāmir and ʿAfār; they were captured by the Bani Qitab and put into Shārjah prison. A brother of Shaikh Shakhbūṭ, Shaikh Hazzāʿ, intervened and obtained their release.

Āl Murrah Some members of the numerous and powerful beduin tribe of Āl Murrah[55] (singl.: Murri) who are based in al Ḥasā and Jabrīn in Saudi Arabia have frequently visited Abu Dhabi territory. Earlier this century about 15 of their families owned date gardens in the Līwā, and according to Shaikh Shakhbūṭ they were asked to pay the customary tax on their crop although they were otherwise not considered to be subjects but rather visitors. They nevertheless used to expect the Ruler or his *wāli* to try cases which involved a Murri and occurred in Bani Yās territory. In the 1940s one Murri visited Dhafrah every year with camels which belonged to the ruling family in Qatar and other Qataris. During the winter of 1948/49 some Āl Murrah came with their camels to the vicinity of Abu Dhabi town and their headman Aṭyār bin Muḥammad al Murri presented Shaikh Shakhbūṭ with three camels.

Expansion of Bani Yās territory

Longstanding possession of Dhafrah and the Līwā oases

The history of Abu Dhabi is an example of how a coherent beduin tribe over several generations extended its area of undisputed dominance, and while remaining under the leadership of one and the same ruling family it built what amounted to a small "nation-state". By the time the disputes over the exact geographical limits of the Eastern Arabian Rulers' authority had sprung up as a result of the signing of oil concessions, the *dār* of the Bani Yās could be considered as the territorial extent of the State of Abu Dhabi.

The Bani Yās were with 10 to 12 thousand members the largest of the 40 or so tribes which made up the population of the Trucial States at the beginning of this century. They were described in the *Gazetteer* as "one of the most compact and powerful tribes of Trucial Oman; their range is practically co-extensive with the territories of the Shaikh of Abu Dhabi."[56] Unlike most other equally coherent tribes on the Peninsula, the Bani Yās do not have one common ancestor who figures in the recorded genealogies of Arab tribes. However, some Bani Yās claim that the tribe was in the past one with the ʿAwāmir and that both descended from ʿĀmir bin Ṣaʿṣaʿ, one of whose sons was called Yās. Both tribes have been mentioned as integral branches of one tribe,[57] but although they are both Hināwi in the political division within the tribes of Oman and the Trucial Coast, their immigration routes into the area which they now share, Dhafrah, have been quite different. The ʿAwāmir spread from Hadhramaut eastwards along the edge of the Rubʿ al Khāli, while the Bani Yās came from Najd, north-west of their present homeland.

Such uncertainty about which tribe actually forms an integral part of the Bani Yās and which does not, indicates that the tribe is a confederation which was welded together by a common history rather than by the ties of blood relationship. They were probably a number of beduin groups which gradually extended their seasonal migration in search of grazing, from the areas in and around Najd[58] into the relatively well-watered Dhafrah, returning to the familiar wells of the area where they customarily spent the summer with their camels. The decisive factor for forging together and keeping intact such strong links between the various groups which shared this pattern of migration and for growing into a confederation using one name, was most probably the establishment of a centre close to Dhafrah where they all spent the summer. This centre is the string of Līwā oases, where water from dew and occasional rain gathering in the huge sand-dunes is sufficient to provide relatively sweet water in quantities enough to raise date palms and to water large herds of camels in the vicinity. A legend which is told by some Bani Yās may point to the fact that the newly found (or redeveloped) settlement area, the Līwā, became so strong a common bond that a common tribal leader was also recognised, most likely at a time when the tribes' new settlements had to be defended against invaders. This legend has it that someone by the name of Yās dug the first water-hole in the Līwā and all the tribes who came to use it called themselves after his well. For most of these beduin groups it was probably the first time in generations that they had built themselves a home near their date gardens to which they returned at least during the date harvest in the summer.[59]

The occupation of Dhafrah with the Līwā oases was a gradual process which may have coincided with the formation of the Bani Yās confederation. Its beginning cannot be dated with accuracy but there are several records which confirm that the Bani Yās were certainly in possession of most of the territory of the contemporary State of Abu Dhabi by the middle of the 17th century. The Arabic chronicle with the misleading title of *Kashf al Ghumma* ("Dispeller of Grief"), which describes the history of Oman from the earliest times until the year 1728 AD, mentions an incident occurring some time after 1633 when Nāṣir bin Qaḥṭān raided every year the borderlands of Oman, and the *wāli* of the Imām of Oman, together with a force of beduin and settled tribesmen, fell upon him in a fort in Dhafrah where the Bani Yās had afforded refuge to Nāṣir.[60] The fact that the Bani Yās possessed forts in Dhafrah, which could only be in the Līwā part of it because of readily available water supply, is mentioned elsewhere, and another source confirms the theory that the Bani Yās had become the dominant tribe in that area more than three hundred years previously.[61]

Increasing presence on the coast

The earlier generations of the Bani Yās who lived in and around Dhafrah were beduin, as had been their fathers in and around Najd.

But with a fairly undisputed domination over Dhafrah, the tribe also came to appreciate the economic opportunities which the district's shallow coastline had in store. Maybe the reason why some of the Bani Yās tribes took to the waters of the Gulf was the one given by an official of the Government of India sometime before 1856: "The larger portion was composed of beduin residing in the interior, and tending their flocks; but some few individuals, reduced to poverty through loss of their cattle, took up their abode on the shores of the Persian Gulf."[62] There was, however, no permanent settlement on the coast because of the lack of potable water. The pattern of life for many of the Bani Yās sections changed considerably after some water was discovered in 1761 on Abu Dhabi Island, which also happened to have a sheltered anchorage, as good as any on the shallow coast between Dubai and Khaur al ʿUdaid. Within the course of two years a village of some 400 houses sprang up on the island. This first permanent settlement on the island developed rapidly, although the shaikhs of the Bani Yās continued to reside in the interior for several decades. The successors of D̲iyāb bin ʿĪsa Āl Bū Falāḥ, who died in 1793, made Abu Dhabi their place of residence and thus the capital of the Bani Yās.

The Bani Yās seem to have gradually adapted their lives to make the best possible use of the economic opportunities which the country afforded. Many groups of the Bani Yās built themselves palm frond houses near their date gardens in the Līwā as a permanent abode. Others returned to their Līwā possessions only during the date harvest. Their camels were taken to graze in the winter in Dhafrah proper and Khatam, and even as far away as Qatar and al Ḥāsā. Most of the Bani Yās engaged in the seasonal pearling, and at the beginning of the 20th century over 400 boats on the pearl banks of the Gulf belonged to the Bani Yās. They sailed from Abu Dhabi and its sheltered harbour of Baṭīn[63] as well as from other landing-places on the shallow coast nearer to the Līwā. The many islands adjacent to the coast of the shaikhdom of Abu Dhabi were also used in various ways by the Bani Yās. Dalmā, Ṣīr Bani Yās, Ghāghah and a few others have been permanently inhabited and served as supply centres for the pearling communities. Other islands were used during the winter to fish, dry the catch, collect guano, or even to graze camels which were taken across by boat. A more detailed description of the way in which the inhabitants of the shaikhdom of Abu Dhabi made use of the resources of the coast and the hinterland will be given in

Chapters Five and Six. At this point it suffices to state that the Bani Yās of the twentieth century have come to depend for their livelihood as much on their boats as on their camels and palms, and that in order to make full use of all three resources they developed a pattern of seasonal movements for at least part of the family unit.

Sharing the area with other tribes

The dominance of the Bani Yās over all of Dhafrah, which after all could manifest itself only in the undisputed right to the use of the area's resources, was maintained and at times successfully defended by the tribe under the leadership of successive Rulers from one family within the Āl Bū Falāḥ subsection of the Bani Yās. However, possession of Dhafrah was never exclusive, for all parts of it were shared with other tribes—perhaps with the exception of the islands close to the shore where only some Bani Yās sections knew their way through the reefs and shallows. The Manāṣīr seem to have for a long time and at least throughout the 19th century considered the entire territory of the Bani Yās as their rightful abode as well. Other beduin tribes such as the ʿAwāmir, Āl Murrah, Manāhīl and ʿAfār came frequently enough to the area, for the purpose of grazing, to be counted by some observers as subsections of the Bani Yās.[64] Unlike some other areas of the Arabian Peninsula, which were known "homelands" of certain tribes, the wells of Dhafrah (but not all of those actually in the Līwā) are and probably always have been free for the use of any group of beduin and their camels. They were not the exclusive possession of the family or tribe who originally dug them.

The extent to which the Bani Yās and other tribes shared the area and its economic opportunities varied from one group to another. The Manāṣīr, for instance, have, for as long as their presence in Dhafrah has been recorded, which is throughout all of the 19th century, shared this area with the Bani Yās as their principal abode. Being mostly beduin, their way of life differed in some aspects from that of, for instance, the Rumaithāt subsection of the Bani Yās who owned no date gardens and were predominantly fishermen. But unlike the also exclusively beduin ʿAwāmir, the Manāṣīr did own date gardens in certain parts of the Līwā, though none were occupied the whole year round. Of the tribes with whom the Bani Yās share all or part of their territory, the Manāṣīr were the first ones to become loyal subjects to the Āl Bū Falāḥ Rulers, certainly as far as contacts with third parties were concerned. On numerous occasions the Manāṣīr fought alongside their Bani Yās allies and neighbours, and the Āl Bū Falāḥ Rulers in turn were often held responsible for the behaviour of the Manāṣīr.[65] One of many examples of this mutual responsibility was the protracted war between Abu Dhabi and Qatar from 1876 until 1891, one of the causes of which were raids by Manāṣīr camel-riders into Qatar territory as far as the immediate vicinity of Doha. In counter-attacks by Shaikh Jāsim of Qatar, Manāṣīr and Bani Yās suffered alike when some 400 camels were carried off from settlements in the Līwā. This special relationship, which causes any Manṣūri tribesman to call himself an Abu Dhabian in the 1990s, has thus been in existence for several generations regardless of the fact that some Manāṣīr, as some sections of the Bani Yās and other tribes who visited Abu Dhabi territory once in a while, spent several winters away in Qatar or al Ḥasā. The Manāṣīr are, however, still a distinct tribe of their own, and have not become a subsection of the Bani Yās even though at times they have referred certain disputes to the Ruler of Abu Dhabi. The usual practice, however, was that justice was expected first and foremost from the shaikhs of the subsections of the Manāṣīr and from their own *muṭawwaʿ*.[66]

The first stage in the establishment of the shaikhdom of Abu Dhabi as one of the important tribal powers in the region was thus the appropriation of all of al Dhafrah by the Bani Yās. They may not have had exclusive domination of the neighbouring grazing areas as far as Oman and Qatar, but even there Bani Yās influence was sufficiently strongly felt by the middle of the 18th century that in the *Bombay Selections* they are mentioned as follows: "The original seat of the Beniyas, . . . was in Nujd, but on leaving that part of Arabia they settled in the tract of country extending between Biddah [old name for Doha in Qatar] and Brymee."[67] The standing of the Bani Yās and their Rulers was further enhanced by the fact that the close links which developed between the Bani Yās and the Manāṣīr meant not only some increase in the tax income of the Āl Bū Falāḥ Rulers but was a most welcome addition to the fighting force of the shaikhdom, which was deemed by the already-quoted Captain Taylor in 1818 to have been about "twenty thousand excellent musketeers".[68]

The foothold in the Buraimi area develops into the town of al ʿAin

At the present time, the territory of the Emirate of Abu Dhabi is divided into three administrative units, of which Abu Dhabi Town, the capital, is the most densely populated. It is, however, closely followed in size and importance by the area comprising al ʿAin and the other five non-Omani villages of the Buraimi Oasis: Jīmi, Hīli, Muʿtiriḍ, al Muwaijʿi, and al Qaṭṭārah. The rule of the Āl Bū Falāḥ over parts of the economically and strategically desirable oasis is the result of the expansion of Bani Yās influence in this area over several generations by both warlike and peaceful means.

Early developments As described in the first part of this chapter, Buraimi, the ancient Tu'ām, was a favoured target for the tribal groups which migrated from Yemen and settled in Oman before the Hijrah. The now second most numerous tribe in the oasis, the Dhawāhir, may have come to the area in this wave of Azdite immigration. Their name suggests a long and close relationship with the Dhāhirah, which has been the name of the mountain foreland to the south of the oasis for many centuries.[69] The most numerous tribe in the oasis, the Naʿīm, came in a later wave from Yemen along the edge of the Rubʿal Khāli. The almost consistently bad relationship between the two tribes may indicate that the latter dispossessed the former of much of their property in this area.

The Bani Yās played a part in the politics of the oasis as early as 1633, when the already-mentioned Omani shaikh Nāṣir bin Qaḥṭān, who had established himself in al Ḥasā, attacked the fort of the Imam's *wāli* in Buraimi with the help of "Bedouins of el-Dhafreh", that is, the Bani Yās. On this occasion the Omani possession was saved by the intervention of the "chief Wāli . . . with an army from Nezwa", who "ordered the demolition of all the Forts of el-Jow, except that of the Imam, and the enemies were dispersed."[70]

One may assume that those of the beduin Bani Yās who visited the vicinity of Buraimi from al Khatam, and who almost certainly used the markets of the oasis, were comparing the size of the crop on the date palms watered by *falaj* in Buraimi with that on their palms in the Līwā, which had to survive on the water which could be reached by the roots. The idea of selling a few camels for the possession of a date garden in the Buraimi oasis may have been in the mind of many a Bani Yās tribesman, and a number of such transactions at least with the Dhawāhir inhabitants of the oasis must have taken place already early in the 19th century.

The Ruler of Abu Dhabi used a dispute between the Naʿīm and the Dhawāhir to join forces with the latter because, as he put it in a letter to the Political Resident in Bushire in 1839, "you are aware that the country of Zuweir (Dhawāhir) belongs to my father Shakbooṭ, and that the date groves are common to them and us."[71] But for the period from 1800 until 1869, the political conditions in Buraimi were anything but inviting for such ventures. The reason was the five successive invasions of Wahhābi troops into parts of Oman, which affected Buraimi first and foremost.[72] During the interim periods when the Wahhābis were forced to withdraw their garrison and while the Sultan was hard put to reassert his authority over this distant part of his large territory, other powers in the area tried to gain influence in the oasis and over its inhabitants. Thus, for instance, the Ruler of Shārjah, Sulṭān bin Ṣaqr, the traditional rival of the Ruler of Abu Dhabi for influence over the beduin of all of Trucial Oman, broke an agreement which he had concluded with the Sultan regarding the neutrality of the forts at the oasis. Another agreement was, however, forced upon him in 1824, of which the Ruler of Abu Dhabi, Shaikh Ṭaḥnūn bin Shakhbūṭ, was a signatory. Furthermore, Shaikh Ṭaḥnūn's rightful interests in Buraimi were implicitly recognised in the conditions of this agreement. The Ruler of Shārjah was obliged to destroy the forts he had occupied in the Imām's territory in Buraimi in exchange for the destruction of a fort which the Ruler of Abu Dhabi had built on the fringe of Shārjah's territory in Dairah with the intent of counteracting Shārjah's expansion in the direction of al Jau.[73]

Meanwhile the town of Abu Dhabi had continued to grow, and attracted an increasing number of tribesmen from the hinterland including the oasis of Buraimi and its vicinity. They flocked in large numbers before the beginning of the pearling season, but at other times of the year there was also an increasing amount of coming and going between Buraimi and Abu Dhabi. Caravans brought dates[74] and other goods from the interior of Oman to the growing coastal market and took dried fish and imported goods back to the hinterland. This increasingly close contact and the fact that some Bani Yās already owned gardens in the oasis made it necessary for the Rulers of Abu Dhabi to involve themselves in the affairs of the oasis; over and above that, successive Rulers of Abu Dhabi from the 1820s onwards deliberately worked at increasing their influence in the oasis. Thus, by 1829 the Ruler of Abu Dhabi had effected peace between the Naʿīm of the oasis who had been in alliance with their relative, the Ruler of ʿAjmān, and the breakaway Āl Bū Shāmis section.[75]

During the rule of Shaikh Khalīfah bin Shakhbūṭ, who succeeded his brother Ṭaḥnūn in 1833 (after he and his brother Sulṭān had killed Ṭaḥnūn), the emigration of the Āl Bū Falāsah section of the Bani Yās to Dubai, repeated attempts at secession by the Qubaisāt section of the Bani Yās, and a prolonged war with Sulṭān bin Ṣaqr of Shārjah, stretched the resources of Abu Dhabi to their limits. Nevertheless Khalīfah availed himself of the opportunity presented by a quarrel between the Na'īm and the Dhawāhir in the Buraimi oasis to intervene on the latter's behalf and try to evict the Na'īm from the oasis in 1839, justifying his intervention by saying that the date groves "are common to them (Dhawāhir) and us".[76] A peace was effected in 1840 when the British Political Resident, at that time Captain Hamerton, visited the oasis under the protection of the Āl Bū Shāmis shaikh.[77] Soon after that a dispute arose between the Bani Yās, supported by the Manāṣīr, and the Bani Qitab, a tribe living immediately to the north of the oasis along the communication line between it and the towns of Shārjah, Dubai and 'Ajmān. In a subsequent agreement between Shaikh Khalīfah and the shaikhs of the tribes in and around Buraimi, Shaikh Khalīfah accepted full responsibility for the Bani Yās and the Manāṣīr and for the first time also for the Dhawāhir. In August 1841 Commodore G.B. Brucks reported to the Political Resident, Persian Gulf, on the news regarding the coast from Abu Dhabi to Ra's al Khaimah and the interior. According to his information some Manāṣīr were in particularly close relationship with the Dhawāhir, who afforded them refuge at times; he referred to the Dhawāhir as "belonging to Khalīfah and occupying six or seven villages in the neighbourhood of Brahamee, and under the immediate control of his Father", Shaikh Shakhbūṭ.[78] By 1844 the picture of tribal allegiance in the Buraimi area presented itself to the Residency Agent in Shārjah, Mullah Ḥusain, as follows: "Sheikh Khuleefa bin Shackbooṭ and his forces consisting of horsemen and Camel men set out from Aboothabee on the commencement of the hot weather. I heard of their being at Brymee and that all the Naim tribes, the Al boo-Shamis and Al boo Khureyban and the other Beduin Tribes such as the Beni Kuttub [Qitab], Beni Kaab, Ghuflah and Zowahir [Dhawāhir], the whole had entered into engagements with him and became united with him as one. It appears to me that at the present time there is not throughout the interior one Beduin tribe opposed to him."[79] Shaikh Khalīfah's successor Sa'īd bin Ṭaḥnūn (1845–55) proved equally successful at rallying the tribes of the area around him, in this case to counter another attempt of the Wahhābis to resume their occupation of Buraimi. He captured his own two forts back from the Wahhābi commander in 1848 with the help of Dhawāhir as well as ʿAwāmir tribesmen. Under his command the Bani Qitab, the Ghafalah, the ʿAwāmir and the Bani Yās assembled in Khatam and the Manāṣīr and the Mazārīʿ section of the Bani Yās from the Līwā waited in Dhafrah to fall upon the relieving Wahhābi force under the command of Saʿad bin Muṭlaq. When the Wahhābis were eventually evicted from their positions in the oasis itself by 1850, Shaikh Saʿīd again had all the tribes of the area behind him, including the Naʿīm, and he cooperated closely with the Sultan of Muscat and—for once—also with the Ruler of Shārjah.

The last attempt of the Wahhābis to invade Oman in 1853 resulted in failure in 1869 and in a further consolidation of the Ruler of Abu Dhabi's influence in the oasis. The Sultan of Muscat, ʿAzzān bin Qais, who had together with the Naʿīm defeated the Wahhābi garrison of Buraimi, appointed his *wāli* to the fort of Buraimi, which was held by the Ruler of Abu Dhabi on behalf of the Sultan for a short while. The other forts were returned to the Naʿīm. Shaikh Saʿīd obtained an allowance from Sultan ʿAzzān in return for his defending this distant area of the Sultanate. This allowance, called *farīḍah*, continued under the successors of the Sultan and the Bani Yās Ruler, and during the rule of Zāyid bin Khalīfah (1855–1909) amounted to 3,000 Maria Theresa Dollars. The money was collected by the Sultan from the people of Ṣuḥār and the Wādi Jizi as a tax called *shūfah*, because they were the people who benefited from this arrangement.

The role of Shaikh Zāyid bin Khalīfah It was under the most remarkable and long-living Ruler, Shaikh Zāyid bin Khalīfah, that the Āl Bū Falāḥ influence on the politics of the oasis developed into undisputed possession of a large part of it. Thus the foothold which was gained during the first half of the 19th century became a position of pre-eminence for at least some of the Bani Yās, their allies and certainly their Ruler. The strongest lever to obtain political and strategic gains for Abu Dhabi's Ruler was still the hereditary feud between the Dhawāhir and the Naʿīm, as it had been throughout at least a century with brief periods of cordial relations *vis-à-vis* a common enemy. The actual annexation of those parts of the oasis which had previously belonged to the Dhawāhir was, however, effected peacefully by purchase. Shaikh Zāyid and his sons, especially the eldest, Khalīfah, bought up various gardens and a large proportion of the water rights, if not whole *aflāj*, and also later founded the new settlement of Masʿūdi. At least until 1887 Shaikh Zāyid seems to have followed a persistent but peaceful policy in his take-over bid and there are no records of enforced eviction of Dhawāhir and subsequent distribution of the land to all and sundry among the Bani Yās.

However, when this general trend of the Āl Bū Falāḥ policy to want both to own and to rule the oasis first became unmistakably obvious during the latter decades of Shaikh Zāyid bin Khalīfah's rule, the Dhawāhir rebelled. Shaikh Zāyid was determined to continue on this road to success, and having at last arrived at a state of peaceful co-existence with the Naʿīm[80] he went to war. in 1887 with those Dhawāhir who opposed him. It took him one month to subdue them, and he felt the necessity to take two of the Dhawāhir shaikhs as hostages against further opposition. In 1891, however, he had to march on the oasis once again, this time supported by the Shaikh of Dubai with 30 horsemen and 300 camelmen. He captured the main village of the Dhawāhir, then known as ʿAin Dhawāhir (now simply called al ʿAin), and underlined the changed situation by building a fort there which was completed in 1897. The other four Dhawāhir villages, Jīmi, Hīli, al Qaṭṭārah and Muʿtiriḍ came automatically under his domination too, although even at the time of his death in 1909 the population in all these villages was still predominantly Dhawāhir. Masʿūdi on the other hand was exclusively inhabited by Bani Yās, while Jāhili, of which the Āl Bū Falāḥ took possession in 1897, consisted of several date gardens. These gardens were rapidly expanded, but only the shaikhs' gardeners lived there.

As a symbol of his successful annexation as well as for practical administrative purposes Shaikh Khalīfah appointed the paramount shaikh (*tamīmah*) of the Dhawāhir, Aḥmad bin Muḥammad bin Hilāl, as his representative in the oasis. He was called *wāli*, and this step therefore brings the oasis, or at least the largest part of it, in line with the so called "dependencies" which other Trucial Rulers and the Sultan maintained under the administration of *wālis*. He collected taxes from all the villages under Āl Bū Falāḥ rule; in addition, the Dhawāhir also had to pay a subsidy to the Āl Bū Falāḥ Shaikh.[81]

The other villages—Buraimi village, Ḥamāsah, and the village of Ṣaʿarah—were still mainly inhabited by various branches of the Naʿīm, who continued to receive a regular subsidy from the Sultan.

Their *tamīmah*, Sulṭān bin Muḥammad al Ḥamūda, of the Āl Bū Kharaibān section, was the Sultan's *wāli*. But being irrevocably split into two sections, the Āl Bū Kharaibān and the Āl Bū Shāmis,[82] the Na'īm were weakened by constant internal strife. The *tamīmah* needed support in asserting his authority over the other elements of the Na'īm in Dhāhirah, at the western end of the Wādi Jizi, in the Wādi Ḥattā and in the region adjoining al Jau in the direction of Shārjah and 'Ajmān; the latter was being wrested from their hands by the Bani Ka'ab and the Bani Qitab. Occasional support came from the Ruler of 'Ajmān and the headman of Ḥamrīyah on the coast, both of whom were members of a Na'īm subsection; Sulṭān bin Muḥammad al Ḥamūda became, however, very much dependent on the assistance and friendship of Shaikh Zāyid bin Khalīfah, who had married one of his daughters.

The Na'īm of Buraimi were certainly not in a position to make independent policy decisions within the oasis or outside it during Zāyid bin Khalīfah's rule. On every move they consulted him either personally or through his Dhawāhir representative Aḥmad bin Hilāl.[83] In 1895, for instance, the 'Awāmir declared war against the Na'īm, and Sulṭān bin Muḥammad al Ḥamūda wrote to Aḥmad bin Hilāl: "We could not do anything against them because our interests and yours are one. . . . Whatever you decide please let us know because they [the 'Awāmir] are with you." When in 1905 the Bani Qitab built a fort in the traditionally Na'īmi-controlled Wādi Ḥattā and attacked caravans moving through this important pass between Dubai and the Bāṭinah, and took the village of Masfūṭ, the *tamīmah* of the Na'īm appealed from his fort in Buraimi village to Zāyid for help, through Aḥmad bin Hilāl: "We are relying on God and on him in all matters . . . for as you know we are [in Zāyid's hand] like an article in the hand of its maker." At a meeting of the Trucial Shaikhs in Dubai in April 1905 to settle this dispute, Zāyid stood up for the Na'īm, and Masfūṭ was returned to them.[84]

The meeting in Dubai is an illustration of Zāyid's successful pursuit of the two closely related aims. First, several villages in the Buraimi Oasis paid tax and had become entirely loyal to the Āl Bū Falāḥ. As Captain P.Z. Cox, who travelled to Buraimi in 1902 and 1905, put it: "The real power in the neighbourhood is the Shaikh of Abu Dhabi, whose material possessions and consequent influence in the oasis are yearly increasing."[85] Secondly, he had been able to increase his influence over both settled and beduin tribes outside the oasis to the extent that his opinion had to be consulted on matters concerning even distant areas such as the Wādi Jizi, the Bāṭinah in Oman, and Fujairah on the coast of the Indian Ocean. This state of affairs was no coincidence or mere filling of a power vacuum, but the deliberately pursued aim of Shaikh Zāyid bin Khalīfah; and ". . . the Shaikh of Abu Dhabi was still anxious to convince the Bani Qitab of the impossibility of opposing his wishes and the Shaikh of Umm-al-Qaiwain of the folly of attempting to compete with his influence in Bedouin affairs".[86] The other Trucial shaikhs could see the necessity to curb Zāyid's ambitions, and in April 1906, after another clash of vital interests, negotiated with him a formal agreement on spheres of influence over the beduin tribes.

This agreement was, however, soon quite far from reality, because most of the tribes concerned had not even been consulted, and the additional influence which Zāyid had, with the Sultan's blessing and continued payment of a regular subsidy, over the beduin and the settled tribes of the Dhāhirah as far as ʿIbri[87] and over tribes under the administration of the *wāli* of Ṣuḥār, in turn increased his standing with those beduin who lived chiefly in Trucial Oman and whose alliance and assistance in case of war were constantly sought after by the Rulers of the coast.

Developments since the first decade of this century After the death in 1909 of Zāyid bin Khalīfah, four of his sons followed him in such quick succession that a less well-founded system of maintaining the newly-established Āl Bū Falāḥ authority in the oasis would have collapsed. As it was, only the extent of the political influence over the tribes in Oman fluctuated considerably, but the possession of the six villages was not contested by any of the concerned parties from the area—only by a renewed claim from Saudi Arabia.

The Abu Dhabi part of the oasis was administered on behalf of the Āl Bū Falāḥ by Aḥmad bin Hilāl al Dhāhiri until his death in 1936, well into the period of Shaikh Shakhbūṭ bin Sulṭān's rule. During the latter's long rule from 1928 to 1966 more Bani Yās bought property in the oasis, which had finally become the favourite retreat during the hot humid summer months for those families who otherwise lived in Abu Dhabi town. Many other families of the Bani Yās and the Manāṣīr could not afford to move permanently into the Buraimi oasis, and retained the old pattern of returning to their houses in the Līwā for the summer if they were not on the pearl banks.

The ascendancy of al 'Ain and the other Abu Dhabi villages in Buraimi had a lasting effect on the way in which the shaikhdom functioned. Not only was the emigration of several sections of the Bani Yās from the Līwā into the Buraimi oasis, usually by way of Abu Dhabi town, the expression of a social regrouping on the strength of relative prosperity (from pearling or work in an oil company abroad), but it went hand in hand with a considerable decline in the interest of the ruling family in matters concerning the Dhafrah and the Līwā. Already the sons of Zāyid bin Khalīfah, with the exception of Ḥamdān, hardly ever visited the Līwā, and even Shaikh Shakhbūṭ and his brother Shaikh Zāyid, who regained the influence which their grandfather had had over so many tribes outside the limits of what came to be the territory of the State of Abu Dhabi, turned their full attention to this ancestral homeland of the Bani Yās only when it was seriously threatened by the Saudi claims. Shaikh Shakhbūṭ made a tour of the Dhafrah, Līwā and neighbouring districts in 1951 and Shaikh Zāyid accompanied the Assistant Political Agent through that area in 1952; on both occasions the inhabitants of the Līwā villages voiced their discontent with the apparent neglect they experienced from the Āl Bū Falāḥ Rulers. This, however, did not influence the basic opinion of the Bani Yās that they were and always had been subjects of whoever was the Ruler of Abu Dhabi.

But the closely-allied Manāṣīr took exception to some of the Āl Bū Falāḥ Rulers in Abu Dhabi. This was demonstrated by the hostile reaction of the Manāṣīr towards those sons of Zāyid bin Khalīfah who did not recognise the longstanding privileges of the Manāṣīr and their entitlement to subsidies. The Na'īm of Buraimi were also much less firmly under the influence of the Āl Bū Falāḥ Rulers after Zāyid's death. They eventually gained virtual independence from everyone, including the Sultan in Muscat, and claimed in 1949 *vis-à-vis* the oil company, which had concluded agreements for all the territory of both Abu Dhabi and Oman, that they should sign their own agreements as independent Rulers.

Following the concessionary agreements concluded in the late 1930s, the use of a particular area by a certain tribe was translated into territorial possession. Tribal allegiance to one Ruler or another—at all times the most important issue in tribal politics—became the subject of a great deal of probing and research. In particular, the so called "Buraimi Dispute",[88] although it was the cause of a regrettable period of bad relations between the two camps, was a blessing in disguise as far as the historiography of the tribes in the disputed area is concerned. The last concerted effort at collecting material on the tribes had been some on-the-spot investigations during 1904–7 to update the archival material available to the Government of India for the compilation of the *Gazetteer*.[89] The dispute over large parts of Dhafrah and over the oasis of Buraimi, which came to a head in the early 1950s, made it essential for all the concerned parties to collect as much evidence as possible on the wandering habits and the allegiances of the beduin tribes of the areas, and on the number, habitat, occupation, tax payments, seasonal movements and other questions regarding the settled or semi-nomadic population. Such research brought much of the information contained in the *Gazetteer* up to date. The changes which took place during five decades in the life pattern of the tribes were recorded. Some of the initial reports of these meticulous investigations carried out by government officials as well as oil company employees on both sides in the dispute remained confidential. Material which stood up to repeated probing and historical correlation was eventually used in the memoranda submitted by each side to an arbitration tribunal which was convened for the first time in Nice on 23 January 1955. These memoranda became known as the "UK Memorial" and the "Saudi Memorial".[90] Both have been used and quoted extensively by scholars who adopted the history of this dispute as the subject of specialised research.

Thus the shaikhdom of Abu Dhabi became a well-studied model which illustrated the different types of tribal claims to a particular area and the relationships between a Ruler and the various tribal groups, which could take any form from unconditional submission to traditionally-established loyalty, to alliance or just temporary respect. The expansion of the influence of the Āl Bū Falāḥ Rulers went hand in hand with the appropriation by the Bani Yās sub-tribes, first of all of Dhafrah and the Līwā, then of the coast and islands, especially of Abu Dhabi and later Dubai. In all these areas the Bani Yās did not have to compete with the established rights of previously settled people, but they shared these rights with the Manāṣīr and some sections of migrating beduin tribes. Extending Āl Bū Falāḥ influence into the area bordering Oman meant competing not only with the incumbent owners of the settlements, mainly Dhawāhir and Naʿīm, but also with the nomadic and settled tribes of the neighbourhood, who had to be kept sufficiently well under control so that they would not be a threat to the Bani Yās ascendancy in the oasis. Hence the Āl Bū Falāḥ's growing interest in the affairs of all the other settled and nomadic tribes which were in any way associated with the Buraimi oasis. Inevitably, the latter interest brought the Āl Bū Falāḥ Rulers into conflict with the interests of the other Rulers in the area.

Conclusions

The number of beduin splinter-groups actually living in Abu Dhabi territory during any one winter has always been impossible to ascertain. The fact that some Āl Murrah as well as Rashīd, Manāhīl and ʿAfār groups and some individuals from other Omani and Dhufāri tribes came to the Buraimi oasis for the summer or to the desert of Abu Dhabi for the winter shows that until the advent of oil transformed the beduin way of life, the only really lasting authority was the capricious climate. If rainfall was plentiful in the Dhafrah and was scanty elsewhere, many beduin from far away would converge on it; and the traditional users of that *dār*, the Bani Yās and the Manāṣīr, knowing full well that they might have to move a long distance to another tribe's *dār* some other winter when there would be little rain in Dhafrah, would not object as long as the visitors did not engage in raiding. The desert version of law and order was enforced by rules common and known to all nomadic and semi-settled people of Eastern Arabia. The few disputes which were not settled among the tribes themselves were brought to the Āl Bū Falāḥ Ruler or his *wāli*. The Āl Bū Falāḥ Ruler usually saw to it that the visits even of small groups from the beduin tribes were good opportunities to befriend people whose help might one day be very useful indeed.

Once the Buraimi oasis, this focus of tribal interests, had been firmly added to the territory over which the Āl Bū Falāḥ had undisputed tax-authority, they needed as wide a screen of "non-hostility" as could be created by influencing the inter-tribal politics of the whole region. Some of these beduin groups were of only peripheral importance while in Abu Dhabi territory, but were numerous and powerful elsewhere and had powerful friends, or enemies.

Tribal politics were concerned with authority over people, not over territory with boundaries. One of the most instructive illustrations for this is the Buraimi oasis in its strategic position.

The establishment of a "state" and the delineation of the state's "territory" were very much out of tune with the traditional conduct of local politics. Since the sovereignty over people was far from permanently binding, sovereignty over territory was even less tangible in the tribal politics of which Abu Dhabi was still part in the 1950s. It is also not enough just to enumerate the tribes and subtribes which made up the population of the state of Abu Dhabi. Their mutual relationships, their political loyalties, as well as the extent to which their economic pursuits depended on the use of particular geographical locations, and how all these factors changed over the first five decades of this century, will have to be taken into account.

3 The tribes on the fringe of the Trucial Coast

Their role *vis-à-vis* the coastal shaikhdoms

The statement in the *Gazetteer* that "Buraimi is independent" seems at first sight to be quite out of date considering the expansion of Abu Dhabi's authority over the largest part of the oasis during the 19th century. But a closer look at the tribes which are intimately connected with the oasis and the country between it and the ports of the Trucial Coast reveals that for all of the 19th century and most of the 20th century few of them were so steadfast in their allegiance to any one of the Rulers as to justify calling them his subjects. They rather formed an aggregate of potential allies which each one of the area's Rulers tried to bring under his control. The Āl Bū Falāḥ were successful in the case of the Dhawāhir living in the oasis; however, the loyalty of the other important tribe in the oasis, the Naʿīm, to the Sultan of Oman was at times only nominal. Many of the tribes and tribal sections inhabiting or frequenting the mountain foreland and the *wādis* between the Buraimi oasis and the oasis of Ḏaid were virtually independent of any of the Rulers of the Trucial Coast and also of the remote power of the Sultan in Muscat. This fact is also borne out time and again in the way in which the officials of the British Government of India carefully avoided getting involved in the tribal politics of this part of the hinterland.

Yet the disputes, alliances and ascendancies of some tribes over others in that region greatly influenced politics on the coast. Not only because most of these tribes, as for instance the Naʿīm, had both settled and beduin sections in the hinterland as well as sections living in the ports of the Trucial Coast; but also the tribes of the hinterland relied on the coastal towns for many needs in their precariously-balanced economy. Some beduin came to the coast to work on the pearling boats, others needed supplies from there such as dried fish; the carrying trade which formed the livelihood of some camel-breeders depended on a healthy trade between the ports and the villages in the interior. Buraimi or D̲aid could play their role as centres for trade and barter for the tribes only if supplies could come through unhindered.

Since none of the Trucial Rulers had more than at the most a few dozen armed men permanently employed, among other duties, to look after their security, the only further source of fighting-men available to any of the Rulers in a dispute were the beduin groups. The Āl Bū Falāḥ usually were in a position to rally large numbers of beduin armed men to help them to fight their wars without formal arrangements regarding remuneration. The Rulers in the other shaikhdoms could sometimes rely on voluntary tribal fighters, but on most occasions they had to find the money to pay beduin to fight for them. This necessity to hire fighting-men, rather than to persuade them by more subtle means of tribal politics to adopt the cause, seems to have come to the fore during the first decades of the 20th century.

The Sultan in Muscat was equally interested in the politics of the tribes in the hinterland of the Trucial Coast. Almost all these tribes declared at one time or another their loyalty to him and paid taxes to the authorities in Muscat. Some remained for decades steadfast subjects of the Sultan; others exploited the fact that communications between Muscat and the western slopes of the Ḥajar mountains were difficult, and they called themselves subjects of Muscat mostly in order to discourage other Rulers from trying to exert authority over them.

During the time under consideration, life in this area was very deeply affected by the inter-tribal politics of three distinguishable "circuits". One was the shaikhdom of Abu Dhabi, where tribal politics were largely concerned with the two settled inland centres, the Līwā and the Buraimi villages. Abu Dhabi was also concerned with the politics of tribes living in the Dhāhirah or roaming as far as Hadhramaut, the Rubʿ al Khāli, and Qatar. The second "circuit" consisted of the settlements of the north-eastern Trucial Coast and the mountainous areas close by, which were within relatively easy reach of each other and formed a socio-economic entity with a distinctly maritime character. Their internal politics became interwoven with their interest in maritime peace, which the British Government of India pursued in this region for many decades. This "circuit" can be labelled the "Qāsimi Empire" because almost all the territory north of the line between the creek at Dubai and Khaur Kalba was much of the time dominated by the Qawāsim Rulers. The third "circuit" was the western foreland of the mountains with Buraimi, D̲aid, and some small oases forming focal points for the very involved tribal politics. Now, this district is partly Omani territory and partly in the United Arab Emirates, but at the time when the material for the *Gazetteer* was being compiled, it was deemed that the most suitable term for this district was "Independent Oman".[91]

Na'īm

Most tribes which made up the population of the coastal towns or villages on the Gulf proper had beduin sections who shared parts of this semi-desert *dār*. The most important tribe in the hinterland used to be the Na'īm, not only because they were the most numerous tribe and considered this district as their headquarters, but also because they were widely dispersed throughout Trucial Oman and the Sultanate. The total strength of the beduin and settled members of the Na'īm after World War II was estimated at 5,000. They could muster about 2,000 armed men. According to the Gazetteer the tribe was about 13,000 strong at the turn of the century, but its strength and their political influence had been on the decline for decades because the tribe was torn by constant in-fighting among its subtribes.[92]

The Na'īm are divided into three sections: the Āl Bū Kharaibān, the Khawāṭir, and the Āl Bū Shāmis. The latter section has, however, become almost independent during the last five decades and associated itself very frequently with the Āl Bū Falāḥ. Its shaikhs have nevertheless stated from time to time that the section still recognises the *tamīmah* of all the Na'īm.[93] Having gained a predominant position in the Buraimi oasis area mostly at the expense of the Dhawāhir, the Ghāfiri Na'īm resented the inroads made by the Bani Yās and their allies the Manāṣīr, both of whom were Hināwi in Omani political terms.

Unlike most of the tribes in the area they adopted the Wahhābi doctrines. But later the Na'īm were among those tribes who assisted the Āl Bū Falāḥ Ruler Khalīfah bin Shakhbūṭ in 1848 and the Sultan ʿAzzān bin Qais in 1869 to evict the Wahhābis from Buraimi.[94] The Naʿīm were subsequently allowed to occupy most of the forts in the oasis which were in or near Buraimi village. The *tamīmah* of the Naʿīm took up residence in the fort of Buraimi village and was considered to be the representative of the Sultan in the area, receiving a regular allowance in the same way as other *wālis*.

At the turn of the century 5,500 people were living in the Buraimi oasis; there were about 300 houses in Buraimi village, Ḥamāsa and Ṣaʿarah occupied almost exclusively by Naʿīm. To the south-east of the oasis the Naʿīm villages are mostly of the Āl Bū Shāmis section; they are Ḥafīt and Qābil at the southern foot of Jabal Ḥafīt, and Dhank in Dhāhirah. Others lived in Sanainah, south of the entrance to the Wādi Jizi, which leads through the mountains to the Bāṭinah coast, where there were some Naʿīm in Ṣanqar. In the other direction settled Naʿīm were found in ʿAjmān town, where they had some 25 houses; the ruling family of ʿAjmān belongs to the Āl Bū Kharaibān section of the Naʿīm. In the small port of Ḥamrīyah, a dependency of Shārjah, the headman and some 250 of its 300 houses belonged to the Darāwishah subsection (Āl Bū Shāmis division). The same subsection dominated Ḥīrah, another Shārjah dependency (also 250 Naʿīm houses). The Naʿīm formed a substantial part of the settled population in Shārjah town, with 100 houses (Darāwishah), and elsewhere in Shārjah territory, such as Ḏaid, with 30 Khawāṭir houses.

Of the 2,500 nomadic Naʿīm, about 1,600 were usually somewhere in Trucial Oman and its hinterland, and considered the district of al Jau as their headquarters. They shared the Dhāhirah with many Omani tribes and Khatam with the Bani Yās and the Dhāwahir. Although the Naʿīm were not settled anywhere in the Wādi Ḥattā, the beduin Naʿīm and their *tamīmah* at Buraimi usually protected the inhabitants of the village of Masfūṭ in the *wādi*, who were at enmity with the Dubai-protected people of Ḥajarain. In what came to be considered as Ra's al Khaimah territory, beduin of the Khawāṭir section shared the use of the Jiri plain with the Ghafalah and others. In other parts of that district between the mountains and the coast the beduin Naʿīm had lost their once undisputed predominance to the Bani Kaʿab, who together with the Bani Qitab became their great rivals. The beduin Naʿīm had camel herds as well as flocks of sheep and goats, and since grazing and water were plentiful even near their date gardens, they never needed to go far afield and did not venture into the sands. The *U.K. Memorial* therefore calls them "pastoral" rather than beduin.[95]

The Na'īm of Buraimi sporadically professed their loyalty to the Sultan in Muscat. The paramount shaikh, Ṣaqr bin Sulṭān al Ḥamūda of Buraimi, who personally owned half the date gardens at Dhank,[96] visited Muscat in 1938. The question of allegiance of the various factions of the Na'īm became an important issue after the Sultan of Muscat had signed an agreement in 1937 with Petroleum Concessions Ltd. to explore for oil in all the territory under his authority. The Na'īm saw that they had the option of professing themselves subjects of the Sultan in Muscat, the Imām who ruled in the virtually independent mountainous area of Inner Oman, the Āl Bū Falāḥ Ruler of Abu Dhabi or one of the other Trucial Rulers, or else to try to maintain their own independence. With the exception of the last alternative, all other options had at different times different attractions because the Na'īm could expect a subsidy of some kind from any one of the Rulers in the area in exchange for their allegiance, although the Na'īm no longer had a fighting force as big as before, consisting in the 1940s of a mere 300 to 400 rifles. Whichever course the shaikh decided upon, he could never be sure of the complete loyalty of all the Na'īm to the chosen overlord. This possibility of a choice further deepened the rift between the various factions of the Na'īm and between the shaikhs of subsections, headmen of villages each becoming that much more independent themselves. Thus at times during the later 1940s the nominal *tamīmah* of the Na'īm lived in fear of losing his position to the Na'īm Ruler of 'Ajmān, Rāshid bin Ḥumaid, who had already seized the Na'īm-dominated village of Masfūṭ in 1948 from Shaikh Ṣaqr bin Sulṭān al Ḥamūda, who had been unable to oppose Rāshid's forces because he could not raise any armed men. Some of the shaikhs of the subsections, such as Aḥmad bin Saif al Ṣalf, of the Khawāṭir at Ḥafīt, could muster about 100 armed men at the time. Shaikh Ṣaqr's influence obviously did not match that of his father, who had been responsible for the Na'īm holding their own in the Buraimi oasis during a period of growing influence of the Āl Bū Falāḥ there.

The Sultan in Muscat recognised that in order to gain genuine and lasting authority over the territories and villages inhabited by the Na'īm, he had to weaken the position of the dissenting shaikhs of the various sections by assisting the *tamīmah* to assert overall authority over the tribe. For a brief period in 1948 his Minister of the Interior,

Aḥmad bin Ibrāhīm, succeeded in this, and most of the shaikhs signed an agreement pledging recognition of Ṣaqr bin Sulṭān.[97] But the Sultan's success was short-lived, as the Na'īm shaikhs soon asserted their independence by trying to grant their own petroleum concessions. Shaikh Ṣaqr bin Sulṭān and Shaikh Rāshid bin Ḥamad, who had become the most important shaikhs of the Āl Bū Shāmis section of the Na'īm in Ḥamāsah, both insisted, first on an agreement with the oil company covering the exploration period only and guaranteeing them Rupees 2 lakhs (£15,000 Sterling); and secondly, on the omission of any mention of the Sultan or of the State of Muscat and Oman in the document. The Sultan insisted on his part that a clause referring to his sovereignty over part of the Buraimi oasis should be included in any agreement with an oil company. However, he offered to allocate to the Na'īm shaikhs a share of one Rupee per ton of the three Rupees per ton which he could expect if oil were ever to be exported from this area. But this did not prove to be a way out of the deadlock.

Thus it came as no surprise that the Na'īm, as well as the other half-independent tribes of the Trucial States hinterland, also responded to the overtures of other powers in the area, namely the representatives of the Saudi King in al Ḥasā, and later his representative in the Buraimi oasis itself. During the 1950s, Rashīd bin Ḥamad of the Āl Bū Shāmis of Ḥamāsah, Muḥammad bin Sālmīn of the beduin Āl Bū Shāmis and 'Ubaid bin Juma'h of the Bani Ka'ab confirmed in letters to the governor of the eastern region of the Saudi Kingdom "our territories are yours".[98] Some of the shaikhs in and around Buraimi assisted and welcomed the Saudi force which established its presence in the Buraimi village and Ḥamāsah in 1952. Considering the past history of virtual independence of the Na'īm and the other tribes in that area it would indeed have been quite out of keeping with the normal function of tribal politics if, in view of the remoteness and intransigence of the Sultan in Muscat, these shaikhs had not responded in some way or other to the approaches of an even greater power in the neighbourhood. Such seemingly contradictory statements as the assertion of allegiance to both the Sultan and Ibn Jalūwi in al Ḥasā within a short span of time were legitimate means frequently used in tribal politics either to come to terms with the powers that be or to try to force the traditional overlord to grant larger subsidies.

The historical-political perspective of this episode of the "Buraimi

Dispute" will be discussed in Chapter Eight; in the present context it illustrates the degree of independence which some tribes of the interior were able to reserve for themselves right up to the time oil was being exported from Oman and Abu Dhabi.

Āl Bū Shāmis

The Āl Bū Shāmis section of the Na'īm had, during the general disintegration of the homogeneity of the Na'īm, established an almost completely separate identity. Originally they represented the beduin section of the tribe and the nomadic element was still dominant during the 1950s, when their total strength was estimated at about 1,000 people including 400 armed men. The shaikh of the beduin at that time was Muḥammad bin Sālmīn bin Raḥmah, who lived either at Sanainah or Qābil south of the Buraimi oasis.[99] The settled Āl Bū Shāmis, although few in numbers, lived in important oases and coastal settlements, and their headmen were accordingly rated as prominent figures. Some owned portions of Dhank, others under Shaikh Rāshid bin Ḥamad al Shāmsi lived in Ḥamāsah. A sizeable section of the population of the ports of Ḥamrīyah and Ḥīrah, both dependencies of Shārjah, has always been Āl Bū Shāmis, and the headmen traditionally come from families within that tribe. The Āl Bū Shāmis came to the coast after they were temporarily driven out of Dhāhirah early in the 19th century. As with the other Na'īm sections, the sovereignty of the Sultan was generally accepted as long as this remained a matter of the usual tax payments on crops, but otherwise did not involve many mutual commitments. The question of who should benefit from the granting of petroleum concessions gave the leaders of the many independent tribal sections strong bargaining positions. For instance, it was alleged that the leader of the beduin Āl Bū Shāmis visited the Sultan in Muscat in about 1948 and offered complete loyalty of his followers for the sum of 10,000 Maria Theresa Dollars, but that the Sultan turned the deal down while giving a considerably smaller sum as a present to the shaikh.

Usually the Na'īm were on bad terms with most of their neighbours, particularly the Bani Ka'ab, the Bani Qitab and the Āl Bū Falāḥ. But the Āl Bū Shāmis, although Ghāfiri like the rest of the Na'īm, came to be steadfast allies of the Āl Bū Falāḥ, possibly since Shaikh Ṭaḥnūn bin Shakhbūṭ had helped them to regain Qābil and Sanainah in Dhāhirah some time before 1833. The Āl Bū Shāmis were usually also on good terms with most of the other tribes of the region, including the Durū' and the Bani Qitab.

Balūsh

The Balūsh of Dhāhirah formed an important element of the settled population in the land between the Trucial Coast and the Sultanate. These Balūsh are not to be identified with the people who had come from the former Omani possession Makrān, now part of Pakistan, to serve in the Sultan's army as mercenaries, nor are they descended from the Balūchis who settled in Muscat, the coastal towns of the Bāṭinah and the Trucial States (according to the *Gazetteer* the latter had about 1,400 Balūchis) as traders and fishermen. While these groups retained the use of their language, the Balūsh of Dhāhirah have a tribal organisation, an exclusive *dār* around their capital Mazīm; they are Sunni and speak Arabic.[100]

On his journey from Abu Dhabi to Muscat in 1902, Major Cox noted particularly that the Balūsh of Dhāhirah had no communications with the Bāṭinah but that their import and export trade was conducted entirely with Abu Dhabi and Dubai. This explains their usually good relationship with the Bani Yās and in particular their shaikh's co-operation with the Āl Bū Falāḥ in the Buraimi area.

At a time of realignment of tribal loyalties during the first decade of this century, the Balūsh of Mazīm had a dispute with and were attacked by their erstwhile protectors the Bani Qitab. When the beduin Bani Qitab converged on Mazīm and hostilities there had claimed some victims, the Balūsh turned to Zāyid bin Khalīfah for help.[101] In February 1906 he collected his forces with the intention of supporting the Balūsh of Mazīm and extracting blood money from the Bani Qitab on behalf of the Balūsh. The Bani Qitab had difficulty finding support, but the young Rāshid bin Aḥmad of Umm al Qaiwain eventually adopted their case as an opportunity to challenge Shaikh Zāyid's influence over the tribes in the hinterland. A general war over the Balūsh dispute was, however, prevented by a meeting of Trucial Rulers and shaikhs of the hinterland, convened in Khawānīj near Dubai in April 1906. It resulted in the written agreement, already mentioned, regarding the Rulers' spheres of influence among the beduin. Shaikh Zāyid bin Khalīfah assumed the responsibility for following up all the claims, "important or trifling", which the Balūsh had against the Bani Qitab, and he instructed his *wāli* Aḥmad bin Hilāl accordingly.[102] In the 1950s, however, the Balūsh followed the example of neighbouring tribes and tried to use as political bargaining points or to obtain handsome subsidies, the keen interest which the Sultan of Oman and the King of Saudi Arabia had in the allegiance of these tribes at a time when prospecting for oil commenced in their *dār*.[103]

Bani Qitab and Bani Kaʿab

The Bani Qitab and the Bani Kaʿab both form very much part of the political scene in the hinterland of the Trucial Coast. Both tribes are Ghāfiri, as are the Naʿīm with whom they share some areas. But the three tribes have rarely been on as good terms as the three principal tribes which share the deserts of Abu Dhabi.

The Bani Kaʿab have the *falaj*-irrigated village of Maḥadhah north of the Buraimi oasis as their centre, but some also live on the Bāṭinah coast, in the Wādi Ḥattā and at the head of the Wādi al Qūr, which joins the sea at Khaur Kalba. The entire sub-tribe of Shwaihiyīn, numbering about 1,000 souls, and according to the *Gazetteer* one other small subsection are entirely nomadic. Another 5,000 people were settled mostly around Maḥadhah and in the neighbouring *wādis* draining towards the Trucial Coast. Some were settled in the Sultanate of Oman, but none lived in the ports of the Trucial Coast. The Bani Kaʿab had displaced the Naʿīm from the desert area south of Shārjah but they in turn had to give way to the Bani Qitab.[104] Although the Naʿīm and the Bani Kaʿab were rarely on good terms, their shaikhs did act in unison for a brief period when it seemed possible to them that they might obtain independent petroleum agreements at the end of the 1940s.

Although the Bani Qitab are numerically weaker than the Bani Kaʿab they have always played a very important part in the tribal politics of Trucial Oman due to their large beduin contingent. The beduin Bani Qitab were 2,100 strong, whereas their settled families numbered only 2,700 people.[105] The former roamed a large part of the Oman promontory on either side of the Ḥajar mountains. The areas in Trucial Oman which they frequented mostly were the tract between the Buraimi oasis and the Jiri plain north-east of Shārjah, the eastern foothills between Wādi al Qūr and Wādi Ḥām, and the good grazing plain around D̲aid. In recent decades this northern section of the tribe separated almost completely from the southern section in Dhāhirah which had the village of Aflāj Bani Qitab as a centre.

While the tribe was still more unified it was more than once in recent history the catalyst for a general re-arrangement of spheres of influence between the Trucial Shaikhs. For instance, in the Wādi Ḥattā dispute of 1905, of the two villages in the Wādi Ḥattā, Masfūṭ and Ḥajarain, the latter had become a virtual dependency of Dubai while the former was under the protection of the Na'īm of Buraimi.[106] With the consent of the people of Masfūṭ, the Bani Qitab built a fort at the head of the *wādi* and stopped passing caravans. The Na'īm of Buraimi and the Ruler of Dubai understandably objected to this interference, while the young Ruler of Umm al Qaiwain, Shaikh Rashīd bin Aḥmad, saw his opportunity to gain a voice in the beduin matters of the Trucial Coast's hinterland. At a meeting of the Rulers in September 1905 in Dubai the actions of the Bani Qitab were condemned by the participants, but Shaikh Rāshid bin Aḥmad's challenge of the venerable Shaikh Zāyid bin Khalīfah's leadership in beduin affairs continued and flared up again at the next outbreak of hostilities in the region. This also involved the Bani Qitab, and it was their previously-mentioned dispute with the Balūsh of Māzam which led to the written agreement, between the Rulers, of April 1906 in which the Bani Qitab were among the tribes assigned to the Ruler of Umm al Qaiwain. But the contest between the Rulers of Umm al Qaiwain and Abu Dhabi smouldered on. The British Government of India, contrary to its general policy, let itself be drawn into this dispute, which had its roots in the hinterland; in February of 1907 the Political Resident in Bushire, Major Cox, arrived off Shārjah in *HMS Lawrence* and mediated between the two parties, who were by then once again at daggers drawn near Umm al Qaiwain's oasis of Falaj al 'Ali.

In more recent years the northern section of the Bani Qitab established its headquarters near D̲aid, and for a time Shaikh Muḥammad bin 'Ali bin Huwaidin obtained an allowance of 2,500 Rupees from the Ruler of Shārjah. The Ruler of Dubai also endeavoured to establish friendly relations with the northern section of the Bani Qitab, which shows that even during the 1940s a strength of 200 to 250 armed and mounted beduin was still an important factor in the reckoning of each of the established local powers. The Bani Qitab section in Dhāhirah was usually on friendly terms with the Sultan, but did not obtain an allowance from him during the 1940s and seemed to have been more closely connected with the Imām of Inner Oman, who maintained a *wāli* at 'Ibri.

The wife of the President Shaikh Zāyid and First Lady of the UAE is from the Bani Qitab.

A new aspect of the old question of allegiance

The period from the end of the Second World War, when the search for oil was taken up in earnest in the Sultanate and on the Trucial Coast, until the end of the war between the Sultan and the Imām in 1959, was a time when the question of the allegiances of the tribes in the hinterland of the Trucial Shaikhdoms and on the western fringe of the Sultanate rose again almost to unprecedented importance. When war broke out between Dubai and Abu Dhabi in 1945, there were again the usual bids for the allegiance of the beduin of the entire area.

Unlike Abu Dhabi, Dubai had no large beduin population within the State, and had to recruit some as mercenaries, at the same time hoping that others would adopt the cause of Dubai of their own accord. After the end of the war in 1948 the oil company began to make use of its pre-war agreements. In the hinterland, where the various interests of the region's powers merged, the shaikhs of non-aligned beduin tribes now saw an opportunity to become independent Rulers. The authority of the Ruler of Abu Dhabi in the Buraimi area was well-defined, but the Sultan of Muscat and Oman, with whom the pre-war agreement was negotiated, was not in a position to guarantee that the exploration parties of the oil company could proceed with their work undisturbed in the territory of the Na'īm and Āl Bū Shāmis. The Sultan did not accept their virtually independent status but nevertheless encouraged the company to negotiate directly with some of the local shaikhs. There was after all a real possibility that the shaikhs of the Buraimi area might sign agreements with another company, and the Sultan and the British Foreign Office, whose responsibility it would have been to see that the 1920 agreement with the Trucial Rulers[107] was enforced, would have found it difficult to stop such a move by the shaikhs. When the "Buraimi Dispute" became fairly acute in August 1952, the attitude of the "independent" tribes in and around the oasis was again a matter of great interest to all parties. The death of the Imām Muḥammad bin Aḥmad bin 'Abdullah al Khalīli in 1954, and the deterioration of relations to the point of open warfare between the new Imām and the Sultan in Oman[108] again brought to the fore the question of allegiance of the tribes in the territory west of the Imām's mountain stronghold. The establishment of a boundary in the Jabal Ḥafīt area recognised by both the Sultan and the Ruler of Abu Dhabi in May 1959 put an end to the independent tribes' opportunities to tip the scale of local politics to any large extent.

4 The multitribal Qāsimi Empire

General Appraisal

In contrast to Abu Dhabi, where the ruling family's position evolved within the already coherent and numerically dominant tribe of the Bani Yās, the Qawāsim were a clan which had succeeded in imposing its authority over a large number of diverse tribes. The name Qawāsim or "Joasmees" was often applied by the British administrators in distant Bombay to all Arabs living on the shores of the Gulf.[109] The reason was that this section of the Hūwalah tribe, who occupied many ports on both sides of the Gulf including Qishim, Lingah, Lāft, Shināṣ and Ra's al Khaimah, had attained prominence. Most Hūwalah sections who engaged in maritime activities were directly or indirectly ruled by the Qawāsim shaikhs. Their capital during the 18th century was the port of Ra's al Khaimah, in the vicinity of the old Julfār. They had a sizeable share of the profitable trade centering on Qishim and Lingah,[110] but such a prominent position antagonised other major powers in the area, notably the Persians, Omanis and later on the British.[111]

On the Arab shore of the Gulf the Qawāsim shaikhs ensured that their authority was not confined to the ports, but included all creeks and coves from which a rival power might otherwise present a challenge, and extended into the hinterland. It cannot have been an easy enterprise to bring under their domination the many tribes, and even some subsections of Omani tribes, living along both coasts of the Musandam Peninsula and in the forbidding mountains of the Ḥajar range.

In the absence of reliable records of this internal alliance it is probably not too far-fetched to assume that most tribes were not subdued by force, but that in particular those who lived on the coast could see the opportunities open to them if they joined in the successful maritime enterprises of the Qawāsim. This assumption is borne out by the fact that the consolidation of the Qāsimi sovereignty over most of the Arab coast north and east of Dubai was completed before the Qāsimi prominence on the waters of the Gulf was dramatically reduced by British intervention, and before the subjects of the Qawāsim Rulers, in common with the inhabitants of other ports on this coast, made pearling their most important source of income. Soon after the beginning of the 19th century the Qawāsim shaikhs confined themselves to administering the area under their sovereignty on the Arab side of the Gulf. The nomadic population as well as the few tribal sections who lived in the *wādi*-oases in the mountains needed to be on reasonably good terms with whoever dominated the ports on which they relied for a market as well as for occasional employment.

The Qāsimi domination over the Musandam promontory was repeatedly contested by the Sultans of Muscat. But from 1850 onwards the sovereignty of the Qawāsim shaikhs was firmly established in the entire coastal and mountainous area north of a line between Shārjah town and Khaur Kalba. The notable exception was the inaccessible terrain inhabited by the various sections and allies of the Shiḥūḥ north of Shaʿam and Dibah. Since this administrative entity soon broke up again into independent shaikhdoms, it may seem arbitrary to use the extent of this former Qāsimi empire as a basis for the enumeration of the tribes in the northern part of the Trucial States. But the Qāsimi-held territory, if Umm al Qaiwain and ʿAjmān are also included, represents in fact those areas of the present State of the UAE which are either mountainous or dominated by the vicinity of inaccessible and barren heights and their water-providing *wādis*. Therefore living conditions in that area are very different from those in the sandy desert of the Bani Yās shaikhdoms. Thus the authority of the Bani Yās shaikhs in Abu Dhabi or Dubai stopped short of the mountains beyond al ʿAin and elsewhere, although their influence extended from time to time into these areas.[112]

The different tribes who have for many generations lived among or near the mountains either as nomads or in a settled existence have developed a common socio-economic pattern; having a descendant of the Qāsimi family as overlord set the political stage. On it a continuous play developed of disputes and changing alliances between the many neighbouring ports, villages, rulers, *wālis*, headmen, tribal shaikhs and independent nomadic groups. As was shown earlier, at times when Abu Dhabi was particularly strong, such as during the rule of Shaikh Zāyid the Great, it also played a part. But the almost continuous tug-of-war between the shaikhs of Abu Dhabi and the Qawāsim shaikhs for dominance over the usually 'non-aligned' beduin tribes was often carried out by proxy; for instance when beduin shaikhs took one side or the other in a local dispute. The description in Chapter Three of the decentralised administration of the Qāsimi Empire gives some insight into this particularly closely

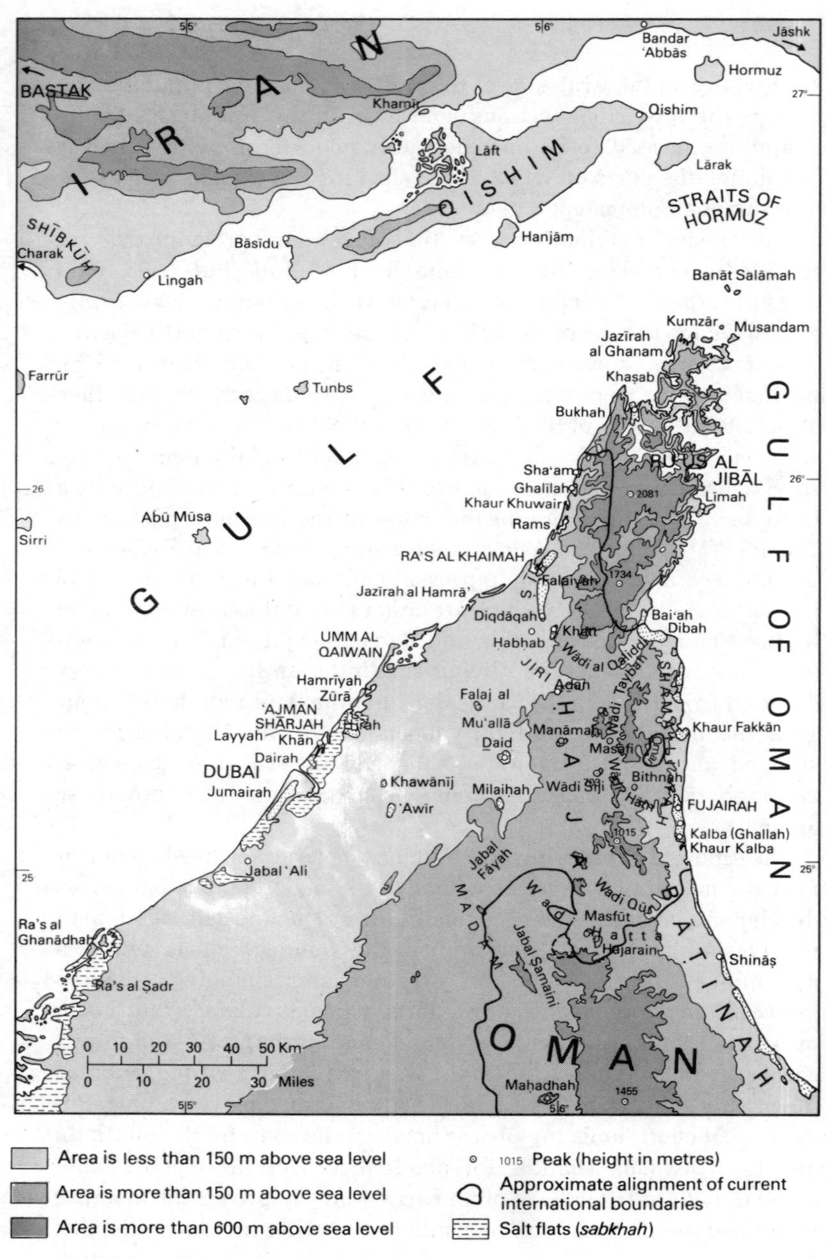

Map 5a The Northern Area (geography)

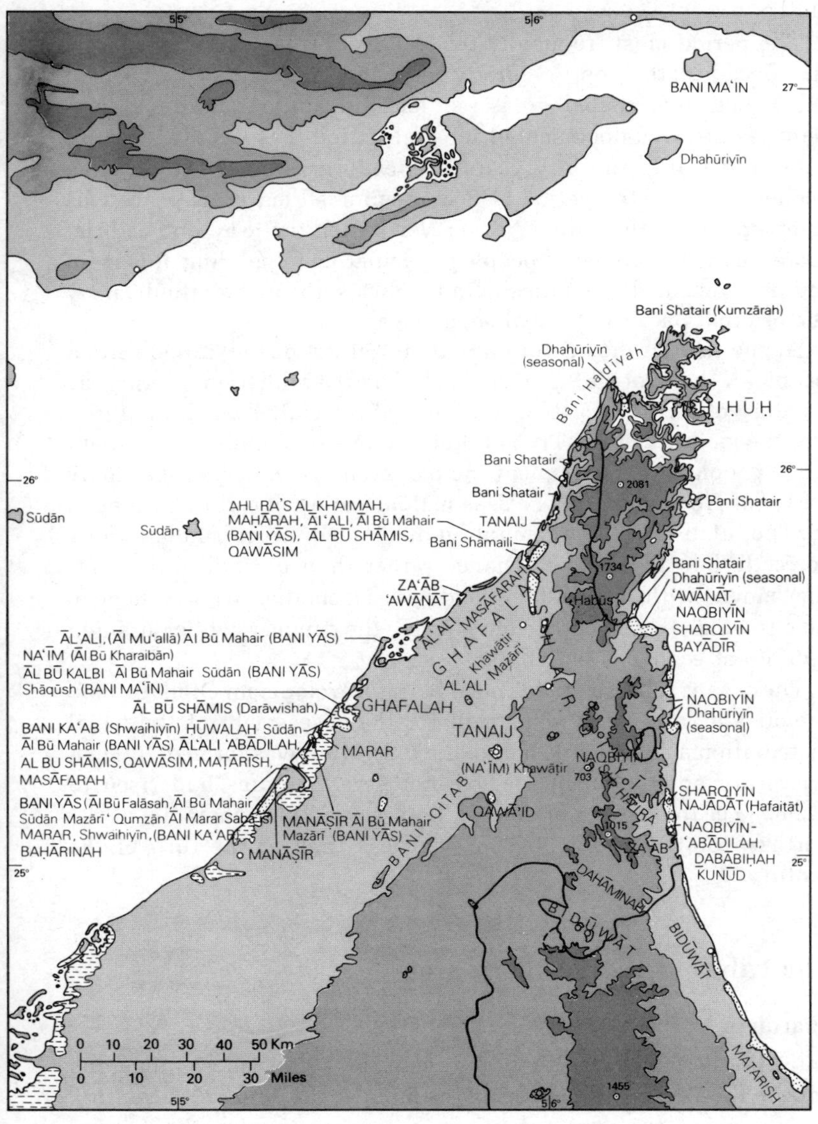

SHIHUH **Tribal name**
Dhahūriyīn **(Subsection)**

Map 5b The Northern Area (the tribes)

interwoven political scene north of, but at times also including, Dubai.

The period most frequently referred to in this description is the first decade of this century: firstly because the number of members of the tribes, their tribal areas, settlements and occupational preferences are well-documented for that period;[113] secondly, because soon afterwards the fifty years of steady growth of the pearling economy during the period of British-enforced maritime peace was interrupted by the First World War. After the war and a brief increase in the number of people participating in pearling, this main industry declined dramatically in the 1930s, throwing into disarray the original pattern of tribal economies.

At the turn of the century about 50,750 out of the 72,000 settled people in the Trucial States lived in the area which now forms the territory of the five northern Emirates of the United Arab Emirates. But the majority of the Trucial States' nomadic population of about 8,000 people did not frequent the mountains so much as the sandy desert of Abu Dhabi.[114] The seasonal migration of certain groups of the population in the mountain-dominated areas should more correctly be called transhumance rather than nomadism, because they moved with some of their belongings from their winter abode to homes which they occupied only during the summer, while pursuing a different economic activity.[115]

The census taken by the Trucial States Development Office in 1968 provides a very useful document for the assessment of the tribal distribution a short while before the federation was formed. By then the entire population of the five northern Emirates had risen to 74,880. Yet the tribal population, both settled and nomadic, of the northern States was at 44,668 even less than at the turn of the century.[116]

The tribes of the northern area

Sharqiyīn

After the Bani Yās the Sharqiyīn were the second most numerous tribe in the Trucial States during the first decade of the 20th century. They resided without exception in territory under the Qāsimi jurisdiction. The eastern part of the promontory was their stronghold for several centuries and there is hardly a village in Shamailīyah, that is the Eastern Coast between Dibah and the border with the

Sultanate of Oman, where they do not form the majority of the population.[117] They are also found in the Wādi Ḥām on the Jiri plain and in and around Dibah. Altogether about 6,000 Sharqiyīn shared this district with another 4,000 members of more than half a dozen other tribes. The entire strength of the Sharqiyīn was estimated in the *Gazetteer* at around 7,000 people.

Fujairah became, under the leadership of subsequent headmen of the Sharqiyīn, their main focal point, and it was from there that the secession of most of Shamailīyah from Qāsimi Shārjah was perpetrated a number of times. The Sharqiyīn of Shamailīyah and the small number of tribal groups living within their eastern habitat had been ruled as an independent shaikhdom since soon after the forceful Ḥamad bin ʿAbdullah of the Ḥafaitāt, the tribe's established leading section, became the headman in 1879. This situation was not recognised by the British authorities in the Gulf until 1952. It was realised then that the Ruler in Fujairah of this particularly coherent tribal shaikhdom of the Sharqiyīn had to be given the same status as the other Trucial Rulers if attempts to obtain concessions for oil exploration were to be successful. On many occasions before this step, the Ruler of Fujairah tried to play off the Sultan of Oman against the British authorities by declaring his allegiance to the former. But such declarations were not then followed up by arrangements such as allowing tax collectors from Oman to come to the villages of the Sharqiyīn. They could therefore be considered merely as diplomatic moves on the part of a Ruler whose urge for independence was supported by his tribal followers. Similarly shortlived were declarations of Sharqiyīn subordination to the authority of the Shaikh of the Naʿīm of Buraimi in 1904 and to that of Shaikh Zāyid bin Khalīfah of Abu Dhabi in 1906.[118] Although the Sharqiyīn had frequent and prolonged disputes with their immediate neighbours such as the Shiḥūḥ, the Khawāṭir, the Naʿīm and the Naqbiyīn, the shaikhs usually managed to rally the support of these neighbours whenever they attempted to shake off the Qāsimi rule.

By the time of the 1968 census, comparatively few of the Sharqiyīn had yet followed the growing trend to leave Fujairah territory for work in the oil industry of Abu Dhabi or Dubai. Of the total of 8,729 Sharqiyīn counted in the northern Trucial States, 8,372 lived in the State of Fujairah, only 116 in Shārjah, and 82 were counted in Ra's al Khaimah. In turn, less than 10 per cent of the tribal population of 9,138 of the State of Fujairah belonged to tribes other than the Sharqiyīn.

The nature of the hand-to-mouth economy of this tribe, which had never depended to the same extent as others on pearling, remained very much the same even into the 1970s. Agriculture and fishing, both on a modest scale, were the major occupations of the economically active section of the population. This situation is further illustrated by the fact that in the State of Fujairah by far the greatest number of households continued to live in *barasti* houses in the late 1960s.

Āl ʿAli

Another Trucial shaikhdom where almost the entire population belongs to one tribe which also comprises the ruling family is Umm al Qaiwain.[119] The Āl ʿAli were about 6,750 strong when the *Gazetteer* was compiled;[120] some 5,000 of them lived in the town of Umm al Qaiwain on the coast. They were also the only tribe at Falaj al ʿAli, an inland oasis belonging to the ruling family of Umm al Qaiwain. Some 200 families of the Āl ʿAli lived at Shārjah and 150 families were in Ra's al Khaimah. There was also a small beduin faction of about 140 families who frequented the country between Umm al Qaiwain and Jazīrah al Ḥamrā', and who were, together with a varying number of beduin from other tribes, always ready to fight for the Rulers of Umm al Qaiwain. The Āl ʿAli ruling family is called Āl Muʿallā, a name which is also attributed to the entire tribe by their kinsmen the Arab tribe Āl ʿAli, which settled in the Shībkūh district of Persia.

The census of 1968 showed that a considerable number of Āl ʿAli had settled in Ra's al Khaimah, where 1,445 were counted (Umm al Qaiwain 2,862). This tribe, too, had suffered a decline in numbers during six decades, totalling only 5,058 in 1968. Most of the Āl ʿAli used to participate in pearl diving, but only one seagoing merchant vessel belonged to Umm al Qaiwain in 1905. The majority of the date gardens which were tended by Āl ʿAli tribesmen belonged to the ruling family.

Zaʿāb

The Zaʿāb, although not very numerous, have at times played an important role in the internal politics of the Qāsimi realm. Their stronghold is the peninsula of Jazīrah al Ḥamrā', also called Zaʿāb in the past because the entire population of the 500 households belonged to that tribe, according to the *Gazetteer*. The inhabitants of Zaʿāb owned some date gardens at Khatt in the Jiri plain, and their families spent the summer there while the men went to the pearl banks. Another 150 Za'āb families had settled on the east coast at Khaur Kalba. While the first group was always heavily involved in, and often antagonistic to, the politics of the Shaikhdom of Ra's al Khaimah, the Za'āb of Khaur Kalba usually supported the shaikh of Kalba against the overlord in distant Shārjah. In 1968 the Za'āb population remaining in Shārjah territory was only 710, a very much larger number of 2,455 being in Ra's al Khaimah, that is at Jazīrah al Ḥamrā'. However, late in 1968 the shaikh of the Za'āb had various disagreements with Shaikh Ṣaqr of Ra's al Khaimah, as a result of which a large part of the population of Jazīrah al Ḥamrā' accepted the invitation of Shaikh Zāyid of Abu Dhabi to settle there. The Za'āb of the Trucial States have continued to maintain close links with their relatives on the Bāṭinah Coast in Oman.

Ṭanaij

The Ṭanaij, although numerically a small tribe, were at times of no small importance in the politics of the northern part of the Trucial Coast, because they represented by far the largest beduin element in that area. In the *Gazetteer* the total number of Ṭanaij is given as 4,000 of whom 1,500 were beduin; this meant a beduin contingent of about 500 fighting-men whose allegiance or support the Rulers coveted when conflict was brewing. The nomadic section of the Ṭanaij used D̠aid as a centre; like the Na'īm community at D̠aid, the Ṭanaij too had a fortified tower for the defence of their quarters numbering about 70 houses. Other settled Ṭanaij lived at Rams in Ra's al Khaimah; all the 400 houses of Rams were inhabited by that tribe, but they had only a few houses at Ḥamrīyah. Most of the settled Ṭanaij on the coast used to go pearling. According to the 1968 population census only 424 Ṭanaij were left in the northern Emirates and Dubai.

Naqbiyīn

The Naqbiyīn, who numbered about 1,800 souls in 1905 and 1,889 in 1968, were the natural rivals of the Sharqiyīn, with whom they lived at close quarters almost wherever they settled in Shamailīyah, the Wādi Ḥām, Khatt, and in the vicinity of Dibah. Only in Khaur Fakkān the Naqbiyīn in 1905 constituted the tribal majority (150 houses), dominating a non-tribal immigrant minority from the Persian coast. In Kalba (earlier called Ghallah) the Naqbiyīn lived with Sharqiyīn,

Kunūd, ʿAbādilah, Balūchis and Persians, but they became the principal "power behind the throne" in Kalba's successful bid for independence in 1937.[121] There were no nomadic Naqbiyīn; the entire tribe was engaged in the settled occupations of fishing and agriculture.

Ghafalah

In 1968 only 197 Ghafalah were counted in the five northern States. At the time when the *Gazetteer* was compiled, this entirely beduin tribe was described as follows: "A nomadic tribe, inhabiting the plain country inland of Rās-al-Khaimah and Umm-al-Qaiwain but not extending into the hills; the Jiri plain and its immediate neighbourhood are their favourite habitat. They are a small tribe and probably do not number more than 500 souls. In politics they are Ghāfiriyah and they are generally well disposed to the Shaikh of Abu Dhabi, whom they have frequently assisted in warfare, but at the present time their closest relations are with Umm-al-Qaiwain; . . . they own camels and live by selling firewood and charcoal in the coast towns. They are credited with the possession of 700 camels, 40 donkeys, 100 cattle, and 1,000 sheep and goats."[122]

Other tribes

All the tribes which have been described above lived almost exclusively within the territory of the former Qāsimi Empire.[123] Only a few members of these tribes had even by 1968 left that area to settle in Dubai or Abu Dhabi. Some of the tribes of the northern shaikhdoms, such as the Zaʿāb, have close links with another branch of the same tribe living in the Sultanate of Oman. Others, such as the Āl ʿAli, are related to Arab tribes living on the Persian side of the Gulf.

An enumeration of tribes in the Trucial States has always met with the hazard of omitting some tribe or faction which considers itself independent or of citing names which according to some local people represent only a subsection of a tribe. Therefore the alphabetical lists of tribes of Trucial Oman in the *Gazetteer* and in Table (d) of the census published by the Development Office in 1968 are not identical.[124] The minor tribes and splinter-groups whose names have not been mentioned in this chapter are of little importance, and to list them all would not add to the understanding of the tribal system of the Trucial States.

It is, however, necessary to recall that although the majority of the northern, mountain-bound tribes did not move into either Dubai or the desert shaikhdom of Abu Dhabi, some of the principal tribes of the latter two Bani Yās shaikhdoms have had tribal relatives in many of the towns and villages of the northern area. There were Sūdān at Shārjah town, on Abū Mūsa island, in ʿAjmān and on Sirri island; Mazārīʿ, who in Abu Dhabi were regarded as part of the Bani Yās, were widespread throughout the entire Qāsimi area and Dubai. As mentioned earlier, some Manāṣīr and ʿAwāmir and other beduin groups were at certain times quite numerous in the north.

Shiḥūḥ and Dhahūriyīn

The life-style of the inhabitants of the mountains and shores of the Musandam peninsula, where the precipitous mountains of Ru'ūs al Jibāl in the north reach some 1,700 metres only a very short distance from the sea, is very different indeed from that of the beduin tribes in the desert and on its fringes. The differences are, in fact, so marked that the inhabitants of the inaccessible and inhospitable parts of the promontory are believed by many to be of non-Arab origin. This tribal group is collectively called Shiḥūḥ, and is distinguished from all the other tribes in the area by social, economic and linguistic characteristics. The Dhahūriyīn share these characteristics but are nevertheless a separate tribe which claims to be related to the Dhawāhir of the Buraimi area.

Research by anthropologist Walter Dostal and geographer Wolfgang Zimmermann helped to dispel the legends which have been in circulation among Arab tribes and European travellers regarding the origin, behaviour and language of the Shiḥūḥ.[125] It is now fairly well established that the Shiḥūḥ are a composite tribe, essentially of Arab origin, which has absorbed elements of Persian origin. The latter component, which forms the entire Kumzārah subsection of the Bani Hadīyah section of the Shiḥūḥ, speaks a dialect similar to the language used by the Balūchis. The Shiḥūḥ do not claim to have one common ancestor, but the Arab majority element is linked by historians to the immigration wave which brought Mālik bin Fahm groups from Yemen to south-east Arabia in the second century AD.[126] In trying to trace the origin of the name "Shiḥūḥ", Dostal supports the theory that the behaviour of these people, who had to eke out a meagre existence in an inhospitable environment, made them appear avaricious in the eyes of other Arab tribes; the Arabic root of their name, SH Ḥ Ḥ, means "to be avaricious".

At the turn of the century the Shiḥūḥ were estimated to number about 21,500 people; this was almost certainly an over-estimate.[127] They are divided into two main sections, the Bani Hadīyah and the Bani Shatair. Both sections are further divided, such as the Kumzārah and Ḥabūs, and the latter is sometimes considered as a separate tribe. Under the leadership of their *muqaddām*, the subsections are probably more independent of the leaders of the two main sections than would be the case in most other tribes of Oman. The reason is probably the sheer physical problem of co-ordination between the isolated communities. In order to gain the maximum benefit from the meagre resources which the country offers, most Shiḥūḥ families seasonally change their domicile. During the cooler winter months, when the infrequent rainfall can be expected, they live high up on the few fertile terraces on gentle slopes and shoulders of the otherwise barren limestone mountains. There they have rough stone houses, the floors of which are often dug into the ground. Such winter settlements are often occupied just by one extended family; in other cases a community of several related extended families forms a larger settlement.[128] Nearby are a few terraced fields for the cultivation of wheat and barley. As far as is known there are no springs anywhere in the mountains and valleys of Ru'ūs al Jibāl, and wells are not sunk because the limestone does not retain the little water there is. Thus rainwater, stored in man-made underground tanks and fed into the fields along channels, has to suffice for men, beasts and crops during the winter months. In the vicinity of the hamlets goats graze on the sparse vegetation of the slopes.

During the summer the entire family or village community moves down to the coast into *muṣaif*; these are summer settlements consisting of palm frond huts erected in the vicinity of date gardens either on the coast north of Ra's al Khaimah, or near Dibah, or in the few *wādi* mouths of the northern Ru'ūs al Jibāl.[129] Some Shiḥūḥ go to the shore nearest to their winter settlement and then proceed by boat to their date gardens. During the height of the pearling industry many Shiḥūḥ participated in the seasonal dive, but only as hired hands on boats belonging to Ra's al Khaimah, Rams or Sha'am. Very few Shiḥūḥ live entirely off fishing, but many do go fishing during the summer months while living on the coast. Recent research into the seasonal movement, *taḥwīl*, and the economic pattern of the people inhabiting the Musandam Peninsula also verified that there are no purely beduin sections of the Shiḥūḥ. Almost the entire population moves twice a year; because of the scarcity of water in the mountains during the summer months crops cannot be grown and neither man nor beast can live there.

Dostal also found that in this poor region any surplus production is offered firstly to the neighbours. Only if this surplus is not required by any of the communities within reach is it taken to the market at Khaṣab, Ra's al Khaimah or Dibah. A surplus of dates is produced most years, and goats are also one of the few items from which Shiḥūḥ families can earn cash; wheat and barley never have been grown in such quantities that they can be exported.

Since the small terraced fields which a family owns in the mountains and the date gardens on the coast form the precious narrow base of its existence, such property is not lightly given away to other families through marriage. Therefore the custom of *bint ʿamm* marriages is even more rigidly adhered to among the Shiḥūḥ than among most other Arab tribes.[130] The intrusion of foreigners who might damage the water cisterns and terraces is met with suspicion and even hostility.

By far the larger part of the Shiḥūḥ and Dhahūriyīn do not reside within the territory of the former Trucial States, but are subjects of the Sultan of Oman. Because they dominate a strategically important enclave of the Sultanate of Oman, because of the economic necessity to come down to the coast, and because of tribal bonds with Shiḥūḥ who reside in Ra's al Khaimah, Shārjah and Fujairah, they have throughout most periods of recent history been the cause of numerous incidents. In very recent years the number of Shiḥūḥ who live in the United Arab Emirates has increased because they could find work even as near to home as Ra's al Khaimah.[131]

The tenuous Omani suzerainty over the Shiḥūḥ was established during the 19th century as a result of the long struggle between the Qawāsim Rulers and the Sultan of Oman. Being of the Hināwi political faction,[132] the Shiḥūḥ welcomed any support against the Ghāfiri Qawāsim. As we have seen, they even, for a time, recognised Zāyid bin Khalīfah of Abu Dhabi as an overlord. The frequent disputes between the Qawāsim Rulers and the headmen of the various Shiḥūḥ sections usually concerned the coastal markets, villages and beaches where the Shiḥūḥ could sell their produce, buy provisions, beach their boats, and go fishing. Friction also rose at Baiʿah and Dibah, where many Shiḥūḥ lived during the summer. In 1859 when the British Political Resident visited Bukhah, Khaṣab,

Kumzār and other places on the coast of Ru'ūs al Jibāl ". . . the impression which he derived from intercourse with the people was that they had a predilection for the Government of the Saiyid of Masqat and were animated by an implacable hatred of the Qawāsim."[133] It is therefore not surprising that the Shiḥūḥ headmen repeatedly and actively supported the secession of the Sharqiyīn of Fujairah from Shārjah. However, when it came to negotiating directly with the British authorities over allowing a telegraph station to be built in their territory, the Shiḥūḥ shaikhs repeatedly denied that they owed allegiance to the Sultan, although he had a *wāli* stationed in Khaṣab. In general the British Government has supported Omani authority over Ru'ūs al Jibāl. The Sultan's *wāli* has for several decades now resided in Khaṣab; he also has representatives in Dibah and Līmah.

The inability of the Qawāsim Rulers to dominate the inhabitants of Ru'ūs al Jibāl, while they were prepared to accept the sovereignty of the distant and rather ineffective authority of the Sultan, demonstrates the tenuous nature of government before modern communications. In the absence of armies, there was little a Ruler could do to keep a tribe or an area under his domination if the people thought that they would be better off without him. Thus the Qāsimi Empire never was a very coherent political entity and it disintegrated quite readily. In comparison the social interdependence which existed between the desert and the coast in the case of the Bani Yās and their associates provided a better base for a territorially extensive but nevertheless quite coherent political unit.

Chapter Three

Administering a Tribal Society

1 The "decentralisation" of the administration in the *wāli* system of tribal shaikhdoms

General

At a time when communication was slow between the scattered settlements of the shaikhdoms, each Ruler maintained permanent representatives, usually called *wāli*, in the more important population centres of his shaikhdom.[1] The fact that his representative was in control in that place meant that the Ruler's authority was at least *de jure* recognised by the population of that remote area and by the neighbouring shaikhs. But often enough control over the representative himself slipped from the Ruler's hand and he declared himself an independent Ruler.

The institution of a *wāli* carried more political weight, the more a shaikhdom was geographically spread out. Cars and motorboats were first brought in any number to the Trucial States by the oil companies and became the predominant means of transport only in the early 1960s.[2] While camels and sailing boats were still the principal means of communication, the administration of a large shaikhdom such as Abu Dhabi or the Qāsimi realm could not easily be centralised. The extent to which a Ruler's personal influence was felt in the distant settlements under his sovereignty depended on the geographical and economic situation as much as on his choice of a *wāli*. The closer the ties of genuine mutual trust between Ruler and *wāli*, the more it was possible to delegate authority without running the risk of secession. This is a reason why most Rulers put a brother or a son in charge of an important "dependency",[3] but this was not always a sure safeguard against secessionist movements, either led by the *wāli* or perpetrated by the inhabitants themselves.

In the following paragraphs the history of decentralisation, direct rule, secession and annexation of the population centres of the Trucial States will be sketched. Local history is examined to show the working of the modest but adequate institutions for the administration of ports, date groves, and markets throughout the country. An occasional spotlight is turned on to detail, to illuminate the extent or the deficiency of administration within the tribal organisation.

Because of their relatively small hinterland, Dubai, ʿAjmān and Umm al Qaiwain do not furnish much information in this respect.[4] Abu Dhabi, the territorial power which derived most of its strength from its interests in the desert hinterland and the remote oases, needed a minimum of institutional administration carried out by *wālis* because the all-important factor which held the shaikhdom together was good management of the tribal relationships. At the other end of the spectrum there were the Qāsimi Rulers, who at times merely claimed and at other times really exerted full control over a geographically disjointed and economically unequal territory. An account of the administration of the important population centres by *wālis* can therefore not be given by neatly examining each of the Emirates in turn, but rather by describing the position of *wālis* in the important population centres while their political affiliation changed over the decades.

The Qāsimi Empire

Rise and disintegration

The Qawāsim, not as a tribe but as a ruling clan[5] with its centre at Shārjah or Ra's al Khaimah, gained domination over most of the tribes of the Musandam promontory with the exception of the Shiḥūḥ and their allies. Before 1760 Qawāsim shaikhs had also established a foothold on the economically important island of Qishim off the Persian Coast. After a compromise had been reached in 1850 between Sayyid Saʿīd of Muscat and Shaikh Sulṭān bin Ṣaqr (1803–66), Qāsimi rule was undisputed in the area north of the line connecting Shārjah town on the west coast with Khaur Kalba on the east coast, but excluding the almost inaccessible territory north of

Sha'am and Dibah. At the turn of the century an estimated 45,500 settled people of a great number of different tribes lived in the two main centres, Shārjah town and Ra's al Khaimah, and in a fair number of smaller ports and in villages in the *wādis*.[6] They were all under the administration or *ḥukum* of members of the Qāsimi family, then numbering only about 20 males. There was also a fluctuating number of beduin in the area, whose relationship with the Qawāsim rulers depended on the political situation of the moment.

The patriarch of the Qawāsim Rulers, Sulṭān bin Ṣaqr, did not reside permanently in either Shārjah or Ra's al Khaimah. He moved around the area, including Qishim, and delegated the administration to his brothers and later to his sons, many of whom figured prominently in the history of the Qāsimi empire for many decades after Sulṭān's death.

In Shārjah, Ṣāliḥ bin Ṣaqr,[7] a half-brother of Shaikh Sulṭān, was *wāli* until 1838, but to the regret of the British authorities, who saw in him one of the most enlightened shaikhs on the coast, he was replaced by Ṣaqr, son of Sulṭān bin Ṣaqr by a Qāsimi wife. Since it was the duty of the *wāli* to levy the pearling tax on behalf of his father, the temptation was considerable to gain popularity by supporting those who wanted a reduction in the annual pearling tax, then 7 Maria Theresa Dollars per diver. Thereby Ṣaqr also obtained some popular support for a move to make himself the independent Ruler of Shārjah. In order to avoid fighting, his father the Qāsimi Ruler agreed to hand over complete control to his son in exchange for part of the revenue of Shārjah as a tribute. It seems, however, that Ṣaqr bin Sulṭān's rule did not please all the inhabitants of Shārjah, but with his father's tacit toleration Ṣaqr remained the virtually independent Ruler of Shārjah until his death in battle in 1846.

However, Shārjah had not achieved permanent independence, for Sulṭān bin Ṣaqr appointed as the next *wāli* another of his sons, 'Abdullah, whose mother belonged to an Āl 'Ali family from the Persian side of the Gulf. He also was killed in battle, in 1855, whereafter the reins of government in Shārjah changed hands several times between relatives of Sulṭān bin Ṣaqr. He was himself too aged to interfere, and died in 1866 at the age of over eighty-five. For a brief two years another son of Shaikh Sulṭān, Khālid, who had for some time held control of Shārjah, was able to reunite Shārjah with Ra's al Khaimah and rule both as one Qāsimi empire. After his death in 1868 the two principalities were once again separated.

Shārjah, which became the more important, was eventually ruled jointly by the two half-brothers Sālim bin Sulṭān, whose mother was a slave woman, and Ibrāhīm bin Sulṭān, whose mother was from the Marāzīq, a Bāṭinah tribe; the latter had been *wāli* of Ra's al Khaimah for a long time under his father Sulṭān bin Ṣaqr. Their nephew Ḥumaid bin ʿAbdullah, who became the *wāli* of Ra's al Khaimah after Ibrāhīm bin Sulṭān, proclaimed himself independent of Shārjah in 1869, and in spite of attempts by the Rulers of Shārjah, Ḥumaid remained in absolute control of the town of Ra's al Khaimah as well as some of the hinterland until his death in 1900. One of the reasons why the Qāsimi realm continued to be divided was the preoccupation of the shaikhs in Shārjah with problems caused by its smaller dependency, Ḥamrīyah.

In 1883 Shaikh Ṣaqr bin Khālid forcibly took Shārjah from his uncles Sālim and Ibrāhīm. On the death of Ḥumaid bin ʿAbdullah in 1900 Ṣaqr bin Khālid also gained control of Rās al Khaimah and placed his son Khālid there as *wāli*.[8] After the latter's death in 1908 the Ruler of Shārjah asked the people of Ra's al Khaimah whom they wanted as *wāli*. When they chose his uncle Sālim bin Sulṭān whom he had earlier ousted from Shārjah but to whom he was obliged to pay an annual subsidy, he anticipated that Sālim would proclaim independence from Shārjah, and, having a lot of popular support, might succeed. Ṣaqr bin Khālid's nominee, yet another son of the deceased Sulṭān bin Ṣaqr, Nāṣir, was made *wāli* of Ra's al Khaimah, but in 1910 Sālim bin Sulṭān succeeded in assuming the government there. Considering the varied career of Shaikh Sālim—exile on Abū Mūsa and minister (*wazīr*) to his usurping nephew Ṣaqr bin Khālid—the British authorities assumed that his rule in Ra's al Khaimah would be of short duration. This was the reason why, unlike Ḥumaid bin ʿAbdullah, who had also initially been a self-styled independent Ruler, Sālim was never given formal recognition of independence and never quite achieved the status of a Trucial Shaikh.[9] His younger son Sulṭān, who succeeded him upon his death in 1919 with the consent of the people of Ra's al Khaimah, was fully recognised in 1921 by the British Government. Since that time Ra's al Khaimah has remained an independent shaikhdom.

In Shārjah Ṣaqr bin Khālid died in 1914. He was succeeded by his cousin Khālid bin Aḥmad; but in 1924 Sulṭān bin Ṣaqr, who had been a minor at the time of his father's death, made use of discontent among the pearling community of Shārjah and took the rule from his uncle Khālid. When Sulṭān bin Ṣaqr died in 1951 his brother Muḥammad failed to become the Ruler, and Ṣaqr bin Sulṭān was recognised by the British Government in 1951. He was deposed in 1965 and lived in exile in Cairo. He returned in early 1972 and in an unsuccessful attempt to wrest the leadership from his nephew Shaikh Khālid bin Muḥammad in a *coup d'état* he killed the incumbent Ruler of Shārjah. Since February 1972 Shārjah has been ruled by Shaikh Sulṭān bin Muḥammad Āl Qāsimi.

Ra's al Khaimah as a *wāli's* seat and as an independent Trucial State.

The importance of Ra's al Khaimah stems from its natural harbour, which has, however, been silting up within living memory; from the long narrow peninsula parallel to the mainland on which the town is built and which is easy to defend; and from an extensive well-watered fertile plain opposite the town on the mainland. Most of the population of the town of Ra's al Khaimah, 1,000 households at the turn of the century, used to engage in both agriculture and pearling.[10] The latter industry was, however, with 33 boats, on a much smaller scale than in Shārjah or in Abu Dhabi; a certain amount of trade in rice, sugar and other goods was carried on by some 15 sailing *baghlahs* and *sanbūks*, hence the necessity for a customs house. The *sūq* served also as a centre for the population of the mountainous hinterland, but trade was less lively than in Shārjah or in Dubai; there were no resident Hindu traders, and apart from seven Khojahs[11] all the merchants were Arab.

The revenues of Ra's al Khaimah during the first decade of this century amounted to some 6,300 Rupees from pearling and 800 Rupees from customs duties, as compared to 23,400 Rupees from the former and 8,000 from the latter in Shārjah. There was also the tax in kind on dates, which was of considerable value since there were an estimated 15,600 trees belonging to the inhabitants of the town of Ra's al Khaimah alone.

According to one local source there was, at least during the rule of Sālim bin Sulṭān in Ra's al Khaimah, a *wāli* appointed to supervise day-to-day administration within the town, including the collection of taxes and customs duties by the *muṭārzīyah*, and to organise the defence of the town against attacks by plundering beduin or during disputes with other shaikhs.[12] The main task of the Ruler of Ra's al Khaimah himself was to be available to the inhabitants to deal with their grievances and disputes, and to dispense justice in consultation with a *qāḍi* and the *muṭawwa'*. The diving court, *sālifah al ghauṣ*, was responsible for settling disputes arising out of the preparations for the annual diving season and the many debts and claims which usually followed it.

Throughout the decades when the *wāli* of Ra's al Khaimah was sometimes *de jure* dependent, sometimes *de facto* dependent, and sometimes independent of the Ruler of Shārjah, the contentious issues usually concerned economics rather than status. Whoever was governor of Ra's al Khaimah levied the customary taxes, chiefly on pearling, but also on dates (one twentieth of the crop in kind) and on animals, and collected customs duties (1.5 to 2 per cent). Such income was primarily used for the administration of Ra's al Khaimah, which included maintenance of the fort and towers, salary for some 70 armed guards, hospitality and subsidies to beduin tribes of the area. The rest was given in allowance to the members of the Qāsimi family who lived in Ra's al Khaimah and at the time of the *Gazetteer* numbered eight males.[13]

More than once in the history of the Qāsimi realm and of other shaikhdoms, an ex-Ruler attempted to regain control of part or all of a shaikhdom because he could not see any other way out of his obligations to his debtors, his family and his supporters. Ra's al Khaimah was in this respect not as coveted as Shārjah, which had a substantial income from pearling: according to the *Gazetteer* 23,400 Rupees were collected there as tax in 1906.[14] The *wālis* of Ra's al Khaimah were usually not required, and the independent Rulers not inclined, to remit any of the revenue from Ra's al Khaimah to Shārjah. The income to be derived from the former therefore helped to solve the economic problems of Sālim bin Sulṭān, ex-Ruler of Shārjah, who managed to install himself as Ruler in Ra's al Khaimah in 1910.[15]

In 1917 Sālim bin Sulṭān's eldest son Muḥammad took over most of the affairs of Ra's al Khaimah because his father had become partially paralysed, but after Sālim's death in 1919 the younger son Sulṭān gripped the reins of government and was recognised as Ruler of Rās al Khaimah by the British Government in 1921.

During the meagre years of the Second World War and after, Shaikh Sulṭān alienated his subjects by unduly neglecting their welfare, and his brother by signing an oil concessions agreement with PCL in secret. Thus it was possible for his nephew Shaikh Ṣaqr bin Muḥammad to take over as Ruler of Ra's al Khaimah in March

1948 with popular support. Ra's al Khaimah has been under Shaikh Ṣaqr's rule since then, and became a member of the UAE in February 1972.

Ra's al Khaimah's dependencies

Whether Ra's al Khaimah was an integral part of the Qāsimi empire or a dependency of Shārjah, a number of small population centres were usually under some form of administrative supervision from Ra's al Khaimah. In most of these places, however, the Shiḥūḥ and their allied tribes presented a continuous challenge, either because they formed the majority of the population, as in Sha'am, or because they were able to exert their influence over the local tribal shaikhs, as was often the case in Rams and Jazīrah al Ḥamrā'.

Nominally all Shiḥūḥ were subjects of the Sultan of Muscat, whose *wāli* resided at Khaṣab. But many Shiḥūḥ owned property and had customary rights in places both in the mountains and on the coast which were accessible only from Qāsimi-held territory. Sha'am is the best example of a Shiḥūḥ village becoming and remaining a dependency of Ra's al Khaimah through geographical circumstances and economic need.[16] All its inhabitants were Shiḥūḥ of the Bani Shatair section. Two miles north of Sha'am the coastal plain, which becomes progressively narrower, is finally sealed off from the ports and coves further north by a spur of the Ru'ūs al Jibāl which drops into the sea. Sha'am consisted at the time of the *Gazetteer* of about 300 houses, and the population lived off fishing, date palms and fodder and vegetable cultivation and diving for pearls, mostly in boats belonging to other ports, since Sha'am itself had only 2 pearling boats. Sha'am exported firewood, charcoal and dried fish to the 66 miles-distant market of Shārjah, transported thither by small coastal craft. In view of the economic dependence of this village on its southern neighbours it is not surprising that repeated attempts to rid itself of Ra's al Khaimah's control could not last for long. A revolt in December 1885, for instance, was brought under control by the Ruler, Ḥumaid bin 'Abdullah, and the village even had to pay a fine of 1,600 M.T. Dollars.

Jazīrah al Ḥamrā', also called Jazīrah al Za'āb, is a small port on the Gulf coast which was usually a dependency of Ra's al Khaimah rather than Shārjah, since a formal division was made between Khālid bin Aḥmad of Shārjah and Sulṭān bin Sālim of Ra's al Khaimah in 1914. All the inhabitants are from the Za'āb tribe, whose 500 houses were divided between two villages on the long and narrow sandbank southwest of Ra's al Khaimah. The Za'āb of Jazīrah al Ḥamrā' were the only community of any size in Ra's al Khaimah territory which was almost exclusively dependent upon the sea; they owned only a few date palms in Khatt, inland in the Jiri plain.

The Rulers of Ra's al Khaimah were not often in the position to appoint a *wāli* of their own choice, but they were usually able to restrict the independent ambitions of the Za'āb headman of the time and make him declare his acceptance of the Ruler's supremacy. Thus, the Shiḥūḥ and the Za'āb were often enough natural allies and Jazīrah al Ḥamrā' was also a convenient refuge for opponents of a Ruler in Ra's al Khaimah.

The same may be said of Rams. This port, eight miles north of Ra's al Khaimah, is also situated beside a creek, but the harbour is not nearly so deep, nor are its date plantations inland so extensive. At the turn of the century the town had 400 houses, only one shop, one seagoing *sanbūk* and only three pearling boats. Since the inhabitants were all from the settled section of the Ṭanaij,[17] they had their own tribal leaders who dealt with most affairs in their community and reluctantly owed allegiance to the Ruler of Ra's al Khaimah.[18]

Dibah

One of the most important of the Qāsimi dependencies was Dibah, a sizeable settlement on the east coast dating back to pre-Islamic times.

One mile north of Dibah lies its twin village of Bai'ah, inhabited by Shiḥūḥ and subject to Muscat. During the early 19th century Dibah usually had closer ties with Ra's al Khaimah's *wālis* and Rulers than with Shārjah.

In 1855 the *wāli* of Dibah was Mashari, whose father Ibrāhīm bin Sulṭān was *wāli* at Ra's al Khaimah at the time. Mashari was killed in that year by Shiḥūḥ tribesmen, an incident which illustrates the key issue throughout the history of the Dibah dependency: that is, rivalry between the inhabitants and their Shiḥūḥ neighbours. While Shaikh Sālim bin Sulṭān was Ruler of Shārjah (1868–83) his younger brother Aḥmad was granted in 1871 the revenues of the village of Dibah as an allowance, which at that time was enough to meet his expenses. In subsequent decades this was no longer the case, because "Salim bin Sultan had a good influence with the Kawasims villages . . . but now in the present rule of Shargah the tribe of the Shahiyain residing at Baia near Deba have taken to encroach upon the revenues of Deba and Ahmed bin Sultan cannot see his way to check their encroachments and hence the revenues of the place are now insufficient for his expenditure."[19]

Unlike certain other *wāli* posts within the Qāsimi territory and throughout the Trucial States, the importance of holding Dibah lay not so much in the need to have a trusted man there to control the tribal inhabitants (ʿAwānāt, Naqbiyīn and Sharqiyīn)[20] but in its function as a fiefdom. The *wāli* usually was an important member of the Qāsimi family whose claims to a share of the ancestral empire had to be considered; he was not often an absentee fief but usually resided in Dibah.[21]

In 1919 the Ruler of Shārjah, from 1914 Khālid bin Aḥmad, appointed his brother Rāshid bin Aḥmad bin Sulṭān as *wāli* in Dibah. After Khālid's deposition[22] in 1924 his successor Sulṭān bin Ṣaqr appointed a negro slave, Bakhīt bin Saʿīd, but in spring of 1926 the son of the previous Qāsimi *wāli*, Aḥmad bin Rāshid (bin Aḥmad bin Sulṭān) ". . . with the concurrence of the inhabitants has been appointed the Shaikh of that place and has occupied the forts there."[23] Aḥmad bin Rāshid at once informed the Ruler of Shārjah, Sulṭān bin Ṣaqr, and the other shaikhs as well as the Residency Agent at Shārjah, of this *fait accompli*. Soon the father, Rāshid bin Aḥmad, regained control of Dibah for himself and remained the *wāli* there until his death in December 1937.

When Shaikh Khālid bin Aḥmad, ex-Ruler of Shārjah, became the strongest power in the eastern area after being appointed Regent of Kalba in 1937, the affairs of Dibah were closely supervised by him rather than by his rivals in Shārjah or Ra's al Khaimah, and he again set up his nephew, Aḥmad bin Rāshid (bin Aḥmad bin Sulṭān), as *wāli* of Dibah in January 1938. But when during his old age he delegated that power to his nephew Ḥumaid bin ʿAbdullah, the latter's mismanagement paved the way for re-integration under the authority of the Ruler of Shārjah. In 1950 Ṣaqr bin ʿAbdullah, a nephew of the ex-Ruler of Shārjah, Khālid, became *wāli* of Dibah, and held the post until he died in 1958.

The wealth of Dibah was not in trade, although it had a small *sūq*, nor primarily in pearling, but in dates from an estimated 10,000 trees. Tax collected in Dibah as well as in the two neighbouring little villages of Wamm and Muḥtarqah was all paid to the *wāli*.

The *wāli* in Dibah often had to contend with encroachment by the Shiḥūḥ. He therefore needed powerful allies or else had to hold them at bay by impressing them. The young Aḥmad bin Rāshid therefore began his tenure in 1926 by assuming the role of mediator between the Shaikh of Kalba and the Naqbiyīn, some of whom resided in Dibah although most of them were subjects of Kalba.[24] For a time Rāshid seems to have been able to establish a reasonable relationship with his counterpart, the headman of the Shiḥūḥ at Baiʿah, Ṣāliḥ bin Muḥammad;[25] they concluded a treaty in 1926. After Salih's death in 1932 the new headman in Baiʿah, Zāyid bin Sinān of the Kumzār,[26] could not restrain the beduin Shiḥūḥ, and allegations of Shiḥūḥ raiding and interference when they visited the *sūq* of Dibah were frequent.

The most that Rāshid bin Aḥmad could do was to request direct action against the Shiḥūḥ by the Sultan in Muscat. Therefore he went personally to Muscat on the occasion of the accession to rule of Sultan Saʿīd bin Taimūr in October 1932, stated his problems, asked for the Sultan's help (or formal protection) and later went as far as hoisting the Sultan's flag on his fort in the hope of getting help from that direction. As an unexpected side-aspect of his request for protection from incursions by the Shiḥūḥ, Rāshid bin Aḥmad received a letter from the Sultan on the occasion of the introduction of a new Omani *wāli* at Khaṣab[27] in 1934, saying: "my object is that you should be obedient to him" (meaning the *wāli* of Khaṣab, who was responsible for the whole of Muscat's possessions on the Musandam Peninsula) "and submissive to his orders . . ."[28] The Ruler of Shārjah clearly saw that he was about to lose Dibah to Muscat altogether, and communicated these matters to the Political Resident in Bushire. Later, the British Government obliged the Ruler of Shārjah by corresponding with the Sultan of Muscat, stating that Dibah was part of Shārjah territory.[29]

Since the recognition of the Sharqiyīn territory of Fujairah as an independent State in 1952, the Shārjah dependency of Dibah looks on the map like a tiny button in between large tracts of Omani and Fujairah territory, the latter starting a mere mile or two south and west of the fort of Dibah. The two other Shārjah dependencies on the east coast, Khaur Fakkān and Kalba, are 32 kilometres and 68 kilometres respectively south of Dibah. But until passes were blasted through several rocky headlands, Dibah was in any case connected to these southern coastal tracts only by sea; the other communication route to Dibah was down the steep Wādi Ṭaybah from Masāfi, which was opened for Landrovers at about the same time as the coastal route in 1968.

At least since formal independence in 1952, the Shaikh of Fujairah has maintained a *wāli* at Dibah at al Ghurfah. Already in 1969 before the federation was established, the *wālis* of both Shārjah and Fujairah could proudly point to a school and a clinic in Dibah, organised by the Development Office in Dubai and paid for by Abu Dhabi. The *wāli* of Bai'ah, himself not from the Shiḥūḥ tribes but from the interior of Oman, bitterly resented the relative opulence of his neighbours, while Sultan Sa'īd bin Taimūr offered to do even less for this outlying exclave of his State than he did for the rest of his country.

Shamailīyah—Kalba

The administration of Dibah by and on behalf of the Qāsimi ruling family has always been relatively undisputed and straightforward compared to the administration of the remainder of its east coast possessions, the Shamailīyah.[30] Early in the 19th century this district changed hands several times between the Sultans of Muscat and the Qawāsim Rulers, and even after the "final annexation of Shamailīyah to the Shārjah Shaikhdom"[31] in 1850, Muscat's claims were frequently revived, on most occasions at the request of the Shaikh of Fujairah. The periodic restoration of Qāsimi sovereignty over the Sharqiyīn part of Shamailīyah usually meant that the Qāsimi *wāli* was once again entitled to the revenues of Fujairah, which in 1900 amounted to 2,000 M.T. Dollars.[32]

As in Dibah, the fort at Ghallah (Kalba) was occupied by a consecutive line of progeny of the original grantee, Mājid bin Sulṭān bin Ṣaqr Āl Qāsimi, who obtained the Shamailīyah as fief when his brother Sālim bin Sulṭān was still Ruler of Shārjah. His son Ḥamad bin Mājid shared his position as shaikh of Kalba with his brother Aḥmad bin Mājid. His son Sa'īd bin Ḥamad[33] succeeded him in 1902 at the critical time when Ḥamad bin 'Abdullah al Shārqi, the headman of the numerous tribe of the Sharqiyīn, had managed to establish and maintain virtual independence. Ḥamad bin 'Abdullah was assisted by the Shiḥūḥ at Bai'ah under their long-lived leader Shaikh Ṣāliḥ bin Muḥammad, supported by some of the Trucial Shaikhs, and received the tacit backing of the Sultan of Muscat. From 1903 the Qāsimi *wāli* of Kalba, Sa'īd bin Ḥamad, usually resided with his family in 'Ajmān, leaving the administration of the fiefdom in the hands of a slave by the name of Barūt. By the 1920s he had taken up permanent residence again in Kalba.

In 1936 Sa'īd bin Ḥamad was recognised by the British Government as a Trucial Ruler, as an incentive to granting landing rights on an emergency air-strip. But he died suddenly at the end of April 1937 during a visit to Khaur Fakkān, while his eldest son Ḥamad was still a minor. His daughter ʿĀ'ishah bint Saʿīd took immediate steps to protect the shaikhdom from usurpers. Even before her seriously-ill father had actually died she rushed back to the fort in Kalba, organised its defences, put the slave Barūt in charge, and sent a message to her husband Shaikh Khālid bin Aḥmad (ex-Ruler of Shārjah), who had become the most powerful member of the Qāsimi clan, and who was visiting Ra's al Khaimah at the time.

The question of succession in Kalba soon developed into a drawn-out dispute involving everybody who was anybody in politics north and east of Dubai: the Ruler of Ra's al Khaimah, Sulṭān bin Sālim, (brother of Saʿīd bin Ḥamad's widow); the Ruler of Shārjah, Sulṭān bin Ṣaqr; the ex-Ruler of Shārjah, Khālid bin Aḥmad; the *wāli* of Dibah, Rāshid bin Aḥmad; the leader of the Naqbiyīn, Sālim bin ʿAbdullah;[34] the *wāli* of Ṣuḥār in Oman and the Sultan of Muscat; all the notable residents of Kalba and its neighbourhood, and last but not least the representatives of the British Government: the Residency Agent in Shārjah, Khān Bahadur Sayyid ʿAbdul Razāq al Razūqi, his superiors, the Political Agent in Bahrain, the Political Resident in Bushire, and the Senior Naval Officer.

At the insistence of the British Government, the notables of Kalba, who had already stated that they wanted to have the twelve-year-old boy Ḥamad bin Saʿīd as successor, were required to choose a Regent for him. In the presence of the Residency Agent they selected in June 1937 the slave Barūt, a choice which was not acceptable to some of the British officials.[35] Eventually a compromise was achieved by the election as Regent by the notables of Kalba of Khālid bin Aḥmad, ex-Ruler of Shārjah, husband of the deceased's daughter.

He was allowed to keep his previously allocated fiefdom of D̲aid and he accepted that Barūt was in charge of the day-to-day affairs of Kalba. The Regent Khālid bin Aḥmad set about sorting out the many differences and disputes which had been absorbing the entire tribal population of Shamailīyah and the other eastern tracts of the Qāsimi realm. Since he did not have enough funds to pay off tribal leaders he had to rely on his diplomacy. When he succeeded in gaining influence over most of the tribes of that area, even over the Sharqiyīn, his relatives and rivals in Shārjah and Ra's al Khaimah did not support him for fear of his becoming too powerful. During the 1940s Khālid bin Aḥmad delegated many of the affairs of the eastern area to his nephew Ḥumaid bin ʿAbdullah, who gained a corrupting influence over the young Ḥamad bin Saʿīd in Kalba. The Regent Khālid bin Aḥmad was by then too old and ill to interfere in the deteriorating state of affairs. When Ḥumaid bin ʿAbdullah died in 1950 the British Government favoured Ḥamad bin Saʿīd as Ruler of Kalba; but he was murdered in 1951, probably by the secretary of Ṣaqr bin Sulṭān bin Sālim. The last of the descendants in the male line of the Qawāsim headmen and Rulers in Kalba having died, it seemed the most convenient arrangement to let Kalba revert to direct administration from Shārjah, of which it has been a dependency ever since.

Shamailīyah—Fujairah

The most important single factor causing the decline of the influence of the shaikhs of Shārjah in the eastern part of their realm was the fact that within the conglomerate of settled tribes in the Shamailīyah one tribe was disproportionately more numerous than any of the others. The Sharqiyīn were about 6,000 strong in a population of about 10,000 while of the other tribes in the Shamailīyah or the Naqbiyīn none was more than 1,000 persons strong.[36] The administration of Shamailīyah was arranged in the same way as that of Dibah, that is, that the Qāsimi *wāli* was a fief and entitled to the use of the revenue, some 2,000 M.T. Dollars in 1905; he did not have to remit any of the revenue to the Ruler in Shārjah.[37] So long as the Qawāsim had a *wāli* on the east coast he had his seat in Ghallah (Kalba) or at the long established natural port of Khaur Fakkān, which has always been more important economically and had a mixed population of Naqbiyīn tribesmen and Arabised Persians.

Because of the distance and difficulty of access of the Shamailīyah from Shārjah the district could be held by Qawāsim Rulers only with the co-operation of the big tribes. As long as the leading shaikh of the Sharqiyīn considered himself and his tribe as subjects of the Shaikh of Shārjah, the rest of the Shamailīyah could be administered by the *wāli* in Kalba. Several times in the 19th century the Sharqiyīn leaders withheld their co-operation, but they were always brought back into the fold of the Qāsimi rule by the various means of pressure available to strong Qawāsim Rulers of either Shārjah or Ra's al Khaimah.

The Qawāsim Rulers had discovered early on that it was not easy to maintain their own appointee as *wāli* in the village of Fujairah.[38] There the tribal leaders of the Sharqiyīn were in a strong position to withhold allegiance as well as tribute, and from 1866 control over Fujairah gradually slipped from the Qawāsim's hands.

In 1901 Shaikh Ḥamad bin ʿAbdullah, the headman of the Sharqiyīn in Fujairah, declared his independence, and this time this move was recognised as an irreversible fact by everyone concerned with the exception of the British Government.[39]

Other leaders of tribes in the Shamailīyah also played important roles in local politics. The support of the shaikh of the Naqbiyīn was an essential factor in the protracted process of settling the succession in Kalba in 1937. By that time the position of the *wāli* in Kalba had become that of an independent Ruler recognised also by the British Government, but the extent of the territory had been diminished because Ḥamad bin ʿAbdullah now ruled all the surrounding Sharqiyīn territory and was in possession of Bithnah in the Wādi Ḥām, which commanded the direct route between Shārjah and the east coast. While asserting their independence, successive leaders of the Sharqiyīn in Fujairah antagonised each of the Qawāsim Rulers in turn,[40] but relations with Kalba were particularly bad because the Rulers in Kalba resented their loss of sovereignty over the Sharqiyīn, while the shaikhs of Fujairah still felt that they needed to consolidate their positions particularly vigorously so near home. Thus, despite the intermarriage during the first decade of this century between the shaikhly families of Fujairah and Kalba,[41] there was constant tension between the populations, which often erupted into acts of violence, accusations, half-hearted agreements and reconciliation, followed by another round of disputes. In the British Government's records of incidents involving the subjects of these two Rulers during the present century, Fujairah frequently appears to have taken every opportunity to provoke its neighbour. This may be partly due to the fact that the single-minded Ruler of Fujairah repeatedly alienated the British Government, which in turn may have been influenced in its reporting of the incidents. However, Fujairah had in fact become powerful enough to deny Kalba, the seat of the rightful *wāli* of all Shamailīyah, any right to the territory adjacent to the town of Kalba.[42]

The formal recognition of the Ruler of Fujairah (then Muḥammad, the son of the forceful Ḥamad bin ʿAbdullah) by the British Government in 1952 almost coincided with the extinction of Kalba as an independent shaikhdom. Like Dibah, the towns of Kalba and Khaur Fakkān have remained dependencies of Shārjah until today.

D̲aid

The most important of the villages of the Qāsimi Empire which are not located on either of the coasts is D̲aid. Strategically it is important because it commands the entrance to the Wādi Sīji, which together with the Wādi Ḥām forms the easiest of the natural routes between Shārjah and its eastern dependencies. There is abundant grazing in a wide area around D̲aid; "the water supply is excellent and ample,"[43] which makes D̲aid a place of great economic importance for the beduin of the whole region. The date groves form an oasis of about one mile in diameter, watered by one *falaj* which divides into channels. According to the *Gazetteer* the village consisted of about 140 houses, 70 of which belonged to the settled section of Ṭanaij, a tribe otherwise found chiefly in Rams near Ra's al Khaimah. The Bani Qitab and a subsection of the Na'īm, the Khawāṭir, owned between them the remainder of the palm-frond houses; both the Ṭanaij and the Khawāṭir had fortified mud-brick towers. The main characteristic of D̲aid is that it is the meeting-point of the settled and the beduin sections of the three tribes. The shaikhs of 'Ajmān and Ḥamrīyah, both belonging to subsections of the Na'īm, own gardens in the oasis.[44] The fort of the Qawāsim overlords, built on the standard pattern with two round and two square towers forming its four corners, was built across the vital *falaj*, but the flow of the *falaj* is so strong that it would be difficult to interrupt it forcibly to coerce the inhabitants of the village.

D̲aid was at the turn of the century a perfect example of a *wāli's* seat. Whoever administered the oasis on behalf of the Ruler of Shārjah collected for him dates, which were paid in kind as a royalty (100 *jirābs* in 1906), and the cash derived from the *falaj* water rates (about 228 M.T. Dollars in 1906). The income was not for the use of the *wāli*, who was at that time a trusted old negro retainer of the Qāsimi family, but was remitted to the Ruler of Shārjah.

The revenues derived from D̲aid featured largely in the financial claims and counter-claims after the deposition of Shaikh Khālid bin Aḥmad of Shārjah in November 1924. In June 1927 an agreement was reached between him and his nephew the new Ruler, Sulṭān bin Ṣaqr, regarding compensation and upkeep of Khālid's family.[45] The latter obtained in this agreement certain subsidies, the fort of D̲aid as the residence of his and his brother 'Abdullah's families, and permission to collect for his own use the customary and other revenues in D̲aid. Khālid did not take up residence there but remained in Umm al Qaiwain, sending some of his men to D̲aid to look after his property. The reason for his absence was that the beduin who had previously manned the fort on behalf of Shaikh Sulṭān were still being supported by him with arms, ammunition and supplies, while Khālid did not have the means to pay enough retainers nor did he have many volunteer followers or powerful friends.[46]

He could not perform the *wāli's* function of enforcing law and order, in particular in the disputes between the Bani Qitab and the Khawāṭir inhabitants of D̲aid and their beduin brothers. The Khawāṭir gained the upper hand unexpectedly in the summer of 1927, and it is reported that the date crop was not as good as in other years, pointing in this context to interference with the water supply to the gardens. In April 1928 the two paramount shaikhs of the Na'īm, who normally resided in Buraimi, together with Sālim bin Dayīn of the Bani Ka'ab, went to D̲aid and effected a peace between the inhabitants, arranging that authority over this village should be restored to the Qāsimi family. The same shaikhs then proceeded to Ra's al Khaimah, and asked the Ruler, Sulṭān bin Sālim, to come with them to Umm al Qaiwain, then the residence of Khālid bin Aḥmad. There the arrangement was agreed by all that the Ruler of Ra's al Khaimah should possess D̲aid "on behalf of Khālid bin Aḥmed". All the shaikhs then went to the Ruler of Shārjah.[47]

The Ruler of Ra's al Khaimah, however, was not very happy about this arrangement, for several reasons: he could see that Khālid, being "penniless", would not be able to guard the fort and his possession, and that he might have to intervene on behalf of Khālid, which would have been a costly and for him totally useless operation. Also, the Ruler of Ra's al Khaimah would hardly have enjoyed responsibility for D̲aid when it was conferred on him by the grace of the shaikhs of the beduin, who clearly saw this agreement as a way to weaken the Qāsimi rule in D̲aid. Last but not least he would have antagonised the customary overlord of D̲aid, the Ruler of Shārjah.

Eventually Khālid did take full possession of D̲aid, in July 1928, and neither the Ruler of Ra's al Khaimah nor the Ruler of Shārjah raised any objection.[48] He still did not reside there permanently, but visited the fort frequently between sojourns in Umm al Qaiwain, visits to Ra's al Khaimah and even to Bahrain. He kept possession of D̲aid when he was appointed Regent for the minor Ḥamad bin Sa'īd of Kalba in September 1937.

Ḥamrīyah, Khān and Ḥīrah

The three remaining Shārjah dependencies, Ḥamrīyah, Khān and Ḥīrah have always had a quite different relationship with the Qawāsim Rulers from that of the more distant fiefdoms. As shown above, the latter depended in their economy on cultivation, and, with the exception of Ḏaid, on fishing and some pearling. But Ḥamrīyah, Khān and Ḥīrah, all in the immediate neighbourhood of Shārjah town, had too similar a geographical situation, were too near, and had too much in common not to be a threat to Shārjah's economy. Therefore it was very important to the Ruler of Shārjah that he should control these towns.

Khān is situated on a sand-spit beside a creek three kilometres west of Shārjah and eight kilometres east of Dairah (Shaikhdom of Dubai); Ḥīrah is on the eastern outskirts of Shārjah and a short distance from the Shaikhdom of 'Ajmān. Ḥamrīyah, also on a sand-spit, lies between 'Ajmān and the next shaikhdom to the north east, Umm al Qaiwain. The four shaikhdoms and the three Shārjah dependencies therefore shared a strip of coast not more than 35 kilometres in extent. Their economies were based primarily on the pearling industry, which in itself generated a fair amount of interdependence between these neighbouring ports, not least because time and again debtors absconded and took refuge with a neighbouring shaikh. The three Shārjah dependencies were obviously very much part and parcel of the constantly changing political scene of an intricately interwoven pattern of economic rivalry and vacillating alliances. The backdrop to this 35-kilometre-long stage, where so much of the Trucial States' day-to-day politics were acted out, was the sporadic interest shown by the beduin tribes of the interior in these ports. The majority of the settled population there was after all either related or allied to them.

In dealing with his three nearby dependencies, every Ruler of Shārjah could even less than elsewhere regard these matters as purely domestic affairs. Every dispute, attempted secession or new agreement brought neighbours on the scene, and not infrequently the representatives of the British Government too. A brief account of the history of the relationship between Shārjah and these dependencies, therefore, is inevitably more than just an account of their relative economic importance and of how each was administratively tied into the Shaikhdom of Shārjah.

The dependency which was most frequently bent on secession and nearly obtained the full status of a Trucial Shaikhdom was Ḥamrīyah. The majority of the inhabitants of Ḥamrīyah were a settled section of the Āl Bū Shāmis division of the Na'īm tribe called Darāwishah. Successive leaders of this tribe were appointed *wālis* of Ḥamrīyah. Through the *wāli*, the community had to pay a tax on pearling boats and on dates to the Ruler of Shārjah. In turn the Ruler of Shārjah was expected to act on behalf of Ḥamrīyah. Frequently there were cases of debtors from among the diving community absconding to a neighbouring port to evade their creditors, and the Ruler should have exerted his influence to help recover the loans. Alleged negligence of this duty on the part of the Rulers of Shārjah was at the root of Ḥamrīyah's attempts to gain independence during the latter part of the 19th century.[49]

Out of consideration to the Ruler of Shārjah, at that time Ṣaqr bin Khālid, the British Government on the occasion of Lord Curzon's visit to the coast in 1903 stopped short of granting recognition to Saif bin 'Abdul Raḥman of Ḥamrīyah as a Trucial Ruler. This shaikh, and later his son, 'Abdul Raḥman bin Saif, were in many respects treated like Trucial Rulers and often asked to mediate, and they invariably attended the official *majlis* held when the Political Resident visited the coast. In 1923 Ḥamrīyah came again within reach of complete sovereignty, when Khālid bin Aḥmed, Ruler of Shārjah, in a letter to 'Abdul Raḥmān bin Saif granted independence to Ḥamrīyah on 9 August, and renounced all claims on taxes and revenues from that port. The following year, however, Khālid was deposed, and his successor, Sulṭān bin Ṣaqr, did not honour this undertaking.[50]

In 1922 and again in 1925 attempts were made by 'Abdul Raḥman bin Saif's son Ḥumaid to take the leadership from his father. Both times the Rulers of Shārjah and Umm al Qaiwain rallied to the support of the *wāli* of Ḥamrīyah. When 'Abdul Raḥman bin Saif was killed in April 1931 he did not die at the hand of his son Ḥumaid but at the hand of his nephew, Saif bin 'Abdullah, whom he had brought up in his household. Saif and his brother claimed that 'Abdul Raḥmān bin Saif had kept for himself their father's property. Saif bin 'Abdullah held the leadership in Ḥamrīyah for some months but he did not satisfy the creditors of the former *wāli* as expected; the murdered uncle 'Abdul Raḥman bin Saif had left some 21,500 Rupees of debts to merchants of Ḥamrīyah and neighbouring ports. Ḥumaid, the son of the deceased, with the support of 'Ajmān and Umm al Qaiwain tried to oust his cousin Saif bin 'Abdullah. He was at first unsuccessful, but when the increasingly suspicious and oppressive Saif lost the support of the population of Ḥamrīyah, Ḥumaid was able to take over with their help when Saif was away in August 1931. Saif's attempt to reverse the outcome and murder Ḥumaid came to nothing.[51] Ḥamrīyah remained under Ḥumaid's leadership but did not gain independence, although the matter was discussed again in 1937 at a time when oil concession agreements were being negotiated for the Trucial Coast.

The village of Khān, being so near to Shārjah town, even within reach of the fort's guns, was administered usually by a tribal leader. There were Āl Bū Mahair, Mazārī' and Manāṣīr living in the village, owning about 75 pearling boats and a number of fishing boats. During Khālid bin Aḥmad's rule in Shārjah, relations between him and the headman, Muḥammad bin 'Ubaid bin Jarash, suffered because of arguments arising from the problems posed by debtors absconding and seeking refuge in another pearling community. In 1917 the Political Resident intervened, arriving on a man-of-war because disturbance of the peace at sea and loss of British Indian lives and property had been feared. In the subsequent agreement Muḥammad bin 'Ubaid undertook to give at the beginning of each diving season 50 bags of rice to the Ruler of Shārjah.[52] In a letter to the Political Resident in August 1920, however, Muḥammad bin 'Ubaid complained that Khālid bin Aḥmad had frequently failed to fulfil his part of the deal between the Ruler and the *wāli* of the people of Khān,[53] and that, when Khān had been plundered three times, Khālid had made no effort to protect the inhabitants nor to retrieve the stolen property of Khān citizens. As a result the people of Khān also became dissatisfied with their *wāli*, Muḥammad bin 'Ubaid.[54] A reconciliation was effected between Khālid bin Aḥmed and Muḥammad bin 'Ubaid in August 1920, and the Residency Agent reported that "the Headman now takes part in the hostilities between Shaikh Khālid and the Manāṣīr tribesmen . . .," which was obviously to be understood as a sign of at least temporary good relations.[55]

In September 1931 Muḥammad bin 'Ubaid died in Bahrain, but the Ruler of Shārjah, then Khālid's nephew Sulṭān bin Ṣaqr, was simply informed by letter from a certain Jarash bin 'Ali bin Rāshid that the inhabitants of Khān had accepted him, Jarash, as their headman in place of the deceased.[56] This obviously separatist course did not promote good relations between Shārjah and its nominal dependency. Sulṭān bin Ṣaqr found it necessary to bring Khān firmly under his control by appointing his brother Muḥammad as *wāli* there after Jarash had been murdered in September 1934, allegedly by a messenger of Sulṭān bin Ṣaqr. The new *wāli* consolidated his hold on Khān by marrying the niece of the late Jarash bin ʿAli.

The village of about 250 houses on the beach on the eastern outskirts of Shārjah town called Ḥīrah was inhabited exclusively by Darāwishah, a subsection of the Āl Bū Shāmis part of the Naʿīm tribe. Because his community consisted of one tribe alone, the leader was in a very strong position to pursue his individualistic activities, as was the case with ʿAbdul Raḥman bin Muḥammad, headman for many years during this century. Some aspects of his relations with the Ruler of Shārjah and other Trucial Rulers will be described elsewhere.[57]

2 Other means of exercising authority

Although the population in the Qāsimi realm in general had little say in the choice of a *wāli*, particularly in areas which were treated as fiefdoms, the tribal structure left room for grass-root democracy for both the beduin and the settled inhabitants. In most villages, hamlets, or quarters of a town, each tribal group had its own leaders, and they would be the channels of communication between the heads of families and the *wāli* or the Ruler himself. Such a person would lead a delegation of his people to the local *wāli* in case of a grievance, and he would also pass on the *wāli's* instructions to them. Usually there was no formal appointment nor a regular salary, but the local *wālis* or the Rulers themselves rewarded services rendered to the *ḥukūmah* by gifts or favours.

Usually tribal bonds manifested in loyalty to the tribal shaikh took precedence over the identification of an individual with the central administration of the *wāli* or the Ruler.[58] Therefore, if a Ruler sent a brother or a son or even a trusted slave or a secretary to represent him when problems in a distant region became particularly acute, the usefulness of such a person's mission was often limited by the delicate balance of local politics, which could often be handled only by a locally known and respected tribal leader.

So far the description of the Qāsimi administration has addressed itself only to the settled population. With the exception of the handful of Hindus, Persians and other foreign minorities living in the towns of the Trucial Coast, that population was tribal. This meant that the people lived, worked, made politics and fought in units which could be identified by the names of the subsections, sections and tribes. It also meant that they were as a rule affiliated to the beduin population of the hinterland, because most of these tribes also had nomadic branches.

Whether people lived in the coastal towns near Shārjah or Ra's al Khaimah, or in a small hamlet at the head of a steep *wādi*, they went about their daily life, hardly aware of government or of administrative interference wherever it might come from. Only the annual payment of taxes would have reminded them once a year of the distant overlords.

An authority higher than that of the village headman would become obvious to them only at times of crises, raids, disputes over wells, gardens or fishing rights.

In most intra-community law cases, offences, and disputes, and in almost everything else concerning the economic, social, religious and moral behaviour in these tribal communities, the people referred first to the family, then to the sub-tribe and the tribal group, not to a distant, albeit sometimes useful, political unit headed by a Trucial Ruler.

A tribal group did not recognise a spokesman just because he declared himself leader, nor only because he belonged to the family which had produced the community's leaders in the past; he had to be outstanding in more than one respect, in strength, determination, or in wealth to distribute, and thus appear to the majority of the community to be a better choice than anyone else at hand. Any tribesman who did not agree with this choice was, in theory, free to use "the democracy of the feet" and to go to live with a community whose leader he could accept. However, in practice each family depended much more on the entire tribal group for their well-being than on good relationships with whoever was the tribal leader, so such an exodus of individuals or families to another community did not happen often; whereas the exodus of an entire subtribe under its leader has always been a feature of politics on this coast.

The same spirit of intrinsic independence coupled with voluntary submission under certain circumstances dominated the relationship between a Ruler, whether recognised by the British authorities or not, and the tribal population living under what might be termed his jurisdiction. The authority of any Ruler over tribal groups has always implied a certain amount of give and take. A community which has been harassed and raided by another tribe looks around for the most likely help, but if a shaikh who came to their assistance, using either force or diplomacy, then tried to dominate that community by imposing one of his men as *wāli*, or by levying a new tax, the relationship would be short-lived and the community would soon be seeking another protector. The Ruler who is strong and wise, who is wealthy but not greedy, who is influential with many neighbouring tribes, who is patient and generous, and who has a reputation of personal courage is a Ruler who does not find it difficult to increase his influence among the tribes and thereby to enlarge the territory of his realm. When a tribe was subdued by force, it was always difficult for any Ruler to maintain permanent control by force, because none of them had more than a few salaried guards (*ʿaskars*). In a major armed conflict a coastal Ruler usually had to rely on mercenary beduin tribesmen, thus being faced again with the necessity to establish and maintain good relations with important neighbouring tribal groups, in competition with other Rulers.

To facilitate the administration even of undisputed outlying districts, a Ruler had to try to establish, if not complete sovereignty over them, at least a *modus vivendi* with the beduin tribes which frequented the area. The beduin in turn needed access to markets to buy their provisions and to sell camels, goats and their few other products. In the northern part of the Trucial Coast few nomads owned pearling boats, but a large number of them signed on as divers and haulers with boats belonging to one of the villages along the coasts, and while the pearling industry was expanding during the first two decades of this century, beduin from the hinterland were a very welcome additional source of labour. In order to gain the support of beduin tribes the Rulers of the northern Trucial States had to rely to a large extent on subsidies and favours, while most of the Bani Yās Rulers were able to command at almost any time the loyalty of large beduin contingents.

3 Abu Dhabi: a tribal confederation's means of absorbing change

The setting

The shaikhdom of Abu Dhabi provides a number of examples of how remote areas were administered in the tribal society of the Trucial Coast. The key to the lasting cohesion of Abu Dhabi as a shaikhdom under one Ruler was good management of the beduin and the semi-nomadic tribes. As was described above, the largest number of beduin in the Trucial shaikhdoms lived either permanently or very frequently in territory which the subjects of successive Rulers of Abu Dhabi claimed as their *dār*. When in the 17th and 18th centuries the confederation of the Bani Yās was developing, the Āl Bū Falāḥ shaikhs probably exercised their influence chiefly through the age-old system of agreements for mutual assistance between themselves and the heads of the tribal subsections; one may also assume that at least the larger of the permanent Līwā villages also had a headman. In the 1950s the Bani Yās were still one of the least settled of the major tribes on the coast because of their diverse economic interests in various parts of the shaikhdom. The Āl Bū Falāḥ authority had been accepted by most of the settled Dhawāhir in and near the Oasis of Buraimi, and a varying degree of influence was exercised by Abu Dhabi's Rulers over the visiting nomads such as the Manāhīl, Āl Murrah, ʿAfār, or Rashīd, and also over tribes settled even in Dhāhirah, at some distance from the Buraimi Oasis.

Because the majority of these people changed their habitat at least once during the course of a year, there developed two sometimes quite separate ways of administering the shaikhdom. There was the system dictated by the geography of the country: a *wāli*, here usually called *amīr*, was appointed for the main population centres, the Līwā, the Buraimi Oasis, Dalmā and later Ṭarīf, Dās Island, and Jabal al Dhannah. Another system addressed itself to the people as members of tribal units regardless of their actual abode at any point in time. The relationship between these tribal units and the Ruler of Abu Dhabi varied: subsidies were demanded from some of them as a sign of submission, occasional gifts or regular allowances were given to others, and for some the regular taxes were waived. Both systems were necessarily interrelated, because often the same people were involved at different times in different places.

The methods of administering the shaikhdom in use at least until the late 1950s will be described firstly by listing the successive incumbents of certain posts, and secondly by looking at the manifestations of sovereignty such as tax collection, jurisdiction and subsidies.

The Ruler's representatives

Dhafrah

Some time after 1793 the shaikh of the Āl Bū Falāḥ exchanged a village in the Līwā for the growing coastal settlement of Abu Dhabi as his permanent residence; it then became necessary to put someone in charge of daily affairs in the Līwā, which was several days' camel journey away. At the beginning of the 20th century the Ruler, Shaikh Zāyid bin Khalīfah, appointed his eldest son Khalīfah to be his representative and to live in the Līwā every summer during the date harvest. When his brother Ṭaḥnūn bin Zāyid became the Ruler in 1909, a representative by the name of Bin Ya'arūf officiated in the Līwā and continued during the rule of Ḥamdān bin Zāyid (1912–1922). While Sulṭān bin Zāyid was Ruler (1922–1926) Abu Dahām was *wāli* in the Līwā, and he remained in office until the death of the next Ruler, Ṣaqr bin Zāyid, in 1928.[59] At times of war with neighbouring Qatar and when raiding Saudi tribes threatened Abu Dhabi's western borders, a number of watch-towers overlooking the approach routes (as on the island of Ṣīr Bani Yās and at Ra's Ghumaish) were manned by tribesmen. During the rule of Zāyid bin Khalīfah their commander (*amīr al jaish*) was Suwaidān bin Za'al al Maḥairibi, and until many of the members of this Bani Yās sub-tribe dispersed to neighbouring countries in the 1950s, the sons and grandsons of Suwaidān appear to have maintained a prominent position and obtained payment for their services from the Ruler. Shaikh Shakhbūṭ's first *wāli* in the Līwā was Hilāl bin Sa'īd al Ghāfiri, an Āl Bū Falāḥ, who was replaced in 1949 by Aḥmad bin Faḍil al Mazrū'i of the Bani Yās. In 1955 Rāshid bin Jābir al Hāmili was appointed to the Līwā.

Rāshid bin Jābir was succeeded in 1964 by Saif bin Mūsa al-Hāmili, who until the early 1980s looked after the affairs of the inhabitants in the Līwā villages. As in past generations the last *amīr's* residence was in al Māriyah, which was not among the few fortified settlements in the Līwā. Like all other houses in the Līwā until about 1977, when the first concrete buildings went up, the government post in al Māriyah was a palm-frond hut on a gentle sand dune, distinguishable only by the flagpole outside and a few rifles in canvas bags inside, ready for use by the handful of part-time tribal *'askars* who were attached to the post. Each of the larger villages has also always had its headman, who would act as spokesman and receive visitors who might be passing by.

When during the final years of the 1960s Bida' Zāyid was built, some 40 kilometres north of the Līwā, as a modern centre where the population of Dhafrah could obtain medical facilities and formal schooling, the *amīr* of the Līwā established a second residence there.

Eventually most families of Dhafrah were allocated a house in Bidaʿ Zāyid constructed for them by the government; women and children of school age and the elderly took up residence there during most of the year while some of the men were either supervising the camels on the winter grazing or looking after the gardens in the Līwā. Eventually the majority of the men established transport businesses either in Abu Dhabi or in Bidaʿ Zāyid, or they found employment with the military, police or one of the many companies operating in the area.

Since the early 1970s Saif bin Mūsa had ceased to report directly to the Ruler in Abu Dhabi, but had referred to the representative in the western region, Shaikh Muḥammad bin Buṭi al Ḥamad. This was the effect of a far-reaching change in the nature and function of *wāli* administration in the shaikhdom of Abu Dhabi after the establishment of new population centres associated with the activities of the oil company.

Ṭarīf

Since the 1950s the activities of the oil companies have required the concentration of a work-force of local inhabitants in new settlements in places previously insignificant in the local economy. The men obtained regular employment, wages were paid, and they were subject to the authority of the foreign company. The relationship between the company, the Ruler and his people in these various locations had to be arranged to suit the new requirements. Thus a total transformation was brought about in the method of administering the shaikhdom.

When preparations for drilling the first well on the Trucial Coast were being made late in 1949 by PD(TC) at Ra's al Ṣadr, men from all areas of Abu Dhabi State found employment with the company. The Ruler, Shaikh Shakhbūṭ, kept in touch with every development regarding the recruitment of labour, the payment of wages, and the conditions of employment; but he also appointed his nephew Shaikh Ḥamdān bin Muḥammad as his representative at the drilling site, to be present as and when required. Routine liaison between the tribal work-force and the company was entrusted first to Aḥmad bin Faḍil al Mazrūʿi, then to the *wāli* in the Līwā, who was at times assisted by Aḥmad bin Jumaʿh.

Under the terms of the agreement of 1939 between the Ruler and the company, the former was obliged to provide guards for all company camps established in his territory. The company refunded to the Ruler the cost of the guards' wages, and only rations were given directly to the guards at each camp. In the first camp at Raʿs al Ṣadr the head guard was Thāni bin Murshid, who was the elder of the Rumaithāt section of the Bani Yās; he became the contact between the company and the guards and eventually also between the entire local labour force and the Ruler.

After drilling a well at Jabal ʿAli in Dubai territory, PD(TC) in 1953 moved their camp to Ṭarīf, west of Abu Dhabi, to drill the first well on the Bāb structure. The head guard Thāni bin Murshid remained the link between the government and the company, living for most of the year in Ṭarīf, although he had by then opened a shop in the *suq* in Abu Dhabi. But he was never styled *amīr*.

In 1955 the main camp was moved again, first to drill a well at Jazīrah, west of the Sabkhah Maṭṭi, then on to al Ḥamrāʾ to drill another well on the coast near to Jabal al Dhannah.[60] A temporary camp was also constructed for drilling at Juwaisah in Shārjah territory in 1957. At the end of 1958, the camp at Ṭarīf, which had never been entirely dismantled, was refurbished because drilling on the Bāb dome was resumed. Guards were required at all these drilling locations as well as at the camps of the seismic survey parties and at the various places on the coast where materials were off-loaded from barges. Where the Ruler's guards were used in any of these locations, Thāni bin Murshid appointed head guards who acted as his deputies in all matters concerning the guards as well as the entire local labour force.[61] In those years Thāni bin Murshid therefore held a very powerful position, being able to decide who among the tribesmen would obtain employment with the company, and in turn he could influence the relationship between the men and the company.

During those early years the head guard in Ṭarīf was directly responsible to Shaikh Shakhbūṭ. But he remained closely identified with his own tribal group and his influence over some of the labour force, which was recruited from almost all of Abu Dhabi's tribes, was not always sufficient to settle disputes and avoid stoppages of work. In these situations only a member of the ruling family commanded the necessary authority to make the men accept the conditions which had been negotiated with the oil company's representatives.[62]

After the announcement of the discovery of oil in commercial quantities in October 1960, the company's activity increased dramatically, and as a result of this the Ruler appointed in June 1961 a labour representative at Ṭarīf. Aḥmad bin Ḥasan, of the Sūdān tribe, who had previously been head guard at various camps, occupied this position in 1963. By this time Thāni bin Murshid had entered into a partnership with a foreign company, African and Eastern, to provide various maintenance services in Ṭarīf.

The expansion of company activity in the western part of Abu Dhabi coincided with the start of oil exports from an offshore field in 1962. At the same time the Ruler started to delegate some authority through the introduction of a rudimentary administration in Abu Dhabi town. The beduin too were subject increasingly to new administrative processes, particularly where they took up employment.

In 1964 Aḥmad bin Ḥasan was the Ruler's representative with the drilling contractor Santa Fe at their base camp near Ṭarīf, but eventually his authority was further increased and he became known as the *amīr* of Ṭarīf. The appointment of Ruler's representative was conferred on a member of the ruling family, and in 1964 it was the Ruler's nephew Muḥammad bin Khālid, who was not resident in Ṭarīf. The Ruler also often delegated his son Sulṭān, head of the police detachment at Ṭarīf and at times also head of the municipality in Abu Dhabi, to have overall responsibility in the entire area where the oil company and its contractors operated. He was present at many a meeting between the company's personnel officers and the beduin when disputes were discussed and on occasion he visited the rigs to smooth out differences. At times his brother Saʿīd was also involved in such tasks.

After Shaikh Zāyid became the Ruler of Abu Dhabi in August 1966, overall responsibility in the oil company's areas remained for some time with his nephew Muḥammad bin Khālid, while Aḥmad bin Ḥasan was still in charge of day-to-day labour relations.[63] In November 1968 a labour inspector was installed in Ṭarīf to observe the implementation of the labour law which had been promulgated on 1 January 1967, and to represent the labour department which had been set up recently in Abu Dhabi under the chairmanship of Shaikh Aḥmad bin Ḥamad. In the summer of 1968 Shaikh Muḥammad bin Buṭi, the Ruler's cousin on his mother's side, was appointed Governor of Ṭarīf. As the senior government official in the area he ensured that the local labour force was treated by all contractors according to the labour law and to the practices laid down in a code by the oil company.

During the 1970s, when employment with the contractors of the oil company became less attractive to the beduin population because many of them gravitated towards Abu Dhabi town and al ʿAin to start businesses of their own or to take up employment with the government, the Governor's "job description" changed too. From being primarily concerned with the employment and working conditions of the beduin, Shaikh Muḥammad became eventually responsible for many aspects of life of the beduin population in the area. He was responsible for the construction of the new town of Bidaʿ Zāyid, between the Līwā and the coast, as a permanent home for families from the Līwā and elsewhere in Dhafrah. The oil company moved out of Ṭarīf in 1972 and Shaikh Muḥammad moved to Bidaʿ Zāyid to supervise the allocation of houses, the provision of water, the planting of desert vegetation and gardens, and generally to lead the population of the area in striking a balance between the traditional way of life and the new amenities which the government could now offer. At the same time as his responsibilities were thus enlarged to cover an increasing number of functions, the extent of his authority too, which originally included only the locations of oil company activities, increased to include all the western desert and after 1990 also Jabal al Dhannah.

Jabal al Dhannah

During the height of the construction work on the oil terminal at Jabal al Dhannah some 4,000 men of different nationalities were based there. Most large projects were completed simultaneously with the completion of a degassing station at Ḥabshān, and the labour force had to be drastically reduced in early 1964. The Ruler visited Jabal al Dhannah to see for himself how many beduin who wanted to continue working were being laid off. He ordered that a committee should be set up to investigate the employment of foreigners, particularly by labour contractors who had brought large numbers of workmen from the Indian subcontinent. The committee consisted of Shaikh Sulṭān bin Shakhbūṭ, Aḥmad bin Ḥasan, and a Jordanian from the Palace in Abu Dhabi. After the terminal was commissioned some construction work was from time to time resumed as the facilities expanded; a steady number of beduin, mostly Manāṣīr, have been working in Jabal al Dhannah to man the mooring launches used by the marine contractor to berth the tankers, and they also work for other companies rendering other services around the terminal. At the height of construction in 1962 Jabal al Dhannah was made the seat of another Governorate. Shaikh Sulṭān bin Surūr al Dhāhiri from the important Dhawāhir tribe of the Buraimi oasis was the representative of the Ruler at Jabal al Dhannah from that time until his death in 1990.[64]

Dās Island

Having followed in detail the impact of changing economic opportunities and working habits of the population on the administrative structure in the desert, it is necessary to mention only a few events in the history of the previously uninhabited island Dās. When the oil company, Abu Dhabi Marine Areas Ltd., started drilling in 1958 it built a service camp on the island, and in due course established all its oil-export and related facilities on the approximately 2.5 square-kilometre island, 160 kilometres from Abu Dhabi town. In July 1962 the State's first cargo of crude oil was exported from there. The Ruler's nephew, Shaikh Ḥamdān bin Muḥammad, became his representative there, being resident on the island for most of the year. When he was called upon by Shaikh Zāyid early in 1967 to head some of the newly-established departments in Abu Dhabi, his assistant on Dās, Mubārak bin Ḥādhr, became the Ruler's representative; he retired from this post in 1992.

Buraimi Oasis

The appointment of his own *wāli* in the Buraimi Oasis, in 1896, put the seal on Shaikh Zāyid bin Khalīfah's endeavours to dominate the oasis.[65] After an increasing number of Bani Yās, and particularly the Āl Bū Falāḥ, had acquired date gardens in several of the villages, some Dhawāhir, the original owners of the oasis, tried unsuccessfully to shake off this Āl Bū Falāḥ domination. But after the last armed clash in 1891 Shaikh Zāyid was in a stronger position than ever, and enforced his sovereignty by extracting a tribute from the Dhawāhir villages and by collecting the customary taxes from the villagers. Shaikh Zāyid was, however, able to avoid resentment among and alienation of the Dhawāhir, who had previously been his allies against the Na'īm, by making the *tamīmah* of the Dhawāhir his *wāli* responsible for all the villages under Abu Dhabi domination. Aḥmad bin Muḥammad bin Hilāl al Dhāhiri resided in Jīmi and served efficiently and faithfully as the representative of Shaikh Zāyid bin Khalīfah, of his four sons who ruled after him, and of his grandson Shaikh Shakhbūṭ bin Sulṭān. Aḥmad bin Muḥammad was vested with considerable power over the lesser headmen of the villages, and due to his personality as much as to the Āl Bū Falāḥ power he represented, his influence over the tribes in the vicinity of the oasis usually far exceeded that of the Na'īm shaikhs of Buraimi and the representatives of the Sultan of Muscat and Oman. Like other leading personalities, the Dhawāhir shaikhs obtained subsidies from the Āl Bū Falaḥ with whom they also intermarried. Now the Dhawāhir occupy prominent positions in the political and economic life of the emirate and of the federal government.

After the death of Aḥmad bin Hilāl in 1936, the *wāli* of al 'Ain, Ibrāhīm bin 'Uthmān, succeeded to this position of extensive responsibility, while the post of *wāli* in al 'Ain was filled for a few years by 'Abdullah bin Ghanūm al Hāmili, whose standing was similar to that of tribal headmen of villages, such as Sulṭān bin Muḥammad al Darmaki in al Qaṭṭārah. Soon after the death in 1946 of Ibrāhīm, and after the war between Dubai and Abu Dhabi in which the younger brother and right hand man of the Ruler, Shaikh Zāyid bin Sulṭān, had proved his ability as a leader, he was formally appointed *wāli* over all the oasis. When Shaikh Zāyid bin Sulṭān became Ruler of Abu Dhabi in 1966 he appointed his son Khalīfah to the post he had vacated.

In August 1970 Shaikh Ṭaḥnūn, one of the sons of Muḥammad bin Khalīfah, was entrusted with the affairs of the fast-growing town of al 'Ain and of the other villages, as chairman of a municipal council. A large part of his responsibility as the Ruler's representative in the Eastern Region is the development of agriculture and the settlement of beduin in al 'Ain and the entire region.

Dalmā

The island of Dalmā, 160 kilometres almost due west of Abu Dhabi town, has been of vital importance to the pearling community of Abu Dhabi. Every year it became the centre for the pearling fleet of the Bani Yās and other boats, initially because they could obtain fresh water there. A seasonal market also developed and many pearl merchants visited the island themselves during the pearling season. The administration of this island on behalf of the Ruler of Abu Dhabi was in the hands of an *amīr* who was also responsible for all the other islands belonging to Abu Dhabi except for the town of Abu Dhabi itself. An *amīr* usually lived on the island only during the summer months, collecting the pearl taxes and settling disputes. He was an employee of the Ruler, and therefore although it was a prestigious position it was different from that of a *wāli* in Shamailīyah or of a headman or semi-independent shaikh in Ḥamrīyah. The Ruler's representative on Dalmā was paid a salary; he was not entitled to a share of the taxes he collected, as was the case in some of the Qawāsim ports where a *wāli* was so frequently a local tribal shaikh or a political figure in his own right.

During the later years of the rule of Zāyid bin Khalīfah, *amīrs* on Dalmā were Ḥamad bin Dismāl, Aḥmad bin Qumbar, and eventually the Ruler's fourth son Sulṭān.[66] In Ḥamdān bin Zāyid's time (1912–22) and that of his successors a permanent resident on the island, ʿAbdul Raḥman bin Ḥamad al Najdi, was *amīr* on Dalmā. He died in the summer of 1932 and the Ruler's brother Shaikh Hazzāʿ bin Sulṭān took over for the remainder of that season, assisted by a secretary of Iranian descent, ʿAbbās bin ʿAbdullah. Between 1933 and 1937 ʿAbbās bin ʿAbdullah shared the responsibility with ʿAli bin Shaibān al Khamīri. After that the latter went alone to the island for the following seasons until 1942 when Rāshid bin Jābir al Suwaidi took over for two seasons. Then ʿAli bin Shaibān returned to Dalmā again for the season of 1945 to 1949. ʿAbbas bin ʿAbdullah succeeded ʿAli and remained the *amīr* for Dalmā until his death in 1951.

An *amīr* on Dalmā usually had an assistant tax collector, *muzakki*, and throughout the year a customs official collected the $2\frac{1}{2}$ per cent customs dues on behalf of the Ruler. The diving court[67] for Abu Dhabi's pearling community has in this century always consisted of just one man, appointed by the Ruler; he was concerned with all pearling-related disputes arising in Abu Dhabi waters, and commuted between Abu Dhabi and Dalmā. During the off-season the few permanent inhabitants on Dalmā settled small disputes themselves. Important matters could be referred to a relative of the ruling family residing on the island for communication to the Ruler in Abu Dhabi.[68]

The increase in oil company activities eventually diverted most of the manpower away from the pearling industry, which was already at a low ebb in the 1950s. With this the importance of Dalmā also declined. In the later 1970s the small community of tribal fishermen was given new incentives to stay there by the establishment of government-financed houses, schools, new mosques, a market complex, and a small hospital; free transport to and from the island by helicopter was organised by the army; several construction projects are proposed for the island. Thus, Dalmā, like the Līwā and Bidaʿ Zāyid and the al ʿAin area, entered the era of departmentalised administration, co-ordinated by government institutions in Abu Dhabi town.

Nowadays the authority of government is manifest in a multitude of administrative measures effected by anonymous civil servants. In the days when the Ruler's representatives (*wāli*, *amīr* or *nā'ib*), the tax collector, a customs official and a *qāḍi* were all appointed and maintained personally by the Ruler, his sovereignty in times of peace was manifest in a limited number of rights, privileges and duties which his tribal subjects would have found difficult to deny him. In the event of an armed dispute the extent of a Ruler's authority became measurable in the amount of fighting support he obtained from his own people and from neighbouring tribes.

4 Manifestations of administrative sovereignty—with an emphasis on examples from Abu Dhabi[69]

Taxation

In every community the Ruler's right to impose taxation is a symbol of his authority. The different relationships between the tribes and the Trucial Rulers were illustrated by the fact that some tribal groups were never expected to pay tax while others had to pay taxes and some even paid an additional tribute. Some of the collected tax was used to provide funds for community projects such as maintaining the *falaj*, but the income from most taxes became the property of the Ruler, and a wise Ruler would know well the value of being generous. The Ruler was expected to reciprocate the payment of taxes by supporting the cause of his subjects, be it a just one in his eyes or not. In more loose relationships where no regular taxation was collected, a Ruler was not necessarily obliged to involve himself in a dispute.

The principal source of revenue for all the Trucial Rulers throughout the 19th century and the first half of the 20th century was the pearling industry. The growth of the town population was in step with the economic growth and decline.[70] This in turn was reflected in the income of the Ruler of a pearling port. In all the ports of the coast the shaikhs derived revenues, not from rent or royalties on the pearl banks but from taxes imposed on their own subjects and on persons resident under their jurisdiction. A passage in the Gazetteer implies that taxation by the Rulers was an innovation of the 19th century.[71] But Ibn Baṭūṭah's description of the Gulf, which he visited during the second half of the 14th century, gives a very similar picture of the contemporary pearling industry in places such as Basra, to what it was during the 19th century on the Trucial Coast; the taxation levied by the Sultan was one fifth, which was much higher than that levied by the shaikhs of the Trucial Coast.[72]

There were over the decades several kinds of taxes connected with the pearling industry. Some were designated contributions, such as for defence or the maintenance of communal buildings, others were taxes which the shaikh levied. Dues of the first category were originally called *ṭarāz*, and were used to pay a few beduin to protect the towns and villages during the absence of most men on the pearl banks in the summer, and to guard the pearling boats which were beached during the winter in remote parts of the coast while the owners were in the desert.

The amount of the various dues, the method of collecting them, and the way in which the Rulers used the funds either for themselves or for the benefit of the tribal community varied from port to port and from one shaikh to another. In some instances dues were paid in kind, such as the payment of one bag of rice per boat to be handed to the shaikh before the season began. In Shārjah the semi-independent headmen of the dependencies were usually expected to remit a certain share of their ports' income from pearling to the Ruler of Shārjah.[73]

As a basis for assessing the different dues, the boats, the individuals, as well as certain pearls were used. During the time that the Gazetteer was compiled the dues which were imposed on the entire boat were called *naub*, regardless of whether they were taken in money or in kind. Between one and four bags of rice[74] were taken from the small, medium and large boats in most ports of Shārjah in the spring as *naub*, except for Ḥamrīyah, where it was one hauler's (*saib*) share per boat in the autumn. In Umm al Qaiwain it was 20 Rupees and 2 bags of rice per large boat in the spring plus one hauler's share in the autumn. A tax called *shūfah* was collected at irregular intervals when funds were needed for a particular community project, for an emergency, or to pay a fine imposed on the shaikhdom. In Abu Dhabi one diver's or one hauler's share was paid in the autumn depending on the size of the boat. There was also a royalty of 75 Rupees on every pearl that was worth more than 1,000 Rupees, and a commission was taken by the Ruler on the sale of all pearls at Dalmā island.

During that same period *ṭarāz* was the tax collected usually in the spring at the rate of between $2\frac{1}{2}$ and 10 M.T. Dollars per diver/hauler team (called *qalṭah*) at all ports except Ḥamrīyah and Ḥīrah. However, relatives, friends, officials and servants of the Ruler were exempt from paying taxes. In Shārjah town these exemptions represented one third of the gross revenue of the port, amounting to 30,700 Rupees because 71 boats and 1,317 men were exempt. In Dubai more than half the revenue due to the Ruler was waived, but the 210 exempted boats (out of a total of 335 boats) had to pay for the cost of 100 beduin employed to guard the town. In Abu Dhabi only 21 boats and 315 men were exempt, which meant a loss of 2,000 Rupees in revenues; in this case the Ruler paid for the cost of maintaining guards, which amounted to 1,450 Rupees.[75] The system of taxation did not only vary between one port of the Trucial Coast and another, but it was also subject to significant changes due to the local changes of regime as well as to fluctuations in this important industry. In the case of Abu Dhabi these changes are well documented.

The system of taxation in use during the first decade of the 20th century on Dalmā island was described, in even more detail than in the Gazetteer, by the Residency Agent in Shārjah in a memorandum in the following sentences: "Dalma island is thickly populated during diving seasons, being visited by the natives of Katr, Bahrein, Lingah and the towns on the Arab Coast, who are dealing in pearls and miscellaneous goods. They pay the Chief of Abu Dhabi a tax (at the rate of) 40 or 30 M.T. Dollars for every merchant and 10 or 6 M.T. Dollars for every petty pearl dealer (Tawwash) whose capital amounts to Rupees 1000/- more or less. The Chief of Abu Dhabi also levies a tax, 'Arziyeh', of one M.T. Dollar on the lodging of every pearl dealer. He also takes one half of the profit gained by pearl dealers who buy precious pearls from the subjects of Abu Dhabi. For instance, if anyone bought 2 or 3 pearls for Rupees 10,000/- and sold them for Rupees 12,000/- a half of the profit will be for the Chief of Abu Dhabi. This [rule] applies to the pearls on which people of Abu Dhabi have no claims (that is to say, on which they have paid no advance). As regards the pearls on which there are claims by the people of Abu Dhabi, the Chief himself settles with them as regards profit. He does not recover anything on pearls which are not precious, except the usual diving tax."[76]

In the early 1950s Dalmā island was still very much the centre for pearling of the desert based population of Abu Dhabi; of the 40–50 houses only 8 were inhabited the year round (by Qubaisāt families), the others belonging mostly to people who also owned houses and date gardens in the Līwā. Some Bani Yās owned houses on other islands; they also converged on Dalmā for the pearling season.[77] Most of the approximately 65 boats reported to be based on Dalmā belonged to Līwā-based Bani Yās. A statement made in 1954 by a Qubaisi pearl-boat owner from Quṭūf shows that of the 14 crew in his boat several of the divers were either Qubaisi or other Bani Yās from Quṭūf, one was a Mazrū'i from Maqab where some of the haulers came from, and one of the haulers was the servant of a Qubaisi of Dalmā. This particular *nūkhaḏā* had taken on some Manāṣīr as crew in previous years.

In 1955 the previous *amīr* of Dalmā gave a written description of the taxation system which was then still in use on the island.[78] It involved six types of dues: 1. At the beginning of the pearling season a sack of rice, *junīyah*, and four Rupees *tūmān* were collected from every boat: half of both amounts were taken from small boats. 2. A share equal to the season's income of one rope-puller, *saib*, was collected as *ḥāṣilah*. This amount was calculated. The remainder was shared between divers and *saibs* at the proportion of three for the former and two for the latter, after adding an imaginary *saib*. The share of that *saib* was the tax due to the Ruler of Abu Dhabi. 3. At the end of a season a tax of two Rupees was levied on every *qalṭah* (pair, a diver and a hauler). 4. On every pearl valued 2,000 Rupees or more a tax of 200 Rupees was taken by the Ruler. 5. *Naub* was at that time the term for the tax levied on every pearl merchant or other merchant in Dalmā or the islands and coastal tracts administered by the *amīr*. The tax varied between 2 and 200 Rupees a year for an individual, depending on the size of his business. 6. *'Azīmah* was a voluntary contribution of the pearl merchants towards the cost of a feast traditionally given in honour of the Ruler when he or a close relative came to Dalmā at the end of every diving season.

Compared to the taxes relating to the pearling industry, taxes on agricultural produce amounted to very little almost everywhere in the Trucial States. This type of tax was collected in kind, so that the Ruler or in some cases the *wāli* could feed the members of his household and his retainers, extend hospitality and maintain his camels, horses, sheep and goats. The rate of agricultural taxation varied between 5 and 10 per cent, the former being the figure given in the Gazetteer for the entire area under Qāsimi rule.

At times the majority of owners of date gardens were exempt from this taxation because throughout the Trucial States a modification of the system obtained whereby no tax was demanded from those who produced less than the *nisab*, a minimum which varied according to time and place and was set at 3,600 lbs of dates for the Līwā during the 1950s.

During the first decade of the 20th century, when the owners of the date gardens in the villages of the Buraimi Oasis dominated by the Āl Bū Falāḥ were still Dhawāhir, the income of the Ruler of Abu Dhabi from the eastern part of the shaikhdom was almost exclusively provided by this tribe. According to the Gazetteer the Dhawāhir paid a fixed tribute of 5,000 *jirābs* of dates worth one M.T. Dollar per *jirāb*, and were also obliged to supply lucerne worth some 3,000 M.T. Dollars for the 100 horses which the Āl Bū Falāḥ kept in the oasis. The remainder of the population in these villages, such as some Najādāt, did not own land, or if they did their gardens were insignificantly small. An increasing number of date gardens which were no longer owned by Dhawāhir families had become the property of members of the Ruler's family, and they were exempt from taxes, although not from the dues collected to maintain the *aflāj*. At that time the Bani Yās who owned date gardens in the Līwā were taxed on their crops. This income was then worth some 2,500 M.T. Dollars.[79]

In later decades when the sovereignty of the Āl Bū Falāḥ was consolidated in the eastern area and when many Bani Yās and other Āl Bū Falāḥ subjects who earned enough money from the pearling industry bought date gardens in the Buraimi area, the tribute of the Dhawāhir was abolished and everybody except members of the ruling family paid taxes at the rate of one *jirāb* for every 10 *jirābs* of dates harvested. A Buraimi *jirāb* weighed 70–80 lbs, less than half a Līwā *jirāb*, so that in effect the tax rate for the *falaj*-irrigated gardens of the Buraimi villages was at least double that of the date gardens in the desert.[80]

During the 1950s the tax return from agriculture also declined. Only about 40 *jirābs* were collected in a good year from Līwā. During the summers of 1950 and 1951 only 10 people in all were taxed on their production in the Līwā. During 1952–4, when locusts had earlier invaded the Līwā, none of the producers came up to the *nisab* of 10 *jirābs*, and the Manāṣir date gardens had not been taxed for decades—possibly because none produced more than 10 *jirābs*. Therefore the tax collector only visited the oases to the west of Tharwānīyah. The tax income from gardens in al ʿAin and the other villages in the Buraimi oasis did not amount to more than 1,200 *jirābs* in the 1950s. There the annual taxation on dates and crops was 1/10th of the crop if the plot was watered by a *falaj* and 1/20th if the water was drawn from wells.

The owners of date gardens in every *falaj*-irrigated oasis contributed to the maintenance of these channels; but not everywhere were they asked to pay a tax on the water to the Ruler. In the oasis of Ḏaid, for instance, the owners of date gardens paid a tax on dates to the Ruler of Shārjah amounting to 100 *jirābs*, but were also taxed on the use of the *falaj* water, for which 228 M.T. Dollars were collected in cash per year on behalf of the Ruler.[81] Such water tax (also called *naub*) was no longer paid by anyone in Muʿtiriḍ, al Qaṭṭārah, Jīmi, Hīli and al Muwaijʿi during the 1950s, because the *aflāj* in these villages were owned by members of the Ruler's family and in Masʿūdi water was provided only from wells. The *falaj* taxation system in al ʿAin was simplified in the early 1950s and the owners of date gardens eventually paid a flat rate of one Rupee for three hours and the proceeds were used to maintain existing *aflāj* and to help to refurbish those which had fallen into disrepair.[82]

Another taxable asset was domestic animals, and some shaikhs in the Trucial States levied this kind of *zakāh*. But the Āl Bū Falāḥ did not collect taxes on camels or any other livestock. In the rare incidents when individuals living in Dhafrah or even in the vicinity of Buraimi paid *zakāh* on camels to tax collectors from Saudi Arabia, there were either political reasons behind this or it was because it was impossible for the scattered beduin families to oppose the well-armed party which sometimes accompanied the tax collector.[83] Because only a few very small gardens exist in Bainūnah, Dhafrah proper and Baṭn Līwā, the Āl Bū Falāḥ did not have any occasion for a yearly visit of their tax collectors. For several years the beduin in this area, whatever the tribe, paid the customary 10 Rupees per head of camel they owned—if and when a tax collector from al Ḥasā came.

The collection of taxes or *zakāh* was a very important factor in the frontier dispute between Saudi Arabia and Abu Dhabi.[84] The preparation of their cases for arbitration consisted to a large extent of the collection of evidence that taxes or *zakāh* had been paid by certain groups or individuals to either of the two powers. Although it is some manifestation of sovereignty if a Ruler can collect tax from nomadic and settled tribal groups, this does not necessarily always mean that his authority is therefore any more acceptable to them. As many of the cases collated in the UK Memorial and the Saudi Memorial, both digested in J.B. Kelly's book *Eastern Arabian Frontiers*, show, taxes were paid when it was difficult to refuse, or as Bertram Thomas puts it: "It is an insurance premium, and by no means signifies a voluntary or lasting acknowledgement of sovereignty."[85] Particularly in respect of people such as the beduin Manāṣīr or the semi-settled groups of the Bani Yās in Dhafrah, the Āl Bū Falāḥ Ruler's authority was manifest not so much in the latter having the power to collect taxes as in the tribes turning to him for protection, subsidies, jurisdiction and the feeling of identity.

Customs duties

Within the confinement of a community, such as the coastal settlements, it is not difficult for a Ruler to exert authority over groups and individuals, even over those who are reluctant to fall in line. There he could enforce unpopular rules and regulations with the help of a few armed guards (*ʿaskar* or *fidāwi*), and he could for example prohibit the construction of a house on a particular site, he could control the rent of shops in the *sūq* and interfere in many aspects of the daily life of the people.

The imposition of customs at the major ports has always been a Ruler's undisputed right. On trade overland, however, no customs dues were collected, such as on the transport of earthenware pots or camel-saddles from ʿIbri to the Buraimi villages. Nor was the market at D̲aid subject to customs duties for goods from Oman. In the Trucial States dues varied between 1½ per cent recorded earlier this century for Shārjah and 2½ per cent current in Abu Dhabi during the 1950s. There were customs collectors at Shārjah as well as Raʿs al Khaimah even before the complete separation into two shaikhdoms. The Rulers of Abu Dhabi maintained a customs collector in Abu Dhabi and on Dalmā.[86] A duty of 2½ per cent of the value of imports except for pearls was levied in both places.[87]

On first sight it seems that there was a lot of room for argument over the value of cargoes on local craft carrying firewood from Iran or dates from Basra. But whether there were proper shipping documents or not, the range of imported goods was, even after the Second World War, so limited, and the selling price of each item was so well known to everyone that the customs official had little difficulty in establishing the correct amount of duties to be paid in almost every case. During the later 1950s, when the oil companies started to import goods which were never previously seen in the Trucial States, such shipments were accompanied by formal documentation. Equipment for the oil industry was imported free of customs duties.

Export duties were not normally collected anywhere on the Trucial Coast, but when a German firm, Robert Woenckhaus and Co., sent a representative to Dalmā in 1899 who wanted to export oyster shells, he was refused residence there until he had obtained permission from the Ruler in Abu Dhabi. He was then allowed to export shells after agreeing to pay 13 M.T. dollars per 100 sacks.[88]

Reservation of rights

There were many good fishing areas along the coastline of the Trucial States and among the many islands, but fishing along much of the coastline was restricted by a system of licences. These licences were issued by the Rulers and were an additional source of revenue; to protect this revenue the Ruler had to be able on the one hand to enforce the collection of annual rents and on the other hand to protect the fishermen from poachers.

In the case of Abu Dhabi, examples can be found of individuals who held the fishing rights for as far along the coast as from Khaur al 'Udaid to Ḥamrā' (about 100 kilometres), which included four islands. Most such concessions were taken by the Rumaithāt.[89] The holder of fishing rights might allow other tribesmen to fish off his shores but he could demand one fifth of their catch in payment. There was no tax on fish caught or on the sale of fish.

The collection of almost any saleable commodity found on the land or in the sea within the jurisdiction of the Ruler could be subject to licensing. Examples are guano, dried sharks and turtles, oyster shells and red oxide.[90] It was thus recognised that the Ruler had the right to issue such licences and himself to benefit financially from them. Therefore, when the oil companies came to negotiate concessions it was consistent with previous practice that they should sign agreements with the Ruler in which all royalties and taxes would be payable to him.

Subsidies and other manifestations of authority

The payment of subsidies by a Ruler to a tribe is as much a manifestation of authority as the collection of taxes and the letting of concessions. It had, for instance, become customary for the *tamīmah* of the Naʿīm, living in Buraimi village, to obtain a share of the tax collected in kind on the dates of the Dhawāhir villages, and another share went to the shaikhs of the Dhawāhir.[91] Other tribes, subsections or even individuals were also paid subsidies, but this did not necessarily develop into an institution which was observed by subsequent Rulers.

Shaikh Zāyid bin Khalīfah used subsidies extensively for his policy of *arrondissement* of his influence over non-Bani Yās tribes. Not all of his sons followed this policy, and by withholding the by then customary subsidies some lost the support of important tribes such as the Manāṣīr.[92] It was known that during the 1950s Shaikh Zāyid bin Sulṭān regularly paid subsidies to the ʿAwāmir, which they called *shafiyah*. The fact that a tribe as large as this could and did expect these subsidies from the Ruler of Abu Dhabi, and in turn offered allegiance, shows that such payments played an important role in maintaining the authority of the Ruler—just as much as routine administration.

A similarly intangible and yet quite important manifestation of administrative authority over a tribal group was the provision of retainers. Each of the Āl Bū Falāḥ shaikhs had a retinue who stayed with them wherever they went. They were mostly armed but untrained tribesmen who received a regular payment about twice a year. At a time when the pearling industry did not bring in the cash that it used to, and when there was not yet enough work with the oil company, it was an important privilege for a tribe to lodge many of its men in the retinue of the Ruler or one of his family.

In the 1950s the Ruler of Abu Dhabi had as many Manāṣīr retainers as Bani Yās, if not more. According to one source he had 85 regularly-paid retainers from the Manāṣīr and 24 from the Mazārīʿ section of the Bani Yās. Another source claims that he had 12 Manāṣīr and 20 Bani Yās. The difference is most probably that the latter estimate included the two dozen or so close confidants (*muṭārzīyah*: originally from *ṭarāz*, tax) who were always with him, served as falconers and even made the coffee and cooked when the party was in the desert hunting, while the former estimate included people who kept the peace throughout the desert of Abu Dhabi, an area which was usually much safer to travel in than the rest of the open country of the Trucial States. Some 15 men were permanently stationed at Muqṭaʿ ford between Abu Dhabi island and the mainland.

From among the large number of retainers the Ruler also selected people to work as guards at oil company sites and the company paid for them direct to the Ruler. Any one of his personal retinue could be entrusted with special tasks such as accompanying the judge on his round of Dhafrah, collecting the tax, bringing a camel thief to the Ruler, or guiding a party of oil company employees to distant parts of the shaikhdom.

When the oil company wanted to employ local labour, the Ruler or one of his representatives selected initially from among his retainers, and then from among the tribes in general, the men whose turn it was to get the jobs; and he collected their wages on their behalf. This practice became in the late 1950s and early 1960s one of the most important manifestations of the Ruler's administrative authority over the people who lived within the area which by then had been defined as being the PD(TC) oil concession area.

Jurisdiction

In the European context the individual is subject to the authority of the State as the sole source of legislation and jurisdiction in the land, and this exercise of authority is one of the most significant manifestations of a sovereign's rule.

But in most parts of the Trucial Shaikhdoms the families, tribal groups and communities were accustomed to dealing themselves with most disputes among their members without reference to the Ruler. Only if they could not agree among themselves would one or another of the parties involved bring the case to the Ruler. This makes the administration of justice largely an act which is requested rather than enforced. Prosecution for the sake of seeing the law enforced, that is, without some plaintiff actually seeking justice, is rare in this system. Disputes concerning property being stolen (animals, rifles, and the like), being damaged (water-courses, gardens), being eaten by someone's domestic animal (date trees, plantations), or being infringed upon (*aflāj*, *hammām*, buildings), were usually dealt with by the family heads or the tribal leaders concerned, or by consulting an *ʿarīf*, someone well versed in the customary law of that community. If two parties in a dispute came to the Ruler to ask for his verdict, this implied that they were both prepared to accept his ruling; it might also indicate that the case had already been heard before some authority whose ruling the parties had not been willing to accept. In an Arab tribal society people often preferred to request a powerful, wise, and popular shaikh to give his ruling in their disputes; similarly, an oppressive ruler was kept busy with endless disputes because people found it difficult to avoid transgressing his many rules and regulations.[93]

In this type of jurisdiction it is not altogether relevant whether the judgement is in conformity with the stipulations of a specific and quotable law; what is important is whether both parties and the observers perceive the judgement as fair in the circumstances and whether they all accept the verdict. The legal principles which guided this process of arriving at a judgement were first of all the customary law, *ʿurf*, which developed within a particular group of tribes, was known to and recognised by its members, and was peculiar to that group. One was also guided by common sense, and often by impartiality and a lack of concern with the question of who was at fault: a major consideration was which of the parties could better afford to concede or to pay the cost. Since the verdict had to be acceptable to everyone involved it had almost always to be a compromise.

Because all the people concerned were Muslim, their personal lives and social behaviour, and therefore these legal principles too, including *ʿurf*, were moulded by Islam. Yet such verdicts were not founded on specific precepts of *sharīʿah*, the Muslim code of law,[94] unless the parties turned to a *muṭawwaʿ*,[95] a man who had studied the Quran, was known to be religious, and was often even called *qāḍi*.

Recently most Rulers on the Trucial Coast have found it necessary for religious reasons to give their subjects the benefit of jurisdiction by bringing to the shaikhdom someone who has undergone formal training in Islamic law, and they have appointed a qualified *qāḍi*. A Ruler will often listen to the complaints of the parties and will then send for the *qāḍi* to deal with the case, or he will send the parties away to consult the *qāḍi* in his house. Any such proceedings take place in the *majlis*, where everyone who cares to attend or who happens to be present may give his view.

In Abu Dhabi the position of *qāḍi* was held during the rule of Shaikh Ḥamdān bin Zāyid and some of his successors by Muḥammad al Kindi of the Qumzān section of the Bani Yās. During the rule of Shaikh Shakhbūṭ, Muḥammad's son Shaikh Mijarin bin Muḥammad al Kindi and afterwards ʿAbdul Rahīm al Gharīb were *quḍāh* in Abu Dhabi town. The *qāḍi* in al ʿAin was the father of Shaikh Shakhbūṭ's secretary, Sayyid ʿAbdullah, who was an Arab from the Persian coast. In the Buraimi area there was a *muṭawwaʿ* in most of the villages, each of whom was partly maintained by the Ruler and partly lived from the fees he obtained in kind from such functions as officiating at marriages and certifying divorces. The brother of the *qāḍi* in al ʿAin was *muṭawwaʿ* in MuʿtiriḌ. The authority of one of the *muṭawwaʿ*, Thāni bin Aḥmad, who co-operated most frequently with the Ruler's *wāli* in the area, extended as far as Khatam. The most respected *muṭawwaʿ* in Dhafrah was called Aṭṭāhir bin ʿAli al Murri. He was succeeded in about 1966 by his nephew Muṣaba.

Some time during the 1940s Shaikh Shakhbūṭ appointed Yūsuf al Badr from Bahrain as *qāḍi* for all of Abu Dhabi. He usually resided in Abu Dhabi town, but was at times sent by the Ruler on a circuit to settle cases in the desert and on the islands. He married in Ḥafīf in Līwā some time before 1955, and owned date gardens in that village.

In March 1951 Shaikh Shakhbūṭ spent several weeks in Bainūnah, north of Līwā, with a large retinue. During this time many people, mostly beduin because there were no permanent settlements in Bainūnah, came to pay their respects, and also to refer their disputes to him for settlement. But he did not himself give a verdict. After his return to Abu Dhabi he sent the *wāli* of Dhafrah, Aḥmad bin Faḍil, and his *qāḍi*, Yūsuf al Badr, who spent more than three months in that area settling disputes; they listened carefully to each case, sometimes taking up to three weeks on one of them.[96] Few of the cases were disputes between members of the same tribe, but mostly between a Manāṣīr, an ʿAwāmir or a Manāhīl on the one side and a Bani Yās on the other side. The Manāṣīr had their own *qāḍis* or *muṭawwaʿ* and preferred to settle their disputes among themselves; but some cases, in particular serious criminal cases and disputes with non-Manāṣīr neighbours over camels or the ownership of date gardens were referred to the Ruler of Abu Dhabi, his *wāli* or his *qāḍi*.[97]

While the fact that cases were brought by the Ruler's subjects themselves to him or his *qāḍi* testifies to a certain amount of practical, administrative authority over them, the extent of his sovereignty may be assessed particularly well if, in a dispute between a member of a beduin tribe which inhabits the fringes of his shaikhdom and a member of a tribe living under the authority of another shaikh, the former turns to him for protection and justice. This would indicate that the former considers himself to be a subject of that Ruler, and such cases were extensively used to prove that the Āl Bū Falāḥ Rulers and their representatives had authority over all the tribes living in the area which was claimed by Saudi Arabia. It proved that the extent of Āl Bū Falāḥ jurisdiction was well known to and respected by the other Trucial Rulers and local shaikhs.[98]

The decentralised system of jurisdiction, where the majority of cases were never brought to the *ḥukūmah* (government) of a Ruler, demonstrates most impressively the tribal structure of the society in the Trucial States. The families, tribal units and village communities are basically self-sufficient and self-reliant; but there are occasions when they are compelled to turn to a more distant tribal leader or a Trucial Ruler for peace within the community, for external assistance or for new economic opportunities.

In an industrialised society certain obligations may be undertaken by the State within the social security system, whereas in the society under discussion such matters are dealt with in the first instance within the family and the tribal structure. Orphans, widows and disabled people would usually be provided for by their relatives or by members of the tribal unit. In the rare cases of failure in this system the responsibility for the welfare of such persons would devolve on the *wāli* of the district or even on the Ruler himself.

5 Conclusion

To sum up the manifestations of administrative authority over a small population, spread over a large area in a tribal shaikhdom, one may enumerate the 'civil servants' within the system: there is the *wāli* (or *amīr* as in Dalmā or *nā'ib* as he was often styled in al ʿAin), a general representative of the Ruler, sometimes one of his relatives, but in the case of Abu Dhabi not a fief; there is the *muzakki*, who collects the taxes and customs duties; there are the *muṭārzīyah* (or *fidāwīyah*) who are the Ruler's own retainers and may be sent on special missions of all kinds; there are the *ʿaskars*, salaried but untrained armed tribal men; there are the guards at the gate to the fort, *ḥaras*; there is a *dūri*, a camel guard in the Līwā;[99] there is a secretary, frequently an educated man from the Iranian coast; there is the *ʿarīf* who is paid by the community of people using the *aflāj*, there may be some one to supervise business in the *sūq*; and lastly, in many respects the most important, there is the *qāḍi*.

Chapter Four

The Islamic Basis of Society

1 The Islamisation of the area

Religion in the area before Islam

There are no known records of exactly how and when Islam came to the tribes of Trucial Oman, but it was probably simultaneous with the well documented conversion of Oman and al Baḥrayn to the faith.[1] As elsewhere on the Arabian Peninsula before Islam, the majority of the population were probably worshippers of the moon or the stars[2], others may have been under the influence of the beliefs of the frequent Persian invaders, while animistic religions were also widespread. As in Oman and al Baḥrayn, communities which had been converted to Christianity were among them.

The Christianisation of Yemen must have greatly enhanced the position of Christians in other parts of the Arabian Peninsula. The first mission to the Yemeni tribes was led by the monk Frumentius.[3] In the second half of the fourth century AD the ruling élite of the Himyarite empire were converted to Christianity by Theophilus Indus. He was born near Karachi and taken to Rome as a hostage, but he later became a missionary on behalf of Emperor Constantine II and built three churches in the region under Himyarite rule, one of which may have been at Ṣuḥār.

Oman had a bishop from the 5th century; the first was John and the last one mentioned was Stephan (Etienne), in AD 676. There was certainly a large Christian population in Oman at the end of the 6th century. The conversion to Christianity of a famous shaikh of the ʿAbs, Qais bin Zuhair, and a large part of his tribe in AD 563 was not an isolated incident; there was at that time a church in Ṣuḥār, whither he retired as a monk. Neither the Julandā' princes ruling the interior from Nizwā, nor the Sassanian governor who resided with a large occupation force on the Baṭinah coast had been converted to Christianity.

After a crisis in the Christian church of Persia during the first half of the 6th century, the Bishop of Dārīn,[4] then the principal town of al Baḥrayn, situated on the bay of Qaṭīf, took the opportunity to declare himself the Metropolite of the "Bait Qaṭrāyah"; this included all the churches on the Arabian side of the Gulf in the dioceses of Dārīn, Mazūn (Oman), Mashmāhaq (Muḥarraq) on Bahrain Island, Ḥajar in Yamāmah (hinterland of al Baḥrayn) and Ḥaṭṭa (al Ḥasa). In AD 676 this hierarchical structure was still intact when the bishops from these dioceses met in Dārīn with the Catholicos Georges I.[5]

Accepting Islam

When the western part of the Arabian Peninsula was seized by the religious, political, military and economic revolution of the early spread of Islam, the tremors were soon felt as far as the extreme corners of the then Arabic-speaking world. The direct impact of what was happening in the Ḥijāz on Oman, al Baḥrayn and the remainder of eastern Arabia was not long in coming. According to the Arab historian al Nawawi, someone by the name of Abū Bashīr bin ʿAṣīd or ʿUṭbah, who had embraced the new faith, came as a refugee to Oman, but the few followers he collected around himself did not succeed in spreading Islam in Eastern Arabia.[6] Omani tradition is that the first native of Oman to go to Medina and swear allegiance to the Prophet Muḥammad was Māzin bin Ghaḍḍūbah.

The Prophet's letter[7] which was brought to the joint Rulers of inner Oman, Jaifar and ʿAbd, at Nizwā by ʿAmru bin al ʿĀṣ in 630 AD, the ninth year after the *hijrah*, only confirmed what was known already even in Oman, namely that the new powerful Arab government at Medina could not be opposed lightly and with impunity, but also that it might be their best ally if the Omani tribes were to rise to expel the Persians from their coasts.[8] A council of the shaikhs of *Nizāri* and *Yamāni* tribes in Nizwā considered the Prophet's letter and decided to adopt the new faith, and to pay *zakāh*, which was already customary for all Muslims. A group of tribal leaders was sent on behalf of the people of Oman to Medina, and before they returned they learnt a great deal about the inspiring personality of the Prophet, about the coherence of the new State, and about the new religion itself. Omanis such as they and their tribal followers probably became the enthusiastic and truly Muslim leaders of the Omani revolt against the unpopular Sassanian suzerainty, because the latter's governor in Oman had repeatedly refused to adopt Islam. The rising against the Sassanians was morally supported by the Prophet's messenger ʿAmru, who had stayed in Oman as a missionary and teacher of the new faith. The revolt was successful in expelling the entire occupation force in the middle of the 7th century AD.

According to Fiey the conversion of al Baḥrayn to Islam began between AD 627 and 629, when the Christian Ruler of the area, Mundir bin Sāwā, became a Muslim at the written request of the Prophet. Allegedly he did it largely to remain in power, and he took it upon himself to collect the taxes due from his Christian subjects, who had become *ahl al kitāb*, "People of the Book". The conquest of al Baḥrayn for the expanding empire centred on Medina was completed in 633 AD, although the continued existence of the taxed Christian communities indicates that not all the population had yet adopted Islam.

When, after the death of the Prophet Muḥammad, the new empire threatened to disintegrate due to regional dissent, in Oman too an Azdite Shaikh Dhul Taj Lakit bin Mālik became the leader of an insurrection against the Muslim Julandā' princes and their tribal supporters. However, the Caliph Abū Bakr dispatched three of his generals with their armies to Oman. "After a long and weary desert march from Bahrain and Yemama [they] reached Towwam (Buraimi, or Al-Riyam, as Tabari has it), from whence they sent orders to the Julanda chiefs, ʿAbd and Jeifar, to meet them at Sohar, under the walls of which fortress the combined Moslem army was soon assembled."[9] They marched on Dibah, where the rebellious tribes had taken up their position, attacked them and fought throughout the day, but were victorious only after an opportune reinforcement arrived: ". . . some of the Beni ʿAbdul Kais and Beni Najia tribe forming part of the Khalif's army, which had apparently been delayed on the march across the Dahna and Sabkheh from Bahrain."[10] According to some historians nearly 10,000 people lost their lives in the battle of Dibah. The thriving market town and port was sacked and one-fifth of the booty and prisoners were despatched to Medina with one of the Caliph's generals, while another proceeded to bring to heel Dhufār and Hadhramaut, and the third, Ḥudaifah, stayed in Oman to help to consolidate the régime of the Muslim Julandā' princes and to make the Omanis more aware of the meaning of the new faith.

As has been mentioned, during the very early years of Islam the old approach routes to Oman, namely the one from al Baḥrayn along the edge of the *sabkhah*, through Tu'ām (Buraimi) and the Wādi Jizi, and the route from Julfār (Ra's al Khaimah) along the mountains as far as D̲aid or Buraimi before a crossing through the mountains was attempted, were as much in use as ever. The armies of the Caliph are not reported to have encountered hostility on that leg of their long march from Medina, and it may be assumed that the majority of the tribes living to the west and north-west of the Ḥajar were either already all faithful supporters of the new régime in Medina or certainly were not militantly opposed to it. Those who were supporters of the Omani seceders and of Dhul Taj Lakit had probably all marched to Dibah to swell his ranks.

To what extent the tribal population, during the first decade of the conversion of Eastern Arabia to Islam, had already grasped how profoundly this would change their way of life, their social and domestic customs, and above all their concept of right and wrong, cannot be easily determined. But it was a fortunate circumstance that after the battle at Dibah there was for several decades no more fighting necessary in the name of the new faith in Eastern Arabia. Once the military and political aspects of Islamisation of the region were settled,[11] the moral values and the spiritual scope of the religion could unfold gradually, become appreciated and whole-heartedly adopted by the population. Miles describes aptly the slowness of this process: "We hear of no religious persecutions or tumults in Oman. No martyr suffered in the cause of heathenism. The people simply ceased to adore idols openly and to frequent the temples to worship the graven images . . . Probably the people long maintained the existing order of things and offered an inert resistance to the encroachments, while nominally accepting the change; but their feelings and interests were not much affected, and it was only as time went on that the . . . invasion of Islam swept away that old system. It was by degrees that the people acquired pride and enthusiasm about Islam and its founder and stamped out paganism as an accursed thing."[12]

The radical change in customs and ideas probably took more than one generation, but the merits of Islam became eventually self-evident to people who had previously known only their own internal tribal laws. Before Islam they had not had much sense of security and fair justice in the face of constant encroachment on their property by other tribes. Their insecurity even extended to their beliefs, because they were confronted with such a variety of different gods worshipped by themselves and by neighbouring tribes. They were people whose communities were divided from one another by different moral values, by different habits and codes of practice in their daily lives, in marriage and divorce, in the treatment of ill-health and burial rites, and in the laws of inheritance.

Although the original dispensation granted by the Prophet to Oman releasing the people from the obligation to remit the annual *zakāh* to Medina was withdrawn after the battle of Dibah, the political sovereignty of the Caliphate over the south-eastern part of the Peninsula was at first sufficiently unobtrusive to permit the traditional structure of tribal rule to continue undisturbed. The General Ḥuḏaifah administered Oman for three years before the Julandā' princes Jaifar and ʿAbd resumed their positions as tribal Rulers. Their status was now greatly enhanced, because they were also leading in the adoption of the new law, the new faith, the novel sense of togetherness in an Islamic society, and, above all, the expectation of a life after death. The Rulers in Nizwā[13] and probably elsewhere in Eastern Arabia were placed under the distant supervision of the Caliph's governor of al Baḥrayn, Ḥajar and Oman, resident in al Baḥrayn.

In Oman the growing enthusiasm for the new faith was not dimmed by any particularly obvious political exigencies, and Islam probably helped the development of Omani nationhood at that time.[14]

2 Influence of the Ibāḍis' struggles against the Caliphate

It is not surprising that most of the survivors of the attack on the Khārijites in the battle of Nahawan in West Persia in AD 657 (AH 37) fled to Oman, where they soon found new supporters, and where a modified version of Khārijite thinking became the basis of the Ibāḍi State. The Khārijites maintained that none of the contenders for the Caliphate should rule over the peoples who had adopted Islam merely because they were closely related to the Prophet Muḥammad or were his companions or of his tribe, the Quraish. They believed that the most pious and respectable and the most politically and militarily able man from among the Muslims should be elected Imām.

The Caliphs and the pretenders to the Caliphate rose repeatedly to meet this uncompromising attack on their very existence, but their persistent efforts to subdue the Kharijites of Oman over a period of three centuries only helped to strengthen the regular Ibāḍi school. On the occasions that a Sunni Caliph managed to conquer the natural fortress of Inner Oman he was unable to maintain control so long as the large majority of its inhabitants did not sympathise with the cause of his army. But the frequent and fierce contests with the Caliphate at times weakened the support for the Ibāḍis in the country, and the Sunni element gained influence. Yet even when the Caliph won a decisive battle such as in AD 752 (AH 135),[15] he did not manage to maintain full administrative control for long. Whenever Oman was ruled by an *amīr* of the Caliph, tribute was remitted to him, and the Sunni portion of the population got the upper hand in the internal strife and the tribal feuds, which were further embittered by religious animosity. Yet over the centuries the Ibāḍi community in Oman prevailed as the strongest element in the country, and while it was not always able actually to establish an Ibāḍi State as it was conceived in the teaching of the Khārijites and perfected by ʿAbdullah bin Ibāḍ al Tamīmī (who lived between AD 685 and 750) and by numerous subsequent Omani scholars, there was for most of the time until AD 1783 an Ibāḍi leader who was accepted by the community as Imām, although he was frequently not elected from among the tribal leaders nor the scholarly *ʿulamā'* but acquired the position by hereditary succession.

Few of the tribes living west of the Ḥajar mountains seem to have permanently turned to Ibāḍism, but the upheavals and the bitter struggles between the Caliphate and the Imāmate could not fail to involve them, and indeed, several of the decisive battles were fought at places which were later part of the Trucial States. In AD 750 (AH 133) Abū al ʿAbbās's General Shaibān lost the battle and his life at Tu'ām (now Buraimi); two years later Khāzim bin Khuzaimah was victorious over the Ibāḍites at Julfār (Ra's al Khaimah); in about AD 696 (AH 78) the Imām Sulaimān went with 3,000 horsemen and 3,500 camelmen to meet the very much larger army of the Caliph ʿAbdul Mālik, which marshalled near Abu Dhabi, arriving by land and by sea; he repelled the invaders.[16] It is probable that the population of al Gharbīyah in the area which later became Trucial Oman was from time to time ruled by the authorities in Oman, but it was at other times quite independent.[17] However, the strategically important port of Julfār and the equally important oasis of Tu'ām probably always formed part of an Omani State, and were also considered to be within the province of Oman when it was administered by the Caliph's *amīr*.[18] But the tribes of the mountain foreland and the desert beyond it were, although involved in the politics of Oman, not always an integral and taxable part of it. The arrival, probably during the 16th century AD, of Sunni tribes such as the Bani Yās confederation, became an important enough factor on the eastern Arabian scene to give al Gharbīyah (Sāḥil ʿUmān) a political character of its own, so that it could no longer be automatically regarded as an integral part of Oman.

3 The religious communities in Trucial Oman at the turn of the twentieth century

Muslim and other communities

At the turn of the century the population of the Trucial States was not only entirely Muslim—with the exception of the few Hindu merchants living in some of the towns—but was also predominantly Sunni.

The homogeneity with regard to religious practice was not disturbed by the fact that three of the four schools of jurisprudence which are recognised by Sunnis were adhered to by the tribal population. These *maḏāhib* were the Ḥanbali, the Māliki, and the Shāfi'i *maḏhab*. The three schools do not differ in the fundamentals of religious belief, but only in minor rules concerning the performance of the religious rites and certain legal interpretations of concern to the learned and the experts in Islamic jurisprudence.

Because there was not even a formally trained *qāḍi* in each of the towns of the Trucial States, and a learned man, *muṭawwaʿ*, acquired his knowledge from a very limited number of written sources besides the Koran, arguments about finer points of difference between these schools could never form part of jurisdiction in this society. Thus, rather than consciously following in one shaikhdom a *maḏhab* which differed from that followed by the neighbours up or down the coast, each community continued to accept most readily the judgements which were in conformity with earlier judgements in identical or similar cases. These judgements, which were thus bound to take precedents and analogies into account, almost inadvertently perpetuated the adherence to a particular *maḏhab*. But for the people themselves these differences did not exist.

What counted more was the fact that the division between those communities who adhered to the Ḥanbali and those who adhered to the Māliki *madhab* was almost identical with the long-standing political division of the tribes of Oman and the Trucial States into Ghāfiri and Hināwi sections.[19] The majority of the tribes which were under the authority of Qawāsim Rulers were Ghāfiri, and having at times co-operated politically with the Wahhābis, the more orthodox *madhab* of Ibn Ḥanbal was generally followed. Māliki Sunni were all Hināwi tribes of the Trucial States, i.e. the Bani Yās, Manāṣīr, Marar, Dhawāhir and Zaʿāb, although the latter then still all lived in Qāsimi territory. Most of the people who immigrated from the Persian coast were also Māliki Sunnis.[20] The Hināwi Shiḥūḥ and some of the Hūwalah living in Shārjah were Shāfiʿi.

Apart from the ʿAwāmir, the predominantly beduin Hināwi tribe who frequented Abu Dhabi territory, and a few Kunūd in Shamailīyah, there were no Ibāḍis in Trucial Oman. However Ibāḍism had an important effect on the affairs of the coastal shaikhdoms and the hinterland because these tribes inevitably took sides in the frequent and deep-rooted internal disputes and the all-out Civil War of the 18th century in Oman.[21]

The differences between Sunni and Shīʿah go beyond the slight variations of religious ritual and legal interpretations. They extend in particular to the concept of the leader in the Islamic community. At the turn of the century only a few people such as the Baḥārinah of Abu Dhabi town and Dubai and some people probably of Persian stock were Shīʿah. This contingent was considerably increased with the influx of merchants from the Persian ports in the 1930s. Along with building-land and the right to pursue their trade from Dubai, the immigrants who were Shīʿah were also given the right to build their own mosques in Dubai, to bring their *mullah* and to celebrate in the accustomed manner the anniversary of the death of Ḥusain bin ʿAli at Karbalāʾ on the 10th of the month of Muḥarram.

In the early decades of this century the Khojah community in the Trucial States was more important than the contingent of ordinary Shīʿah, both socially and numerically. Khojahs are a sect whose ancestors were Hindus in origin and who converted to the faith of the Shīʿah Imāms of the Ismāʿīlis in the 15th century. The Khojahs, who were to be found in many ports around the Gulf, were descended from Hindus originating in Sind and Kach.[22] The Khojah community on the Trucial Coast at the turn of the century numbered about 220, with the largest contingent, 158, residing in Shārjah town; this was a relatively small community compared to the over one thousand Khojah merchants living in Maṭraḥ, the coastal trading centre of Oman.[23]

The Hindu community was even smaller, barely 200 at that same time, who were all immigrants from Sind and Gujarat. They mostly engaged in the pearling trade and therefore their numbers rose seasonally when more of them came for this business, particularly to Dubai and Abu Dhabi. They left their families in India and visited them frequently; thus they did not become integrated into the society of the Trucial States. They also did not mix easily with the Khojah communities either, and in some instances the presence of one appears to have excluded the other: there were about 65 Hindus in Abu Dhabi around the turn of the century, but no Khojahs at all, while Ra's al Khaimah town had 33 Khojah merchants with their families, but no Hindus. In Shārjah the Hindu community numbered about 50.[24] In the 20th century Hindus are usually referred to as "Banians" by the Arab population of the Gulf.

There were no Sabaeans nor any Oriental Christians, Nestorians or other Christian communities living in Trucial Oman at the turn of the century. Some members of the American Arabian Mission, working in Basra, Bahrain and Muscat, had visited Trucial Oman in 1896 and claimed to have sold "more than 100 portions of Scripture" there,[25] but the object of their work and travels being of an evangelistic, philanthropic and medical nature, they did not solicit the conversion of Muslims to Christianity.

It may be seen from this enumeration of religious communities that the society of the Trucial States was quite homogeneous. The only substantial non-Muslim group of inhabitants, the Hindus, demonstrated by constantly travelling back to their Indian homes that they did not want to be integrated fully into the local society. Thus the all too common struggle for cultural supremacy between two different religious groups was wholly absent. The political complications which arose out of the British protection of their Indian subjects will be discussed later.[26]

The unifying force of Islam in this society

As far as the overwhelming majority of the ordinary inhabitants of the Trucial States was concerned, the differences between the various schools, Māliki, Ḥanbali, Ibāḍi, within their Sunni Muslim faith were rarely realised and were certainly never reasons, in recent decades, for religious strife among the tribal population. Whenever in the last century there were bitter fights between adherents of the Wahhābi reform movement and the other Sunnis, the sword was unsheathed only when tribal politics were also involved. The minor differences of observances, of moral strictness or leniency, or of ways of applying *sharī'ah*, did not detract from the fact that Islam was the very basis of life both public and private in the society of the area. Islam was the indestructible, lasting fabric into whose even structure the pattern of local historical events was printed. Islam being, in the words of Alfred Bonné, "not only a system of religious elements or religious and political doctrines, but above all, that civilisation which . . . has created . . . a common culture and philosophy of life based on a uniform creed and a framework of ideas, political, social and State, derived therefrom,"[27] it provided also the basic rules for family relationships, marriage and burial, prayer and caring for the poor, how to dress and how to respond to the authority of the State, and how to rule and to dispense jurisdiction.

The different parts of the Islamic world have developed different adaptations from the same common source of Islamic heritage. In the Trucial States the modest economic opportunities and the prevalence of the tribal structure of society fostered the uniformity which was characteristic of this Islamic society. The first Muslims lived in a tribal environment in the Ḥijāz which was very similar to the tribal society of the Trucial States, whose very direct, undiluted, unrefined application of their understanding of the Koran and *sharī'ah* to all situations in life both public and private came quite naturally, although it may have appeared to be unsophisticated in the eyes of the complex Islamic communities of Iraq and Iran.

Islam is not merely a religion in the western sense of the word; divided into secular and religious spheres, it comprises the purely spiritual and the speculative, the form and content of devotion and the order of authority in all matters concerning the faith; Islam also dominates the cultural, moral, social, economic, legal and political spheres. Thus, Islam is the inescapable common denominator for life in a Muslim society; the illiterate nomad, the learned *qāḍi*, the successful pearl merchant and the widow claiming her inheritance, they all consciously or unconsciously turn many times during a day to the same moral, legal and religious authority.

Despite some obvious differences in the way of life in the desert, in the mountains or by the sea, and the resulting differences in economic political and cultural aspects, the communities living in the Trucial States were all moulded by the same Islamic "system of life".[28] In the following paragraphs an attempt is made to trace the many manifestations of this Islamic basis of society through the institutions, customs and ways of life of the people who lived in Trucial Oman before the changes due to outside influences following the discovery of oil.

4 The Muslim system of life on this coast during the first half of the 20th century

In and around the mosques

The mosque

There is no ecclesiastical hierarchy in Islam and no administrative and canonised authority such as "The Church". The many mosques in the Trucial States were not linked together under any regional supervisory body, but were places of worship built by and for small communities. It was customary for leading families in a settled population to build mosques near their family compound for their own use in daily prayers and for the use of the neighbourhood. Whenever a mosque was built, some other property (*waqf*) was attached to it which brought in a regular income to pay for its maintenance. In the villages of the Buraimi area and in other predominantly agricultural settlements of the Trucial States this property consisted of a date garden or two. In the towns it was usually a row of shops in the *sūq*, rented to merchants. The income was used to pay for someone to clean the mosque regularly, to replenish the water containers if there was no running water nearby, and in the case of a larger mosque to pay a salary to the person who led the prayers.

Every larger population centre had a main mosque where people from the whole town congregated on Friday for the midday prayer and the address of an *imām*. The "Friday mosques" were not usually built by a Ruler nor by the community as a whole but by individuals. In Abu Dhabi the old "Friday mosque" was built by the richest pearl merchant and boat owner, Aḥmad bin Khalaf al Otaibah, who also built a small mosque near his large family compound by the sea.

Mosques in the Trucial States were built in different styles and with different materials depending on the wealth of the founder or of the community who built it. There were very simple palm-frond mosques[29] which could hardly be distinguished from the neighbouring *barasti* compounds, because they could not exceed the other buildings in height and they had no minarets. The only immediately distinguishing feature externally was the *qiblah*, the niche orientated towards Mecca. Often, however, the mosque was the only brick building among the houses of a village or of a tribal quarter in a town, and near the coast this would usually be a structure of coral stones bound together with mud. This construction allowed the mosque to have two or three open arches in the long wall opposite the *qiblah*. A few low-level windows in the shorter walls, and on either side of the *qiblah*, allowed enough air to enter the building, which might well be filled to capacity at prayer times. A rectangular courtyard in front of the mosque and facilities for ablution completed such a typical small mosque.

Often there was no minaret, although some mosques had a small elevated platform a little higher than the roof on one side of the building. The more elaborate mosques had one minaret; the arches and the gallery, for the *mu'a̲d̲dīn* who calls for prayer, would have some decorative plasterwork or carved wood. The interior of the mosques was very simple; the floor was usually covered with rush-mats or, rarely, with woven rugs.

The number of mosques in use in the Trucial States during the first two decades of this century can only be estimated, because written records were not even kept for the *waqf* which existed for the maintenance of a mosque. There seems to have been a great increase in the number of new mosques being founded during the height of the pearling industry, and the majority of those mosques which were still in good repair and use during the 1950s and early 1960s had been built within living memory of the people who still prayed there then.[30]

As already mentioned, each mosque was provided for by the *waqf* attached to it. There was no need anywhere on the Trucial Coast for a special person or organisation to administer all the *waqf* property of one town, as the communities were small enough for it to be common knowledge who built and endowed a mosque, and what it cost to maintain it. Either the founder of the mosque or a member of his family or the *imām* who was attached to the mosque supervised the collection of the income and the use of it.

At the main mosque of the larger towns an *imām* was employed who led the prayers and delivered the *khuṭbah* on Fridays. In most other mosques the *imāms* were not specially-trained people who had no other occupation, they were *muṭawwa'* who led the prayers—as in fact in the absence of an *imām* anyone could do. But by unspoken common consent the eldest, most respected or best-read person in a congregation would do this. In mosques which were built by or for ethnic or religious communities, for instance the Balūch communities on the east coast or the Shī'ah of Dubai,[31] the leader of that community was often also the leader in prayer. Such minorities did not necessarily gather in their own mosque on Friday morning, but also came into the town's big mosque—with the exception of the Shī'ah of the Bastakīyah in Dubai.

Religious theory and practice

The ways in which the manifestation of the Islamic faith are woven into the daily life have not changed. As elsewhere and in other religions, women are probably the most devout members of the community, strictly observing the correct times for prayers and praying for longer. Traditionally they are not expected to pray in mosques.[32] If men did not find themselves near a mosque at prayer time, they spread out a rug or their headcloth on the ground to perform the *ṣalāt* (prayer) there and then. If several men happened to be together, they might pray individually or else line up behind the most respected among them and follow him as *imām*. Unless travelling or far from a house, perhaps out in the desert, women prayed inside a house, either at home or wherever they happened to be visiting at the time. Even while visitors and children were present in the same room, they each got up in turn from the circle where they had been sitting talking; they would leave another member of the female gathering to entertain the guest and to keep an eye on the children. After the ritual ablutions women took off their masks and embroidered veils (*shailah*) and wound a simple cloth round the head and shoulders before beginning their often prolonged prayers.

If at all possible everyone performs the prescribed ablutions with water before praying, but in the desert, where men lived off the milk of their camels and water was not always available, sand was a permissible substitute.[33]

Few of the people living in the Trucial States before the advent of oil could afford to dedicate their lives entirely to religious studies; yet some of those who were comfortably looked after by their family members spent a lot of time reading in their old age. Books were not easy to come by and a great scholar would not often have had the necessary companionship of others who could also dedicate that much time to religious studies.

The deep religious devotion of people in this area was very much a practical matter; few people were particularly concerned about minor points of interpretation which in other times and places had torn Muslim communities apart in debate and strife. People who live their faith practically, rather than analysing it, are rarely fanatical. To an outsider who came into the Trucial States a few decades ago, it would have been instantly clear and obvious that every family, every individual in this community was Muslim—not only from the comparatively large number of mosques he would count but also from the many instances when he could see men praying either in the crowded mosques or anywhere convenient. He would also find in the Ruler's *majlis*, in an ordinary house, and even around the camp-fire of the hard-living beduin, that some of the day-to-day conversation consisted of stories about the Prophet and his companions, about Moses, about Paradise and even about the Virgin Mary and her son Jesus. He would also find that in many houses during the holy month of Ramaḍān a member of the family would read the Koran aloud for the benefit of the others. He would also notice that people gave generously for the sake of God to a poor pilgrim on his way to Mecca or to a wandering *darwīsh* or to a destitute person. He would find that although everyone was convinced that without a shadow of doubt Islam was the last revealed and therefore the right religion, and that they wanted dear friends who had been brought up in another religion to join them, they would still prefer to deal with a true, believing Christian than with an unbeliever.[34]

"Superstitions"

Islam was never felt to be in conflict with some practices which an outsider might readily call "superstition". It was, in fact, frequently the *muṭawwaʿ* who was requested to write an appropriate verse of the Koran on a piece of paper which was inserted in a silver charm and hung round the neck of a sick child, one who cried too much, or had been affected by the evil eye. Some individuals were credited with the power to transport people magically from one place to another many miles away, and there was a widespread fear of *jinn* haunting certain trees, water holes, water courses, and the date gardens.[35] Likewise the practising of cauterization as a treatment against almost any kind of illness was considered, like circumcision,[36] to be the natural thing to do. But nowhere did superstitions or relics of pre-Islamic tribal rites and healing practices encroach on Islam to the extent of overshadowing it.[37]

Art in religion

The meagre resources available to the people of the country in earlier times did not allow them much scope for artistic creativity. The materials commonly used in other parts of the world for artistic expression such as in sculpture, painting and architecture do not naturally occur locally; another limitation was that in Islam the portrayal of human and animal forms is not permitted. The Trucial States did not bring forth many works of Islamic art; paying reverence to God by embellishing a mosque or copying a religious book usually had to remain very simple. Although there were no beautifully illuminated manuscripts produced locally, there were some people—in one reported case in as remote an area as the Līwā—who copied by hand religious tracts which were not otherwise available. Some of the local traditional poetry is about religion, but the majority of poems described historical incidents, battles, or the generosity of shaikhs, or they were moulded on the pattern of classical beduin love poetry.[38]

Music for dances, played on variously sized drums, tambourines, cymbals, and flutes, did not form part of religious ceremonies, but it was enjoyed at weddings or in honour of an important guest and on the Islamic feast days. During the month of the Prophet's birthday, Rabīʿ al Awwal, people gathered to perform or watch *al maulid*, a religious recital: two rows of up to twenty men each kneel opposite each other. The men on one side wear their *sufrah* (white head cloths) also called *ghutrah*, wound round their heads, and are generally people from the less well-to-do groups of the community or of slave origin; they perform in unison a ritual which includes movement of the right hand, bending their heads to the floor and rising to an upright kneeling position. Those on the other side all have large, shallow drums in their right hands and wear their traditional white *sufrah* with the *ʿaqāl* (the black twisted rope). One drummer recites in the traditional fashion in a forceful voice, without taking a breath until the end of the line or even of the paragraph is reached. When the chorus of both rows responds, singing, chanting and exclaiming, the drums accompany the human voices; the enthusiasm of the performers and the rhythm of the music may leave the beholder spellbound.

In another ceremony, which is traditional for the same time in this area, men gathered in a *majlis* take turns reading aloud the description of the birth of the Prophet Muḥammad written in the 18th century by ʿAbdul Raḥīm al Barzanji. The reading culminates in a prayer and exclamations, at which moment everybody, including the women who have gathered behind the curtain wall to listen, rises to their feet.

Burials

Simplicity and absence of pomp and ceremony also marked the traditions for burial of the dead. The deceased was buried as soon as possible, and certainly before sunset of the day he died. His body was taken to the graveyard, which was recognisable only by the many stones pointing up out of the ground, marking the head and foot of each grave. Relatives and friends carried the body, which was wrapped in a white cloth, to the grave, accompanied by only the male mourners. Near the grave they would line up for a prayer, which in the absence of a *qāḍi* or *muṭawwaʿ* could be led by any respected man in the group, and after the body was lowered into the grave it was filled again with stones and sand and the head and footstone were placed upright. After another prayer the mourners would disperse. The wife and close female relatives might relieve their grief with a few spontaneous wailing shouts, but otherwise the family accepted the death of one of its members composedly as the very will of God, being confident that the deceased would remain in the hands of God.

Pilgrimage (*Ḥajj*)

The pilgrimage to Mecca at least once during a lifetime is one of the five obligations which a Muslim should endeavour to fulfil. But for people living in the eastern parts of the Peninsula the *ḥajj* was an extremely arduous and long journey, and on account of this not many people undertook it in the days before motorisation.[39] There were various routes to Mecca: one could take a boat to Aden and then another boat from there to Jiddah; or else one went by boat to Basra and joined the Iraqi pilgrim caravan travelling on foot or by hired camel all the way across Arabia. Towards the end of Shaikh Zāyid bin Khalīfah's rule a group of some twelve to fifteen people from Abu Dhabi went together by boat to Ḥaifa and from there to Jerusalem and on to the Holy City of Mecca; this pilgrimage is well remembered by the community to this day. After the Second World War an ever increasing number of pilgrims found a seat in one of the desert taxis and buses which private tour companies were operating from the main centres such as Baghdad, Riyadh and Damascus. But to travel even as far as these cities from the Trucial Coast was no easy task, particularly for the women.

Few people from the Trucial States ever set out to cross Arabia alone or in small groups; they preferred the security and companionship of an organised pilgrim caravan. The only people who could have undertaken the journey alone were some of the beduin who were sufficiently familiar with the Rubʿ al Khāli and the other deserts of Arabia. The pilgrims from among the settled population of the coastal towns and villages of the Trucial Coast were familiar with the climatic and geographical conditions of the entire Peninsula, if only through listening to poetry and the accounts of beduin; therefore they did not set out without adequate preparation and they kept to the commonly travelled routes.

On the other hand, for centuries the Trucial States have seen faithful Muslims from further east land on their shores and in their ignorance of the geography attempt to reach Mecca on foot; these people were usually ill-prepared, carrying only a little water, few provisions and a little bundle of their seamless clothes for the festivities in the Holy City. It was usually impossible to deter the pious pilgrim, to turn him back, or to suggest he took another route on account of his being so ill-equipped for the lonely journey along sparsely populated coasts and through the empty deserts. Pilgrims believed that if they failed to reach Mecca, it was at least meritorious to die on the way.

It was in the nature of the pilgrimage that usually the older people would undertake it because they could see that their time in which to obey the Holy command was running out. On their return from the pilgrimage the entire family and all the neighbours would rejoice, celebrate and listen avidly to the *ḥajji*'s often-repeated accounts of the festivities in the Holy City, and the hazards of the journey, and the people he encountered.

But neither the performance of the pilgrimage nor any other deed which was of religious merit made a person so honoured as to accord him a special place in society. Life in the Trucial States was usually hard for everybody and the majority of those who could not go on the pilgrimage did not have to face accusations of neglect of their duty from over-zealous religious groups.

Conclusion

The common faith, which provided all the inhabitants of the area with the same understanding of justice and law, and with a common way of life, did not depend on the mosque and the religious institutions as the only places where the sincerity of a Muslim's belief was manifest. The institutions were only a part of the Muslim system of life which was shared by the whole population and gave this society its homogeneity.

Religion and family life

The absolute necessity for any locally born individual to be and to remain integrated into a clan and a tribal system stems from the tribal rather than the Islamic basis of society. But the way in which the members of the family arrange their lives together, and incorporate other members of the society into the family unit by marriage, is to a very large extent prescribed by the tenets of Islam. To describe the family life of the traditional society on the Trucial Coast only in terms of the influence of Islam on it would be inadequate, because the origin of the traditions and the very basis of tribal society, both of which rule family life, are also inter-twined with the tribal roots of Islam itself.

The *Ḥarīm*[40]

The form that family life takes is largely moulded by the role of the women in it. To the outsider this role is obvious in the way in which the family accommodation is built and allocated to the members of the family and to the various functions. In the Trucial States every house or tent provides for a segregated area called *ḥarīm*. An extended family in a typical household lives within the confines of a rectangular *barasti*-fenced compound including a courtyard; most of the *barasti* buildings opening onto the courtyard are used by all the family and therefore form part of the *ḥarīm*. The *majlis*, which is open to visitors, usually occupies one side of the courtyard. Sometimes it has a door directly to the outside but in many houses access to it is through the courtyard and a few yards from the main front door.[41] In the *majlis* male visitors are received by the male members of the family and no females who have reached the age of puberty may enter the *majlis* while there are guests. If the guest is a distant relative, a neighbour or a very close friend of the head of the family, he can speak to the women of the household through the door or by raising his voice while sitting inside the *majlis*.

Only the father, a brother, a son and possibly other very close male relatives and also a foster-brother[42] may proceed beyond the *majlis* to sit and speak face to face with the women of the house.[43] The courtyard, the kitchen area, the separate room or rooms for the older generation of the family and the room where the women of the household gather and the head of the family sleeps at night are thus part of the *ḥarīm*. In densely built up areas none of these rooms nor the courtyard walls have windows at eye-level to the outside; in towns there is often a curtain wall opposite the rear door to guard against people seeing into the yard when the door is opened. In this way, rather than being confined to one room or a small area, the women go about their daily routine within the family compound even while strangers are visiting.

There are many different patterns of separation between the *majlis* and the *ḥarīm* area, depending on the type of accommodation which the family can afford, on the social status of the family, on the number of non-related visitors which the family can expect, and on the importance which the head of the family attaches to strictness of segregation and the necessity to guard against the possibility of a stranger catching a glimpse of the women's faces.

The institution itself, the *ḥarīm*, is largely a symbol of the position of women within society: they are not members of the community as much as they belong to the private lives of the man on whom they depend most at a particular stage in their lives (father, husband or brother). Within the domestic scene, as anywhere else in the world, however, women often dominate. In particular an older woman who is known to be a devout Muslim may become very much the person who lays down the rules for the entire household with regard to strict observance of praying and fasting, concerning marriages of members of the household and the social contacts of the family, which in some cases amounts also to the measure of political involvement of the family in the affairs of the community. Women are protected from the male world by the institution of the *ḥarīm*; they are secure within its boundaries and this security they carry with them in the form of the mask (*burqaʿ*), the veil (*shailah*) and the black coat (*ʿabāʾah*) when they leave their houses. They thus keep themselves apart wherever they are from the men of their society. But by means of the same institutions they also withhold from male participation a large part of the world about them. Many things that women talk about, think about, worry about, and enjoy are not discussed with the men. Among the male members of society it is considered to be improper when enquiring about the well-being of the family to ask more than the stereotype questions. More specific information about members of the family is not exchanged unless someone is known to be very ill, or if a dispute develops into a case where outside adjudication is required.

The fact that women do not participate in the public life of the community as seen by men does not necessarily mean that they have an inferior position to men. In this aspect of family and social life, the necessity to preserve the cohesion and protect the family through the co-operation of the male members falls completely in line with the spirit of early Islam which endeavoured to restore to women their honour as members of the family rather than as objects of exchange.

Marriage and divorce

In the traditional society of the Trucial States the customs relating to marriage and divorce are in accordance with Islam, and they are at the same time the very backbone of the tribal system. By and large, girls are given in marriage only to members of the family, the more closely related the better, starting with first cousins. Compared with some other societies on the Arabian Peninsula, marriage with the *bint ʿamm*, daughter of the paternal uncle, does not, however, have the same predominant position, and the eldest son does not have an institutionalised claim on a *bint ʿamm*, nor can he claim compensation if that girl is married to someone else. Marriages of first cousins from either side, paternal or maternal, are equally welcome, but if there is no suitable partner to be found even within the wider family circle, the ladies who negotiate in such matters may be able to persuade a neighbour or a family which is socially of the same standing to agree to give their daughter in marriage. The parents of the girl require a considerable incentive (social status or economic advantage) if they are to agree that their daughter should live in a family whose members she does not know well, and where she might fear that she would always remain a stranger. But if such a marriage is lasting and successful, this is usually the beginning of further marriages between the families in subsequent generations.

It was customary to marry girls off as soon as possible after they had reached puberty; they were brought up to see marriage and childbearing as the most desirable status, which they should attain as soon as possible. Parents and brothers seemed to fear that a marriageable girl in the household was a liability, because there was always the very faint chance that she might succumb to someone's seduction and bring disgrace to the family. Once she was married, her conduct became the responsibility of the husband, although misdemeanour was seen as a blot on the honour of her father's family, and it was up to them rather than to the husband—who would probably divorce her—to punish or to forgive. Many girls were therefore married at the age of thirteen to husbands who were themselves only about sixteen years old; but because such marriages usually took place within the fold of the extended family the girl remained within that family group. She might continue to live with the same female relatives as before the marriage, she might even continue to live in the same household as her mother, but in any event she would be living near to the family that she had grown up with, the female members of which would help with the problems associated with setting up a new household or with pregnancy and child-bearing. Finding suitable partners for marriage, contacting the respective parents and arranging the economic aspects of a marriage was customarily done within the female world of related and friendly *ḥurum*. On some occasions, however, the services of known female go-betweens (liberated slave women, servants, midwives or healers) were employed. A girl was always asked for her consent to the marriage in front of the *muṭawwaʿ* or another trusted and well-known male witness or before a group of people.[44] But very young girls were usually too dependent on their fathers and too obedient to their parents and brothers to withhold this consent. In many cases the two partners grew up playing together when they were children, and had a good idea of each other's personalities.

If the arranged marriage was not successful, it was in principle the husband's privilege alone to initiate divorce proceedings. He could even just tell his wife that he wanted to divorce her, in which case she had to take her own belongings and her smaller children and go back to her father's house; usually boys over the age of seven stayed with the fathers, and girls remained with the mothers until puberty.

However, there are very many cases when a wife who found life intolerable with the husband or her in-laws, and being unable to divorce her husband, behaved so obstreperously towards him that he was forced to divorce her to save face in front of his relatives. The majority of such cases happen before the couple have any children, and both partners emerge from such a broken marriage without any social stigma, often marrying again soon afterwards.

In the traditional society of the Trucial States divorce has nowhere the stigma which is attached to it particularly for women in a European society. The economic aspect of divorce rather than the moral or social aspects may spell problems for women. Because if—as happens frequently—she is divorced at an advanced age, maybe because she cannot have any more children and the husband wants to have a younger wife, she may no longer have a father or a family to return to. She may have to live in the house of her brother or her eldest son. One of the reasons why a woman wants to have many sons, apart from pleasing her husband, is the hope that they will provide for her in the event of divorce or death of her husband. It is considered the duty of the sons to give support to their mother if she needs it, to give her a house and the means of livelihood or else to take her into their own homes. There are, however, many instances to be found, particularly in Abu Dhabi state, as well as among the tribes of Dhāhirah, where a divorced or widowed women lives in the household of one of her daughters and therefore at the expense of her son-in-law.

Some women have sufficient independent means from an inheritance to set up their own houses with servants and to engage in a small business such as in one case buying perfume and incense in large quantities and selling it to a small circle of female relatives and friends. Others may even buy property in the *sūq* and live off the income of one or several shops which they let out. It is always with an eye to the possibility of divorce that a wife keeps a separate account of her own money and her possessions including domestic animals, her jewellery and her date gardens.

For the same reason the bride-price plays a very important part in the negotiations which precede a marriage. The total bride price is made up of various components: firstly the money to be handed to the father of the bride, who often gives this to his daughter, but it has also been known to be used by the father to obtain for himself another wife or a new car; secondly jewellery, dress material and other gifts which the bride receives from her husband; thirdly, the cost of the wedding festivities, which may include food for many guests as well as money to be given to a group who are engaged to sing and dance, and prizes for the winners in camel races.

The most important part of the marriage contract is, however, the money, or animals or real estate, which the girl is given and which she should keep separate from the rest of the household income to be available for her use in case of divorce. It is important to stress here that, however close the family ties between the bride and bridegroom, a formal contract, which may not always be in writing, is almost certainly worked out between the two parties. It is very much part of the Islamic tradition that society as a whole ensures that the rights which are accorded to women are strictly safeguarded, this is facilitated by the fact that everyone in the community is told the details of the contract.

Polygamy

Although many men in the Trucial States have more than one wife during their lifetime, this is not necessarily due to widespread polygamy nor to a high rate of divorce. The most frequent reason for a divorce is if a husband wants more children and the wife is barren. It is rare that the husband divorces his wife in anger, because apart from the emotional aspect of losing the small children he has to consider the cost if he wishes to marry anew. The bride price has always been very high relative to the income which the various levels of society could reckon with at any particular period in history. To have more than one wife at a time was common only among the well-to-do families of the coastal towns who were involved in the pearling industry, and among the ruling families and leading shaikhs. Shaikh Zāyid bin Khalīfah, who died in 1909, had six wives; one of the leading pearling-boat owners in Abu Dhabi was said to have had eighteen wives, but neither had more than three wives at a time and death ended a marriage more frequently than divorce. A Ruler often used marriage for political reasons: by taking the daughter of a leading tribal shaikh he could hope to consolidate the allegiance of that tribe.

There was an unusually high rate of death in childbirth before modern medical facilities were introduced in the Trucial States; it has been estimated that some 40 per cent of the women in the Trucial States died during child-bearing age as a result of problems during pregnancy or while giving birth.[45] This is one reason why in every family one finds that several children are only half-brothers and half-sisters. Another reason is that if a man had more than one wife at a time he often kept the households well apart or even in different locations in the country. Half-brothers and sisters also did not see much of each other if a mother died young and her children were brought up by their grandmother, while their father married again.

In the case of multiple marriages of members of the ruling family the first wife was usually herself a member of that family. Later wives were often daughters of shaikhs of important tribes or tribal sections with whom the Ruler wanted to establish closer relationships. A separate household was set up for each one of the wives unless she stayed with her parents. Thus the children of the respective marriages were unlikely to meet each other very much, if at all, while they were young, and they were quite naturally influenced by their family's and tribe's domestic situation and ambitions. Shaikh Zāyid bin Khalīfah had one wife who was the daughter of the shaikh of the Manāṣīr, two of his wives were from the Āl Bū Falāḥ family, one was from the ruling Āl Maktūm family in Dubai, one was the daughter of one of the shaikhs of the Na'īm in Buraimi and one was also a Na'aimi whose only child died very young. Some of his marriages were arranged for political reasons to foster his steadily growing influence in the Buraimi area and among the beduin tribes. After his death in 1909 the various tribal and political interests influenced his sons to the extent that they committed fratricide while aspiring to become Rulers.[46]

With the exception of the wealthy and the politically influential families, monogamy was the common pattern of marriage in the Trucial States until the changes in the economic and cultural conditions brought certain changes in this pattern, too. In some cases when a man could afford to do so he might not want to divorce the mother of his children and yet he wanted a younger wife in order to have more children. The majority of men had one wife at a time; when she died or he divorced her he would take another.[47]

The social role of women

The preceding paragraphs demonstrated how the internal structure of the family is very largely the result of the role which women play in this Islamic and tribal socio-cultural context. Although the social rating of women in the public sphere was different from that of men (some men maintained that God created men, women, and animals,— in that order), inside the family such statements do not hold good. There, in her role as daughter, sister, wife and mother, a woman can mould her personality in the daily contact with other members of the family. As a sister she can at an early age replace her mother in the care for the younger children. As a wife she is very often the driving force behind many economic decisions, such as what should be bought for the household or whether the house should be extended, and in very prosperous houses a wife may become a formidable catalyst for local politics. A touching and often quoted example was Shaikha Salāmah bint Buṭi, mother of the Abu Dhabi Shaikhs Shakhbūṭ and Zāyid and the other sons of Shaikh Sulṭān bin Zāyid, because she not only made her sons promise not to harm each other if one of them were to be deposed by another as Ruler, but she was also the most important "éminence grise", with whom both her sons consulted almost daily while they were Rulers.

In the domestic sphere many women, particularly those who had learnt to read the Koran, were the most steadfast practising Muslims. As was mentioned earlier, most women do not miss any of the prescribed prayers, and they often fill idle moments, such as when the conversation with a visitor has lapsed into silence, to murmur a *ṣūrah* from the Koran or a prayer. To have an older woman in the family who is a devout Muslim without being bigoted or self-righteous, who has the humility, kindness and all-embracing nature of truly religious people, gives that family a spiritual leader; members of the family learn from her example how to cope with adversity, to be loyal to one another and tolerant towards strangers. During the month of Ramaḍān the older women may sometimes press the men to be steadfast in observing the fast, keeping a record of the days missed and to be made up later. Other women have become quite formidable tyrants over the entire extended family, dictating on all matters big and small, from marriage arrangements even to the size of the eyeholes in the mask (*burqaʿ*) which each mature woman of the household has to wear.

Men's social rating

While for all practical purposes the role of women within the household is frequently that of decision-maker, the male head of the family is the provider, spokesman and representative. He is the upholder of the Islamic norm of conduct in the eyes of the outside world. He embodies the social standing of the family *vis-à-vis* other families, and if he is of true local tribal origin his children will never be considered anything less than full members of the local tribal society, even if their mother was of foreign origin. The social rating of an individual male—and through him of the whole family—depends first and foremost on the purity of his tribal Arab descent; since the tribal genealogies, along with some long-established legends thereof, are common knowledge to most tribal Arabs, the kinship relationships cannot be invented.

But this does not mean that someone of pure tribal Arab stock will invariably be rated higher than a wealthy man of uncertain tribal background. The indicator for the social rating on the basis of a man's wealth is the level at which he can expect to arrange marriages for the members of his family. The flourishing pearling industry of the early decades of this century has provided in the capitals of the larger Trucial States several examples of immigrants who became wealthy and so acceptable enough to intermarry with the ruling family of the state. Both the pearling-boat owners and the merchant communities of the coastal towns established their own social rating largely on wealth. Eventually the status on account of tribal descent and the status on account of wealth and property were rated on a par, and intermarriage became possible at the highest levels of both pyramids, although it was less common at lower levels. But in every case the social rating of the male head of the family is the rating that counts.

Thus, the dominant position of the man, both within the family and *vis-à-vis* the outside world, was a given factor and not one which could be attained. As has been shown earlier, a woman had no position *per se* in the world outside the house, while her position within the family circle was a reflection of her personality and depended on the way in which she used this confined scope for the development of her abilities. In this structure of society not the individual but the family is the smallest unit. Neither man nor woman has an identity except in the context of the family to which he or she belongs.

Other members of the household, servants and slaves

In the Trucial States, family (*'ā'ilah*) never meant the family nucleus of father, mother and children only; even in the rare cases where these were the only occupants of the household, such an arrangement would be considered temporary or a result of force of circumstances such as death or absence of other kin while taking their camels grazing. The family which shares one compound usually consists of three generations: grandparents, father, mother and their children. It frequently happens that a widowed or divorced sister of the old generation or an unmarried sister of the man in the middle generation also live in the same household. Often the male of the middle generation has taken over from his father as the effective head of the family and bread-winner. It was not very common for two or more brothers to remain with their wives and children within the one family compound of the father. Usually one of them built his own house, which would soon also become the home for other members of the family.

Domestic servants were also considered to be part of the family. They used to be almost exclusively slaves, later liberated slaves and their offspring. Most of them—or their parents—were originally brought during the last century from pagan east and central Africa by Omani slave-dealers to Oman, where they were needed to work on the land. On the Trucial Coast very few families could afford to have domestic slaves as opposed to locally available helpers for work in the date gardens.[48] During the 20th century slaves were more frequently imported from Makrān and Balūchistān. Only the growing wealth of the families living in the coastal towns, due to the boom in the market for pearls, enabled them to purchase and keep several slaves.

The institution of slavery has existed in Arabia since before Islam;[49] according to the Koran and other Islamic sources it is in principle lawful to have slaves, but the relationship between the master and his slaves is clearly defined. The master is responsible for the well-being and humane treatment of his slaves; the giving of alms to slaves, liberating them or assisting them to buy themselves free are praiseworthy actions.[50] Within the family of his master the slave had a home and all the necessities of life provided for; like other members of the family the slave participated in the economic activities of the family, and most male slaves in the coastal towns worked on the pearling boats during the summer months. Their share of the dive was quite legitimately taken by their masters.

The very wealthy pearling entrepreneurs not only owned boats but also a considerable number of slaves to work on them, and of course the slaves would not earn a share as a free diver or hauler would have done.[51] But when the boom in the pearling industry began to wane the slaves still depended on their master to provide for them, while the free men who had to rely exclusively on their share in the annual dive became destitute. In the later 1930s it became increasingly difficult for the few households where there was a considerable number of slaves to provide for them; to liberate them seemed a ready solution to the master's problem. In the bigger population centres of the coast quite a few people thus suddenly found themselves without a home or any means of support, and work was not easy to come by.[52]

In most cases families had only one or two slaves as domestic servants, whose status changed very little when they were liberated. They were then free to go and seek employment elsewhere, but hardly any of them ever did. They remained in the families of their former masters where all their daily needs were still cared for as before, even if it meant tightening the belt for the entire family. Before and after they were liberated most domestic servants of slave origin were part and parcel of the family, and as such were also part and parcel of the same tribal affiliation. The difference in status usually mattered only when it came to marriage; the tribal Arab did not normally marry a slave girl, but the head of the family could quite legally become the father of a female slave's children, who were then brought up with the other children and treated as equal—except, again, when they came to marry.

It has been mentioned above how in the Trucial States, as elsewhere in Arab countries, slaves could rise to important positions on the political scene, as trusted servants of Rulers or as important individuals.[53] Being Muslims and often very devout indeed, the descendants of slaves were easily integrated into the Arab society through their integration into their master's family.

Local Muslims at home

The ordering of one's family life in the way described above was the norm and was therefore hardly ever questioned. If it were questioned, people would have been quick to observe that this was the way in which a Muslim was expected to live. For the majority of people it was quite inconceivable that any other social order or any other type of relationship between the individual in his family and the outside world could be at all in keeping with the spirit of Islam. This absolute certainty that there is no conflict between their concept of life and the spirit of Islam precluded the need to reflect on how and why things were the way they were and why most people did things in a certain manner. The daily routine of people of this area was abundant in manifestations of a universal deeply felt identification with the spirit of Islam. The humble manner in which people accepted even the most grievous afflictions and the many invocations of God throughout the day, before and after meals, before climbing into a vehicle, when promising or planning anything: these were not mere words but were often really meant.

Several years ago a European couple visited the family of a beduin with whom they had made good friends in his encampment in the desert. They found that their only girl was very ill and too weak to be transported to a doctor. The mother was quite beside herself, worrying, consulting people, crying and praying. When the couple returned to the encampment several weeks later and enquired about the health of the daughter, the mother answered with a smiling face that she was well; asking to see the child, the couple were told by the composed and serene woman that it had been God's wish that she should die, "Thanks be to God".

In the traditional society of this area it was not difficult to observe that Islam not only moulded the patterns of social behaviour and the many conventions of the daily life, but also permeated people's minds, behaviour, thoughts and desires in such a way as to make it appear that they were born natural believers. Compared to the western way of separating things religious from things secular, and of making religion a subject of speculation, the spirit of Islam was totally intertwined with the traditions of this tribal society. Thus everything concerning the family's domestic structure, its functions within the community and all its daily routine were part of man's very existence as a Muslim.

Education

Within the family

In the traditional society of the Trucial States formal education was usually understood as being religious education. In the majority of families the education of children consisted of encouraging them to behave like adults as soon and as well as possible. The mother and other females in the family as well as the older children are very tolerant of young children's behaviour up to the age of about five, while fathers and other male relations also did not interfere. The child sleeps and eats largely when and how it wants to, but is constantly in bodily contact with or at least under the eyes of some adult or older child. The child is told many times during the course of the day that it should be *rajul* (a man) or *ḥurmah* (woman) and visitors admire a child by saying *māshā'allah ṣār riyyāl* (by God he became a man) even to a toddler. In this way the children become motivated to live up to this expectation, and a previously quite unruly child under this influence suddenly, within the span of a few weeks, turns into a well behaved boy who accompanies his father sitting in a *majlis*, or into a demure little girl who could be entrusted with the care of a younger child; though left on their own they are as boisterous and mischievous as any other children. These children are taught to behave like little adults; as they grow older they participate more and more in the duties performed by the elder members of the family, until in their early teens they are expected to accept the responsibilities of adult life, including marriage.

Because the growing child is involved in the duties and the activities of the adults in the family, the values of the adults are instilled in the child; it learns by example how to master the very same duties and to conduct its life in the same fashion as the adults. A family of devout Muslims could thus not fail to bring forth a new generation of Muslims, even though very little formal instruction may be involved. Observing the adults perform the *ṣalāt* (prayers), listening to the frequent invocations of God, hearing stories about Muḥammad, his followers, and exemplary Muslims, and witnessing the giving of alms to the poor and of money to the mosques, the children grow up to be practising Muslims themselves before questioning Islamic tenets intellectually. Thus Islam in this society has hardly ever been a formidable array of doctrines and theological interpretations such as had to be absorbed by young people who become believing and practising Christians.

Formal Education

In earlier days most families required the help of the growing children in the household, in the date gardens, on the fishing boats and with the domestic animals, and few would have been able to afford to pay for formal education. Some families did, however, consider it to be important that one should be able to read the Koran, and therefore they sent their children to learn reading and writing and reciting the Koran. A *muṭawwa'*, or even a *qāḍi*, gathered a number of boys and girls in a *kuttāb*, a Koranic school, which could be conducted in his house or anywhere convenient, even under a tree. The scarcity of copies of the Holy Book and the shortage of writing material[54] often restricted the schooling to learning by rote verses of the Koran which the teacher read or recited to the children. A child was often considered to have completed his education only when he could recite the entire Koran.[55] In many *kuttāb* the emphasis was more on reading than on writing, for it was important to be able to read the Holy Book and other religious books; but some people regarded it as being undesirable for girls to be able to write and thereby to communicate with the outside world by letter.

The urban surroundings of Dubai, Shārjah and Abu Dhabi since early this century gave many families the incentive to want their children to be taught basic mathematics so that they could later enter the family business. Because teachers were always respected men in the community, not only for their religious knowledge but also as good honest citizens, therefore the pupils were expected to learn from them *adab*: how to behave responsibly and to appreciate current affairs beyond the confines of their community.

In general the teachers were not formally employed by the ruler nor paid for by endowments of a public benevolent institution. In some cases the *muṭawwaʿ* was also the *imām* in a small mosque maintained by the *waqf*, and as a further source of income he would teach children in the mosque. But more frequently the teacher just used his courtyard or gathered the children under a tree for instruction. The teachers were quite often paid by the parents of the pupils their previously-agreed tuition fees in kind: that is, food, cloth or small domestic animals. As far as the author is aware there were no purpose-built *kuttāb* in any of the Trucial States.[56] There was also no *madrasah* for higher religious studies; the nearest such school for studies of Islam and for the training of *quḍāh* was surprisingly enough in Bukhah in the Ru'ūs al Jibāl on the Musandam Peninsula, and another famous one was on Qishim island.

The role of Sharīʿah

Sharīʿah as a guide for the local Muslim's way of life

Sharīʿah is more than the instrument which enables judges to deal with the cases which are brought to them for trial. "It comprises, without restrictions, as an infallible doctrine of duties the whole of the religious political, social, domestic and private life of those who profess Islam."[57] This collection of principles for all affairs of life, *sharīʿah*, was compiled from all the passages of the Koran which relate to the behaviour of man in respect to God and to his fellowmen, and was supplemented by the traditions (*sunnah*).[58] This very wide role of *sharīʿah* does not, however, concern a person's religious feeling and the individual's inner consciousness of God's existence and is therefore not quite co-extensive with the meaning of the word *Islām* itself.

To be a Muslim implies that one has knowledge of all the basic aspects of *sharīʿah*. This knowledge is not necessarily acquired through reading and studying; because *sharīʿah* relates to all activities of man, this knowledge is handed down from one generation to the next and is the essential, formative agent of the society into which a person in the Trucial States is born. The common knowledge, understanding and acceptance of God's laws has been one of the fundamental reasons for the cohesion of the society in this area. The verbatim application of the totality of *sharīʿah* was not feasible in countries, societies, peoples and ages which were different from that of the Ḥijāz during the Prophet's lifetime. The concept of *sharīʿah* as the one and only code of conduct and of law became limited for practical reasons; and eventually it came to be understood as a system of legal pronouncements for certain matters only, and operating parallel with traditional law, State law and other sources of law and jurisdiction.

Sharīʿah as a source of law for formal jurisdiction

In this narrow sense *sharīʿah* is now understood in most Islamic States as the law which is applied by the *quḍāh* of the special *sharīʿah* courts in the cases which these courts are entitled to handle, that is, cases concerning marriage, divorce, inheritance and similar matters.

Until relatively recently no law courts of any kind existed in this area; the traditional tribal society turned to the family elders, shaikhs, *wālis*, Rulers or *quḍāh* to obtain justice.[59] At these different levels of jurisdiction the deliberations of the adjudicator and the attitude of the parties to the verdict were all based on the *sharīʿah* and the customary tribal law (*ʿurf*), often supplemented by a Ruler's decree. Only at the level of a *qāḍi* specially employed by a Ruler was the division between the formalised and codified *sharīʿah* and any other source of law better defined, for the very reason that *quḍāh* were employed because they had studied *fiqh*, which is the jurisprudence of *sharīʿah*.

Although most *quḍāh* in the main population centres of the Trucial States during this century were born outside the area[60] they also took into consideration the traditional concept of the local population concerning right and wrong, fairness and justice in punishment. In some cases the opinion of the Ruler was of considerable weight and could even be the decisive factor in reaching a verdict.

During the first decade of this century, men trained in the interpretation and application of *sharīʿah* were appointed by several of the Rulers of the Trucial States. This generated competition, not only as to which of the legal principles should be applied, namely *sharīʿah*, *ʿurf* or a Ruler's opinion, but also among the judicial authorities. As has been shown above,[61] most disputes between members of the tribal society never actually reached the Ruler, nor the *qāḍi*; they were dealt with on the family or tribal levels. But cases with domestic or external political relevance were tried by the Ruler: his very title in Arabic, *ḥākim*, was, not for nothing, derived from the same root as another word for judge. Matters concerning the pearling community were tried by an independent diving court, *sālifah al ghauṣ*, manned by respectable members of that community, merchants, captains, and divers alike.

All these *ad hoc* or institutionalised judicial bodies, while not necessarily referring to particular paragraphs of the relevant books on *fiqh*, nevertheless were imbued with the spirit of Islam and *sharīʿah* in the wider sense, even though they might in the end base their decision on the *ʿurf*. It is significant, however, that for a period earlier this century when there was increasing alienation between the various groups residing in the coastal towns, due to immigration from abroad and from the desert, there was also an increase in disputes over property and over money, there was more fraud and theft, and there were more marriages between non-related families. This made it necessary to engage judicial authorities who had no local tribal links and were separate from the existing hierarchy. Their jurisdiction was based exclusively on the universally acceptable interpretation of *sharīʿah*.

The Rulers in the coastal towns, with increasingly diversified and sophisticated societies, were eventually expected to delegate to the *quḍāh* judicial cases which were brought to their attention. An example has already been cited above[62] of Shaikh Shakhbūṭ, who did not try any of the cases which were brought to him during his visit to Bainunah in 1950s, but sent the *qāḍi* to do this. In the course of the continued opposition of members of the ruling family and an influential group of citizens of Dubai to the Ruler, Shaikh Sa'īd bin Maktūm, his judicial competence did not remain unchallenged either. A group of erudite citizens, obviously realising the conflict between judgement according to *sharī'ah* and that according to other standards, "called on the notables and the Ruler to take notice of the fact that crime is on the increase in Dubai and to punish perpetrators according to the *Sharī'ah* law and not as is done by the Ruler and his officials at present."[63]

A Ruler's reason for wishing to deal himself with certain cases, particularly if they involved non-tribal inhabitants of the town, such as slaves or foreigners, was two-fold: he could thereby continue to exercise his authority as the source of law and order within the tribal society, and he was seen to be reacting to novel political situations. When the Ruler of Dubai, Shaikh Sa'īd bin Maktūm, ordered that the punishment recommended by the *sharī'ah* court for theft was carried out and the hand of a certain Sālim bin Fairūz was cut off, the British Resident in Bushire was prompt to criticise the Ruler severely for condoning this type of punishment. Sa'īd bin Maktūm tried to keep such cases away from the *sharī'ah* court because he did not want to alienate his British support; afterwards he justified the court's decision by saying that the Trucial Shaikhs could not afford to maintain men in prison and therefore had to punish culprits in this way.[64] The furore about this case shows that such severe forms of punishment as are recommended according to *sharī'ah* for theft, adultery, murder and so on, were not normally administered in this tribal society, where the offender was usually known in the community. Criminal acts, such as murder or sexual assault were avenged by the family, either by killing the offender if he could be caught or by negotiating blood money if he managed to take refuge with some other tribe or community. For petty theft and other minor offences a local culprit who was found out had to pay compensation or he was imprisoned, which usually meant being shackled for a couple of weeks in the local fort, albeit sharing the lives and the food of the Ruler's guards.

The increasing number of criminal offences during and after the economic recession of the early 1930s most frequently proved to be committed either by immigrants who had come during the pearling boom or by desperate, impoverished beduin raiders. Neither group was really part of the communities in the coastal towns which were mostly affected by this development. The call for jurisdiction by the *sharīʿah* judges rather than the Ruler in such cases signified that *sharīʿah* became universally accepted because it could overrule the temporal Ruler's whims and was binding on all Muslims no matter where they were born.

The dualism, and in some instances even polarisation, of customary jurisdiction and *sharīʿah* became more acute from the 1930s on. People were aware that not all cases and not everyone should be subject to the traditional jurisdiction. The development during the 1940s of a set of regulations for the trial of foreigners on the one hand and the necessity to introduce laws to deal with novel offences such as traffic accidents, labour and contractual disputes on the other hand, led to the limitation of the jurisdiction of the *sharīʿah* in the Trucial States, in the same way as it is limited in most Muslim countries. Already during the late 1940s the *sharīʿah* courts in Dubai operated a register of marriages which took place in the town, and became the authority which handled all matters relating to personal status, family affairs and inheritance, while criminal offences reverted to the political authorities, both local and British. Regulations were devised for new situations by way of Rulers' decrees and His Majesty's Order in Council.[65]

The fact that *sharīʿah*, in the narrower sense of the law such as is administered by specialised graduates from foreign law schools, has not been the exclusive legal and judicial authority anywhere in the Trucial States, does not preclude the important role of the spirit of *sharīʿah* as the common guide for relationships between the people. It is therefore not surprising that the current efforts of federal and regional authorities in the UAE to create a new code of laws, which suits the vastly transformed society of the present day, do not only try to adapt other Arab or European laws, but also follow the growing trend throughout Muslim States to base laws on the *sharīʿah* by re-interpreting *fiqh*. The very undoctrinal religiousness of the local society, rather than legalistic deliberations concerning the reconciliation of different sources of law, helps to pave the way for the ascendancy of *sharīʿah* in legislation and jurisdiction in the UAE at the present time.[66]

Zakāh

The giving of *zakāh* (alms-tax) is one of the five duties incumbent on every true Muslim. This institution gradually developed from voluntary giving away of worldly possessions to the poor, into an obligatory contribution in the form of taxation to the expansion and maintenance of the early Islamic State under the Caliph Abū Bakr. In later centuries the governments based the rate of taxation and the assessment of taxable items on the traditional system for the giving of *zakāh*, and even the term *zakāh* was retained,[67] although the revenue was not always used for distribution among the poor nor for the cause of spreading Islam.[68]

In the Trucial States certain taxes and dues were paid to the Rulers on produce, possessions and imports,[69] for which the word *zakāh* was sometimes used among other more specific terms. But the true meaning of *zakāh* in this area, which after all had not remitted tax to the central Caliphate for many centuries, was the giving to the poor. While the worldly authorities are entitled to tax a person on his visible and assessable property, the undisclosed wealth (*bāṭin*) of a person, such as his gold and silver coins and his merchandise in his store, is estimated by himself and he has to put aside a fixed percentage to be given away. This assessment is made annually; for example, if someone held 1,000 gold sovereigns on a certain date and did not make use of them for a year, he had to put aside 25 sovereigns as *zakāh*. It was neither the Ruler's, nor the *qāḍi's*, nor indeed anybody else's business to monitor this yearly payment. It was entirely up to the individual's conscience to fulfil this duty of Islam very carefully, including even the little heap of unsold pearls tied up in a cloth, or the stock of wood in the shop.

It was also for the individual to decide how he distributed this *zakāh*, but if someone had relatives who were less well-off than himself, it was considered meritorious to give generously to them first and only then to turn to the poor strangers or to send the *zakāh* to Mecca for distribution to the poor. Many people who did not understand the method of assessing *zakāh* consulted a *muṭawwa'* or the *qāḍi*, who had access to the legal interpretations of this obligation. Judging from the more easily visible manifestations of the unquestioning, deep religiousness which was practised in the traditional society, it may be assumed that the obligation to give *zakāh* was generally observed.

5 Conclusion: The tribal system of the Trucial States and Islam

Traditionally, social differentiation in the Trucial States stemmed from the tribal structure rather than from class distinction and material well-being. The various levels of identification—family, sub-tribe and tribe—allocated to a person his particular place in society; thus even the poorest member of a powerful tribe could have more social prestige than a prosperous trader without tribal connections in the shaikhdom.

The role of Islam was that of levelling many of the differences which are inherent in any society's structure. When it came to observing the tenets of Islam there was only one set of behaviour for rich and poor alike, symbolised for instance in the way in which all men make the same movement simultaneously when praying together.

In pre-Islamic times the Arab tribal structure of society evolved in parallel with the development of the means to exploit the meagre resources of their homeland. The tribal structure became the backbone of nomadic existence. The settled and the nomadic existences of the population were often forced by circumstances to be interchangeable; even village life in Eastern Arabia, after it had been colonised by the various Arab tribes, remained for centuries based on tribal bonds rather than on neighbourhood affiliations. This strongest of social bonds, the tribal structure, survived more or less intact in Inner Oman and on the coasts of Oman from pre-Islamic times until the present day, weathering foreign invasions, temporary subjugation by Persian overlords, religious strife, civil war and the threat of colonial rule from the Portuguese and the British.

The historical evidence of this is readily available in the *falaj*-irrigated towns and villages of Inner Oman and the Ḥajar mountain range. As for the tribal population of the mountain foreland and the desert to the west, the sparse water resources from wells dug in the sand did not favour permanent settlement. The majority of the population there remained nomadic until quite recently, and like all nomads they depended vitally on the system of group identification, mutual assistance and hospitality which the tribal structure provided.

Islam, itself moulded by and grafted onto the tribal society of the Ḥijāz, therefore did not disrupt tribalism in Eastern Arabia, but rather solidified it and enhanced its strength, enabling this tribal society to withstand adversities of wars and economic crises. As for the political aspect, the most intimate synthesis of tribal and Islamic principles evolved in the form of the Imāmate in Oman. At times of peace and economic prosperity the tribes of Oman rallied round their Imām—wherever he happened to spread his prayer-mat and make the seat of government—in the same way as tribesmen rally round their shaikhs and different factions accept the leadership of the *tamīmah*. During periods of strife, occupation and destruction of economic resources, the population endeavoured to survive such times by rallying to the tribal entity, and in the case of the settled population, to the tribal neighbourhood. For the non-Ibāḍi tribal Muslim of Eastern Arabia, Islam was also so intertwined with the tribal structure that even there the political focus, the shaikh of the tribe or the Ruler of a federation of tribes, is expected to be a leader and an example in religious matters.

Islam has taken the sting out of the pre-Islamic tribal system of compulsory revenge for any and every injury, by introducing forgiveness as a praiseworthy act. It has levelled the difference between members of different tribes by making them brothers in the same creed; it has changed the status of women, who in pre-Islamic times were often considered merely as objects of possession. Above all, Islam has brought to the tribal society a law which has its point of reference outside the tribal structure; it is undoubtable, uninfluenceable and eternal. The all-embracing character of the Islamic system did not conflict with the tribal basis of society, as both enhanced the way of life which characterised the society of the Trucial States before the discovery of oil.

Chapter Five

The Traditional Economies

1 General

The development of the one major natural resource, petroleum, found within the territory of the Trucial States depended on people and technologies imported from abroad; this together with the flow of oil revenues produced an instantaneous increase in the area's capacity to accommodate a rapidly-growing immigrant population. This radical change is in stark contrast to the period immediately preceding the discovery and export of oil. The estimates of the population figures in all the Trucial States in the first half of the 1950s show a decrease in numbers of almost every tribe and coastal settlement as compared to the figures in the *Gazetteer*. The obvious reason was the emigration of many of the able-bodied men to neighbouring countries where they found work. The underlying cause of this exodus was, given the lack of natural resources other than pearls, the decline in this industry hastened by the opportunities for men to work in the oil industry of neighbouring countries. There was no alternative source of income for them at home. The effects of the decline of the pearling industry since the 1930s show how delicate the balance was between the local resources and the number of people who could live off them.

The traditional economies of the region had not been static for centuries, and there was a considerable movement within the society. During the 18th and early 19th century, communications with India improved considerably, opening greater opportunities to sell pearls in this expanding market. Also the Perpetual Treaty of Peace signed in 1853 meant that pearling communities could pursue their seasonal occupation in greater security. A number of local factors combined to decrease the percentage of predominantly nomadic families and to increase the settled population. This trend was particularly obvious in Abu Dhabi, where the originally beduin Bani Yās first established the Līwā settlements and later Abu Dhabi town as centres for a semi-settled existence; in due course whole sections of the tribes no longer accompanied their camels to the grazing grounds, but placed them in the care of beduin. The other ports of the Trucial Coast also grew in size and importance over the same period, drawing primarily on the nomadic population of the entire eastern Arabian promontory. The influx of nomads into the pearling communities on the coast was supplemented by immigrants from the predominantly Arab ports on the opposite shore of the Gulf, such as Lingah or Bandar ʿAbbās.

The total of 8,000 beduin among the 80,000 inhabitants of the Trucial States, as estimated in the *Gazetteer*,[1] probably decreased further over the following two decades due to the boom in the market for pearls. But statements on the relative percentages of settled and nomadic people remain highly speculative, even after a census carried out in 1968, because of the way in which both modes of existence were intertwined. It is equally difficult to state accurately how many people were engaged in any one particular economic activity. As was emphasised previously, the versatile tribesman was often himself a camel-breeder, a date grower, and a pearl diver, or else those skills were shared among the members of one family.

2 Husbandry in the Trucial States

The camel has always been and still is the most important domestic animal raised on this coast and its hinterland. In the 1990s some households even in the towns still keep a female camel in the yard for her milk. Throughout the Arabian Peninsula the only known type of camel is the one-humped dromedary. Of the tribal people who inhabit permanently or visit the Trucial States very few are exclusively camel-breeders; even the almost entirely beduin Bani Qitab and the Manāṣīr own date gardens. However, most of the ʿAwāmir and splinter groups of the Rashīd, Manāhīl, ʿAfār, Āl Murrah and others who also roam the entire area between their homelands to the west and north of the Hadhramaut and Dhafrah, used to organise their entire lives around the requirements of their animals.

In all of Eastern Arabia camels have usually been owned by individuals, not by the family or the community. Since every Arab recognises his own animals from among the hundreds in a herd, a large group such as a whole subtribe or even a tribe can use one and the same mark or *wasm*, which is branded onto the flank or chest of the camel.

Some tribes specialise in certain breeds of animals, and some of the hardiest though not the most beautiful camels of Eastern Arabia were bred by the Rashīd.[2] The camels of the Hadhramaut-based fully beduin families are among those which can endure the longest journeys consuming very little water. On a journey such as crossing stretches of waterless desert the beduin of Eastern Arabia travelled as lightly as possible, carrying a rifle, and a dagger, a cooking-pot, a coffee kettle, and as much water in goat-skins and as many dried dates in rush bags as could be carried by the animals. The well-being of the camels is always considered first; when arriving at a well they were all watered before the people could take their first sip. Camels were allowed to stray and forage for small pieces of vegetation even if the rider was in a great hurry; camels would be hand-fed on dates when there was no other food for them. They would be given the last drop of water from the skins, because the safe arrival of its rider depended entirely on the strength of his mount. There is no hard and fast rule as to how long a camel from south-eastern Arabia can go without water, as this depends on many factors; the type of plant it grazes on, the load it is required to carry, the speed of travelling, the ground it walks on, and above all the time of year. A long and arduous journey such as crossing the Rubʿ al Khāli can only be undertaken during the winter.

During the summer, beduin such as the Rashīd went to wells which were within relatively easy reach of sufficient grazing. They split up into very small groups so that the vegetation would not be depleted too quickly. The camel-herders would prefer the gravel *wādis* to the sands because the occasional acacia tree gives shade to animals and humans;[3] but often these coveted areas were not safe for beduin who might be at feud with another tribe, and therefore they often decided to stay near a well in the sands. Sometimes the wells are too bitter for human consumption, and although the camels, reluctantly and with their nostrils closed by the owner's hand, drink the water, the people have to mix it with camel milk for their own consumption. In the desert and the borderlands there are no ponds or artesian wells, and the animals cannot be left to drink by themselves.[4] The water in a well is usually found several feet down and has to be drawn by skins attached to a rope and tied at the four corners to form a bag. Since camels may drink ten to twelve gallons each at a time, watering a herd of them during the summer is extremely arduous work, especially since they have to be taken further and further away for grazing as the vegetation in the vicinity of the well is eaten up. Under such conditions a camel is usually watered every two to three days.[5] During the winter camels may go for six or seven months without any water, provided that the grazing is plentiful and of the right kind. The beduin families would themselves live on little other than camel milk and dates during that time.

Under these conditions it is understandable that, although each animal is valuable as a source of meat, of dung for fuel to cook on, of wool and skins to make rugs and containers,[6] as a rule only the female camels were raised, with the exception of a few stallions to serve the mares. In general most male calves were slaughtered on occasions such as a wedding or to celebrate the arrival of an important visitor.

Beduin who also owned date gardens divided their time between that property and their camels. There are differences among the population of the Trucial States as to how much of the time such people led a nomadic life. Very few of the Manāṣīr, for instance, resided in their houses in the Līwā all the year round, and the bulk of the tribe was usually somewhere in Dhafrah, or even as far away as Qatar and Dhāhirah, seeking the best grazing for their large herds of camels. Most Bani Yās except for the Mazārīʿ were more inclined to stay in the Līwā and entrust their camels to other Bani Yās or to Manāṣīr tribesmen to be looked after during the winter. In the summer, when even many Manāṣīr wanted to be in their Līwā homes for the date harvest or to go to the coast for the pearling season, the camels had to be kept near the wells in the Līwā.

The grazing in the Līwā and to the south in Baṭn al Līwā is plentiful, but the predominant plant is *harm* (zygophyllum) which is salty and acts as a purgative, so that the camels need to be watered three or four times a day. When the camels were kept near date gardens there was also the additional problem of supervising them, because if they strayed into the small oases and ate from the date trees the consequence was inevitably a dispute between the owners of the camel and those of the date palms.[7]

All along the coast some tribes who had undisputed rights to certain islands used to ferry their camels across the sea by boat to make use of the winter-grazing on the islands.

Because the camel-owners among the tribes living in or at the foot of the Ḥajar mountains found both grazing and water in the immediate vicinity of their settlements, few of the beduin sections of the tribes of the Trucial States outside Abu Dhabi territory needed to lead a fully nomadic life, nor did they confine their pastoral activities always to camels. Most beduin families of the Na'īm, Āl Bū Shāmis, Bani Qitab or Sharqiyīn used to own many goats or sheep, which could graze in the vicinity of their settlements, sometimes together with the camels; but more often the camels were taken by some members of the family out into the plains.

Camels were raised primarily for their milk, and also to provide a mount for their owner and his family and as beasts of burden. Secondly, they were the only item which a beduin had to sell if he wanted money to buy the few necessities in life: a rifle and ammunition, clothing material, cooking implements, camel-trimmings, rice, coffee, sugar or even jewellery for a wedding. Probably the most important camel market of the area used to be 'Ibri in Oman, but Buraimi village and to some extent D̲aid and the coastal settlements were also places where camels changed hands.

The importance of camels for the carrying trade is obvious in a sandy and waterless terrain. An age-old caravan route passed from the ports on the western coast through Buraimi to Ṣuḥār. With the expansion of trade into Dubai, when it became a port of call for the British Indian Steamship Company early in the 20th century, this town developed into an important caravan terminal as well.

The route between Abu Dhabi town and the Buraimi oasis became increasingly busy after the Bani Yās and other subjects of the Ruler of Abu Dhabi consolidated their interests in the oasis. A large number of families left Abu Dhabi during the summer for the drier climate and the date harvest in the oasis. Few of those families who normally lived in Abu Dhabi town owned enough camels to move their entire households. They used the services of tribesmen who specialised in this seasonal carrying trade between Abu Dhabi and the oasis in about the month of May and back again in the autumn. The Āl Bū Khail subsection of the Manāṣīr and occasionally some Dhawāhir acted as the principal carriers for this annual summer migration. At other times in the year these camel owners carried the charcoal they made themselves, and firewood and dates, limes, wheat, and other products from the oasis gardens to Abu Dhabi, Dubai or Shārjah. The journey to the Buraimi oasis, which was usually undertaken by three or four families together, took about fourteen days; messengers and fighting men could cover the 160 kilometres in about three days.

The inhabitants of the Līwā owned enough camels to carry everything and everybody on their own animals for their frequent journeys to Abu Dhabi town or to the coast where travellers used to meet local coastal craft to take them to Abu Dhabi or Dubai. In the days before Landrovers, camel-riders were coming and going between the Līwā or the Buraimi oasis and Abu Dhabi almost every day.

Besides camels, donkeys played an important role as beasts of burden almost everywhere in the Trucial States. They were as useful in the mountains for short distances as in the narrow lanes of the *sūq* and the living quarters of the towns. They carried the rider as well as a load of animal fodder, crops for the market, or drinking-water for sale. It is not certain whether the donkey used throughout the Trucial States was locally bred from the wild asses which were until very recently found in the foothills of the Ḥajar range, or whether it was imported from abroad.[8]

Horses were never widely used in the Trucial States, either for carrying or for agriculture or warfare.[9] The ground is frequently too soft for their pointed hooves and, because feeding and watering them presented problems, they were not used very much in raids where their speed might have been an asset, nor for journeys in the mountains and *wādis* over the rough terrain. However, since every Arab has learnt to appreciate the value of horses, which figure so prominently in written and oral Arab poetry, most shaikhs would like to own some. A good horse has always been considered to be an appropriate gift between shaikhs. In Dubai, Shārjah and Abu Dhabi merchant families also owned horses and rode them within the towns.

Among the domestic animals traditionally kept by the population, cattle rank very low on the list, but a number were raised in oases where lucerne could be grown under the date palms, therefore excluding the Līwā and other oases without *falaj* irrigation. Cattle were kept primarily for milk, but in the oases such as Buraimi where wheat was planted, oxen were used for ploughing the fields.[10] In the Shamailīyah, where cattle were also used for ploughing, they were fed on dried sardines boiled with old dates, leaves and other vegetable refuse found in the date gardens. There, oxen were also used to draw water from wells; the bucket was lowered on a rope which passed over a pulley mounted about two metres high on the well frame. As the oxen walked away from the well down an incline, the full bucket was pulled up and caught by the attendant, who emptied it into the irrigation channel or into a tank.

Both sheep and goats used to be kept by most settled and beduin families in the Trucial States. During the last few decades the number of goats has increased at the expense of sheep. The reason which the owners give for this preference is that goats are easier to keep because they are less particular in their diet. The goats are usually tended by women and children in the vicinity of the settlements. When the tribes who roamed the foreland of the Ḥajar mountains left their settlements and adopted a nomadic life during the winter months, they took the goats and sheep with their camels. The nomadic tribes in the desert of Abu Dhabi sometimes left the goats with members of the tribe in the Līwā during the winter because they took their camels to an area without wells from which the goats could be watered. In the past there were not many goats nor sheep in the Līwā villages.

The goat was useful in a variety of ways. The milk was turned into curds (*makhīḍ* or *rā'ib*), the hair was spun and woven by the women into tent material and tent ropes, or knitted into socks to protect the feet in the burning hot sand of the summer. Goatskins and the skins of an edible lizard, *dhabb*, were favoured for making bags to transport water or clarified butter. The skins were cured with salt, worked and sewn together; sometimes the extremities of the skins were neatly knotted to form tassels and handles.

3 Hunting, fishing, collecting

Wildlife and hunting

Within living memory there was never enough game for a family to live off the hunt anywhere in Eastern Arabia, but until recently there was enough wildlife in the mountain foreland and even in the desert to justify a beduin carrying a rifle even if he did not expect to meet an enemy but hoped to spot some game for the pot. In the Trucial States there used to be many gazelles, not only in the outwash plains of the mountains and in those parts of the desert which were fairly green, such as Khatam, but even on the shallow inshore islands and sandbanks off the coast. The name Abu Dhabi means place of (or father of) the white gazelle.[11] Beduin on the move used to kill gazelles for the pot if they chanced upon them. With the introduction of automatic weapons and four-wheel drive motorcars, the gazelle population everywhere in the Peninsula was dramatically diminished. But fortunately it is not on the verge of extinction and is now protected in the United Arab Emirates, in common with all other wild life. Arabian oryx, now very rarely found anywhere in the wild, were once abundant in Manāṣīr country in the western Trucial Oman.[12] Ibex were never recorded as far east as the Trucial States or the Ḥajar mountains; the nearest place where ibex are reported to have been sighted is on the Jabal al Akhḍar, in Oman proper.[13]

Only a few of the beduin groups could afford to keep *salūqi* dogs for hunting. These slender dogs are fast enough to keep up with gazelles. But when there was no wild life to hunt, the dogs had to be fed on left-over scraps of meat, which most nomadic groups just did not have, since their daily staple diet was milk and dates. A few *salūqi* were kept by people in the Līwā and some shaikhs liked to hunt with them, but the most popular method of hunting bustard (*ḥubāra*), foxes, rabbits and other small animals was and still is with falcons. Two types are used in this area, the *ṣaqr* (Latin *falco cherrug*) and the *shāhīn* (Latin *falco peregrinus*).[14] Both types used to visit south-eastern Arabia on their migration routes. To catch the wild bird and to tame, train, feed and groom it is a time-consuming exercise, and for this reason the owners of several falcons employ people specially to look after their birds. The Rulers' retainers, *muṭārzīyah*, served as their falconers during the winter.

Apart from the *ḥubāra*, rabbits, lizards, gazelles and foxes were also sometimes hunted for food; wild cats, eagles, ravens and any other birds were invariably hunted when sighted, but if they were caught or shot they would only be eaten in extreme cases of near-starvation, because they were considered to be unclean. The foxes of the desert and wolves which took refuge in the mountains were a constant threat to small domestic animals such as chickens and kid goats, and if one was reported in the neighbourhood of a village the entire community was mobilised to kill it. Neither hyena nor jackal are reported to have ever been seen in this part of Eastern Arabia, but leopards living in the Ḥajar mountains and on Jabal Ḥafīt have been seen, even recently. A particular type of wild goat (Latin *capra aegagrus*) which was otherwise not known to occur on the Arabian

Peninsula was caught alive near Masāfi at the head of the Wādi Ḥām, and presented to London Zoo.[15] Its local name could not be verified. Another type of mountain goat, Arabian taher or *wa'al* (Latin *hemitragus jayakari*) has been reported to live on the Jabal Ḥafīt as well as the Jabal al Akhḍar in Oman. Lions used to live in the area, particularly in the mountains, but have not been reported during the last few hundred years. The shells of ostrich eggs are found occasionally in the desert but it is believed to be some fifty years or more since ostriches have been seen alive.

Fishing

Between them the seven shaikhdoms have 540 kilometres of coastline. The east coast facing the Gulf of Oman consists of long stretches of sweeping beaches and sandy bays intersected in places where the barren Ḥajar mountains reach into the sea. A few rocky islands are within sight of the coast. The chief characteristics of the western coast facing the Gulf proper are shallow waters near the shore, islands, sandbanks, lagoons, reefs and tidal channels which rendered much of the coast before the construction of modern harbours inaccessible to all but the people who regularly fished in that area.

The fishing potential on both shores is very high. The southern part of the Gulf is particularly productive during September to March, when cooler, less saline and biologically enriched waters from the Indian Ocean penetrate through the Straits of Hormuz for about 160 kilometres along the coast from Ra's al Khaimah to Dubai. The water brings with it large numbers of pelagic fish such as tuna, bonito, mackerel, sardines and anchovy.

The Gulf of Oman coast is even richer in fish because there is a constant upwelling of water from deep down in the contiguous Indian Ocean which helps the abundant growth of plankton. Fishermen do not need to go out very far to secure a good catch; consequently deep sea fishing has not been developed. Trawling for demersal fish is not so productive because the continental shelf is narrow and the grounds are not suitable. For most people in the Trucial States fish has often been almost the only source of protein. There have been fish markets and auctions in most towns and villages on the coast, where fresh fish could be bought by those who did not go fishing themselves. But a large amount of fish protein reached the population in the hinterland only in rather inferior sun-dried form. Dried fish for human and animal consumption and in the case of sardines for fertilizer was and still is a major export item from all the Trucial States. It was estimated that during the 1950s and early 1960s about 10,000 tons of fish were produced annually, of which 6,000 tons were exported.[16]

It is almost impossible to estimate the number of people who used to be involved in the fishing industry. For many people fishing was a seasonal or an occasional occupation, while some depended entirely on the sea for their living even after the decline of the pearling industry. In 1969 the Trucial States Development Office estimated that "there are about 30,000 people, all Arabs of local origin, who depend wholly or partly upon the catch of fish for their cash income."[17] It was also stated that the methods of fishing had not changed, which meant that oars and sails were still in use as they had been for centuries.

On the east coast there were several traditional ways of fishing. The fisherman who operated on his own used a craft called *shāshah* which was made entirely from the branches of the date palms; the space between the hull and the deck was filled with palm-fronds, which gave the boat just enough buoyancy to stay afloat with one or two persons on board, who while sitting on the often partly-submerged deck, rowed themselves through the surf to lay out their weighted nets. Sometimes wooden rowing boats were used which could hold about ten people. The large surf boats called *ʿāmlah* were fitted with sails and oars and could hold 25 to 30 crew; they were used to set beach seines (nets laid out parallel to the shore) sometimes up to 100 metres long. Usually such nets would have been very much shorter and could be laid out by any of the local types of fishing craft, which after several hours pulled both ends of the net in to the shore. The crew and other helpers, while chanting rhythmically, would pull the net up onto the beach and shake the catch, sardines and anchovy, on the sand. The fish was laid out and dried in the sun before being collected into baskets by the women and children. The dried sardines were sold locally as fodder for cattle and even for camels, or to be used as fertilizer; a considerable amount was also exported to neighbouring countries.

On the east coast fishing and agriculture could be easily combined as an occupation because the sea and the palm groves are both within easy reach of the villages; the same applies to the coast of Ra's al Khaimah. But elsewhere on the Trucial Coast the oases are a considerable distance inland and therefore people could not engage in agriculture and fishing at the same time. This was particularly true in Abu Dhabi where the oases of Līwā and the Buraimi area are a long way from the barren shores and islands, the homes of fishermen. Fishing therefore became, together with pearling, the exclusive occupation of a small group of people in the shaikhdom of Abu Dhabi.

Some of Abu Dhabi's islands were permanently inhabited by fishermen, mostly Rumaithāt and also some Qubaisāt, both subsections of the Bani Yās. Those people who lived on islands in the west such as Ṣīr Bani Yās had to fetch water from Dalmā Island, where there was a permanent source of fresh water. An alternative means of obtaining water was to trap the occasional winter rain by supporting, on a number of poles, large sails with a hole in the middle, but the winter rains were unreliable and the supply could not last for very long. The Ghaghah group of islands also, in the west, had a village with stone huts on one of the islands; the inhabitants built cairns on the islands to guide their boats through the shallow channels. To the east of Abu Dhabi Island, too, some of the neighbouring inshore islands such as Saʿdiyāt had permanent fishing villages on them, inhabited mostly by Rumaithāt. Dalmā, in the open sea in the west, was the most important of the inhabited islands but was not used as a base for fishing; some of its permanent inhabitants went to other islands in the winter to fish from their more protected shores.

Fishing on the entire coast of Abu Dhabi and its islands was undertaken on the strength of fishing rights which were rented from the Ruler. For example, the area between Khaur al ʿUdaid in the far west up to just west of al Ḥamrā', about 100 kilometres of coast with many islands and sandbanks, was at one time in about 1940 rented to Darwīsh bin Ḥaddād of the Rumaithāt, who paid 350 Rupees per year to the Ruler.[18] Families who lived from fishing on the islands and on the coasts paid one-fifth of the catch to the main holder of the fishing rights. Such rights were held primarily by Rumaithāt, but were also held by some of the Qubaisāt, Āl Bū Falāsah and Rawāshid sections of the Bani Yās. Inhabitants of the Līwā who went fishing during the winter did not themselves obtain fishing rights but gave the customary one-fifth of the catch to the holder. Many Bani Yās from the Līwā left their pearling boats pulled up on the shore for the winter months if not in use for fishing. No Manāṣīr, ʿAwāmir or Āl Murrah tribesmen went fishing because few of them owned boats, but some of them joined in the pearling dive as crew; they did not have as intimate a connection with the coast as the Bani Yās.

The different methods used for fishing off the coast of Abu Dhabi did not require a communal effort, as pearling did. The fishermen knew which kind of fish came to feed on the type of vegetation available in a particular spot. Some of the best fishing was done by setting two nets (*masākir*) across the mouth of a small creek, or along the beach, at high tide. The nets were placed one on each side of a central pole in the water and extended at a right angle to the tidal movement, so that as the water receded the fish were trapped. This method is called *iskār*. *Yāl* is the name of another method by which one man alone could catch fish. He would wait on the shore until he heard or saw a shoal in the shallow water, whereupon he fastened one end of the net to a pole on the shore (*mākhir*), and took the other end of the weighted net in a wide circle through the water to another point on the shore, using a small boat or a dug-out. The net had an opening in the middle for which the fish would make when the net was slowly pulled in to the shore; behind the opening was a trap in which all the fish were gathered. Even sharks were caught in this way. A similar method called *idfārah* required two or three people; instead of having a trap behind the net one man held the middle of the net down with his feet as it was drawn into the shallow water. Some fishermen used to wade in the shallows stalking the fish and catching them by throwing over them a circular net, weighted at the edge and with a rope attached to the middle; this method is called *salīyah*. The people also set fishtraps, *qarqūr*, which used to be made of palm fronds, lowering them to the bottom of the sea with the entrance on the downstream side. The crews on pearling vessels would put opened shells in these traps to entice the fish, frequently leaving them on the seabed all day in the hope of obtaining a good catch.

On the western Gulf coast, too, most of the catch was dried and exported. Merchants from Qatar, Bahrain, Qaṭīf or Dammām would visit the islands occasionally to purchase fish. Fresh fish was sold in the markets of Abu Dhabi and Dalmā, or direct for consumption in the oases, even as manure for the date palms. At one time dugong (Latin *sirenia dugong*) were probably more plentiful in the Gulf than now, but on the rare occasions when one was caught in a net it would be killed and eaten as a delicacy.[19]

Collecting guano

Some of the islands in the Gulf have considerable deposits of guano. Dās, Zirkū, Qarnain and Arzanah in the open sea, and Umm Ḥaṭab,

Maḥammilīyah near the shore, and others were rich enough to make it worthwhile for a Kuwaiti by the name of ʿAbdullah al Ṣanʿāwi to pay for a concession to collect guano in 1949 from these Abu Dhabi islands. In the following year a certain Rāshid bin Aḥmad of Dubai obtained a similar concession from Shaikh Shakhbūṭ.

4 Agriculture

Date cultivation

The cultivation of the date palm has always been by far the most important form of agriculture in the area. The date palm (Latin *phoenix dactylifera*) provides its owner with a fruit which is higher in calorific value than almost any other.[20] Boiled and packed into bags made of dried palm leaves, dates can be kept for a long time and therefore were used as a staple food for men and beasts on long journeys through the desert. When the families gathered in the oases during the date harvest in the summer they consumed a fair amount of the crop while it was fresh; another big share of the harvest went straight to the many pearling boats which were at sea at the same time. Throughout the year in every household, on board ships, or when travelling in the desert, either fresh or conserved dates were eaten at least as a supplement to other food, but often they were the main source of nourishment other than milk.

Apart from its fruit the date palm provided the tribal communities with a variety of other useful materials; the dead tree-trunks, although too fibrous for most carpentry, have always served as beams in the construction of houses;[21] the branches, stripped of their leaves and spikes were bound together into mats which formed the walls of the houses,[22] while the *shāshah* used for fishing on the east coast is made entirely from palm branches. The leaves of date palms were used to make fans, baskets, bags, food trays and their covers, and a variety of other household implements. The fronds were also bound together and lined with pitch to form water tanks, or even boats. The fibrous bark which grows at the bottom of the tree is suitable material for making ropes and for such purposes as stuffing camel saddles, mattresses and cushions.

Date palms can grow from a stone, but the usual way of obtaining a new tree is by transplanting a shoot which comes up by the foot of a mature tree. If well watered, such new plants may bear fruit after three years. Because only female date palms bear fruit, very few male trees are planted in a garden. Therefore pollination cannot be left to insects or to the wind; it has to be done every spring by hand.[23]

A date palm growing in the wild is a bush, not a tree. It is only by cutting off the outside branches that the successive new inner branches are forced to sprout at an ever greater height. Eventually a trunk is formed on which the stumps of the cut-off branches form convenient footholds for the men who have to climb up to the crown of the mature tree to pollinate the panicles or to harvest the dates.

The size of the tree, the quality of its fruit, and the time of ripening all depend on the variety of palm, on the geographical location of the date garden, and above all on the amount of water available. Countless varieties are distinguished by Arab date cultivators, while within the Trucial States people had according to the *Gazetteer* names for over three dozen varieties.[24]

Even under the more favourable conditions in Buraimi and Ra's al Khaimah dates are picked before they are fully ripe because they would shrivel up in the intense heat and not retain their juicy plumpness if left to ripen on the trees. Therefore most locally grown dates are eaten fresh when about half the length of the fruit has turned transparent and sweet. Dates can be preserved by boiling for use later in the year. The total production of dates in the Trucial States rarely met the requirements of the population, particularly when in the first decades of this century an ever growing proportion of the population took up pearling as an exclusive occupation, established themselves in the coastal ports and no longer took any interest in the date palms. According to the *Gazetteer* during the six years from 1899 to 1905 dates were imported representing an annual value of over £20,000 Sterling. They came mostly from Turkish Iraq and from Persian ports. But a small percentage of the date crop of the area was "exported" in the sense that some of the nomadic tribes such as the Manāhīl and Rashīd, who only occasionally visited the Trucial States, bought dates from the Buraimi oasis and even from the inhabitants of the Līwā. Nomadic groups such as those Manāṣīr who did not own gardens came to the Līwā villages during the summer and helped with the date harvest in exchange for payment in kind.

Gardens irrigated by *aflāj*

Throughout the Trucial States the majority of date gardens were planted in locations where irrigation by a *falaj* (pl. *aflāj*) was possible. The important oases such as Buraimi, Maḥadhah, D̲aid, and a string of date plantations on either side of the mountains could not exist without this age-old system. The *falaj* distributes water among various gardens along surface channels where the flow can be directed and regulated. The water comes through a tunnel usually several kilometres long and originating where the elevation of the water table is higher than the ground elevation in the gardens. The alignment of the underground channel is clearly marked above the ground by heaps of excavated rubble dumped around the openings of vertical shafts through which the original builders and the maintenance teams have access to the water course. Water for domestic use is taken upstream at convenient points, preferably before the water comes into the open; the tunnel is reached by a flight of stairs. Further downstream bath houses are built over the stream. The *aflāj* in Trucial Oman are not as long, deep or elaborate as some in Inner Oman, but they function everywhere in Eastern Arabia in the same way.[25]

Very few if any new *aflāj* have been built within living memory; indeed most *aflāj* in all of Eastern Arabia were probably constructed in pre-Islamic times. The maintenance and restoration of existing *aflāj* is a specialised and dangerous technique practised by a few people in the oases.[26]

Over the last century and a half about a dozen *aflāj* have been in use within the Buraimi oasis; some were from time to time damaged by flash floods or destroyed in wars, but most were in due course re-activated. During the 1950s a special effort was made by the Ruler of Abu Dhabi's representative in the oasis to restore a number of dilapidated *aflāj*; by the end of the 1960s seven were used to irrigate gardens in Abu Dhabi territory and two in Omani territory. At that time an area of about 280 hectares was cultivated with the waters from these *aflāj*, which delivered about 16.6 million cubic metres of water per year.[27] The average *falaj* in the Buraimi oasis is about seven kilometres long. The more compact oasis of D̲aid has only one *falaj*; it is, however, an exceptionally good one. It comes from some wādis to the south-east of D̲aid. Where the stream runs in the open in a lined channel it is about one metre wide and over half a metre deep, and has a strong flow before being divided up into various channels for irrigation. Before entering the oasis the *falaj* passes through the precincts of the Ruler of Shārjah's fort in D̲aid. The *falaj* used to irrigate all the date gardens in the oasis, which formed a circle of about one and a half kilometres in diameter, before the introduction of mechanically pumped water wells made a dramatic expansion of the cultivated area possible.

Whereas tunnels are characteristics of the *aflāj* which serve oases in the plains such as Buraimi, D̲aid or Mazyad, and which are also an essential feature of all major villages in the mountain zone of central Oman, another type of *falaj* is in use in the upper reaches of the *wādis*. This type of *falaj*, also called *ghayl*, derives its water from the streams running through the gravel of the *wādi* beds, frequently just below the surface, which soak away to waste before reaching the area suitable for cultivation. By building a dam across the *wādi* some water is diverted into open channels either cut into the rock or cemented with mud. These channels flow down either of the *wādi* sides, sometimes crossing over through inverted siphons, and where the *wādi* bed falls with a steeper gradient than is necessary to maintain a good flow of water in the *ghayl*, the latter forms a gallery rising relative to the *wādi* bed.[28] Particularly in Shamailīyah, where many small settlements were actually in the *wādis* or very close to the foothills, the *ghayl falaj* was often the predominant if not the only source of water for the gardens as well as for domestic consumption.

Wherever there is a *falaj* in the Trucial States it is used to irrigate more than one garden. Soon after a *falaj* enters the area of date plantations the open channel reaches a place where it is divided into several channels of equal width. Passing under the mud-brick walls which enclose the individual gardens, each channel carries water in a different direction and to other places for further division into shallow trenches. Usually a whole garden is completely flooded during irrigation; in some parts the earth is built up in little mounds a few inches high dividing portions within a walled date garden from one other.

The water of a *falaj* is distributed by ʿ*urafā*'; every so often the ʿ*arīf* on duty blocks one of the channels with a stone slab and opens up another one to let the water flow into the gardens belonging to someone else. In principle the water was shared equally between all the owners of date gardens near that *falaj*, all of whom contributed towards the cost of its upkeep by paying a fixed sum called *māshā*. But some partners who owned larger, or several gardens, and required more water to irrigate them could buy irrigation time for a fixed sum per hour because other people had only a small garden which was irrigated in a short time. All such payments were collected by the ʿ*arīf*, and what was left of it after he and his helpers were paid their salaries was used for repairs on the *falaj*. In the Buraimi oasis, for instance, a *māshā* of two Rupees for three hours in the summer and one Rupee in the winter was paid by the owners of date gardens in Muʿtiriḍ, al Qaṭṭārah, Jīmi and Hīli, until the municipality took over the maintenance of all *aflāj* in the territory of the oasis controlled by Abu Dhabi.[29] The work of *ʿarīf* required not only a conscientious person but also someone who could determine very accurately when to divert the flow from one channel to another, using a sundial by day and the movement of the stars by night.[30]

Some date gardens in the *wādis* and in the vicinity of the mountains are irrigated exclusively from wells, but in general a well in a date garden is used to supplement the supply of water during the periods between *falaj* irrigation. Oxen were usually used to draw water from these wells but in some cases even agricultural well-water was hoisted manually.

In *falaj*-irrigated gardens a few other fruit trees grew among the date palms. Citrus trees, (oranges, lemons and limes) were the most common; but mangoes, figs, mulberries, bananas, and pomegranates seemed to do well in among the date trees; grapes were sometimes grown over vertical trellises. Underneath the trees the soil produced some seasonal crops, the most important of which was lucerne, producing several crops per year and, if irrigated every three to five days, continuing to grow through the summer. Water-melons, sweet potatoes, beans, garlic and onions used to be the only other crops obtained from the date gardens until the introduction of other vegetables to the daily diet induced the oasis farmers to plant tomatoes, carrots, cucumbers and other vegetables during the winter months. Pulse, cotton, wheat and barley grown in the spring and *juwāri* and millet sown in autumn were the principal crops obtained from fields outside the date gardens.[31] This description is applicable throughout the oases of the Trucial States, regardless of whether they are situated on the coastal plains or in the interior.

Desert gardens

The date gardens in the Līwā and in other locations in the desert grew without *falaj* irrigation and with little irrigation from wells. There only the newly-planted date palms were watered regularly, usually by the owner carrying bags full of water from the well to the plant. The roots of date trees raised without irrigation tend to grow vertically rather than spreading laterally. They soon reach the water table, which is not very far down in the Līwā hollows and various other small desert oases. From then on the tree is self-supporting even if, as in some parts of the Līwā, the water is fairly brackish. Under the harsh desert conditions and because of the scarcity of water only certain varieties of date palms thrive, and their fruit is always much smaller than that of trees grown in the oases where water is plentiful.

In the desert the owner of a garden was well satisfied if he managed to replace dying palm trees by new growth and even add a few young trees every year. Diversification of crops was not possible; thus neither fruit trees nor animal fodder or vegetables were planted among the date palms. In a very few locations a well might have sustained the regular offtake needed to irrigate an entire area—as opposed to giving a bucket full of water to each young plant individually. But the lack of suitable material for the construction of irrigation channels and above all the absence of proper top-soil prevented agriculture on a general scale in the sands.

Since the early 1970s some owners of date gardens in the Līwā have started to extend and diversify their gardens by building water-tanks and cemented wells with imported materials, and by using mechanical pumps. More recently the government of Abu Dhabi has undertaken to transform agriculture in the area altogether by preparing with the use of bulldozers on a frightening scale plantations in which the date palm is still dominant but grows side by side with some other fruit trees and many trees and bushes which provide windbreaks for previously unimaginable acres of vegetable fields.

The problem of protection from wind and foraging animals has always been difficult in desert gardens. Before the advent of barbed wire some date gardens were surrounded by fences made from palm branches, but these would soon keel over and be buried in the sand. Drifting sand is a formidable enemy to the desert garden. The best protection was a strong low fence made of palm branches to run along the entire crest of the high dune to the windward side of the hollow in which the garden was situated.

Modern equipment such as steel sheeting and pipelines can now be used to deal with this problem, too. A garden no longer has to be in a hollow right by the best place for a well; it can be established on flat ground at some distance from the dune.

But time will tell whether such modern aids, which make it possible to farm in the desert on a very much larger scale, will not also lead to a rapid depletion of the limited sweet-water resources of these areas.

5 Pearling

Economic importance

Agriculture in the Trucial States was inadequate to guarantee self-sufficiency even for the families participating in it; therefore, a source of cash to purchase additional supplies was required for the subsistence of most families. The nomadic and semi-settled groups could fall back on selling some of their famous breed of riding camels for cash. The population in the ports of the Trucial States came to depend to a large extent on the pearl-fishing industry for their livelihood. The following quotation from the *Gazetteer* demonstrates the importance of this resource at the end of the 19th century: "Pearl fishing is the premier industry of the Persian Gulf; . . . besides being the occupation most peculiar to that region . . . Were the supply of pearls to fail, . . . the ports of Trucial ʿOmān, which have no other resources, would practically cease to exist; in other words, the purchasing power of the inhabitants of the eastern coast of Arabia depends very largely upon the pearl fisheries."[32]

Pearls have no intrinsic value, in the way that gold does, therefore the requirement for them in the rest of the world and the growth in that industry depend entirely on the demand for such luxury goods. In India, the age-old market for Gulf pearls, Pax Britannica brought economic growth in its wake, and pearls were ever more fashionable among the traditional ruling and wealthy classes as well as among the new group of officials in the British Government of India. Victorian Britain and the rest of Europe saw in pearls a tangible symbol of the romantic Orient. This predilection was taken up by society in the United States, and during the first two decades of the 20th century New York became the second biggest market for Gulf pearls after Bombay.[33]

The share of the Trucial States in the pearling industry of the Gulf is illustrated by some of the figures given in the *Gazetteer*: the number of pearling boats in Trucial Oman was over 1,200 carrying an average crew of about 18 men. This meant that during the summer most able-bodied men, numbering more than 22,000, were absent on the pearl banks. The largest number, 410 boats, was under the protection of the Ruler of Abu Dhabi; the figure for Shārjah, 360 boats, included Ra's al Khaimah, Ḥamrīyah, Ḥīrah and Khān since all these ports as well as Fujairah, Khaur Fakkān and Kalba were nominally under the shaikh of Shārjah. Dubai had 335 boats, Umm al

Qaiwain 70 and 'Ajmān 40. The average annual value of pearls exported from the Gulf at the turn of the century was estimated at £1,434,399 and £30,439 was earned from the export of mother-of-pearl.[34]

Within the Trucial States the techniques used in pearling did not vary from one port to another. There were, however, considerable differences in the socio-economic context of the industry; the tribal groups subject to the Ruler of Abu Dhabi, for instance, operated more frequently as genuine co-operatives, while in some of the ports in the northern Trucial States entrepreneurs played an important part in the organisation of the industry.

The oyster

Three types of oysters which grow at different depths between the low water mark and about 36 metres water depth and prefer different types of ground are all possible sources of pearls in the Gulf. Where conditions such as light, sea bed, currents and feeding materials are right these oysters are found, sometimes forming extensive banks. A pearl is formed by the secretion of nacreous matter inside the oyster after a minute parasite or another foreign particle has penetrated the shell. Subsequent layers of this secretion may form within a sac and if this sac is located in the mollusc's body and is not subject to deforming pressure it becomes globular or pear-shaped, and the pearl that develops inside it also becomes round or pear-shaped. If this cyst is lodged in muscular tissue or between the shell and the mantle, an oddly shaped pearl (baroque pearl) is formed in the first case and a blister pearl, which has to be scraped off the hard outer shell, is the result in the second case. Mother-of-pearl is thick layers of nacreous material often covering the entire inside of the shell.[35]

Pearl banks

The majority of the pearl banks of the Gulf are situated nearer to the Arabian than to the Persian shore. Their positions have been known to the inhabitants of the Arab littoral for millennia, and individual banks have their own place-names.[36] But none of them were actually claimed as belonging to any particular shaikhdom and their use was free for all pearling boats from Arab ports. Until the latter half of the 19th century most pearling boats made their way to a particular pearl bank of their choice without charts and compass, the latter being fitted only on the big trading *baghlahs*. The captain of a boat used the sun, the stars and the colour and depth of the water as navigational aids. Most pearling boats were *sanbūks*, but *batīls*, *baqarahs*, *shū'ais*, and *zarūqahs* were also used; all types were propelled by sails but also had oars for moving short distances, while on the banks the sails were used to provide shade for the men on board.[37] Once the boat reached the bank of the captain's choice it might stay anchored for a whole season by the same pearl bank; although some captains preferred to move frequently from one bank to another. Since the more perfect pearls in general came from greater depth the captain with a number of very good divers would go to a different bank from the one who had a motley collection of untried divers of whom he could not expect above average performance.

The dive

The captain and crew of a pearling boat formed an unusually close unit during the months they were at sea. Each individual's economic well-being depended so much on the co-operation of all aboard the boat that most disputes and animosities were shelved at least until after the dive was over. A boat carried on an average 8 divers (*ghāṣah*, singl. *ghaiṣ*), 10 haulers (*saib*, pl. *siyūb*), an apprentice whose duty it was to catch fish, to serve coffee, cook and scrub the deck. Some of the very big boats also carried a *muṭawwa'*, who could lead the prayers and start off the rhythmical chants which the Arabs on this coast often use to ease a common strenuous effort. The captain, *nūkhaḏā*, was responsible for the location of the dive and the sale of the catch, but not for the date of sailing to the banks or of returning from them; the Ruler in each port appointed an "admiral" of the local pearling fleet, who was responsible for fixing these dates.

The age-old *modus operandi* of the actual dive was as follows. After a light breakfast of dates and coffee the divers started work about an hour after sunrise, having opened some of the oysters which were caught the previous day. Diving continued without intermission until about an hour after midday. After prayers, coffee and a rest, diving continued until about an hour before sunset when prayers were again said. The evening meal usually consisted of fish and rice followed by dates and coffee. Due to the heat and humidity none of the crew on board slept anywhere but on deck, even where there was room below. During one day each diver would dive up to sixty times, staying submerged usually for less than one and a half minutes.[38]

The diver sped his descent by attaching a heavy stone to his foot, which was pulled up on a rope by the attendant *saib* as soon as the diver reached the bottom. With his nose plugged by a peg made of bone (*faṭām*) his ears protected with wax and his fingers capped with leather tips he would quickly gather shells into a basket (*diyyīn*) which he carried attached to his waist. When he could no longer hold his breath he gave a tug on the rope tied to his belt and the *saib* hauled him up as fast as possible. The contents of the *diyyīn* were taken aboard, while the diver rested in the water holding on to a rope, and after a few minutes he descended again. The accumulated heap of oysters was opened in the very early morning under the supervision of the *nūkhaḏā*, who immediately registered in a book any particularly good pearl which might be sold individually, and he weighed and registered at intervals the collection of smaller pearls.

All the boats belonging to the same port under the authority of one shaikh departed to the pearl banks as one fleet. One of the *nawākhiḏah* was formally appointed leader of the fleet; he co-ordinated mutual assistance if a boat was in trouble, and he decided upon a date for the return of the entire fleet; no boat was allowed to return before all the others were ready to set sail for home. If someone was taken ill he was sent to Dalmā Island or to the nearest port on one of the small craft used by the visiting pearl dealers.

The diving season lasted for about 120 days, from early June to the end of September. During that time most boats returned only for one or two brief visits to their home ports but would put in a number of times at Dalmā, where drinking water was available free of charge to all pearling boats and where supplies of rice, dates, coffee and tobacco could be bought in a seasonal *sūq*. Apart from this *ghauṣ al kabīr*, many boats used to put to sea earlier for a forty-day period called *ghauṣ al bārid*, the cold dive, because the waters of the Gulf were still cold. The exact date of the beginning and the end of each season was not the same each year, especially if the fasting month of Ramaḍān, when diving is not permitted, occurred during the summer months.[39] Each shaikhdom set different dates for the departure to and the return from the pearl banks.

In certain places, for instance, in the far west of Abu Dhabi, pearls were obtained by wading (*mujannah*), and during the winter all along the coast people would search for oysters in the shallow waters.

Pearling by foreigners

As has been mentioned earlier, the pearl banks near the southern shores of the Gulf were considered by all the Arabs as common property; they did not belong to individual shaikhdoms. This situation was respected by the pearling communities from the Persian Coast, some of whom, by virtue of their also being of Arab tribal origin, might have come to fish on the Arab pearling banks but for the great distance from home.

When the demand and the price for pearls increased, complete outsiders were not slow to come in with the intention of securing for themselves a share of this obviously quite profitable industry. Many individuals and companies who tried to get a foothold in the pearling industry in the Gulf reckoned that by using modern diving equipment they would make the process of collecting the oysters from the sea-bed faster and therefore more profitable. The first such attempt was made in 1857 by two British people resident in Bombay; when an enquiry about the possibility of their participating in the pearl diving reached the British Political Resident in Bushire, his reaction was to advise strongly against such an attempt because the Arab pearl-diving community could not be expected to suffer such interference with their prime source of income.[40] Throughout the latter half of the 19th century several more such enquiries reached the Government of India, whose policy remained unchanged, and in cases where boats of Indian or foreign origin arrived on the pearl banks without first contacting the Government's representatives such intruders were removed from the scene by a naval escort.

The question became more complicated when other foreign powers were involved. In 1899/1900 the Turkish Government was considering selling a concession for part of the pearl fisheries in the Gulf, a step which, besides harming the economy of the littoral Arab communities, would have seriously undermined the British position in the Gulf and once again have set in motion the discussion over the issue of declaring the Gulf a *mare clausum* for the purpose of pearl diving. But ever since this formula had been first considered in 1862, the Government of India time and again decided against such a formal announcement, because such a declaration would only have drawn unnecessary attention from America and European powers.

After various firms had made numerous attempts to enter into this industry, it became necessary that a clear line of policy should be laid down. The Law Officers of the Crown were consulted and in a finding dated 11 February 1905 their opinion was that within the three mile limit and in "any other water which might justly be considered territorial, the tribes of the Arabian Coast were entitled to the exclusive use of the pearl fisheries. As regards pearl banks outside territorial waters it was held that, as a matter of international law, such banks were capable of being the property of the tribes to the exclusion of all nations."[41] The Law Officers pointed out that the question of ownership of the banks could be raised at the Hague Tribunal, but because there was no guarantee that its decision would be in favour of exclusive Arab ownership of all the banks on the southern part of the Gulf, it would probably be better to avoid raising the question internationally, and that as far as possible indirect measures of diplomacy should be used by the Government to protect the Arab tribes from intruders into the pearling industry.

On the strength of this recommendation it became easier for the authorities in Bombay and Bushire to foil subsequent attempts of companies to enter into this industry. At times this firm policy of the British authorities was endangered by the underhand attempts of people seeking concessions, in that they went straight to the Arab shaikhs. In one instance in 1900 a British Indian merchant settled in Muscat managed to obtain a concession from the Ruler of Abu Dhabi and made arrangements with some Bani Yās regarding boats. The British Political Resident in Bushire immediately enquired from the other shaikhs of Trucial Oman and Bahrain whether they consented to this arrangement. The general opinion was, however, that the banks were the "common property of the coast Arabs, that no Shaikh had the right to grant permission for diving to foreigners, and that the appearance of divers equipped with European diving dresses would probably not be regarded with equanimity by the local operatives."[42] So ingrained was this conviction that the pearl banks belonged to the people of the Arab coast and islands that even in the post-oil era Rulers do not find it worth their while to antagonise the tribal population over this matter of principle by granting concessions to anyone, local or foreign, for the exploitation of the pearl banks with modern diving equipment. The few attempts to bring together local Arab and foreign interests in such ventures in the Gulf have all come to nothing.

6 Trade

Trade in pearls

It may safely be stated that trade other than barter would have hardly existed in the Trucial States but for the proceeds from the pearling industry. Pearls and mother-of-pearl constituted almost the only export. The importation of foodstuffs and other goods grew along with the growth of the pearling industry during the last decades of the 19th century and in the 20th century, until in 1928 and 1929 a peak was reached which was followed by a very sharp decline.

The exportation of pearls involved a certain amount of internal trade which is worth describing in some detail because it also offers an interesting insight into the social stratification of the ports of the Trucial Coast.[43]

The first link in the line of pearl traders is the *ṭawwāsh*. In the context of the trade in Abu Dhabi most *ṭawāwīsh* visited the pearl banks from Abu Dhabi or Dalmā in boats while the dive was in full swing. They bought there and then pearls from the *nūkhaḏā*. Other *ṭawāwīsh* waited ashore for the boats to return. Exceptionally large or perfect pearls were sold by the *nūkhaḏā* as separate items; all other pearls were sorted by the *ṭawwāsh* in the presence of the *nūkhaḏā* according to their sizes. For this process a number of brass or copper bowls (sieves) with standardised holes in the bottom were used. The five sizes which were commonly used throughout the Arabian pearling ports all have names,[44] but some dealers also used more sieves to sort their pearls into very finely graded lots. Not every *nūkhaḏā* sold the season's catch to a *ṭawwāsh*, because some made contact direct with a pearl merchant, *tājir* (pl. *tujār*), and others were under an obligation to transfer the whole season's take to a financier at a prearranged rate.[45]

A *tājir* is a wholesale pearl merchant; he does not obtain the pearls by going himself to the boats, but they are offered to him either by the *ṭawwāsh* or by the *nūkhaḏā*, often through contacts made by a middleman, *dallāl*, who gets a commission from both parties. The *tājir* used to pay in cash, and he also received cash when he parted with the pearls. But during the 1920s it became quite common for pearls to be taken on credit and the *tājir* was paid after the pearls had been sold in India, and, with luck, before the following season.

The pearls of the Gulf used to be bought up by *tujār* from Bahrain and Lingah. But after new customs regulations on the Persian side of the Gulf, introduced during the first decade of this century, made trade on that coast very difficult, Lingah was supplanted by Dubai, which became the centre for the pearl trade, and indeed other trade too, of the Trucial States.

The actual export of pearls and mother-of-pearl was effected by the *tujār* selling to the Indian pearl merchants who came for the season, mostly from Bombay. None of the dealers resident in Arab pearling ports could dispose freely of the pearls themselves in either Bombay or Baghdad, because the receiving markets were closed to anyone but the community of Indian pearl-merchants or the traders in Baghdad. For a few seasons in the 1920s jewellers from Paris and New York came to Bahrain to purchase pearls.

The trade among the various types of dealers as well as the sale to visiting Indian merchants involved rather complicated systems of assessment of the value of pearls, at least for those not quite perfect pearls which were sold by size and weight. The specimens of over about 30 grains troy (two grammes) were bought and sold singly, and there seemed to be no precise method of assessing their value. There were recognised differences between the basic unit of dealers' systems in Bahrain, Qatar and Bombay because the *chau* (a formula), although in itself standard to all, is derived mathematically, using for instance 150 grains troy for the weight factor in Bahrain and only 74 in Bombay. Within the local trade every dealer was usually well able to cope with the rather complicated mathematics of these deals, and he could also make use of people who specialised in the mathematics of the trade. No *ṭawwāsh* or *tājir* parted with his pearls before having sounded out the market completely and having offered his precious merchandise to several of the visiting pearl merchants. A great risk was involved in buying a *majhūlah*, an "unknown" pearl, that is one with a very imperfect surface. Underneath this first layer might be a perfect pearl worth a great deal of money or there could be a shapeless mass of sandgrains and nacre. Some Bahraini *dallāl* was usually prepared to buy such a pearl and "operate" on it.

While the pearls changed hands within the Trucial Shaikhdoms both Arabs and resident Indians participated in these transactions. The pearling trade was the only reason why Hindu and Khojah merchants initially took up residence on the coast, whereas some of the Persian residents in the towns of the Trucial States were content to trade in ordinary merchandise. Indians were engaged in the pearl trade at all levels, as *ṭawāwīsh*, as *tujār* and as exporters, but in each section they were nevertheless out-numbered by the local Arabs in the trade by about 4 to 3. For Abu Dhabi, for instance, the *Gazetteer* states that there were about 70 shops in the *sūq*, of which 40 were kept by Persians, 19 by Hindus and 10 by Arabs;[46] assuming that all the 19 Hindus also participated in the local pearl trade at one level or another, there were then at least another 30 Arab pearl traders in the town. Some time during the first decade of this century seven Khojah traders also became residents in the town. Most of the Indian traders, in particular the Hindus, had established permanent residence only shortly before the turn of the century, a move which came in the wake of the boom in the pearling trade. Most of them had families with them, but they still used to take an annual leave in India and did not consider their place of residence and work to be their home. During the pearling season the number of Hindus in all the coastal towns of the Trucial States more than doubled.

General trade

The volume of imports into the Trucial States was a reflection of the growth of the proceeds obtained from the export of pearls, and the bulk of the goods was bought by the pearling community and the many people who depended on this industry for their livelihood. Comparatively few of the imports were used by the population of the hinterland, and some of their requirements came to them by way of Ṣuḥār. As already mentioned, the *sūq* of the village of Buraimi, which was supplied with imported goods from Shārjah, Dubai and Abu Dhabi, or Ṣuḥār, was the most important place upon which the settled and nomadic communities of the hinterland of the Trucial Coast converged to buy commodities such as rice, coffee, sugar, and cotton cloth. There were also a few shops at Dibah, Khaur Fakkān and Kalba which primarily served the population in the surrounding countryside.

The total value of the goods imported through the ports of the Trucial Coast was worth an average 2.5 million Rupees per year at the turn of the century, the biggest items being grain and pulse from India.[47] With the exception of dates from Iraq and some piece-goods such as pottery for cooking in and for storing water, rugs to decorate the walls and floors of homes, wood and a few other items, the bulk of the imports came from India or via India, as did for instance coffee from Yemen. During the 19th century most imports were carried on sailing vessels belonging to the ports of the Trucial Coast. Some went to India, but many made use of the entrepôt trade of nearer ports such as Bahrain and Lingah. Dubai was already then leading in the number of trading vessels: out of the 90 vessels whose home port was somewhere on the Trucial Coast, 20 belonged to Dubai, 15 to Ra's al Khaimah, 18 to Shārjah town, 10 to Abu Dhabi.[48]

Only some of these sailing vessels were of the type called *baghlah*, which had a capacity of 80 to 300 tons and a crew of 20 to 50 men. The majority of the vessels were *sanbūk*, a smaller sailing craft handled by a crew of 15 to 20 men. Most local craft could enter the shallow creeks, which were a feature of the principal ports of the coast, at least at high tide and beach inside to be offloaded. The largest sailing vessels or steamers had to be offloaded onto coastal craft in the roadstead a few kilometres offshore. This is why calls by European vessels were not worth their while, considering the small amount of carrying trade to be had, particularly in view of the competition from the considerable number of local merchant vessels plying between the ports of the coast and the entrepôt ports. But when Lingah lost its importance and Dubai took over as the distribution centre for imported goods on the Arabian Coast between Ru'ūs al Jibāl and Qatar, it became a worthwhile proposition for the British India Steam Navigation Company to call regularly at Dubai. From 10 June 1904 a steamer called every fortnight on its way up the Gulf, and if required called again on the return journey. In 1905–6, 34 British steamers called at Dubai, discharging a total load of over 70 thousand tons.

Customs duties paid on imports were a major source of revenue for the Rulers of all the Trucial States. They were usually levied in two ways: 2 per cent for merchandise where the value could easily be assessed, such as the standard bags of dates or sacks (*kīs*) of rice, and a flat rate for piece-goods which worked out at about 1½ per cent of the total value. Some of the imports landed by coastal craft were not taxed, because during the 19th century the only customs posts were at Shārjah town and Ra's al Khaimah town on the western coast of the Qāsimi empire. The annual revenues collected at the turn of the century were about 8,000 Rupees in the case of Shārjah and 800 Rupees in Ra's al Khaimah.[49]

An interesting aspect of imports into the Trucial States was the increase in the trade in weapons and ammunition, which assumed sizeable proportions towards the end of the 19th century. A rifle being the most treasured possession of every tribal Arab, the market for more up-to-date models was considerable, especially among the beduin, but many weapons were re-exported and sold to tribes in Makrān and elsewhere on the Persian Coast. For a time these imports came mostly through ʿAjmān, but the trade shifted to Dubai and Shārjah. For example 120 rifles were imported during September 1902 and 200 more in October into Dubai; some also came into other ports. Later in the same year the rulers desired to put an end to these arms imports and together with the Political Resident in the Persian Gulf the Rulers of Dubai, Shārjah, Umm al Qaiwain, ʿAjmān and Abu Dhabi made the importation, re-exportation and the sale of new arms illegal.[50]

The relationship between the traders, the financiers, and the various local, Indian and Persian participants in the pearling industry will be dealt with in more detail in the following chapter.

7 Manufacturing

General

Very few people were engaged in manufacturing items for sale either within the community of the Trucial States or abroad. Various items were manufactured for domestic use from the materials that were at hand. The principal items made from camel or goat hide were waterbags, sandals, hanging cradles and containers for making curdled milk. The many uses that the various parts of the palm tree were put to have already been described.[51] Normally none of these items was made for sale but only for the use of the maker or members of his family and tribal kin. A communal effort is required to put up structures such as a frame over a well or to build a *khaimah*; this palm-frond house with palm trunks as beams was the predominant type of house used by most families both on the coast and in the interior.

Boat building

The most important manufacturing industry was boat building. Pearling boats, trading vessels and fishing craft, either with sails or with oars, and of all sizes from the *sanbūk* downwards were built in most ports of the coasts. Early this century Umm al Qaiwain was an important boat-building centre; about 20 boats were built there during the course of a year while only about 10 were built in Dubai. The wood for boat building was imported from Malabar or East Africa, ropes of all sizes came from Zanzibar, and the canvas for the sails was usually imported from Bahrain or Kuwait, although some lengths were produced locally. Smaller craft and the dug-outs which were made from one single tree trunk were imported ready-made from India; it was not uncommon for a large trading vessel to carry wood and a ship-builder who made a small boat during the course of the journey, which he sold in one of the ports. Only the *shāshah*, which was usually made by the man who later used it, was constructed entirely from parts of the local date palm.

Pottery

Some household pottery used in the towns and villages was imported from Iran, such as the large water storage vessels and big earthenware cooking-pots; other pottery came from further east via India. There is moderately good clay in some *wādis* near Ra's al Khaimah town and around the Buraimi oasis. Bahlah in Inner Oman was and still is an important source of household pottery. The items which were manufactured in these three places and on a smaller scale in other villages of the Trucial States were brought by boat or camel caravan to the markets and sold to the communities in the area.[52] Much of the locally-made pottery consisted of storage jars of about 1 metre in height, used for storage of water and sometimes oil; then there were water jugs with a round bottom and a long neck which were hung up in the breeze, so that evaporation through the pores kept the water cool. A conical pottery beaker was used for drinking. A speciality of the potteries near Ra's al Khaimah and the Buraimi oasis was incense burners, which consisted of a bowl with slits in the side, set on a broad stem and with a handle; sandalwood (*ʿūd*) on top of charcoal embers was burnt in this vessel.[53]

Metal-work

Most pots, pans and kitchen implements were made of copper and brass. Coffee-pots were in constant use in every household throughout south-eastern Arabia; in the Trucial States as in Oman they were made of copper and usually had a band of decorated brass around the neck. Most coffee-pots imported into the Trucial States came from the coppersmiths in Nizwā or ʿIbri by camel caravan.[54] There used to be at least one coppersmith in each major port in the Trucial States;

they made little else but the large trays covered with zinc on which food is placed. The copper cooking-pots, up to a metre in diameter, which were also covered with zinc, were usually imported from Iran. Other items of daily use were made of brass, such as the mortar and pestle used to grind coffee and spices. Blacksmiths, who were found in the *sūqs* of the ports and also in the Buraimi oasis, made chiefly locks, nails and tools which were needed for building and repairing boats.

Jewellery, most of which was made of silver, played a very important role in the life of women, as part of the marriage price. In the 19th century, Maria Theresa Dollars became the only accepted currency among both the settled people of Inner Oman and the nomadic population of Eastern Arabia, because they could rely on the high silver content being consistent. The dollars (Thaler) were also melted down to make large arm-bangles, anklets, necklaces, hair ornaments and rings. In some of the traditional necklaces the dollars themselves were attached to chains in the same way as was common with other coins throughout the Middle East. Much of this traditional silver jewellery was imported into the Trucial States from the age-old craft centres in Nizwā, Bahlah and elsewhere in Oman.[55] There were also some silversmiths in the ports of the Trucial States, whose number, particularly in Dubai, increased when the pearling industry was prosperous. *Khanājr* were made in Ra's al Khaimah; the blades for these curved daggers, which were carried by most men, were imported from India and Iran.

Woodwork

Apart from the boat builders there were few carpenters in the towns of the Trucial States. The locally-obtainable wood from the date palm or acacia is unsuitable for carving and shaping. Most items of furniture such as four poster beds, cooking stands, kitchen cupboards, large chests for dresses and small chests used by pearl merchants were all imported. These items were almost exclusively used by the section of the population which came into close contact with India through trade and had adopted certain fashions which were otherwise uncommon in the majority of households in the Trucial States.

Wood for making doors also had to be imported. These doors, which were decoratively carved, frequently have sentimental value, and if people construct a new house they may well take with them a door from the old house. The doors are usually made of two equal parts dividing vertically in the centre. A small door with an arched opening is often built into one part of the main door. On forts the doors are particularly splendid, made of thick wood, studded with large iron spikes and fitted with intricate locking devices. A verse from the Koran may well be carved into a panel above the door.

Weaving

Very little cotton grew locally; the yarn, which was mostly imported from India, was dyed locally with indigo and other natural dyes.[56] In Buraimi, Ra's al Khaimah, and possibly some of the larger settlements, there used to be professional weavers. The weaver sat in a pit in the open air in a courtyard with a wooden weaving frame at a convenient level above the knees.[57] The finished product was sold to customers in the vicinity and also found its way into the local *sūqs*. As mentioned earlier, the other locally-woven items such as tents made of goat hair and sheep wool were not made by professional weavers and were not for sale but were woven by the women as required.

According to the *Gazetteer*, an industry of weaving fine sheep wool *ʿabā ah*, presumably with gold braid, had been developed in Shārjah, but not enough were made to meet local demand so they were also imported from Bahrain and al Ḥasā. Most of the cloth used by the population of the Trucial States was not made locally but imported from India and elsewhere. As recently as the early 1920s there was no tailor in Abu Dhabi town; the women of each family made the clothes for everyone with the exception of the men's *ʿabā'ah*, while the shaikhly families and the well-to-do merchants had servants to do this work.

Camel-trimmings

On first sight it seems surprising that camel-saddles and camel-trimmings were not always made by the camel-breeders on the Trucial Coast themselves, because the locally used *ḫawlāni* saddle is easily made; it requires very little wood, a small amount of woollen material and date palm fibres for stuffing.[58] The descendants of the nomads who originally developed this type of camel-saddle are the full nomadic tribes roaming the areas to the west and south of ʿIbri and as far as Hadhramaut. ʿIbri was a centre for the trade in camel-saddles and trimmings made by these beduin, from whence the *sūq* of Buraimi was supplied.

Fuel

Before kerosene became widely used as a fuel, wood, charcoal, camel-droppings and even date-stones were the only types of fuel available to most households in the region.[59] Therefore perhaps the biggest strain which traditional Arab hospitality imposed on the economic situation of a nomadic family was not the camel which was slaughtered in honour of the guest nor the expensive coffee that was served afterwards, but the effort required to provide enough fuel to cook both of them.

In the Buraimi oasis, near Ra's al Khaimah, along the coastal plain facing the Gulf of Oman and in the *wādis*, it was possible for the families to meet all their fuel requirements from brushwood which the women collected in the vicinity of the houses. Some types of acacia, particularly one called *ḥuwaif* (*prosopis juliflora*) are quite numerous in the outwash plains. But if too much firewood was collected by the people and the goats were permitted to graze on the new shoots, the supplies in the neighbourhood of settlements would be depleted. Eventually the effort needed to gather firewood from further and further away became too great and the families had to buy it. There were people who collected wood from other areas which they sold in the *sūqs* or converted to charcoal, also for sale. In the Buraimi area the leading group in this trade were the Āl Bū Khail section of the Manāṣīr, who both manufactured charcoal and took it by camel to Abu Dhabi.

In the northern shaikhdoms it was the Bani Shatair from Ra's al Khaimah and Ru'ūs al Jibāl who made charcoal and took it by coastal craft from their port of Shaʿam to Dubai and Shārjah with firewood and fish, selling these goods themselves in the markets.[60] The firewood that was brought from the interior (*al barr*) was mostly *ḥaṭab ghāf* (*prosopis spicigera*). This species is also found near the coast, and people from Abu Dhabi town used to go to neighbouring islands and collect this wood for themselves or for sale in the *sūq*.

Because there was no firewood on some of the inhabited islands further west of Abu Dhabi the fishermen exchanged fish for firewood with the beduin. The *ḥaṭab samar* (*acacia tortilis*) was exclusively used by the crews of pearling boats for cooking rice and frying fish; although this tree grows on the Arab side of the Gulf, most Rulers and particularly the Rulers of Abu Dhabi forebade the felling of them, and the entire supply of this wood required by the pearling boats was imported from Iran. Charcoal was not generally used for cooking but only for making coffee and tea, and as embers for the incense-burner. In a well-off household where guests were expected frequently, the coffee pots, for several are required for the best result, would be kept hot all the time on the charcoal embers contained in a metal tray.

8 Conclusion

In the settlements of the Trucial States the few locally-made items were almost all consumed within the community itself. There was no surplus of resources from which to manufacture exportable goods. A quotation from Lorimer can be used to summarise this chapter on the traditional economy and lead into the next chapter on the social implications of this situation. "In face of the facts it does not seem unreasonable to hold that all sources of profit here are subsidiary to pearl diving, and that if the pearl banks were to fail this coast would shortly be depopulated."[61]

Chapter Six

The Social Aspects of the Traditional Economy

1 The changing occupational and social pattern of Abu Dhabi's tribesmen

The traditional economic basis: desert and sea

When the Bani Yās moved into Dhafrah at least three centuries ago, occupied Līwā and eventually spread to the adjacent coast, they did not take over unoccupied land; there were tribes already there who were, like them, nomads, and therefore easily assimilated. It was not the classic situation of nomadic people competing with an established village population[1] for the use of land and water, as had been the case in the mountainous parts of Eastern Arabia before the advent of Islam and during the eviction of the Persians. One may safely assume that the Bani Yās confederation of tribes and their Manāṣīr and other associates were an egalitarian society at the time when they started to create their own date gardens in the hollows beneath the dunes of the Līwā and to settle there. Initially, cultivating remained a sideline in a basically camel-oriented way of life. Eventually almost all the Bani Yās families became semi-settled and attached to certain places in the Līwā or on the coast. When many members of this community took up pearl-diving as a regular occupation, it was undertaken as a communal effort. At that time the boats belonged to the community and the proceeds of a season's catch were distributed fairly among the crew: "fair" meaning that the divers and the captain (*nūkhaḏā*), who had the greatest responsibility, got bigger shares than the haulers (*saib*).

Most Bani Yās tribesmen became of necessity versatile; they were as good camel-breeders as any other nomadic Arabs of Eastern Arabia; they grew date palms under very unfavourable conditions in the Līwā and in various other parts of the desert; and they became a leading pearling community in the Gulf. This does not mean that all Bani Yās men participated in all these activities; as the above description of the sub-tribes shows, there were whole groups who never went diving and others, in particular the Rumaithāt fishermen, who in recent generations never went to the Līwā. Because these seasonal occupations overlapped—the date harvest taking place during the *ghauṣ al kabīr*, the great dive—there had to be a great deal of co-ordination of activities in the family and within the tribal society as a whole.

The slightly different economic inclinations of the Manāṣīr, who did not own many pearling boats, facilitated a system of caretaking. For a fixed fee a tribesman from another Bani Yās sub-tribe or from the Manāṣīr was paid to look after camels during their owners' absence. Since most people were still in the desert and did not return to the Līwā at the time for pollinating the date palms in March, some of the permanent residents in the oases were paid to do this, usually in kind when the dates were harvested.

Tribesmen who own, organise and operate a number of different economic means which secure their livelihood are a common phenomenon of all the eastern Arabian tribal societies. Many who live near the mountains have date gardens as well as camels and herds of goat; some of the fishermen of the east coast also tend their own date gardens; some camel-breeders such as the Āl Bū Khail of the Manāṣīr have gardens, engage in the carrying trade, and sell firewood and charcoal.

In the Buraimi oasis and the northern Trucial States there were few individuals who were involved in more than two of the traditional occupations in the same way as most Bani Yās. The population living in the vicinity of the mountains did not have the same egalitarian participation in all the available economic resources of the country, because where arable land is scarce and supplies of water are limited the structure of society is such that there is a contest for the ownership of these resources, and a wage-earning class is required as labour.[2]

Occupational specialisation in Abu Dhabi

The impact of the pearl boom

The communities of versatile tribesmen, all sharing a frugal way of life, which were characteristic of the shaikhdom of Abu Dhabi, became more structured by specialisation towards the end of the

19th century. The growing foreign demand for pearls at that time meant that ever-increasing profits were being made. Beduin who participated in a pearling co-operative organised on a tribal basis also earned more cash; whereas previously the season's savings were just enough to purchase the few imported commodities required, now there was extra cash available. The beduin could either buy more camels, and pay for them to be looked after in his absence, or he could buy established date gardens and arrange for them to be tended by other tribesmen. Others put their money back into the pearling industry, thereby speeding the transformation from an industry of tribal co-operatives to an industry with entrepreneurs and a whole strata of participants who became locked into a system of financial interdependence. Most pearling boats of Abu Dhabi town were eventually owned by individuals, who because of the cost of fitting out the boats and financing their food supplies in advance, required a system of loans which was adapted from the practices which were already well established in some other ports of the Trucial States.

This system led to a new stratification of the society of the desert shaikhdom of Abu Dhabi. A growing number of families could afford to buy their own pearling boats and even make enough profit in a season or two to build a good two-storey house in Abu Dhabi town. They spent less and less time at their traditional property in the Līwā, gradually becoming absentee landlords, and some even saved enough to buy a date garden in one of the villages in the Buraimi oasis. This change for the better in the economic situation of these families meant also that they now had the means to employ others to work for them. Some of the tribesmen who remained in the desert were paid to look after the camels, tend the gardens, bring firewood to the town and provide transport for the seasonal move to the oases. During this period of increasing prosperity a shortage of labourers developed which was covered by importing slaves. They worked as domestic servants and were employed to tend date gardens,[3] but they were used most profitably by their owners as divers.

Changing population pattern of Abu Dhabi town

Abu Dhabi town grew in size with the expansion of the pearling industry. Many of the formerly beduin tribesmen took to staying there for the winter and lived off the money they earned from pearling during the summer, or they obtained advances from their captains on the share they could expect to earn from the dive of the following season. The population was further increased by people who came from other areas of the Gulf to Abu Dhabi and other towns of the Trucial Coast because the pearling industry itself, or the ancillary trades, attracted them. An example is the 120 Baḥārinah who came to Abu Dhabi town before the turn of the century and were mostly pearl divers or craftsmen such as blacksmiths; some were traders and used the connections they had with other members of this tribe in Bahrain, al Ḥasā, Qaṭīf and Qatar and in some districts on the Persian Coast.[4]

About 500 Persians also immigrated into Abu Dhabi town during the course of barely a century and a half after the founding of the town in 1761. About 120 members of an originally Arab tribe from Khamīr in Persia, the Khamārah, and other splinter-groups of people from neighbouring coasts also settled in Abu Dhabi town. The retail trade within the *sūq* was mostly in the hands of Persians who owned about 40 of the 70 shops, according to the Gazetteer.[5] All trades and crafts were also in Persian hands, such as forging copper, brass and iron and building houses; the more elaborate houses of the town were built of coral taken from the sea-bed and covered with mud; the most suitable mud was obtained from the far side of the neighbouring island, Saʿdiyāt. During the first half of the 20th century, Arabs from the Persian shore supplied the clerical services which were increasingly needed such as the teacher in the Koran school, the *kuttāb*; the Ruler's secretary; the secretary of the *wāli* on Dalmā; some learned men, *muṭawwaʿ*. The *qāḍi*, however, was either from Abu Dhabi, Bahrain or al Hāsā.

These non-tribal Sunni Muslims were assimilated without great difficulty while this process of relative urbanisation[6] continued and the economic expansion lasted, creating the need for more divers, more shopkeepers, and more craftsmen; even tailors, bakers, butchers and builders were now required. Although domestic servants were usually slaves or at a later date their freed descendants, Balūchis from Makrān were also employed in increasing numbers.

Perhaps the biggest change in the socio-economic structure of the towns of the Trucial Coast was the presence from about the mid-nineteenth century of a number of Hindu merchants. They were reluctant to make the places where they earned their livelihood their homes; most of them went back to their families in India from time to time. In the case of Abu Dhabi they all came from Tatta in Sind province, which contributed to making their small community of about 65 very inward-looking. The Hindus were all involved in the export of pearls and were for some time also the chief importers of cloth, rice, coffee and sugar. Since the trade in both directions was almost exclusively arranged in India, the Hindu merchants had the edge over their Arab colleagues particularly in the wholesale marketing of imports. The resident Hindu merchants usually sold their pearls to Hindus who came only for the pearling season to the Trucial Coast and Bahrain. Their religion, eating habits, customs and dress marked them as aliens. They remained aliens even after several generations had lived in the country, and their men were not allowed to marry a Muslim girl, although marriage of a Muslim man to a Hindu girl was acceptable.

The integration of non-tribal Muslims, even if they were Shiites, was much less of a problem because the town population of tribal and non-tribal origin mixed quite freely, although not at all social levels. There were instances of immigrants from Khamīr who did so well in the pearling industry that they owned several boats within a few years of their arrival, and they became not only well accepted but leading citizens; and in due course their families married into the ruling family.

Quite apart from the sociological and cultural barriers, the integration of Hindus was practically impossible because their status as aliens was perpetuated by their being British subjects. There were many moments in the history of the Trucial States when even the notion that British-protected lives and property might be in danger was sufficient to bring a British man-of-war on to the scene. This status, which must have appeared akin to diplomatic immunity, did not endear the Hindus to the population of their host shaikhdoms.

Entrepreneurs in the Abu Dhabi pearling industry

As time went by, some entrepreneurs in the pearling industry in Abu Dhabi town became more prosperous and eventually they owned several pearling and trading vessels. One of the most successful of these businessmen was Khalaf Otaibah. The share in the industry of the Līwā-based beduin tribal co-operatives was not affected, because the growth of the industry could absorb the additional boats, and, as was pointed out earlier, immigration and the employment of slaves provided enough people to man the boats. Eventually the entrepreneurs came to dominate the whole spectrum of the pearling industry: they owned boats, employed *nawākhidah* and crews and bought and sold pearls. Some branched out into financing the yearly advances to the owners or *nawākhidah* of other boats. Following the example of the Hindu merchants who were involved in both the trade in pearls and the trade in other goods, many Arab entrepreneurs also started to import merchandise. When the pearling industry started to decline in the 1930s some of the merchants were bankrupted while others managed to remain in business under very difficult circumstances in a rapidly-declining market for pearls. The people whose livelihood depended directly or indirectly on the pearling industry also suffered, through losing their business or through being unable to find work. The entire social-economic structure of the pearling community in the ports was thrown into confusion.

The effect of the decline of the pearling industry on the desert tribesmen

By contrast, the way of life of the tribal population in Abu Dhabi was not affected so radically by the decline of the pearling industry, because the families who had retained their roots in the desert concentrated again on utilising its resources. The material collected for the *U.K. Memorial* shows that the multi-skilled tribesmen still existed during the first few years of the 1950s. This material is supplemented by information given by local people who have described the life of the non-urban population of Abu Dhabi at that time. This picture then changed very rapidly after the search for oil began.

During the early 1950s, 42 date groves of the Līwā were still inhabited during the summer months;[7] a great number of other places in the Līwā had small groves but no houses. The owners used to camp there, collect their dates and either return to their parent settlement in the Līwā or, like many Manāṣīr who had no permanent houses, return to the desert. In all, about 620 to 750 houses were occupied in the Līwā during the date harvest; if it is correct to assume that about five persons belonged to each house the temporary population of the Līwā was still about 2,500 to 3,000 during the 1950s.[8] Some 13 settlements were at that time inhabited throughout the year, the most important one being Muzairaʿah.

During the summer months the representative of the Ruler for all of Dhafrah went to the Līwā and collected the tax due to the Ruler. For the harvest of every 10 *jirābs* (one *jirāb* in the Līwā was 180 lb., and in Buraimi 80 lb.), one *jirāb* was paid as tax; but people who harvested less than 20 *jirābs* from all the trees they owned were exempt. The latter circumstance obtained in most of the gardens east of Tharwāniyah, which is a village situated near the centre of the crescent-shaped string of oases. The Manāṣīr were exempt from paying tax on dates to the Ruler of Abu Dhabi, thus the *wāli* did not need to visit any of the oases east of Tharwāniyah because they either belonged to Manāṣīr or were in any case too small. In 1950 45 *jirābs* of dates were collected from the Līwā, but, due to an invasion of locusts in June 1951 the crop was very poor in that year and only 15 *jirābs* were collected as tax. According to the statement made by the *wāli* of Dhafrah at the time only ten people were taxed in the Līwā in 1950 and 1951.[9]

The Ruler of Abu Dhabi did not collect tax on animals, but some of the Manāṣīr, Āl Murrah, and a few of the Mazārīʿ section of the Bani Yās who at times left Dhafrah to find grazing further west were visited by Saudi tax-collectors, who obtained from them 10 Rupees tax per camel per year in the spring of most years between 1937 and 1951. This shows that the importance of camels as the most valuable property had not yet declined among the traditional nomads of the area. Among the people who owned property in the Līwā in the early 1950s about three dozen owned a pearling boat—in a very few cases even two boats, manned by their relatives and neighbours.[10] Although these boats might be left at various places along the coast during the winter months, most of them were regarded for purposes of administration and taxation as being based on Dalmā Island, the remainder being based on Abu Dhabi Island. Dalmā was an important trading centre during the summer, but many families in Dhafrah used the *sūq* in Dalmā all the year round, rather than travelling all the way to Abu Dhabi town.

Within the context of the tribal society of the Līwā, owning a boat frequently meant that the proceeds from this property—just like the date gardens—were shared between the members of an extended family; some probably assisted in the building of the boat and its maintenance, and many relatives helped as crew. The proceeds of the season's catch were therefore not divided up in the same meticulous fashion as had to be the case among hired crews of unrelated town-dwellers. Although resources were usually shared within the extended family, an individual was always identifiable as the owner of a garden, a boat or a camel. He was the person who dealt with the tax collector or the *qāḍi* in case of a dispute.

Alternative sources of income after the Second World War

The preceding paragraph illustrated that for more families than might have been initially expected the old order of life continued well into the 1950s, with dates, pearls, camels and fish being still modest but eagerly exploited resources. These desert-based people did not rely to the same extent as did people in town on obtaining certain imported foods such as rice and sugar, but they produced almost enough of their own accustomed staple diet of dates and camel milk. They therefore did not feel the full impact of the devastating increase in food prices which hit the Trucial Coast ports during the Second World War and which did not significantly decrease afterwards.[11] The tribal people of Abu Dhabi, did however, become painfully aware of the high prices and the shortages when they came to buy the provisions for the pearling season.

Although few of the families with a base outside the town of Abu Dhabi were threatened by starvation during and after the war, additional sources of income in the form of paid jobs were very much sought after. The position of retainer with the Ruler or one of his brothers was therefore welcome even if it did not bring in a high or regular salary. It meant that at least a rifle, food and clothing were provided; besides, a shaikh's retainers are always fed when and wherever he himself eats. The employment of retainers was based on the mutual trust and good rapport between certain tribes or tribal groups and the shaikh, the former seeing it as an honour to protect and even to serve the Ruler or a member of his family, and the latter regarding retainers as representatives of that tribe, giving occasional presents, favours, and opportunities to earn some money on special missions and deals. The Āl Bū Falāḥ maintained a body of over 100 such armed but untrained retainers. They were used as guards at the various forts and check-points, as escorts for members of the Āl Bū Falāḥ when on the move and for the Ruler's representatives, *wālis* and *qāḍi* on duty visits to the Līwā and other places in the desert. They were also guides through their own *dār*. During the winter many of them acted as falconers and accompanied the shaikhs on hunting trips where they would even prepare the meals and serve the coffee because ordinary servants were rarely taken on such outings.[12]

When an important guest such as Thesiger, or a representative of the British government, or as happened frequently in the 1950s a party from the oil company wanted to travel to a particular part of the country the Ruler usually sent one of his brothers or another relative to accompany that party together with guides and a group of armed retainers.[13] About fifteen retainers were always on duty to guard the southern end of Abu Dhabi island; a small fort was constructed on the mainland in addition to the watch-tower in the middle of the ford. The *amīr* of Dalmā island and the customs official there were also assisted by a number of the Ruler's retainers.

When the oil company started drilling in 1950 tribesmen and townspeople of Abu Dhabi could hope for regularly paid employment. From the very beginning of the activities of PD(TC) in the country the company employed some of the Ruler's retainers on a regular basis as guards. In the 1950s there were never less than sixteen guards at the company's camp, paid by the company and nominated by the Ruler, and they were periodically rotated as all other guards in the country. In consequence it was reported by the European employees of PD(TC) that the security throughout Abu Dhabi territory was very good, and better than in other parts of Oman or Trucial Oman which was then all part of the concession area of PD(TC). The shaikh's guards were said to be loyal and "in their bedu fashion disciplined". The majority of the Āl Bū Falāḥ retainers were Manāṣīr, the second largest group being Mazārīʿ, all of whom received regular payment twice a year for their services.

During the late 1940s and in the 1950s, an increasing number of people from the desert and in particular many Manāṣīr went to Saudi Arabia and Qatar to work with the oil companies there, but they returned frequently to their property in the Līwā. According to some estimates made in 1952 nearly one-third of all the male Manāṣīr were in al Ḥasā during any one winter, either with their camels or working for ARAMCO. The Ruler of Abu Dhabi at that time knew of about a hundred Manāṣīr who worked there. When the dispute between Abu Dhabi and Saudi Arabia over the border between the two countries came to a head and the movement of the tribal subjects was carefully recorded by both sides, such migration, even if performed only in pursuit of improving one's living, was discouraged. Eventually the palm trees of the inhabitants of Dhafrah who had resided for more than one winter in Saudi Arabia or Qatar were confiscated. When during the early 1960s the number of tribal Abu Dhabi men employed by the oil companies then established onshore and offshore in Abu Dhabi territory reached a peak, the Ruler took measures to prevent the return[14] of the people who had been employed elsewhere in the Gulf, because those who had stayed behind were afraid that they might lose their jobs to those who came back armed with experience in oil-field work.

In the middle of the 1950s the traditional pattern of the life of the Līwā based on the multiple-skilled tribesman of Abu Dhabi was still recognisable, but for an increasing number of people the traditional seasonal routine had changed. According to the information collected by an oil company employee and those who helped him during interviews in almost every inhabited village of the Līwā in April 1955,[15] only about one in ten of the people who used to go pearling still participated during that year. They were generally only those who owned pearling boats and their relatives who had a direct interest in them. More people went pearling during the summers of the early 1950s because of the bad date harvest following locust attacks.

The availability of outside employment influenced the traditional pattern of life of the multi-skilled tribesman, but at the same time did not necessitate drastic changes in his lifestyle. Most tribesmen initially took a job with the oil company, regarding it rather like one of the traditional seasonal occupations, returning to the dates or camels or to fishing at any time they saw fit. The traditional routine arrangements with regard to the rest of the family, the camels and date palms remained unaltered even though the able-bodied men now went to work for the company.

By 1955, of the Līwā-based men who went away to seek work with an oil company the largest number was employed by PD(TC); others remained in Qatar, Saudi Arabia, Kuwait and Bahrain. Employment opportunities for retainers and guards with the oil companies remained important aspects of the increase in numbers of regularly paid jobs available for local people. After the establishment in 1951 of the Trucial Oman Levies, some young men from the Līwā enrolled as soldiers and trainees. Some Līwā-based families were also among those subjects of the Ruler of Abu Dhabi who went to live and work in Doha, Dubai or al Ḥasā in Saudi Arabia.

Abu Dhabi, the Trucial shaikhdom with a large beduin population among whom the versatile tribesmen were predominant, proved to be an example of the relative ease with which these people who had a base in the hinterland fell back on their other resources—dates, camels, fish—when pearling was no longer as profitable as before. For the majority of the inhabitants of the other Trucial States ports, however, the pearling industry and associated trades represented the only means of earning a livelihood.

2 The pearling communities in the other Trucial States

The economic structure: interdependence and debts

Among the urbanised pearling communities of the Trucial States many of the egalitarian aspects of the tribal society were replaced by differentiation of social groups on the basis of a system of financial ties. A unique type of community in the ports of the Trucial States emerged in parallel with the growth of the pearling industry. It should not, however, be forgotten that many aspects of these communities were also found among the pearlers of the Persian Coast. The way in which this predominant industry was organised had an all-pervading influence on the structure of the society of the coastal towns of Trucial Oman and even on external politics of these shaikhdoms. It is significant that in a table in the *Gazetteer* listing the taxes which were levied by the authorities in the ports of the Trucial States, two local terms are used which denominate the two ways of operating pearling boats: *ikhluwi* was the system in which the crew and the *nūkhaḏā* shared all the net profit of the season, distributed according to the recognised system depending on the type of work each individual performed. *ʿAmīl* (or *marbūb*) was the system in which the boat was owned and fitted out by an entrepreneur who received a large part of the take at the end of the season, leaving the rest to be divided among the crew.[16]

The *ʿamīl* type of arrangement developed because a large capital outlay was required before the boat could be manned and sail. For boats which were operated by a group of tribal men who were all related to each other and which set out from a cove or port near to their date gardens, much of the provisions, which consisted largely of dates, were brought from these gardens. The group paid for rice and other essentials out of the proceeds of the previous year. But there were many divers and haulers who lived in the towns, who had no date gardens, and an increasing number of them did not even belong to a tribal group represented in the town. They were individuals who presented themselves to a *nūkhaḏā* who engaged them as crew; the crews of such boats often consisted of people of different tribal and ethnic provenance who could not put up the money to fit out and provision a boat between them. Others in town had enough cash in hand to advance the necessary sums and thus obtained a share in the proceeds from the season's catch.

The forms of contract between the participants in the pearling industry varied from one town to another along the Trucial Coast. As the industry expanded rapidly the increasing competition for capital to pay for fitting out the boats meant that financiers could more and more state their own terms. In this situation the form of contract and the rights of all participants were subject to continual change, and the often very complicated systems were far from uniform throughout the area. The general principles, however, remained in force even during the decline of the pearling industry in these towns.[17]

The *nawākhiḏah*, who were the central figures in the industry in the towns, were originally the owners of the boats which they commanded. In later years more captains commanded hired boats or were employed by a boat owner; in Abu Dhabi town Aḥmad bin Khalaf Otaibah had several captains working for him during the 1930s. When money had to be borrowed to fit the boats out before the season began, the services of a *musaqqam* were enlisted. Often the *musaqqam* himself did not have adequate funds and he acted as a broker, obtaining the cash from Arab and Indian pearl merchants or from general traders. The interest involved in the latter deal (between the merchant and the *musaqqam*) was 10 to 25 per cent. If the *nūkhaḏā* was financed in this fashion by a *musaqqam*, the season's catch of pearls and mother-of-pearl became the latter's security and was handed over to him at about four-fifths of the market value. Because not every *musaqqam* was an expert in judging the value of the catch, the *nūkhaḏā* could also dispose of the catch to the highest bidder among the *ṭawāwīsh* and *tujjār* and then give the *musaqqam* his share. But if a catch was poor due to stormy weather or to disease among the crew, or because not many pearls were found, the *musaqqam's* share might be much less than the amount he advanced at the beginning of the season, and the *sālifah al ghauṣ* (diving court) then arranged for the remainder of the debts of the *nūkhaḏā* to be deferred until after the following season. This was often the beginning of real financial problems for a formerly quite independent *nūkhaḏā*, who after a series of bad years became increasingly indebted to the *musaqqam*. The poor yield of one season meant also that his share as *nūkhaḏā* or as owner was small, and from this share he had to live until the next season. Often during the years of decline in the industry the divers' shares were totally inadequate for them to meet their commitments. The *nūkhaḏā* who did not want to lose good divers to other boats gave them advances on their shares of the following season's catch. Thus after a series of bad years the divers too became increasingly indebted.

During the half century when the pearling industry was relatively prosperous, men were attracted to this industry, settling in the coastal towns and abandoning their traditional economic activities. They earned enough in the summer to see them through the winter when little other employment was available in the towns. Although they generally did not become sufficiently wealthy to enter into business themselves, a sequence of good seasons thus encouraged them to adopt a slightly more extravagant life style which however did not better the lot of the divers and their families in the long run. Sometimes following a poor season a diver might request even larger advances from his *nūkhaḏā*, gambling on the hope that the next year would be good again. In the event of the death of a diver a *nūkhaḏā* sometimes lost considerable sums of money which he had lent.

Depending on how powerful a particular group within the pearling community was at a particular time and how well connected it was to the shaikh, the rules governing intricate debt relationships could be changed in favour of one or another group. Thus at times in the ports of the Trucial States the *nawākhiḏah* were free to recover the debts of a deceased diver from members of his family or by employing his son as a diver without pay until the debt was repayed. The son was treated like a diver who owed money to the *nūkhaḏā* and he was not normally allowed to take up employment with another *nūkhaḏā*, or if he did the second *nūkhaḏā* had to pay all the diver's debts to the first one.

After some bad seasons or as a result of excessive speculation a *musaqqam* or even a merchant might experience financial difficulties which made it imperative for him to insist that the *nūkhaḏā* repaid his debts in full or in instalments arranged by the *sālifah al ghauṣ*. Sometimes when a *nūkhaḏā* was insolvent he was forced to sell his boat and other property; only the family's house and other private belongings were exempt from seizure.

In the Trucial States the pearling industry provided the most important reason for continuing to keep slaves. Because some of them had been on the pearling boats every season since they were young, they became the most expert of the divers, while many tribal Arabs who may not have been able to leave their camels or their date gardens every summer worked as haulers. Slaves thus played an important role within the industry, and while it expanded slaves were still bought and sold in the main markets although their importation had already been outlawed in the 1870s.[18]

Some of the wealthy Arab pearl merchants who owned several boats usually also had a number of slaves who would make up the majority of the divers on their pearling boats, while the *nawākhiḏah* and other members of the crew would be hired hands. The slave divers of a boat owner in town did not usually have arduous tasks to perform during the off-season, but they would often help with the repair of the boats while being housed and fed with their masters' family. In many of the less well-off families the one domestic slave would help like any member of the family in the date garden or with the fishing nets, to cut firewood, look after the animals, or work in the house during the winter; during the summer he would be sent to join a pearling crew. His master was entitled to the slave's share of the catch. However, since he was part of the master's household this arrangement was often not considered in the least unfair, and it frequently continued when the liberated slave remained as a servant in his master's family.[19]

Absconding debtors

People who carried debts over from one season to another eventually found it necessary to borrow money from a number of lenders. When debts became very large and the creditors combined their efforts to get their money back, usually by going to the Ruler, the temptation for the debtor to abscond was great. Since most of the ports of the Trucial Coast are only a few miles apart, it was easy for someone who could see that trouble was brewing to take whatever cash he had left to another port where he could reside with a relative and start up again as *nūkhaḏā* or diver or *musaqqam*. This practice, together with emigration in order to avoid taxes, was one of the most frequent causes of friction and open warfare between the shaikhs of Trucial Oman. Therefore when the benefits of the British-supervised ban on war at sea had been enjoyed for several decades after the Treaty of Peace in Perpetuity of 1853, the detrimental effects on the peace between shaikhdoms when absconding debtors were pursued over land became obvious. Because the pearling industry became increasingly based on credit in all the ports of the Trucial States, the Rulers themselves felt the necessity to come to a common understanding over the problem of absconding debtors. This move was encouraged by the British Resident in the Gulf, who even accepted the position of arbiter.[20]

In 1897 all the Trucial shaikhs signed an agreement which provided for the surrender of fraudulent absconders, especially pearl divers and sailors, from the sovereignty of one shaikh to that of another. Each shaikh became responsible for the debts of a runaway if he failed to hand him back to the Ruler of the shaikhdom he came from, and he was fined 50 M.T. Dollars for harbouring a fugitive. If there was a dispute over the facts pertaining to such a case, a council of Rulers was to convene, whose decision was final if the British Political Resident also agreed.[21]

Position of British subjects in disputes over debts

While the pearling industry continued to expand, its annual returns attracted an increasing number of Indian merchants, both Hindu and Khojah, who lived permanently in the towns of the Trucial Coast, but they were still British and entitled to the protection of the British Government of India. Inevitably these Indian merchants were in an even better position than local merchants to lend money, because of their financial backing in India, but they were less well-placed than their Arab colleagues to retrieve it, as they were unable to exert much pressure on the local Ruler. The effect which disputes over debts could have on regional politics, and many aspects of the political role played by Indian merchants, are illustrated in the case of a family called Bin Lūtāh, which figures prominently in the correspondence between the Residency Agent in Shārjah and the Political Resident in Bushire for about two decades.[22] Aḥmad bin ʿAbdullah and his cousin Nāsir bin ʿUbaid[23] were called the "Bin Lota", a term which is believed to be a variation of "Lūti", the Arabic word for Khojah. During the first decade of the 20th century the Bin Lūtāhs resided in Dubai and must have been well placed to participate in the growing business carried on in that town, but they became progressively more antagonistic towards the Ruler of that shaikhdom, and at the same time appeared to act as go-between in local disputes such as that between the Rulers of ʿAjmān and Umm al Qaiwain in 1911, thus interfering with the role which the Residency Agent in Shārjah intended to reserve for himself.[24]

The Political Resident, at that time Sir Percy Cox, deemed it very undesirable that British subjects should take sides in any conflict of interests between local Rulers or between any Ruler and the British

Government of India. After such a dispute the two Bin Lūtāh were made to pay a fine of 5,000 Rupees for their behaviour, which was considered "incompatible with their status as British subjects engaged in commerce".[25] However, in their answer to the Political Resident they maintained that since they had pearling interests in ʿAjmān and Umm al Qaiwain as well as in Dubai, they naturally tried to mediate between the three Rulers when a dispute was brewing among them, because they, the Bin Lūtāh, wanted to safeguard their commercial interests. They also stated that they left Dubai to settle in ʿAjmān because they had felt unwelcome in Dubai. But in doing so they took a large group of divers with them, an action which led to the usual problems over settlement of their debts. The two Bin Lūtāh had owned three houses each in Dubai, some of which were sold, some were occupied by relatives who remained in Dubai, and others were leased for rent.[26]

The presence of the Bin Lūtāh in ʿAjmān meant an increase in the number of pearling boats belonging to that port, and this attracted a considerable number of divers who had obligations in either Dubai or Umm al Qaiwain. The Ruler of ʿAjmān, Ḥumaid bin ʿAbdul ʿAzīz, did not, however, conform with the common practice of returning divers. For two people,[27] indeed, he asked the Ruler of Dubai to send their belongings. Furthermore, he insisted in several letters that the Bin Lūtāhs' status was that of the people of ʿAjmān "in regard to property and life", a statement which was considered inappropriate for merchants who claimed and were accorded the status of British subjects. But it was not long before the Ruler of ʿAjmān and the Bin Lūtāh also had arguments.

In contrast with the stringent measures taken in 1912 by the British Government, in 1924 the Bin Lūtāh of ʿAjmān, now Aḥmad ʿAbdullah and Nāṣir's son Ḥussain, figured prominently as British subjects on whose behalf the Government of India even sent a man-of-war to ʿAjmān. Shaikh Ḥumaid was then accused of interfering in their diving business by compelling divers who had been maintained by the Bin Lūtāh over the winter to dive for him, and even of sending their divers away to Dubai. The intervention of the Senior Naval Officer, who ordered the Ruler of ʿAjmān and the Bin Lūtāh aboard *Triad* on 21 April 1924, helped the Bin Lūtāh to get their divers back.[28] Thus, in this case, as on many other occasions, the Political Resident in Bushire in the end came out in support of the British-protected party with little regard for the history of the dispute.

Viewed as an isolated incident, the Resident's reaction to the case of the Bin Lūtāh might be explained largely by the fact that Ḥumaid's attitude to the representatives of the British Government was not considered very co-operative at the best of times, and that the Bin Lūtāh affair of 1924 was just one of a great many disagreements between that Ruler and successive Political Residents. Other examples do, however, support the observation that the recovery of debts on behalf of an Indian British subject appeared to be a major concern of the officials who represented the British Government. The obligation to "safeguard the lives and property of British subjects", a phrase which was used time and again in this context, offered a convenient pretext for influencing local disputes, the majority of which arose over debts, and frequently therefore involved Indian creditors. The affairs were further complicated by the fact that the subjects of one Ruler, if they could not obtain sufficient credit in their home port, would go a few miles along the coast and borrow from someone in another shaikhdom.

There are many examples of intervention by the Resident on behalf of creditors who were British subjects. Particularly illustrative is the case of ʿAbdul Raḥman bin Muḥammad, a shaikh of the Āl Bū Shāmis who resided in Ḥīrah in Shārjah territory. On 15 June 1920, in a surprise attack he evicted Ḥumaid bin ʿAbdul ʿAzīz al Naʿaimi, the Ruler of ʿAjmān, from his fort in an unwarranted attempt to re-establish the Āl Bū Shāmis leadership, which had been eclipsed some generations previously by Ḥumaid bin Rāshid al Naʿaimi, originally shaikh of the Buraimi village of Ṣaʿarah.[29] Ḥumaid bin ʿAbdul ʿAziz, assisted by the Ruler of Shārjah, Khālid bin Aḥmad, and the Residency Agent in Shārjah, ʿĪsa bin ʿAbdul Laṭīf, persuaded the intruders to leave the fort after promising them safe conduct. But the Ruler of ʿAjmān threatened to avenge the deeds of ʿAbdul Raḥman bin Muḥammad if he returned to his house in Ḥīrah, because he had lost some personal property in the incident, some of his subjects had lost their lives in the fighting, and the shops of others had been burnt down. The Ruler of Shārjah, too, was indignant at so insubordinate a subject.

But when it transpired that ʿAbdul Raḥman bin Muḥammad had diving debts amounting to 21,560 Rupees and also that several of the many creditors were British subjects,[30] the Residency Agent completely changed his stance, and took ʿAbdul Raḥman to his house. He afforded the offender sanctuary in order to make sure that the creditors could retrieve their money before he went north to Ru'ūs al Jibāl.[31] The Political Resident in Bushire feared that the claims which "British and foreign subjects have against him . . . will be lost if he goes to live in the interior". He therefore requested Ḥumaid bin 'Abdul 'Aziz in October 1920 to allow 'Abdul Raḥman to reside temporarily in Khān,[32] in the hope that he could earn enough money in one pearling season to be able to pay his debts.

In December 1920 'Abdul Raḥman returned to Dubai from Bahrain, where he had unsuccessfully tried to obtain a foothold in the local pearling business. When he was joined by some of his men from Ḥīrah and they all returned to his family there, the shaikhs of 'Ajmān and Shārjah prepared to attack 'Abdul Raḥman and his men, who barricaded themselves in the fort.[33] The Senior Naval Officer, on board *Triad*, was ordered to sail to Shārjah and try to effect a truce because "'Abdul Rahman owes money to British subjects and his only method of repaying it is by being allowed back to work at Shārjah."[34] On 8 January 1921 a settlement was reached between the Ruler of Shārjah and 'Abdul Raḥman in the presence of the Senior Naval Officer, in which 'Abdul Raḥman agreed to reside in Shārjah town for one month and then to return to Ḥīrah, promising not to cause any more trouble; the Ruler of Shārjah pledged to protect the former offender, who thus formally returned to the status of loyal subject of Shaikh Khālid.[35]

The Ruler of 'Ajmān ignored the invitation of the Senior Naval Officer to join the discussions on board *Triad* and was not a party to the subsequent agreements. Thus he once again antagonised the Political Resident and was cautioned in a letter "not to harm Abdor Rahman. If you do, by the terms of the agreement the Shaikh of Sharjah and the people of Hira will probably fight you and, if there is a fight, damage will probably be done to the lives or property of British subjects, for which I shall hold you strictly responsible."[36] The same 'Abdul Raḥman was again the cause of a major clash between the British Government and several of the Rulers of the Trucial Coast because he was suspected of having attempted to murder the Residency Agent in October 1925.[37]

It appeared within the pearling communities that the concern of the British officials in the Gulf for the British subjects in the Trucial Coast ports made life somewhat easier for these Hindu and Khojah merchants. The latter knew that if a debt was not paid back and the debtor absconded to another shaikhdom, the Residency Agent supported by the Political Resident would exert pressure on that shaikh for the recovery of the debt. This meant that these merchants could take greater risks and their gains were that much bigger. This reassurance frequently more than made up for the disadvantages of not being members of the local Arab society. However, since most people who claimed to be British subjects were involved in the pearling industry, they were part and parcel of that community and had to abide by the rules.

The status of immigrants

The immigrant merchant communities from the Persian coast—as opposed to the Indians—often had a more difficult time trying to recover their debts. They sometimes tried to claim protection from the British Government and sent petitions to the Residency Agent in the same way as some British subjects, but without success.[38] The ports of the Trucial States provided ready melting-pots for people from neighbouring areas who often came without their families hoping to earn some money as divers or in such other jobs as were open to them, sometimes because the local population would not do them.

Although these immigrants remained socially and legally outsiders they were economically fully integrated. This is demonstrated by the case of three subjects of Mīr Barakāt Khān of Biyābān in Persian Makrān. They had lived for seven years in Ḥīrah, one had become a diver for ʿAbdul Raḥman bin Muḥammad, one was a diver who was not attached or indebted to anyone, and the third worked as a water carrier. They carried arms and were sometimes engaged as watchmen in the tower of Ḥīrah. When they were being accused of planning an attempt on the life of the Residency Agent—possibly at the instigation of the banished ʿAbdul Raḥman bin Muḥammad—the Ruler of Shārjah, Sulṭān bin Ṣaqr, disclaimed responsibility for their behaviour and suggested that they should be deported.[39]

In the 1920s it became increasingly clear that if the influx of people into the ports from the desert on the one hand and from neighbouring countries on the other hand had continued, the local institutions, such as they were, namely Rulers, *quḍāh*, diving courts and a few armed guards in place of a police force, would soon have been inadequate to cope with the less and less cohesive society and with its security and its judicial needs.[40] Already then the society at least in the larger towns of the Trucial Coast was affected by the consciousness of divisions between local tribal, immigrant Persian, and British-protected Indian communities. This consciousness turned easily into resentment of one group against another's privileges when the economy started to decline. Signs of such resentment became therefore more obvious during the later 1920s and may be detected, although in a not entirely unbiased version, in the reports which the Residency Agent sent to the Political Resident.

An attempt was made in Dubai in the 1930s to introduce a new socio-economic balance between the various old and new interest groups in that town.[41] This came to be known as the Dubai reform movement, which is described in the next chapter.

The divers' court

During the fast expansion of the pearling industry up to the 1920s the demand for cash to equip and provision boats also grew, and entrepreneurs, both Arab and foreign, not only earned a high and relatively risk-free return but also were in a strong position to lay down the terms for giving credit. The very complicated system of financing the pearling industry also called for stringent regulations to safeguard the rights of all the people involved, including the financiers without whom the industry could not continue to grow. Such rules differed from place to place and changed considerably with time, circumstances, and the nationality and experience of the participants in the industry. Deviations from the current code in any one shaikhdom were not tolerated, regardless of the status of the offender within the community. In each pearling port a tribunal constituted of members of the pearling community was set up to deal with such complaints. The financiers, captains and divers all stood on an equal footing before this tribunal, called *sālifah al ghauṣ*.

It usually consisted of several members of the diving community, particularly *nawākhiḏah* with a reputation for fairness and good judgement. The Ruler appointed the members of the diving tribunals, but neither he nor the *qāḍi* could interfere in their judgement. In matters which required an oath, however, the disputants had to go before the *qāḍi*. In Abu Dhabi, throughout the present century there has invariably been one person appointed by successive Rulers: only three in eighty years.[42]

During the early years of the decline in the pearling industry, when the accumulated debts which could not be recovered were leading to the ruin of many families, an increasing number of cases were referred to the *quḍāh*, particularly if all parties involved were

Muslims. The Rulers usually dealt with cases which were neither strictly diving claims nor within the usual routine of the *sharīʿah* courts, because these cases had a political aspect.

Members of ruling families interfering in the pearling industry

The growth of the pearling industry in all its aspects, that is the number of boats, participants, and merchants, of pearls fished and marketed, the duration of the year's diving season and the total income of the industry, meant a steady growth in tax receipts for the Rulers. Frequently a Ruler further increased his income by introducing new forms of taxation or by changing existing practices and regulations. In some shaikhdoms the Ruler himself or the headman had a share in the pearling business as the owner of boats or as a pearl merchant. Such direct interest and involvement in the industry inevitably led to disputes between these Rulers and leading merchants in town, and increasingly so when the industry started to shrink from 1929 onwards.

When ʿAbdul Raḥman bin Saif of Ḥamrīyah was murdered by his nephew Saif bin ʿAbdullah and his brothers in May 1931, he left 20,000 Rupees-worth of debts to merchants and others in Dubai and Umm al Qaiwain, some of the creditors being Indian; he also owed 1,500 Rupees to Persians in Shārjah. The reason why his nephews turned on him was that they suspected that he had used their inheritance, amounting to about 10,000 Rupees, as security for his own business, but instead of being a successful pearl merchant he got further and further into debt and was unable to restore the boys' property when they became old enough to claim it.[43] Saif bin ʿAbdullah and his brothers were themselves "engaged in a pearling venture which did not turn out a success and ended in leaving them in much reduced circumstances".[44]

In 1927, when Shārjah was already in a state of turmoil due to the fact that the deposed Ruler, Khālid bin Aḥmad, was attempting to regain control by attacking Shārjah town with a number of beduin, the young ruler, Sulṭān bin Ṣaqr, permitted the diving boats to go to the "small dive" before the main season started, an occasion when traditionally all the proceeds after tax were divided between the captain and the crew only, the financiers being excluded. In a report to the Political Resident of 9 June 1927, the Residency Agent noted that the "boatmen were taking the notable's (financiers) divers", who would then be tired out before the main season started, thus diminishing the boats' chances of getting a good catch. Ignoring the protest of the "notables" and even threatening them, Sulṭān bin Ṣaqr stipulated that each boat should pay 75 Rupees in tax; over 30 boats went, and "the amount which the sheikh earned on this occasion was 2,500 Rupees."[45] Similarly the ruler of ʿAjmān, Ḥumaid bin ʿAbdul ʿAzīz, was alleged to have ordered the crews of locals belonging to the Bin Lūtāh who then resided in ʿAjmān, as well as other crews who owed them money, to go diving for him before the proper season.[46] A rivalry had certainly developed in the pearling business between the Ruler and the Bin Lūtāh, which led to allegations such as that the Ruler had forbidden some 160 divers of the Bin Lūtāh to continue to work for them and that they had decamped to Dubai and Shārjah to join pearling boats there.[47]

Effects of the declining demand for pearls

The decline in the demand for Gulf pearls on the world markets had a particularly disastrous effect on the diving communities in towns because of the uncontrolled expansion which had taken place previously. It was reported in July 1929 that "about 60 diving ships of Dubai failed to put to sea owing to financial difficulties. The number of pearling boats has increased out of all proportion to the catch, and the pearl merchants do not find it possible to subsidise all the boats."[48] In the same report several pearl merchants are mentioned as being in severe financial difficulties, in particular Muḥammad bin Aḥmad Dalmūk, who had in 1928 sold pearls worth several lakhs of Rupees to Ḥajji Muḥammad ʿAli Zainal of Bombay but had not yet received his money "owing to delay in disposal of pearls in Paris". In order to re-equip his pearling fleet for the diving season of 1929 he had to borrow 200,000 Rupees from a Hindu at the exorbitant interest rate of 36 per cent per annum. The same leading merchant of Dubai returned from Bombay in March 1930 after selling his stock of pearls at a loss, and it was later reported that he had to "reduce his establishment, dismissing beduins and camels".[49] There must have been many similar cases of sudden loss of employment by retainers, servants and people in lowly jobs who worked for merchants. This bleak story was repeated throughout the Gulf; in Kuwait the catch of 1930 was poor, and prices were 50 per cent below those of 1929.[50] In Bahrain, too, the total value of sales in 1930 was estimated at 28 to 30 lakhs of Rupees, which was one quarter of the 1929 value; there the chief reason for the slackness of the market was the lack of interest of Europeans, who were mainly French buyers. They usually spent about one million pounds sterling per season, but in 1930 they spent only a few thousand pounds sterling in Bahrain.[51]

Hindu merchants were reported to be speculating in 1932 that pearls had reached their lowest price, and they accepted pearls again as security.[52] But the trade remained depressed and in Bahrain pearls fell behind gold, rice and cotton goods in order of importance as the principal export or re-export commodity in the year 1933–4. In a report to the Department of Overseas Trade in London by the Residency in Bushire dated October 1934 it was stated that "for a number of reasons this industry has fallen into a state of extreme depression during recent years and no signs of improvement are as yet visible. In the first place, economic conditions in Europe and America have led to a decrease in the demand for pearls with a result that continental buyers no longer find it worth their while to visit Bahrain every season as they did in former years. Secondly the introduction of Japanese cultured pearls has had an adverse effect on the market for natural pearls, and, thirdly, the quality of the local catch has deteriorated due perhaps to the fact that the pearling beds have been overworked."[53]

This situation did not improve in the remaining years before the beginning of the Second World War and became, of course, even worse during the war. Using as a standard the selling season of winter 1928/9, which was the last one in which prices continued to rise over those of previous years, prices of pearls fell in 1943 to about 10 per cent of that value, and a 10-grain pearl which cost a dealer about 4,000 M.T. Dollars in 1924 dropped to 400 M.T. Dollars after 1929.[54] An added problem was that from 1944 onwards it became particularly difficult to obtain the large quantities of rice which were required as provisions for the pearling crews. It was therefore expected at the beginning of the 1944 season that the diving would be on a much-reduced scale and within a smaller radius than usual because the boats had to return frequently to pick up supplies.[55]

Another threat to the pearling industry during the war years did not, however, materialise. In order to avoid spending sterling on purchases which were deemed inessential, the Government of India was asked by the Treasury in London to prohibit the purchase of precious stones from any country outside the sterling area. During the summer of 1943 some departments of the Government of India acted as though this request included the purchase of pearls from the Gulf, but in the event arrangements were made to allow free import of pearls into India from the Gulf, including parts which did not lie within the sterling area.[56] Immediately after independence in 1947 the Indian Government decided to allow only limited imports of uncut diamonds and unpolished pearls "for the specific purpose of being cut, polished or finished in India and subsequently re-exported without delay".[57] The Ruler of Bahrain and other Gulf Rulers appealed to the Political Resident, who had moved from Bushire to Bahrain, and to other British officials to try to influence the Indian Government to remove these restrictions. But since the overall policy of the British Government was to press the ex-colony to bring her imports and exports into balance these officials were not in a very strong position.

Search for alternative markets for pearls

In this depressed situation attempts were made by institutions such as the British Board of Trade to help open up alternative markets for Gulf pearls and in particular to interest American jewellers in buying more natural pearls again. These attempts failed on two accounts, firstly because the market was dominated by importers in New York who had mostly turned to cultured pearls; secondly, the obstacle to a proposed transfer of the processing and distribution end of the pearling industry, which had been built up over centuries in India, to either the Gulf or to New York was that the Indian workmanship was very good, labour costs were low, and the Indian merchants who imported the pearls into Bombay had all aspects of the trade well organised. The pearls were drilled, bleached and sorted into various qualities, sizes and colours for world distribution. Since the bulk of the pearls from the Gulf were very small, 0.80 to 2.50 grains, the cost of establishing a similarly well-functioning centre for the trade in Gulf pearls outside India even with Indian specialists would probably not have been commercial. For many decades India itself had absorbed only 20 per cent of the value of the annual pearl trade of Bombay; most of the higher quality pearls had been exported to the USA.

The various enquiries made by British commercial officers in embassies in the industrialised countries all had the same negative result;[58] the general public in Europe, the USA, Canada and elsewhere did not appreciate the difference between natural and cultured pearls, and several of the established importers of pearls, rather than trying to emphasise these differences, went along with the market trend and ceased to buy expensive pearls from Bombay.

The cultured pearls had become a threat not only on the distant markets of New York but at home too. In January 1948 the Ruler of Bahrain had a meeting with the leading pearl merchants, who urged him "to take all measures possible, in conjunction with the Ruler of Saudi Arabia and other Rulers of the Gulf States to forbid the entry of foreign pearls into the Gulf States". The reason for this appeal was that Venezuelan and Red Sea pearls had been sent to Bahrain merchants for disposal. It was also feared that even cultured pearls might be brought into the Gulf.[59]

In the event the threat of an embargo on pearl imports to India lasted only one season, and in June 1948 it was announced: "The Government of India have stated that pearls may now be imported into India freely. It is understood however that import licences are still required."[60] But the pearling industry of the ports of the Gulf had by that time already disintegrated almost beyond remedy, because most of the participants in the industry had dispersed, being unable to wait for all these years in the hope that the markets of the world might recover. Many divers had abandoned the seasonal diving and, if they were tribal people from the desert, concentrated on their other activities; or if they had come to these ports from across the Gulf they either drifted back home or found other jobs. Eventually there were the openings for ex-divers in the oil industry abroad and at long last even at home.[61] Many of the erstwhile pearl merchants, if they were Banians, returned to their homes which their families had in any case never left. The Persian and Arab members of this group, many of whom had earlier participated in the import of consumer goods, disengaged from the trade in pearls and concentrated on the import and entrepôt trade. The volume of this trade grew quite significantly from the early 1950s onwards, and, due to the start of oil company activity, the outlook was not as bleak after the Second World War as it would otherwise have been.

But nevertheless for those who had seen the very much better years of the 1920s, the lean years from 1930 onwards must have been extremely difficult. The most trying aspect of this period was probably that the relief from this depressed economic status did not come simultaneously to all the one-time pearling communities of the Gulf ports, but that Bahrain, Kuwait, and neighbouring Qatar seemed for some time to be the only lucky countries.

On the way from Abu Dhabi to the Līwā with provisions in 1958

A beduin family near a Līwā oasis in 1962

Inshore fishing in view of the mountains of Ra's al Khaimah in 1958

Drawing water with a bull in the Dhāhirah in 1954

The fort at Ḏaid in 1937

The fort of Abu Dhabi in 1949, while being enlarged

Shaikh Khalīfah bin Zāyid and members of his family in 1936

Abu Dhabi merchant Aḥmad bin Khalaf Otaibah with his family in 1936

The Ruler of Dubai, Shaikh Sa'īd bin Maktūm and his son Rāshid in 1936

Dubai Creek in 1960

The Ruler of Shārjah, Shaikh Sulṭān bin Saqr, his brother Muḥammad and his son Saqr in 1936

Cars being loaded onto a dhow during the first geological reconnaissance of the Trucial States in 1936

Seismic shot-hole drilling in Shārjah in 1956

Oil company employees going home after their weekly shift in 1961

The Ruler of Abu Dhabi and members of his family in Paris in 1951 at the successful arbitration tribunal concerning off-shore rights

Shaikh Shakhbūṭ and dignitaries at the inauguration of ADPC's oil terminal at Jebel Dhanna in March 1964

Abu Dhabian looking at government-provided modern houses in 1970

Schoolboys on old cannons outside the fort of Dubai in 1960

The Līwā village of the past: palm frond houses and wind barriers (photograph by Ronald Codrai)

Examples of traditional houses; Dubai 1960

The President of the UAE and Ruler of Abu Dhabi, Shaikh Zāyid bin Sulṭān with his brothers Shakhbūṭ and Hazzā' in 1963

3 Socio-economic status of the settled population in the oases

Who owns the land?

For well over a century the key to the socio-economic situation of the society was the material benefit derived from the pearling industry of the urbanised ports. But in many respects the way of life in the villages in the *wādis* and oases remained the cultural backbone of that society. However inadequate the agriculture and horticulture of the oases were in providing for the needs of the local population, the tribal people of these states shared with the inhabitants of the rest of the Arabian Peninsula the fascination for the possession of fertile land and sweet water. Date gardens and the few areas where farming other than horticulture is possible are considered to be very valuable possessions.

The value which townspeople, villagers and beduin alike have always attached to date gardens was at times quite out of proportion to the value in terms of money and of the crop which could be obtained from them. The gardens of the oases with running water from a *falaj* or well have always symbolised for people in south-eastern Arabia relief from the glaring sun of the desert, from the scorching summer heat of the barren mountains, and from the hot unpleasant humid atmosphere which lies heavy over the coastal towns even during the nights in the summer. Life in the oases during the summer was easy, comfortable and entertaining compared to life anywhere else in these shaikhdoms during that season. Dates and other fruit were picked daily and consumed fresh, there was enough food near at hand for everyone including the domestic animals. Men and women could enjoy the luxury of a daily bath in the separate bath-houses (*hammām*) built over the *aflāj*. Families who lived apart during the winter all congregated in the same oasis, and socialising and visiting between families and neighbours was easier than in the desert. Therefore it is not difficult to understand why, when one comes to the question of who owned horticultural and agricultural land, only the remote small *wādi* oases were usually exclusively owned by the people who worked in them and who lived by them. Of the extensive date gardens which line the coasts on either side of the Ḥajar range and the oases on the plains of the mountain foreland such as Buraimi, D̲aid and others, a large part has usually belonged to absentee landlords from the coastal towns.

Social stratification in villages

An examination of land ownership in these oases, together with the question of who does what type of work in the oasis village communities, reveals a social stratification which was partly based on wealth, for the wealthy were those who owned large flocks of camels or who were very successful in the pearling industry and could buy up date gardens in the hinterland. But another basis for this stratification arises out of historical incidents such as the dispossession of the original inhabitants when they were conquered by newcomers, or when a strong tribe gradually supplanted a weaker one, acquiring its share of the land and relegating the former to work as gardeners.

Other groups in village communities such as the *bayāsirah*, who are identifiable at least in the Buraimi oases and who are considered *mawāli* (subservient), indicates that they might be an element of the original inhabitants whom the dominant tribal groups rejected as having no *aṣl* (root, in the sense of a place in the Arab tribal genealogy) or because they initially rejected Islam.[62] The tribal Arabs would not intermarry with *bayāsirah*.

The term *bayādīr* (sing. *bīdār*) was widely used in the village communities of the Trucial States to identify farm workers. They were people who might be the descendants of the Persian village population of pre-Islamic times who were assimilated by the Arab overlords and eventually adopted Arab tribal names. *Bayādīr* were numerically the strongest group among the inhabitants of Dibah; they had about 100 houses there at the turn of the century.[63] They are certainly people who have lowly positions within these tribes now but they are acceptable partners for marriage within the tribe. *Bayādīr* may buy date gardens or boats or accept other work than that of a *bīdār*. As a worker in the gardens, a *bīdār* was never paid in anything but in kind, that is he got one bunch of dates per tree he tended in the garden. A *bīdār*'s duty was to guide the flow of the *falaj* water at the receiving end when the gardens were flooded one by one, to cut off the lower branches of the growing palm trees, to fertilize the female dates in spring and to help in the harvest during the summer.[64]

The same work was also performed by people of slave origin who remained in the households of their masters as servants; but while a *bīdār* performed only these particular duties in date gardens, servants could be asked to do all the other tasks which needed attention in a garden as well as in the houses or elsewhere. In the date gardens of the east coast, immigrants from the Persian coast, there summarily called *balūch*, frequently worked in the date gardens, drew water from wells and helped with building houses. Some of the *balūch* were paid in kind but most of them earned a wage. In most village communities *balūch* could not marry Arab tribal girls.

Trade in real estate

Date gardens everywhere in Trucial Oman could change hands either through inheritance or by being sold. The beduin Bani Yās and Manāṣīr bought date gardens in the Līwā; the members of the ruling families and the families which prospered in the pearling industry bought date gardens in *falaj*-irrigated villages. Zāyid bin Khalīfah's policy of buying up date gardens in the Buraimi oasis before the turn of the century was followed by his eldest son Khalīfah, who, apart from establishing the new group of date gardens called Masʿūdi, also bought many established gardens as they came on the market.[65] Shaikh Muḥammad bin Khalīfah, following his father's example, became probably the individual in all of Trucial Oman who owned the largest number of date palms. Besides buying in al ʿAin and the neighbouring villages[66] he also bought gardens on the Bāṭinah and Shamailīyah.

It was not uncommon for members of the ruling family or other families of one shaikhdom to buy gardens in the territory of another shaikh. The Rulers of Dubai have had gardens in Ra's al Khaimah for several generations. The entire oasis of Falaj al ʿAli, where about 5,000 date palms grew, has been the property of the ruling family of Umm al Qaiwain for a long time. About sixty families who permanently live in that oasis have traditionally worked in the date gardens for payment in kind. The Ruler's representative in that oasis has frequently not been the head of the tribal families who live there, but one of the Ruler's slaves.

Establishing new gardens

There was nothing to stop a tribesman from trying to establish a garden anywhere in the desert if he thought that he could find enough water in that location to sustain the young date palms. He did not have to obtain permission from the Ruler nor from his tribe's shaikh. The same applied to the many still uncultivated hollows between the dunes of the Līwā. But if someone else claimed that there had once been a garden in that location and that he was entitled to its possession, then the *wāli* in the Līwā or the Ruler's *qāḍi*, if he happened to be in the vicinity, dealt with the dispute.

In *falaj*-irrigated oases the ruler or his representative had to be asked for permission if someone wanted to start a new garden; but the principal obstacle to expansion of the oasis was the limited supply of water. A substantial increase in the cultivated area in an oasis such as Buraimi was only possible after the introduction of mechanical pumps. The establishment of new gardens in areas with good soil meant either the rehabilitation of a dilapidated *falaj* or the digging and operation of water wells; both required an immense community effort. For an individual to engage in such a project meant that he would require quite large amounts of money to pay labourers to dig the wells and prepare the land. Therefore the few extensions established since the beginning of this century in the major oases were mostly owned by members of the ruling families.

Summary

For the first five decades of this century there are no statistics to show how many of the date gardens in the Trucial States were owned by those who worked in them. But it appears that the date gardens were owned less and less by the people who worked in them, nor were they even owned by people who lived permanently in the village to which the gardens were attached. The absentee landowners were frequently members of the ruling families who enjoyed having, and could afford, such retreats away from the ports of the coast; their large households and many retainers consumed large amounts of dates provided by the gardens. Some, such as the Āl Bū Falāḥ, used the private acquisition of property as part of a policy of gaining influence in an area. Many gardens were bought up by Arab pearl merchants and traders.

Allowing for many exceptions one may say that in general black servants worked in the gardens near the coastal towns, *balūch* servants in the gardens of the east coast, *bayādīr* in many places including Dibah, Buraimi and Ra's al Khaimah, and tribeless but settled immigrants and original inhabitants of uncertain ethnic background worked in places where agricultural labour, other than date gardeners, was needed.[67] During the date harvest, when a few extra hands were welcome, beduin helped with this seasonal work. Payment for such work was usually only in kind, but in some cases it consisted of a share of the crop as well as money.

The villages of Trucial Oman did not have anything near as rigid a social stratification as, for example, the settled population of Hadhramaut, but within the general cultural homogenity of these village communities there were marked differences between certain groups. These differences were based primarily on tribal affiliation, which usually meant that families of one tribe lived together in one quarter of a village. But within the tribes there were families of higher and families of lower standing; the latter were sometimes even adopted groups of non-Arab origin. Marriage between families of different levels was possible. The men of the tribal families of higher standing frequently engaged in pearling or other enterprises away from home (raising camels, accompanying a camel caravan or serving as a retainer or guide). In cases where a beduin section of the same tribe visited the village during the summer[68] their contact would be with the truly tribal families of the settled section in the village. They shared certain facilities such as the use of wells, of brushwood and dates to the benefit of the beduin, while the villagers would hope for protection in war and a general rise in prestige. This same upper group of families within a settled tribal subsection were usually also those who had the closest contact with the coastal towns, because at least one brother or cousin from each household lived with another branch of the tribe in one of the ports.

Even in the very small villages in the mountains of the Trucial States, some outsiders, such as Balūch[69] and other recent immigrants from the Persian coast, in the case of Buraimi also some Zaṭūṭ,[70] and a varying number of people of slave origin owned houses. Most such foreign elements lived apart from the settled tribesmen in their own quarters of the village, except for the domestic servants, who were largely people of slave origin and resided with and shared the lives of their tribal masters. Another group of outsiders in the village might be the absentee landlords and even the people who worked in their gardens, remitting a large part of the crop to the landlord; this obligation was invariably expressed in terms of a share of the crop and never in terms of a fixed amount.

4 Side-effects of economic stress

The limitations of resources and economic opportunities

The dependable natural resources available to the people of the Trucial States within their boundaries were exceedingly diverse and at the same time adequate to satisfy the requirements of only a modest population. The skill of the beduin tribesman in mastering the rigours of the burning summer desert and in maximising his economic benefits from the various resources in the ages before world trade agreements and instant communications is often overlooked or just not understood today. Baskets are now rarely made from the fronds of the palm, truffles are left uncollected in the sand, and as in most other societies in the world that enjoy the benefits of modern civilisation, the simpler pleasures of the past are rapidly forgotten.

During the last hundred years there were three factors which led to an influx of foreigners, all arising out of new economic opportunities. These were: the years of exceptional prosperity in the pearling industry, particularly during the first two decades of this century; the transfer of trade from Persian ports to Dubai after 1902; and the more recent development of the oil industry. The decline and collapse of the market for Gulf pearls had a devastating effect on the fortunes of the wealthy families and reduced many other people nearly to starvation. This development, which happened within the memory of many living people, demonstrates the extent to which the population, both original and immigrant, had come to rely on one resource which, when it failed, could not be made up for by the conventional use of the territory's remaining natural resources.

Whenever the delicate balance between resources, economic opportunity and the number of people who could live thereby was upset, which happened several times during the recorded history of this region, many people tightened their belts and made do, while others emigrated to neighbouring countries or returned to where they had come from. A period of economic decline also brings forth a few soldiers of fortune, and this area was no exception.

Factors leading to raids and maritime *ghazū*

For several centuries the settled population of the entire Musandam promontory was so small that, even without much trade, the then modest needs of the beduin and the village communities were secured. Under the leadership of the Qawāsim many people of the coastal villages and the hinterland benefited from the growing share of the trade in the area as sailors, boat-builders, and traders in ever-increasing numbers.

The Qāsimi hold over the naturally-favoured trading places such as Qishim and Lāft on Qishim Island, and Lingah and Shināṣ, lasted for only a few decades during the 18th century and their position was weakened by the efforts of their traditional enemy the Sultan of Oman. The absence of any single dominant power in the Gulf was detrimental to trade, and Qāsimi ventures also suffered accordingly. A combination of political, religious and economic factors[71] induced some people under the Qāsimi authority to follow their ships' commanders into numerous adventures in which they pursued Omani, British, Persian and even French and American[72] merchant and naval vessels. They boarded them, sometimes killed or imprisoned the crews, and towed the ships and their cargo, armament and prisoners home to Ra's al Khaimah or to some other port. Genuine religious fanaticism, intimidation by the new Wahhābi overlords, or unquestioning loyalty to the ruling shaikh and his policy towards the Omani enemy and their British supporters, could not have been lasting motivations for the many men who participated repeatedly in such raids over a period of more than half a century between 1778 and 1835. A more probable reason is that there were more seaworthy boats lying idle in the ports of the Qāsimi-dominated area than elsewhere in the Gulf, and many sailors were no longer needed after the trade had declined or changed route.

The majority of the men who manned the large Qāsimi fleet[73] had become dependent on the sea for their livelihood; if trade was no longer possible, the share which they could expect to take home from a plundered foreign vessel became an acceptable substitute. Being tribal people of Eastern Arabia, the idea of *ghazū* was never far from their minds. On land this meant raiding enemy tribes with the aim of carrying off as much of their property as possible, but usually there were only camels and goats to be had. *Ghazū* by sea, capturing the cargo vessels of the tribe one was at war with, was as legitimate as driving off their camels. It was therefore not surprising at all that, once it had become obvious that the success rate was very high even when tackling British ships, and that the reward was high, too, in the form of booty as well as ransom for European and Indian prisoners, the shaikhs of other equally depressed communities followed suit[74] in leading or at least tolerating attacks on passing ships being carried out from their ports.

Piracy was as intolerable for the British government, endeavouring to establish peace on these vital sea routes, as it was for the Rulers whose subjects followed the command of individual pirates. When such ships were apprehended and punished it was usually not only to fulfill the treaty obligations which the Rulers had pledged to observe after 1820, but also to re-establish sovereignty over unruly subjects. The repeated outbreaks of piracy were very annoying, costly, and damaging for British shipping and prestige. But the fact that every dispute between the Rulers, shaikhs and tribes of the entire region was also pursued at sea, by attacking one another's trading, passenger, and pearling vessels, had a devastating effect on the economy of the shaikhdoms. In the long run the families at home were the losers, because many a time the boats could not venture to the seasonal diving or the pearls could not be disposed of because communications with Lingah, Bahrain and India were too dangerous, and provisions could not be brought in. Therefore it was eventually not difficult to enlist the co-operation of the Rulers on the coast to observe and help to enforce the maritime peace which was first agreed in 1835, periodically renewed and then eventually in May 1853 styled the "Perpetual Treaty of Peace". Security on the waters of the Gulf, during the diving season as well as for voyages to neighbouring ports, Iran and India, was essential if the inhabitants of the Trucial States were to obtain the greatest possible benefit from the pearl banks situated off their shores.

Resurgence of raiding

When the pearling industry declined after 1929 people did not take to piracy again as an outlet for the surplus men and ships, but the majority of the tribally-associated people found ways of adapting themselves to their new situation, seeking employment elsewhere. It is however, not surprising that there was a marked increase in raiding in the desert by beduin groups as well as lawlessness among the unemployed who drifted from one port to another in search of a livelihood. On the borderlands of the Rub' al Khāli there was little which one beduin could take from another beyond his camels and his rifle. But in the vicinity of towns and villages raiding beduin stood a chance of being able to carry off pots and pans and jewellery which they could not afford to buy themselves. For, during these years of depression, beduin camel-breeders did not get even a fraction of the price they used to obtain when they sold their camels, because the need for beasts of burden was greatly reduced in the general decline in trade. Many of the raids near the coastal towns and villages formed part of blood feuds and other long-standing disputes between tribal groups and families, while in other raids the element of economic gain and the hope for booty were at least equally strong.

Several such incidents were reported in the year 1931 alone. In March some people from Fujairah received news that their caravan would be attacked by ʿAwāmir beduin; so they sent off the caravan with only three guards, and when the ʿAwāmir attacked, killing one man, the rest of the members of the caravan fell upon the ʿAwāmir, killed three of them, took one prisoner, and saved the caravan.[75] There were many reports of beduin raiding the outskirts of Dubai, Shārjah, and Ra's al Khaimah towns, such as the following: "The Ruler of Ra's al-Khaimah is . . . fighting with Awamir beduin who recently killed one man and carried off another from a garden in the suburbs."[76] In May 1931 a caravan of the shaikh of Buraimi (Naʿīm) was attacked outside Dubai by subjects of the Ruler of Abu Dhabi (either Manāṣīr or Bani Yās). In Umm al Qaiwain some ʿAwāmir were "reported to be looting the suburbs of this place. They cut down the unripe fruit of 20 trees in retaliation for the punishment meted out to them by the Ruler of Umm al-Qawain."[77]

Trading in slaves

While the pearling industry expanded, there was an ever-increasing demand on the Trucial Coast for slave divers as well as for domestic slaves. After the 1847 agreement on the ban on transport of slaves by boat, it became virtually impossible to bring new supplies from the traditional sources. During the first two decades of this century the British authorities in the Gulf began to manumit domestic slaves who applied to the Residency Agent in Shārjah for liberation. The internal trade in slaves remained the occupation for a few daring individuals whose activities were frowned upon by the British authorities but were nevertheless tolerated by the Rulers because the business of many a pearl-boat owner in the coastal towns had grown to depend almost exclusively on slave divers. A new source of supplies had opened because Balūchistān was suffering from a period of internal strife and famine during the 1920s, and many people who emigrated to the coasts of Bāṭinah and Shamailīyah seeking employment in the gardens and on the pearling boats were abducted into slavery.

The decline of the pearling industry put a temporary stop to these activities, and during the early 1930s the British authorities believed that trading in slaves had ceased on the Trucial Coast. But when eastern Saudi Arabia began to prosper with the start of oil company activities there, the demand for domestic slaves in al Ḥasā grew. The economic situation in the Trucial States in the 1940s was going from bad to worse, general security outside the towns was low, and some unscrupulous individuals were tempted to snatch Balūchis, ex-slaves, and even Arabs, and sell them through the channels which soon opened up. Thesiger recounts that while he stayed in al ʿAin in October 1949 a well-known slave dealer from al Ḥasā, ʿAli al Murri, had recently started trading between Ḥamāsah and al Ḥasā, and Thesiger's companions claimed that when ʿAli al Murri visited a well just before Thesiger's party arrived there, he had forty-eight slaves with him.[78]

Many incidents of kidnappings of Balūchis, Persians and negroes and their being transported from or via the Trucial States to al Ḥasā are reported during the period before the Saudi force was evicted by the Trucial Oman Levies in October 1955, thus ending a dispute which had hindered the oil company's activities. During the late 1950s the patrols of the Trucial Oman Levies, who were in 1956 renamed the Trucial Oman Scouts, made the transport of any sort of contraband difficult; however, the quickening pace of the economic development concentrated the minds of people on the new opportunities at home on the Trucial Coast, and the supply of slaves from the Trucial States to al Ḥasā dried up completely.

While these activities were flourishing in periods such as during the pearling boom and at the beginning of the oil industry in Saudi Arabia, the individual outlaw or the beduin raider who kidnapped immigrants and tribal people alike made a quick profit out of selling them to the few inveterate dealers. The "unfortunate victims", as they were usually called in British documents, were not necessarily all that unfortunate. During the 1920s the Balūchis who arrived on the Trucial Coast had fled from strife and famine at home to seek work, food and shelter, all of which were usually more securely provided if they belonged to a master than if they tried their luck on their own in the rough-and-tumble of the expanding pearling ports. As for the individuals who ended up as domestic servants in a Saudi household or working in one of the newly established farms in al Ḥasā during the 1940s and early 1950s, most were more comfortable there than they would have been in the then depressed shaikhdoms of the Trucial Coast. This is the gist of a number of accounts, for when relatives succeeded in tracing their kidnapped kin to where they were living, by then usually as free members of a well-to-do household, they obtained such glowing reports of conditions that they sometimes decided to go and live there themselves.

Thus in general the trading in slaves is a phenomenon which coincided with disturbances of the traditional economic patterns in the Trucial States, and was not what the distant beholder might imagine it to be. The deprivations of a 19th century factory worker, or the distress of the unemployed in Europe after the First World War could cause more individual suffering than when people were taken and forced to work at what they would almost certainly have chosen to do anyway. If not the law of the land then the ethics of the religion protected those who fell prey to the slave traders from inhuman treatment.

5 The role of women in the economy

The description in earlier chapters of the various economic activities in the desert, the oases and on the coasts showed the role played by the men as the bread-winners of the households. The role of women was particularly important in the families and communities where the men were absent during the pearling season, and it was not made any easier for them by the many pregnancies which most women experienced during part of their lives.

Whether the men were there or not, women traditionally performed certain duties in the household, including supervising the servants. They went at least twice a day to the well or the *falaj* to fetch water in earthenware jars; at the same time the clothes of the family were washed and spread on the sand to dry. Beduin women spun camel and goat hair into thread which they used to make clothes for the family, camel trimmings, and the large pieces of material needed for making tents. In the households on the coast or in the hinterland women sewed the family's clothes with the exception of the *ʿabāʾah* (locally also called *bisht*) for men, which came from Bahrain or al Ḥasā. Apart from the daily food preparation which usually included fresh fish for the midday meal on the coast and dried fish in the oases, it often fell to the women to deal with any excess milk production by making it into butter or curds.

During the peak of the pearling industry, when most able-bodied men from the Līwā spent the entire summer on the boats, women were in charge of the organisation of harvesting the family's date crop, which came frequently from several groves scattered in hollows among the dunes. When they were little girls they would have climbed a palm tree without hesitation, just like their brothers or cousins. If nobody else was there to do it the younger women would even go up the trees with the rope around their waist for a secure hold while both hands were used to cut off the branches and put them in a basket. But usually the dates were harvested by the boys who were too young to go diving or by beduin who converged on the Līwā and other oases to help with the date harvest and who were paid in kind for their work. Often the women had to decide which dates were ready to be picked; the many different kinds of dates ripened at different times between May and September and had to be brought down when they were ready. Women often had to supervise the work of the beduin helpers, pay them, deal with the tax collector, and distribute the fresh dates to those to whom a share was due.[79] The women cooked the thick date stew, which was stored in palm-frond containers and was eaten as the staple food (*tamr*) throughout the winter and also on the pearling boats during the summer.

While women might help with watering the camels when beduin families were in the desert, milking the female camels was always the duty of the men or the young boys. Women were in charge of the sheep and goats. In some villages large herds of goat were taken out by a person specially hired by the entire community; otherwise the women or the children took the goats out in the morning to graze at some distance from the camp or the family home if they lived in a desert oasis; in the summer they would usually bring them back before it became very hot, tether them or put them in a pen and give them leftovers from the family meal or greenery which had been collected in the desert or the date garden. Everywhere women would often be required to gather firewood, carrying the heavy bundles home on their heads.

Fishing, too, was an economic activity in which women had a part to play. Where the catch consisted of sardines and anchovies as on the coast of Shamailīyah and in Umm al Qaiwain, the women and children spread the still-quivering silvery catch on the beach and a day or two later they collected the dried fish into baskets. The men, if not out fishing, hauled the boats out of the water and repaired them and their fishing gear. Women would also sometimes help to mend the nets. Where fish were caught by hanging a net across a shallow cove, husband and wife might share all the tasks involved.

Because the catch had to be disposed of quickly, fish was the most common item which women sold in public in the *sūq*, and some still do so today in the modern fish markets of the UAE. Otherwise women did not normally participate very much in trade. But, as mentioned earlier, some women invested their own money in buying cloth, perfumes, combs or any other wares which they could sell to the women of related and neighbouring households. The poorer among them might sell wherever they could or spread their wares of home-made face masks (*burqa'*), fish-hooks, incense burners and other small items on a mat by the *sūq*.

Some women who inherited money, or who after a divorce retained large sums of money from the bride-price, would buy a shop but take no active part in running it. In rare cases a woman did herself engage in business ventures, own and fit out pearling boats, or lend money, or trade in pearls and general imports. She would use a trusted slave or employ a man to function as her agent in all contacts with male counterparts in the business, but the final decision would be hers, and if need be important negotiations would be carried on from behind a door or through a curtain. While the economy in the oil exporting shaikhdoms expanded rapidly, many more female members of ruling and merchant families alike engaged in profitable business, particularly through letting multi-storey buildings.

The fact that women in the shaikhdoms of the Gulf lead a life secluded from public gatherings and hidden from the eyes of strangers does not mean that their role within the family is any less important for the economic prosperity of the household and the entire community than the role of their sisters who live in a different environment.

6 Conclusion: uniformity of life-style due to economic limitations

Before the export of oil from Abu Dhabi began, even the most industrious of the people in the Trucial States could not dramatically increase their wealth or improve upon the overall economic situation in these shaikhdoms. Outside influences such as regional political developments or the opening of new trade routes only brought about minor changes for the community as a whole. Nothing could ever totally transform the way of life as much as the export of oil did later. Whether pearls were the fashion in Europe, whether entrepôt trade with neighbouring countries shifted to the Trucial States, whether there were a few years of good rains or whether the locust swarms destroyed the date crop, the economic base remained the same: pearls, dates, boats, camels, domestic animals, fish, agriculture and trade.

However much the benefits obtained in one field of activity could be improved, they were never enough to transform the entire environment; the desert could not be made to bloom, nor was it possible to avoid exhausting journeys on camel-back or boat under the unmerciful summer sun.

The climate and the natural environment as much as the limitations of occupational variety made for uniformity of life-style throughout the area and for all the people, whatever their private wealth. On the pearling boats everyone from the *nūkhaḏā* down to the lowliest deck hand suffered many weeks of separation from their families under very hard conditions. A diver was also exposed to danger to his health from respiratory problems and sheer exhaustion. Sharks rarely attacked divers, but sting-rays and poisonous jelly fish lurk in the water and the cotton shirts which some divers used were an inadequate protection. The daily contact with salt water and the heat and humidity on board the boats frequently prevented skin irritations from healing during the diving season. Apart from these additional hazards to divers, life was equally hard for everyone on board a pearling boat. The food consisted of rice, fish, dates and occasionally limes. Drinking-water, which had to be fetched from distant sources such as Dalmā island, was rationed, and being stored in skins or bitumen lined containers it went foul all too quickly in the heat. Everyone on board spread their bed rolls on deck for the night; the fact that the *nūkhaḏā* and maybe his first mate slept on the raised poop of the boat provided precious little privacy or extra comfort to their existence either. Even during the summer there are sometimes high seas, and neither sleeping nor eating nor diving was possible, and the entire fleet had to run for shelter near the islands. On one occasion during the first decade of this century some 100 people from the Trucial States alone lost their lives, and many boats foundered in the storm. Such common dangers welded free men and slaves into a close community of people who were content in spite of hardships and enjoyed together the few pleasures which they contrived on board. After the sun had set and darkness relieved the eyes which had suffered throughout the day from glare and salt, they could rest while listening to a poem being recited accompanied by the *rabābah*, or join in a song. As in a community of gamblers, spirits were often kept high by tales about a lucky boat which had fished an immensely valuable pearl and had left everyone rich at the end of the season.

Meanwhile the people who stayed back home in the *wādis* and oases of the hinterland or in the coastal towns were not leading very much more comfortable lives either. The heat of the summer sun was unbearable during the day in the hinterland, while it was extremely difficult to live in the high humidity on the coast. Whatever nature and human ingenuity offered to bring a little respite from the heat was relished; to be able to bathe in the *falaj* or to pour water from the well over the hot body, to reach the shade of the palm groves after a journey through the desert or to sit on an elevated gallery to enjoy the cooling effect of a little breeze.

Although the prosperity of the various communities in the Trucial States varied greatly over the decades, the way of life in the individual households at any one time was comparatively uniform. Exceptions to this did not amount to very much: some families in a town like Abu Dhabi, where the wells produced only brackish water, could afford to buy drinking water which came by boat from further up the coast; in the interior the owners of date gardens often lived in two-storey mud-brick buildings while their gardeners lived in palm-frond huts; some merchants could afford to feed large numbers of people while in other households even the staple food was in short supply. But nevertheless the same type of food was consumed in all homes, and the same style of clothing was common to all.

Chapter Seven

Dubai—Example of a City State on the Trucial Coast

1 Dubai before the 1950s

Introduction

Dubai has in many aspects always been a typical example of the towns of the Trucial Coast which drew their population from the hinterland and which also experienced rapid growth as long as the pearling industry continued to expand. A combination of geographical location, the farsightedness of its Rulers, the astuteness of its merchants, and good fortune led to Dubai's success in defying the limitations of local resources to a greater extent than its neighbours. Following in the footsteps of the Qawāsim who reaped the benefits of entrepôt trade in the 18th century, Dubai became in later years prosperous and also politically important because its merchants exploited the various opportunities to trade with or on behalf of neighbouring countries. Time and again people residing in Dubai spotted ways and means of making a better living than they could have had by relying wholly on the resources which were locally available at that time.

Thus the development of Dubai also stands as an example that, given the right circumstances, it is possible for a community of merchants on the Trucial Coast to reach out beyond the resources of their own immediate environment. In the case of Dubai the means to add to the benefits which could be derived from pearling, fishing, date palm agriculture or internal trade, ranged from entrepôt trade, the circumvention of customs regulations on neighbouring coasts and smuggling, to the establishment of service industries flourishing in the wake of rising oil production in other areas of the Gulf.

Dubai first exported oil in 1969, seven years after Abu Dhabi, and even then the revenues were a fraction of Abu Dhabi's income from oil.[1] Therefore the physical changes (e.g. town planning) and social changes (e.g. population increase through immigration) throughout the 1960s and early 1970s were not directly generated by the new resource, oil. Such changes were then still the effects of the growth of Dubai into a mercantile metropolis. The description of some aspects of the development of that City State in this chapter will therefore be taken beyond the final years of the 1950s, the decade which otherwise is seen in this study as the borderline between an old order fitting the homogeneous society and a new transitional period on which the social as well as the economic systems are superimposed by foreign elements.

Early history

Within recorded history Dubai started as an insignificant fishing village probably some time during the 18th century. It was a dependency of the shaikhdom of Abu Dhabi[2] and its inhabitants were probably mostly Bani Yās. In 1833 a group of about 800 people of the Āl Bū Falāsah subsection of the Bani Yās seceded from Abu Dhabi and settled in Dubai.[3] The leaders of the exodus, ʿUbaid bin Saʿīd and Maktūm bin Buṭi, remained joint leaders until the death of the former in 1836. Maktūm bin Buṭi ruled until he died in 1852, establishing the dynasty of the Āl Maktūm Rulers for Dubai.[4] The newly-established shaikhdom had some difficulty in defending its independence from both Abu Dhabi and its Qāsimi neighbour in Shārjah. Maktūm and most of his successors usually followed a policy of good understanding with the British authorities in the Gulf, probably partly as a safeguard against obliteration of the small State.

Developing into a focal point for trade and pearling

Before they were artificially improved, the ports of most of the coastal towns of the western Trucial States had certain features in common. They were sheltered creeks connected with the open sea, but suffered from sandbars forming at their entrances due to a strong current parallel to the coast. In this respect the creek of Dubai was no exception, but it had the advantage that it extended considerably further inland than any of the other creeks.

Dubai now stands on both sides of the S-shaped entrance of the creek, which was the dividing line between Āl Bū Falāḥ and Qāsimi domination along the coast during the time of Abu Dhabi's

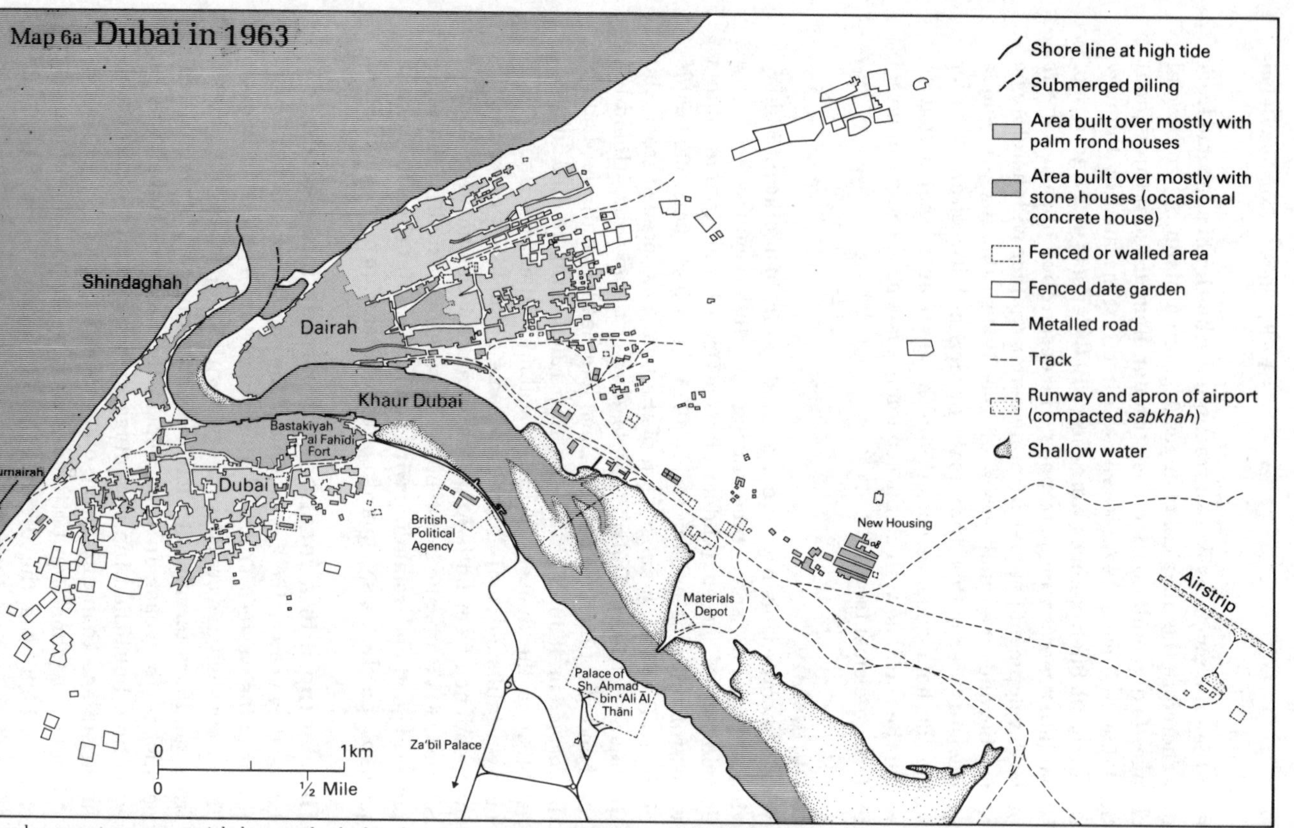

based on a contemporary aerial photograph which is the property of Sir William Halcrow and Partners, Dubai

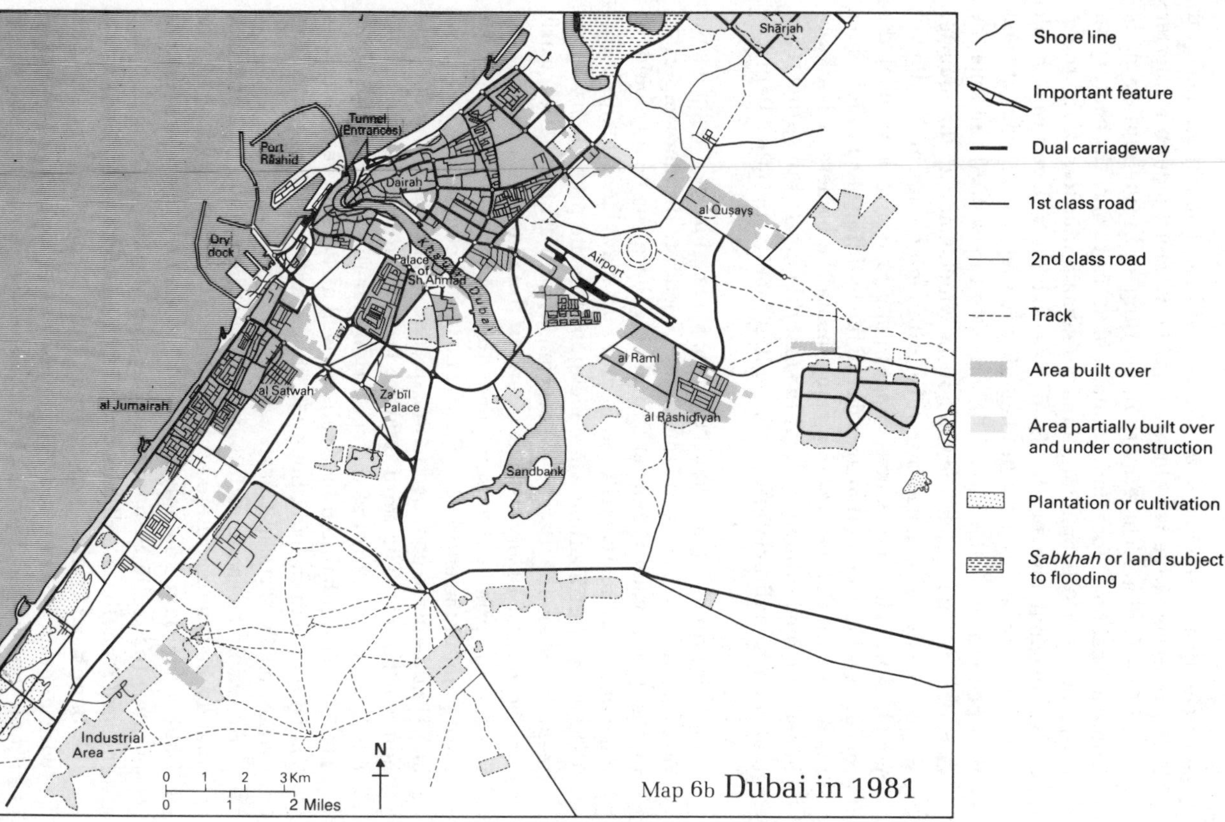

Map 6b Dubai in 1981

sovereignty over the Bani Yās of Dubai village. The fort of the Āl Bū Falāḥ representative was located on the western side in a quarter called Shindaghah. The growth in pearling and trade rapidly made Dubai a focal point for immigration, and at the turn of the century an estimated 10,000 people inhabited three main quarters of the town.

The original site of the Bani Yās fishing village was in all probability the quarter of Shindaghah, situated in a triangle between the open sea in the north and the creek to the east. At the time the Gazetteer was compiled, the 250 houses which made up that quarter were exclusively occupied by Arabs. Although buying and selling of land has brought about some change in this pattern of settlement, the recent development of that area due to the building of a tunnel under the creek and the necessity to compensate the owners of land and houses affected brought to light the fact that most of the property in that quarter still belonged to the ruling family and other Bani Yās families.

Dubai proper is situated on the same side of the creek as Shindaghah, but further inland. It developed into the more important of the two western quarters, probably because boats could be offloaded there more easily. Al Fahīdi Fort may date back to before 1820, when fortifications were mentioned in the preliminary agreement between the Bombay Government and Dubai; it is clearly marked on the 1820/29 survey view. In the nineteenth century the fort and the principal mosque made the quarter of Dubai proper the focal point of the entire City State. The Indian community[5]—Khojah and Hindu—were confined to this quarter, which had about 50 shops and 100 houses. The third quarter, Dairah, on the east side of the creek, was at the turn of the century by far the biggest, with about 1,600 houses, inhabited by Arabs as well as Persians and Balūchis. The *sūq* of Dairah had about 350 shops, and was thus the biggest market on the Trucial Coast.

By the first decade of this century the population of Dubai had already become more mixed than that of Shārjah town or of Abu Dhabi. The Bani Yās only just held the majority, with 440 houses, because the Āl Bū Mahair as well as the Mazārī' of Dubai—unlike those of Abu Dhabi—did not consider themselves as integral parts of the Bani Yās.[6] Arabs from Bahrain, Kuwait and the Persian Coast with another 400 houses, 250 houses of the Sūdān, 30 houses of people originating from al Ḥasā, 30 of the Marar and 10 of the Shwaihiyīn (part of the Bani Ka'ab tribe) completed the Arab element within the town. The remainder of the population was made up of 250 Persian households, 200 Balūchi houses and the Indian British subjects.

The only inland settlement which could be considered as being subject to the Rulers of Dubai was Ḥajarain in the Wādi Ḥattā, which, in its disputes with the inhabitants of the Naʿīm protected village of Masfūṭ, looked to the Ruler of Dubai for support. In later decades the name Ḥattā was adopted for that village, and for some time now rulers of Dubai have had a representative in Ḥattā and services for the village are now the responsibility of the municipality of Dubai. The inland oases of Khawānīj and ʿAwīr, some 17 to 20 kilometres from the coast, in relatively well-wooded dune country, are both more recent developments of gardens and out-of-town houses which became possible with the installation of pumps in water wells.

The data which are available on the economic activity of Dubai in the first decade of the 20th century may not be correct in all details, but they provide part of the general picture of a growing multi-national, sea-orientated pearling and trading community. Dubai had, of all the Trucial States' ports, the highest number of men employed on pearling boats (6,936 according to Lorimer)[7] although it had only 335 boats, while 410 boats belonged to Abu Dhabi. But while many of the people who manned those boats which sailed from Abu Dhabi came in from the desert at the beginning of the pearling season, the crews manning the Dubai pearling boats, and their families, lived in town all the year round. The gross revenue from taxes levied by the Ruler of Dubai at that time, 41,388 Rupees was only surpassed by that of Abu Dhabi, 43,964 Rupees. The number of exempt boats and men was, however, so high (210 boats and 3,813 men) that the Ruler had a net income of only 20,860 Rupees,[8] but the community of exempt people did have to pay for the upkeep of 100 beduin guards to watch over the, by then, no longer walled quarters of the town during the absence of most of the local fighting men in the summer. The exemptions which Dubai accorded at that time, particularly to the majority of the Bani Yās—though they could also extend to others—left the community as a whole much better off. In later decades this relative laxity in taxation encouraged entrepreneurs in the pearling trade to settle in Dubai.

The rule of the liberal and far-sighted Maktūm bin Ḥashar not only covered part of the period during which the pearling industry experienced fast growth everywhere in the Gulf, but also coincided with an incident which was immediately turned to the benefit of Dubai. In 1902 a law introducing very high customs dues for imports and exports going through Persian ports drove away the prosperous entrepôt trade from that coast and especially from the then dominant port of Lingah at the entrance to the Gulf proper. Goods from India for the Trucial Coast were consequently shipped direct to Dubai. This port developed not only into a distribution centre for trade with the interior, particularly the Buraimi oasis, but also became increasingly important as a port where goods from India which came by sailing vessel or by regular steamer service (weekly since June 1904) were re-exported to Persia and other neighbouring countries.

Among the people who tried their hand at becoming financiers or owners of pearling boats or were otherwise involved in the entrepreneur aspects of the industry in Dubai, were a number of minor members of the ruling families of other Trucial Shaikhdoms, some of whom were biding their time until a moment when they could take over as headman or Ruler at home.[9] It was probably the economic opportunities of the day, rather than a particular attitude on the part of Dubai's ruling shaikh in favouring certain individuals in dynastic quarrels up and down the coast, which made Dubai so frequently the temporary home for exiles.

As has been shown above, the pearling industry had continued to be increasingly profitable for participants at all levels until the final years of the 1920s. Thus almost every family in the Trucial States experienced a gradual—or in some cases a dramatic—rise in buying power. During the first decade of this century a very large share of the imports which filled the stalls in the *sūq* and the baskets of pedlars continued to be brought into Dubai, from where they were shipped by coastal craft or camel to the other parts. This meant that the ports on the Persian coast, which had traditionally served as entrepôt ports for the few wares which the families living in the Trucial States expected to have either from India itself or from the Indian market of imports, were replaced by Dubai. Thus the bulk of the re-exports in that early period of Dubai's mercantile boom after 1902 went to neighbouring Arab shaikhdoms.

Already a number of merchants from the restricted, beleaguered southern Persian ports had moved to Dubai, followed by craftsmen, traders and pearl divers. The latter found ready employment and being usually of Arab origin, built up a new existence with their families. The merchants did not necessarily sever their ties with their previous existence—customers in Persia and business connections in India; they took up residence in Dubai but arranged for their goods to reach markets in Persia despite the new customs posts and high import duties. Some also engaged in the pearling business. But the activities of these Persian merchants in and from Dubai were still on a small scale; the prominent merchants were all Arab or Indian.

However, a pattern of re-export to Persia was established in that first decade, and a large number of inhabitants of southern Persia who in 1925 suffered from the economic impact of even more severe import and export restrictions followed this pattern.

Immigration of Arab merchants from the Persian coast

By the 1920s it had become obvious that these restrictions which strangled the economy of southern Persian ports in every respect were no passing whim, but were there to stay. Therefore most merchants who had initially taken up temporary residence in Dubai to keep a foot in the business of importing into Persia decided to accept Shaikh Sa'īd bin Maktūm's offer to settle in Dubai and brought their families over.

A particularly large number came from the Bastak district, a part of the sub-province of Lār in the Fārs Province.[10] The greater portion of the Bastak is at some distance inland, but the district has also about 35 miles of coast with the principal port of Khamīr. The population of the latter place was about 1,800 at the turn of the century. There, and elsewhere in the Bastak district, as indeed throughout the south-eastern coast of Persia with the ports of Lingah, Bandar 'Abbās and Charak, the inhabitants belonged to various Arab tribes[11] and were Sunni, not Shī'ah like most of Persia beyond the mountain range which cuts off this coast from the rest of the Persian Empire. Communication between Dubai and a port such as Khamīr had always been frequent, due not least to the fact that most of the firewood for the entire lower Gulf was obtained from the extensive swamps to the west of Khamīr. The immigrants from Bastak and other areas of the Persian coast were given an area immediately to the east of al Fahīdi Fort in Dubai to build themselves houses. This location is close to the creek where boats could be offloaded and near to the *sūq* of Dubai, which turned out to be very favourable indeed. The new quarter, called Bastakīyah, bears witness to this day to the prosperity which its inhabitants have enjoyed since they became residents of Dubai.

Bringing a new feature to the town—the wind-tower house

These houses were built by masons, who, like a certain Ustād Muḥammad,[12] stood in a line of sons who had learnt from their fathers how to design and construct houses in order to minimise the discomforts of heat and humidity on the coasts of the Gulf. The majority of people on the Arab coast usually lived in palm-frond houses which were cooled by the breeze; those who had to live in a fort or tower used the upper levels to catch the wind during the hot summer months. The influx of people from the Persian coast introduced the wind towers to the ports of the Trucial States. In the Bastakīyah every compound had at least one, while in the other quarters of Dubai, Dairah and Shindaghah, this feature was readily introduced by those inhabitants who could afford to build more elaborate houses.

Wind towers on two-storey buildings rise about fifteen metres above the ground; the upper part consists of four concave inner walls with pillars, arches and often intricate plasterwork to continue the square shape of the tower. Wind from any direction is caught on the concave walls and funnelled down through a chimney to a room beneath, where all occupants of the house seek this breeze for relief from the heat of the summer. Other features of a typical house in the Bastakīyah of Dubai were, as is usual in Arab compounds, an inner courtyard surrounded by rooms, roofed verandas open to this courtyard, and rooftop areas which were screened and walled on the outside, and, in the two-storey houses, galleries overlooking the courtyard. The building materials were, for the foundations, *saruj*, a mixture of red clay from Iran with manure, dried and baked in a kiln; lumps of coral; slabs of limestone; and plaster for decorative screens as well as for overall finishing. *Chandel* wood from East Africa, palm-frond matting, mud and straw were used for roofing.

The expansion of the Bastakīyah, which grew to contain well over fifty compounds for large extended families, can be seen as a symbol for the changing emphasis in the economy of Dubai as well as for the new cultural and social influence and as a new dimension to the social structure of the City State.[13]

In the following paragraph a description of some aspects of the physical environment which obtained in all quarters of Dubai is given in an attempt to convey a more complete picture of life in Dubai in the difficult two and a half decades from 1930 to 1955.

Sketch of the town before work on the creek began

The town and the people

The first house built of concrete blocks was constructed in 1956. A large number of inhabitants of Dubai lived in palm-frond (*barasti*)[14] houses until well into the 1960s. These *barasti* quarters usually contained compounds for extended families grouped together in clusters of related families. Between these groups of two to about five compounds, the alleyways were often just a little wider than those which provided access to the compounds within the group. The quarters of different tribal relationship were usually quite separate from each other, especially in the settlements of fishermen along the shore of al Jumairah and between Dairah and the date gardens. In the quarters where coral and mud-brick houses predominated, the alleys were nowhere wide enough to let a car pass through. There was no need for wide spaces between houses since each house and compound was built to provide the maximum of privacy inside, with high walls connecting the various buildings within the compound; there were no windows, or only very small and high ones, opening on to the street, and there were high walls and screens on the outward-looking side, even on the rooftop terraces. Transport within the town was possible only on donkey or camel until the beginning of the 1960s, when some roads were opened up by the municipality. Traffic between Dubai and Dairah was largely by rowing-boats (called *ʿabrah*). There were, and still are, a number of fixed landing points on either side of the creek. On Fridays the passage was free for people from Dairah who went to attend the midday prayer in the big mosque on the Dubai side of the creek.

The first motor car on the Trucial Coast was imported in 1928 by the Residency Agent, ʿĪsa bin ʿAbdul Laṭif, in Shārjah, for use between Shārjah and Ra's al-Khaimah. The first car in Dubai was brought in about 1930 by Muḥammad bin Aḥmad bin Dalmūk, who gave it to Shaikh Saʿīd bin Maktūm. Cars could be driven over the salt-flats (*sabkah*) and along the beach at low tide, but had to be left well outside the built-up quarters of Dubai. In the late 1930s a taxi service operated in Dubai and between Dubai and Dairah around the eastern end of the creek. Another service, owned by Shaikh Maktūm bin Rāshid, had a monopoly over journeys between Dubai and Shārjah.

In a society where consumer goods in bottles, tins, and plastic containers were virtually unknown, and leftovers from meals and food preparation were given to camels, goats, chickens and cats, all of which had their own area in the yard, there was very little waste to dispose of. The family used to get one of the servants to deposit refuse anywhere outside the house. In some quarters a person would be paid by the community to collect this refuse from the alleys, and it would then be deposited on an empty space outside that quarter for general collection. Proper disposal of refuse was not organised until some time in the late 1950s, when Shaikh Rāshid appointed someone to undertake this for all quarters of the City State.

Throughout that period and even up to the middle of the 1960s the entire population of Dubai lived in identifiable groups. The neighbourhoods within the different quarters of the town had originally grown through a process of immigrants moving in with, or settling next to, their tribal relatives.[15] Therefore each neighbourhood also had a headman, elder or notable who was the spokesman for that group of inhabitants when complaints had to be voiced, when a disaster occurred, or when the Ruler wanted a certain decision to be communicated to all the residents. There was no *wāli* for any quarter of the town.[16] During his rule, Shaikh Sa'īd bin Maktūm used to send his brother Ḥashar almost daily to Dairah to settle disputes among merchants and to hear their complaints and suggestions. The Ruler or his brother acted as arbiters in any dispute which people cared to bring to them for settlement. But disputes regarding inheritance or marriage and divorce were immediately referred to the *qāḍi*.[17]

With no State police, no government-run educational system, nor organised supervision—for instance by a municipality—of land use, buildings and market practices, very little contact with government authority was forced upon the individual. The residents were nevertheless well aware of the presence of the Ruler's authority, of his armed retainers, of his tax collectors and of his duty to act as arbiter. The most effective coercive force in such a tightly-knit community as Dubai was then, was public opinion within the groups and communities.

One of the few services rendered by the shaikhly government to the community was the co-ordination of improvements along both sides of the creek, where wooden platforms were built as landing-points for *'abrahs*, and to facilitate offloading goods from the boats and barges. Because customs dues had to be collected on all imported goods, a system had to be organised whereby boats could not creep into the creek unobserved by night; guardhouses on the creek at Shindaghah and other points were manned throughout the night, and the guards would communicate by shouting to the boat's captain (*nūkhaḏā*) to establish the identity of the boat. All other marine facilities were organised by Gray Mackenzie & Co., shipping agents who have been operating in Dubai since 1891.[18] For example, this company put out buoys to mark the entrance of the creek; and before battery-powered lights and fog sirens were introduced, a man was paid to row with his *'abrah* out to a certain buoy, tie up at it and keep a warning lamp alight all night.[19]

Collection of customs duties

Unlike the various pearling taxes which were seasonally collected by someone appointed and employed by the Ruler, the collection of customs duties in Dubai was not done by an official. The Ruler gave a contract to a merchant who agreed to remit a certain yearly sum to the Ruler; the surplus was his earnings. This system of tax-farming of customs dues was predominant in Iran but was also in use in Muscat and several other Arab ports. The flat rate of 2 Annas on each bundle, sack, case or parcel was changed after the Second World War to $3\frac{1}{2}$ per cent on all imports. A special building called locally the *jumruk* was built on the Dubai side of the creek. The Ruler used as his office the first floor of that building which was next to his creek-side summer palace. The last person to have a tax-farming contract was Muḥammad al Mūsa. Then in 1955 the British Bank of the Middle East, which had opened a branch in Dubai in 1946, was appointed to handle the collection of customs due on goods imported by bigger ships with proper documents. The rate was then fixed at 4.625 per cent, of which 0.025 per cent was generally considered to be the bank's fee.[20] *Dhow* trade and overland trade, however, remained under the old system, which was eventually also streamlined in 1955 by a new customs clerk, Muḥammad Mahdi Tājir, who was seconded through the influence of the Political Resident in Bahrain from the Government of Bahrain.

Fresh food was landed close to either of the two markets and carried over the sand if need be. But everything else, from barges as well as from *dhows*, was landed in the vicinity of the office of the Ruler. In 1951 Gray Mackenzie & Co. found it necessary to put a crane there, and the area where boats could come alongside was gradually extended by building up the bank behind with some rock binding.

Warehouses, godowns and asbestos sheds grew up in the restricted area between the Ruler's office and the Indian consulate, the creek and the built-up quarters of Dubai and the Bastakīyah. The merchants were expected to arrange to have their goods removed to their own storage places soon after clearance.

The Second World War and its aftermath

Within this frame of the physical environment and the general conditions of life, the prosperity of the entire community depended largely on the opportunities for trade abroad. The decline of the pearling trade in the 1930s was a blow which triggered off the decline in the prosperity of Dubai. As alternative trade was being built up, there came the interruption of the Second World War. It not only brought much of the previous trade to a standstill and dashed all hopes of enterprising merchants, but also meant near-starvation for many inhabitants of Dubai. Rice and sugar were in acute shortage. The British Government supplied the Trucial Shaikhdoms with food, which was distributed in rationed amounts through the channels of local governments in co-operation with the known headmen of quarters and neighbourhoods. Sugar and tea formed part of this supply, both commodities being in even shorter supply in Iran. In Bahrain, Dubai, Abu Dhabi and other Arab Gulf ports, people who had bought either of these goods cheaply as part of the ration but did not need all of them, sold them to agents who shipped them to the black market of Iran. The British Government in India severely clamped down on these practices and if smugglers' launches were caught the cargo was burnt or confiscated. Sometimes other non-rationed goods were temporarily plentiful in India or Iran and a black market would develop for these goods in the Trucial States ports. Towards the end of the war, even the black market was depleted, and according to local sources some deaths from starvation did occur in Dubai town, where a large part of the population had no access to any locally-produced supplies such as dates or milk.

Dubai, between the 1930s and the mid-1950s, provides a suitable example of how external economic developments and domestic forces may change the stratification within the society of a town in the Trucial States. The group near the bottom of the social ladder during the first two decades of this century, the haulers and divers on the pearling boats, became either unemployed or had to accept any casual job such as helping to offload ships or build up the bank of the creek. In leaving the pearling industry these people also lost the security and legal protection of the conventions which governed that industry; for however harsh some aspects of the system of inherited debts had proved for some divers, they had been part of a strong community with a common interest, and they had always had access to the Diving Court (*sālifah al ghauṣ*) to obtain justice. When Dubai's economy came to rely almost entirely on trade in the later 1930s the same people who once provided the mainstay of the pearling industry were often the very same people who, as porters, were the ones without whom the merchants could not move their goods. This was realised by the leading merchants of the town, and the porters' status, payment and working conditions became one subject of discussion in the short-lived Council which was set up in October 1938 by the so-called reform movement led by the Ruler's cousin Māniʿ bin Rāshid.[21]

Domestic slaves

The status of the slaves owned by merchant families and employed on their pearling boats was being changed too. Dubai's treaty relations with Britain forbade the importation of slaves into the shaikhdom, but did not actually interfere with the internal sale of people whose status was still that of slaves.[22] During the 1930s the British authorities in the Gulf were under pressure from London to clamp down on the illicit trade in slaves, and manumission of slaves who presented themselves to the British Government was being encouraged. Towards the late 1930s nearly fifty slaves from Dubai applied during one year for their manumission, mostly to the Residency Agent in Shārjah.

The reason for the sudden swell of manumissions in 1937/38 was not necessarily due to increased activity in this matter by ʿAbdul Razāq al Razūqi al Maḥmūd, the new Residency Agent, but most likely reflected the steep decline of the prosperity of their masters, some of whom could no longer afford to provision all or any of their pearling boats for the annual dive, let alone to feed and maintain all the members of the household at the same standard as previously enjoyed. In houses where this was no longer easy to do, some slaves decided to try to obtain a manumission certificate and fend for themselves by finding work of their own.

At that time, when some of the merchants even had to sack most of their beduin retainers, they were obviously not keen to lose their slaves, without whom their pearling ventures would be totally destroyed. Thus, the threat that the British Government might impose a general manumission loomed large, and the influential merchants of Dubai together with the Ruler's cousins further criticised the Ruler for not impressing upon the British Government representatives more successfully that Dubai should not be forced to accept general manumission. In the event this issue was not enforced by the British Government until long after the Second World War.

Some wind of change

Some of the Āl Bū Falāsah and other prominent merchants realised that employment had to be provided for the many people who had been thrown out of work by the decline of the pearling industry. When a scheme to deepen the creek to prepare it for the oil companies was first considered, and when the possibility arose of the construction of an airstrip as a result of an air traffic agreement between the Ruler and the British Government,[23] they suggested that the Ruler should insist on the employment of local labour. Already, then, the principle was formulated that foreign companies operating in Dubai were required to recruit and train local people. Initially this applied particularly to the oil company which had made a preliminary agreement with the Ruler on 22 May 1937.

A latent but important influence on life in Dubai was the rapidly increasing frequency of contacts with the world outside the Gulf and outside British India. The landing of civilian and military aircraft, the increase in steamer traffic, but above all the Second World War itself sharpened the awareness of the fact that the way of life in the industrial countries was spreading fast and had become of some relevance even to the traditional society of the Trucial States. The wish to bring modern medicine to the City State was prevalent among the leading families in Dubai some time before the *Majlis* engaged in the process of recruiting a doctor. Modern education was inaugurated during the short life of that *Majlis* in the atmosphere and spirit which arose from the realisation that there were important developments in the world at large, and from the determination that the society of Dubai should not fail to take full advantage of such of these developments as would benefit the City State. Schools were opened in quick succession, and the introduction of the English language was considered desirable from the beginning.

The economic decline of the 1930s and 1940s caused changes

among the wealthier social groupings as well. These changes were not so radical, because they affected only the economic status but left the original Arab tribal social order intact. The "aristocrats" of the City State had been the members of the Āl Bū Falāsah clan and of other Bani Yās subtribes, among whom a fair number had become relatively wealthy from trading in pearls and running pearling boats. Many of them were far wealthier than the Ruler, who did not participate personally in the industry but could use the tax revenue at his discretion either privately or for public purposes. After the decline of the pearling industry many of the pearl merchants, who were habitually reluctant to deal in foodstuffs and textiles—a type of trading they had always left to the Persian traders—found themselves overtaken in personal and family fortunes by the Persian immigrant merchants on the one side and the Ruler himself on the other. But Shaikh Saʿīd bin Maktūm understood, as did the other Rulers on the coast, that the guaranteed annual rents which were paid by Petroleum Concessions Ltd. and the British Government for exploration and landing facilities were his personal income.[24] By the end of the 1930s, he was financially much better off than the rest of his family. This was a source of much friction between him and some of his cousins, which, as can be seen at a later date, led to their repeated attempts at armed rebellion and eventually to their success in combining the many pockets of discontent and resistance against his rule in Dubai into an organised opposition.

The roots of discontent

As has been shown above, the decline of the pearling industry hit the merchants in Dubai particularly hard because, as times grew worse, most of their boats went to sea loaded down with a complex chain of debts. Returns had been phenomenal for some lucky individuals. Therefore the number of people who borrowed money, fitted out a boat and tried their luck grew out of all proportion, while the debts which people were willing to risk also grew every year. When the decline started, a rising premium was demanded for the risk: up to 36 per cent annual interest was taken in 1929. During that same year, 60 boats from Dubai failed to put to sea owing to financial difficulties.[25] Among the merchants who suffered were Muḥammad bin Aḥmad bin Dalmūk, the cousins of the Ruler, Mānīʿ and Ḥashar the sons of Rāshid bin Maktūm, and Saʿīd and Suhail whose father Buṭi had been the previous Ruler.

While they and a great number of other Arab merchants saw their businesses decline or even collapse, the merchants of the town who had long-standing trading connections in Persia and knew how to avoid the Imperial Persian Customs restrictions had something to fall back on. The opportunities for illicit trading with a black market in Persia were probably even greater in the 1930s than before.[26] The goods which were in great demand and being smuggled into Persia by boat as well as camel caravan from Iraq were sugar, tea, all types of cloth, hides and even cement.[27] An important side-effect of the continued economic depression on the Persian side of the Gulf was the mass emigration which became a severe problem by the 1930s. Statistics kept by the police office at Bushire showed that during the seven months from March to the end of October 1934, 6,000 inhabitants of Bushire and the surrounding district left their homes; at least half of them went to Arab ports.[28]

The loading and unloading of *dhows* at Dubai and at most Trucial Coast ports were concealed in creeks and could not be observed by vessels at sea; and the shaikhs did not welcome frequent visits by British naval officers to their ports. The Persian merchants were accustomed to buying the smaller classes of old *būm* made in Kuwait, and the fact that Persian-made *jalibūts* were not easily distinguished from those built on the Arab coast contributed to the impression that most of the smuggling was done on Arab vessels.[29] This widespread misconception was, however, gradually revised.[30] But this does not imply that none of the native merchants of Dubai had any involvement in or trade benefits from the illicit re-export; merely that the nature of the trade precluded them from playing any leading role in it.

The genuine discontent of the Āl Bū Falāsah and the leading members of the Arab community in Dubai during the later 1930s made them hungrily and constantly seek ever more proof that conditions, privileges and customs were in need of reform, and pursue ideas and ideals which would support as well as sanction their movement. Therefore the news that a similar movement in Kuwait was successful in forcing the Ruler in July 1938 to give power to an elected council provided the supporters of the reform movement in Dubai with the necessary additional backbone and confidence to pursue their cause.

Very many of the suggestions which the Āl Bū Falāsah and their supporters put forward would probably never have met with so much adamant opposition from the Ruler if there had not been such a long history of attempts on the part of his cousins to depose him.[31] At the time Shaikh Saʿīd bin Maktūm could only see another cleverly-concealed attempt to grasp the reins of power, whatever the moves of the Āl Bū Falāsah and their supporters. He was supported in this view by the officials of the British Government, who valued the greatly moderating influence Shaikh Saʿīd and his brother had on the Rulers of the other Trucial States during crises, and did not want to see him replaced.

2 The Reform Movement

The new *Majlis*

During the periods of economic growth the different communities living side by side in Dubai rarely begrudged the customary privileges which some groups enjoyed. But during the 1930s smouldering dynastic squabbles within the ruling family combined with general discontent among the Arab element of Dubai's merchants with their reduced wealth and status. The resulting reform movement was more than a palace revolution, it was an attempt to bring into harmony the paternalistic authority structure of the City State with the requirements of a multinational merchant society.

The background of the movement which culminated in the setting up of the advisory *Majlis* with the power to veto decisions of the Ruler was a combination of four factors: the decline of the pearling industry, the comparative prosperity of those residents of Dubai who engaged in illicit trade with Persia, the influx of egalitarian ideas from outside, and a history of disputes and armed incidents between the Ruler and his cousins.[32]

The development came to a head in October 1938, when the town of Dubai became divided into two armed camps: the Dubai side was held by Shaikh Saʿīd and his followers, and the Āl Bū Falāsah were in Dairah. As was common in cases of confrontation between two parties in the Trucial States, other shaikhs came to mediate. Shaikh Shakhbūṭ, Ruler of Abu Dhabi, and the Shaikh of the Bani Qitab helped to arrange a five-day truce between Shaikh Saʿīd and the Āl Bū Falāsah. When the Political Agent of Bahrain, Weightman, arrived in Dubai on 15 October the Ruler's position had weakened, and after lengthy discussions an agreement was signed on 20 October by which a consultative council, the *Majlis*, was set up. The

Ruler was made the President of the *Majlis* of fifteen, whose names were proposed by leading people of the community.

Not unexpectedly, the question of income was a central point in the agreement which the Ruler was forced to accept in October 1938. "The income and the expenditure of the State had to be spent in the name of the State and had to have the approval of the Majlis. An allowance of one-eighth of the total revenue of Dubai was to be allocated to the Ruler."[33] During the short-lived existence of the *Majlis* this clause was not fully implemented in practice, for the *Majlis* had to remind Shaikh Sa'īd several times to pay up for projects and services which the *Majlis* had taken in hand; this implied that he was still physically in control of the purse-strings. Eventually this issue irritated Shaikh Sa'īd to such an extent that he brought about by force the end of this *Majlis* after it had decided on 3 March 1939 to fix the Ruler's income not in terms of a percentage but to allow him only 10,000 Rupees for his personal expenses, including the traditional subsidies he had to give to beduin, retainers and others.

The *Majlis* began to operate in a very practical manner and tackled many day-to-day problems such as regulating the customs service, for which a list of employees with their salaries was drawn up. The amount of the import duty and the way in which it should be collected, and how the revenues would be used for the benefit of the community were discussed and agreed upon. A Council of Merchants was nominated to watch over these affairs and a Municipal Council was set up to initiate and implement improvements for the port facilities, the roads, hygiene, and security of the City State. Three schools were opened while Māni' bin Rāshid was Director of Education.[34]

The correspondence and the minutes of the *Majlis* show that the members did not want to confine their activities to practical reforms but intended to bring about changes in the political and social structures as well. At least some of the members saw that it was welcomed by the merchant community at large if improvements were made in commercial matters such as organising customs, porter and storage services; but over and above that they saw that their mandate carried a responsibility towards all groups and communities within the State, and that to reform certain aspects of government improved the lot of the common man and was therefore a national duty. It was surprising that these latter ambitions were not acceptable to the Ruler, particularly since he had always been a conciliatory man, who had been prepared to abdicate in 1929 if he would have served the interests of his country best by doing so. The very nature of responsible autocratic rule, based on and supported by *sharīʿah* law, as understood by Shaikh Saʿīd bin Maktūm and other shaikhs on the coast, ran contrary to the new concept of a system where ordinary citizens might also carry responsibility for the State and no longer have only advisory roles. In the Ruler's eyes, a good *ḥākim* should not want to disclaim total responsibility for those people who regarded themselves as his subjects.

The great number of earlier incidents of insurrection, and of opposition for the sake of opposing, completely ruined all possibility of genuine co-operation between Shaikh Saʿīd bin Maktūm and most of his cousins and their followers. There was always the suspicion that their good ideas and innovations were intended ultimately to work for their own private benefit. Shaikh Saʿīd bin Maktūm therefore tolerated the new order for only as long as it seemed necessary; he presided over the first few meetings of the *Majlis* and then ignored all appeals to attend the meetings. The *Majlis* made a point of keeping him informed of its decisions; for some time he chose to ignore them and refused to co-operate in implementing them. But he was not patient for long; on 29 March 1939 he had the entire *Majlis* dissolved by ordering a contingent of beduin who were in town for his son's wedding to attack and disperse the members.

The consequences of the existence of the *Majlis*

Although Shaikh Saʿīd bin Maktūm chose not to accept any of the suggestions of the *Majlis*, the efforts of its members during their extremely short term of office were not all lost. In these six months, examples were set of the ways in which the City State could be governed; it was demonstrated that institutions such as a Municipal Council were both necessary and useful; a community spirit, a feeling of pride in and optimism for the well-being of the State was generated; and official, rather than religiously-motivated, concern for the poor became acceptable. The seeds had been sown both in the minds of the leading personalities among the population of Dubai and in the mind of the Ruler, who, consciously or subconsciously, adopted several of these ideas when he improved certain aspects of commerce and life in Dubai in the 1950s.

But Shaikh Saʿīd bin Maktūm never entirely regained his political self-confidence, and after 1939 delegated a lot of the responsibility for domestic affairs of the City State of Dubai to his son, Rāshid. The latter had the reputation of being a good fighter, and on more than one occasion he had swiftly retrieved stolen camels or caught up with runaway bandits. Shaikh Rāshid bin Sa'īd seems to have sympathised with a great many of the reform movement's proposals for the improvement of the State, although he was politically opposed to its leaders. Shaikh Rāshid bin Sa'īd became Ruler in 1958, and when funds became available to improve conditions in the shaikhdom he initiated changes which had much in common with those proposed in 1938.

3 Development of a modern infrastructure in Dubai

First step: improving the creek

At the beginning of the 1950s it became obvious that the activity of Petroleum Development (Trucial Coast), which held the concession to explore for oil in all the Trucial States and Oman, was about to increase substantially. Even if no oil was found, exploration still necessitated the import of large amounts of heavy equipment, of food and other requirements for all the employees of the company.[35] Whichever port on the Trucial Coast offered the best facilities for handling these imports and for accommodating the new services was bound to be able to develop local business in the wake of the activities of the oil company. These opportunities were pointed out to several of the Trucial Rulers, but Shaikh Sa'īd bin Maktūm, together with his son Rāshid, were more ready than the others to take advantage of the developing situation.

Thus the old idea of improving the port facilities was revived. In 1954 a British firm of consultants working in Kuwait, Sir William Halcrow and Partners, was asked to advise on whether and how the silted-up entrance of Dubai creek could be deepened. "Creek Bonds", which the Ruler asked the various merchants to buy, provided the money for a survey to investigate the sea bed. With the help of some British Government officials resident in Kuwait, a loan of half a million pounds sterling was arranged, to pay for an Austrian company, Overseas Ast Co. Ltd., to dredge the creek between the end of 1958 and June 1959. The improved creek offered sheltered anchorage for local craft and coastal steamers up to about 500 tons.

Dubai very quickly gained an advantage over Shārjah, which, due to the activities of the RAF and the Trucial Oman Levies within its territory, had drawn equal with Dubai in volume of trade by about 1950.[36] Imports came largely on steamers which still had to be off-loaded about two miles out at sea, but the barges of the shipping agent, Gray Mackenzie & Co., could now enter the creek at all times and did not have to wait for high tide. Similarly the local craft on which a large part of the merchandise was re-exported to Iran, Pakistan, and India, could enter and leave the creek regardless of the tide.[37]

Improving the town

In 1958 Shaikh Sa'īd bin Maktūm died, and his son Rāshid, who had already been largely responsible for government in Dubai, became the Ruler. Twenty years after the first short-lived attempt, a new Municipal Council was set up in Dubai, and the nucleus of a municipal administration was organised, for which task a qualified clerk was recruited from the Sudan. By 1961 the three sections of this municipality employed 40 staff and 120 labourers, and had a budget of 300,000 Rupees of which 40,000 Rupees were subsidies and 260,000 Rupees were derived from tax revenue. Also in 1958 the nucleus of a police force under the command of a British police officer took over the duties of the Ruler's guards.

The necessity to widen roads and plan the further development of the town led to the engagement of a British firm of architects and town planners, John Harris, to draw up a town plan for Dubai. Shortly afterwards, a survey was started to search for a better supply of water; this survey was paid for by Shaikh Aḥmad bin 'Ali Al Thāni of Qatar, son-in-law of the Ruler of Dubai. The hub of all this activity remained, however, the development of the creek and its wharfs, loading facilities, and warehouses.[38] This development was promoted by the Dubai Port Committee, which counted amongst its members not only the prominent merchants but also bank managers, representatives of consultancy companies, of Gray Mackenzie & Co., and the British Political Agent. Because most of the other development of Dubai was linked to the development of the port, this Dubai Port Committee became the co-ordinating body for many subsequent projects and eventually served as a general advisory committee to the Ruler.

Between 1959 and 1961 the foundation was also laid for a system whereby most community services were undertaken by private companies; this feature helped in later years to make the economic structure of Dubai appear very different from that of the other members of the federation. Many of the services which had become desirable or necessary for the City State were not provided or organised by government or municipality but by private companies. The Dubai Electricity Co. was owned from its inception by a number of local merchants and the Ruler, who was chairman of the board;[39] the majority shareholder in the Dubai State Telephone Company was International Aeradio Ltd., the Ruler held the rest of the shares and was also the chairman of this board. Similar arrangements, whereby the Ruler set up private companies in which he held a sizeable share were made later as the need for other services developed.[40]

Between 1959 and 1961 an airstrip was built with *sabkhah* which was brought from the salt flats along the coast;[41] it could take Dakotas and Herons, and in 1962 Viscounts of Kuwait Airways started a service three times per week. In December 1963 work started on an airport extension, and since the area is low-lying and liable to flooding it was desirable to provide protection and to stabilise the shore line of the inner creek. When approached to consider establishing a weekly VC 10 flight to Dubai, the British Overseas Airways Corporation was reluctant to commit itself because the company thought that there would not be enough demand. An inquiry among the foreign firms operating in Dubai and among the Trucial Oman Scouts showed that there was great interest in such a flight, and the Ruler guaranteed BOAC that a certain number of seats would be occupied from Dubai on each flight. In fact the demand for seats on these flights grew much faster than he had anticipated, and even before the runway was completed in June 1965, other airlines approached the Ruler of Dubai for landing rights.

The other big communications project was the construction of a bridge across the creek to save cars travelling between Dubai and Dairah the long detour around the head of the creek. A study was prepared by a consultant to find the cheapest way to build this bridge at a convenient crossing point. But Dubai's financial commitments were already approaching the limit of what was then considered to be a prudent assessment of the State's ability to pay back the various loans in the foreseeable future. Shaikh Rāshid bin Saʿīd therefore approached his son-in-law, the Ruler of Qatar, to pay for a bridge more expensively designed than had originally been intended. After only one year in construction, the bridge was opened to traffic in May 1963, rising twenty-five feet above mean tide level, thus allowing vessels to pass beneath to the still undeveloped banks of the inner creek.

Both these communications projects, the airport and the bridge, showed clearly that in Dubai infrastructure planning was hardly ever just a response to the immediate needs of the community: it was clearly linked to ambitious ideas about the future development of Dubai. Much of this development seemed to foreign experts to be over-optimistic at the time of conception but in the event the economic situation changed very rapidly during the time it took to implement the projects; the influx of foreign companies, the growth of imports and of turnover realised by businessmen more than justified this daring optimism.

Land management

The economic growth, however, including some large projects, brought in its wake many administrative problems which were tackled by the establishment of new institutions. One of these problems was land management, the resolution of which was fundamental to the further development of the State.

Outside the built-up areas, most land belonged to the Ruler, who could, therefore, to some extent control the price of land by responding to a growing demand for building land by supplying, that is selling, this virgin land outside the town. The greatest demand was for land along the shore of the creek on which merchants constructed houses close to where local craft were unloaded and also loaded with goods for re-export. The creek was deepened by dredging, which proved to be not a costly convenience but was turned to good advantage because the spoil was deposited in a low-lying area nearby to create new building land. The sale of this land paid for the cost of dredging. The value of reclaimed land became an integral part in the assessment of all marine projects; no amount of dredging work seemed too large when the cost of that work was already debited against the expected commercial value of the new building sites. The Ruler personally became the owner of such reclaimed land. Since he also often personally guaranteed loans raised for certain projects, the money he would eventually realise from selling the land was taken into consideration when negotiating such loans.[42]

The need for land management inside the built-up areas was

realised as early as 1959, when a Land Department was set up. It began with the very difficult task of determining the ownership of land within the older built-up tribal quarters. This was particularly important when trading in this land accelerated and more merchants realised the benefits to be derived not only from possessing, as in the past, shops, warehouses and a comfortable family house, but also from investing in land and constructing on it tall buildings with flats and offices to rent. It was equally essential to establish the ownership of property which the municipality had to demolish while widening roads for vehicular traffic. The roads which were constructed were winding and narrow to minimise the costs of demolition and compensation, because at that early stage very little money was available. The Municipality and the Ruler paid some compensation, but wherever possible only half of one compound was expropriated; the other half then rose in value because of the commercial opportunities which easy access by car had brought.[43]

There were no written regulations governing land ownership in Dubai, but the accepted pattern is based on the principle that land outside the built-up areas, and reclaimed land, belongs to the Ruler. Certain areas in the town have also traditionally belonged to the Ruler and his family, and the rest of the built-up land is owned by individuals who either obtained it as a gift from the Ruler or bought it. A lively property market has developed, and citizens of Dubai, Kuwaitis, Bahrainis, Iranians and Indians buy and sell land among one another. Land may also be owned by Europeans provided that they reside in Dubai. Property as an object of speculation and for the purpose of letting may not be owned by foreign individuals nor companies. Foreign companies are expected to take out leases on land and to build offices and houses or else to rent ready-built accommodation.

Much of the land which is owned by the Ruler is managed as an asset of the State; some of it is allocated to public purposes, such as roads, parks and schools. The funds which the Ruler derived from selling or leasing land were used for financing public projects, which were, however, not subject to formal public authorisation. Leases to foreign companies had usually about eight to twelve years' duration; after that period the land and all immovables would revert to the Ruler, but in many instances the leases were extended under the old terms even though the value of the land and the building had risen considerably.

The harbour project, leading to large-scale industrialisation

In about 1964 it became obvious that before very long there would be more sea-borne traffic than could be handled in the creek. The number of local, Iranian, and Pakistani *dhows* entering Dubai Creek was increasing rapidly; ocean-going vessels were calling in ever-increasing numbers and still had to be off-loaded onto barges out at sea; the barges then unloaded in the creek. To add to this growing congestion, industrial enterprises such as McDermott, building off-shore oil platforms, and Oilfield Supplies Co. were also based in the creek. When it became apparent that oil would soon be exported from Fatḥ, Dubai's off-shore field, Halcrows were commissioned in 1965 to undertake a feasibility study for a deep water harbour. The plan chosen was for a harbour to accommodate four ocean-going vessels, which could be expanded to berth nine ships. It was not difficult to arrange for foreign credit, as Dubai's off-shore oil-field was soon to come on stream. The contract for the construction of the four-berth harbour, worth about £9 million, was signed on 6 June 1967, but the start of work was delayed for several months due to the outbreak of the June war.

Meanwhile congestion in the creek became ever more acute as the building boom in both the public and the private sector accelerated; the expansion of the RAF base at Shārjah in 1967 also contributed to the quickening pace of economic growth. Therefore Shaikh Rāshid decided to have the design of the extension to the harbour altered to include fifteen berths; the £23 million Port Rāshid project was officially opened on 5 October 1972.

When people's attention was turned from merely improving facilities at the creek to building a deep water harbour in 1967, the population of Dubai numbered some 59,000.[44] In 1973, when the City State enjoyed the benefits of the new harbour, the population had grown to an estimated 120,000, and by 1981 to well over one quarter of a million, due to immigration from abroad. The rapidly developing infrastructure serving the needs of the local community was progressively overshadowed by the very diverse requirements of the many nationalities who came to Dubai in such large numbers; their different life styles and habits, their requirements for medical services, schools, power and water all had to be met. Within a space of 25 years Dubai was transformed: multi-storey buildings now overshadow the fine wind towers, the old fort has been converted to a museum, and now, within the range of its Portuguese cannon, hotels catering for businessmen from all over the world stand on the other side of the creek. A road tunnel has been driven under the creek, and a second bridge constructed near the inland end of the creek. Spoil from dredging has been used to reclaim land on the seaward side of Dairah for the development along a Corniche road; while on the Dubai side the harbour was eventually extended to 35 berths, and dry docks to rival any in the world were constructed.

Up to the end of 1973 the growth of Dubai as reflected in these ambitious development projects was partly in response to the conditions created by an astute merchant community with a network of foreign contracts. The other part of the growth was, however, the result of a deliberate policy to attract additional business to Dubai. Neither the activities of the oil company nor the income from oil itself actually generated the greater part of the economic growth in Dubai. Since trade is concomitant with communications, all significant development projects up to the end of 1973 were concerned with communications in one form or another. But after the economic upheaval following the 1973 October War and the enormous increase in oil revenues, it was decided to embark on a programme of industrialisation; Dubai's future was not to be based on trade and services alone but also on manufacturing industries.

Dubai's new industrial centre at Jabal 'Ali, 22 miles south-west along the coast, leads the emirate's economic diversification. As with the development of Dubai itself, the Jabal 'Ali project revolves around an imposing harbour with 67 berths for ocean-going vessels. The 'Jebel Ali Free Zone' comprises over 650 industrial and trading enterprises. The most important one is the aluminium-smelter DUBAL, where some 300 thousand tons are produced each year, making it the largest in the Middle East. The waste-heat from DUBAL is used to produce fresh water, originally about one third of Dubai's requirements. This and any other large industrial project depends on the supply of cheap energy: it is supplied by gas from Dubai's fields and the rest comes from Shārjah. The constantly increasing activity in Dubai's two harbours and the growing industrialisation, all of which entails growth in all other economic sectors of the city, in turn necessitate periodic expansion of Dubai airport, which has become a major cargo handling centre and is also home base of Dubai's new airline 'Emirates', founded in 1985.

Since the first modest attempt to improve the entrance of the creek early in the 1950s and thus to influence fortune, successive Rulers of

Dubai have led the development of the City State with single-minded determination, to provide facilities, to encourage existing business, and to attract new business. Shaikh Maktūm bin Rāshid, who succeeded his father in 1990 continues this tradition.

4 The Development of Community Services

Background

A conscious effort to develop the physical environment which went hand in hand with the economic development could not fail to change fundamentally the living conditions of most long-standing residents of Dubai, but more time was required to develop social services. Neither the government of Dubai nor the British Government was financially in a position to do more than initiate health care, epidemic control, and educational projects during the early 1950s.

From the beginning of the 1950s the efforts which were made in Dubai, to create a basis for modern social service organisations, benefited from the fact that the British Government decided to upgrade its representation in the Trucial States and to move the newly created Political Agency to Dubai in 1954. Dubai became the headquarters of the limited development and social services programme which the British Government decided to organise.[45] Before 1956 assistance was given piecemeal to selected projects; the first five-year plan with a budget of £450,000 was drawn up in that year. Selection, planning and supervision of development projects were until 1965 the responsibility of the British Political Agency in Dubai. The example of what was being done for one shaikhdom often aroused the interest of the rest of the Rulers in the Trucial States.

The Development Office of the Trucial States Council was established in 1965 with its headquarters in Dubai, and a number of agricultural, medical and technical experts were provided by the British Ministry of Overseas Development. The presence of a group of foreign specialists stationed in the then small town of Dubai, where few other Europeans resided, gave Dubai an advantage over the other States, as development projects could be discussed informally in the *majlis* and the achievements of the Office could be observed at close quarters. Perhaps this gave some impetus to many projects in Dubai which were initiated with money provided by Shaikh Rāshid bin Saʿīd or donated by the Rulers of Qatar and Kuwait.

Medical facilities

In 1949 an Indian Muslim, Dr Muḥammad Yasin, practising in Dubai, who had been employed by the British Government in India, was succeeded by Colonel D. McCaully, a doctor who had retired from the Indian Army. Dr McCaully was engaged by the British Government to run the first hospital on the Trucial Coast (the Maktūm Hospital, opened in 1950 with 38 beds), built in Dubai for the benefit of the population of all the Trucial States. The cost of the initial building with 38 beds and the cost of a doctor were borne by the British Government; the running costs were shared among all the Rulers of the Trucial States, the biggest share being paid by the Ruler of Dubai.[46] All the Rulers were members of the Āl Maktūm Hospital Committee.[47]

The impact which the development of the health services has had on the quality of life in the City State for almost every one of its residents is illustrated by the fact that before the Second World War a sick person who needed modern medical help had to travel by boat to India, which few inhabitants of Dubai could afford. Now people travel to Dubai from neighbouring countries to obtain treatment in its various hospitals. Yet a large hospital does not provide the full answer to health care among the local and immigrant communities whose health problems were and sometimes still are the result of draughty homes, indigenous pests, and a lack of appreciation of hygiene.

In parallel with the building of hospitals all the other aspects of a modern health service were being attended to. The government of Dubai, the Trucial States Council and international agencies such as the World Health Organisation organised mass vaccination,[48] regular checks on school children, and public health education programmes; the municipality improved on rubbish collection, pest control and food-handling standards in the market and the slaughterhouse; and eventually the new media, radio, television, and newspapers, were used to instil an awareness of the causes and the remedies of ill-health. In the planning of health care facilities in Dubai it was essential to take into consideration the structure of the society and the difference in attitude between the local and the various immigrant communities. Even after the well-equipped Rāshid Hospital was opened,[49] many people still preferred to go to the old-established, centrally-located, smaller Maktūm Hospital or to an outpatient clinic built in the centre of Dubai. During the 1970s neighbourhood clinics were established to relieve congestion in the central facilities and to meet a popular requirement for treatment at clinics among people of the same background and living in the same neighbourhood. Many families even prefer to pay for a visit to a private practitioner,[50] but they often fail to establish a "family doctor" relationship with him because there is a tendency to change from one to another, sometimes merely because of a feeling that the first did not prescribe enough medicine.

In a community of people with such a variety of backgrounds as a Dubai merchant, a beduin from the desert, a Pakistani immigrant, an Egyptian teacher, or a British engineer, the approach to and appreciation of health services are very different indeed. A large section of the population had even to be made to want doctors and hospitals, because old practices, which passed as cures before the arrival of modern medicine, cannot easily be eradicated among either the local or the immigrant communities. In previous times a knowledgeable old woman or the *muṭawwaʿ* was called in to provide their age-old concoctions and charms, to cauterize and to write verses from the Koran on paper inserted in amulets.

The health service is only one example of a number of fields where the provision of modern social services has to be implemented and promoted at several levels: firstly, the provision of adequate buildings, secondly, the establishment of procedures; thirdly, the recruitment of qualified and suitable staff; fourthly and most important, educating the public to appreciate and to use sensibly the facilities which are made available.

Education

In this description of the social development of Dubai from the early 1950s to the end of the City State's predominantly mercantile and pre-industrial phase in the early years of the 1970s, it is not possible to list all the changes which were effected by official bodies and through commercial enterprise. But some details of the development of education are essential to give a good picture of the transformation of Dubai from a predominantly Arab traditional town to a multinational community serving many interests. With the exception of al Aḥmadīyah, the schools which were established in Dairah and Dubai by the *Majlis* of the reform movement in 1938/9 were closed again during the World War for lack of funds, education remaining largely the domain of the *muṭawwa'*, who ran a *kuttāb* where children, boys and girls, learned the Koran by rote and also learnt to read and write.

Modern schooling on the Trucial Coast was first provided with the help of the British government in Shārjah in 1953. From 1954 onwards the government of Kuwait built, equipped and staffed several schools in the six northern Trucial States.[51] The government of Dubai was not inactive, the Ruler even turned his summer palace into a temporary school for the winter months in 1958. The Ruler asked the education authorities in Cairo for more teachers, who came under the control of a United Arab Republic's educational mission which had been established in Shārjah. Dubai's own school-building programme started during the 1960s, and by the time education was handed over to the Federal Ministry of Education of the UAE in 1972, 16 boys' schools and 12 girls' schools had been built and were in use.

It is significant that in the development of education in Dubai emphasis has been given to technical education. A trade school with an initial intake of boys mostly from Shārjah and Dubai opened in Shārjah in 1958[52] and was funded by the British Government. Shaikh Rāshid bin Sa'īd, who foresaw the benefit of a technical education for his young citizens and for the future development of the town, put up the sum of over £30,000 to have a trade school and accommodation built in Dairah under the supervision of the principal of the school in Shārjah. The running costs of the school were shared equally between the Ruler of Dubai and the British Government until March 1967, when all the expenditure became the responsibility of the Trucial States Development Fund. The Dubai Trade School was extended in early 1966 to allow a commercial course to be added to the curriculum,[53] and further additions, with pre-technical courses and two extra post-technical years at secondary school level, brought the entire curriculum to twelve years of education. At the end of 1968 there were 194 students enrolled at the Trade School in Dubai. The accelerating economic development of the City State in the late 1960s already gave a foretaste of the employment opportunities that lay in store for young local people who had gone through a practical education and were willing to apply their knowledge and skills.

Police force

The establishment in 1956 of a police force was a significant step in the process of transforming Dubai into a well-organised State prepared to develop an ever more diversified economy and an increasingly mixed society. Although under the command of a British major until 1975,[54] the policy was to avoid recruiting mercenaries, and only citizens of the Trucial States and the Sultanate of Oman were recruited. The force started with some 80 men and expanded to over one and a half thousand by the time command changed hands in 1975. Initially recruiting presented no problems, as the regular salary was a strong incentive for young men; also the prospect of useful training often rated high on the list of reasons why young men wanted to join the Dubai police. In later years both these points lost their attraction because of better pay in alternative employment and other educational opportunities; the attraction of the police force for certain young men then became rather the pride of working in a growing, well-organised institution providing scope for promotion and for learning specialised skills, and giving a challenge to men who were prepared to take on responsibilities.

5 Analysis of the achievements

To record the City State's achievements in the field of social services merely in figures does not necessarily indicate the real impact they had on the community in Dubai. However impressive the number of hospital beds, schools, fire brigades or police cars may be, the outstanding characteristic of Dubai from about 1955 onwards has been the way that the entire community has coped with the enormous growth of population. Not only during the 1970s, when the rate of growth accelerated beyond all expectation, but throughout this period, many a planned development, once executed, already fell short of the requirement. The magnitude of this problem of planning adequate social services is indicated by the fact that the population of Dubai doubled between 1968 (census: 59,000) and 1974 (estimated 120,000). Planning for such an immense increase is difficult enough in an ethnically, culturally, and economically homogeneous community; but in Dubai the increase, apart from a normal annual rise of 3 per cent in the birth rate, was caused by immigration, and thus was always unbalanced in its composition and its structure. Many of the immigrants, particularly those from nearby countries, came initially to Dubai without their families, and they were not expected to reside permanently in Dubai. Yet, over the years, many of them have stayed and have been joined by their families, coming from Arab and neighbouring Muslim countries, from India, from South East Asia, from Europe, and from the USA. Consequently their demands on the State and on society have changed: no longer do these men live as bachelors in a construction-camp cared for by their employer; they now have their families with them in flats or in villas, and they require the services of a modern State.[55]

Throughout the period of its pre-industrial development, which may be considered to end with the decision to build the tanker dry dock in 1973,[56] the economic tendencies and the social changes which have characterised the period since the turn of the century in the towns of the Trucial States are seen most clearly in Dubai. The impact of the expansion as well as of the decline of the pearling industry was most pronounced in this City State without its own tribal hinterland to fall back on. The early business activities in the area helped Dubai to have a head start over the neighbouring shaikhdoms, and the move of the British Political Agent for the Trucial States to Dubai both directly and indirectly helped it to embark on planning a new economic order, and on setting up social services, which were to be for some time an example to the other shaikhdoms.

The pattern, seen throughout the recent history of Dubai, of maximising all possible means for economic expansion and diversification remains firmly in place. Even while his health was failing, Shaikh Rāshid continued to lay down the guidelines for the emirate's development. His sons Maktūm, Ḥamdān, Muḥammad and Aḥmad each took on specific responsibilities in the 1980s. On 8 October 1990 Shaikh Maktūm became the Ruler of Dubai and Prime Minister of the UAE upon the death of his father. With the help of his brothers, who all have positions in Dubai government, Shaikh Maktūm continues to facilitate the ever increasing role of Dubai as the regional centre for trade, re-exportation, services, exhibitions, conferences, sporting events and latterly also tourism. Shaikh Muḥammad bin Rāshid, who has served as UAE Minister of Defence since the foundation of the federation was confirmed in this position in the new cabinet of November 1990. He was proclaimed Crown Prince in January 1995. Shaikh Ḥamdān bin Rāshid remains Minister of Finance.

Chapter Eight

The External Influences

1 Before the 19th Century

The Portuguese on the Arab coasts

Whereas the conversion to Islam of the entire area was an historical event which over the centuries remained the most important and constant factor forming the society of the UAE from its very roots, there are certain outside influences which were important enough at the time, but which had nevertheless only limited impact on the subsequent course of history in these shaikhdoms, as well as on the people who lived there and on the generations who followed. The arrival of the Portuguese as the first distant power to dominate certain parts of the Gulf and Oman completely transformed the regional power structure from the beginning of the 16th century; but they were expelled from all the Arab and Persian ports by the middle of the 17th century, and they left no religious and hardly any cultural imprint, except for their cannons and the ruined forts of their garrisons. The political consequences of their intrusion were the temporary re-uniting of the tribes of Oman under the Yaʿāribah dynasty, and the building up of an Omani East African colonial empire as they chased the retreating Portuguese to their garrisons at Mombasa, Kilwah, Pemba and elsewhere.

Before the arrival of the Portuguese in the Gulf, wealthy City States developed around favourably-situated harbours on or near the Persian coast such as at Sirāf, Qais and Hormuz. These cities, inhabited mostly by Arab tribes, often under a ruling family of Omani origin, came to dominate the entrepôt trade between India, the Arab countries and Europe, which passed through Mesopotamia or the Red Sea. Usually one such trading empire was built upon the decline of another. The control of the trade often meant that attempts were made also to dominate the population in the distant ports of one's trading partners. It was not just a group of daring Portuguese adventurers who conquered the traditional trade emporia of the Gulf and parts of the Indian Ocean; this was the result of carefully-prepared strategy at the Court in Lisbon aimed at taking over by any means possible every sector of the very profitable trade between the Indian Ocean coasts and Europe.[1]

None of these major trading ports were located in the territory which later became known as the Trucial States. But minor ports on the Arab coast were occupied by the Portuguese from time to time to ensure that Arab trading communities could not set up rivals to their trade emporium. Thus the port at Khaur Fakkān, which at the time was probably paying tribute to the king of Hormuz, was destroyed in the first expedition against the Arab trade in the Gulf in 1506 by Alfonso de Albuquerque.[2]

In 1625, after being defeated near Bandar ʿAbbās by Dutch and English vessels, the Portuguese commander took refuge with the remainder of his vessels at an anchorage on the Arabian coast, probably Khaur Khuwair near Ra's al Khaimah, and established a temporary base there. Khaṣab near the tip of the Musandam Peninsula also served as a Portuguese base at times.[3] The Arab coast, as well as the nearer islands on the Persian coast, was sometimes visited to obtain shipments of water for Hormuz. The Portuguese built a fort at Julfār near Ra's al Khaimah in 1631, when their power was already on the wane and after the key position at Hormuz had been irretrievably lost to a combined Persian and English force. There may have been other minor Portuguese fortifications elsewhere on the coast between Dubai and Khaṣab as well as on the east coast in the vicinity of Khaur Fakkān. The inadequate harbours and few watering places of the Arab coast of the Gulf were not in themselves important to the Portuguese, nor did they figure prominently in the struggle of English and Dutch trading companies to replace the Portuguese. While the latter's attention was focused on the Persian coast the Arab tribes were able to regain control of their ports. But the continuous conflict between the Portuguese and the Dutch, the English and occasionally the Turks[4]—with the Persians trying to promote their sovereignty over important trading places—endangered and at times all but eliminated the trade undertaken by Arab vessels. During this struggle the Imām of Oman, Sulṭān bin Saif, was able to wrest Bahrain from the Persians in 1717 or 1718 and take a number of islands near the Persian coast, including Qishim; but the Omanis soon lost most of these places again to Nādir Shah, who overran and occupied Oman until 1744. Yet the claim of the Omanis—under an Imām or a Sultan—to a dominant position in the area including the Gulf proper during the 18th century had thus been established.

The Qawāsim

Many of the Arab tribes inhabiting the Musandam Peninsula and Sāḥil Oman were so closely linked with the affairs of Oman[5] that the Omani attempt to dominate the Gulf proper by occupying parts of the Persian shores, islands and trading places, had it been more lastingly successful, would have meant almost complete encirclement for the independent tribes and probably total integration of the whole area into the Omani State. However, the Omani successes were followed by setbacks and defeats at the hands not only of the Persians but of the new Arab power which had emerged at the head of the Gulf during the period of general confusion in the Gulf in the 1720s. The Qawāsim,[6] the shaikhs who ruled from their stronghold Ra's al Khaimah over much of the northern coast of the Arab littoral of the Gulf, took possession of Bāsīdu on Qishim Island and established there a centre for trade which seriously affected the customs receipts of Bandar ʿAbbās, where the British East India Company had already established rights granted by Persia. The Qawāsim had a considerable influence on the course of the history of the Gulf during the 19th century. Their frequent clashes with the Omanis and the subsequent involvement of the East India Company had consequences which shaped events even in the 20th century.

The polarisation of Eastern Arabian tribes into Hināwi and Ghāfiri factions

The Civil War in Oman

The Yaʿāribah dynasty, which had successfully combined the tribes of Oman to expel the Portuguese and which had built the Omani maritime empire, collapsed less than a hundred years after its founder, Nāṣir bin Murshid from Rustāq, had been elected Imām in 1624 AD. When the Yaʿāribah Imām Sulṭān II bin Saif died in 1718 AD, his son, who was only twelve years old, became Imām through a pseudo-election which was organised to support the dynastic principle of succession. The election of a minor as Imām antagonised the religious leaders of all tribes as well as the leading members of the other branches of the Ya'āribah clan, and sparked off a competition for an alternative Imām. The most successful of the contenders for the Imāmate was the *tamīmah* of the Bani Ghāfir, Muḥammad bin Nāṣir.

The Bani Ghāfir were supported in this choice by most of the tribes who were, like themselves, of Nizāri (Adnāni) descent: that is, they had come to Oman in about the fourth and fifth centuries AD from central and north-eastern Arabia. The election of Muḥammad bin Nāṣir in 1724 AD was opposed by Khalaf bin Mubārak of the Bani Hina (hence the name Hināwi), who led a confederacy of most of the Yamāni (Qaḥṭāni) tribes, who were the descendants of the first Arab tribal groups to conquer Oman from south-western Arabia, as early as the 9th century BC.[7] Neither Imām was generally recognised, and a fierce competition commenced for the Imāmate and the leadership, which developed into a rebellion against the Ya'āribah dynasty and ended as a full-scale civil war involving all the tribes in Oman, splitting the country into two bitterly opposed camps, labelled Ghāfiri and Hināwi.[8] When the Nizāri tribes had arrived in the 4th century AD they had found the mountain heartland of Oman already occupied by Yamāni tribes, and because of Yamāni opposition they were primarily confined to the fringes of Oman and to the north; this Shamāl (north) province of Oman later became the northern Trucial States. Being of Nizāri descent the majority of the tribes of al Shamāl supported the Ghāfiri camp in this prolonged Civil War in Oman.

When the Hināwi candidate, Imām Saif II bin Sulṭān, had grown to manhood, he resorted in 1737 to the desperate step of calling upon Nādir Shah of Persia for help in the Civil War. The Persian army lost no time, landed in Julfār and Khaur Fakkān and marched on the Buraimi oasis. The current proponent of the Ghāfiri camp, Bil'arab bin Ḥimyar, met the Persian army on his home ground in the Dhāhirah, but was heavily defeated. The Persians did not retire completely after gaining victory for their protégé, but retained Julfār, thus being in an even better position to invade the area and prepare for the total subservience of Oman to Nādir Shah when his assistance was sought once again by Saif bin Sulṭān in 1741.

The Persian occupation was all but complete when the last pocket of desperate resistance formed the rallying point for all the elements in Oman who had become aware of the danger that neither of the contestant parties would emerge from this internal strife as victorious ruler of Oman, but that a third party, and an intruder at that, was about to carry off this prize. The *wāli* of Ṣuḥār, Aḥmad bin Saʿīd of the small Hināwi tribe of the Āl Bū Saʿīd, who chiefly resided in Adam, refused to hand over to the Persians the Ghāfiri contender for the Imāmate, Sulṭān bin Murshid, who had taken refuge at Ṣuḥār. By 1749[9] the coalition of Hināwi tribes of ʿ*ulamā*ʾ from the interior who opposed the Shīʿah Persians, and of merchants from the Bāṭinah coast who dreaded Persian control over their trade, had become a strong enough national movement to evict successfully and permanently the invading Persian army. The Hināwi Aḥmad bin Saʿīd became the Imām, and although his rule did not gain the wholehearted support of all Ghāfiri tribes nor of all the religious men (ʿ*ulamā*ʾ) of the interior, this decision marked the end of this prolonged period of fierce fighting among the tribes of Oman.

The Āl Bū Saʿīd dynasty founded by Aḥmad bin Saʿīd has to this day provided the Rulers of Oman; for some time they have not pretended to base their rule on the principle of the Imāmate but have dropped this title in favour of "Sultan".[10] The Āl Bū Saʿid source of power shifted from the spiritual and the military support which an Imām could muster from the tribesmen, to the reliance on wealth gained from maritime and commercial enterprises with which the ruling Sultan could recruit a mercenary army of Balūch or African soldiers. Aḥmad bin Saʿīd and his successors were therefore neither the "national leaders", which previous strong Imāms have been styled because they could rely on the voluntary support of almost every tribe in eastern Arabia, including al Shamāl; nor were they territorial rulers of the coastal region without any claim to sovereignty over the hinterland. With the change in the means of gaining and retaining sovereignty came a change in the character of the State of Oman. Eventually it had in many ways more in common with States such as Persia, where a regular army had usually been the principal means of exerting sovereignty.

The tribes on the northern and western fringes who had for so many centuries identified themselves with the events of Inner Oman now adopted a more independent attitude, making alliances at their convenience, or being forced to accept the rule of the strongest man in the area.

The Civil War had weakened the central authority in the State, and the Āl Bū Saʿīd Sultans, even at the height of their strength and popularity, could not equal the most popular Imāms, who in their times were leaders of all of Eastern Arabia. The Sultans' State had also become more formalised through having a regular army. The division of the population into Ghāfiri and Hināwi might sooner or later have become a thing of the past once a new Imām was finally in command, but the Civil War had been so violent and prolonged that it had re-kindled the latent struggle between the earlier settlers and the newcomers for predominance throughout Oman. Since the Civil War each tribe has been identified as being either Ghāfiri or Hināwi, and there are only a very few cases of a tribe changing sides.[11]

Until this very day every local tribesman of the UAE, too, knows which faction his tribe belongs to and usually also knows where most of the important tribes between Ra's Musandam and Dhufār stand. On innumerable occasions since the middle of the 18th century the forming of alliances and the outcome of disputes among the tribes of the Trucial States and neighbouring Omani territory have been decisively influenced by the division of the land into the Ghāfiri and the Hināwi groupings. Therefore, in order to understand better many aspects of the history of the Trucial States, it is necessary to include the following catalogue of the tribes on the coast and in its hinterland.

Enumeration of Ghāfiri and Hināwi tribes of the area later called "Trucial Oman"

The Ghāfiri tribes of the area live either in the territory of the "Qāsimi realm" or in the hinterland of the coastal States where it merges with Oman. Like the Qawāsim of Ra's al Khaimah and Shārjah, the inhabitants of Ḥamrīyah and Ḥīrah, of Dibah and Umm al Qaiwain and the Naʿīm of ʿAjmān are all Ghāfiri.[12] The beduin Ṭanaij of D̲aid and the Jiri plain, their neighbours the Mazārīʿ and the Ghafala, the Dhahūriyīn of Ru'ūs al Jibāl (but not their allies, the Shiḥūḥ), the Bidūwāt of the Wādi Ḥattā and the Dahāminah in Ra's al Khaimah territory are all Ghāfiri, making the area north of the creek of Dubai and to the west of the mountains a natural stronghold of the Ghāfirīyah. In Shamailīyah the principal Ghāfiri tribes are the Naqbiyīn, the Kunūd and the Najādāt. In the Buraimi area and in Dhāhirah the Ghāfiri balance was held by the Naʿīm and their relatives the Āl Bū Shāmis, the Bani Kaʿab and the Bani Qitab, the

Bani Kalbān of Dhank and the Bani Kalaib east of Buraimi, together with a few minor tribes of the area and the more remote powerful tribe Durū'.

The Hināwi tribes of the Trucial States, the most prominent of whom are the Bani Yās, live chiefly in Abu Dhabi, Dubai and Shamailīyah. The traditional allies of the Bani Yās are also Hināwi, the 'Awāmir together with the 'Afār and the Manāṣīr. The Dhawāhir of the Buraimi oases and northern Dhāhirah, who declared their loyalty to the Āl Bū Falāḥ leading sub-section of the Bani Yās in the 19th century, are also Hināwi; so are the Bani Ghāfir of Dhāhirah and several other smaller tribes in the same area, such as the Aḥbāb. The important tribe of the Bani 'Ali who traditionally supported the Hināwi Āl Bū Sa'īd Sultan, live in the Wādi Dhank and Yanqul near the Āl Bū Falāḥ-dominated area of al 'Ain. The Balūsh of Dhāhirah have also traditionally supported the Hināwīyah. Outside this strong Hināwi grouping west of the Ḥajar range, there was an important link with tribes in the north, because the Shiḥūḥ, the Ḥabūs and the Za'āb[13] are also Hināwi, but the largest Hināwi tribe apart from the Bani Yās are the Sharqiyīn of Fujairah on the east coast.

Outside the Sultanate of Oman the division between Ghāfiri and Hināwi, although relevant politically, was not associated with the dispute concerning temporal or religious leadership. At times of peace this division was dormant and alliances were made considering only the economic advantage to each party. But in periods of general strife and unrest, an alliance within one's own faction was considered the safer arrangement, in particular because over decades of strife between tribes of the opposing factions, it became inevitable that unresolved cases of blood feud overshadowed any more practical approach to a political alliance.

Wahhābi influence on the area[14]

Another development which shook the foundations of a neighbouring society and could not fail to influence the history of the Trucial States was the religious reform movement in the centre of the Arabian Peninsula led by Muḥammad bin 'Abdul Wahhāb. He was born at the beginning of the 18th century in 'Ayainah in the uplands of Central Arabia. After studying at Medina and travelling to several other centres of Islamic teaching such as Baghdad, Isphahan and Qūm he became very critical of what he considered to be the lax way in which Islam was being practised wherever he went, and he began to formulate his fundamentalist doctrines in his book *Kitāb al Tauḥīd* (the Book of the Unity of God). He spoke of the need to purify the minds of Muslims from polytheistic habits of invoking the help of saints, angels, the dead, and prophets. He attacked all philosophical and legal innovations introduced into Islam after the third century AH, and tried to abolish certain abuses. When Muḥammad ʿAbdul Wahhāb tried to urge his views on the citizens of his native town he was banned from there, but he found refuge and an open ear for his reformist religious ideas and a powerful supporter in Muḥammad bin Saʿūd of nearby Daraʿiyah. Together they convinced the tribes of the area of the new doctrine—or else forced them to accept it in an alliance of the spirit and the sword not unlike in the early days of the expansion of Islam. The movement gained in strength under ʿAbdul ʿAzīz, the son of Muḥammad bin Saʿūd as the "leader of a Beduin Commonwealth", according to Jacob Burckhardt, one of the earliest European observers of this movement.[15]

By the end of the 18th century the Wahhābis had overrun al Ḥasā and reached the Gulf coast, having also taken possession of both Karbalā' and Mecca. There were vigorous and numerous attempts to bring all of Eastern Arabia and particularly Oman under their sovereignty. Many tribes needed little persuasion to become followers of this strict and austere form of practising Islam, which was after all not remote from strict Ibāḍi observance, while other tribes joined in for political reasons, and others soon found that armed resistance was punished severely.

In 1800 Buraimi was seized by a force of 700 cavalry and camel-riders, forcing the Naʿīm and Dhawāhir population to capitulate. The Wahhābis built a new fort in the oasis, which served as a vantage point from which to make inroads deep into Oman.[16] An obvious means of gaining sovereignty over Oman was to form an alliance with the Qawāsim, who were the traditional rivals of the Omani Sultans and merchants. In due course, the Qawāsim became staunch allies of the Wahhābis, but they did not consider themselves to be completely under the rule of the Amīr at Daraʿiyah to whom they paid *zakah*, since they did not remit the customary one-fifth of the value of booty. Partly due to this support by the Qawāsim, the Wahhābis established supremacy over the whole Arabian coast of the Gulf by 1803, and continued to try to conquer all of Oman. After the severe but temporary set-backs to Wahhābi domination by the victorious campaign of Muḥammad ʿAli (the Viceroy of Egypt from 1812), the death of the Amīr 'Abdul 'Azīz and the fall of the capital Dara'iyah in 1818, the Wahhābi forces under the new leader Turki bin 'Abdullah regained the whole empire, including the Gulf coast. The same sequence of defeat and victory followed again between 1835 and 1840, when the Egyptian forces once more occupied al Ḥasā and Najd.[17] The Wahhābi movement then entered a phase of spiritual consolidation, having lost much of its militant zeal, and direct Wahhābi influence over the seaboard tribes of the Gulf was also restricted by the activities of the British.

2 Qawāsim, Oman and Great Britain at the beginning of the 19th Century

Early English trading interests in the Gulf

The English traders were at first interested only in the Persian coast of the Gulf, in the same way as the Portuguese and the Dutch before them.

The initial foothold in the Gulf was gained by traders who were partners of the British East India Company.[18] Having obtained the lease for the establishment of a factory[19] at Surat in India in 1613, the manager found that the market there could not absorb the quantities of cloth which had been ordered from England. Persia seemed the most promising alternative market, and eventually Shah 'Abbās, who was at the time at war with Turkey and was trying to expel the Portuguese (then under Spanish domination) from the ports of his empire, sought the help of the highest bidder among the European nations interested in the trade in silk and other goods. Expecting that the English would help him to achieve his objective he gave permission to the representative of the company to establish a factory at the fort of Jāshk in 1616.

It was soon realised in London that competition for such privileges was acute, with the Spanish and the Dutch still waiting in the wings. If the Government in London was expecting to reap benefits from English trade in the East it had to give official, royal, and prompt support to the pioneers who promoted this trade. If the Shah was to be requested to grant lasting monopolies to the English traders, correspondence with King James was a prerequisite. The privileges which were eventually granted to English traders in a *firmān* of 1617 confirming the concession at Jāshk thus already signalled the political character of such agreements. It provided for the residence of an English ambassador at the Persian court at Isphahan, spelled out the jurisdiction of the latter over English subjects, and the conditions under which disputes with a Persian subject came under Persian jurisdiction. It also mentioned the right of the English to practise their religion.

Thus from the very beginning the promotion and the protection of the English trading interests in the Gulf inevitably involved the Crown. Not only was the Crown a party to the negotiations with the local potentates but also it inevitably became involved militarily. This first happened when in 1621/2 the Persian army required the assistance of the naval force of the East India Company at Surat to expel the Portuguese from Hormuz.[20] During subsequent decades the Indian subcontinent proved itself to be the far more rewarding target for commercial enterprise, while the unstable relations with Persia never allowed complete British domination of its markets. The East India Company's governing body developed into the Government of India, ruling from Bombay with full powers conferred on it by the Crown. But just as English commercial enterprise in India could not be successful, nor even survive for long, without political support from London, it also required military might to protect both the trade in neighbouring regions and the shipping to and from India. By the end of the 18th century the British in India had become a regional power, and as such were involved in various economic, political, and military interactions with other regional powers including the Persians and the Arabs. Britain was also locked in power struggles in Europe notably with revolutionary and Napoléonic France which led to the British endeavours to exclude such powers from Oman and the Gulf.

Initial contacts with the Arabs of the southern shores of the Gulf also began through the medium of trade. In about 1720 the Ruler of Ra's al Khaimah seized Bāsīdu on the island of Qishim and established a trading centre there. This new entrepôt port seriously affected the customs receipts which were previously shared between the English and the Persians. In 1727 the East India Company's agent at Bandar ʿAbbās led a naval expedition in company ships and recovered the share of the customs dues which were estimated to belong to the Company.

Qawāsim clashes with English shipping

Decline of Qāsimi trade

By the end of the 18th century the Qawāsim had lost much of the trade and the political influence which they had built up in previous decades in spite of the opposition of the rulers of the Persian coast and in spite of the fact that Oman not only claimed sovereignty over the Qawāsim but had also tried to expand its own possessions within the Gulf proper. Partly due to the decline of the central power in Persia, the struggle for supremacy in the Gulf reverted after about 1778 to inter-Arab warfare, during the course of which trade as well as pearling suffered considerably, particularly for the Qawāsim. Having a much narrower economic base than their Omani enemies, they relied more and more on the supplies which they captured from Omani trading vessels passing through the Gulf to and from Basra. With their forts on either side of the narrow entrance to the Gulf, the Qawāsim were able to intercept vessels and retreat to the safety of numerous *khaurs* and lagoons of the shallow coasts which were known only to them. Eventually this behaviour, while still attempting to regain their lost trade through wars against the Omanis, led the Qawāsim to attack and capture even ships flying British colours.[21]

It has been alleged that the influence which the Wahhābis exerted over the Qawāsim instilled in them the religious fervour of the new puritanical Muslim movement, giving them a licence not only to convert by force to the Wahhābi persuasion but also to kill fellow Muslims who resisted, and in the Gulf to attack and plunder British Indian ships. However, the explanation of the extraordinarily daring and also often cruel attacks on ships flying British flags[22] is probably more complex than that, as the Wahhābis did not influence the Qawāsim to such a great extent.

Although the authorities in Bombay probably thought otherwise, the status of British merchant ships and naval vessels in the Gulf had long since ceased to be that of uninvolved passers-by. Their very presence caused resentment among the littoral powers; yet they were welcome in the area to the people who could do good business with them or could induce them to give support in time of war. But their presence was resented even more because they were Christian; they represented the quasi-local power of British India and the foreign power of distant Great Britain. Their superior ships and armaments, their strange language, and their foreign habits all helped to antagonize the Arab and Persian Muslims of the Gulf. Ships in the Gulf flying the British flag were usually commanded by captains born in the British Isles, while most of the crew were people from the Indian subcontinent. If these British Indian subjects were Hindus or Buddhists they were nevertheless rivals or enemies even though they were protected by the British flag; if they were Muslims, some of the Arab crews felt justified in giving them the choice of conversion to Wahhābism or punishment.

The memory of the Portuguese conquests

A factor which has to be taken into consideration when discussing the acts of piracy committed by tribesmen on the Arab coast against British shipping, is the longevity of memories among the population. The first Christian power which came to the area behaved in an unnecessarily cruel fashion towards anyone who opposed it in its bid to take over the eastern trade. The path of Albuquerque and the Portuguese commanders who succeeded him is stained with the blood of many thousands of Arabs. If a coastal settlement did not hand over the harbour, shipping, and fortifications at once, the entire population risked being put to death or mutilated.

In contrast to this, traditional Arab warfare was rarely carried to such extremes; the losing side could admit defeat and a peace was usually arranged before the victorious side had time to annihilate its adversaries. In general the Arab's concept of war was of a contest of man against man. The civilian population was not considered to be a target in an honourable war between tribesmen; they suffered only to the extent that they were considered to be part of the belongings of the defeated enemy. Thus women and children were as a rule never harmed in a military encounter, but they were sometimes carried off together with the domestic animals and household goods as booty.

The memory of the indiscriminate killing of women, children and the old, and the mutilations inflicted on their prisoners, by the Portuguese[23], became engraved in the minds of Arabs living anywhere between the Red Sea and the Persian coast, and were remembered as the deeds of Christians. There was usually little understanding of the differences between one European power and another, particularly among the people on the Arab coast where there had not been an established trading post. They could hardly be expected to be aware of the profound differences in behaviour arising out of the development of Humanism and Protestant ethics. In their eyes there was no guarantee that English merchants in pursuit of trade on the Persian shores would not kill and plunder indiscriminately on the Arab shore if they had a chance.

Qawāsim resentment of British-Muscati rapprochement

Such deep-rooted resentments against a Christian and European presence in the Gulf were enhanced by the practical consideration on the part of the Qawāsim Rulers that whoever helped their enemies had to be considered as an enemy himself. The rivalry between the Qawāsim-dominated tribes and the Omanis under the Āl Bū Sa'īd rule became acute by the end of the 18th century, and so the growing co-ordination of policies between the authorities in Muscat and Bombay was a cause of anxiety for the Qawāsim.

Muscat was the most flourishing entrepôt port of the entire area by the end of the 18th century because most traders from the gulf called there to take on water and provisions or to trans-ship their cargoes to square-rigged vessels for transport to India or elsewhere. The larger and slower vessels did not dare to make the long voyage within the Gulf to and from Basra and Bushire. Thus for example the entire trade in coffee between Yemen and Iraq was trans-shipped at Muscat.

Apart from desiring a share in this profitable trade for the British merchants in India, the British Government needed a sympathetic ally who could be relied upon to oppose the interests of Napoléonic France. To this end the Sultan of Muscat and Oman signed an agreement for political and commercial co-operation with Britain in 1798.[24] The British expedition to punish piratical attacks by the Qawāsim on British vessels which culminated in the destruction in 1819 of the entire Qāsimi fleet was a triumph for Omani merchants, who could once again expand their trade in the Gulf unopposed.[25]

The implications of the 1820 treaty

The objectives of the British authorities

Even before the British naval expedition of 1819/20 there was a considerable controversy among those who prepared it in Bombay as to the military and political objectives of the expedition, particularly with regard to the question of who was to enforce and police a maritime peace agreement.[26] It was, however, laid down by the Governor-General, Francis Rawdon, (later first Marquis of Hastings) firstly, that a permanent military establishment in the Gulf was undesirable unless the cost of the upkeep could be recovered from the Omanis or from other local sources and secondly, interference in the internal affairs of the Arab States was to be avoided at all cost. Yet at the same time both the authorities in Bombay, in particular the new Governor, the Hon. Mountstuart Elphinstone, and the Commander of the expedition, Sir William Grant Keir, displayed enough of the spirit of a great power to insist on their right to search the entire Gulf, the Arab as well as the Persian shores, for piratical hideouts;[27] and they insisted on the right to recognise, depose, or replace any of the Rulers of the maritime Arab tribes as they saw fit. Thus the outcome of the expeditions of 1819/20 and indeed of the policy of the following years was not one of straightforward retribution and punishment of those who had attacked British shipping but one of preparing the ground for seeking and retaining influence over the tribes by a show of force as well as demonstrating sympathetic leniency and offering co-operation and friendship.

As the British forces made contact with one shaikhdom after another, preliminary agreements were made with each Ruler. The content of these agreements varied from case to case, but all served the general objective of securing the surrender of vessels, fortified towers, guns and British Indian prisoners, while the tribes were at the same time assured that pearling and fishing vessels would be restored to them. Such an agreement was signed on 6 January 1820 by Sulṭān bin Ṣaqr, Ruler of Shārjah since 1803.[28] He signed also on behalf of ʿAjmān and Umm al Qaiwain. On the 8th, Ḥasan bin Raḥmah signed a preliminary agreement by which he also renounced his rule over Ra's al Khaimah town, which became the British garrison, while he remained Ruler of Khatt and Falaiyah at some distance from the coast. The Hināwi Rulers of Dubai (on whose behalf the Hināwi Sultan of Muscat intervened) and of Abu Dhabi signed preliminary agreements, as did the Rulers of Bahrain, where some Qawāsim had frequently found a market for plundered goods.

The agreement of 1820 between the Government of Bombay and the various shaikhs of the Arab coast was therefore not a document in which defeat was ratified as a basis for the future relationship between the British interests in the Gulf and the Arabs; but its aim was to minimise possible conflicts of interest between the two parties. Fortunately the interests of the tribes were considered in its formulation, and so it also did not disillusion those among the Rulers who were trying to exert their independence from the Qāsimi overlord.[29]

These Rulers had hoped that, with the assistance of the British, an end could be brought to the constant disturbance to trading and pearling which had embroiled most ports of the Gulf and Oman in an inescapable sequence of strike and counterstrike which were usually *ad hoc* piratical attacks on the current enemy. The treaty outlawed as piracy violence on the high seas without a formal declaration of war (articles 1 and 2). This promised a welcome breathing-space for the hard-pressed tribes in the Gulf who had not enriched themselves by attacking merchant vessels but who had been attacked themselves. They in turn, either to save face or to try to recoup their losses, had themselves turned on their attackers or had chosen an easier target. The provisions of articles 3 to 6 were an attempt to enforce the treaty by obliging the captains to identify themselves as coming from one of the ports whose Rulers had signed the treaty. Each Ruler had a different flag which his captains were required to fly, all were to use a combination of red and white; they had to keep a log-book to show where the ship was registered, the nature of its business and the nationality of the crew; and they had to hold a clearance certificate signed by the Ruler. Article 7 stressed again the condemnation of piratical activities among themselves and called on the "friendly Arabs" to take counter-measures, and it vaguely promised what could be interpreted as a British obligation to police the Gulf.[30] As well as a more detailed description of the acts which were to be considered outlawed, such as carrying slaves from the East African coast,[31] the treaty also contained an incentive to improve relations with the British by stating that "the vessels of the friendly Arabs . . shall enter into all British ports . . ."

The treaty was signed in January 1820 by nine Rulers, including those who had first signed preliminary agreements: Ḥasan bin Raḥmah signed on the 8th at Ra's al Khaimah, as did Qaḍīb bin Aḥmad of Jazīrah al Ḥamrā' two days later; Shakhbūṭ bin Ḏiyāb of Abu Dhabi signed on behalf of his son Ṭaḥnūn on the 11th; Ḥusain bin ʿAli of Rams signed on the 15th. They all came to Ra's al Khaimah for the occasion, but the uncle of Muḥammad bin Hazzāʿ of Dubai signed on the 28th at Shārjah and the ruling shaikhs of Bahrain of their own accord sent a representative to Shārjah who signed on the

5th of February; the Rulers of ʿAjmān and Umm al Qaiwain went aboard ship to sign on the 15th of March when Keir was already on his way to the Persian coast. The Shaikh of Rams soon lost the support of most of his people, and he and the Shaikh of Jazīrah al Ḥamrā' were later deposed by the British authorities, and Sulṭān bin Ṣaqr was eventually recognised as the Ruler over all the ports of the Qawāsim, which did not include ʿAjmān nor Umm al Qaiwain. Sayyid Saʿīd of Oman, although benefiting most from the downfall of the Qawāsim, did not participate in the drafting of the treaty, nor did he stay in Ra's al Khaimah for long enough to witness its signatures.

Impact of the treaty on the relationships between Arab Rulers

The general treaty laid down the foundation for a new type of relationship between the British Indian Empire and the Arabs of the lower Gulf. This treaty was only one of many which the authorities in India concluded over the generations with tribal societies on the fringes of the empire.

More significant is that this treaty began to change the relationship among the littoral Arab Rulers themselves: they had now made a truce with each other through making a truce with the British authorities. It was expected by both parties that the British would police the Gulf to prevent violation of the treaty. This was, however, not very effective because the British authorities lacked the means to patrol constantly in the Gulf. They also avoided the resentments which close observation would inevitably have created among the Arabs of the Gulf. As it was the Arab Rulers became accustomed to the idea that there was a British "fire-brigade" which any one of them could call in if a settlement could not be reached by diplomacy or by war. It therefore needed little effort on the part of the British authorities to persuade the Rulers to depend more and more on the outside guarantor in the subsequent treaties of 1835 and 1853. For the small price of maintaining five cruisers at Bushire, which gave the impression that prompt diplomatic and naval action was forthcoming if the treaties were violated, the British authorities eventually gained a position from which they could shape politics on these shores if they so wished, under the pretext of any of the wide range of issues covered by the treaties.

Practicalities of peace-keeping

The General Treaty of Peace of 1820 was important not so much because it was an attempt to bring about complete peace, for in this it failed, but as a precedent for further treaties in which the British, as an alien power, were able to assume the role of catalyst for neutralising the regional rivalries. The British authorities in India were not well prepared for this role of mediator in the Gulf: even after the naval force had left for the Gulf in 1819 to subdue the Qawāsim, few of those in authority in Bombay had given much thought to the problem of what should come after a military victory, and how the adherence to the terms of the treaty, which formed part of the instructions for Keir, could be brought about. The early involvement of the Government in Bombay in the affairs of the Arab coast therefore was not the result of neatly planned strategy, but the consequence of the need to respond to violations of the treaty and to enforce in particular the clauses about registration of Arab vessels.

The first step towards political intercourse between the littoral shaikhdoms and British India (as opposed to a superior military force held in awe by the defeated tribes) was the visit of the Resident in Bushire, Lieutenant J. McLeod to all the signatories of the treaty during 1823 to conciliate them. He explained that the role of the small naval force in the Gulf after the evacuation of Qishim[32] was to search the ports for hidden warlike vessels and to arrange for the registration of merchant vessels. The marine survey, which took in 1822/23 a hitherto unsurveyed passage between Shārjah and Doha, symbolised the Arab coast's transition from independence to becoming the minor ally and dependent of the colonial power in India. Sometime between 1823 and 1825 the Government of Bombay appointed a Native Agent to reside in Shārjah and to represent British interests, in the same way as such Native Agents were appointed elsewhere on the fringes of the empire.

During the decades which followed the conclusion of the General Treaty minor incidents of piracy still occurred, which were comparable to the desert raids (*ghazū*) of tribes at war with each other; they were not, as before, expeditions organised purely for material gain, and outright warfare between the Qawāsim and the Omanis decreased markedly. The more the British influence over the Trucial Rulers and the Sultan in Muscat grew, the more the former became extricated from the Omani scene. After 1820 the Qawāsim had to opt out of the struggle for supremacy in the Gulf because of the loss of their powerful fleet. Under Sulṭān bin Ṣaqr, re-established in 1820 as Ruler of Ra's al Khaimah as well as Shārjah, the Qawāsim set out to make the most of the new situation in which the more peaceful atmosphere in the Gulf encouraged a revival in trade. Pearling was on the increase everywhere in the Gulf and soon became the primary source of income for all the tribal settlements on the coast.

Culmination of the maritime peace policy in 1853

As the pearling industry flourished, new types of disputes between the subscribers to the treaty became more prominent, such as disputes over absconding debtors. Eventually the shaikhdoms of the southern coast of the Gulf became so preoccupied with these disputes that they all but ceased to play a significant role in the regional power struggles.[33] This inward-looking preoccupation with the purely domestic Trucial Coast scene and its pearl banks was further enhanced by the first Maritime Truce of 1835, an agreement between the British authorities and the Rulers of Shārjah, Dubai, ʿAjmān and Abu Dhabi. The truce was for one pearling season, banning all hostilities at sea between 21 May and 21 November. Similar treaties, initially covering a few months and later the entire year, were concluded annually thereafter. In June 1843 a truce was signed for a ten-year period; the prospect of undisturbed pearl fishing year after year did much to stabilise relations between the Qawāsim and the Bani Yās, who as the leading proponents of the Ghāfiri and the Hināwi factions had carried out a series of raids on land and had declared war against one another at sea. At the end of this period the Government of India supported the proposal of the Political Resident in Bushire, Captain A.B. Kemball, to make a permanent truce. All the Rulers appear to have agreed spontaneously to this, and they signed the Perpetual Treaty of Peace between 4 and 9 May 1853.

3 Growing British military and political involvement

Anti-slavery treaties

The British Government of India, once so reluctant to commit itself to binding responsibilities in the Gulf, itself generated during the course of the 19th century a number of issues which required a more comprehensive system of British political and military involvement in the affairs of the littoral states of the Gulf. The first such issue, which had nothing to do with the original aim of preventing disturbances to trade and communications, was the slave trade.

Capturing, transporting, selling and owning slaves had been as profitable an enterprise for many British individuals as it had been for other Europeans and for Arabs, Turks and Africans. But during the 18th century the growing moral indignation, fanned by reports of the terrible sufferings endured particularly by the people captured and transported to the American continent, led to the outlawing of slavery in the British Isles. Against many vested interests, the legal campaigning proceeded until in 1838 proprietary rights in slaves were abolished throughout the British dominions. The Government of India, too, had to support the anti-slavery cause, and tried to persuade the rulers of the littoral States of the Indian Ocean and the Gulf to abandon slavery voluntarily.[34] In Arabia the Africans contributed a necessary source of labour. When slavery was outlawed, the consequences were not only felt by the entrepreneurs who had profited from transporting slaves on their ships and selling them at an Arab port, but were also obvious in the fast decline of agricultural output in Oman, where the area under irrigation and cultivation was reduced considerably during the 19th century partly because of the growing labour shortage.

The age-old institution of slavery is treated as a fact of life in the Koran; it does not advocate it and it does not outlaw it. But people in Arabia were aware of the need for a Muslim to observe many rules in his relationship with a slave, and it was considered a deed worthy of merit to free a slave or to assist him to buy his freedom. It was therefore not too difficult for the British authorities to obtain support, if not enthusiasm, for their anti-slavery regulations.

The earliest example of an attempt on the part of the British to curb slavery, Article 9 of the General Treaty of 1820, did not, however, spur the Government of India into action against violators of the article. But soon afterwards, in 1822, a treaty was concluded with Sultan Saʿīd of Muscat,[35] which forbade the selling of slaves to Christian nations. The Government of India intended to enforce this treaty and they obtained the agreement of the Sultan to place an agent on the East African coast who could monitor the adherence of Omani shipowners to the treaty. The authorities in India continued to concentrate their anti-slavery efforts on Oman,[36] concluding several further agreements, and tried also to persuade the other littoral States of the Gulf to sign similar agreements.

In 1838/39 the Trucial Rulers conceded to British Government vessels the right to detain and search at sea ships from their ports which were suspected to be carrying slaves. An agreement which all the rulers signed in 1847 made it illegal for any vessel belonging to the territory of a signatory to export slaves from any place whatever; detention on suspicion and confiscation of the vessel in case of guilt were also agreed upon. In 1856 the Rulers also promised to seize and deliver up to the British authorities in the Gulf any slaves which were brought into their territories.[37] The previous undertakings concerning this issue were reiterated and reinforced in an agreement signed by the Rulers of Shārjah and Abu Dhabi in 1873.

The littoral shaikhdoms under British eyes

These agreements concerning slavery and other agreements which were concluded after the Perpetual Treaty of Peace in 1853 all demonstrate that the British authorities found it increasingly advantageous to be able to compel the Rulers of the littoral States to comply with their wishes. The British also became more interested in the internal affairs of the coastal shaikhdoms, and did not hesitate to intervene if they felt it was necessary. The Native Agent in Shārjah,[38] who acted on instructions from the Political Resident in Bushire, was expected to report all important incidents and developments on the coast, whether they affected the treaties and agreements, or British interests. A new Ruler was always closely scrutinised to determine whether he was likely to adhere to the treaties; only at the turn of the century, however, was a system introduced whereby a new Ruler received formal recognition by the British Government in India by being sent a copy of the treaties which previous Rulers in that shaikhdom had signed. If a Ruler incurred the displeasure of the British Government by harbouring pirates or slavers in his ports or by building up his defences when he had agreed not to, he ran a serious risk of fines, or of bombardment by a British cruiser, although this was usually resorted to only after warnings and negotiations had brought about no change in attitude. Usually the inhabitants of the port backed their shaikh in his defiance of the British Government, but there were also occasions when Rulers lost popular support because the pearling communities just wanted to get on with their work. Thus an atmosphere was slowly created in which both the Rulers and the tribal population of the Trucial Coast were conscious of the degree of British support or displeasure with regard to any political event.

In later decades this distant British presence stifled the possible incorporation of smaller principalities into one or two powerful tribal confederations dominated for example by the Bani Yās or the Qawāsim. The inevitable British preoccupation with the maritime Rulers affected the natural balance between the tribal powers on the coast and those in the hinterland. Because the affairs of the Buraimi area, the Ḥajar mountains, and Inner Oman came to the attention of the British authorities usually by hearsay through the Agent in Shārjah and the representative in Muscat, they were generally considered to be of little consequence. Eventually this attitude also became locally adopted to the extent that both parties to the treaties, concluded at the end of the 19th century and during the first decades of the 20th century, easily kept up the pretence that a coastal Ruler had authority over all the territory that lay between his coastal stronghold and the land considered to be under the sovereignty of the next coastal Ruler, or even of the Sultan in Muscat. Thus it was as much due to the deliberate British strengthening of the coastal rulers as to the pull of the growing economic opportunities which the Gulf's pearling banks offered to the pastoral tribes of Eastern Arabia, that the traditional power struggle between nomadic and settled Arabs was decided in favour of the coastal settlements.

British-inspired agreement concerning absconding debtors

Much as the British Government benefited politically from the various agreements of the 19th century, which allowed in later decades the imposition of political restrictions, the shaikhdoms on the coast also benefited substantially in economic and human terms, mainly because the increasingly important pearling industry could continue to grow and flourish with a minimum of disturbance. Such disturbances as there were almost always stemmed from the fleeing of debtors from one principality to another, where they were afforded asylum and could resume their work. Each Ruler wanted to have as many pearl merchants and pearling crews under his jurisdiction as possible, and, not being averse to turning to their own advantage the tribal customs of affording hospitality and refuge, they did not relish the idea of having to give up this conduct. But the disputes over runaway debtors became so numerous, adversely affecting every shaikhdom in turn, that the British Political Resident in Bushire, at that time Colonel Pelly, was eventually able to persuade the Rulers to sign an agreement for the mutual surrender of fraudulently absconding debtors.

This agreement, which was signed by the Rulers of Shārjah, Ra's al Khaimah, 'Ajmān, Umm al Qaiwain and Abu Dhabi in 1879, can be seen as another significant step towards moulding the shaikhdoms on the Arab coast of the lower Gulf into one political frame which separated them from the other littoral shaikhdoms, Bahrain, Qatar and Kuwait. The agreement provided for an arbitration council to be convened on behalf of the Trucial Rulers to hear cases concerning disputes over debts. The agreement also demonstrates that for the sake of peace and economic prosperity the shaikhdoms had accepted a considerable measure of British tutelage. Not only did the agreement stipulate the imposition of fines, 50 dollars to be paid by a Ruler who did not deliver up a runaway debtor, and 100 dollars if a Ruler allowed such a person to proceed to the pearl banks or take up his business in the shaikhdom,[39] but it also established the British Government's authority in this matter of debtors, although this was understood at the time to be only the function of an arbiter: "These fines are only to be enforced when Her Britannic Majesty's Resident in the Persian Gulf has satisfied himself that the Chief complained against is really in fault and fairly liable."[40]

Intervention in internal matters

Even after the agreement was signed, many a dispute arose over debtors between the shaikhdoms of the coast. The above-quoted clause obliged the Resident in Bushire to keep a closer watch on affairs in the shaikhdoms all the time. It also furnished a good pretext for intervention if a Ruler seemed to be preparing to break out of the British-enforced peace arrangements.

In practice, control was exercised by the Residency Agent living in Shārjah. He communicated with the Rulers on many day-to-day matters, sent reports back to Bushire and received instructions on how to handle each particular problem. In important matters the Resident in Bushire addressed a letter to the shaikh himself, but such direct correspondence was also routed through the Agency at Shārjah. Whenever there was any sign of disturbance of the peace at sea, and in later years even if there was a strictly internal dispute, such as over succession, the Resident or his deputy used to come in the Residency cruiser, styled "man-of-war", to the troubled shaikhdom; he stood off on the roadstead and sent word that the culprit or the disputants should come aboard.

On many occasions when an infringement of an agreement was

proved, the Resident made the Ruler pay compensation to the aggrieved party and he might threaten to levy a fine. In some instances a fine was even collected from the Ruler there and then, but usually only a first instalment was required immediately, the rest being waived for subsequent good conduct. In extreme cases of what was termed "insubordination", such as when a shaikhdom built up its fortifications and threatened war with its neighbours, the cruiser's cannon would after several warnings bombard fortifications, watchtowers and even the town. In later decades, when the growing trade in pearls attracted an increasing number of merchants from the Indian subcontinent, many of whom settled in a town on the Trucial Coast, the protection of these British Indian lives and their property became one of the most frequent pretexts for intervention.[41]

4 Political benefits of the British influence

Although the British Government of India had established a strong hold over the Trucial Coast[42] primarily to rid British shipping from danger in the Gulf, this turned out to be very much to the advantage of the British towards the end of the 19th century, when the empire at its zenith was threatened by France and Russia agreeing to curb British influence in the Gulf. While France tried to wrest the Arab States from British influence, Russia concentrated mainly on Persia. As previously in Napoléonic times, Oman was again the object of an Anglo/French diplomatic race for influence and the British experienced several set-backs.[43] Not so with the Trucial States, where hardly a foreigner who was not a British subject had set foot ashore.[44] The Rulers were easily persuaded to sign an agreement similar to the one which was signed by Sultan Turki bin Faiṣal in Muscat in 1891. In this treaty, which was signed by the Rulers of Abu Dhabi, Dubai, ʿAjmān, Shārjah, Ra's al Khaimah and Umm al Qaiwain between 6 and 8 March 1892, they agreed on behalf of themselves and their heirs and successors "not to enter into any agreement or correspondence with any Power other than the British Government". They bound themselves not to let a representative of another government reside in their territory and on no account to "cede, sell, mortgage or otherwise give for occupation any part of [their] territory except to the British Government".[45] These agreements were ratified by the Viceroy of India and subsequently approved by Her Majesty's Government in London.

This so called Exclusive Agreement integrated the Trucial States into the screen of semi-independent States and principalities which was created right across the British Indian Empire's northern frontiers and western seaboards and along its vital communication lines with Europe. It was designed to impede the progress into any of these areas of the rival powers France, Russia, and the German-Turkish alliance of interests.[46] For the shaikhdoms in the Gulf this agreement made it virtually impossible to conduct their own affairs with outside powers or even with their Arab neighbours, such as the Wahhābi State, without the close scrutiny of the British authorities. Thus the British Government secured enough exclusive influence and practical political leverage over these shaikhdoms without formally making them protectorates.[47] During the first decades of the 20th century this predominantly political and military leverage[48] was turned to economic advantages. In 1911 the Trucial Shaikhs pledged not to give concessions for pearling and sponge-fishing without consulting the Political Resident.[49] Practical matters such as safeguarding the telephone cable across the Musandam Peninsula and the construction of a lighthouse on Tunb Island were also regulated by agreements.

5 British anticipation of economic benefits

Move to exclude non-British economic interests

By the time the First World War broke out, the prime objectives of the "cordon-sanitaire" policy of the British Government with regard to the Arab principalities in the Gulf had been achieved. Formal treaties and undertakings as much as informal political tutelage had made it impossible for these principalities to respond to any diplomatic overtures from the Turkish and German enemies or from any other rivals to the British position. This, in turn, also secured the British military objectives by preventing the establishment of foreign bases. Even the economic benefits which could be derived from these shaikhdoms, though they were considered to be meagre enough in the case of the Trucial States, were put securely out of the reach of any outsiders and made almost inaccessible even for British subjects.[50]

With the signing in 1922 by all the Trucial Rulers of undertakings not to give oil concessions to any company which was not supported by the British Government,[51] their privileged position in these States was being turned to potential economic advantage. This move was made not because there was any evidence of oil deposits in the territories bordering the Gulf, but, after the traumatic experience which British companies had had in securing exploration rights in Turkish Arabia (later Iraq) where oil deposits were known to exist,[52] it was deemed judicious to ensure that if there was any hope of finding oil in the territories belonging to the semi-independent Arab Rulers, Britain should have the first option. The Trucial States were thus simply brought into line with Kuwait and Bahrain, who had signed similar agreements regarding oil concessions in 1913 and 1914 respectively, and with Oman, which signed such an agreement in 1923. As for the principalities of south-western Arabia, the possibility of obtaining the first option for oil concessions was taken for granted because of their colonial and protectorate status.

But the British monopoly over the granting of oil concessions did not arouse much interest among the British oil companies already working in Persia and elsewhere in the Middle East. Eventually some geologists of the Anglo-Persian Oil Company (a predecessor of British Petroleum) visited parts of the Ḥajar mountain range within Oman and the mountains of Dhufār in search of surface evidence of oil-bearing rock structures. The result was not encouraging enough to initiate negotiations for concessions anywhere in eastern Arabia until after oil had been discovered in commercial quantities in Bahrain in 1932.[53] Surface rock structures similar to those of the Bahrain field were observed near Dhahrān in al Ḥasā and on the Qatar Peninsula. By default, a concession for the former did not go to the British company, while prolonged negotiations for the latter resulted in an agreement in 1935 between the Ruler of Qatar and the London-based multinational Iraq Petroleum Company (I.P.C.).[54] This company, which was in part owned by the Anglo-Persian Company (later BP), had been established specifically to develop the resources of Iraq. In order to prevent other companies from entering the area, the IPC formed in October 1935 a wholly-owned subsidiary called Petroleum Concessions Ltd., which secured concessionary agreements with the Rulers and governments of the entire Arabian Peninsula, excluding only the newly-proclaimed Kingdom of Saudi Arabia.[55]

Negotiations between Petroleum Concessions Ltd. and Trucial States Rulers

During the early 1930s representatives of the D'Arcy Exploration Co., a major shareholder in the Anglo-Persian Oil Company, obtained options from most of the Trucial Rulers.[56] Petroleum Concessions Ltd. took over these options and began after 1935 to negotiate concessions with the Rulers. This proved in some cases exceedingly difficult, because, much as some Rulers might have wanted to be obliging over issues which were then foremost in the minds of the British authorities, and great though their interest was in securing a steady income from rentals for oil concessions, their subjects were generally opposed to the change and disturbance which an influx of Europeans would bring. Each Ruler watched carefully to see that the terms he obtained were as good as those of any of his neighbours.[57] The negotiations were further complicated by the fact that sovereignty over certain territories was disputed by some of the Rulers.

In 1936 Saʿīd bin Maktūm, the Ruler of Dubai, who had usually shown himself receptive to proposals by the British Government and in turn had relied heavily on the support of the Political Resident in a series of internal power struggles, was the first to initial an agreement with PCL (Petroleum Concessions Ltd.), which was ratified in May 1937. In September of the same year the Ruler of Shārjah signed a similar agreement. Approaches to the Ruler of Ra's al Khaimah failed to bring results before the beginning of the Second World War, because the dispute over the succession in Kalba had precipitated a head-on collision between the British authorities and Shaikh Sulṭān bin Sālim of Ra's al Khaimah.[58] He had already been very uncooperative over the granting of refuelling rights for the RAF and civil aviation requested by the British authorities. The recognition of Kalba as a separate Trucial State by the British Government through the signing of an agreement with Saʿīd bin Ḥamad in August 1936, allowing Imperial Airways to land there in an emergency, meant that a separate oil-concession agreement could also be concluded and was signed in 1938 by the Regent of Kalba Khālid bin Aḥmad, after Saʿīd's death.

The only other agreement concluded before the war was that with Shaikh Shakhbūṭ in Abu Dhabi in 1939. In Ra's al Khaimah, Umm al Qaiwain and ʿAjmān the options were converted into concessions only in 1945, 1949, and 1951 respectively. The Ruler of Fujairaḥ, who had for many years tried to obtain formal recognition from the British Government, finally succeeded when PCL put pressure on the British Government, as they wanted to have a free hand for oil exploration throughout the entire east coast; thus in 1952 Fujairah became a Trucial State and the last of PCL's agreements for this area was signed with Shaikh Muḥammad bin Ḥamad. This brought the number back to a total of seven Trucial States after Kalba had been re-incorporated into Shārjah in 1951.

The use of other facilities

The signing of oil concessions turned out to be the most significant of the considerable number of activities which the British Government had introduced on the coast since the turn of the century. Over the centuries the British interests in India grew from trading posts to an empire with all its complex requirements for supply and communications with the mother country. In the course of this process it became increasingly desirable to have the use of territories adjacent to the approach routes to India for the establishment of coaling stations, watering points, secure harbours and more recently telegraph communications.[59] Facilities were also required for the British Indian Post Office[60] and the Royal Navy to position markers for surveys, and possibly to use some of the creeks as bases. The British India Steam Navigation Company's calls on the coast after 1902 also became symbolic of the British presence.

The facilities which the British authorities had acquired, together with the continued British involvement in the prevention of armed incidents at sea and the special protection which the Government gave to Indian merchants, enabled the British Government to intervene in the affairs of any Trucial shaikhdom whenever it wished. Because of the increasing variety of its interests, it did indeed intervene quite frequently after the turn of the century. This was facilitated primarily by the continuous contact of the Residency Agent in Shārjah with everything that went on in the coastal towns. Supporting him, there was the authority of the Political Resident with naval power at his disposal.

As had been the practice for many decades of the 19th century, on occasions when it was considered to be the only way to affirm British authority, the prominent buildings and the fortifications of a coastal Ruler's possessions were bombarded in the 20th century too. On other occasions fines were imposed and payments obtained under threat of naval attack. The authorities became increasingly intolerant of any type of warfare between coastal Rulers, whether declared or spontaneous. There are many instances of British diplomatic, military, and economic intervention after the turn of the century, as in the disputes between Ḥīrah, ʿAjmān, and Shārjah, between Rams and Ra's al Khaimah, and between Fujairah and Kalba.

During the late 1920s the British authorities realised that peace upon the waters of the Gulf did not suffice; the strips of coastal territory themselves became objects of British interest in the area because of the necessity to establish land bases for military and civil aircraft *en route* between India and England. Refuelling facilities for RAF Wapiti seaplanes were sought, and the best site, the creek of Ra's al Khaimah, was selected. As mentioned above, the Ruler, Sulṭān bin Sālim, proved unco-operative; his anti-British attitude had already manifested itself in his refusal in 1926 to surrender ʿAbdul Raḥman of Ḥīrah,[61] and it was suspected that he was supported in his attitude by the Wahhābi Governor of al Ḥasā. Despite pressure from his own people and other Rulers, he continued to object to the presence of a refuelling barge which was put in the creek in 1929. The air route along the Arabian shore was eventually established, but, as an added precaution, another refuelling facility was built on the island of Ṣīr Bani Yās, towards the western end of the coast of Abu Dhabi State. In 1933, the RAF required more elaborate facilities and the establishment of a better fuel depot; also, the buoys which they wanted to place in the creek to mark the landing area could only be maintained if the local Ruler was willing to co-operate. The Rulers of Dubai and Abu Dhabi were approached but both shunned the idea at first, fearing serious repercussions from some of their tribal subjects, who objected strongly to receiving British aircraft on their land. Eventually both Rulers were ready to make compromises, and in January 1934 the first military seaplane landed on the creek in Dubai, while an emergency landing-place was made available at Abu Dhabi.

The civilian aircraft of Imperial Airways also needed an airstrip somewhere on the Trucial Coast after the agreement with the Persian Government for a route along the northern shore of the Gulf expired in 1932. Several Rulers were approached for this civil air link, but Sulṭān bin Ṣaqr of Shārjah actually offered the facilities in 1932, partly because he hoped to obtain a handsome annual remuneration. In the agreement, which was reached on 22 June 1932, it was arranged that he should receive 800 Rupees a month as rent for the landing-strip, landing fees, and a personal subsidy of 500 Rupees. The Ruler had to build the rest-house for the crew and passengers.[62]

Emergency landing facilities for British Imperial Airways were secured by an agreement with Saʿīd bin Ḥamad in Kalba in August 1936; he had been recognised as a Trucial Ruler precisely for that purpose.[63] Eventually Imperial Airways' flying-boats were also allowed to land on the RAF landing area in Dubai creek. During the Second World War Britain made quite liberal use of its facilities, and the number of landings as well as the number of military personnel living in Shārjah increased dramatically. In 1949 a new agreement was negotiated between the British Government and the Ruler of Shārjah regarding the use of the airport and other facilities as a RAF base.

Territorial sovereignty during early oil exploration

With the establishment of the air facilities at Shārjah, there was for the first time a physical British presence on the coast; a Residency Agent had been there since 1829 but he was never an Englishman. The safety and maintenance of the airstrip, the fuel depôt, the guest house and the route to and from the airport had to be guaranteed. The Rulers who agreed to the establishment of such facilities on their territories realised that this was a political burden for them, because the semi-independent tribes in the hinterland were liable to use these facilities as a pretext for disputes with the Ruler. In the event of serious trouble, the British Government had to step in to protect the facilities and sometimes the host Ruler.

The new British interest in parts of the coastal strip thus promoted the first step towards the abandonment of the principle of non-involvement in the interior. Before the Second World War the British Government of India tried to avoid negotiating with representatives of the tribes in the hinterland by diplomatically supporting the actual, or the claimed, authority of the Trucial Rulers over these tribes. The administration in Bushire rarely stirred when a dispute arose between a Trucial Ruler and a neighbouring beduin or settled tribe of the interior. Not only was there no legal basis for British intervention in disputes which were not fought at sea, but some British authorities may even have regarded it as a welcome development that the coastal shaikhs should seize every opportunity to assert their influence over the people in the interior. We have already discussed in Chapter Three the need for the tribes in the hinterland to have access to markets, the use of pearling boats and ports, and the gradual growth of the political predominance of the coastal Rulers recognised by the British, resulting in, for instance, the establishment of the territorial State of Abu Dhabi and its Ruler's authority over the Buraimi area.

Yet the degree of authority or mere influence remained tenuous even during the first decades of the 20th century. The vagueness of political sovereignty and territorial identification suited all sides, and, as far as the hinterland was concerned, even the British authorities. The conclusion of concessionary agreements put a sudden end to this state of affairs. Now it became necessary to define precisely the boundaries of a concession area and therefore the limits of a Ruler's authority; but this very necessity provoked disputes and disturbed the peace which was essential if any foreign company was to search for oil.[64] The prospect of the discovery of oil could have fed a potentially explosive situation.

The Political Agent in Bahrain, who from 1934 had been directly responsible for the Trucial States, urged the Political Resident in Bushire to initiate official contacts with the shaikhs of the interior and at the same time to try to ascertain the actual territorial extent of the sovereignty of each of the Trucial Rulers. During the summer of 1937 the Residency Agent was sounding out each Ruler about his territorial claims. On the strength of this evidence PD (TC), supported by the Political Agent in Bahrain, tried to obtain access to areas in the interior, notably around Buraimi, with the support of the coastal Rulers. But the latter did not agree among themselves over who could claim authority over the various tribes of the hinterland; and the tribes themselves, despite overtures and payments by most of the Trucial Rulers in turn, could not be moved to recognise any one of them as overlord. A party of PD (TC) geologists who tried to collect information in the Buraimi area in 1937 was not very successful because their movements were restricted. Whereas the Trucial Rulers argued amongst themselves over the extent of the territories for which some had already signed concessionary agreements, the shaikhs of the tribes in the hinterland, notably the Bani Qitab, Bani Kaʿab, Āl Bū Shāmis and Naʿīm, wanted neither agreements nor money from the oil companies but were chiefly concerned with their independence from any coastal Ruler, or the Sultan of Oman, and above all from the British Government. The Second World War delayed any further exploration and deferred the need to solve the thorny question of territorial sovereignty. Those British officials who were closely concerned with PD (TC)'s tentative moves to assert their concessionary rights did, however, realise well before the War the problems which lay ahead if the search for oil was to be pursued under such difficulties.

After the War, the oil company resumed exploration, geological parties examined the rock outcrops, and gravity survey parties traversed the desert. In 1946/47, most of the areas in Dubai, Ra's al Khaimah, and Abu Dhabi which had been visited before the War were examined again; and this time it was also possible to send a party as far inland as Jabal al Fāyah, a solitary mountain west of the Ḥajar range. The party was again harassed by tribes of the interior because the coastal shaikh's letters and guides were not recognised. Great difficulties were also encountered in the Buraimi area in 1948. The Ruler of Abu Dhabi, Shaikh Shakhbūṭ, assisted the company in organising surveys in the territory under his jurisdiction, but the shaikhs of the Āl Bū Shāmis and others refused to recognise his influence, and they ignored the Sultan's claim that they were under his sovereignty and that their tribal *dār* should be treated as part of the concession area which he had granted in his agreement with Petroleum Development (Oman) in 1937.[65]

A dispute over the boundary between Abu Dhabi and Dubai near the coast overshadowed the otherwise usually very cordial relationship between the two shaikhdoms dominated by the Bani Yās. Shaikh Sa'īd bin Maktūm of Dubai had been the first of the Trucial Rulers to sign an agreement with PD (TC) in 1935 for a concession to explore for oil in the territory "under his sovereignty". Shaikh Shakhbūṭ of Abu Dhabi, wanting to prevent a misunderstanding with regard to the extent of his territory, delineated his claims in a written message to Shaikh Sa'īd in the summer of 1936. In Shaikh Shakhbūṭ's view, Abu Dhabi extended as far north-east as Jabal 'Ali, while Shaikh Sa'īd held the opinion that his State included Khaur Ghanādhah, some 40 kilometres south-west of Jabal 'Ali. Although both Rulers were anxious to resolve this difference amicably by discussion and exchange of letters, no agreement was reached before the War. The problem lingered on and grew again in importance when exploration parties of PD (TC) returned to the area after the War.

Partly because such territorial disputes over concessionary

boundaries were boiling up everywhere, and partly because the semi-settled tribes of the interior felt the economic depression of the 1930s and the War years most acutely, the hinterland fell into a state of almost constant warfare. Raids by beduin groups against one another or against the coastal settlements became more frequent. While the Rulers, Shaikh Shakhbūṭ and Shaikh Sa'īd in particular, were trying to secure influence over the inland tribes, notably the Bani Qitab, Bani Ka'ab, the Āl Bū Shāmis, the Na'īm and the Bani Yās's traditional allies, the Manāṣīr and 'Awāmir, both states got drawn into these incessant feuds. In September 1945 the increasingly hostile atmosphere beteween the Rulers of Abu Dhabi and Dubai—the latter State was by then very much under the control of Shaikh Rāshid bin Sa'īd—over the border problem and the beduin raids developed into open warfare.

War meant still, as it had always done in this region, a series of raids and counter-raids continuing over several months and even years. Camels and other property were carried off, but human casualties hardly ever exceeded single figures. In this war, which lasted until 1948, other tribal leaders tried unsuccessfully to mediate, but even the Rulers on both sides failed to restrain the beduin groups from fighting, and had to dissociate themselves from them. Jabal al Fāyah and the Līwā area became the scenes of the most serious fighting. The British Political Resident was altogether powerless to intervene when the intermittent fighting occurred in the desert.

When, early in 1948, fifty-two Manāṣīr were killed at Ruweiḥah located between the Līwā and Abu Dhabi and many more were wounded, the entire population of the coast became apprehensive at the unprecedented scale of this war, and a movement to restore peace became strong enough to bring about lasting agreements in 1948 and 1949 between all parties concerned. The British authorities made use of the general demand for peace, and more or less dictated the frontier between Abu Dhabi and Dubai, drawn on the strength of their own inquiries into tribal use of the area. For the first time the British Government involved itself deliberately in affairs on land in the Trucial States.

6 The Buraimi issue up to 1955

It was inevitable that as soon as PD (TC) exploration recommenced in the late 1940s, this would lead to a revival of the dispute over the entire length of the border between Abu Dhabi and the Kingdom of

Saudi Arabia. During the 19th century the Wahhābis had from time to time dominated all or part of the Buraimi oasis, where they built a fortress.[66] But their occupation was not permanent, and they had been dispossessed of the fort several times. On occasions the Wahhābis' claim to the oasis was used by Muḥammad ʿAli Pāshā, who had eclipsed the Wahhābis' power, as the reason for trying to wrest the Buraimi area from the Naʿīm.[67] The last occupation of the oasis by a resident Wahhābi garrison in the 19th century ended in June 1869 after the Naʿīm had expelled them with the assistance of ʿAzzān bin Qais, Sultan of Muscat.

Saudi interest in the oasis was revived in the 1920s, when inter-tribal fighting led some tribal leaders who lived in the Buraimi area and to the west of it, to travel to al Ḥasā and seek help from the Governor, ʿAbdullah bin Jalūwi. In 1925 and in the years up to 1929, Wahhābi tax collectors were received by some of the tribal shaikhs in the area and obtained *zakāh* on camels and sheep.

In July 1933 King ʿAbdul ʿAzīz ibn Saʿūd granted a petroleum concession to the Standard Oil Co., of California for: ". . . the eastern portion of our Saudi Arab Kingdom, within its frontiers."[68] These frontiers were not further specified, and the United States Government was obliged to inquire about the actual extent of this concession from the British Government, who stated that the eastern frontier of the Kingdom was the so called Blue Line, agreed upon by the British and Turkish Governments in the Convention of 1913/1914; constitutionally Ibn Saʿūd succeeded the Turkish authorities as sovereign of the area. However, the Saudi Government did not accept the Blue Line as the eastern frontier, and an extended series of meetings and exchange of notes between the Saudi and the British governments followed. The last of these contacts before the Second World War was an exchange of notes in December 1937; this marked the end of this series of negotiations because no agreement could be reached. After the War the chance of an amicable settlement was more remote than ever because the search for oil was taken up again. Newly-developed exploration methods nourished new hopes that oil-bearing strata might be found beneath parts of the disputed territory.

In 1949, survey parties of the Arabian American Oil Company (ARAMCO) traversed the coastal strip of Abu Dhabi's territory as far east as Abu Dhabi Island. This action triggered off another series of protests and counter-representations, and the agreement between the British and the Saudi governments of July 1950, to establish a joint technical commission to investigate the tribal loyalties and the sovereignties of the Rulers in the disputed areas, came to nothing. In due course a round-table conference was held in Ḍammām in Saudi Arabia in January/February 1952 on the proposal of the Amīr Faiṣal bin ʿAbdul ʿAzīz. The British delegation for this conference was led by the Political Resident in the Gulf, Sir Rupert Hay, accompanied by the Rulers of Abu Dhabi and Qatar.[69] The conference was adjourned, without agreement being reached, on 14 February 1952, never to be re-convened.

In August 1952 the Shaikh of the Āl Bū Shāmis in Ḥamāsah, one of the three Omani villages of the Buraimi oasis, brought a contingent of forty *fidāwis* under the command of Turki bin ʿAbdullah bin ʿUṭaishān from Saudi Arabia to Ḥamāsah. Turki carried letters for several of the tribal leaders of the area from the Governor of al Ḥasā, inviting them to consider themselves as subjects of the King.[70] When the Sultan of Oman heard this he prepared for a military confrontation, and at the same time the Saudi contingent in Ḥamāsah was reinforced with men and vehicles. Armed confrontation was, however, avoided by a "standstill agreement" which was negotiated in Jiddah between the Saudi and British Governments, with the mediation of the US Ambassador in Jiddah, in October 1952.[71]

In November 1952 the British Government voiced its view that, because the disputed area was so large and the prospects of a negotiated settlement seemed so remote, the question should be submitted to an international court for arbitration. An agreement on the terms of the arbitration was signed in Jiddah on 30 July 1954.[72]

The tribunal opened its hearings on 11 September 1955 in Geneva.[73] The members of the tribunal were Sir Reader Bullard, a retired British diplomat and former Ambassador to Jiddah (1936–9); Shaikh Yūsuf Yāsīn, Deputy Foreign Minister of Saudi Arabia; Dr Ernesto de Dihigo from Cuba; and Mr Muḥammad Ḥasan from Pakistan. A former judge of the International Court of Justice, Dr Charles de Visscher from Belgium, presided over the hearings.[74] On 16 September the British member of the tribunal, Sir Reader Bullard, resigned, accusing the Saudi member of partiality and improper practices, alleging that the Saudis had, in contradiction to the arbitration agreement, before, during and after the tribunal was sitting, airlifted military supplies into Buraimi and continued to try to win over the local tribal leaders by various means. This led to the breakdown of the tribunal, which was never reconvened.

This phase of the dispute was brought to a sudden end when, with the full backing of the British Government, the forces of the Sultan of Muscat and Oman and those of the Ruler of Abu Dhabi, supported by the Trucial Oman Levies,[75] moved into the oasis on the morning of 26 October 1955 and forced the bloodless surrender of the Saudi detachment. The British Prime Minister, Sir Anthony Eden, explained his Government's reasons for this action to the House of Commons that same day.[76] The Riyadh Line,[77] as amended in 1937, was unilaterally declared the frontier between Abu Dhabi and Saudi Arabia. This *fait accompli* laid the entire issue to rest only for as long as the British Government remained formally and legally the spokesman for the emirate of Abu Dhabi. The question of the frontier between the two States came up again as a major factor while the support of Saudi Arabia was being sought for the new federation, which was being created in the wake of the British abrogation of the treaties with all the Trucial States in 1971.[78]

The surprisingly firm line adopted rather abruptly by the British Government in October 1955, after years of half-hearted diplomatic defence of what she nevertheless regarded as the indisputable rights of the Rulers of Abu Dhabi, Qatar and Oman, marked the end of an era. For over a century from the 1820s, Great Britain had gradually extended its influence over the coastal Rulers of the Gulf while taking elaborate precautions against getting involved in their affairs in the hinterland. From the 1920s this stance, reiterated innumerable times in the correspondence between the British administrators in India and in the Gulf, was thrown to the winds to defend the territorial extent of the oil concessions. From this time on the coastal Rulers who had signed concessionary agreements were supported in their efforts to assert their sovereignty over the tribes of the hinterland.

When the concession-holder, PD (TC), was able to start exploration for oil after the Second World War, these concessions soon took on a real commercial meaning and value. Protecting the interest of the London-based consortium of oil companies was seen by the British Government to be its duty even if this meant abandoning the long-standing policy of strict non-involvement in the internal affairs and in the hinterland of the Trucial States. The so-called Buraimi Dispute became eventually the turning point where, at first hesitantly, but eventually using even military force, Britain fully adopted this change in policy.

7 British involvement in the 1950s and 1960s

A change of attitude

While the British authorities had kept the closest watch for possible infringements of Britain's confirmed rights and privileges, her duty towards the people of the area was seen in India to be confined to keeping the peace at sea. A few years after the Second World War Britain's policy towards the Trucial States changed to include a novel feature: it was maintained by many of those who then influenced Britain's policy towards its weaker protégés that she should assume a certain amount of responsibility for the betterment of the welfare of the population in those areas.

This voice of social conscience was stirring throughout the western world of the post-war decades, strongly enough to arouse bad feelings if such responsibility was not shouldered and no development assistance was rendered. Yet reality always fell short of this idealistic notion of brotherly responsibility for the weaker partners, for no nation can sustain for long a largely altruistic foreign policy. Development help of all kinds necessarily also serves in the first place the donor nation's interests, be they the need to secure the supply of raw materials, to guarantee the stability of a vital region or to pacify pressure-groups at home. Great Britain, too, was in the event able to make only the minimum contribution to the social development of the people in the Trucial States: a minimum as compared to the requirements of the then impoverished and backward region; a maximum if looked at in the light of British commitments to similar tasks in its overpopulated former colonies. During the decades while Britain's former wealth, resources and world power were vanishing fast, her development assistance to the Trucial States had to be fairly accurately tailored to match whatever benefit she could hope to derive in return for maintaining her influence over this area.

Growing financial commitments of the oil companies

In the 1950s, the commencement of large-scale oil exploration channelled relatively vast amounts of foreign investment into the Trucial States for the first time. The two main oil companies were British-based, although some of the shares were held by foreign companies,[79] and this placed the British authorities under some obligation to safeguard the investments. After a winter of seismic work in the Trucial States in early 1949, Petroleum Development

Trucial Coast PD (TC) decided to start drilling at one of the more promising locations which was not in an area under dispute, neither claimed by Saudi Arabia nor the shaikhs of the hinterland tribes. The site of this first well, which was spudded in February 1950, was at Ra's al Ṣadr in Abu Dhabi territory, about half-way between Abu Dhabi town and Dubai. Preparation of the site entailed the construction of a jetty, a road and a landing strip, importation of the drilling equipment, building materials and a power generation plant. The well was abandoned as a dry hole at the then record depth for the Gulf of 13,000 feet. The second well was drilled at Jabal ʿAli in Dubai territory, and the entire back-up organisation had to be transferred from Abu Dhabi to Dubai. More wells were drilled in various locations in Abu Dhabi and one in Shārjah; camps were set up, and the total investment over this decade of unsuccessful exploration amounted to many million pounds Sterling, until the announcement was made on 28 October 1960 that oil had been found in commercial quantities at Murbān in Abu Dhabi.

The financial commitment of the companies in this area went hand in hand with an ever more intensive personal involvement. In previous decades it was the Residency Agent who alone dealt with the Rulers on the Gulf Coast, and, as required, with their relatives and the leading merchants, making rather infrequent visits to the remoter shaikhdoms. Now the Arabic-speaking representatives of the oil companies were seen in some of the Rulers' *majlis* almost every day, regulating a multitude of details concerning the day-to-day requirements of the company. At the same time hundreds of local inhabitants were recruited, and during training and employment they came into contact with the Europeans and Americans working with them.[80] It was as desirable for the company to develop some continuity in their workforce and to train the labourers as it was for the local population to move forward through education, better health, and new contacts with the outside world. Comparisons with nearby Qatar, which had had such contacts since the 1940s and was already benefiting from the income from its oil exports during the 1950s, further whetted the appetite of the people of the Trucial Coast for a general improvement in their living conditions.

The political representation

During the 1930s the mutual trust between the British authorities in the Gulf and the local Rulers and their people had declined to a very low level. The Government of India, being in great need of landing and refuelling facilities for aircraft, had advanced her own interests regardless of the adverse effect upon the naturally rather xenophobic population. This attitude had in turn produced stubborn refusal by some Rulers, in particular Sulṭān bin Sālim of Ra's al Khaimah and the two Bani Yās Rulers of Dubai and Abu Dhabi, and reluctance on the part of others to co-operate on any of the issues which were then still unresolved. The outstanding issues concerned the expulsion of piratical individuals, such as a certain Mirza Birkat, originally from Makrān; punishment of people who were involved in taking slaves from the coastal towns to Saudi Arabia via Ḥamāsah; compliance with British standards in jurisdiction over thieves; and last but not least the signing of agreements with the oil company.

While the rather distant British presence, maintained during the first decade of this century, had been appreciated because the peace at sea still held and thus the income from pearling was secured for all the shaikhdoms, the British objectives in the area during the 1930s and the 1940s clashed with the feelings, needs, and inclinations of the population and their leaders. A gradual change in this atmosphere of mutual mistrust came about when, during and after the Second World War, the Political Officers helped to organise the import and distribution of food for the population of the coast and the hinterland. The restrictions on the export of food from India, which came into effect soon after the beginning of the War, could have had disastrous effects on the Trucial States, whose population had not been self-sufficient in food for many centuries and could not suddenly start growing adequate supplies. Permits were granted for the export from India of rice, tea, sugar, and other items, and the distribution of rationed supplies was undertaken by local merchants supervised by local committees. The Political Officers set up a workable system and acted as the final arbiters in disputes. While doing so they came into daily contact with a large part of the population in the coastal towns and even in the hinterland. Their personal efforts were appreciated by the people, and thus the image of the British in general was considerably improved. Other activities, such as vaccination during epidemics and the establishment in Dubai of a dispensary with an Indian doctor did not fail to demonstrate to the population that these British civil servants were not bent solely on serving the interests of a waning empire.[81]

Some changes had already been made during the 1930s in the arrangements to guard the British interests on the coast. The Political

Resident in Bushire, who had been directly responsible for this area and was assisted by the Residency Agent in Shārjah, a local servant of the Indian Government, handed the routine supervision over to the Political Agent in Bahrain in 1934. The reason for this change was that the establishment of landing facilities for RAF and Imperial Airways planes in more than one of the shaikhdoms required closer local liaison than previously. This routine work grew so rapidly in volume and in importance that the Government of India eventually recognised that the local Residency Agent could no longer cope with it alone. Therefore the first British-born Political Officer, appointed in 1937, was Captain J. B. Howes, formerly an employee of the oil company IPC, which was then seeking concessions from the Rulers of the Trucial States; he resided in Shārjah only during the winter months. This arrangement continued until 1948,[82] when Mr P. D. Stobart became the first Political Officer to live in Shārjah throughout the year.[83] The post of local Residency Agent was abolished in 1949.

A gradual change in style of administration and in emphasis of the objectives of the British presence in the lower Gulf was to be expected when the British Indian Empire ceased to exist in 1947. For just over a year the conduct of relations with the Gulf States was the responsibility of the India Office in London, which eventually became part of the Commonwealth Relations Office. But since neither the Trucial States nor any of the other Gulf States had ever been as directly linked to Britain as the former colonies and protectorates of the Commonwealth, the Foreign Office, not the Colonial Office, became ultimately responsible in 1948. Initially this did not mean a complete set of new faces for the various posts in the Gulf: the Residents, Agents and Political Officers were still mostly appointed from among the people who were taken over by the Foreign Office from the Indian Civil Service. But the overall considerations which guided the Foreign Office in its policy towards these states were more influenced by world opinion about Britain's colonial past, and by UN resolutions on Britain's current duties in respect of its former dependents, than had ever been the case when the affairs of the Gulf were primarily linked to Britain's interests in and around India. Thus the British officers serving in the area had to work hard at an acceptable compromise between serving the British interests, by then mostly of an economic nature and focused on oil, antagonising the local Rulers over thorny problems such as cases of slave trading into Saudi Arabia, and carrying out the humanitarian duties of assisting the local population to partake of some of the amenities which the industrialised nations took for granted.

It was the increase in both the activities of the oil companies in the region and the more intensive involvement in the internal development of these shaikhdoms which prompted the Foreign Office to raise the level of the post on the Trucial Coast to that of Political Agent in May 1953. By the end of the 1940s Shārjah's importance had declined, while Dubai, which was the thriving trading centre of the 1920s, had weathered the two subsequent difficult decades fairly well and had eventually caught up with Shārjah. The Ruler of Dubai had also accepted British requests for air facilities, and had been the first to sign a concession agreement for oil exploration. In the 1950s, the oil companies using Dubai as their headquarters on the coast generated through their activities the need for certain facilities such as postal and banking services and an improved harbour. At that time Dubai therefore seemed to be the natural centre for the British representation in the Trucial States, and in 1954 the Agent moved from Shārjah to Dubai. Until 1961 the Political Agent in Dubai was responsible for all the Trucial States;[84] he was assisted from 1957 onwards by a Political Officer residing in Abu Dhabi, where the increase in oil company activities, the number of British subjects working in the State, and above all the revival of the Buraimi issue made this immediate presence necessary. In 1961 the Abu Dhabi post was itself promoted to a full Political Agency, because the discovery of oil in commercial quantities had been announced in 1960 and it was anticipated that there would be a surge in development and in commercial activities.

The increasing interest shown in the area by the British Government can also be seen from the change in the length of time which most appointees served in their posts on the Trucial Coast. The first Political Officers stayed usually for only one season or one year, in what was then regarded as a hardship-post, not long enough to get involved in long term planning for the development of these States. Since the move away from Shārjah, living conditions improved to the extent that British civil servants were required to spend an average of three years in their posts.

The considerable increase in the responsibilities of the British officials went hand in hand with the increase in the British Government's involvement in the internal affairs of the Trucial States. From 1950 onwards the Political Agent was also the Judge of

Her Britannic Majesty's Court for the Trucial States.[85] He presided over the Trucial States Council from its creation in 1952 until 1965, after which the chairmanship rotated among the seven Rulers. The Political Resident in Bahrain became the "Commander-in-Chief" of the Trucial Oman Levies, the British-officered force which came into existence in 1951.[86] The British initiative in identifying and implementing development schemes for these States involved their representatives in various ways: the Political Agent or his deputy usually presided over or at least participated in the hospital and trade school board meetings, and various other committees engaged in development projects.[87]

Although British representation was thus substantially upgraded during the 1950s and 1960s to enable the new policy of greater involvement in affairs of these States to be carried out, the Political Agents did not as a rule force the views of the British Government upon the shaikhs. In spite of this, they did expect that their advice would be heeded by the Rulers.

Making the countryside secure

When the tribes were at war with each other it was never very safe or easy for strangers to travel in the hinterland.[88] The state of war which existed between Abu Dhabi and Dubai from 1945 until 1948 made it dangerous, even for tribesmen who had no part in the quarrel, to travel in the desert of the Trucial States. British officials and geological parties were certainly not welcome in the desert during that time, and even the well-adjusted desert traveller, Wilfred Thesiger, and his beduin companions had initially to keep clear of the parties involved in the war.

The continued economic depression of the post-war years added to this natural insecurity because a growing number of tribesmen were driven to make a living by lawless means. Raiders fell upon unprotected villagers and stole their animals and belongings[89] or they held up caravans and vehicles.

The old problem of arms and ammunition being smuggled through the Trucial States to Balūchistān and to Oman also obliged the British Government to step up control, or else to risk being accused of tacitly assisting the secessionist movements in Balūchistān and Makrān against the Persian Government and in Oman. The source of the relatively old arms was usually East Africa, from whence they were shipped to the Bāṭinah or to Saudi Arabia and reached the coastal towns, particularly Dubai, from Ḥamāsah in the Buraimi oasis, to be shipped north across the Gulf. Probably the most compelling reason for the British Government to involve itself in the problem of security in the Trucial States, to the extent of setting up a British-officered force, was the odium attached to the slave trade, which had again become very profitable during the late 1940s. News of incidents in which former slaves from Africa and Balūchistān and even free people were taken to Ḥamāsah, and sold to be domestic servants in Saudi Arabia,[90] had leaked out. Britain, already somewhat on the defensive before a world audience which had made anti-colonialism and the responsibility of former colonial powers for newly independent States a burning issue, felt compelled to concern itself with these internal matters in those States for which she was responsible in the eyes of the outside world.

If exploration for oil was to commence seriously in the country, the security of the Europeans involved had to be guaranteed. Similarly, if the country was to be gradually modernised, the hinterland as well as the coastal settlements had to be made secure enough for development to be carried out. A security force, initially called the Trucial Oman Levies (the name was changed to Trucial Oman Scouts in 1956), was established by the King's Regulation No. 1 of 1951 under article 82 of the Trucial States Order in Council of 1950. The duty of the force was to maintain peace and good order in any part of the Trucial States, particularly outside the coastal towns, and to provide an escort for the British representative.[91] Because the latter lived in Shārjah at the time when this force was created, it seemed to be the most logical location for the headquarters of the TOL. The first commander, Major Hankin Turvin, was seconded from the Arab Legion with two Jordanian officers and several other ranks. Most of the soldiers were initially recruited from among the people of the Trucial States to whom the steady income and the prospect of training were considerable incentives during the 1950s. Of the 200 men in the force in 1953 many belonged to Abu Dhabi tribes, because Shaikh Zāyid bin Sulṭān, the Ruler's *wāli* in the Buraimi area, who had a great deal of influence with the tribes, encouraged enrolment and supported the TOL. During the 1960s recruitment for the TOS in Abu Dhabi proved rather less successful because the oil company paid considerably more and the men could more easily leave the company at their convenience, whereas this was not so with the force.

In the first year of its existence the force was successful in stamping out the lingering security problems such as occasional abductions, highway robberies and tribal hostilities against the foreigners who increasingly needed to move around in the country.

When the border dispute concerning parts of the Buraimi area and the southern desert of Abu Dhabi became acute again in 1952, the British Government decided to strengthen the TOL which by 1955 numbered about 500 men in three rifle squadrons. After the Levies participated in the eviction of the Saudi force from the disputed area, the force was built up further to reach the strength of five squadrons, which were distributed throughout the Trucial States, moving frequently from one location to another.[92]

During the time of rapid expansion of the force the percentage of Trucial States recruits fell because there were better job opportunities, or at least the expectation thereof, in the oil industry. Only the soldiers from the northern Trucial States stayed in any number. The force was by then largely made up of Omanis from the tribes living on the fringes of Oman. One squadron consisted entirely of Dhufāris, who also manned up to one third of other squadrons. Men from Dhufār had left their homes in search of employment in Bahrain, Saudi Arabia, Kuwait and Qatar. They worked for the oil companies and then for the police forces and became well trained in various skills, but were gradually edged out of such employment when the locals of these states grew to resent their presence in such relatively large numbers. In the TOS the Dhufāris presented problems because they did not mix well with the other soldiers on account of their different tribal background, and because many of them speak a language of their own.[93]

Because of the mixture of nationalities in the force and the involvement of Omani tribesmen from many parts of that country, it was a bold decision on the part of the British Government to send the TOS to assist the Sultan's forces on their final assault against the rebellious Sulaimān bin Ḥimyar of the Bani Riyām and other supporters of the Imām.[94] The force fought with a good military record in Oman from November 1957 until January 1959, when the Imām's natural bastion the Jabal al Akhḍar was taken by the Special Air Service regiment of the British Army.

The TOS were not required to fight again outside the territory of the seven States. They concentrated on the maintenance of law and order, which still occasionally meant that they had to step in when small-scale fighting broke out between tribes over the ownership of a well or a *wādi* bed. The force, often assisted by the British forces stationed in Shārjah and in particular by the Royal Engineers, undertook many civilian tasks such as blasting motorable tracks through the Ḥajar mountains and along the east coast, assisting with the evacuation of sick people and with surveys of various kinds conducted for the Trucial States Development Office. Thus most of the country was opened up at least for rugged vehicles and became safe to travel in. The population came to appreciate the role of the TOS in this and did not normally appear to resent the force's powers to arrest and to search any suspect person, although these powers were conferred on the force by virtue of British Government legislation.[95]

In deference to the Rulers of the seven shaikhdoms, the TOS were instructed not to operate in the towns except with the explicit consent of the Ruler concerned. In the towns where law and order had originally been enforced by the Rulers' guards, the increase in population and change in its structure made it necessary to form police forces. Shaikh Saʿīd bin Maktūm created a police force in 1956 in Dubai under a British commander.[96] The Ruler of Abu Dhabi followed suit in 1957. When the Rulers of Abu Dhabi, Shārjah, Ra's al Khaimah and Dubai began to build up their own defence forces during the late 1960s, they were largely officered by seconded and contracted British officers. Thus, over two decades before the withdrawal in 1971, the British Government became formally and informally almost completely responsible for the internal and the external security of the Trucial States.

Foreign jurisdiction

The framework

Throughout the 19th and the first half of the 20th century the British Government of India had made it increasingly obvious that British subjects in the Trucial States enjoyed British protection. This came to be interpreted as meaning that the local Rulers should not have jurisdiction over these people, be they Muslim, Christian or of any other faith. Yet British jurisdiction in the territories of the Trucial Rulers had not been specified or codified. The reason was that there had been very few cases other than the disputes between Indian merchants and local inhabitants over debts and lost property. With the influx of foreigners to the Trucial States and increasing contacts with the outside world, a legal code was required to cover the activities of British aircraft, their crews and passengers, British oil experts, businessmen and civil servants. It was considered to be necessary to state explicitly that these people as well as various other foreign groups should not fall under the jurisdiction of local courts and Rulers. This principle was established in the Trucial States Orders in Council of 1946 and 1949. The further Order in Council of 1950 became the basis for the execution of British jurisdiction in the Trucial States for two decades, to which the Rulers gave their formal consent.[97]

The legal system which was applied throughout the duration of this foreign jurisdiction was drawn from a variety of sources; for all general purposes the Indian Legislature and the Bombay Legislature were used. Provision was made for Acts of Parliament and Orders in Council to be applied for specific purposes. A further source of law were the provisions set out in the Third Schedules of successive Orders in Council of 1950, 1956 and 1959. Provision was also made for King's Regulations (Queen's Regulations) under Article 82 of the Order in Council of 1950; the most important such regulations were those concerning the establishment and functioning of the TOL. In the Orders in Council, rules for the administration of the courts were laid down.[98]

The courts

A number of courts were established, arranged in hierarchical order to allow for appeals. The first instance in all cases was the Court for the Trucial States, under the Political Agent as judge. The Assistant Political Agent, the Political Officer in Abu Dhabi or persons appointed by the Secretary of State in London acted as assistant judges. A Chief Court for the Persian Gulf, under the Political Resident as judge, served as an appeal court in civil and criminal matters, as well as the court of the first instance in certain criminal cases which were assigned to it by the Order in Council. The Full Court of the Persian Gulf was the higher appeal court, composed of "not more than three and not less than two members nominated by the Political Resident from among the following: the Political Resident, the Assistant Judges of the Chief Court, the Judges of the High Court of Kenya, the Judges of the High Court of Cyprus or members of the Bar . . . of not less than 9 years' standing."[99] Both the latter courts could sit either in the Trucial States or within the limits of the Bahrain, Kuwait, Qatar and Muscat Orders in Council. The nomination of registrars, court procedures and conditions for appeals were all regulated in detail in the Orders in Council on the model of British Courts abroad elsewhere. Little was changed throughout the period of the courts' functioning.

Persons under this jurisdiction

Very considerable changes were, however, made over the years with regard to the persons to whom this jurisdiction applied. In the 1950 Order in Council it was envisaged that it should apply to all persons (as well as corporations and matters) within the limits of the Order, except for subjects of any of the Trucial States Rulers other than those who joined the TOL or were employed by a person or company which was itself subject to this order.[100] In the 1956 Order in Council a clause was introduced which provided for the transfer to the shaikhs of jurisdiction over certain non-native groups of people. In 1960 the first such transfer was agreed between the Rulers and the British Government regarding the nationals of most Muslim states (except Muslim Commonwealth Countries). This agreement specifically mentioned the "stateless persons of Palestinian origin". In 1962 the nationals of Syria and in 1963 those of Algeria became excluded from British jurisdiction.[101]

With the formation of the federation of the United Arab Emirates in 1971 came the transfer to the new State of the jurisdiction over all people and institutions, national or foreign, residing within the limits of the UAE.[102] The agreement for the final transfer of jurisdiction made provision for a period of grace in which cases pending could be settled, appeals could be made, and the new State also bound itself to recognise the findings of the Trucial States Court and the appeal courts.

Matters under this jurisdiction; adapted and new legislation

In 1963 provision was made for the transfer of jurisdiction over certain matters, a parallel to the provision for the transfer of jurisdiction over certain groups of people.[103] The provision for the transfer of matters grew in importance as the individual States progressed with formulating their own legislation on a number of issues during the 1960s. Dubai and Abu Dhabi led in introducing a number of regulations concerning, for example, customs, income tax, road and air traffic.[104] After the announcement in January 1968 of the British Government's intention to withdraw its military presence from the Gulf and abrogate the treaties which had established the special relationship, the enactment of local legislation accelerated, not least because of constant prodding by the British officials who were on the scene and could see clearly that these small States were inadequately equipped with institutions, laws and administrators. In some cases it took a considerable time for the transfer of jurisdiction to be promulgated in a Queen's Regulation, because not all decrees issued by the Rulers were published in such a form as to come automatically to the notice of British officials. Only Dubai and Abu Dhabi adopted the habit after 1966 of publishing all decrees and regulations. British officials who saw the need for these regulations often helped by advising the Rulers to instruct their expatriate Arab legal advisers to draft such laws.

During 1971, the final year of British jurisdiction in the area, a number of existing decrees of the Rulers, which had been overlooked, and a multitude of new decrees passed between 1968 and 1971 were adopted in hastily-prepared and published Queen's Regulations. A total of 31 enactments in Abu Dhabi State during 1969 and 1970 were recognised in June 1971 as amendments to the "Trucial States Transfer of Jurisdiction (Miscellaneous Matters) Regulation 1971".[105] An agreement between the Ruler of Ra's al Khaimah and the British Government regarding four enactments (Workmen's Compensation Law, Income Tax Law, a Penal Code and a Law of Criminal Procedures) was published as a Queen's Regulation in May 1971.[106] More such agreements were made throughout 1971 either with the individual shaikhdoms or with the Trucial States as a whole.

During the two decades of formal British jurisdiction in the Trucial States a great number of special regulations were made to suit particular circumstances. Some of them have been mentioned before as being of major importance; others included an Alcoholic Drinks Regulation (No. 1 of 1954), a Prison Rules Regulation (No. 5 of 1957), an Aircraft Accident Regulation (No. 1 of 1958), a Fire Arms and Ammunition Regulation (No. 1 of 1955), an Orient Airways Accident Regulation (No. 3 of 1953),[107] the Abu Dhabi Port of Jebel Dhanna Regulation (No. 6 of 1967) and the regulation regarding the Traffic in Cultured Pearls (No. 2 of 1952).[108]

Apart from the regulations specific to the area, jurisdiction was applied according to laws and codes which were applicable elsewhere where Britain had extra-territorial jurisdiction in the Gulf (for example the Penal Code and the Code of Criminal Procedures). Some issues which had initially been regulated by laws in use in other areas of British jurisdiction (for example the Indian Contract Law)[109] were covered by a new regulation which was eventually formulated specifically for the Trucial States.

The effects

Thus the Trucial States were exposed for two decades to British legislation, jurisdiction and legal thinking in three ways. Firstly, legislation created for British colonies elsewhere was applied unchanged; secondly, British law was modified to suit the conditions of the entire Gulf area or just the Trucial States; thirdly, English legal thinking exerted in some instances a strong influence when the local authorities of the day formulated their own regulations and laws. But compared to most countries which had been former British colonies, the influence of British legal thinking was nevertheless only skin-deep. The duration of the influence was too short to create a tradition which might have made recourse to British legal principles the most obvious and automatic reaction even after the ties with the British legal system were severed. As will be seen later,[110] when the process of drafting new laws, at a local as well as a federal level, was accelerated after 1971, the new laws were most frequently modelled on Egyptian, Sudanese and Jordanian examples, where an assimilation of mostly French and British law with the principles of *sharīʿah* had already been made. However, for practical purposes, because there was in some cases a long delay in either local or federal legislation, many of the earlier regulations remained in force for several years. Matters concerning commerce and contracts in particular were for a long time regulated according to the Indian Code or the code formulated especially for the Trucial States, because both parties in a civil contract agreed to follow these rather than any other codes equally foreign in a State which had not yet formulated all the relevant commercial regulations of its own.

From the outset of formal British jurisdiction in the Trucial States there was provision for co-operation with the existing local bodies of jurisdiction, and in practice the British officials often helped to strengthen local jurisdiction by suggesting the establishment of local courts for various specialised matters in all the States, and the recruitment of legal advisers from Arab or Muslim countries.[111] Provisions were made to allow for cases which concerned people not subject to the Orders in Council to be tried either in a joint court or to be referred to a tribunal of the shaikhs.[112] The Trucial States Order in Council of 1959 made provision for the transfer of jurisdiction in such "cases as may be agreed from time to time between Her Majesty's Government and the Trucial Sheikhs".[113] But the British Government endeavoured to save non-Muslim persons involved in a criminal case from being tried in the Ruler's court.[114] In practice a joint court was rarely set up, and the mixed cases were dealt with in such a way that the accused could defend himself in the court by which he would be tried in a non-mixed case.

The impact of two decades of limited British jurisdiction within the Trucial States was not very great at the time, because the number of cases were few and often involved matters which were not of much relevance to the local scene, such as international agreements concerning air traffic control and postal services. But the actual process of receding jurisdiction on the part of the British Government helped considerably to stir the local authorities into action, formulating their legislative policy on a federal level, and this actually speeded the promulgation of a number of regulations. It made the Rulers and the new federal government very aware of the various fields in which a legal vacuum existed. The machinery for legislation thus gained greater prominence in the new State than it might have done without the necessity to replace certain British-made regulations.

The Development Office

General

By describing the efforts of the Development Office of the Trucial States Council in detail, the intention is not to over-emphasise the British-patronised development efforts, but rather to provide a well documented account of the state of affairs in various fields of development before the federal authorities began. Longterm, the influence on the population as a whole, of the practical achievements of the Development Office, may be less important than the seeds which were sown in the minds of young people,[115] when they were first made aware by their Arab teachers of the cohesion of the Arab culture and of the trends in Arab nationalism. The establishment of the Egyptian educational mission in Sharjah in 1958/9 was in some ways the turning point, at which the influence of the British Government, companies, and individuals, became overshadowed by the influence which the Arab World rapidly gained on people and politics in these seven shaikhdoms, both in its own right and as the vehicle for assimilating the influences from the industrialised world.

The role which Britain eventually played in the field of development in the Trucial States was not spectacular in financial terms, but it was significant not least because most of the planning and much of the work were done by British officials. The new British policy of assuming some responsibility for the welfare of the people of these States was readily adopted by most of the British civil servants in the Gulf during the 1950s and 1960s because many of them had previously been involved in development work for the Indian or the Sudan Civil Service. They easily singled out the fields where help was most needed, and they often tried their very best to prod the British Government into spending more money for development in the Trucial States, as the sums of money which were channelled in this direction usually fell short of the hopes and expectations of these officers. But a number of specific schemes were realised even before a plan for the overall development was prepared. The lack of medical facilities locally made this field the most obvious one to be tackled first. In 1939 the British Indian authorities opened a dispensary in Dubai with a resident Indian doctor; this was a forerunner of the hospital which had been planned since 1941. The war years delayed these plans until 1949, when an Irishman, a former doctor in the Indian army, was sent to Dubai to prepare for and later to run the first hospital on the coast.

In the years 1954/56 the British Government spent a total of £50,000 on small development and welfare projects, including the restoration of a *falaj* in Abu Dhabi's sector of the Buraimi oasis,[116] on drilling water wells in Ra's al Khaimah, on building the first school in Shārjah, and on adding to the hospital in Dubai. In 1955 the then Political Agent in Dubai, J.P. Tripp, together with the Political Resident in Bahrain, Sir Bernard Burrows, convinced the British Government of the necessity to commit herself to finance a Five Year Plan in the sum of £450,000. This plan was conceived to bring long-term benefits to these states by specifically helping to create institutions and administrative bodies which could themselves implement further development. In the event the Five Year Plan did, however, provide more immediately visible results at the expense of the less spectacular work of laying solid foundations for future projects. The establishment of the agricultural trial station at

Diqdāqah falls into this period, and the medical and educational facilities were improved out of this budget.

A second and much more ambitious Five Year Plan for 1961 to 1966 was proposed by the Political Agent, D. F. Hawley; however, the sum of £550,000 which was eventually approved by the British Government fell far short of expectations. Some extra grants were made, such as £100,000 for capital and £40,000 for recurrent expenditure for improvements on the hospital.

In 1965 the British Government decided to increase aid to the northern Trucial States considerably by the allocation of £1 million spread over three and a half years and an annual provision of £200,000 for current development expenditure. This decision came after Abu Dhabi had already started to export oil and could, even more than before, go its own way in development matters. The British contribution was made to the already existing Trucial States Council and was, together with contributions from other countries, administered by the Trucial States Development Office.

This Development Office grew from the modest organisation which had been set up to run the agricultural trial station in Diqdāqah in 1955 and the headquarters of the office were moved to Dubai in 1965. The office of the Secretary General of the Fund and the Development Office supervised the various departments and projects. By 1969 the Services of the Development Office consisted of:

1. Running the headquarters of the Trucial States Council;
2. Providing agricultural services based on Diqdāqah;
3. Trade and Technical Schools at Shārjah and Dubai;
4. Scholarships abroad for Trucial States subjects, and courses of instructions for Council Staff;
5. Health services centred on the Maktūm Hospital in Dubai, a touring doctor service operated in collaboration with several rural clinics, and a small hospital in Ra's al Khaimah;
6. A department to survey and develop the fisheries resources of the States;
7. A Public Works Department to execute the capital works programme with over-all responsibility for the development of water resources, building, plant and road maintenance, and supervision of public utilities.

The Development Office represented an important step in the process of making development assistance to these States a permanent institutionalised concern with long-term planning. British aid began with single donations channelled through the Political Agency in Dubai, the Agent supervising the execution of such projects. Gradually the Trucial States Council which was set up under the chairmanship of the Political Agent in 1952 earmarked development projects and suggested priorities. Some of the British political officers serving on the Trucial coast were eager to encourage the Rulers and the people in positions of responsibility to become more involved themselves in planning a long-term development strategy. To this end a committee of local delegates was formed in 1964. Its task was to formulate in detail suggestions for the most urgent projects and advise the members of the Trucial States Council in this respect.[117]

During 1965 several steps were taken to separate planning and execution of development from the Agency in Dubai. On 1 March the 21st meeting of the Trucial States Council was held and the Rulers approved the following resolution: "The Council welcomes unconditional aid from any source for the development of the Trucial States and is grateful for the interest shown by the Arab League and others in contributing to this development. In order to avoid duplication of effort and in order that the Governments of the Trucial States may jointly plan the development of the area for the common good, the Council resolves:

(a) to open an account in the name of the Trucial States Development Fund to which all sums contributed, whether from outside or inside the area, in addition to those already received, should be credited;
(b) to appoint additional staff as required to its central Development Office, so that the Office, under the Council's control, may be capable of handling the Fund and carrying out development programmes approved."[118]

This meant that not only was future development to be co-ordinated by an administrative body set up for this purpose and to be supervised by a number of specialists hired specifically for this work, but it also meant that all prospective donors including the British Government could turn to a single organisation through which to channel their assistance to these relatively poor and backward States. As expected, aid from the richer neighbouring countries flowed in more readily when the Development Office was established. Abu Dhabi, the only member to be exporting oil, contributed £100,000; Qatar and Bahrain gave £250,000 and £40,000 respectively to help set up the

Development Fund. Further generous contributions from these and other governments followed in subsequent years.[119]

When Shaikh Zāyid bin Sulṭān became Ruler in Abu Dhabi in August 1966 he immediately gave £500,000 to the Development Fund. He contributed a further £365,000 in April 1967, one million pounds Sterling in September 1967 and another £300,000 in August 1968. Until the end of 1972, when the Fund was disbanded and the duties of the Development Office were transferred to the new federal ministries, Abu Dhabi's contributions rose steadily until they covered 80 per cent of the total budget.

From 1965 more long-term projects could be budgeted for because considerably larger sums of money were available. Although one might expect that the Fund would be primarily concerned with the implementation of capital projects, it also had to contribute to maintenance and running costs of installations already constructed. With the exception of Dubai, the northern States had no budgets of their own to pay for the running costs of water-distillation plants and electric generators. Such services were provided at low cost to the consumers and had to be heavily subsidised by the Fund. In the 1971 budget there was also a sharp increase in the cost of health services following the establishment of new health centres at Ra's al Khaimah, Dibah, Shārjah, and D̲aid.[120] Subsidies for running-costs were largely responsible for the fact that the Fund's money could not be evenly distributed to benefit all the northern States equally. The statistics show that the smaller and the less developed the State, the greater was the annual per capita assistance. To the end of 1970, BD 1,300,772 had been spent by the Fund on Shārjah (population 31,500), which was an annual average of BD 6.90 per inhabitant; while the annual average was BD 27.90 for the 3,700 inhabitants of Umm al Qaiwain, and BD 0.80 for 59,000 inhabitants of Dubai.[121] The biggest single item in every budget, of great benefit to all the States, was the provision for the construction of roads, and the Trucial States Council always agreed to give priority to the improvement of communications.[122]

The most obvious advantage of channelling assistance through the Development Office, as opposed to promoting individual development projects either through the Political Agency or through the individual Rulers' courts, was that a number of people could be employed whose specialised training and experience in other developing countries gave the Office the necessary expertise for long-term planning. Many of the senior staff in each department of the Office were British specialists who had undertaken similar projects in the Sudan, India, the Hadhramaut or East Africa. By May 1970 twenty-six British citizens were employed by the Development Office,[123] ten of whom worked in the field of technical education, six in the Public Works Department, five in the health services and three in agricultural services. A fisheries specialist and the Senior Development Officer were also British. Several of them were seconded from the Ministry of Overseas Development and could therefore call on the specialised expertise of people working for that organisation, as well as for the Food and Agricultural Organisation of the United Nations.

Many of these men recognised the challenge to achieve under very difficult conditions, and they brought with them a wealth of experience which they were keen to apply. They were faced with what was for many of them an ideal planners' "grass roots" situation: they could start from scratch. They were working for a relatively small organisation in which they could to a certain extent use their own initiative, and they could see the results of their efforts among an appreciative population. In this atmosphere a team spirit could grow, often also drawing in officials working in administrative functions in Dubai itself and throughout the northern shaikhdoms. This also meant that voluntary assistance was often offered by individuals working for companies who were operating in these States. In the small and close circle of expatriates who were based in Dubai everyone took an interest in the efforts and problems of the Development Office, and in particular the Political Agency remained a focal point for the discussion of development matters. The advisers who were employed by some of the Trucial Shaikhs and municipalities in various capacities were often instrumental in informally co-ordinating the work of the Development Office with the projects of the individual Rulers.

Formally the Development Office was independent of the British Political Agency from 1965, when the chairmanship of the Trucial States Council was taken by Shaikh Ṣaqr bin Muḥammad of Ra's al Khaimah. But the Political Agent remained a member of the Council, sat in on all its meetings, and was still very much involved in steering the Rulers, often individually, towards accepting British views on development priorities. Thus Britain played an important part in the commencement of developing the Trucial States by providing expertise rather than large sums of money.

After the federation was established in 1971, development projects began to transform the northern Emirates beyond recognition, thanks to the almost unlimited funds which Abu Dhabi provided. The visible impact of the modest beginnings which the Development Office had been able to afford was soon all but obliterated by federal development projects, by the Rulers' realisation of some of their dreams, and by the building boom of private entrepreneurs. But beyond these achievements which are measurable in miles of asphalted roads and in kilowatts of installed electrical capacity, one can detect in many cases the lasting effects of the groundwork which had been laid by the Development Office. Particularly useful were the many technical surveys which were made on behalf of the Development Office often in co-operation with the British Ministry of Overseas Development and with British universities.

The population of the Trucial States had to wait painfully long, compared to some neighbours, for the first clinics, schools, piped water and other amenities. The financial aid which was forthcoming was inadequate to pay for the many projects which all seemed to be equally urgent. The fact remains that outside assistance came late and piecemeal. But the work which the Development Office was able to carry out in these circumstances, both by providing immediate betterment in the living conditions of the population and by laying the foundations for future planning, by gathering vitally necessary information, deserves recognition.

Health services

Before the Development Office was established in 1965, considerable progress had already been made in providing some medical services for the people of the Trucial States. The Maktūm Hospital in Dubai was opened in 1949 and in due course enlarged several times; the hospital at Ra's al Khaimah was opened in 1963; a number of clinics were set up, and touring doctors were organised who sent their more serious cases to the hospital in Dubai.[124] In 1964 the Senior Medical Officer, Dr McCaully, departed; he had been appointed by the British Government and had until then co-ordinated all the health services and run the hospital. The increasing number of organisations providing health care[125] made it necessary to appoint a medical administrator to co-ordinate all these activities and to advise the Council. Dr ʿĀṣim Jamāli, a national of Oman, was appointed to this post in 1967.

After the Development Office had assumed responsibility for health, more clinics were opened or rebuilt (Shārjah, D̲aid, Jazīrah al Zaʿāb, Umm al Qaiwain) and existing facilities were upgraded. The hospital in Ra's al Khaimah was enlarged to 60 beds. Soon after the health adviser was appointed, a smallpox vaccination campaign was organised after an outbreak in the summer of 1967 in Dubai. A longer-term task was the organisation of malaria control. "The incidence of malaria, particularly in Ra's al Khaimah, the East Coast and the mountain areas, has been a cause for concern, and in May 1967 the W.H.O. Regional Malariologist, Dr H. J. Van der Kaay, paid a visit to various areas of the Trucial States. He reported that malaria definitely existed in certain areas and was responsible for about 50 per cent of the illness in the Fujairah and Kalba regions of the East Coast. He considered that whereas a complete eradication program would be difficult without a similar campaign being launched in Muscat, certain control measures could be adopted and that a survey team from W.H.O. should carry out a more intensive survey."[126] This team arrived in early 1969.

From April 1967 to the end of 1970 the Development Fund shared with the Ruler of Dubai on a fifty-fifty basis the expenses of running the Maktūm Hospital.[127] In 1970 responsibility for the clinic and the maternity ward in Umm al Qaiwain was handed over to the Government of Abu Dhabi.

During the late 1960s the Development Office increasingly used its resources to co-ordinate and organise interstate projects. In August 1970 some cases of cholera were diagnosed in Dubai and Umm al Qaiwain, and a campaign was organised by the Maktūm Hospital in which some 60,000 people were vaccinated.

Agriculture

Traditional agriculture in the Trucial States did not pay much attention to gardens other than date groves. Some limes, mangoes, tobacco and lucerne were grown, but vegetables did not form part of the diet and were not grown. One of the reasons for establishing the agricultural trial station at Diqdāqah in 1955 was to find out which crops could best grow under the difficult climatic conditions in the silty soil and using local ground water. Owners of date gardens were encouraged to use uncultivated land near their gardens or to develop new areas to grow suitable fruit, vegetables, and animal fodder for marketing in the villages and towns. This meant that better communications and marketing facilities had to be prepared and the people had to grow accustomed to consuming vegetables. By 1970 the trial station comprised permanent offices, a veterinary clinic, the agricultural school, a mechanical workshop, stores and stables. The station had gardens at Diqdāqah, the main experimental centre (60 acres), Falaj al Muʿallā (5 acres) and Kalba (7 acres). At all three gardens farmers were encouraged to discuss their own extension projects, to buy at cost price seedlings, seeds, fertilisers, and insecticides, and to hire agricultural machines. Demand was such that by 1970 one field assistant with a staff of six village agents were insufficient to give advice to the growing number of farmers, and the demand for the hire of tractors could hardly be met by the available plant.

The trial station also experimented with raising various imported breeds of animals. A herd of 28 cows and two Friesian bulls were brought in by air in 1969, and by the end of 1970 the herd had grown to 51. It became clear that during the hot season special bedding and cooling had to be provided for such imported animals if they were to survive, and therefore they were not suitable for a family keeping only one or two cows; but it was found that it could be commercially viable to keep large herds of them if fodder could be grown cheaply. A herd of Damascus goats and various poultry were also reared at Diqdāqah for sale to farmers.

In September 1967 a qualified veterinary officer was employed by the Development Office. In 1970 his territory was divided into a north section comprising Ra's al Khaimah and the east coast with a veterinary surgeon based at Diqdāqah, and the remaining southern section with a surgeon based at Shārjah. Over 600 head of stock were treated monthly by the specialists and their assistants, meat inspection was carried out on alternate days in Ra's al Khaimah and other towns. This veterinary service was still only a modest beginning, for example it had no laboratory. Also because the roads were only dirt tracks and through the mountains they were particularly difficult to negotiate, a lot of time had to be spent on travel, and the east coast, not easy of access, was less well served than the rest of the area. The Development Office started to formulate regulations to prevent the introduction of animal diseases, but this task was eventually undertaken some years later by the federal government.

In 1968 the Milaiḥah agricultural scheme was created near Jabal

Fāyah in Shārjah. Three hundred acres of land were irrigated, and planted with fruit trees, lucerne and vegetables, with the intention of handing over sections to tribesmen of the area, many of whom would continue to lead a semi-nomadic life. But the latter part of the Milaiḥah project was not achieved during the lifetime of the Development Office. The federal Ministry of Agriculture and Fisheries, which took over this project, inherited the technical inadequacies of the scheme; they found that there was no assured market near enough and that most of the settlers preferred to earn a regular wage rather than face the risks inherent in owning their own plot.[128]

Perhaps the most useful contribution which the Development Office made to the improvement of agriculture in the area was through its agricultural school. This was established in September 1967 in place of the primary school which had been run by the Diqdāqah station since the 1950s. The school ran a two-year course in agriculture for students who had completed intermediate schooling. In 1970 five students graduated all taking posts with the Development Office, and in the following school year, the last under the Development Office, there were 24 students and 3 Palestinian teachers at the school.

Surveys

Before any large-scale agricultural projects could be undertaken in the area it was essential to commission surveys to determine the nature and availability of ground water, and to investigate the various soil types of the area. Therefore the first sum of money which the British Government gave for development in the Trucial States in 1952 included funds for a Water Resources Survey; a second survey in 1959 was carried out under the auspices of the UN Technical Assistance Branch. Any local farmer would himself classify the various areas bearing in mind the availability of water. The properties of the soil in the mountain foreland, the *wādis* and the desert borders play an equally important role in the siting of new farms and the selection of crops to be raised there.

From the outset the Development Office concentrated on gathering information in surveys before engaging on a project, and inevitably the majority of these surveys were hydrological.[129] The British firm of consultants, Sir William Halcrow and Partners, which had worked in Dubai since the 1950s, made another groundwater survey in 1965 which was commissioned by the British Government. This firm became specialised in hydrological surveys of the area and issued several hydrological yearbooks for the Development Office. The first mineral resources survey was undertaken in 1966 by Mr J. E. G. Greenwood, of the Overseas Division of the Institute of Geological Sciences in London. The University of Durham first became involved in soil surveys in 1967, and published an assessment of agricultural potential both in the northern Trucial States and in Abu Dhabi; the latter was usually not included in such surveys because the State could by then pay for them itself.[130] Studies were also made of the feasibility of constructing roads and tracks through difficult sandy, rocky or mountainous terrain, bearing in mind the limited financial resources. Fishing on both coasts of the Trucial States was also studied with a view to expanding this industry. Because all these surveys were often also of interest to other development agencies and universities, the Development Office had little problem in obtaining assistance, other than financial, from universities, the Food and Agricultural Organisation, and other United Nations organisations, and from the British Ministry of Overseas Development with its regional headquarters in Beirut.[131]

Roads

Until the late 1960s if anyone in Abu Dhabi or Dubai considered travelling to Fujairah he would usually take a boat all the way round Cape Musandam. There were no roads, and the tracks through the sand and over the mountains were either so rough as to require rugged vehicles, or were only passable by donkey or camel. If the new institutions such as the hospital in Dubai or the marketing facilities in the towns on the Gulf coast were to play a role in the lives of the people on the east coast and in the interior, communications had to be substantially improved.

When the Development Office was established in 1965 no road had been built except some town roads in Dubai, and the 13.5 kilometre road between Dubai and Shārjah became the first major project to be executed by the Development Office. The road was opened in October 1966 by the then chairman of the Trucial States Council, Shaikh Ṣaqr bin Muḥammad of Ra's al Khaimah. The continuation of this road from Shārjah to Ra's al Khaimah was eventually not built by the Development Office, but the Saudi Arabian Government decided to finance and execute the project independently, with a revised route and specifications, and to include an extension from Ra's al Khaimah to Diqdāqah. Work started in 1967 and the road was finished in 1969.

The Development Office built the four kilometres of road from Shārjah to Khān. But the important link from Shārjah to D̲aid, which was to form part of the transpeninsular road, was built at the expense of Abu Dhabi. After a study had been prepared by Sir William Halcrow and Partners in 1967 on the feasibility of such a road across the mountains, the Development Office initiated the first stage of this project.[132] Work commenced in 1967 on improving the very rough track through the mountains. The Royal Engineers stationed in Shārjah assisted with blasting rock off the steepest hills along the track and opening up three mountain passes on the coastal stretch between Khaur Fakkān and Dibah, which was until mid-1968 only passable on foot or donkey. The tracks, culverts and gradients were constructed in some places with a view to asphalting in the future, whereas much of the track followed the easier and cheaper routes through the *wādi* beds. The Development Office had ceased to function when this latter project was completed by the federal Ministry of Public Works. Much of the track through the Wādi Ḥām was redesigned to take it above the *wādi* bed, because funds were then available to build the necessary high bridges.

The proposal to build a road to link Ra's al Khaimah, Manāmah and D̲aid with the al ʿAin and Buraimi area, a distance of about 175 kilometres was studied by the Development Office. This road was considered to be of high priority, not only to link these similar tribal areas but also because it passed through the main existing agricultural areas and a considerable amount of potential agricultural land. In a report on roads prepared by the Development Office in September 1970 this project was described: "By its careful siting to the east of agricultural lands (present and future) and by its being structurally designed in the form of a flood barrier, the following additional results are expected: (a) the protection from floods of existing areas such as Dhaid, Mileiha and Hamraniyah as well as sizeable other areas not yet developed (b) by retaining waters to the east of the road barrier and having it diffused over the gravel plain to percolate into the subsoil, the progressive improvement of the quantity and quality of all groundwaters westward to the sea (c) in the necessary maintenance works of removing silt washed down at flood times, to keep the gravel plain surface open to percolation, the winning of top dressing soils for garden areas."[133]

The Development Office did not start on this project; like many others it was adopted by the federal Ministry and paid for by Abu Dhabi; the last few kilometres were completed in asphalt during the summer of 1978.

The large amount and high quality of road construction which was completed, in particular during the first five years of the existence of the United Arab Emirates, completely overshadows everything which the Development Office had achieved during its lifetime. However, using limited funds it had opened up the country sufficiently to enable even the outlying communities to benefit from new facilities offered in the towns, such as medical care, and to bring markets within reach of agricultural producers. The Development Office had also identified priorities and with the help of specialised surveys laid the foundations for the speedy implementation of various projects by the federal authorities.

Education

A development organisation which concentrates only on changing the physical environment without endeavouring to adapt the way of life of the people to the new conditions does not bring lasting benefits to the country. Before the Development Office was established, the British Government built in 1953 the first school in Shārjah, and in due course initiated further educational projects through the Political Agency.

Technical education was given high priority when funds became available, and in 1958 the British Government started building the first Trade School in the Trucial States in Shārjah. The school began with one class of 18 boys, many of whom left after the first year because the skills which they had already acquired made them valuable staff for firms which operated in the Trucial States. Of those who remained at school, four were sent in 1960 to Sudan for further education and training as teachers and instructors for future employment in the Trade School. By 1964 the school had been expanded several times and accommodated 48 students, taught by 6 instructors; the courses included Arabic and English language, mathematics and engineering drawing. Technical education was greatly encouraged by the Ruler of Dubai, who paid for a new Trade School in Dairah, and by the principal of the Shārjah school, who planned and supervised this new project.[134] In 1965 the Development Office took over from the British Government the financing of the Shārjah School and half a share of the Dubai school until 1967, when all the expenditure became the responsibility of the Office. Shārjah had then an intake of 48 students for a 3-year course and Dubai had 80 students for a 4-year course. In 1964 for the first time all new entrants were already literate, which meant that the standard of the school improved. Specialised training could be carried to a higher level and a link was established with further education centres in Khartoum, Kuwait, Bahrain or Beirut and, from 1965, the U.K. By the beginning of 1969 there were 298 students receiving technical training in the Trucial States, excluding Abu Dhabi.[135] In September of that year the Trade School in Ra's al Khaimah opened.

The Development Office did not involve itself in general education, as this was a field in which Kuwait was particularly active. Since 1954 the Ruler of Kuwait had paid for the construction and running of schools in the Trucial States. Qatar and Saudi Arabia also contributed financially to educational projects, while Bahrain helped by providing some of the teachers who were paid for by the other states.

Analysis of British Development Efforts

In the field of education the successes of British development assistance as well as its shortcomings show up particularly clearly. Under the strong influence of the British Ministry of Overseas Development the British Political Agent and from 1965 the Development Office faced their task in the Trucial States employing the same principles as they would have adopted in any other developing country. They therefore sought to motivate the young to undergo technical and commercial training, and did not try to create a cadre of administrators. This order of priority seemed to be correct for a country with a very small population and the prospect of a rapidly increasing number of technical jobs with oil companies. Trade was expanding in the bigger population centres in the wake of the oil company activities, and it became obvious to the Rulers that it would be beneficial to their States if students were trained in skills which would be needed in a booming economy, so they in turn welcomed and promoted this policy in the Trucial States Council.

The question may be asked in hindsight whether the very limited manpower should not have been trained to a greater extent for public administrative careers. Could and should people involved in development work in the Trucial States in the late 1960s have foreseen that this was not the ordinary "developing country", but a country where financing a project was soon to be no longer a problem? Some form of political union was anticipated, and therefore more effort might have been made to provide these states with national administrators to run the country in the future.[136]

Whichever route might have been followed, that is to provide an education predominantly in the technical or predominantly in the administrative field, the outcome would have been rapidly overtaken by events. After all, education is a long-term process. Even after the discovery of oil in commercial quantities in Abu Dhabi in 1960 it was impossible to predict that the resultant economic boom would be so great, and would build up so rapidly. It was also not possible for people to obtain training, in the time before the boom and before the union in 1971, in the management of the new situations that were themselves a product of the economic and political changes.

British involvement in development in Abu Dhabi was always of a different nature from that in the rest of the Trucial States. It was consultative, not active. One of the reasons why a British Political Officer was sent to Abu Dhabi in 1957 and the post was upgraded to Political Agent in 1961, and why the British Government took great pains to find suitable British advisers for the Ruler, was that they wanted to encourage the Ruler to speed up development himself. These advisers were directly employed by the Ruler of Abu Dhabi, and therefore took their instructions from him and not from a development agency or from the British Government. As in the case of the employees of the Development Office, or other expatriates working in Dubai, they frequently made a valuable contribution to development in their special fields. But they could not be expected to be particularly interested in the problems concerning the co-ordination of development efforts throughout all the Trucial States. In the late 1960s Abu Dhabi had become wealthy and was making a considerable financial contribution to the development of the northern Trucial States; the standard of living of the people in Abu Dhabi improved dramatically compared to the changes in the other states. The long term significance of this imbalance was not recognised at the time, even by the advisers. Yet its rectification would have facilitated the transition to a unified State which sooner or later was to replace the anachronistic array of small shaikhdoms.

The Ruler of Abu Dhabi, Shaikh Shakhbūṭ bin Sulṭān, repeatedly turned down offers from the Political Agency to include Abu Dhabi in assistance programmes and surveys. But it was Shaikh Shakhbūṭ who asked the Americans running the Dutch Reformed Church's Hospital in Maṭraḥ, in Oman, to establish medical facilities in al ʿAin. In so small a population every person is needed. Thus, the lives which were saved by Mr and Mrs Kennedy, Surgeon and Gynaecologist respectively, and by their staff, since the Oasis Hospital opened in 1960, count in the local society of today. In al ʿAin and other areas where this mission built up by medical facilities, before any government could do so, most local families had no other contact with the world outside, and the success or failure of western medicine, as well as the personalities of those who administered it, became the yardstick for many people's expectations of Europe and the New World. The establishment of the Development Office in 1965 almost coincided with the change of rule and policy in Abu Dhabi, because after 1966 the new Ruler, Shaikh Zāyid bin Sulṭān, pushed ahead with a multitude of development projects and social services, for which he could easily pay from his ever-increasing oil income. While there was a great deal of co-operation between most officials, advisers, consultants, specialists and political bodies concerned with the development of Dubai on the one hand and the northern Trucial States on the other, there was usually a certain amount of rivalry between these people and those working in Abu Dhabi. The former were justifiably proud of their achievements with limited financial resources, and criticised Abu Dhabi for pushing ahead rapidly with many costly projects simultaneously. In Abu Dhabi, both expatriates and nationals alike were exhilarated by the long-awaited opportunity to "do things", and were prepared to accept some costly flaws in the detail.

It was primarily due to the activities of the London based PD (TC), "The Company", and later to ADMA and to the efforts of the British Government that the population of the Trucial States experienced really dramatic changes in their lives during the 1950s and early 1960s. Much conscientious planning and hard physical work was done during these two decades by scores of oil company employees, development officers, and British Government officials. Perhaps the very intensity of the good will generated and the personal engagement at all levels meant that they sought satisfaction in immediate results which could be seen in the particular field which concerned them. By the late 1960s life on the Trucial Coast looked a great deal less grim than it was at the end of the Second World War. There was employment for many with the oil companies. Commerce was building up incredibly fast in Dubai and Abu Dhabi. Security, communications, and social services were improving every month, and the general economic boom was itself enough to promote the constant upgrading of the infrastructure.

There was no longer the obvious need for the "social conscience approach" which the British officials and Government had adopted in the 1950s. Once it had been recognised that Britain ought to do something to improve the quality of life of the population in the Trucial States, it was not too long before action was taken because the task of organising health services, education, communication, security, had been performed many times over by British officials under similar conditions. The biggest problem in post-war Britain was lack of funds.

There was, however, no such common consent about the extent of British responsibility for the political future of the Trucial States. Not many British politicians ever questioned during the 1960s whether the chance of history which had made this distant coast an appendix to the British Empire should remain the basis of its political existence. While some might have wished that these small shaikhdoms had long ago become integral parts of one of the big political units in the neighbourhood, others envisaged the continuation of political tutelage together with humanitarian assistance as a bounden duty of Great Britain for many years to come.

In the event it did not make much difference what approach those officials took. The fate of these small shaikhdoms was decided by developments which were completely outside their scope, namely the reappraisal of Britain's role in the world and in the western defence system. Britain was withdrawing from its commitments East of Suez.

Chapter Nine

The Formation of the Federation

1 British withdrawal

The Labour Government's economic measures

The event which redirected the course of history in the Trucial States and led to the creation of the UAE was a result of totally unrelated events taking place in British domestic politics. The rank and file of the British Labour Party had for several years been very critical of the annual increase in defence spending. The Labour Government under Mr Harold Wilson therefore undertook to reduce this item of expenditure, and in a White Paper published on 16 February 1967 further cuts were envisaged. One of the central features of this policy was to liquidate almost all British military bases east of Suez, withdrawing tens of thousands of men and their families. Part of this plan was the withdrawal of all British troops from South Arabia by 1968, when Aden and the protectorates were to form an independent federation. Yet this White Paper did provide for "generous financial assistance" to strengthen the South Arabian federal forces; arrangements had been made, and "practical preparations were under way for the small increase in forces stationed in the Persian Gulf which would be needed by Britain to fulfil her remaining obligations in the area after leaving Aden."[1] However, the parliamentary debate on defence made it clear that even this drastic change of Britain's role in the world did not satisfy a large number of Labour MPs, who were determined to speed up the withdrawal. Thus it was also taken for granted that the number of troops in the Persian Gulf would be decreased,[2] and by May 1967 the Government was seriously considering withdrawal from the Gulf States as well as from Aden. This intention was strongly criticised by the late King Faisal of Saudi Arabia during a visit to London in mid-May.[3]

Following the devaluation of the pound sterling in autumn 1967, withdrawal from east of Suez appeared to be inevitable, yet the British Government still intended to meet its treaty obligations *vis-à-vis* the Gulf States. In November 1967 a Foreign Office Minister, Mr Goronwy Roberts, visited the Shah of Iran and the Rulers in the Gulf, assuring them that in the interests of stability in the Gulf region the British military presence would be maintained at all its traditional bases. But in a speech in the House of Commons the Prime Minister announced on 16 January 1968 further drastic expenditure cuts and the intention to withdraw completely by the end of 1971. He said: "We have also decided to withdraw our forces from the Persian Gulf by the same date."[4] In the meantime between 8 and 11 January Mr Goronwy Roberts had returned to the Gulf to break this news to his incredulous hosts.

Thus, internal British and Labour Party politics, not the initiation of a particular foreign policy, brought about this completely new situation in all the Gulf States.

The technicalities of withdrawal

Initial despondency over the decision was felt as intensively by the British diplomats serving in the area as by the Rulers. The latter had just experienced two decades during which the attitude of Britain had developed from aloofness and an occasional show of gunboat power to a humanitarian interest in these States. The Rulers could then look forward to enjoying the new wealth from oil under British protection and guidance. On the diplomats, many of whom had endeavoured for years to understand the Arab way of life, fell the unenviable task of explaining what was seen as the British Government's breach of written agreements and the unwritten Arab law of trust and friendship. They also had to grapple with the technicalities of handing over military, political, legal and administrative responsibilities; in some States there were as yet no appropriate institutions to assume these responsibilities.

The British Government hoped that in spite of the tight withdrawal schedule the transition from British tutelage to complete autonomy would be effected smoothly in all the States. It was considered by some that localised unrest was probably a bigger risk at that time than the risk of upsetting the global balance of power, and of the Soviet Union gaining access to the Gulf. A number of disputes had to be settled before the British Government could claim that the withdrawal would not cause the disruption which was predicted by the opposition in Britain and by many people who knew the area well.

A fairly straightforward problem was the so-called "defence agreement", which was a clause in the British-Kuwaiti Agreement of 19 June 1961 promising British assistance in the event of Kuwait being attacked. By May 1968 an exchange of letters resulted in the removal of this defence clause from the agreement, with effect from 13 May 1971.[5]

The Bahrain predicament

The biggest single problem which had to be resolved to ensure orderly withdrawal was that of sovereignty over Bahrain.[6] As soon as the British withdrawal was announced Iran reiterated its claim to the islands of Bahrain, which it called a "crown jewel" and counted as one of its provinces although it did not exercise sovereignty over it. However, the common concern for peace and stability in the area prevailed, and the Iranian Government ventured on a course which led eventually to total Bahraini autonomy. Bahrain has always been opposed to a formal plebiscite, but eventually agreed to the British proposal to ascertain public opinion on the island under the auspices of the United Nations.[7] The Secretary-General sent as his personal representative Mr Vittorio Winspeare Guicciardi, Director-General of the UN Office in Geneva, who arrived on 30 March 1970 and stayed until 18 April. He conferred with organisations, societies, institutions and private citizens. An office was set up where anybody could meet him and discuss the issue. Mr Guicciardi reported to the UN on 2 May: "My conclusions have convinced me that the overwhelming majority of the people of Bahrain wish to gain recognition of their identity in a fully independent and sovereign state free to decide for itself its relations with other states."[8] This report was endorsed by the UN Security Council on 11 May. The UN endorsement of Bahrain's independence was ratified by the Iranian Majlis on 14 May by 186 votes to 4, and unanimously by the Iranian Senate on 18 May. Thus Iran renounced her claim to sovereignty over Bahrain.

Considering the fact that the Iranian State contains within its borders a fair number of ethnic and religious minority areas, it was a bold and statesmanlike decision initially to agree to Mr Guicciardi's mission and subsequently to renounce the claim without further ado. It demonstrates that the Iranian Government was at that time well aware of the possible dangers in British withdrawal, and while preparing to assume the role of the major military power in the Gulf, it was ready to make this sacrifice for the sake of stability and of good relations with Arab neighbours. But having climbed down once, it would have been very difficult for Iran to renounce its claim over the islands Abū Mūsa and the two Tunbs.[9]

Bahrain had been the test case for Britain's ability to settle any outstanding disputes within the area before vacating and leaving the governments and people to their own devices. Thus after summer 1970 the outlook was brighter and the various parties gained confidence while preparing themselves for the future after December 1971. The replacement of the oppressive and unco-operative Saʿīd bin Taimūr, Sultan of Muscat and Oman, by his son Qābūs also contributed to the air of optimism.

Speculation that the Conservatives might reverse policy

If the establishment of the federation combining the small Gulf States into an internationally-recognised politically viable entity was being delayed, this was again largely due to domestic politics in Britain. The Labour decision to withdraw from east of Suez was strongly criticised by most Conservatives. Withdrawal from the Gulf in particular was portrayed by many leading opposition politicians as an error in all respects: military, economic, and political. It was seen as an invitation to the Soviet Union to extend its influence to the waters of the Gulf. In Parliament and elsewhere the decision to withdraw from the Gulf in unseemly haste was described as a stab in the back of the pro-western governments who, it was feared, would fall prey to Cairo-orientated left-wing propaganda. Many Conservatives also pointed out that the argument that Britain could not afford the cost of maintaining troops in the Gulf was not valid. The cost to Britain of maintaining its military, naval and air presence in the Gulf was then some £16 million, while British investment in the area, particularly by petroleum companies, was many times that figure. Also in 1966 Britain imported almost half its requirements of oil from the Gulf. The Deputy Leader of the Opposition, Mr Reginald Maudling, visited the area early in February 1968. Other Conservatives followed and in April Mr Edward Heath himself held talks with Arab and Iranian leaders. This activity left the impression that the Conservatives were so deeply opposed to the withdrawal that they would reverse the decision if and when they came to power.

It is therefore not surprising that many of the political leaders in the Gulf area nourished hopes of the restoration of the *status quo ante* in the event of a Conservative election victory. This frame of mind of at least some of the people did not encourage those attempting to finalise the establishment of the federation of Gulf emirates. Following the surprise victory of the Conservatives in the election of 18 June 1970, the new Government was pressed for a decision on their policy regarding the Gulf.

Although it soon became obvious that the decision to withdraw could not and would not be reversed by the Conservative Government, it took another nine months for the formal announcement to be made. On 1 March 1971 the British Foreign Secretary, Sir Alec Douglas-Home, told the House of Commons that Britain had offered the Arab Emirates of the Gulf a treaty of friendship to replace the existing defence treaties, which were scheduled to be terminated by 31 December 1971. During all this time the Conservatives were sounding out the practical implications of their own bias towards keeping a presence east of Suez and in particular in the Gulf. Sir William Luce, who had been Political Resident in the Gulf from 1961 to 1966, was brought out of retirement to be the Foreign Secretary's special adviser. At the same time it was announced that Sir Geoffrey Arthur, Britain's Ambassador in Kuwait at the time of the 1968 announcement, was appointed successor to Sir Stewart Crawford as Political Resident in Bahrain. Earlier Sir William Luce had advocated that Britain should proceed to withdraw from the Gulf. He spent five weeks in August and September 1970 in discussion with leaders of all the countries bordering the Gulf and also of other Arab countries. During his visits to Iran he ascertained that the British withdrawal was already treated as a *fait accompli* and that Iran was aiming at becoming the major military and political power in the area.[10] Although the Iranian attitude may have been reassuring for some in Whitehall, Iran's intransigence over its claim to the islands of Abū Mūsa and the Tunbs cast a shadow over the federation negotiations.

Sir William Luce returned twice to the area, in October 1970 and again in January/February 1971, before his recommendations to the Foreign Secretary were finalised and the latter announced the Government's long awaited decision on 1 March 1971. Since the deadline for Britain's withdrawal remained the same, 31 December 1971, time was fast running out for finalising the structure of the Union of Arab Emirates.

2 Local response to the new situation

Early stages in co-operation

While the withdrawal of the British military presence forced all the Gulf States, including Iran and Saudi Arabia, to reconsider their defence requirements, the January 1968 announcement meant that Bahrain, Qatar and the Trucial States would soon have to conduct all their external relations themselves. In some of these states educational and development projects as well as much of the day-to-day administration and internal security was run directly or indirectly with British Government assistance. At the time of the surprise announcement of the British intention to withdraw, few of the states appreciated the formidable task of establishing at home viable governmental machinery, while at the same time finding the right balance in regional and global power politics. The problem of security was obvious enough, and the legacy of unresolved territorial disputes added to some Rulers' problems. The immediate reaction to the British announcement was disbelief because of recent British assurances to the contrary, followed by apprehension when the truth became clear.

The resultant state of mind among the Rulers certainly encouraged them to draw more closely together, aided by some strong lobbying on the part of the British Foreign Office. However, some British diplomats were cynical because they had seen the recent failure of the British-engineered South Arabian Federation.[11]

The Ruler of Bahrain, Shaikh ʿĪsa bin Salmān Āl Khalīfah, was the first of the Rulers to state publicly that the establishment of a federation between the Gulf Emirates was "a national issue which we will decide and which will not be decided by anyone for us."[12] He made official visits to Saudi Arabia and Kuwait during January and February 1968 to discuss the future of the Gulf, while the Kuwaiti Minister of Foreign Affairs, Shaikh Ṣabāḥ al Aḥmad al Jābir Āl Ṣabāḥ, demonstrated his country's support for Gulf-wide co-operation by visiting all the Lower Gulf States at the end of January.

An important step towards realising some form of institutional union resulted from the statesmanlike decisions of the two Rulers, Shaikh Zāyid of Abu Dhabi and Shaikh Rāshid of Dubai. They met on 18 February 1968 on the border between their two States and formally agreed to merge the two shaikhdoms in a union, conducting jointly foreign affairs, defence, security, and social services, and adopting a common immigration policy. This agreement became possible after a dispute regarding the off-shore boundary between the two shaikhdoms was settled to Dubai's advantage. Dubai relinquished its claim to a further stretch of coastline but did obtain full sovereignty over the whole of the off-shore Fatḥ oil-field.[13]

The two Rulers invited the neighbouring Rulers to participate in a larger federation. On 25 February the Rulers of the seven Trucial States and of Bahrain and Qatar convened in Dubai to hold a constitutional conference. This quick response and willingness to co-operate, no matter how grave some of their differences had been, was partly due to the fact that before the British announcement British officials had been encouraging the idea of forming a federation. The Trucial States Council of the seven Rulers established in 1952 by the British Government already gave the Rulers a say in the British-run development projects and it also provided a means of institutionalising consultation and co-operation between them.[14] There is also a tradition of meetings of all or some of the Trucial Rulers, usually convened by the strongest Ruler at the time, to settle a particularly disruptive dispute between two shaikhdoms or tribes or to counter a general threat. The Trucial States Council meetings which took place at the invitation of the Political Agent resident in Dubai, which were at times addressed by the Political Resident in the Gulf, never developed much of an organisational working routine, but they did help in that the seven Rulers met at least twice a year to discuss and to agree on matters concerning development work.[15]

The meeting of the nine Rulers in February 1968 in Dubai was organised neither by the Trucial States Council nor by a British-sponsored constitutional conference. The invitation was extended by the Rulers of Dubai and Abu Dhabi, who each had their own reasons for wanting to expand the scope of the meeting, and hopefully of the federation itself, beyond the circle of the seven Trucial States. Thus it was probably the idea of Shaikh Rāshid of Dubai to include Qatar, which was then ruled by his son-in-law, Shaikh Aḥmad bin ʿAli Āl Thāni, who had helped generously with loans and grants for development projects in Dubai; on the other hand Abu Dhabi had always had close relations with Bahrain, whose currency, the Bahrain Dinar, it had used from 1966 to 19 May 1973; also the Government of Bahrain had literally provided teachers and civil servants for the expanding Abu Dhabi administration.

The first federation meeting

When the nine Rulers gathered in Dubai in February 1968 they probably supposed that it would be a preliminary meeting to sound out the possibility of forming a federation of their nine Emirates. But the Government of Qatar had already prepared the draft of an agreement for the creation of a federation there and then.[16] This draft formed the basis of the discussions between the nine delegations, and much of the original text became in the event the text of the first agreement between the nine.

The most noticeable difference between the Qatari draft proposal and the agreement was that the number of participants was not reduced, as proposed by Qatar. The draft had envisaged that the five small shaikhdoms (Shārjah, ʿAjmān, Umm al Qaiwain, Fujairah and Ra's al Khaimah) should establish a union among themselves, to be known as the United Arab Coastal Emirates, in which each of the five shaikhdoms would be a province, ruled by a governor, namely its Ruler, while the presidency of this new Emirate would rotate among the five governors.[17] This construction would have cut the number of member States of the anticipated federation from nine to five, which would have been more nearly equal in terms of population and economic resources. However, the idea of signing away their sovereign rights was totally unacceptable to the five Rulers concerned and was also rejected by the rest as being unworkable.

The meeting in Dubai of the nine Rulers with a number of relatives, advisers and retainers in attendance, lasted from 25 to 27 February 1968. Much to the surprise of some of the participants, who might have expected a rather vague declaration to "strengthen brotherly ties" and of the intention to look into the possibility of forming a union, the draft constitution on the table compelled them to concentrate their minds on the practicalities of creating a federal State. A great deal of the bargaining was between the expatriate Arab advisers of the Governments of Qatar and Abu Dhabi. The nine Rulers finally signed a version of the agreement which differed in a number of points from the original draft.[18]

The draft deals in two places with procedures for settling disputes among the member States, but both references were dropped in the final version to avoid reference to such disputes and to assume a sense of cohesion from the outset.

The agreement of February 1968 was inadequate as an instrument for welding the nine shaikhdoms into a political organism functioning as one federal State or union. It was not a constitution but more the expression of an intention. There was no provision for a cabinet of ministers, either in the draft or in the agreement. The legislative power was reserved to the Supreme Council, consisting of the nine Rulers.[19] The Supreme Council was to draw up a constitution, to formulate the policies of the State, to "legislate federal laws required in this connection"[20] and to prepare an annual budget.

The executive body of the federation was to be the "Federal Council".[21] In the draft this Council was intended to resemble a parliament, and three councils concerned with defence, economy and culture were to report to it. In the agreement the role of the Federal Council was considerably reduced, and it was to operate under the close supervision of the Supreme Council.[22] The composition of the Federal Council was to be left to be decided by law.[23]

The part of the agreement, entitled "General Rules", addressed itself first to the need to co-operate in defending individual Emirates and the State as a whole against external agression; secondly to the Supreme Federal Court, whose functions were specified only in the draft; thirdly to the need for the Supreme Council to decide on its permanent headquarters; fourthly to the reservation to each Emirate of the right to manage its own internal, non-federal affairs; and finally to a provision that the Supreme Council could amend the agreement "particularly if the amendment tends to make ties among the member Amirates stronger."[24] As proposed in the draft, it was decided that the agreement should come into force on 30 April 1968 and remain in force until superseded by a permanent charter.[25]

The comparison between the draft and the eventual text of the agreement shows that, while the draft avoids rash unification of administrative powers and abstains from aiming at a textbook constitution which would have had no prospect of being adopted by the nine Rulers, let alone of being implemented by the administration, the three days of bargaining by the Rulers and their advisers in Dubai resulted in an even more vague document. All participants in the Dubai meeting were very much in favour of seeking strength in unity, but some had reservations about signing away their prerogatives and sharing their own State's achievements and wealth. Others realised that although this agreement did not provide for the enforcement of members' participation, it was a foundation on which to build, in time and with much patience, a functional federal State.

The signature of the Dubai agreement on 27 February 1968 by all the nine Rulers[26] was immediately welcomed by Kuwait and favourably greeted by many other governments.[27] Saudi Arabia, after an official visit by the Ruler of Qatar, stated on 3 April that it welcomed the federation, and made an offer of economic aid.

Iran, the other State with territorial claims *vis-à-vis* a member of the federation, broke its silence only on 1 April, stating that it "reserves all its rights in the Persian Gulf and will never tolerate this historic inequity and injustice . . . The British Government cannot relinquish and give away land which according to history was taken from Iran by force."[28]

But it appears that some of the participants of the meeting, particularly the Rulers of the smaller Emirates, began to have second thoughts. Thus 30 March 1968, the date for the agreement to come into force, came and went without the Supreme Council meeting and without any further explanation, leaving open the question as to the practical function of the fledgling federation. There was, however, a great deal of discussion among some Rulers and their aides at that time.

3 The three-year construction period

Discovering the realities of federal life

The advisers take stock

Eventually a meeting was convened in Abu Dhabi on 18/19 May 1968 of the advisers[29] to the Rulers of the nine member States, which was to prepare the ground and draw up an agenda for the planned meeting of the Supreme Council of Rulers. At this meeting it became clear that the differences between the member States, which emerged after the February agreement, although considerable, were nevertheless only differences of priority and emphasis. All nine states were in favour of a federation, some wished it to be loose, others hoped for strong central powers, and others saw the federation as the vehicle for the evolution of democratic representation. The background and the temperament of the different advisers were reflected in the position taken by an Emirate on any particular issue. Throughout the two days of meetings many of the arguments were reduced to a discussion of the extent to which the advisers had authority to take the initiative and to reach decisions on technical issues which the Rulers might choose not to dispute. It also emerged that some participants preferred to leave many subjects until after the adoption of a constitution, which was tantamount to prolonging the transition period until the federal authority could assert itself. Qatar particularly strongly advocated forging ahead with establishing the various organs necessary for the new state to function; it insisted that fourteen new items were included in the agenda, ranging from the selection of the first President of the Federation to the unification of the currencies and a discussion of the establishment of ministries.

One of the important topics discussed at this meeting was the drafting of the permanent constitution for the federation. The delegation of Abu Dhabi proposed that several experts in constitutional law should prepare the draft and a committee from the nine emirates should liaise between the experts and the nine governments; but the advisers agreed that two Arab experts on constitutional and public international law should be appointed.

When the matter of the election of the President was discussed, Ra's al Khaimah's proposal of a popular referendum was supported by Bahrain but rejected by the others, who considered as premature the election of the President before a permanent constitution was agreed upon. Equally, the proposal to recommend to the Supreme Council the choice of an administrative seat for the federation was rejected by 6 to 3 votes. Qatar's proposal concerning the formation and function of the Federal Council was rejected by 8 to 1, and Bahrain's proposal was adopted to form a follow-up committee to implement the resolutions of the Supreme Council of Rulers. The advisers agreed, with one abstention, to recommend the formation of four committees of five members each: the follow-up committee (seat in Bahrain), the currency committee (Qatar), the liaison committee (Abu Dhabi), and the postal services committee (Dubai). The Qatari proposals to recommend the discussion of ministries, an official gazette and various financial matters were rejected in favour of Bahrain's suggestion to assign all of this to a follow-up committee. It was agreed that unanimity on all matters within the Supreme Council of Rulers should be superseded by a system of majority votes. In the Dubai Agreement the Rulers had settled for unanimity because the smaller Emirates feared that in any other system they would be dominated by the larger States.[30]

The meeting of advisers accentuated three quite different approaches; Qatar argued all along that the preparation of the permanent constitution was only one item of many in the Dubai Agreement which should be activated and its authorities established; a President and a capital city should be decided upon. Qatar bombarded this meeting and subsequent Supreme Council meetings with suggestions, legal opinions, memoranda and draft agreements, all aimed at actually making the federation start functioning.

Abu Dhabi advocated proceeding slowly, allowing time to adjust to the new situation and to anticipate the consequences of each move. Abu Dhabi adopted a very cautious attitude towards the establishment of institutions at that time, realising how very difficult it could be to change certain functions once they had become institutionalised. The Abu Dhabi delegation wanted to concentrate on creating the right federation with, in due course, the right constitution on the basis of the experts' drafts and informal consultations among member States. It was less concerned about how the union would function in the interim period. Bahrain went along with Abu Dhabi in wanting to leave all decisions of importance to the constitution-making period, but it had already indicated that it had very definite views on certain issues.

Three meetings of the Supreme Council of Rulers

If we consider the meeting of the nine Rulers in February 1968 as the first session of the Supreme Council, the second session was convened in Abu Dhabi on 25 and 26 May 1968. It held four closed meetings, from one of which even the closest advisers of the Rulers were excluded. The final communiqué was merely a statement of the intention to strengthen the Union. However, the meeting had been unlikely to make many decisions, for some of the issues were being put in front of the Rulers, with any clarity, for the first time. The majority (excluding Qatar, Dubai, and Ra's al Khaimah) preferred not to proceed with establishing the institutions proposed in the Dubai agreement, but reiterated the desire to obtain a legal expert from outside the area to draft the constitution. In the event, no decision was taken on that either.[31]

The third meeting of the Supreme Council of Rulers, scheduled for 1 July in Abu Dhabi, eventually took place a week later, giving time for more last-minute consultations. The Government of Qatar had decided to refer this matter of the tardiness of the members in building the Union's institutions to two legal experts of their choice.

As might be expected the experts[32] fully supported Qatar's view, and some unofficial support for that view was expressed by the Government of Kuwait. Under the chairmanship of Shaikh Zāyid, Ruler of Abu Dhabi, the Council agreed to elect from among its members a chairman for each session who was also to supervise the implementation of the Council's decisions for the entire period up to the next session, which he should convene at the request of any of the Council's members.[33] No permanent seat for the federal institutions was agreed upon; instead the Supreme Council was to decide each time on the venue for its next meeting. At the Abu Dhabi meeting the Council also agreed to invite Dr ʿAbdul Razāq Sanhūri, the Egyptian author of the Kuwaiti constitution, to draft the Union constitution. The committee responsible for liaison between the adviser and the local authorities included some of the legal advisers in the Emirates and some citizens.[34]

The most important step taken at this meeting was to implement Decisions 8 and 9 of the Dubai Agreement by setting up a Temporary Union Council (sometimes translated as Provisional Federal Council). With the exception of Bahrain, each Emirate nominated a member of its ruling family to the Council, and a maximum of three aides each.[35] The duties of the Union Council were to review the affairs of the State in general, to propose federal laws and supervise their implementation, to prepare the draft budget, to set up committees to assist in the performance of its duties, and to submit a progress report every year. Shaikh Khalīfah bin Ḥamad Āl Thāni, the Deputy Ruler of Qatar, was elected first chairman of the Temporary Union Council. It was also agreed that this Council was to reach agreement on the basis of a two-thirds majority, each Emirate having one vote. The Temporary Union Council held its first meeting in Doha on 8–9 September 1968, and decided to set up a number of committees, including one to deal with the unification of currencies, and one to draft the regulations for the Council's functioning.[36]

The July meeting of the Supreme Council of Rulers had helped to settle the differences which had developed between some members since the February Agreement. In subsequent months the general mood was constructive even though there were rumours that some Rulers intended to ask Kuwait to join the Federation, to house its capital and to counterbalance Bahrain.[37] Most of the Rulers or their deputies used the summer lull for visits to London, where they invariably held talks with Foreign Office officials; some Rulers visited Iran, while Qatar maintained close contact with Saudi

Arabia, either the Ruler or Shaikh Khalīfah visiting monthly.

In an interview with *The Times* in London, published on 9 October 1968, the Ruler of Abu Dhabi maintained that in his view the ideal federation was that of the nine States, but if that proved too difficult to realise at present, a federation of the seven Trucial States was still better than a union of only three or four of them. Yet, initially, even a smaller union comprising Abu Dhabi and two or three other Emirates would be better than nothing.

The routine autumn meeting of the Trucial States Council was held on 13 October 1968. The seven Rulers discussed, under British auspices, development projects, and agreed on a budget of £2 million and a supplementary budget of £300,000.

A constructive atmosphere was maintained at the fourth meeting of the Supreme Council of nine Rulers in Doha on 20 to 22 October 1968. It was agreed to set up six more committees, such as for education, health, immigration and nationality problems, each based in one of the larger capitals. The most important agreement was to form federal land, air and naval forces under a unified command to replace the British forces after their withdrawal at the end of 1971. Two military experts were to advise on this organisation. The individual States could retain their own national guards.[38]

By now the Rulers, their families and their advisers had accepted that by joining in a federation they had to acknowledge the authority of federal institutions. Frequent declarations by the Ruler of the richest member state, Shaikh Zāyid, stressing that "Abu Dhabi's oil and all its resources and potentialities are at the service of all the Amirates,"[39] encouraged the poorer member States on the Trucial Coast, who could testify that such words were often followed by generous deeds. To have such a fervent advocate and generous supporter of the federal idea greatly benefited the Union, particularly in the eyes of sceptical foreign observers. It also counterbalanced Qatar's persistent pressure to proceed more rapidly with the formalities of building the federation.

On 26 to 28 November the Temporary Union Council met in Shārjah[40] and decided to ask the World Bank for help in preparing an economic study of the member States and Britain for expert military advice on the Union's defence needs. A former Commander of British Land Forces in the Middle East, Major-General Sir John Willoughby, was invited in December to become senior military adviser to the Union.

There was a lapse of more than half a year before the Supreme

Council of the nine Rulers met for the fifth time in May 1969. During the interim period some progress was made towards unifying routine administration in several working sessions of the specialised committees and at three meetings of the Temporary Union Council.[41]

A period for clarifying bilateral relations

More important was that almost all the Rulers keenly sought to clarify outstanding issues with their neighbours and with other members of the Union. In early November 1968 the Rulers of Abu Dhabi, Dubai and Qatar and the Crown Prince of Ra's al Khaimah went separately to Iran; a few weeks later the Deputy Ruler of Qatar, Shaikh Khalīfah bin Ḥamad, visited Iran again.[42] The consequences of British troop withdrawals as well as the Iranian reservations about the proposed federation were among the topics of common interest.[43] The frontier agreement of February 1968 between Abu Dhabi and Dubai was slightly amended in Dubai's favour at talks between some Rulers in a village on that border from 17 to 24 February 1969. This agreement, reached between the Rulers of Abu Dhabi and Dubai, was witnessed by Shaikh Aḥmad bin ʿAli, Ruler of Qatar. The Ruler of Ra's al Khaimah joined the meeting later in the week[44] and some outstanding issues were discussed.

After a three-day visit to Kuwait in March 1969, his first to an Arab country since he became Ruler in 1966, Shaikh Zāyid went to Qatar to sign an agreement on the continental shelf between the two States, and joint exploitation of the border-zone Bunduq oilfield. He also visited the Ruler of Bahrain a day after the latter had declared that Bahrain might "go it alone" and apply for UN membership if the federation did not develop to Bahrain's satisfaction.[45]

Qatar and Iran agreed to demarcate the limits of the continental shelf between their two States on 7 April 1969. The almost 200-year-old dispute between Qatar and Bahrain over territorial waters and islands was also tackled at an official visit of the Qatari Ruler on 3 to 6 May 1969.

The Federation in suspension

The Rulers' advisers and some members of the Temporary Union Council met to try to settle as many as possible of the outstanding differences of approach to the federation; but in spite of this and other intensive diplomatic activity in the Gulf before the fifth meeting of the Supreme Council of Rulers between 10 and 14 May 1969 in Doha, this session made little headway.

Once again it looked as though Qatar's well-meaning zeal only alienated the delegates from the less well prepared member states and from Bahrain; the latter by virtue of its long history of overseas trade and formal education claimed that it should be the federation's natural "think tank". Being host to the meeting, the Government of Qatar presented a 20-item agenda designed to compel the Supreme Council of Rulers to discuss steps which would enable the federation to function as one body even before the adoption of the new constitution, which had still not been drafted. The majority of the other emirates rejected this agenda and one day was spent trying to agree on a new one. The communiqué issued on 14 May indicates the dilemma facing the federation of nine emirates. The members supported the idea but the majority were hesitant over putting these principles into effect, and the meeting adjourned without having decided upon a President, the names of the ministers to replace the Temporary Union Council,[46] a flag, a capital, or a centralised military command.

One of the stumbling blocks was that Bahrain insisted that the members of the proposed parliament (Federal Assembly) should be selected on the basis of proportional representation. This was opposed by all the other emirates because this system would have given Bahrain, with its large and well-educated population, an overwhelming advantage.

At this stage, preparation of the draft constitution had not commenced, the British withdrawal was still two years away, there was even a hope that the Conservatives might reverse the decision, therefore the majority of the delegates to the Supreme Council meeting seemed tacitly to agree to disagree, gaining more time to consult on the final shape and size of the federation. Yet most delegates had already become much more conversant with the realities of political life in a federation; and they realised that the spirit of the constitution had to be derived from the political relationships between the member States, not introduced as theories by outside experts. At the Supreme Council meeting in May 1969 a committee of the Rulers' own advisers and legal experts was set up to prepare in two months the first draft of the constitution to be submitted to outside legal experts for comments and recommendations.[47] The Egyptian legal adviser, Dr Waḥīd Ra'fat, who had been asked a year earlier by the Government of Qatar to give a legal opinion, was appointed to study this draft during the month before it was presented to the Rulers. The expert who had been appointed in

July 1968, Dr Sanhūri, had fallen ill soon afterwards; his assistant, Dr Ḥasan Turābi, had so far only prepared a questionnaire and visited the governments of member States.[48] This slow progress of the constitutional experts contrasts with the increasing activity of the Rulers' advisers and local political figures.

The inconclusive May 1969 meeting of the Supreme Council was followed by a long summer recess. It was no coincidence that the Rulers of the bigger Emirates again all visited London during that summer; Shaikh Zāyid[49] and Shaikh Rāshid went on official visits at different times, the Rulers of Bahrain and Shārjah and the Deputy Ruler of Qatar were on private visits. They all had talks with Foreign Office officials, invariably including the Minister of State, Mr Goronwy Roberts, in which the British Government made it clear that it attached great importance to the success of the federation plan.[50]

A comprehensive agreement—never signed

On 21 October 1969 the nine Rulers came to Abu Dhabi for the sixth meeting of the Supreme Council. The communiqué[51] of thirteen points included the election of Shaikh Zāyid as the first President of the Federation and of Shaikh Rāshid, Ruler of Dubai, as its Vice-President; the establishment of Abu Dhabi as the temporary capital; the decision to build a permanent capital on the border between Dubai and Abu Dhabi and the appointment of Shaikh Khalīfah bin Ḥamad, Deputy Ruler of Qatar, as Prime Minister of a thirteen-member cabinet to which each Emirate could propose up to three candidates.[52] Contrary to the intention voiced at the May meeting, the Supreme Council did not after all consider the constitution in detail, partly because it was presented in two different drafts, one prepared by the committee set up in May and one written by Dr Waḥīd Ra'fat. The communiqué stated the Council's decision to refer both drafts to a committee of senior officials and legal advisers for it to report on both.

Due to some last-minute disagreements this communiqué was not signed as scheduled on 24 October by the nine Rulers. While a further session, to iron out these disagreements, was in progress on 25 October 1969, the British Political Agent in Abu Dhabi, Mr James Treadwell, unexpectedly arrived and interrupted the discussions. He read a three-page message from the British Political Resident in Bahrain, Sir Stewart Crawford, which contained rather patronising passages such as ". . . but I have been most disturbed to hear that serious difficulties have now arisen. My Government will be extremely disappointed if these difficulties cannot be overcome. I strongly urge all the Rulers to do their utmost to find a way of resolving their difficulties . . ."[53]

Nobody in the assembly doubted the honourable intentions of the Political Resident, whose message was just one link in a long chain of meetings and exchanges between officials of the British Foreign Office and Rulers and officials in the Gulf. However, at this particular moment the message served as a convenient pretext for some participants to break up the meeting and not to sign the communiqué, which was also—as became immediately obvious—strongly opposed by Iran. The Rulers of Ra's al Khaimah and Qatar walked out of the meeting while the British Political Resident's message was being read, claiming that it was an offensive interference and that the British were trying to impose the Federation. After a short time the Ruler of Qatar rejoined the meeting, which was adjourned without the communiqué being signed, to be reconvened two weeks later.

The reason why some delegations balked at this stage was their apprehension of the reaction of neighbouring powers with claims on parts of the area, in particular Saudi Arabia and Iran. Whether Iran had in fact issued a warning to some members during the Abu Dhabi meeting,[54] or whether the increase in Iranian statements regarding Bahrain and the other disputed islands was enough discouragement, a declaration of the Iranian Foreign Ministry, issued a day after the Abu Dhabi meeting broke up, proved correct the fears of those who wanted to avoid antagonising Iran. It emphasised that "so long as the future status of Bahrain has not been legally clarified the Federation will under no circumstances be acceptable to Iran . . . The Imperial Government expresses its regret at the decision taken by the Abu Dhabi Conference without consideration of Iran's views."[55]

The October 1969 meeting did not reconvene in November as planned, ostensibly because two States did not reply to the invitations, but more likely because a great deal of further consultation was going on privately.[56] The nine Rulers never met again as a Supreme Council.

Preparing for the possibility of withdrawal from the federation

In the meantime both Bahrain and Qatar continued to build up institutions, preparing for the moment when the British umbrella would be withdrawn. On the eighth anniversary of his accession, 16 December 1969, the Ruler of Bahrain, in a move to forestall increasing pressure from educated Bahrainis, promised to reorganise the government, giving the people a greater part to play in the country's affairs.[57] On 19 January 1970 the new cabinet (called Council of State) was announced, and of its twelve members only five were members of the ruling family.[58] While still pledging its support for the Federation, Bahrain consolidated its administrative structure, and preparations were made in case the Federation of the nine did not come about in time.[59] In the Spring of 1970 it was expected that Bahrain would declare its independence during that year and that it was already applying for membership of the Arab League and the United Nations. Kuwait established a Government Office in Bahrain which would pave the way for an exchange of diplomatic representation. After the report of May 1970 by the UN Secretary's special envoy to Bahrain[60] became public, stating that the people were "virtually unanimous in wanting a fully independent sovereign state" and after the threat of Iranian annexation of Bahrain was removed, an almost festive atmosphere reigned throughout the Gulf area.[61] After congratulations and deep sighs of relief the issue of the federation of the nine was tackled with renewed enthusiasm.

Perhaps influenced by Bahrain's progress, Qatar on 2 March 1970 promulgated a provisional constitution. In several of its seventy-seven articles reference is made to the "Union of Arab Emirates".[62] In both, this document and in the law dealing with the Determination of the Powers of Ministers and the Function of Ministries and other Government Organs,[63] the sovereign rights of the State of Qatar *vis-à-vis* the Union are emphasised. Such references clearly indicated that Qatar envisaged a confederation rather than a progressively more integrated Union. On 29 May the Ruler nominated the seven members of Qatar's first cabinet, three of whom were not from the ruling family.

Half-hearted revival of the federation of nine emirates

The June 1970 meeting of Deputy Rulers

While Bahrain and Qatar were engaged in consolidating their government apparatus, bilateral consultations and regional state visits continued, and the revival of the Iranian claim to the small Gulf islands of Abū Mūsa and the two Tunbs made headlines. During the summer of 1970 all nine members made further concerted efforts to promote the federation. The nine Deputy Rulers convened a meeting on 13 June 1970 in Abu Dhabi in order to prepare an agenda for a Supreme Council meeting, but in the event three days were spent in discussing means of solving some of the differences which had led to the breakdown of the last Supreme Council meeting in October 1969.[64] The Deputy Rulers agreed to recommend that federal ministerial portfolios should not be allocated to particular Emirates and that instead the Prime Minister should select the federal cabinet from a list of candidates composed of three nominees from each State. A financial committee based in Bahrain should advise on a federal budget and the members' contributions, and as agreed by the Rulers in the October meeting the establishment of a legal committee in Dubai was also recommended to comment on the two draft constitutions which had been submitted.[65]

Just as at the October 1969 meeting of the Supreme Council of Rulers, the June meeting of the Deputy Rulers demonstrated that intensive formal discussions as well as behind-the-scenes lobbying would eventually produce a workable compromise on most issues. Yet at that moment the federation was in many peoples' minds still just one alternative among several solutions which appeared possible. To some members the federation appeared more vital or at least more attractive than to others, and some were preoccupied with other political issues. Bahrain had to consider the popular mood after the Iranian gesture, urging total independence, while Shārjah and Ra's al Khaimah had their own worries because Iran had earlier in the summer of 1970 repeated its claim to Abū Mūsa and the two Tunbs. Shārjah sought compromise and tried to establish special links with Iran,[66] Ra's al Khaimah gravitated towards Saudi Arabia, hoping to enlist its assistance in a possible confrontation over the Tunbs while continuing to benefit from some development projects paid for by Saudi Arabia.[67] Abu Dhabi had its own worries because the border dispute with Saudi Arabia was heating up again, which possibly held back some of the Emirates from associating themselves too closely with Abu Dhabi in case Riyadh would be offended.

A new British Government—will it withdraw or not?

The Conservative election victory of 18 June 1970 added to the uncertainty, raising hopes that Britain would call off withdrawal. While the upshot of official consultations in July 1970 between Iran and Kuwait, Saudi Arabia and Iran, Kuwait and Iraq was a general consensus along the line of the statement of the Kuwaiti Prime Minister, Shaikh Jābir al Aḥmad, "We will neither welcome nor accept any foreign presence in our area, whether British or otherwise,"[68] and while the British press interpreted the meeting of the new British Foreign Secretary, Sir Alec Douglas-Home, with the Shah in Brussels, as a cautious move towards continuing the British presence in the Gulf, most of the Rulers of the Trucial States intimated to the British Government that they would welcome the retention of British forces in the Gulf.[69] The Conservative Government considered that the entire question of British presence in the Gulf was still open, and therefore deemed it necessary to send Sir William Luce on his fact-finding mission to Iran and the Arab States of the area in August 1970.[70]

Thus most of the members of the federation were more anxious than ever not to pre-empt the situation or to forestall developments which they hoped for, by making firm decisions on important federal issues. The next meeting of Deputy Rulers, scheduled for 22 August, was postponed until 12 September, only to be deferred again until 24 October.[71] Meanwhile Sir William Luce, after discussing with the Rulers of Bahrain, Qatar, Abu Dhabi and Dubai the draft proposed by the second constitutional committee,[72] sent a constitutional adviser, Mr Holmes, to try to bring these four Emirates to a consensus on outstanding constitutional issues. On his arrival Mr Holmes proposed that he should meet the legal advisers of the four Emirates together at the British Residency in Bahrain.[73] The legal adviser of Qatar said that the venue was inappropriate for an Arab constitutional discussion; the joint meeting therefore did not take place. It is probable that certain points, in particular regarding the capital and representation in the Union Council, might have been agreed upon.

The thorny issue of representation in the Union Council

The Deputy Rulers of the nine Emirates met on 24 October 1970 in Abu Dhabi; the host, Shaikh Khalīfah bin Zāyid, opened the meeting, and Mr Aḥmad Khalīfah Suwaidi acted as Chairman for the duration of the three-day discussions.[74]

The second constitutional committee's draft had been circulated and amendments agreed during negotiations between July and October 1970. Unfortunately these changes were not properly inserted into the draft presented to the Deputy Rulers, who therefore had no alternative but to adjourn, after lengthy discussions, and to request that the constitutional committee produce an integrated version of the entire text. It took this committee all evening of the 24th and part of the morning of the 25th of October 1970 to agree on the fair copy of the drafts and to decide that five controversial items should be referred to the Committee of Deputy Rulers for further discussion.[75] These items were 1. The siting of the capital, 2. Representation in the Union Council in the permanent constitution, 3. The method of voting in the Supreme Council of Rulers, 4. Representation in the Union Council while the provisional constitution was in force, and 5. Provisions concerning aviation.

At the insistence of Bahrain, representation in the Union Council was discussed first. Although Bahrain had agreed at the Supreme Council meeting in October 1969 to equal representation, that is, four members from each of the nine Emirates, as recorded in the communiqué which was never signed, it now insisted on representation on the basis of the size of the population of each Emirate.[76] It became obvious during the course of the long and heated debate about this point that Bahrain had modified its position in the light of the recent survey of public opinion conducted by the UN emissary and in response to the popular requests for more democratic institutions. When it became clear that Bahrain's formula for the mode of representation was not acceptable, it changed its stance, proposing that a further paragraph be inserted requiring that, before the four-year period for the provisional constitution expired, a census should be conducted and that provisions should be made to introduce proportional representation on the Union Council. As before, Qatar led the opposition to this provision and persuaded Dubai and the smaller Emirates, except for Shārjah, to vote likewise;[77] Abu Dhabi, usually given to conciliation, abstained. The Bahraini delegation maintained their position; they abstained from voting for the rest of the meeting and at the end declared their unwillingness to take any further part in the discussions "before ensuring that the Constitution guarantees the rights of the people of the Union, particularly in so far as the representation of the people in the Union Council is concerned."[78] The delegations decided not to propose a date for the Supreme Council of Rulers' meeting, realising that the plainly-visible rift between some members made a great deal of informal discussion and probably some outside mediation advisable.[79]

Attempts at mediation

Being very anxious to keep Bahrain in the federation, Abu Dhabi was first off the mark trying to make it change its stance. At the beginning of November Shaikh Zāyid sent two envoys to Kuwait to explain to the Foreign Minister the position of Abu Dhabi and to enlist Kuwait's help as mediator. They arrived in Bahrain from Kuwait on 5 November and met with the Ruler, Shaikh 'Īsa. On 21 November 1970 a Saudi delegation headed by Prince Nawāf bin 'Abdul 'Azīz went to Kuwait to discuss the breakdown of the federation talks; he stressed that Saudi Arabia was strongly in favour of a nine-member federation.

Meanwhile Bahrain, taking counsel from Britain, refrained from declaring independence at the Ruler's accession anniversary on 16 December 1970, but a constitution was promised on that day with a hint that there might be elections in Bahrain to enable every "citizen to shoulder his responsibility to serve his country."[80]

Even after the conclusion of Sir William Luce's second tour of the Gulf in October 1970, the British Government did not state whether the plan to withdraw or the timetable set out for this would be followed.[81] The Rulers however were probably well aware that the Conservative Government was also preparing for an early end to the British protective role in the Gulf. In a message not unlike the one sent to the assembled Rulers in October 1969 by the British Political Resident in the Gulf under a Labour Government, the Conservative Foreign Secretary, Sir Alec Douglas-Home, strongly advised the nine Rulers to go on with building the federation, saying that their "continued inability to decide on a federal structure now seriously threatened international credibility of its future success."[82]

Omani participation in the federation?

On 24 July 1970 a completely new dimension opened for the federation when Sa'īd bin Taimūr was replaced by his son Qābūs as Sultan of neighbouring Oman. Although the logistics of integrating the large and very different country would have been formidable, the idea to include Oman in the federation appealed at least to some of the nine-member Emirates. Shaikh Zāyid, Ruler of Abu Dhabi, was the first to make personal contact with the new Sultan in a spontaneous visit to Muscat on 9 August. The new regime in Oman was probably nowhere greeted with more genuine joy and relief than in Abu Dhabi. The many changes which took place during the first few months of the new era were all observed with great interest and Oman was assured of Abu Dhabi's readiness to help.[83] Oman's new Prime Minister, Ṭāriq bin Taimūr, declared on 20 October 1970 that Oman would not join the federation at present although it might be prepared to form an association with some of the Emirates at a later date.

The last resort

Saudi-Kuwaiti mediation efforts

By the end of 1970 prospects for a workable federation of the nine were less encouraging than ever, although many of the operational details had already been agreed. Persistent though polite acrimonies continued to be exchanged between Qatar and Bahrain, the former being given as much as ever to lengthy explanations of its views in memoranda and letters.[84]

In January 1971 a delegation, headed by Prince Nawāf of Saudi Arabia and the Kuwaiti Foreign Minister Shaikh Ṣabāh Aḥmad al Jābir Āl Ṣabāḥ, went to Bahrain and then to the other Emirates with proposals to resolve the stalemate over seven points. Four of them had already been agreed in October 1969 but had subsequently been raised again by Bahrain; they were the representation in the Union Council, the site of the permanent capital, the method of voting in the Supreme Council of Rulers, and the members' contributions to the Union budget. Three new subjects, about which disagreement had arisen since then, were the role of the Emirates' local armed forces, legislation concerning air traffic, and the membership of individual Emirates in international organisations such as OPEC.

During the course of January the nine Emirates communicated their views on the Saudi-Kuwaiti proposals. Qatar did not wish to re-open discussion on matters already agreed. It also concurred with the Saudi-Kuwaiti proposals for the three other subjects at the same time, insisting that the sentence "the regulation and the exploitation of natural resources" should be deleted from the list of matters over which the Union should have exclusive powers of legislation.[85]

After the comments and criticism of the other emirates were received the joint Saudi-Kuwait delegation prepared new proposals:[86] 1. To return to the original text of the draft constitution allocating four seats to each State in the Union Council. 2. To decide on the permanent capital when the permanent constitution had been prepared. 3. To permit individual emirates to retain or to acquire membership of OPEC and OAPEC. 4. To add in Article 122 that the Union should legislate on the limits of territorial waters on the high seas. 5. To give the individual Emirates the right to establish armed forces ready to join the Union forces to repel outside aggression. 6. To require a majority of seven for voting in the Supreme Council on substantive matters. 7. To require that each emirate should contribute a fixed proportion of its annual revenue with due regard to the income and number of citizens.

These proposals were presented to the nine emirates during a second joint Saudi-Kuwaiti mission in April 1971[87] led by the under-secretaries in the two countries' Foreign Ministries. All nine Rulers accepted the proposals 1, 3 and 4. Qatar opposed point 2 because it wanted an immediate decision on the location of the capital, point 6 because it still favoured unanimity or at least the qualification that the big four emirates should be among the seven who agreed, and point 7 supporting the original clause that each emirate should contribute 10 per cent of its income from oil without regard to the size of the population.[88] Other emirates disagreed on other points; for example, Abu Dhabi was reported to be reluctant to merge its 3,500 strong defence force with the federal army.[89] Bahrain reiterated on 22 April that it accepted the proposals, but there were reports that Bahrain was preparing for independence on its own and was seeking King Faiṣal's concurrence to this course by sending a delegation to Saudi Arabia on 27 April, 1971.

The Conservative Government moves

After Sir William Luce's third visit to the Gulf between 26 January and 14 February 1971, the long awaited formal statement of the Conservative Government's intentions was made on 1 March. Sir Alec Douglas-Home told the House of Commons that the British forces would be withdrawn by the end of December 1971 and that Britain had offered the Emirates a treaty of friendship.[90]

The first of the nine Rulers to comment on this decision was Shaikh Rāshid of Dubai, who told *The Times* quite plainly that he was disappointed and that he thought that this feeling was almost certainly shared by most of the other Rulers, although they might not all wish to express it so clearly. In Shaikh Rāshid's view the federation had to include Qatar, while he thought that Bahrain "simply does not want the Union."[91] On 11 March the Rulers of

Dubai, Qatar and Abu Dhabi met informally to discuss the future of the Union.

The British Government sent Sir William Luce on his fourth visit to the Gulf, starting in Teheran in May. He was primarily concerned there with negotiations regarding the ever more persistent Iranian claim to the islands of Abū Mūsa and the two Tunbs.[92] He also paid several visits to Bahrain and the other Emirates, following which the Residency in Bahrain circulated a memorandum to all the nine Rulers containing Sir William Luce's suggestions for compromises on the four points which were still in dispute after the second Saudi-Kuwaiti mission. His proposals met the same fate as those of the mission in that they failed to bring about agreement on these points. After his return to London a new round of visits and frantic deliberations recommenced in the Gulf.[93]

Bahrain and Qatar opt out while Abu Dhabi prepares for the worst

During early 1971 Bahrain became increasingly preoccupied with normalising its relationship with Iran. The continental shelf between the two countries was demarcated in an agreement signed on 17 June. The Iranian Foreign Minister, Ardeshir Zahedi, arrived on 23 June, from the start reiterating Iran's claim to the three islands near the Straits of Hormuz and emphasising that his country would oppose the federation if the question of the islands was not settled first. It was rumoured that the big neighbour tried to impose certain conditions[94] on Bahrain in return for allowing it a free hand in choosing its political destiny.

It became increasingly obvious that the authorities in Bahrain were still hoping that their country would be part of the federation and thus be less vulnerable to Iranian pressure. But the majority of the educated population of Bahrain did not really want to be integrated with a society which in their eyes still had some way to go to reach Bahrain's sophistication. By June 1971 it became clear that Bahrain could be reasonably secure on her own, enjoying peaceful co-existence with Iran, Saudi economic and moral support, as well as the prospect of close technical co-operation with other Gulf States. So, the would-be partners in the federation of nine Emirates were privately informed that Bahrain would soon "go it alone". The declaration of independence was broadcast by the Ruler, Shaikh ʿĪsa, on 14 August 1971 after the formation of the United Arab Emirates, comprising the seven Trucial States, had been agreed upon in July of 1971. On 1 September Qatar followed suit.[95]

Meanwhile Abu Dhabi, apprehensive of the outcome of the further deliberations and realising that Dubai was hesitant to join a federation without Qatar, prepared for the eventuality that the federation would not take shape before time ran out by announcing on 1 July the formation of the first cabinet in its history.[96] The organisation of its governmental and administrative structure had been in preparation for several months in the hands of local and other Arab civil servants and outside advisers. The Ruler also set up a National Consultative Assembly with fifty members. They were representatives of Abu Dhabi's tribes and main tribal sub-sections and of the most important merchant families in the town nominated by Shaikh Zāyid in consultation with the leading members of society.

One of the first acts of the new cabinet was to establish on 8 July the Abu Dhabi Fund for Arab Economic Development with an initial capital of 50 million Bahrain Dinars. The very generous assistance which Abu Dhabi already gave to Arab, African and Islamic countries was institutionalised in co-operation with a similar fund in Kuwait and with the IMF. This timely gesture also demonstrated once again that the Ruler of Abu Dhabi and the new government really considered the wealth which this State derived from oil to be an asset for the entire, formerly so desperately poor, coast and for the needs of other countries. Shaikh Zāyid remained determined that Abu Dhabi should do its utmost to foster the Federation, but there was still the uncertainty over which Emirates would join.

4 Agreement to establish the UAE

The UAE agreed upon

On 10 July the seven Rulers met in Dubai as members of the Trucial States Council. The urgent task before them was to work out the formula for the transfer of a number of functions which had hitherto been performed by the British Government, such as jurisdiction over foreigners and control of immigration.[97] While progressing through a 22-point agenda, measures were agreed for the co-ordination of police activities and the unification of various duties by modifying existing organisations of the Development Office.[98]

During informal consultations of the Rulers and their aides

agreement was reached at long last on the real topic of the meeting, which was the Federation. A communiqué was issued on 18 July 1971 announcing the formation of the State of the United Arab Emirates, comprising six of the Trucial States. Ra's al Khaimah was not yet ready to compromise on the issue of representation in the Union Council. The Rulers approved a revised version of the constitution which had been intended for the now defunct nine-member Union of Arab Emirates. This constitution was now referred to as "provisional", to come into effect on a date still to be determined by the Rulers and to be superseded by a permanent constitution.

In their joint communiqué the Rulers expressed their hope "that this Federation will form the nucleus of a complete federation which will include the remaining members of the brotherly family of emirates."[99]

Delegations were sent to various Arab countries to explain the structure and the policy of the new State; Shaikh Zāyid and Shaikh Rāshid sent personal representatives to London to confer with the British authorities over the actual process of transferring certain authorities to the new Arab State. Membership in the UN, the Arab League, and other international organisations was sought.

Making it workable

The July agreement was a milestone in the creation of the UAE, providing the framework within which the governmental institutions could be evolved in the discussions during subsequent weeks.[100]

The withdrawal of Bahrain and Qatar from the federation meant that a large number of experienced civil servants were no longer available to set up and run the federal administration. The six Emirates were forced to look more closely at the availability of such people within their own borders. Also their attention was more closely focused on their own domestic problems, as opposed to those of the larger federation. These problems were accentuated by the poor communications which still existed then between the Emirates, as illustrated by the absence of an asphalted road across the hundred miles of desert between Abu Dhabi and Dubai or across the mountains to Fujairah. At that time, too, the telephone system linking the Emirates was still rudimentary and only available to a few in the larger population centres. The authorities who had hitherto conducted the federation discussions could only begin to tackle the very much greater logistical problems of establishing an administration.

Fortunately, during the four months available, agreement was reached on an adequate number of measures required to enable the UAE to present a unified face to the world,[101] and to achieve a certain degree of internal cohesion. Thus, it was not a failure on the part of the authorities in the Emirates to set their own house in order, that might have led to a delay in the declaration of the federation. Two complicating factors were the British requirement to hand over certain responsibilities to recognised federal authorities and the issue over Iran's claim to the three Gulf islands, which was largely outside the control of the main architects of this federation.

The issue of the islands

Iran had given up her claim to Bahrain to avoid a possible showdown with the Arab World at a time of uncertainty over how the British-provided security of the Gulf would be replaced. After accepting Bahrain's independence the Shah and his government were determined not to bargain over their claim to Abū Mūsa and the two Tunbs. The larger Tunb had a population of up to 100 people, while the small Tunb was normally uninhabited; they both lie nearer to the Iranian coast than to Ra's al Khaimah, but had for some time belonged to the Qawāsim Rulers. Abū Mūsa has been permanently inhabited by a few subjects of the Ruler of Shārjah for generations while many more have used the island for winter grazing for their camels.[102] Rulers of Shārjah have granted concessions to various foreign companies (British and German)[103] to mine the red oxide which used to be in demand in Europe before the introduction of chemical paints, the revenue from such concessions was at one stage important as the compensation granted by a new Ruler to his deposed predecessor.[104]

Iran argued that all three islands had belonged to it until early last century, when the British Government of India arbitrarily assigned them to the Qawāsim Rulers; Iran's intransigence would not permit reasoning on historic, demographic, economic or any other grounds. Very much preoccupied with its new role as self-appointed protector of the Gulf and the north-western shores of the Indian Ocean, Iran decided it just had to have these three islands with their strategic positions near the entrance to the Gulf. When the Arab governments of the region saw this and remonstrated, Iran did not alter its stance but reiterated its determination.[105] The Iranian Foreign Minister

Zahedi insisted that it was a matter to be decided between Britain and Iran alone, and threatened that Iran would oppose the federation of Arab Emirates if this question were not settled to Iran's satisfaction. The Shah as well as Prime Minister Hoveida repeated that Iran would use force if necessary.

Anxious to resolve this problem, which the respective shaikhdoms were not expected to negotiate themselves,[106] Britain engaged in an intensive dialogue with Iran, and Sir William Luce never missed out Teheran on his frequent visits to the Gulf. He presented various British compromise proposals to the Iranian government, Shārjah and Ra's al Khaimah, as well as some other members of the projected federation. The British Foreign Secretary, Sir Alec Douglas-Home, frequently consulted with the Iranian Ambassador to Britain, Amir Afshar. The British government maintained, without being explicit, that the islands belonged to the Arab shaikhdoms, but in the face of Iranian intransigence, Britain eventually sought to soften the impact of the Iranian blow and negotiated certain conditions for condoning a compromise. Both Britain and the Ruler of Shārjah, in the interests of stability in the Gulf, resigned themselves to the fact that Iran's determination to have a military presence on Abū Mūsa could not be ignored.

The Ruler of Shārjah, the late Shaikh Khālid bin Muḥammad, took an active part in the search for a solution, visiting Iran in early 1970 and agreeing to set up a joint committee, which, however, did not materialise.[107] Instead Iran's conditions were conveyed to Shaikh Khālid by Sir William Luce. These conditions were unacceptable to Shārjah mainly because sovereignty over the island was to fall to Iran after two years; the only positive aspect of the deal was Iran's offer of economic aid to Shārjah.

To demonstrate to Arab governments the extent of the Iranian claim and the reality of the threat on the one side, and his own inability to deal with this situation alone, Shaikh Khālid sent, on 23 August 1971, a lengthy memorandum to a number of Arab States in which the history of Abū Mūsa's connection with Shārjah is chronicled and the steps in the negotiations are described. The text of the memorandum culminated in an appeal to the Arab States for support in at least averting loss of sovereignty: "Shārjah appreciates that it is not appropriate at this stage to request its Arab brothers to use force against Iran to prevent it from occupying the island. However, we hope that all the Arab States will support us in our position and will attempt to bring pressure on Iran . . . and that they will not permit it to act freely in occupying the island by force."[108]

An agreement between Shārjah and Iran was announced by the Ruler of Shārjah on 29 November 1971 which was substantially more favourable to Shārjah when compared to previous Iranian demands.[109] Shārjah retained sovereignty over the island except for a part to be handed over to Iranian forces. In the event of oil being produced on the island, Shārjah and Iran would have equal shares of the revenue, but until Shārjah's own revenue from oil reached £3 million a year Iran was to give aid to Shārjah amounting to £1.5 million annually.[110]

While the issue of the Iranian claim to Abū Mūsa was concluded in the nick of time, the dispute over the two Ra's al Khaimah islands was not resolved. On 30 November, an Iranian task force took possession of the allocated part of Abū Mūsa and was greeted by the Deputy Ruler of Shārjah in accordance with the spirit of the peaceful settlement. On the same day Iranian troops took over the two Tunbs by force and a number of people, both Iranian troops and members of Ra's al Khaimah's police force, were killed on the Greater Tunb.

Although Britain was legally still bound to defend the Trucial State's security she did not intervene. The Ruler of Ra's al Khaimah had been advised by Britain to accept an agreement similar to that reached between Shārjah and Iran. Shaikh Ṣaqr bin Muḥammad of Ra's al Khaimah refused such a deal to the last, and had instructed his police force to shoot if Iranian troops attempted to land.

Reaction both against Iran, who had given a first demonstration of its new power politics *vis-à-vis* an Arab country, and against Britain ran high in some Arab countries. Iraq immediately severed diplomatic relations with Iran and Britain.

Most Arab States condemned the Iranian move; Libya, going one step further, nationalised the interests of BP in Libya, handing them over to the newly founded Arab Gulf Exploration Company.[111] Throughout the Emirates of the lower Gulf, in particular in Ra's al Khaimah and Shārjah, Iranian banks and other institutions were the targets of stone-throwing youths. The Deputy Ruler of Shārjah who had greeted the commander of the Iranian garrison force on Abū Mūsa was shot at and wounded in Shārjah. These were the storm clouds which cast long shadows over the formal inception of the long-awaited Federation.

The UAE proclaimed

While issues beyond the control of the six Trucial States thus came to a head, the terms of reference for the federation were at long last finalised during November 1971. On the 14th the legal advisers of the six States met in Abu Dhabi; on the 23rd the Ruler of Dubai had discussions with the Ruler of Abu Dhabi and on 2nd December the Rulers of Abu Dhabi, Dubai, Shārjah, ʿAjmān, Umm al Qaiwain and Fujairah, who had signed the provisional constitution in July 1971, proclaimed the creation of the new State, the United Arab Emirates. After this ceremony the Rulers met in their capacity as members of the Supreme Council and elected Shaikh Zāyid bin Sulṭān as the first President, for a five-year term. Shaikh Rāshid bin Saʿīd was elected Vice-President, and his son Shaikh Maktūm bin Rāshid was appointed Prime Minister.[112] The door was left open for Ra's al Khaimah, and the hope was expressed that Bahrain and Qatar would also join in due course.

A week later an eighteen-member cabinet was appointed,[113] in which each Emirate was given portfolios roughly equal in number to its weight in the federation: Abu Dhabi had six ministerial posts, Dubai four, Shārjah three and the other three Emirates had one each. Some important members of the seven ruling families had to be accommodated within this frame, while the still small group of technocrats were also eligible for ministerial posts—themselves all members of prominent families in Abu Dhabi, Dubai and Shārjah who had sent their sons abroad for further education. Eventually a number of Under-Secretaries and Deputy Ministers were also appointed to the various ministries,[114] whose task was to co-ordinate the activities of the already well established departments of some emirates with the embryonic federal ministries.

On 6 December 1971 the UAE joined the Arab League and on 9 December 1971 it became a member of the United Nations.

On 1 December the protection treaties between Britain and the seven Trucial States were terminated. The following day Sir Geoffrey Arthur, the outgoing Political Resident in the Gulf, and Shaikh Zāyid, President of the newly proclaimed state of the UAE, signed a treaty of friendship in Dubai; Queen Elizabeth and the British Prime Minister were among the first to congratulate the President and the new State. The British Political Agent in Abu Dhabi, C.J. Treadwell, became the first British Ambassador to the UAE, while the British Political Agent in Dubai became the Consul-General there.

Because of the absence of institutions to which certain authorities could be handed over, some aspects of the abrogation of the treaty relationship with Britain could not be dealt with promptly on the final day. The command of the Trucial Oman Scouts passed, on 2 December, from the British Political Resident in the Gulf to the President of the UAE after the appropriate military law had been issued in Dubai; but the actual handover of day-to-day responsibility was only possible on 22 December.[115] Similarly, the retrocession of jurisdiction over certain foreign subjects which, in theory, had to be completed before the 2nd of December was a long and difficult process because new federal courts had to be set up and a number of federal laws had to be passed for which Britain continued to press.[116] Even after the British Political Residency in Bahrain was closed on 26 March 1972, some unsettled appeal cases were still pending, and for this purpose the British Ambassador in Abu Dhabi retained a brass plate engraved "British Political Residency" which was put up when he dealt with the few cases which dragged on beyond that date.

Thus, by necessity, Britain served as midwife at the birth of the federation. Britain had all along had doubts about a federation which included Bahrain and Qatar; it could now be satisfied that the infant was of the very shape and size it had anticipated. Because of the protracted handover procedures, the new legal requirements, and the need to allocate the duties of the Trucial States Development Office,[117] Britain still helped to smooth the path for a few months while the federation took its first steps. However it was not long before the British Embassy took its place among the rapidly-increasing number of embassies opened in Abu Dhabi.

Britain had not succeeded in tidying up all the loose ends quite as neatly as had been hoped. In particular the border dispute between Saudi Arabia and Abu Dhabi was unresolved. In December 1970 Saudi Arabia had repeated a territorial claim which would have cost Abu Dhabi much of her territory and most of her onshore oil-fields.[118] But Britain was by then confident that a solution could best be worked out between the two governments, possibly with the mediation of other Arab governments. This belief was justified and an agreement was signed in August 1974.

Ra's al Khaimah – last but not least

This State in the extreme north probably had three major reasons why it did not sign the July 1971 agreement between the other Trucial

States, and did not join until some time after the Federation had been proclaimed.

Firstly, Ra's al Khaimah had resented that throughout the negotiations between the nine States it did not rank equal with the big four in matters such as the number of delegates and voting rights, and that neither the British officials nor the Arab mediators consulted as frequently with Ra's al Khaimah as with the larger States.[119] To Ra's al Khaimah it appeared to be not in keeping with the historic role which the shaikhdom had played in the past. When the federation was reduced to seven members Ra's al Khaimah saw all the more justification for making its presence felt and insisting on its own terms for membership.

This attitude was reinforced by the persistent rumours which were circulating to the effect that Union Oil of California, who held the offshore concession of Ra's al Khaimah, had made a promising oil strike. The third exploration well had reached the target zone, a structure in the lower Cretaceous Thamama limestone from which oil is produced in Abu Dhabi.[120] Two earlier holes had to be abandoned because the drilling platforms could not be used for such extreme depths, much deeper than in Abu Dhabi. The third well did encounter hydrocarbons, and by mid-December 1971 tests had established that the amount of oil present was too little to justify production. The hope of finding oil in the onshore concession held by Shell Hydrocarbons was still more remote, because so far only a seismic survey had been carried out. The possibility of Ra's al Khaimah joining the federation as an oil-rich shaikhdom was the second reason for its hesitation.

The third problem involved the claim of Iran to the two Tunb islands. The Ruler of Ra's al Khaimah refused to sign an agreement similar to the one which Shārjah eventually accepted. On 30 November 1971 Iranian forces seized the two Tunbs. Ra's al Khaimah did not want to arouse a military confrontation between Iran and the Arab countries, some of whom might have been prepared to provide troops, but instead appealed to Arab heads of States for moral support.[121] Ra's al Khaimah sent a delegation, led by Shaikh ʿAbdul ʿAzīz bin Muḥammad Āl Qāsimi, to the emergency session of the Arab League on 6 December 1971. He said that his Emirate would like the problem to be solved peacefully and indicated the possibility of an appeal to the International Court of Justice.

From the beginning of December Ra's al Khaimah re-opened the negotiations for membership of the UAE, one of her conditions being that the other Emirates "should adopt the question of Iranian occupation of the islands", to which they agreed.[122]

Ra's al Khaimah formally joined the UAE on 10 February 1972. Like Shārjah, Ra's al Khaimah was allotted six seats in the assembly, thus falling short of being ranked with Abu Dhabi and Dubai, who have eight seats each. Ra's al Khaimah was assured of substantial federal assistance for her development projects. Having participated actively in the discussions during the three years of preparing for the nine-member federation, Ra's al Khaimah's leaders integrated into an already familiar political system. Thus it is not surprising that a member of one of the leading Ra's al Khaimah families was nominated Deputy Foreign Minister on 6 February, some days before the seventh State formally joined the federation. He was the late Saif Ghabāsh.

5 The Constitution of the UAE

A constitution made for the nine Gulf emirates

The document which was signed on 18 July 1971 by six Trucial States and on 11 February 1972 by Ra's al Khaimah was entitled "Provisional Constitution of the United Arab Emirates".[123] It was to be valid for five years only, during which period a permanent constitution was to be prepared. However, this first constitution is still in force today, 1996. This may indicate that the realities of federal political life at times encouraged a very flexible interpretation of some provisions of the constitution for the sake of maintaining a workable consensus, particularly within the Supreme Council.

The predominant reason for the unexpected longevity of the first constitution, however, is found in the main characteristics of this constitution itself. Although many of the 152 articles, particularly the majority of those which deal with the Fundamental Social and Economic Basis of the Union, could be found in similar wording in the constitutions of many countries, there are certain key provisions which are tailor-made by and for the federating shaikhdoms. These are the results of the long drawn out deliberations which preceded the formation of the federation. But even beyond the date of signature nothing but a delicately balanced compromise would be acceptable to some parties with regard to certain issues, a fact which makes the constitution remain, despite all its inadequacies in other respects, a very workable constitution. But in some cases a subject which was hotly disputed while the constitution was being prepared became an integral part of the political life of the country, and far from raising further objections to such a provision in the constitution, such a subject was soon treated as the only sensible way of dealing with that particular matter.[124]

Political life everywhere depends on this phenomenon of political dynamism which constantly renders the outcome of yesterday's controversies today's commonly accepted principles. Thus for a long time it was not seriously disputed that the oil-exporting member States may have full sovereignty over this natural resource, as in turn the other Emirates enjoy a surprisingly free hand in the development of their resources, which may, as in the example of Shārjah, be special conditions for attracting commerce or tourism.

Containing as it does a fair number of still relevant and respected compromises, it is all the more interesting to dwell on the fact that the entire constitution, in particular its compromises, might have had a very different emphasis if it had been worked out and agreed upon just by the seven emirates alone which are now bound by it. It has been demonstrated on the previous pages that a great deal of the spirit of the constitution is the result of deep engagement in these matters in particular by a number of people in Doha and Bahrain. For the three years during which the Federation of the nine Emirates existed on paper, the Qatari delegation left no stone unturned in an attempt to mould the federation to make it conform to certain principles which were first propagated in Doha government circles early in 1968; they remained quite inflexible throughout this entire period, more out of preference for certain principles than out of practical political necessity. Bahrain was more dynamic, ready to rescind old grievances, once decisions had been taken and agreements reached; its delegations were open to novel proposals and additional compromises as the discussions proceeded; Bahraini flexibility was, however, instantly suspended when the general consensus on certain issues cut across vital political interests of the State of Bahrain.

Both Emirates raised a great number of issues which might never have been thought of, had the seven Emirates been on their own in the process of constitution-making. Many compromises which now form part of the constitution of the UAE would have been settled very differently without the presence of Bahrain and Qatar.

Important as the role of these two governments was for the genesis of the constitution, it was possibly even more significant once they were absent; having had ample demonstration of the room for disagreement between these two States, the governments of the Trucial States suddenly appreciated the common ground which had always existed between them.

The rather more extreme positions taken so often by either Qatar or Bahrain thus eventually turned into catalysts for a relatively painless final operation of constitution-making, during which each of the seven Emirates sacrificed some treasured views. Thus with only a few changes, most of which had already been discussed during the previous months, the draft which had last been reviewed in full during the meeting of the nine Deputy Rulers in October 1970 became the constitution of the UAE.

Centralistic and federalistic elements

It is not by chance that the Arabic name of the new State became the rather more active derivation of the root *waḥada*, by calling it *dawlah al imārāt al ʿarabīyah al muttaḥidah* (*United* Arab Emirates).[125] The federation of the nine had been called *ittiḥād al imārāt al ʿarabīyah*,[126] *Union* of Arab Emirates. This change of emphasis, which helped to tilt the balance further towards a more unified, if not even a more centralised State than that envisaged earlier, was in keeping with the concepts which were being developed at the time by citizens who had become intimate advisers to the Rulers in Abu Dhabi, and Dubai, particularly H.E. Aḥmad Khālifah Suwaidi and H.E. Mahdi al Tājir, who had taken over most of the responsibility for the finalisation of the federation talks, and who were then given important positions in the new State, which they had helped to create. In their view, the new State had more chance of consolidating itself the more it played down the individuality of the Emirates and strengthened the hand of the central authorities. It was difficult to administer shaikhdoms of such different sizes and stages of development from one centre during the first few years of the nascent State. This prevented over-enthusiastic *ad hoc* unification which could have suffocated some of the enthusiasm for the federation. The realities of political life in the UAE did not encourage rapid unification in every aspect, and this helped to maintain the integrity of the various local systems. It was eventually realised that these systems still had a very valuable role to play because of their immediate proximity to the citizen.

While the centralistic tendencies had only qualified success in practice, they featured prominently in the text of the constitution.[127] Part Seven (Articles 120–125) deals directly with the balance of centralistic and federalistic elements and is entitled "Distribution of legislative, executive and international jurisdiction between the Union and the Emirates". Article 120 contains a catalogue of nineteen matters for which the central authorities shall have exclusive legislative as well as executive powers.[128] Apart from the obvious ones such as foreign affairs and defence, this catalogue also includes education and electricity services, which in some other federations are under the regional authorities. Exclusive legislative power is reserved for the central authorities in a further catalogue of fifteen points (Article 121), such as labour relations and social security, real estate and expropriations in the public interest.[129] The individual Emirates have jurisdiction over all matters which are not assigned by the constitution to the exclusive jurisdiction of the central authority (Article 122), but Articles 116 to 119, which form Part Six (entitled "The Emirates"), do not give a comparable catalogue of the legislative, executive and judicial powers of the individual Emirates. Yet the vague wording of these articles implies, rather than describes, such powers by saying: "The exercise of rule in each Emirate shall aim in particular at the maintenance of security and order within its territories, the provision of public utilities for its inhabitants and the raising of social and economic standards" (Article 117), and "The member Emirates of the Union shall all work for the co-ordination of the legislation in various fields with the intention of unifying such legislation as far as possible" (Article 118, Part One). The failure to list the powers of the individual Emirates is consistent with the intention of the fathers of the constitution: existing laws and well-established institutions in the Emirates were guaranteed continued existence.

Forthcoming legislation in almost all matters that could be anticipated, as well as the accompanying executive and judicial institutions which could be expected to evolve, were assigned to the central authorities in Articles 120–125. The authors of the constitution could foresee the very obvious situation that in some Emirates, notably Dubai, Abu Dhabi, and to some extent Shārjah, the existing laws and regulations as well as the functioning government machinery could and probably would remain barriers to the process of unifying the public sector. The almost complete lack of legislation and institutionalised administration in most of the other Emirates facilitated the introduction of the overall and comprehensive legislative and executive activities of the new central authorities. Gradually the individual Emirates' governments would need to conform in their legislation and integrate their administration into this evolving central system, if for no other reason than the fact that the constitution does not specifically allow (although it does not forbid) new legislation to be enacted by the Emirates' authorities exclusive of the Union authorities. Local laws and regulations are foreseen by the constitution only within the frame of the implementation of Union laws through the governments of the Emirates (Article 125).

The centralistic intentions of the constitution are evident particularly in the provisions regarding the position of the President of the Union. The powers assigned to him in Article 54 could be interpreted as being in keeping with the representative nature of the head of State, but the President does, in fact, also have the last word in the selection of the entire cabinet, (Article 54, paragraph 6). This, together with his power of "supervising the implementation of Union laws, decrees and decisions through the Council of Ministers of the Union and the competent Ministers", (paragraph 8) augments the centralistic character of the executive authorities.

In practice the amount of central as opposed to regional administration depends very much on the distribution of funds between the central government organs and the local bodies. The constitution of the UAE addresses itself to the financial aspect in Part Eight, entitled "Financial Affairs of the Union". Yet the relevant articles (126–136) do not give guidance; they deal in general terms with the source of the money for the central government's expenses and mention only that the member Emirates "shall contribute a specified proportion of their annual revenues to cover the annual general budget expenditure of the Union" (Article 127). The manner and scale of these contributions were to be prescribed by the Budget Law. Thus the central government has no recourse to the constitution if it is in danger of becoming ineffective through lack of funds. The ability of the central government to finance the exertion of its powers, to the extent which the constitution anticipates, depends in the event on a further compromise. However, a law stipulating the percentage of each Emirates' annual income as its budget contribution is less permanently binding than a clause of the constitution. In the event, the generous budget contributions of the Emirate of Abu Dhabi provided the nascent central government with ample funds to assert itself and eventually to prevail over regional tendencies in many aspects of the new State's political life.

Compared with the constitutions of other federations such as Switzerland or the Federal Republic of Germany, the constitution of the UAE neglects, deliberately, some principles which are most carefully worded and jealously guarded by these federations. In the UAE's constitution one cannot detect a deliberate determination to safeguard federalistic elements *vis-à-vis* the centralistic trends. It was deemed that individual shaikhdoms possessed enough of their original determination for self-assertion to be retained even without particular definition in the constitution.

The division of powers—legislative, executive and judicial

The five central authorities which share political power are listed in Article 45: 1. The Supreme Council of the Union, 2. The President of the Union and his Deputy, 3. The Council of Ministers of the Union, 4. The National Assembly of the Union, 5. The Judiciary of the Union.

The *Supreme Council* is the highest authority in the country; its members are the Rulers of the seven Emirates. It is vested with legislative as well as executive powers. Laws and decrees of the Union are ratified by the Supreme Council;[130] this may not always be a formality, since Article 110, paragraph 3(a), enables the Supreme Council to ratify a law which has been rejected or amended twice by the National Assembly. The Supreme Council's executive power is to exercise "supreme control over the affairs of the Union in general", (Article 47, paragraph 7). The constitution stipulates (Article 49) that procedural matters of the Council shall be decided by a majority vote, with the qualification that "on substantive matters [decisions] shall be by a majority of five of its members provided that this majority includes the votes of the Emirates of Abu Dhabi and Dubai." No catalogue of these "substantive matters" is given in the constitution, leaving the door open for discussion and compromise. Should most members of the Supreme Council feel strongly about a particular issue, no decision would be taken without the agreement of the Rulers of Abu Dhabi and Dubai.

In that the constitution does not stipulate how frequently the Supreme Council shall meet,[131] its legislative and executive powers may prove in practice to be not so supreme as the constitution permits.

The position of the *President of the Union* is defined in Articles 51 to 54. His powers are wide-ranging, both legislative and executive; he also has the traditional power to pardon criminals and to confirm or commute a death sentence.[132] Since he is also the President of the Supreme Council of Rulers, a great deal of its power reverts to him while the Council is not in session.

The President and his Deputy are elected from among the seven Rulers. Their term of office is five years and both may be re-elected. The eleven-point catalogue of the President's powers in Article 54 describes his role as the ceremonial Head of State, appointing members of the cabinet, ambassadors and senior officials, with the exception of the president and judges of the Supreme Court. His function is also to sign "Union laws, decrees and decisions which the Supreme Council has sanctioned," (Article 54, paragraph 4), to promulgate them and to supervise their implementation through the Union's ministries, (Article 54, paragraph 8).

Further powers which may accrue to or be assumed by the President stem from certain provisions of the constitution which do not deal exclusively with his position. The President, in conjunction with the Supreme Council, may overrule the National Assembly's amendments to a bill and promulgate the law in the version which the Council of Ministers originally suggested.[133] Article 113 gives the President, together with the Council of Ministers, the authority to promulgate urgently-required laws in the form of decrees. "Such decree-laws must be referred to the Supreme Council within a week . . . for assent or rejection . . . if they are approved they shall have the force of law and the Union National Assembly shall be notified at its next meeting." The President's legislative powers are further enhanced by the provision that the Supreme Council may authorise him together with the Council of Ministers to promulgate decrees as long as they do not pertain to international agreements, martial law, a defensive war, or the appointment of judges of the Supreme Court. The constitution does not provide a catalogue of those matters which may only be dealt with by law as opposed to by decree. Legislation by ordinary decree does not involve the National Assembly; it requires agreement between the President and the Council of Ministers only.

The *Council of Ministers'* functions are dealt with in Articles 55 to

67 of the constitution. It is described as "the executive authority of the Union, and under the supreme control of the President of the Union and the Supreme Council, [it] shall be responsible for dealing with all domestic and foreign affairs" (Article 60). The catalogue of the powers of the Council, running to ten points, underlines its legislative capacity. A Union law is drafted here and then submitted to the National Assembly before being presented to the President. The Council of Ministers also drafts "decrees and various decisions". The remainder of the catalogue firmly reinforces the executive authority of the Council.

The examination of the powers which the constitution ascribes to the Union's authorities indicates that the parliamentary organ, the *National Assembly of the Union*,[134] is neither the exclusive nor the most prominent legislative authority in the state, but in reality has a predominantly consultative character. It may not initiate bills but it discusses those which are submitted by the cabinet. In this first and provisional constitution the functions of the organ of popular representation are carefully tailored to the requirements of the nascent State. Thus the role of the forty delegates[135] was envisaged to be generally to foster and enhance a growing sense of federal communal awareness and to represent the different regional interests, even though Article 77 states that a member "shall represent the whole people of the Union".

The members of the Assembly do not have to be elected by popular vote, although each Emirate may devise its own system for selection of its quota of Assembly members. Here, too, the constitution is appropriate to the requirements of the new federation, because the nature of the tribal societies in each of the seven Emirates and the earlier absence of formal education limited the choice of suitable representatives to the small number of leading families. The Assembly's main role as a key link to strengthen the Union does not prevent it from developing characteristics of other parliaments, becoming a substantial counter-weight to the executive, and voicing the opinion of a progressively more amorphous population. The constitution is sufficiently vague to allow for the discussion in the Assembly of most subjects, so that pressure may be exerted on the executive authorities of the State.[136]

The provisions of the constitution dealing with the *Judiciary* (Articles 94 to 109) are more in accordance with textbook provisions than the specially tailored provisions dealt with so far. They provide for an hierarchy of courts which culminates in the Union Supreme Court.[137] This court is a constitutional court comparable to the *Bundesverfassungsgericht* of the Federal Republic of Germany. It adjudicates on disputes between the central authorities as well as between these and the local authorities. Above all it acts as the watchdog, ensuring that the constitution is adhered to and reigns supreme. This court is also the highest court of appeal.[138] The independence of its judges and their immunity from removal from office is guaranteed in the relevant articles of the constitution.

Below the Supreme Court of the UAE the constitution stipulates the establishment of one or more Primary Tribunals which have jurisdiction in civil, commercial and administrative disputes between the State and citizens and in cases pertaining to the permanent capital.[139] The Primary Tribunals are expected to be courts of appeal above the local judicial authorities, but the constitution also prepared the ground for transfering all or part of the jurisdiction of local courts to the Primary Tribunals. Little guidance can be found in the constitution on the relationship between local and Union courts.

The division of the legislative, executive and judiciary powers between the authorities of the Union is not meticulously defined, because this is not the primary objective of this provisional constitution. It was intended as the *modus vivendi* which was most acceptable to the seven Rulers and also not unacceptable to the local tribal population and the rest of the inhabitants of the UAE. The emphasis is on providing the basis for integrating seven Emirates and weaving the fabric of a united State. This is why in an analysis of the distribution of powers the figure of the President emerges as the authority actually holding or being able to command more power than any of the other authorities. The tribal society can trust its own means to counterbalance excessive authoritarian tendencies on the part of a powerful central figure. Thus the constitution's emphasis on unification and centralisation, even at the expense of a neater division between the powers, is not out of tune with the political expectations of the society, particularly if the central figure is a charismatic leader.

6 The Provisional Constitution remains

Although the Provisional Constitution stipulates in the preamble that a permanent one should be prepared and specifies in Article 144 that the transitional period should only last for five years, the federation has entered the third decade of its existence with the 1971 document still as its only written foundation. Its text has never been well publicised and is now not readily available; it does not form an essential part of education in the same way as for some nations. But the people trust that the spirit of the constitution serves the uniform development of the whole country.

Over the years, a growing number of people voiced concern about the inadequacy of the constitution. In the early years the task of drafting the permanent constitution was given due attention by the authorities. A committee of ministers and members of the FNC was formed. In July 1976 the Supreme Council was presented with the draft, but decided to extend the Provisional Constitution for a further five years, mindful that such a fundamental revision could jeopardize many of the compromises on which the federation was based. Rather than prematurely enact unsustainable constitutional changes, it was deemed preferable to continue with compromises which had proved their worth during the initial years of the UAE.

Then, the constitutionalists were primarily concerned with the balance of power in the federal system, the relationship between the central authorities and the government of each emirate, standardising of laws and strengthening of the central government's hand. In order to spread the wealth evenly throughout the country, a constitutional formula was sought which precluded the exclusive sovereignty of each emirate over the natural resources within its boundaries. The emphasis was on the formal aspects of structuring the federation, while making the institutions in the constituent member emirates more uniform. Efforts to bring about constitutional changes led to confrontations in the late 1970s, which will be related in more detail below.[140] There were fewer demands for constitutional changes during the 1980s for a variety of reasons, the preoccupation with the Iran-Iraq War, the spread and growth of personal prosperity, and most important the issuing of many new laws which to some extent made up for the inadequacies of the Provisional Constitution.

Those who are nowadays advocating the drafting of a new constitution are above all hoping for a more open society and formalised democratic participation, which would bring in its wake more accountability into the decision-making process. Unless these expectations can be fulfilled, and changes in the structure of the state as well as in the substance of its society can come to pass, there is little to be gained from writing an improved text for a permanent constitution.

Chapter Ten

The UAE in the third decade of its existence

Constitutions do not in themselves make or break a country. A federal state's cohesion does not necessarily depend solely on the written word. In a strong federation, there is enough unwritten common social and political substance on which to rely, when dealing with difficult domestic or external developments. Events and pressures from outside may highlight internal weaknesses, and the inability to withstand such pressures may even precipitate the disintegration of a federation. There can be momentous, disruptive foreign events, which even a well thought out constitution and an entirely satisfactory federal arrangement are unable to withstand, and which can drive the internal situation to breaking point. Since 1971 the world around the UAE has experienced fundamental and unexpected changes, both in the immediate neighbourhood as well as on the global scene. Several of these events might have shaken the UAE to disintegration. Yet, this did not happen – some such events may even have contributed to the strengthening of the federal state.

1 Policy formulation and reaction to external developments

Strategic use of foreign policy

Foreign policy was deliberately used from the very inception of the UAE to help to consolidate the federal state. Recognition by the neighbours, diplomatic ties, initially with selected nations, and the respect of many distant governments were the first very important objectives of the policy makers to the extent that by now the UAE has diplomatic relations at various levels with some 130 nations. Thus, foreign policy was indeed very successful in firmly placing the new State regionally and internationally on the map, from which it could not be erased without provoking an international outcry.

Contrary to the advice of the British Foreign Office, which at the time advocated a period of consolidation at home before venturing onto the international stage, the UAE followed a forward strategy in its foreign policy right from the start. Like Bahrain and Qatar it applied for and obtained membership of the UN and the Arab League at the earliest possible date, partly because this is considered a symbol of statehood. The UAE subsequently joined most UN organisations and affiliates as well as regional Arab and Islamic organisations, even though it could not, for the time being, co-operate fully with them for lack of trained personnel. State visits and the exchange of governmental delegations became frequent occurrences, and the UAE participated in conferences all over the world. It was a step of particular importance, when diplomatic relations were established with neighbouring Saudi Arabia after King Faiṣal and Shaikh Zāyid had signed the border agreement in 1974.[1]

The UAE firmly engraved its name on the minds of officials of many a developing country which benefited from Abu Dhabi's generosity; the aid was given in the name of the Federation. In 1974, after the price of oil had almost quadrupled over a span of seven months, Abu Dhabi reached a record by giving some 28 per cent of that year's income in foreign aid in addition to paying the lion's share of the 1974 federal budget. This aid represented nearly half the total disbursements of Abu Dhabi in that year. In later years the amount given in aid rose in step with the rising revenues from oil, but it did not again reach the high percentage of 1974. Initially aid was given mostly in the form of grants to foreign governments and institutions. It took some years for the Abu Dhabi Fund for Arab Economic Development to start disbursing funds for projects, because of the time taken to evaluate their economic feasibility. The Fund finances up to 49 per cent of projects at favourable interest rates. It had disbursed Dh.1,412.9 million and made loan agreements worth Dh.2,833.5 million up to the end of 1979, and a total of over Dh.6.1 billion up to the middle of 1995. The aid, given to governments and to innumerable international and Arab funds, foundations and charitable organisations assisted many people. It also helped to spread the name of the UAE.

In continuation of the close relationships established between the Gulf States leading up to the formation of the Federation, the UAE eagerly supported any moves which promised closer regional co-operation. This met with success in a number of specialised fields such as aviation, information exchange, oil affairs and currency alignment. It is interesting to note that the member Emirates rarely appeared as individual participants after 1972, but that the federal government had taken over where the seven shaikhdoms used to act individually.

Within weeks of the formation of the Federation the new government's original declared intention of total non-alignment, and therefore implied possible acceptance of diplomatic relations with communist countries, was clarified, and it transpired that the aim was harmony with its like-minded neighbours. A different position favoured by any of its members would have been incompatible with the UAE's conservative inclinations. An important decision taken in this context was that the guerrilla war in neighbouring Oman's southern province of Dhufār was eventually recognised by all the authorities in the UAE as a possible threat to its own security, and the willingness to co-operate more closely among themselves, including in security matters and immigration procedures, promptly followed suit.

The October War of 1973 was a milestone in a great many respects for the self-understanding of all Arab and most Muslim communities. Within the UAE, too, this event engendered a universal consensus endorsing large-scale involvement of the UAE in the common Arab concern. It was a catalyst for the process of rapidly sharpening awareness of a number of issues which are vital for the UAE's prosperity, such as the management of the oil reserves, the need to invest surplus money for the future, industrialisation at home, the role to be assumed in what became known as "recycling the petrodollar", the obligation to assist Third World countries, and last but not least the possible involvement of the State's armed forces in the Arab cause.[2]

The revolution in Iran in 1978/79, causing instability in that country, was then probably the most important external event to evoke reactions in the UAE. This, compounded with the impact of the American/Egyptian/Israeli Camp David agreement, provoked discussion, which served to strengthen the Federation. The crisis of the American hostages in Iran and the Soviet invasion of Afghanistan brought the possibility of a clash of the super powers in the Gulf area very close. It might be speculated that the emirates could then have disagreed among themselves over the position which the State should adopt towards the super powers, in particular if America had offered military protection to the vulnerable oil producers, an offer to which all in the Gulf would have vehemently objected at that time. Up to August 1990 the UAE shared the strong reservations held by Arab countries towards US Gulf policy, including in particular the formation of the Rapid Deployment Force in 1981. The antipathy towards the USA is caused by her policy of underwriting Israel so unreservedly. Whatever the pragmatic necessities, there will always be an underlying uneasiness for as long as this policy remains unchanged.

During the 1970s the UAE succeeded in resolving diplomatically differences with Saudi Arabia and Iran. By the end of the decade, acceptance and friendship throughout the Arab World had replaced the hostile stance of revolutionary and Ba'thist regimes towards the oil exporting shaikhdoms. The UAE's policy of fostering brotherly ties with Arab and Third World countries and of working for an image of financial generosity and political reasonableness paid dividends, giving this new country a high international standing. With increasing self-confidence, the country was by the end of the 1970s less inclined to bend to the policy of any big brother, and in consequence baulked at the high-handedness with which the rules were laid down at the Arab summit in Baghdad in October 1979 after the Camp David agreement, which prescribed the sums to be paid by the oil producing states of the Gulf to the front-line states.

The decade closed with the events in Iran casting ominous dark clouds over the entire region. The UAE had arrived at a comfortable *modus vivendi* with the Shah's Iran during the latter years of the 1970s. The Iranian assistance in bringing the communist-inspired insurrection in the southern Omani province of Dhufār to an end had been appreciated; state visits and exchanges of official delegations, private travelling across the Gulf and growing economic ties between the UAE, particularly Dubai, and Iran helped to foster good relations. The fall of the Shah and the accompanying violence were therefore viewed with regret; but the establishment of the first state in modern times to use Islam as its sole constitutional and social foundation appealed to many people in the UAE. In consequence, recognition of the Islamic Republic of Iran by the UAE was assured. The confused political situation which prevailed in Iran for months after the Ayatollah Khomeini took charge was the cause of much anxiety, not helped by the belligerent media criticism by Teheran of many of Iran's Arab neighbours.

Neighbours at war: 1980–1988

In 1961 Iraq had tried to annex Kuwait. Support for subversive groups in later years in Bahrain and Oman emanated from Iraq, and Ba'thist anti-emirate propaganda was a continuous worry. When, in the aftermath of the 1973 war and the enormous increase in oil revenues, Arabs dreamt of an oil wealthy, unified and powerful Arab nation, the UAE with the other Gulf states was prepared to forget its earlier apprehension of Ba'thist Iraq. During the war between Iraq and Iran, which broke out in September 1980, there were mixed feelings about the consequences for the Arab states of the Gulf if either of the two sides were to win an all out victory. The prospect of the Ayatollah winning religio-political domination at the head of the Gulf filled the UAE's leadership with apprehension, particularly since there were elements in the towns, who had applauded the fall of the Shah and welcomed the establishment of the first modern Islamic state. Few of those who displayed Khomeini's portrait in their shop in the *sūq* in 1978/79 would later have welcomed an Iranian presence on the Arab side of the Gulf. However, many people were equally apprehensive of a victorious Iraq, led by Saddam Hussain, dominating the Gulf and playing a greatly enhanced role in the rest of the Arab World.

The UAE was in danger of being drawn into this conflict, when one of the Iraqi conditions in the ultimatum of 24 September 1980 was the return to the UAE of the islands of Abū Mūsa and the two Tunbs, which Iran had occupied in 1971. Iran ignored the offer, but the episode strengthened Iraq's case in its efforts to persuade a number of Gulf countries to allow Iraqi planes to refuel at airports near the mouth of the Gulf en route for raids in southern Iran. The UAE did not wish to provoke Iran, but was ready to assist Iraq in a number of other ways, particularly during the early part of the war. Damage to Iraq's oil export facilities rendered it unable to deliver oil to its customers. The UAE and other oil producing Gulf states helped to make up the shortfall with production increases and by assigning some of the increased revenue to support Iraq's war efforts with loans and grants.[3] In spite of this financial assistance, which was vital for Iraq, the UAE and other Gulf States were accused of leaving Iraq to stand alone to defend Arab territory. While there was sympathy for the Iraqi position, as the war dragged on, the UAE joined Oman in working to maintain a good relationship with Iran, keeping the dialogue open with Teheran to endeavour to bring about an end to the war. The

UAE was not drawn into the hostilities, but the attack on the Abū Al Bukhūsh production platform, the so called 'tanker war', the drifting mines and other acts of warfare came close enough to both its shores to cause some loss of life.[4] The Iranian Airbus which was shot down on 3 July 1988 by the American warship Vincenne was on a scheduled flight to Dubai with several UAE citizens on board.

Throughout the Iraq-Iran war the UAE advocated keeping the super power rivalries out of the Gulf at almost any cost, calling for a settlement brokered by Arab and Islamic organisations with the support of the UN.[5] In spite of this there was sympathy in the UAE for the Kuwaiti predicament. Kuwait was obliged to assist Iraq with greater financial and practical help than the more distant Gulf states. This provoked the full brunt of the wrath of Iran, which targeted Kuwaiti oil tankers and loading facilities. Kuwait's arrangement with the Soviet Union for the lease of tankers flying the Soviet flag motivated the USA to take 11 Kuwaiti tankers under her flag from July 1987 onwards. The UN-brokered cease-fire which came into force on 20 August 1988 and left the two once-powerful countries in a state of exhaustion was greeted with great relief in the UAE.

The GCC—a new identity

The UAE eagerly supported closer regional co-operation. Politicians in the Gulf capitals were able to build on the personal contacts which they made in the negotiations during the years leading up to the formation of the Federation. This facilitated co-operation during the 1970s in a number of specialised fields such as aviation, industry, information exchange, oil affairs, the environment and currency alignment. Some of the initiative for co-operation came from Iran or Iraq.[6] But the UAE and the other Arab oil producing states of the Gulf remained cool towards Iranian overtures for any kind of formalised joint security arrangement, even though the Soviet Union was perceived to present a common threat.

The October War of 1973 was the occasion, when the UAE first became closely involved with the 'Arab Cause' and experienced for the first time being a fully accepted and integral part of the 'Arab World'. The dramatic increases in oil revenues during the years which followed, enabled the UAE to play an ever more active part. Although it was primarily the country's almost legendary generosity which attracted attention, her voice became more audible and the council and friendship of her leaders were sought by the politicians in the rest of the Arab World. The President Shaikh Zāyid, renowned regionally for his political acumen, rose to this new challenge to lend his charismatic political skills to the solution of greater Arab predicaments. It was fortunate that he was assisted by his astute Foreign Minister, Aḥmad Khalīfah Suwaidi, who had already acquired a high reputation in a number of Arab capitals for his integrity and unwavering devotion to his country and the aspirations of the Arab nation.

The UAE together with the other oil producing Arab states were expected to contribute with their 'Arab petrodollars' to enable all Arab countries to enjoy a higher standard of living, thus helping to bring closer the realisation of the dream of Arab unity. But since victory over the common enemy, Israel, had eluded the Arab side, a large proportion of these funds was diverted to arming the so called 'frontline states' for a possible next round in the Middle East conflict.[7] The people of the UAE have a traditional preference for seeking to resolve conflicts by means of dialogue and compromise. It was therefore not an easy decision for the UAE to join Saudi Arabia and most of the other conservative Arab states in their condemnation of the Camp David agreement, in which Egypt and Israel agreed on 17 September 1978 to proceed to a peace conference. It was largely at Iraq's insistence that Egypt was not invited to the Arab summit in Baghdad in November 1978. Oman, Sudan and Morocco refrained from signing the formal condemnation of Egypt's policy. This somewhat reluctant and unhappy alliance of the conservative states in the Arab World with a radical group of countries resulted in the oil producing countries having to pledge an annual contribution of $3.5 billion to support the 'front line states' for ten years. The oil producing states of the Gulf resented finding themselves cast in the role of paymasters, without being accorded a commensurate policy-making role among their Arab brothers.

Finding themselves set apart in this way, the Gulf countries reappraised aspects of common ground, hoping to establish a formal regional political entity. They are all based traditionally on tribal social structures with very similar economies; their oil-generated wealth and new found political weight are novelties to all of them. But above all, they share a history which makes them different from the rest of the Arab World. None of the Arab countries of the Gulf have been colonies; the extent of their association with a colonial power had never gone further than honouring treaties negotiated by their independent rulers. Therefore they are not in the same way encumbered with the acrimony of the process of decolonisation, and have a much more pragmatic approach in their relationship with western nations.

In the deliberations which preceded the founding of the 'Arabian Gulf Cooperation Council', GCC,[8] there were different views on priorities. Oman asked its partners Saudi Arabia, Kuwait, Bahrain, Qatar and the UAE to urgently consider joint defence arrangements in the light of the ongoing hostilities in the area and the perceived threat from the USSR, but some feared that this would lead to military involvement of western powers, and the proposal was rejected outright by Kuwait. Kuwait wished to first develop economic, social and institutional co-operation among the Gulf countries with a view to eventual integration similar to the EEC. This view prevailed and dominates the Charter which was signed by the six Heads of State at the founding conference on 25 May 1981 in Abu Dhabi.

The GCC's charter stipulates an annual meeting of the six leaders, who form the Supreme Council, taking turns to provide the venue for the meeting and the presidency for the subsequent year. The permanent administrative office is in Riyadh, headed by the Secretary General. The co-ordination of all matters of importance throughout the year and the preparation of the agenda for the Supreme Council Meetings is entrusted to the six foreign ministers, who meet every few months. The ministers for the interior, information or defence also meet regularly. Over the years most matters which are of concern to government bodies in member countries, have been discussed at various levels, resulting in co-operation on topics as diverse as oil, trade, labour migration, narcotics, postal services, internal security, or the environment.

The establishment of the GCC was greeted enthusiastically in the UAE. Having been involved for more than a decade in the process of federal integration, there was the political will to take a further step. There was also an expectation that Gulf-wide agreements might expedite a common approach on matters still unresolved within the federation. The many nationals who participate in meetings and conferences in neighbouring Gulf countries have the chance to test, compare and improve their administrative and management skills. Delegations from the UAE to GCC-committee meetings may face as an additional challenge the problem of balancing their loyalty to their home emirate with the interests of the UAE as a whole. This problem became particularly acute in the various attempts to implement the Unified Economic Agreement, reached in November 1981, an agreement which by the end of 1995 has still not resulted in economic integration to any great extent.[9] The UAE, which is in the process of formulating its federal laws and shaping the future of its society, would benefit if the GCC were more successful in legislating for a greater number of economic and social matters. For many years the formulation of legislative details and their implementation were frequently left to civil servants, who, not being nationals, were unaware of local traditions and customs. Some merely adapted regulations and procedures from their own countries, which were often inappropriate or outdated. As more nationals become involved at all levels of planning and administration, it is hoped that they may use the GCC as a forum to help each other to guide society in their countries into the 21st century, maximising the benefits from their economic wealth while not losing their own identity.

At the December 1992 Supreme Council Meeting in Abu Dhabi a new Secretary General was chosen to replace the Kuwaiti 'Abdullah Bishara, he is Fāhim bin Sulṭān Āl Qāsimi, son of the late ex-Ruler of Ra's al Khaimah; an American-trained lawyer, who has served the UAE in prominent positions in the Foreign Ministry.

The Kuwait Crisis and after

The Arab summit in Bagdad in May 1990 was a personal triumph for President Saddam Hussain and a boost for Iraq after the long years of war with Iran. The regime, while trying to play down its revolutionary aspects and present a pleasant mien to its neighbours and the rest of the world, found support for its position on oil prices, loan repayments and accusations of impropriety in the acquisition of military equipment. The main objective of the meeting was to discuss the Soviet Jewish emigration to Israel. Although the final statement was extremely tough, the UAE was not alone in endorsing it, and in the days after the meetings the President Shaikh Zāyid was feted as he toured Iraq.[10] The Gulf leaders shared the view that all foreign fleets, in particular the American, should stay out of the Gulf for as long as the USA appeared to be so unhelpful in resolving the Palestinian problem. The result was therefore an apparent convergence of views between an Iraq showing a more trustworthy face and the conservative countries of the Gulf.

That trust was shattered on 2 August 1990, when Iraq invaded Kuwait. The UAE President's reaction was swift and uncompromising: rushing back from a visit to Morocco, he met with King Fahad in

Saudi Arabia and President Mubārak in Egypt, advocating an Arab summit. Back home in Abu Dhabi in co-ordination with the other leaders of the GCC he strongly condemned the invasion and demanded the immediate withdrawal of Iraqi troops. The stormy Arab League meeting in Cairo on 10 August, in the course of which 12 of its 21 members agreed to send Arab troops to Saudi Arabia to support American and other troops in protecting that country from Iraqi aggression, made it quite obvious, that the dream of Arab unity had been dealt a severe blow. Pragmatic *Realpolitik* made it now imperative to protect the Arab Gulf countries by whatever means available, even a military alliance led by the USA. While the UAE had always advocated that foreign fleets, and troops and any kind of American Rapid Deployment Force, were best kept out of the Gulf, the UAE now proved one of the most supportive regional partners for the Allied military operations.[11] The presence of foreign forces, 28 nations in all, in the countries of the Gulf was legitimised by 12 UN resolutions and sanctioned by the majority of Arab League states.

From the outset the UAE gave unstinting support to the operation Desert Shield, by making available harbours, airfields, storage facilities and back-up for military personnel. The public saw little of these efforts, which were largely confined to out-of-town locations and the desert. But it was obvious to most residents in the UAE, that the country was hosting sailors, airmen, and women, from many nations who took the opportunity for rest and recreation, to go ashore, to shop, to visit the country, to meet with families, to enjoy sport, and to go to church. Their presence for about six months caused practically no friction with the population of the UAE. Jebel Ali Port in Dubai catered for the largest number of ships at any one time, but the other ports were also used extensively.

The federal government, the local institutions, and the people went out of their way to make 66,000 Kuwaiti refugees welcome in the UAE. Housing, medical care, schooling, even university places, jobs and business opportunities were provided, and their anxieties about their personal future and hopes for their country were shared. There was also a constant stream of displaced persons who had escaped from or were thrown out of Kuwait and were on their way home. The brunt of this exodus hit Jordan and Saudi Arabia, but the UAE also had to cope with thousands of people who came by boat, bus or plane from Kuwait, Iraq or Saudi Arabia and were hoping to return to the Indian subcontinent, the Philippines or other destinations in Asia. Oman and the UAE prepared contingency plans in case even larger numbers of people from eastern Saudi Arabia, Qatar, Bahrain and the UAE had to be evacuated. The cost of this crisis to the UAE is obviously far in excess of the US $ 3.3 billion pledged to the USA, the UK and others.[12]

The UAE's own military contribution, consisting of army and air force units was co-ordinated with other GCC forces. UAE planes flew 123 sorties during the final days of Desert Storm, and ground troops were among the first to enter liberated Kuwait, sustaining some loss of life. Young nationals joined in large numbers in voluntary training. Women and men were encouraged to participate in civil defence exercises, which became very popular, particularly among the girls, leading to the establishment of a women's' military college.[13]

In the wake of the liberation of Kuwait and the failure to bring an equally liberated Iraqi society back into the fold of the Arab family, the six states of the GCC, Egypt and Syria announced at a meeting in March 1991 in Damascus that they would form a peace-keeping force to patrol the Gulf after the non-Arab forces withdrew.[14] This proposed 'six-plus-two' security arrangement was criticised by Iran, whose Vice President Ḥassan Ibrāhīm Habībi said that "If the security of the Gulf and the Sea of Oman is to be safeguarded in the true sense of the word, then Iran's views will have to be considered".[15] Four years after the Damascus meeting no structure has been finalised for this proposed peace-keeping force. Meanwhile relations between Egypt and Iran have deteriorated further and complications have arisen over security in the Gulf. The UAE is in a difficult position because of the dispute with Iran over the three islands and has sought the support of the Arab League members. Whereas the GCC as an organisation has not maintained the pre-1990 momentum towards military co-ordination and a common defence policy, some of the states have since individually concluded defence agreements with the US and the UK; others may follow suit.

Even within the UAE co-operation between the seven emirates in the defence sector had already proved difficult, because before 1971 the various forces had been the traditional manifestation of a Ruler's standing. Therefore, the political price to be paid for trying to enforce amalgamation and thereby alienating some Rulers would have been disproportionate to the fighting strength which these forces would have added to the capability of the newly formed federal forces. Plans for the unification of the forces were formulated in 1977 with help from Saudi Arabia, but it took several more years before the forces were welded together to be able to respond 'as one' to a challenge such as participating in the liberation of Kuwait. Since then the UAE has again responded to the UN's call for assistance and sent about 700 troops to Somalia in January 1993. In all the Gulf States the traumatic experience of the occupation of Kuwait resulted in a massive increase in purchases of defence equipment at all levels of sophistication, and the UAE is no exception.

The gloom and apprehension which prevailed during the crisis have vanished. The UAE's economy has regained almost unprecedented optimism, and in particular the building boom in Abu Dhabi and Dubai has not seen such activity since before the Iran-Iraq war. Trade, in particular through the Dubai ports has recovered its vitality. Goods going to the traditional destinations are continually increasing, while new partners are being found in particular in the countries of the former Soviet Union. The bi-annual Dubai air show resumed with larger numbers of exhibitors, displaying their wares on the ground and in the air. Abu Dhabi held its first international bi-annual defence exhibition in February 1993 with worldwide participation on a lavish scale and in a carnival atmosphere. The UAE has placed very substantial orders for aircraft, ships, tanks and other highly sophisticated modern military equipment. The images of the horrors of Desert Storm brought into the homes daily by CNN satellite television have faded as though it had all been just a bad dream.

The immediate neighbourhood in a new light

The end of the cold war and the break-up of the Soviet Union radically changed the situation on Iran's northern border. In the Gulf her priority remains the elimination of foreign powers, in particular the USA, and peaceful co-existence on her terms to safeguard oil exports and trade.

When the UAE was new, fragile, vulnerable, unknown, disliked by the revolutionary Arab countries and regarded as a rough upstart by many others in the Arab World, it was at the time a wise decision to consider the three islands to be the price to have to pay so that the Shah, who had given in over Bahrain in 1971, could save face.[16] This meant that the UAE had nothing to fear from Iran during the difficult first years of her existence, on the contrary, diplomatic recognition came promptly, helping in the development of cordial relations. Through more than two decades with revolution, religious fervour, war, mines off the UAE east coast and oil policy disputes, there might have been opportunities for the unstable situation on the island of Abū Mūsa to become a major issue between the two countries. Yet, the fragile compromise over sovereignty on Abū Mūsa reached in 1971 survived.

In April of 1992 and again in September of the same year the *status quo* by which the UAE shared sovereignty over Abū Mūsa was infringed by the Iranian authorities on the island. The UAE obtained declarations of support from the GCC,[17] the eight participants in the 1991 Damascus meeting, and the Arab League Council,[18] calling for the three islands, Abū Mūsa and the two Tunbs, which had been taken from Ra's al Khaimah in November of 1971, to be returned to the UAE. A complaint against Iran was lodged with the UN. Not withstanding this, the diplomatic avenues between the two neighbours remain open, and ministerial visits continue. The numerous ties between the two countries, rooted in history and cemented by commercial relations, should facilitate the resolution of disputes through discussion.

The Sultanate of Oman and the UAE together occupy the eastern extreme of the Arabian Peninsula, separated from other countries by vast uninhabited tracts of desert. Throughout the centuries their common tribal, cultural and linguistic bonds have set them apart as an identifiable group of people. The establishment of the UAE in 1971 was warmly greeted in Oman, as had been the accession of Sultan Qābūs in 1970 by the people in the emirates. For decades there seemed to be no necessity for formal diplomatic ties because of the closeness of the numerous personal contacts at all levels. In 1991 the two countries decided to set up the Higher Joint Committee which first met on 4 May in Muscat. Subcommittees were set up to deal with matters of common interest as diverse as water resources, oil, education and investment. The first Omani ambassador arrived in Abu Dhabi in May 1992.

2 Progress in the domestic affairs of the federal state

None of the events, which cast shadows over the young country during the first two decades of her existence, checked the momentum of building the country, a process starting from extremely modest beginnings. Being a small country the UAE has limited influence on developments in the world around, but the authorities can steer domestic developments to cushion the impact of adverse external events on the people.

The UAE's achievements since the foundation of the federation have often evoked the use of superlatives. No attempt will be made here to present a complete catalogue of these achievements which are found in every field of activity. But some developments will be highlighted, which have been of particular importance for the betterment of society in the UAE; others will be included, because their controversial nature calls for an effort to understand the background. The citizens are grateful to their government and justifiably proud of their country; the large multinational expatriate population is also able to appreciate and enjoy the high standard of public services, security, amenities and the pleasant atmosphere in the UAE comparable to the best anywhere in the world.

The economic base

Abu Dhabi's oil wealth was the midwife at the birth of the UAE. The federation's economy remains firmly based on the income derived from exporting hydrocarbons. In 1995 the UAE is reported to have the third largest oil reserves in the Middle East. Three of the emirates are currently oil producers: Abu Dhabi with some 1.9 million bpd (barrels per day) in 1996, far outshines Dubai's estimated production of 300,000 bpd and Shārjah's 8,000 bpd. All three also produce condensate and natural gas.[19] In 1992, at the start of the third decade of its existence, the UAE's income from oil was reported to have been of the order of US$14 billion,[20] with GDP in 1995 at US$37 billion a very wealthy country indeed.[21] Financing the nation's needs should not ever have been a problem since the federation was founded.

In 1972, when the first federal budget, amounting to Dh.200.9 million was announced, Abu Dhabi's revenues had reached Dh. 2,180.8 million. The UAE's budget rose rapidly to a peak of Dh.26.23 billion in 1981. During the latter part of the decade it declined to just above Dh.14 billion, rising again to Dh.17.94 billion in 1995, with a reduced deficit of Dh.1.04 billion to be borrowed from banks.[22] The defense of the nation has high priority for the allocation of funds, but these expenditures do not figure in the federal budget. Some such expenses are met by the individual emirates. In May 1993 the FNC once again drew the attention of the authorities to the long-standing commitment of each emirate to hand over 50 per cent of its oil revenues to the federal state.[23] In the UAE there are several areas, where the public sector economy plays the leading role. The federal government, the governments of Abu Dhabi and Dubai and on a very much reduced scale those of the other emirates all operate somewhat independently of one another. There is a considerable difference in the amount of funding available to the various emirates.

The federal government's economic activity has dramatically expanded, as demonstrated by the 80-fold increase in the budget over 23 years. The relatively low federal expenditure during the early years was due to the lack of federal institutions, which had to be built from scratch. The population increased during two and a half decades from some 220,000[24] to near 2.4 million by 1996, largely due to immigration, creating the need to expand federal services and infrastructure at an ever accelerating rate. A variety of responsibilities accrued to the federal authorities, which had either been carried out previously by the local emirate, or most importantly, had become necessary in the wake of the increasing diversity and sophistication of life in the country. A measure of the growth of these needs is for instance the electricity generation, which grew to 4,250 MW, equivalent to one-third the capacity for the whole of Egypt.[25]

The number of employees in the federal administration increased from a few hundred to a total of 55,000 in 1995.[26] More than half of these civil servants are employed by the Ministry of Education, which has achieved the provision of a uniform standard of service. Priority was given to the establishment of schools throughout the land; initially even prefabricated buildings and tents were used in the outlying villages to provide education for all. National families were given financial inducement to send their children to school. Teachers were recruited from many Arab countries. The number of students rose sharply in the first few years, as children of all ages were enrolled for the first time,[27] and because the pace of development brought in ever more Arab expatriate families. By the end of the first decade almost 110,000 children were studying in schools run by the ministry, in some of the higher classes in secondary schools only about 20 per cent of the students were nationals. The privilege of free schooling for all Arab expatriate children was later limited to the children of civil servants. By the mid-1990s children of all other expatriates and of a growing number of nationals attend one of the 289 fee-paying private schools, which also cater for the different nationalities' linguistic, cultural and religious requirements.[28]

The federal government's economic activity expanded, developing infrastructure and services sometimes in addition to those provided by the individual emirates. The Ministry of Health, for instance, is not responsible for running all hospitals, primary health-care centres, dental clinics and mother-and-child centres in the country. Such institutions are also funded by individual emirates or run by private organisations.[29] Private health-care, which is widely available, is supervised by the Ministry.

Communication was of primary importance in welding together the seven emirates. There were only a few miles of metalled road when the federation was announced. Journeys from the east coast to Shārjah or from the Līwā to Abu Dhabi could only be undertaken in four-wheel-drive vehicles, taking days for distances which can now be traveled in a few hours. Priority was given to building highways radiating from the towns on the coast, connecting the northern emirates and the east coast with Dubai and Abu Dhabi.[30] By the second decade almost every village in the UAE, however remote its mountain or desert location, was connected with a graded track. Telecommunication has for some time been the responsibility of a company, Etisalat, in which all nationals can buy shares. That company's investment in the latest communication technology has been a major factor in making the UAE the preferred location for regional or Middle Eastern company headquarters. It is remarkable that less than three decades ago a message from the Līwā oases to Abu Dhabi town took several days, while now most of the one-time beduin families own four-wheel-drive desert going vehicles, carrying a mobile telephone in direct communication with the whole world.

The strength of the UAE economy depends not only on the financial soundness of the federal state, but even more on the economic activity in the key emirates, in particular Abu Dhabi and Dubai. Over the years the characteristics, which the chance of the geographical setting, the vicissitudes of history and the energy of its population had imparted to each emirate, created differences between them and therefore determine each emirate's economic activity.

Abu Dhabi's salient characteristic is that it has been one of the big oil producers in the Middle East for the last 30 years and can look forward to continuing to reap the benefits of its oil reserves for years to come. The focus must be on how best to employ the income from oil for the greatest benefit of the people of the country today and for coming generations. Wherever one looks today in the emirate of Abu

Dhabi, there is evidence of large amounts of money lavished on the creation of a 'new world' for all its inhabitants to enjoy – functional, comfortable, green, clean and well-lit. The concrete and glass high-rise buildings in the town of Abu Dhabi as well as the acres of newly planted forests in the desert bear witness to the determination to transform the life of the people of Abu Dhabi. This is effected by the government departments of the emirate, guided by the Executive Council. The municipalities of Abu Dhabi and Al 'Ain are responsible for a great number of projects well beyond the confines of the cities. The government bodies share the responsibility for the provision of electricity and water at subsidised rates, free rubbish collection, and the facilities such as parks for the enjoyment of all.

When the government of Abu Dhabi acquired a 60 per cent share from the Western oil concession holders in 1974, and assigned it to the Abu Dhabi National Oil Company ADNOC, that company became a very important 'player' in the economy of the emirate. ADNOC founded a number of subsidiaries and joint ventures, dealing with aspects in the industry beyond merely the production of crude oil. These activities include refining, natural gas processing, chemical production, maritime transportation, exploration and production services and – most noticeable for the general public – marketing of its refined products in the country. The company is a major employer, rapidly increasing the share of national staff, particularly since the appointment of its first national General Manager, Sohail Faris al Mazrui in 1988, succeeded in November 1994 by Yousef Omair bin Yousef, also in his capacity as Secretary General of the Supreme Petroleum Council. That is chaired by the Crown Prince Shaikh Khalīfah bin Zāyid.

The future is provided for with the establishment in March 1976 of the Abu Dhabi Investment Authority, ADIA, to invest overseas some of the oil revenues. The funds are carefully and conservatively spread in equities, bonds, real estate etc. worldwide. The Authority does not publish results, but it is believed that it has accumulated a substantial portfolio of investments over the years. This organisation is controlled by some of the most respected personalities in the emirate. ADIA has given many scholarships for university education abroad and has also functioned as a training ground for Abu Dhabi nationals. Some of its more experienced staff have moved to government posts, including ministerial positions.

In the private sector of the economy of Abu Dhabi the policy is to ensure that, rather than handing money to the nationals, they should be given the opportunity to participate in the economy and thus to *make* money. This aim is pursued by institutionalising a number of privileges for nationals so that they can earn income, for instance from trade agencies, renting property built with government-provided loans on freely distributed land,[31] renting vehicles to companies operating in the desert or competing on favourable terms for projects. The illiterate beduin as well as the urbane chairman of a trading empire are well aware of the benefits of being one of the small number of Abu Dhabi nationals. The distribution of wealth depends to a considerable extent on a person taking the opportunity, commensurate with his tribal and social position; but people who are on the periphery of this society can in time also acquire some privileges. There are many who for one reason or another have not availed themselves of these opportunities; there are others who own considerable property, yet prefer to live as close as possible to their old traditional style. The skyline of the city of Abu Dhabi is rising dramatically as the six-storey buildings of the 1970s are giving way to the buildings of the 1990s reaching up to well above twenty storeys. The popular, government-provided, housing of the late 1960s has been largely replaced by substantial villas often financed by the compensation given when the old houses were demolished. A visitor to modern Abu Dhabi cannot but be impressed by the spacious layout and cleanliness of the roads, the modern buildings and recreational areas.

In Dubai for at least four decades the state has invested in spectacular projects. Shaikh Rãshid bin Sa'īd, the Ruler of Dubai until October 1990, believed Dubai's income from oil, starting in 1969, should be devoted to preparing the emirate for the time when oil production would decline. Oil revenues were dedicated to realising the vision of a latter-day Hormuz, competing with Hong Kong and Singapore. This approach meant that projects were executed which were thought by many to be oversized for their place and time. Yet, one by one these installations became fully utilised and generated further economic activity. The 102 berths of Dubai's two ports were eventually all used for handling much of the UAE's ever increasing imports and Dubai's specialised entrepôt trade. During the Iraq-Iran war, they were very busy, when entering the northern part of the Gulf became hazardous. The ports were essential for the allied forces to maintain their fleets in the area during the Kuwait crisis. In much the same way these developments favoured the use of the Dubai Dry

Dock, once considered a white elephant by many. The time of large surplus capital is passing; increasingly projects will need to recuperate the initial investment in good time; private capital is actively sought also from abroad, such as through the 'offset' arrangements.

The Jebel Ali concept encapsulates Dubai's economic approach: the more ventures, the greater current benefit and the more opportunity for creating further economic activity. The 'Jebel Ali Free Zone', JAFZ, attracts investment from local and foreign companies which rent the warehouses, workshops and factories in a 45 sq. km. industrial park. By early 1996 there were some 900 companies in operation employing more than 30,000 people. Many of these companies require a base somewhere in the UAE and chose Jebel Ali; others have been attracted by the favourable terms.[32] The new harbour was inaugurated in June 1979 at a total reported cost of US $2.5 billion, and there has been further Dubai government investment in enhancement since then. The benefit to the Dubai economy is difficult to determine, but the spending power of the companies in the JAFZ is estimated to be about US $120 million a year in food, commodities, insurance and rentals.[33]

The other emirates also endeavour to develop their particular characteristics or exploit their geographical position. They often find it difficult to secure the necessary capital. Loans and grants from Abu Dhabi, Dubai, Saudi Arabia and elsewhere, as well as borrowing in the financial markets have often helped to start up a project. Fujairah, built a modern port on the east coast, competing with nearby Khaur Fakkān, in Shārjah territory. Both these ports offer access to the UAE and the Gulf countries without the need to use the shipping lanes through the Straits of Hormuz, which may be liable to disruption at times of crisis. An international airport and a free trade zone have been built in Fujairah, linked to the other population centres of the UAE by an excellent road system. Shārjah, which has oil, gas and condensate production, encouraged the establishment of manufacturing industries and financial and trading institutions, which have benefited from the easy availability of building land, and a certain administrative *laissez-faire,* combined with improved port facilities and the proximity of Dubai. Shārjah aspires to be the cultural and intellectual hub for the UAE, even though its modest financial means curtails these efforts. As mentioned elsewhere, Ra's al Khaimah has joined the group of oil exporters, but so far production has been disappointingly small. However, other industries have been successfully established, such as pharmaceuticals, cement and quarrying, and services as well as its long established and flourishing agriculture. The emirates where the economy is not sustained by revenues from oil, are to a very large degree dependent on the wealth of the other emirates to supplement allocations from the federal budget. The clause in the Provisional Constitution which states that each emirate has exclusive sovereignty over the natural resources within its territory results in this obvious inequality. Yet there is reluctance even among the non-oil-producing emirates to remove this clause, because of the hope that one day oil and gas may be found within their boundaries.

The great wealth and the speed of development have brought forth spectacularly successful business ventures in all the emirates, but the biggest names among these family empires are to be found in Dubai, Abu Dhabi and Shārjah. Often from humble beginnings such as being the owner of a hardware shop or a messenger in a bank, some enterprising people seized the opportunities to become the agents for companies providing the commodities and services which were needed to build the country. The founders of such family businesses, which in some cases grew to be empires, have become patriarchal figures in the economic and social life of the country, even though they may have had only a modest education. Their sons, and in due course their grandsons, are frequently sent overseas to study and when they return to join the company, they are well prepared to build on these foundations.

For those nationals who want to start a new business the authorities help them in various ways, in particular through the chambers of commerce and industry in each emirate. They facilitate contacts between national businessmen and foreign companies and together with the municipalities ensure that the various types of joint business ventures comply with current regulations. Exhibitions, trade fairs and conferences have in recent years become popular means of promoting business. The Dubai Trade Centre has several large exhibition halls, which are almost constantly in use, it has established a good reputation for hosting international fairs and conferences. Other emirates have their own organisations and often a dedicated venue for such events. The various municipalities[34] also play an important role in the economic life of an emirate, not only because this is where the allocation of land is effected, property is registered and businesses are licensed, but also because some of the biggest construction projects in an emirate may be undertaken by the municipality.

While the economies of the public and the private sectors grew at an ever increasing pace, it became essential that proper monetary control was institutionalised. As a first step a Currency Board, run by a former employee of the Bank of England, was established and in May 1973 issued the new UAE currency, replacing the Bahrain Dinar, which had been in use in Abu Dhabi, and the Qatar and Dubai Riyal circulating in the rest of the country. The Board was found to lack the authority to regulate the increasingly complicated and diverse monetary scene, particularly after the quadrupling of the oil price in 1974 had caused a big increase in the number of foreign and local banks and in the scope of financial transactions.[35] One of the demands made in the memorandum of spring 1979 was the establishment of a central bank. Federal law No. 10 of 1980 set up the UAE Central Bank, but it was no easy task to regulate and reign in the diverse financial and banking practices to which the liberal economies of the individual emirates had become accustomed. It took a decade of painstaking organisation-building and some spectacular financial failures before the Central Bank was able to assert more wide-ranging regulatory powers over the banks and financial institutions of the country. In December 1991 a new Central Bank Board was appointed, and an experienced national banker was chosen to be Governor. The new board moved quickly to assert greater control and restore confidence in local banking in the aftermath of the BCCI crisis.[36]

Looking back on more than two decades, the UAE's economy has had few financial worries at home while being seen from abroad as a sound business partner. Such a solid financial backbone could not fail to make the young federation a more successful political enterprise than it might otherwise have been. The economic outlook for the future depends first and foremost on the market for and the price of oil and gas, which are outside the country's control. When the income from oil starts to decline, the proceeds from investments will assume ever greater importance and will have to be adequate to cover the cost of running a country whose population has come to expect a high standard of living.

Higher education—investment in human resources

Before the oil age, those who were fortunate enough to receive secondary education traditionally went to India. When the oil revenues started to flow, students chose in increasing numbers universities in Arab and Western countries. To meet the growing demand for higher education, the UAE University was established in Al ʿAin and first opened its doors to 315 male and 205 female students in autumn of 1977. Soon the girls began to outnumber the boys, because the families preferred that the daughters did not go abroad to study far away from their familiar protective home environment. Initially all the teaching staff were recruited from abroad, mostly from Egypt, Iraq and other Arab countries. In July 1983 Shaikh Nahyãn bin Mubãrak Ãl Nahyãn, who had been at Oxford University, became the chancellor of the UAE University. The majority of students graduated in arts subjects, particularly favouring business and administration. The variety of subjects taught grew to include engineering and sciences, and a medical faculty was set up in co-operation with the Taw'ãm Hospital in Al ʿAin, the first batch of medical students graduating in 1993.

In addition to these traditional channels, a new approach to higher education was introduced by the university chancellor, when he established the first Higher College of Technology in 1988. The objective is to provide the country with young national manpower, prepared, trained and motivated to take on a wide range of jobs in industry, banking, government etc. Demands on the students are very high, the media for teaching practical and technical subjects is English, and computer skills are an essential part of all tuition. The growing prestige of the colleges is demonstrated by the government decision to give graduates from the colleges the same grades as university graduates. There are now eight colleges for men and women in Abu Dhabi, Al ʿAin, Dubai and since 1993 in Ra's al Khaimah teaching a total of 2,691 national students in the academic year 1995/96.

For many years it has been government policy in Abu Dhabi that suitably qualified nationals should be given priority in the allocation of positions. It is of great concern to the authorities that the national manpower should be adequately prepared to take up the wide variety of jobs available today in the UAE. The role of higher education was recognised through the establishment of a Ministry of Higher Education in 1990, in addition to the Ministry of Education and Culture. It was very appropriate that Shaikh Nahyãn bin Mubãrak, was appointed the first Minister.

Women as a source of national manpower are seeking higher education in ever increasing numbers. Some, not considering a career, are keen to experience education as a way to improve themselves and to help them play a more meaningful role in the education of their families. As the statistics demonstrate, with 9,148 female university students (as compared to 2,773 men) enrolled for the academic year of 1995/6, the university in Al 'Ain has become a place, where it is possible for a girl even from the most conservative of local families to study, because all precautions are taken to give her the protected environment required by the families, even when she is taught by male professors. The concept of the Higher Colleges helps to go a step further in the direction of integrating women into the world of careers, and in consequence, the women who intend to seek employment after graduation tend to opt for enrollment there. In many cases the students have come through the private education system, where English is the teaching medium. The colleges are so popular, particularly with women, that there are plans to establish several more closer to the homes of national families in the other emirates.

An important feature of education in this country is the variety of educational possibilities at various levels available to students, including the opportunity to study abroad. In some cases the parents send their children to foreign universities. The Ministry of Education and many organisations such as ADIA, ADNOC and banks give scholarships to suitably promising national students; in 1993 1,200 students were sent abroad by ADIA alone. Although the primary function of ADIA is to invest some of the nation's wealth to secure its long term future, it has always served as a training ground for many of the most promising nationals. The most important local and federal economic institutions have drawn from this reservoir of professionals, who have shown themselves to be honest and dedicated citizens.

Unlike some Arab and many developing countries, the UAE's bright young people are not fettered by poverty or self-imposed ideological blinkers. This freedom and the wide range of choice of education at home and abroad should be treasured as a very special privilege.

A country shared with others

Since the foundation of the UAE a census was held regularly every five years until December 1990, when it was canceled due to the Kuwait crisis. The census of 1980 showed that during the previous five year period there had been a population increase of 86.7 per cent. During the next five year period to the census of 1985 the increase for the UAE was 55.7 per cent. The total population in 1985 was 1.62 million, 670,000 in the emirate of Abu Dhabi, 419,000 in Dubai and 29,000 in Umm al Qaiwain, the smallest of the seven emirates. Having cancelled the scheduled census of 1990 because of the Kuwait Crisis, the Ministry of Planning organised the enumeration of all inhabitants in December 1995.[37] The total population was 2.377 million, a ten-fold increase over the estimated population figure of 25 years ago. No breakdown of the population composition has yet been published, except the totals for every emirate and that men outnumber women by two to one.[38]

This phenomenal population increase is only partly due to a high national birth rate, the prime reason for growth is immigration on a very large scale over the last three decades from other Arab countries and from Asia. Many of these immigrants do not expect to settle, but hope to return to their homes wealthier than when they left. They come to work or are dependents of people who work. As the economy of the state has grown beyond all expectation, the requirement for manpower has expanded commensurably. From manual labour in the construction industry, the municipality or in agriculture, to civil servants and teachers, to bankers and consultant engineers, and to people in the growing tourist and entertainment industry, expatriates are essential to the economy. Many people who came to the UAE did not have a particular job waiting for them, nevertheless found employment in due course in the ever expanding economy of the country.

While in the 1960s the labour force as well as much of the skilled manpower came from the Indian subcontinent, in the mid-1990s there is hardly a country in the world, with the exception of Israel, which does not have some of its nationals residing in the UAE. Many teaching, administrative, health care, military and a host of other professional tasks are performed by Arab expatriates; in the service industry south-east Asians are now predominant. Europeans and North Americans usually perform specialised tasks, and they tend to come for a fixed contract of a few years and rarely bring other relatives apart from their own immediate family. Expatriates are also welcome to help to fill the apartment and office blocks and they are valued consumers, without whom the local economy could fall on hard times.

Over the years many federal laws and local decrees have been devised to regulate the coming and going of this vast number of non-national residents, to safeguard their rights as residents, but curtail claims to the privileges which only citizenship can offer. Thus, the composition of the population in the UAE is in a perpetual state of flux. In this unusual demographic situation there are two prominent trends: firstly, the permanently resident national population continues to increase rapidly in number, secondly, the ratio of nationals to expatriates has been decreasing steadily since before the UAE was founded. This state of affairs has been the subject of a great deal of debate, analysis, and even controversy and encouraged the authorities to develop national manpower even more vigorously. Time and again the issue of foreign manpower has dominated the discussions of official bodies, including the FNC, as will be described below.[39] None of the many expatriate communities is numerous enough by itself to antagonise the other communities or to threaten the local society. The sheer number of the many different nationalities represented in the UAE acts to balance the cultural, linguistic, religious and political impact of any one group of expatriate residents. Life in the UAE is liberal and benevolent, which means that every individual and every group of people can live according to its own traditions and preferences, as long as it abides by the law. This makes for an extremely interesting juxtaposition of cultures, rarely observed elsewhere side by side in such variety, and in such harmony.

"My home is my castle"

The English saying "my home is my castle" describes equally well the UAE national's attitude; a castle is meant to keep out intruders, it can be impressive, a measure of the family's importance and influence. For them the house is a retreat, a refuge from the fast changing outside world and the object of the family's pride. It can be one of several houses, the others are either in another town or tucked away in a farm in a scenic rural area of the UAE. Many nationals in governmental or private employment in an emirate other than their own may have to accept living in an apartment; but this is usually just a place to live for the working week, because home is where the extended family lives.

Although an extremely large percentage of the population is temporarily resident, the people of the country share a great number of facilities and often much of the time of day with them. The place where people live, this is where the clearest distinction is drawn between the national and expatriate societies. For a local family, regardless of its social status, the home encapsulates its identity: The family house is in the emirate to which the tribal family has always 'belonged'; this home is where they can decide to what extent change and outside influences are permitted within their own environment; this is where the traditional social values are lived, even though many other features of a foreign lifestyle may have been adopted. Thus, in every local home the *harim*, that is the private family quarters, is separate from the *majlis*, where guests enjoy the traditional Arab hospitality.

The authorities in each emirate are mindful that people attach great importance to house and home. Providing modern housing was the essential first step to be taken by the governments to improve peoples' lives. In the late 1960s as the economy expanded, the wealthier families built villas to replace the *barastis* or mud brick compounds they had previously lived in. The majority of families could not afford to do this, so the government supplied them with new accommodation, built in concrete and provided with electricity, running water and sewage disposal. A scheme to provide "peoples' houses" for nationals was started in Abu Dhabi in 1966, and by 1976 some 5,000 houses had been given to families in the capital, Al 'Ain and many newly created villages, where the beduin population was encouraged to settle in order to partake of the development efforts made on its behalf. Mosques, schools, clinics and markets were constructed at the same time.

Thus, even before 1971 all of the traditional wind tower houses in Abu Dhabi had been replaced by modern houses and office buildings, and suburban villas appeared where previously people had lived in palm-frond houses. Here and increasingly in the other urban areas of the country, the crooked alleys and open spaces between the tribally settled quarters became obliterated by straight dual-carriageway roads slicing towns and the surrounding countryside into neat rectangles with a roundabout at each intersection. In the early 1970s the government of Abu Dhabi also built "peoples' houses" for the population of some towns and villages in the northern emirates. The construction of free housing for low-income groups eventually became the responsibility of the federal Ministry of Public Works and Housing, except in Abu Dhabi and Dubai, where the provision of houses or villas for the less well-off nationals, some civil servants and military personnel is an important obligation carried out by the emirates' governments.[40]

There continues to be a great demand for government-provided housing, because the children of the original recipients now require their own homes. Housing is also needed for the people who have migrated from the northern emirates to the cities and for the recent immigrants from Oman, Yemen and elsewhere, who have obtained UAE nationality. New houses are constructed for the rural communities which now have roads or motorable tracks leading up to their remote ancestral homes. Some have become dormitory villages, because their young men work away from home in the military or the police. There have been several government loan schemes to help nationals to build their own houses. Over the years financial assistance for building private houses has frequently been given by the local governments or through special funds set up by the rulers.[41] Low-cost houses and building loans are privileges which are reserved for nationals.

Similarly, only nationals can own land, with the exception of GCC nationals who are allowed to buy property in some emirates. There are differences in the laws governing the ownership of land in each of the emirates. Traditionally, land is "in the gift" of the Ruler; it used to be allocated by him personally or by people entrusted to follow the unwritten customs and privileges in the shaikhdom's tribal society and to know a community's settlement patterns and historical land use. During the first years of rapid urbanisation and construction in the coastal towns and villages, the families which were already settled there were given priority in obtaining building plots or "peoples' houses". Tribal groups which frequented the towns or had close family connections there, were more likely to be given a house in the town than the tribesmen whose principal abode had always been in the desert or mountain hinterland. The latter were encouraged to settle in their home areas through the gift of houses and services there.

As the oil revenues increased and business flourished, there was a rapidly increasing need to house the influx of expatriates and to provide office, workshop and storage space everywhere. Initially the ensuing property boom was almost exclusively in the hands of the shaikhs and leading families of each shaikhdom. In due course the demand for accommodation was such that an ever increasing number of new units was required, and a government policy was developed to enable more and more nationals to own property for renting out and benefit from the country's increasing wealth.[42]

Land ownership outside the urban areas originally only applied to gardens in oases, which were mostly devoted to the cultivation of the date palm. The traditionally limited cultivation of vegetables and animal fodder for local use formed the basis for a rapid expansion in agriculture, made possible through the increase in public funds. Today market gardens which have sprung up in many desert and mountain areas are used to help the desert population to enrich themselves. Often the land is given free ready prepared and water costs little or nothing, seedlings, manure, insecticides and labour are subsidised and frequently the government guarantees to purchase the produce. Nationals among the town dwellers like to establish gardens away from the main population centres, where they build weekend homes and cultivate fruit and vegetables for their own use and for the market. These properties were originally allocated by the local authority, but in some of the popular locations they are now traded.

In which ever way property is obtained, ownership is a privilege which depends on status within the local society and therefore has little to do with the federal authorities. Such status is usually more closely linked to traditional tribal structures than to newly acquired wealth, but longstanding civil servants do not go unrewarded. The system does not automatically provide every citizen with the opportunity to own his home, the most visible of the privileges which distinguish the national from the mass of other people around.

Constitutional crises of the 1970s, closing ranks in the 1980s

Events in Iran during late 1978 and early 1979 could not fail to have an effect on the political scene in the UAE. One result was an increasing political awareness, with the emphasis on improvement of the existing structure of government rather than on any fundamental changes. The criticism that the Supreme Council of Rulers, the country's highest legislative and executive body, was practically immobilising effective government by meeting too infrequently and by its ponderous ways of proceeding, was made publicly for the first time. This criticism took the form of a memorandum prepared by members of the FNC and the Council of Ministers.[43]

On 13 February 1979 the parliamentary body, the FNC, and the Council of Ministers held a joint session to discuss the developments in the region and their impact on the UAE. They decided to submit to the Supreme Council recommendations for consolidating the Federation.[44]

Predictably the memorandum dealt with problems which had over the previous eight years become, in the eyes of many people, obstacles to a more satisfactory functioning of the federal State. The first of the eleven points called for the unification of the armed forces and an end to arms imports by individual emirates' governments. Another important aspect was the call for the abolition of all internal borders, which implied abolishing the emirates' authority over the natural resources within their territory. Comprehensive planning of immigration and naturalisation policies was called for. Under the heading "conservation of national wealth" the memorandum criticised the unequal distribution of wealth. Abu Dhabi having exclusive authority over its oil revenues, the memorandum called for management of the nation's single resource and the financial benefits derived from it to be handled by federal bodies, a central bank, national rather than foreign banking institutions, a reserve fund, and tighter federal control over what it called foreign "economic invasion". The authors stated that "economic and social justice is a pillar of internal stability."

Probably the most important immediate impact which the memorandum could be expected to have was to improve substantially the functioning of the federal institutions. The memorandum therefore included the following demands: "The Supreme Council, which draws up the state's policy, should meet periodically (regularly) every month . . . The Supreme Council's General Secretariat should have competent cadres to prepare agenda, studies and documents. Ministers should be given (more) powers." A fundamental demand in this respect was that the FNC should be given full legislative powers and cease to be only a consultative assembly. The memorandum also has some direct references to democratisation: where the point of improvement of living standards was raised, a further paragraph stated: "not by bread alone human beings live". The document concluded with the statement that the provisional constitution was now an anachronism and a hindrance to unification attempts and that "the current phase necessitates the immediate start for having a permanent constitution."

There was no direct reference to elections on the basis of one-man-one-vote, because the authors of the memorandum were fully aware that with the existing population structure the application of this principle would be controversial, and that, in the absence of political parties, the traditional leadership groups within the local society could well continue to be used as adequate vehicles of popular representation. Contrary to the conclusions which outside observers reached, the joint memorandum and the Spring 1979 crisis did not primarily focus on Western style democratisation. Nor was criticism of lack of freedom an issue, because in every respect, personal, religious and economic, and with regard to political opinion, the UAE is one of the least restrictive Middle Eastern countries. The central issue in 1979 was the need to make the Federation more governable and its institutions more professional. The nature of the public support for the movement and the reaction of the highest federal authorities indicate that these arguments were part and parcel of the ongoing debate about interpretation of the federal principle; although, to some, unification to the point of centralisation had always seemed to be a much neater solution.

On the day that the memorandum was handed to the Supreme Council a number of citizens from other emirates and students from the UAE University converged on the venue of the seven Rulers in Abu Dhabi. The demonstrations which were organised during the following four days in many parts of the UAE portrayed greater centralisation as the remedy for the Federation's problems. Hand in hand with this went a surge in enthusiastic expressions of support for the President, Shaikh Zāyid, who was seen as the proponent of speedier unification.[45] Such summary unification and virtual abolition of the principles of a federalistic as opposed to a centralistic State were rejected as unconstitutional, rash and ill-timed by some emirates' governments, in particular Dubai. Predictably no decisions concerning the federation could be made during the two days of talks.

Dubai chose to comment on the joint memorandum in a statement, submitted to the Supreme Council's second meeting. In essence it was just as adamant in its dedication to the search for unity within the Federation as was the joint memorandum.[46] But they differed considerably in the means they envisaged to this same end. Dubai favoured unification of some services but otherwise advocated that, because conditions had been different in the various regions of the UAE in the past, an attempt to unify others prematurely would not bring the expected result of better and more equitable conditions throughout the country.

This constitutional crisis coincided with the discussions of sanctions against Egypt, with the proclamation of an Islamic Republic in Iran, and with the execution in Pakistan of former President Bhutto, a frequent visitor to Gulf countries. Thus the attention of the decision makers was divided, but even in a less tense political climate abroad, fundamental issues at home would not have been tackled without the usual rounds of discussions and the invitation of an outside mediator, in this instance the Foreign Minister of Kuwait, Shaikh Ṣabāḥ Aḥmad Āl Ṣabāḥ. The result was the dissolution of the Council of Ministers on 26 April and the announcement that Shaikh Rāshid bin Sa'īd would form the next cabinet. This cabinet was presented on 1 July 1979 and in the event contained only four changes. The process of forming this cabinet involved a good many compromises, most of which were, however, reached between the members of the Supreme Council, who were still concerned primarily with the issue of how centralised the Federation should be, and how much sovereignty should be retained by individual emirates' governments. In the years after 1971 one after another of the original members of the Supreme Council of Rulers died. By 1995 only Shaikh Zāyid and Shaikh Ṣaqr of Ra's al Khaimah can draw on the experience of the founding years of the federation.[47]

The Spring 1979 crisis was an attempt to edge the constitution towards that of a centralised state, because the federal system had not yet attained the necessary balance between input by the member states and output by the central government. The FNC continued to remind the Supreme Council that the federal institutions were still inadequate to cope with the country's needs. Moreover, the precedent was set in Spring 1979 for outspoken criticism and demonstrations, and when a public grievance arose over the price of petroleum products in the northern emirates in February 1980, students again took to the streets, this time to demonstrate against the oil companies and to ask for federal government subsidies.[48] A large number of students from the University met with the President in a televised discussion, in itself a demonstration of traditional grass-roots democracy in action. In the movement of Spring 1979 and in subsequent repetitions of the demands voiced in the memorandum, the issue of democracy formed part of the call for improvement of the structure and function of the federal state, but it has never been a main preoccupation.

In a meeting of the Supreme Council on 29 October 1981, the Provisional Constitution was extended for a further five years without much overt opposition from the FNC. Shaikh Zāyid was re-elected President and Shaikh Rāshid Vice-President and Prime Minister.

The new decade began well for the UAE, the Prime Minister vigorously pursuing the proliferation of services to the distant corners of the poorer emirates and the UAE oil revenues stood at an all-time high of over US$14 billion in 1980. Soon events beyond the country's control hindered the consolidation of the federal institutions and delayed the process of democratisation. The deterioration of law and order in Iran and the hostage crisis, the Iraq-Iran war, the Egyptian peace treaty with Israel, war in Lebanon, the presence of Soviet troops in Afghanistan all caused tension and frustrated efforts to focus on domestic matters.

The situation in the UAE was complicated by the fact that the Prime Minister, in whom people had placed high hopes, fell ill soon after his re-election in 1981, and in spite of temporary improvements in his health never recovered before his death on 7 October of 1990. It would have seemed incorrect to appoint someone else to this position as long as he was alive; the resultant uncertainties slowed or even reversed the process of eliminating the differences between the emirates. With the exception of a memorandum presented to the Supreme Council in 1986, voicing the already familiar grievances, the FNC rarely again took the initiative to press for changes. Towards the end of the decade the assembly seemed to be almost paralysed, and the 40 members spent much time attending meetings with parliamentary delegations, at home and abroad.

There are other bodies, where nationals discuss matters which have a bearing on their daily lives. The most prominent of these bodies is Abu Dhabi's National Consultative Council, an assembly of 50 nominated tribal leaders, influential merchants and some technocrats, who have at times been outspoken, suggesting changes in the way in which their emirate functions.[49] Views voiced in this council influence the decisions which are taken by Abu Dhabi's government, the Executive Council.[50] An arrangement for political participation was promised by Shaikh 'Abdul 'Aziz Āl Qāsimi in his bid to usurp power from his brother in Shārjah in June 1987. After the Ruler regained full control with the help of Dubai's mediation, he himself established a cabinet-like Shārjah Executive Council with 26 nominated members.[51]

There are also the municipal councils. As already mentioned, a municipal council of 12 members was first nominated in Dubai in 1961 and was reconstituted periodically since then, reaching a strength of 30 members in 1980.[52] Abu Dhabi town has had a municipal council since the 1960s; the 30 member council for the town of Al 'Ain was appointed by decree on 21 September 1992.[53] In a similar way the chambers of commerce in the cities of the emirates have committees, which offer opportunities for debate, but the effectiveness of such deliberations is often limited by the lack of formal education of some of the community leaders, for whom it is increasingly difficult to keep abreast of the ever more complicated economic and social developments even in their home towns. Everywhere in the government and in private offices more educated nationals, women among them, are filling middle management positions. They have experienced the challenges of professional discipline, and are proud to be able to lead their country out of its dependence on expatriate expertise. They have to bide their time before they can be considered for one of the various representational councils, which still tend to be associated more with the notions of family, rank and seniority.

While participation in the formal political sense had not progressed far during the 1980s, significant developments have taken place in some important areas of public life. For two decades nationals with the relevant specialised training have been carefully selected for positions in finance, planning, the oil industry, banking and education, to name just a few, and have become very important players in the decision-making process, replacing expatriate management. They command both through birth and by their understanding of the subject matter the trust and confidence of their superiors in the positions of ultimate authority. Decisions in government depend on their input and advice to the highest authorities, who rely increasingly on these national experts to prepare recommendations when a matter is put forward for their signature. In this way competent nationals are more effective and may have more scope for genuine participation in the running of their country than if they were active only through councils and committees.

The 1980s were a period of diminished political activity due to events in the Gulf and the Arab World, which led people to close ranks with the authorities, even if their political system was perceived to be in need of reform. In the 1990s after the Kuwait crisis such quietism appears to be giving way to renewed interest in the domestic political environment. There is a sense of deliverance and much optimism that the Gulf region will now remain a secure area for the foreseeable future, and in most business circles the buoyant spirit has returned. The nationals of the UAE are thinking about new plans, and increased participation in public life is one of them.

While in Saudi Arabia a national consultative council and regional councils are being set up, the existing institution in the UAE is being revitalised. In February 1993 the FNC was reconvened with 27 of its 40 members being newly appointed, the first session was opened by the President. In the reply to the opening address the new speaker, Al Hāj bin ʿAbdullah al Maḥairibi again raised certain points which the FNC considers to be of national importance, in particular that every emirate should provide 50 per cent of its oil revenues to the federal budget. The establishment of a federal housing bank was again suggested and anxiety was expressed over the spread of drugs and the ever growing number of immigrant labourers.[54] During the month of Ramadhan of that year the FNC held question and answer sessions in a tent in the garden of the Cultural Foundation in the capital. These were televised, and they served to give nationals a chance to air their views. In Dubai and Shārjah private citizens held similar outdoor *majlis* events, to which the press were invited.

While some women have strong views on questions concerning their place in society, it was a rare occurrence when a group of 18 primarily professional national women attended an open *majlis* for women and discussed their grievances in public. They criticised the custom that they need the intervention of a custodian for most business transactions, that they are disadvantaged in government service and some demanded that women should become members of the FNC and other representational bodies.[55]

In this renewal, of public debate, the FNC was once again the focal point for many people's expectations. Yet, the establishment in 1993 by Shaikh Zāyid of marriage funds for all the emirates demonstrated that prompt reaction to a grievance is still more likely to come through intervention by the President or a ruler rather than as the result of FNC deliberations.

The Council of Ministers provides continuity, co-ordination and control of the administration throughout the federation. This has increasingly come to be guaranteed through the routine of its weekly meetings in Abu Dhabi under the chairmanship of the Prime Minister, Shaikh Maktūm bin Rāshid or, as happens quite frequently, the Deputy Prime Minister, Shaikh Sulṭān bin Zāyid. This council was appointed on 21 November 1990 after the death in October of the Prime Minister Shaikh Rāshid bin Sa'īd, Ruler of Dubai. There are 26 members, of whom four are Ministers of State; the new Ministry for Higher Education was added. There is a higher number of technocrats than previously, and each emirate is fairly represented in this important body, nine are members of one or another of the ruling families, nine members retained their previous portfolios, several others had ministerial posts in the past; five members, including the Deputy Prime Minister are newcomers to this federal body, but not to government appointments or public duties.[56] The revitalised cabinet of the 1990s and its various committees combine within the team members who have long experience in government, members who advocate the interests of their home emirates and members who, being shaikhs, are well placed to have the ear of the President and the Supreme Council.

Since 1971 the UAE has made tremendous material progress, visible in Dubai's and Abu Dhabi's astounding level of sophistication. In the entire country progress has been made towards spreading material well-being more evenly and providing essential services for nationals and expatriates. This progress was achieved in spite of the fact that there was no great popular ground swell, through which demands were formulated. Progress was almost automatic. The huge influx of people necessitated administrative responses, even if there was no debate about a political one. The administration was continually enlarged and modified to deal with all the requirements of the growing national and expatriate population. From road construction to immigration laws, the response to a host of practical needs inevitably often had to be federal. Thus, unification, too, becomes an administrative inevitability.

Legislation and jurisdiction

When the UAE was founded in 1971, public life did not have to operate in a complete legal vacuum. The individual emirates, Dubai and Abu Dhabi in particular, had in the preceding years already enacted some legislation. Urged by the British officials, who were eager to see matters properly regulated before withdrawal – matters for which British jurisdiction had previously applied – a variety of laws and regulations was hastily prepared and decreed by the Rulers.[57]

The federal constitution gives a mandate to the authorities to provide the framework for equalising opportunities throughout the land. A society's identity is unmistakably expressed in the country's laws and legislative regulations, reflecting the religious, moral and ethic concepts of society. In 1972 the process began of formulating the federal laws and decrees, which make up this framework. During the subsequent two decades, the federal legislative process has not always come up to expectation. Hindered by the shortage of competent nationals to draft the texts and through delays caused by conflicts of interest, important federal legislation, which ideally should have been finalised in the early 1970s, was too long in coming. The arrangements on Emirate level had meanwhile had time to take root, making nationwide implementation of new federal laws more difficult. With the overwhelming majority of the population being foreign, legislation has to balance between the necessity to regulate matters on behalf of the entire population whilst safeguarding the priority interests of the national society.

Since the Provisional Constitution does not permit the FNC to propose bills, federal legislation depends on the initiative and follow-up of the Council of Ministers and its legislative subcommittee, prompted by the ministry which perceives the need for a particular law. The latter prepares the draft, frequently modelling it on legislation already in existence in particular in Kuwait, Egypt, and Jordan. The draft is sent for comments to the Ministry of Justice and to other concerned ministries. While the FNC cannot prevent a law being promulgated in a form it does not approve, the views of the assembly can influence its final version. Checks and balances are brought to bear on a bill, when the draft is taken to the individual Emirates, from where changes may well be demanded in order to pave the way for the law to be sanctioned by all seven members of the Supreme Council of Rulers. Such informal consultation is not specifically prescribed in the constitution, yet it is an essential part of legislation in the federal state. While this can be a cause for the tardiness of some legislation, it provides more opportunity for discussion and practical input from society, than would be possible in some of the centralised states of the GCC. Yet, this opportunity for Emirate related input does not necessarily improve the draft or make the law more universally enforceable. The general malaise of lack of professionally sound judgment available to decision makers may result in all kinds of self-serving, impractical or irrelevant elements being introduced into a federal law with the effect that certain aspects of it are delayed or even ignored by some local governments.

As time goes by every region exploits more successfully its specific economic opportunities, and the differences between the Emirates with regard to their economic, social and demographic circumstances become more pronounced, often with little consideration for the price of development in demographic terms. The individual Emirates, responding to their specific needs, have since before 1971 provided through local laws and decrees a framework in which the many unforeseen changes can be given proper direction. In particular, Dubai requires its own legislation to sustain continued growth as a major trading centre. In some Emirates local legislation is subject to discussion on various levels. In the case of Abu Dhabi this is one of the functions of the National Consultative Council; ideas may also come from the municipal councils, the chambers of commerce, the concerned government departments and informally from the *majlis*.

Legislation, which is passed by the individual Emirates, in most instances still retains the hallmarks of their Rulers, who are used to acting directly and even autocratically, when they perceive the need for their regulatory intervention. While the regulations, which are thus introduced by 'Emiri Decree' might be prepared by competent advisers or even foreign specialists in the particular field, there is often little provision for consultation with the concerned population groups. In these cases the legislative process itself is still part of the era, in which the homogenous tribal society depended on its Ruler to exercise his authority single-handedly and in all matters big and small.

The UAE is a country with a remarkably low crime rate. Unlike Saudi Arabia, this is not achieved by applying a form of *sharī'ah*-based deterrent jurisdiction. The people of this coast have usually shunned extremes and their preference for compromise is reflected in the country's legislation and in the sentences which are passed by its courts. For immigrant offenders the threat of deportation is the most powerful deterrent because it would deprive them of the chance to work in the UAE. On occasions individual judges, often from other Arab countries with different legal backgrounds, have tried to set precedents basing progressively more verdicts on their own interpretation of *sharī'ah*, but in subsequent cases of a similar nature such trends were reversed. More often than not a judge selects the lighter of the possible penalties, while the death penalty has so far only been imposed in extremely rare cases and even more rarely carried out, always in consultation with the President.

The UAE' s system of courts is based on the principle of appeal, with the Supreme Court at its apex for constitutional as well as other jurisdictional disputes. When the Union Courts of First Instance and Appeal were established in 1978 the Emirates of Abu Dhabi, Shārjah, 'Ajmān and Fujairah (and later Umm al Qaiwain) recognised these courts as the higher authorities for their own local courts, which thus became part of an integrated federal court system. Since 1983 this is monitored and co-ordinated by the Supreme Judicial Council. Dubai and Ra's al Khaimah continued to build after 1971 on their existing court systems under the direct aegis of the Rulers, with the Supreme Appeal Court in Dubai being attached to the Ruler's Office. In these two Emirates specific matters are assigned to civil courts, while under the federal court system the division into two chambers, civil and *sharī'ah*, originating from before 1978, is usually maintained.

An ever increasing number of law courts had to be established and staffed to deal with infringements against the law in the multinational society. In many sectors of public service nationals are found, whose general education enables them to replace the expatriate civil servant. The judiciary, however, requires people with a specialised education, and it took time before the first nationals took the oath as judges or public prosecutors. Meanwhile the Ministry of Justice and the legal departments of the individual Emirates have employed Sudanese, Syrian, Egyptian and Jordanian judges and legal advisers. Still, the backlog of cases pending adjudication appears to be growing. The UAE University's Faculty of Sharī'ah and Law as well as law schools abroad are adding to the number of national graduates in the legal profession but it will probably take time for complete 'emiratisation' of the legal sector in public life.[58]

The situation in the legal field is an illustration of the problems which the UAE continues to face. The description in this chapter of some of the effects of the sudden wealth and the huge population influx on the tightly-knit fabric of the local society is meant to bring into proportion rather than detract from the extent of the country's achievements during the last decades.

Conclusion

The extremely harsh climate and inhospitable environment imposed terrible hardship on the people born in the emirates before the oil age; they made the most of their marginal subsistence economy under conditions, such as will never be known again on this coast.

Even though oil exports had already commenced in 1962, there was little revenue available to fund large-scale development until after Shaikh Zāyid's accession in 1966 and the growing production and dramatic price increases of 1973/4, which made it possible to transform the coastal settlements into striking twenty-first-century cities and the oases in the hinterland into lush green market gardens.

The major concern of this study is to establish the structure of society and the predominant influences on peoples' lives before the income derived from oil led to such dramatic changes. Since the beginning of this transformation from the old order revolving around pearls, date palms, camels and fishing, the society of the UAE has moved a generation further on. Some stocktaking of where it now stands must also be attempted. Is the local society losing its identity while the material and cultural imports from many nations are implanted?

The families in the towns who live in close proximity to the overwhelming number of immigrants, with their different traditions, languages and alien habits, became increasingly aware of their own traditional values and live more consciously by them, assisted by the discipline required of a good Muslim. The family structure and the conventions which form part of domestic life, such as marriage patterns and the continued role of the *harīm*, the part of the house reserved for the family and women, were consciously maintained. This is the world one treasures; this is where the roots are, the strength and integrity of which enable people to respond to the radically changing life without losing their identity.

Nationals of a new generation now take in their stride, what seemed unimaginable to their parents. Recently built family homes display in their architecture and furbishment the most modern amenities and an astonishing variety of luxuries brought from East and West. The urge to preserve their identity while also sharing the uniformity of a lifestyle which is defined in terms of 'affordability', results in clinging tenaciously to outward signs of identity, which in a less multinational environment might have been allowed to disappear. Nationals are recognisable by their attire—men invariably wear the *kandūrah* and Arabic headdress, and women traditionally cover themselves in a black cloak known as *abāyah* and a face mask. Because women shun contact with men other than close relatives, cars used by local families are recognisable, having heavy curtains or sometimes tinted glass.

If in certain circumstances the people of the UAE change their way of life and even their values, this is by choice. At other times, in particular while in the abode of the extended family, people still feel most comfortable with the old customs and choose to live by them. Being able to afford either, modernity or to maintain their traditional culture, people hope to 'get the best of both worlds'. It is thus not modernity itself which threatens the national society's identity, it is the fact that all these choices of a hitherto alien way of life can be afforded – but not all these choices are equally beneficial to the individual or to society as a whole.

More than 20 years have passed since the foundation of the federation, the time span of an entire generation. Nationals beginning their working lives now, have never known their country to be anything other than wealthy and employing people from all parts of the world. They have to fit into a society, which is dependent on expatriate assistance in all walks of life. Many nationals are very critical of this situation, and hope to change it by placing the new graduates in positions of authority, but this does not necessarily reduce dependence on expatriate manpower. Frequently they become surrounded by people, who make them feel that authority was achieved by obtaining the title. It is then more difficult for young nationals to accept that they have to fully involve themselves and do the detailed "paperwork" themselves to be truly in command – or else the control will in reality still be in the hands of others. The remarkable efforts being made in the UAE to revolutionise higher education are designed to prevent the perpetuation of such dependence by helping a new generation to learn the skills of continually updating knowledge, so as to give substance to decision making.

The new generation should no longer have to live in a transitional state. The 'period of transition', which has frequently been an excuse for the various deficiencies in evidence throughout the country, can too easily become second nature and be perpetuated by further generations. Two decades are a considerable time for a state to consolidate its institutions and a society to mature enough to make informed choices.

The UAE, like her oil producing neighbours in the Gulf, has the choice of where to turn for assistance in building the country. Currently many countries import UAE oil, others hope to export their goods and services to this growing market. Historically the emirates have not experienced the trauma of post-colonial re-orientation, in the course of which many developing nations used up much of their political energy. Although Great Britain had by the end of the 1950s taken a firm hold of the Trucial States' relations with the outside world and greatly influenced the economic life through the search for oil, in their domestic politics and interaction with each other, these shaikhdoms had remained independent states. The tribes of the southern coast of the Gulf had not been subservient to any power. They owed allegiance only to their tribal leaders, who during the nineteenth century entered into treaties with a distant power, British India. This enhanced their shaikhs' standing and reduced their reliance on the tribesmen for their legitimacy. It never meant colonial rule for the population, but it did keep at arm's length potential encroachments from regional powers. This past experience permits the authorities of the UAE to be pragmatic in the choice of countries with which they entertain close contact.

Flanked by powerful neighbours, the tribal leaders, particularly of the Bani Yas, were wary of the dangers of being drawn into the strife which was prevalent in the Arabian desert and Oman and they managed to preserve their independence. Having thus historically developed, as a necessity, political and religious tolerance, this is now a hallmark of the society and of the authorities in the UAE. It enables the leaders of this small country to play an important role in regional and Arab politics by working for compromise and avoiding confrontation. It is thus no coincidence that when Shaikh Zāyid, as the country's President turned his attention from domestic and regional cares to world matters, he was recognised as an elder statesman. In keeping with this society's approach to political problems, the UAE welcomed the PLO-Israel accord of September 1993.

It was the British decision in 1968 to withdraw the defensive and diplomatic umbrella from the Gulf, which made it necessary for the small shaikhdoms to become fully autonomous states. This necessity set in motion the search for a viable form, into which these mini-states could amalgamate. The decisions preceding the declaration of the federation in 1971 were made by the Rulers with a number of advisors and senior citizens on behalf of the tribal population. The people in the remote settlements did not understand very much of what was going on. This has fundamentally changed over the two decades of the federation's existence. The federal government has extended its authority affecting all inhabitants in many different ways. Gradually it became obvious that betterment in their daily lives increasingly emanated from the federal ministries and came to them as citizens of the UAE, not as belonging to a particular emirate. They could not fail to develop pride in being nationals of a country which was praised for its great development strides. Sharing their country with so many temporary residents further enhanced the local population's loyalty to the UAE as their motherland. This does not conflict with loyalties to one's own emirate, which remain the building blocks for the structure of society, in which the recognition of a true national is still defined by belonging to a tribe which owes allegiance to a particular ruling family. Thus continued allegiance to one's ruler and staunch support of one's emirate are both sources of a UAE citizen's national pride – in this society the one could not exist without the other.

The UAE can proudly point to the fact that it is today the only federal state in the Arab World. The oil wealth plays an essential role in welding together the seven emirates and synchronising the progress of the entire local society, which shares the country with an overwhelming majority of outsiders. Having withstood a quarter of a century, marked by many divisive and potentially destructive events in the region, the UAE is there to stay. Whether the country will continue to be a federation or eventually develop a more centralised political system, the UAE is well placed to remain a viable state – home for its citizens in a multinational society.

Notes

CHAPTER ONE

1 "This set of facts is not given once and for all: between human society and its context there is a constant and necessary interaction. If the physical context in which man lives serves as a set of major conditioning factors for society, so will society exert a moulding impact on its natural surroundings." Nieuwenhuijze, C.A.O. van, *Sociology of the Middle East. A Stocktaking and Interpretation*, Leiden, 1971, p. 47.

2 See Fisher, W.B., *The Middle East: A Physical, Social and Regional Geography*, London, 1950, 2nd edn., 1952, pp. 439–44.

3 This was the average total recorded over 30 years at the longest-established rainfall station at Shārjah (see: Trucial States Council, *Water Resources Survey*, Draft Report, 1967). Between 1965 and 1968 more than a dozen new rainfall gauges have been installed throughout the country (see: passim, *Hydrological Yearbook*, 1967/68, February 1969). Other stations have been in operation for some time at Ṭarīf (Abu Dhabi Petroleum Company) since 1962, in the Trucial Oman Scouts' Fort at Jāhili in the al ʽAin district, at the Political Agency in Abu Dhabi, and in Diqdāqah in Ra's al Khaimah territory. From the combined records it can be seen that 95 per cent of the yearly rainfall is concentrated in the six-month period from November to April, while 50 per cent occurs during December and January. The variations in annual totals from year to year are very great; in Shārjah they ranged from 0.3mm in 1961/62 to 258mm in 1956/57; see Government of Abu Dhabi, Department of Development and Public Works, *Water Resources Survey*. Interim Report by Sir A. Gibb and Partners, April 1969 (quoted as Gibb, 1969), p. 48. In Ṭarīf 0.07mm were recorded in 1967 while 1964 showed 94.1mm (see Gibb, 1969, p. 6ff). The yearly rainfall recorded at the newly-established gauges exemplifies the assumption that rainfall varies greatly in the different regions of the UAE; but even within one region

the measurements frequently differ by 50 per cent, due to the occurrence of localised freak storms which might not bring a drop of rain at the neighbouring gauge. Thus the maximum yearly total for the area in 1967/68 was recorded at Jabal Fāyah in Shārjah territory as 130.1mm; the minimum for that year, 66.6mm, was recorded at Diqdāqah in Ra's al Khaimah territory, only 60km away; (see: *Hydrological Yearbook*, 1969).

4 The importance of this particular configuration for certain characteristics of the country's society is for instance pointed out by Wilkinson, J.C. "The Origins of the Omani State", in *The Arabian Peninsula: Society and Politics*, edited by Hopwood, Derek London, 1972, pp. 67ff.

5 The geographical extent of the desert for which the term Rub' al Khāli applies is not undisputed. Depending on the angle and the distance from which local and foreign travellers and geographers look at it, the whole of the Southern Desert of the Arabian Peninsula is referred to as Rub 'al Khāli when mentioned from far away, while the bedu simply say Al Rimal (The Sand). But the different parts of the desert have many local names. The resulting confusion among geographers is discussed by Bertram Thomas, himself a traveller in the area, in his review of H.J.B. Philby's book entitled *The Empty Quarter*; see *Journal of the Royal Central Asian Society*, vol. 20 (1933), pp. 438ff. He comes to the following conclusion: "Nothing can be clearer than that the area properly called Rub'al Khāli . . . stretches from the Persian Gulf to the Indian Ocean and from the mountains of Oman to the mountains of Aflāj and Nagran, as it has done from time immemorial" (p. 444).

6 The first account which Thomas gave had many observations on the nature of the country; see Thomas, Bertram S. "A Camel Journey across the Rub'al Khāli" in *Geographical Journal*, vol. 78, 1931, pp. 209–42.

7 The Gulf extends for some 830km between the parallels of 24° and 30° North latitude, and the meridians 48° and 57° East longitude. It has an average width of about 200km. For more geographical data see: *The Persian Gulf Pilot, Comprising the Persian Gulf, the Gulf of Omān, and the Makrān Coast*, 6th edn, 1915, London, Printed for the Hydrographic Office; Admiralty, under the authority of HMSO.

8 Not all parts of the area have already been adequately surveyed. Thus, statements concerning the size of the UAE and its member States respectively are approximate and vary between 32,300 sq. miles (83,660km^2) and 29,950 sq. miles (77,570km^2) for the UAE, but even higher figures can be found. The areas of the seven States as given by the statistician Dr Fenelon are:

Abu Dhabi	26,000 sq. miles	67,000 sq. km
Dubai	1,500 sq. miles	3,900 sq. km
Shārjah	1,000 sq. miles	2,600 sq. km

Ra's al Khaimah	650 sq. miles	1,700 sq. km
Fujairah	450 sq. miles	1,100 sq. km
Umm al Qaiwain	300 sq. miles	770 sq. km
ʿAjmān	100 sq. miles	260 sq. km

See Fenelon, K.G., *The Trucial States: A Brief Economic Survey*, 2nd rev. edn., Beirut, 1969, p. 136.

9 For an analysis of coastal and inland *sabkhahs* in the UAE, see Kinsman, David J.J. and Robert K. Park, "Studies in Recent Sedimentology and Early Diagenesis, Trucial Coast, Arabian Gulf" in a paper for the *Second Regional Technical Symposium, Society of Petroleum Engineering of AIME*, Dhahran, 1968; Mr Kinsman's research, which resulted in a PhD thesis of London University in 1964, was followed up by a team of sedimentologists from Zurich University, headed by Mr T. Schneider, during several periods of field work in 1971ff.

10 The groundwater is drawn either from the dunes or from the upper parts of the underlying rock formation. Water can be found at a depth of one metre in some of the hollows between dunes, while the water table might be as far as 25 metres from the surface of a sand dune. The only sources of re-charge are rainfall and dew. Where the sand is of great thickness the water is sweeter than nearer the older rock formation. The latter is extremely rich in water-soluble minerals. Water with 0–1,000 parts per million (ppm) dissolved minerals is considered fresh; most wells in the western and southern areas of Abu Dhabi have over 1,000ppm. The brackish water can be used for domestic purposes and animal watering, but it is not suitable for irrigation because of its high salinity.

11 The dunes of the Līwā do not directly rise from the underlying rock formation which is partly exposed in the Bainūnah plateau to the north. The floors of some of the hollows are formed by compacted older dunes which developed a gypsoferous character through cementation and are also called "inland *sabkhah*".

12 "In 1906 a valuable pearl was found off the extreme end of Musandam Island. The Shaikh of Bahrain claimed that all pearls found in those waters belong to him or should pass through his hands. The Shaikh of Qatar claimed that the pearl was found by one of his followers and it should be disposed through him. A considerable quarrel developed, the result being that the Shaikh of Qatar was murdered, some important additions were made to our geographical knowledge of Trucial Oman, and the publication of Mr Lorimer's book was delayed. The man who actually found the pearl claimed that he came from the village of Shāh in Līwah, and as no one had ever heard of such places, Colonel P.Z. Cox, the then Political Resident in the Persian Gulf, in his endeavour to settle this dispute, discovered that this man belonged to neither Qatar nor

Bahrain, but came from what was apparently the inhospitable wastes of the Ruba'-al-Khāli, the terrible 'Empty House' desert of South Arabia. Continuing his investigations, Colonel Cox was able to contribute a mass of information concerning Bainūnah, Dhafrah Proper, Qufa, Līwah, and other parts of Trucial 'Omān, which went far to fill in a good deal of the white space on the map of Arabia . . ." Hunter F.F., "Reminiscences of the Map of Arabia and the Persian Gulf" in *Geographical Journal*, vol. 54, 1919, pp. 355–63 (pp. 357f).

13 Unless indicated otherwise the geographical term Dhafrah is used here as in the Gazetteer (see Chapter Two, footnote 17) for the entire area between the Rub 'al Khāli and the coast of the Gulf and between the Sabkhah Maṭṭi in the west and Khatam in the east; its five subdivisions are Dhafrah Proper, Bainūnah, Ṭaff, Qufā, and Līwā.

14 Recent population figures, wherever published, were based on informed guesses. See *Statistical Abstract*, 1992, p. 27 (no later edition had come out by 1996). The Ministry of Planning organised a census for December 1995, at which time the population of the UAE was 2.377 million.

CHAPTER TWO

1 Longrigg, Stephen, "The Liquid Gold of Arabia", in *Journal of the Royal Central Asian Society*, vol. 36, 1949, pp. 20–23 (p. 21).

2 Bibby, Geoffrey *Looking for Dilmun* London 1970. He sums up the archaeological investigations which had taken place in the Gulf countries up to that date, and projects a number of not undisputed theories on the interpretation of the finds. Descriptions of the yearly digs are in *KUML*, the Journal of the Danish Archaeological Society in Aarhus, in the years 1956 and after. See also *Archaeology in the United Arab Emirates*, a booklet published in 1979 by the Ministry of Information, with an introduction by Serge Cleuziou; since then the Department of Antiquities has published more reports.

3 See Thomas, Bertram S., "Ūrbār: the Atlantis of the Sands of Rub 'al Khali", in *Journal of the RCAS*, vol. 20, 1933, pp. 259–65.

4 See also Thomas, Bertram S., "Anthropological Observations in Southern Arabia", in *Journal of the Royal Anthropological Institute*, vol. 62, 1932, pp. 83–103 (p. 84): ". . . it may connote that a very early civilisation existed in this region. Indeed caravan tracks of great antiquity were pointed out to me in lat. 18°30′, long. 52° on the very edge of the sands and leading on a bearing of 325° into what is now a drought-stricken waste of sands."

5 Wellstead describes the oasis of Manaḥ, south-west of the Jabal al Akhḍar, as having extensive cultivation in open fields in 1835; Wellstead, J.R., "Narrative of a Journey into the Interior of Oman in

1835", in *Journal of the Royal Geographical Society of London* vol. 7, 1837, pp. 102–13. Bertram Thomas relates in his book *Arabia Felix*, which sums up his travels until the year 1931, that during the preceding six years in Oman, south-east and central south Arabia he had heard from the beduin that the scarce rains had been diminishing within their lifetimes. The date crop of the interior of Oman was then half of what it had been a generation earlier and many plantations had vanished altogether. See Thomas, Bertram, *Arabia Felix*, London, 1932, p. 137. The question which is of importance in the context of this chapter is whether the manifest recession of agricultural land and good grazing ground throughout the area is due only to the desiccation in a climatic cycle which might have begun this phase with a rainy period around the time of the last European Ice Age, or does the loss of productivity of the agriculture in the region between the middle of the 19th and the middle of the 20th centuries originate in a change in the structure of society?

6 Regarding the still-unanswered question of the origins of these early inhabitants, see e.g. Bertram Thomas, *Arabia Felix*, pp. 22f and elsewhere, and Appendix I, pp. 301ff to the same book, written by Arthur Keith and Dr W.M. Krogan, and other remarks by Bertram Thomas (e.g. source mentioned in footnote 4) all supporting the non-Arab theory. The literature about the contradicting theories is dealt with extensively in the footnotes of Dostal, Walter, *Die Beduinen in Südarabien. Eine ethnologische Studie zur Entwicklung der Kamelhirtenkultur in Arabien*, Wien, 1967, pp. 85ff, and in the bibliography on pp. 166–90.

7 A Himyaritic inscription was found on a tombstone in the western territory of Shārjah. The late Ruler, Shaikh Khālid bin Muḥammad, arranged for the inscription to be transferred to paper, and it has since been identified by Prof. A.F.L. Beeston in Oxford; see also Wilkinson, J.C. *Water and Tribal Settlement in South-East Arabia: A Study of the Aflāj* of Oman, Oxford, 1977, p. 135, footnote 6.

8 An example from S.B. Miles' pen may indicate the general trend: ". . . others were Tasm and Jadis, who were sisters of two brothers Thamood and Sohar. . . . The sections of the Tasm and Jadis, who migrated to Oman, appear to have settled in Al-Jow and Towwam giving to those districts the names of the places they had occupied in their old home in Yemama." Miles, S.B., *The Countries and Tribes of the Persian Gulf*, 2nd edn., 1966, p. 4. Tu'ām was for centuries the name of Buraimi, and al Jawf that of the area south of Nizwā; see Wilkinson, *Water*, p. 33 footnote 5 and elsewhere.

9 See for the following: Wilkinson, J.C., *Origins*, pp. 70ff. See also Miles, *Countries*, pp. 9ff, especially pp. 16–28.

10 See also Klein, Hedwig in the annotated edition of chapter 35 of the anonymous Arab chronicle, *Kašf al-Ǧumma al-Ǧāmi ʿli-al Aḫbār al-Umma*, Hamburg, 1938, pp. 21ff.

11 The old name still survives in the alternative name, Tayma, for al ʿAin (ʿAin al Dhawāhir); see Wilkinson, *Origins*, p. 71, and for spelling Wilkinson, *Water*, p. 33, footnote 1.

12 See Wilkinson, J.C. "Arab Persian Land Relationship in Late Sasānid Oman", in *Proceedings of the 6th Seminar for Arabian Studies*, London, September 1972, pp. 40–51, in particular pp. 45f.

13 In its widest possible meaning, the term al Baḥrayn was used for the area including the oases of al Ḥasā and Qaṭīf, the peninsula of Qatar and extending east along the coast to Ruʾūs al Jibāl and south to the Rub ʿal Khāli. In geographical terms Oman was the neighbour of al Baḥrayn to the east, the borderline being approximately identical with the edge between the western mountain foreland and the sandy steppe. The territory of the present day UAE was often called al Shamāl (the North) in Omani context, while the area to the west of Abu Dhabi town up to the Qatar Peninsula was known as al Gharbīyah (the western); see also Miles, *Countries*, pp. 377ff, in particular p. 384.

14 The division of all 200 or more tribes of south-eastern Arabia in the Civil War in the 18th century into Hināwi and Ghāfiri stems almost certainly from the antagonism between tribes of the two main divisions at the time of their arrival in the area. Hināwi is to be identified with Qaḥṭāni (Yamāni) and Ghāfiri with Adnāni (Nizāri).

15 See Wilkinson, *Origins*, pp. 72ff and map 3.

16 For this period of between two and three thousand years the climatic difference was certainly only marginal, as the continuous practice to irrigate with channels (*falaj*, pl. *aflāj*) indicates.

17 See Lorimer, J.C., *Gazetteer of the Persian Gulf, 'Omān and Central Arabia*, Calcutta 1908/15, vol. I Historical, vol. II Geographical and Statistical; quoted as Lorimer, *Geogr. and Histor.* The population of the Trucial Coast was then estimated at 72,000 settled and 8,000 beduin people, *Geogr.* p. 1437. Although frequent reference is made in some parts of the book to the *Gazetteer*, this is not considered as an infallible document. However, it does represent a comprehensive collection of the information on the Gulf, which was available to the British Government of India during the first decade of this century. The copious data should be considered a guide to assess proportions in the communities' development – rather than taken at face value as statistics whose precision frequently cannot be checked.

18 See Lorimer, *Geogr.*, p. 408.

19 See Kelly, *Eastern Arabian Frontiers*, London, 1964 p. 36 from p. 52 of Volume One of the *UK Memorial*, the full title of which is *Arbitration Concerning Buraimi and the Common Frontier between Abu Dhabi and Saudi Arabia. Memorial submitted by the Government of the United Kingdom of Great Britain and Northern Ireland*, 1955. It is in two volumes and is henceforth quoted as *UK Memorial I* or *II*.

20 See: Government of Abu Dhabi, Directorate-General of Planning

and Co-ordination *Statistical Abstract*, vol. I, July 1969, p. 11; the Mazārī' subsection of the Bani Yās were counted separately (1,287 people), the remainder of the Bani Yās in Abu Dhabi at the time were 4,597 people. The main reason for that decrease was that during the late 1950s whole families emigrated to Qatar, Kuwait, and Saudi Arabia because there were many opportunities for work with the oil companies or in construction. When exploration work started in Abu Dhabi the industry had become much less labour-intensive, due to the advance of technology. The emigrant tribesmen returned in large numbers only after the development of Abu Dhabi was well under way a few years after Shaikh Zāyid had become the Ruler. The censuses of 1971 and 1975/76 unfortunately did not register tribal groups.

21 See Lorimer, *Geogr.*, pp. 1932ff; Kelly, *Eastern*, pp. 36ff and *UK Memorial II*, pp. 291f. See also Government of Bombay, *Selections from the Records of the Bombay Government, Historical and other Information connected with the Province of Oman, Bahrain and other Places in the Persian Gulf*, Bombay 1856, New Series XXIV, pp. 462f; see also Kelly, *Britain and the Persian Gulf 1795–1880*, London, 1968, p. 860 and *UK Memorial II*, p. 123. The 19th-century source lists some of the sections which compose the Bani Yās and gives their assumed original descent; according to this source the Hawāmil formed part of the Āl ʻAli and the Maḥāribah were originally Bani Naʻīm. Those major sections which were mentioned by Lorimer and not by Kelly nor the *Memorial* are: Āl Falāḥ, Āl Bū Ḥamir, Qanaiṣāt, Qaṣal, Bani Shikir, Āl Sulṭān. The Marar Rawāshid, and Sūdān are listed separately by Lorimer, while the Nuwāṣir, who are mentioned only in the *UK Memorial*, are not listed at all by Lorimer. The Āl Bū Amīn, Daḥailāt, Ḥalālmah, and Thamairāt, who are listed separately in Lorimer, were then already in the process of merging with the Bani Yās, and are now counted as minor subsections. The bedouin Jabais of the *Memorial* are probably the Sabā'is.

22 See below, page 46ff. Therefore most of the land which belongs to the Āl Bū Falāḥ village of Muwaijʻi belongs now to the heirs of Muḥammad bin Khalīfah, who died in 1979; some belongs to Shaikha Laṭīfah bint Zāyid, the Ruler's aunt, who also died in 1979, and to other members of the ruling family. Shaikh Muḥammad bin Khalīfah also owned most of the gardens of Masʻūdi, some at Hīli, al ʻAin, Qaṭṭārah, and Muʻtiriḍ. Three sons of Sulṭān bin Zāyid, Khalīd, Hazzāʻ, and Zāyid, the present Ruler, inherited and bought date-gardens in Jīmi, al ʻAin, Qaṭṭārah, and Jāhili; see also *UK Memorial I*, p. 53. Shaikh Zāyid and other members of the ruling family founded in recent years new farms outside the traditional villages such as Mazyad.

23 Lorimer, *Geogr.*, p. 1121f: "All the foregoing Āl Bū Mahair are non-nomadic, but a few others, perhaps 20 households, in the Abu Dhabi Principality are Bedouin in their habits. At Abu Dhabi the Āl Bū Mahair

are reckoned a section of the Bani Yas; but they are said to be of Mahra origin and to have come originally from Hadhramaut".

24 See below pages 239 and Lorimer, *Histor.*, p. 772 and 765.

25 About 57 houses according to the *UK Memorial II*, p. 292.

26 See below, pages 286ff.

27 Shaikha Salāma's brother Ḥamad bin Buṭi moved with his sister to Abu Dhabi and married a Suwaidi woman; his son Aḥmed bin Ḥamad became a member of the first Abu Dhabi government and has been Minister of Information in the UAE government from 1971 until 1990.

28 See *UK Memorial I*, p. 53; in the 1950s there were about 80 Hawāmil families in the Līwā.

29 See also below, page 110

30 See also below, page 111. He was also closely related to the Khamārah. an Arab tribal group from the Persian coast.

31 See Lorimer, *Geogr.*, p. 1842.

32 See Lorimer, *Histor.*, p. 750.

33 The other shaikhdom which may be considered a tiny nation-state is Fujairah, but its territory is a fraction of that of Abu Dhabi—450 sq. miles as opposed to 26,000 sq. miles—and is much more uniform in character, being all mountainous terrain within easy reach of the beach.

34 Exceptions were the repeated secessions in the 19th century; see above, page 29.

35 See also for the following Kelly, *Eastern*, pp. 39ff, *UK Memorial I*, pp. 53–8, Lorimer, *Geogr.*, pp. 1162ff.

36 Lorimer lists only three sections while the Āl Bū al Khail are counted as a subsection of the Āl Bū Raḥmah and the Āl Bū Ḥamīr as a section of the Bani Yās; this accounts for some of the discrepancies between the total figures for the tribe in the Gazetteer compared to later counts.

37 See Kelly, *Eastern*, p. 39 and *UK Memorial I*, p. 54. According to the Memorial there were about 50 individuals living in Abu Dhabi town, 30 were settled in Qatar and 550 in Dubai.

38 See Kelly, *Eastern*, p. 40. But these figures differ slightly from those of other authorities also concerned with the study of the Līwā in the 1950s; see *UK Memorial I*, p. 18 for summary.

39 See below, pages 116f.

40 See below, pages 45f and footnote 65.

41 See below, page 46f.

42 Lorimer, *Geogr.*, p. 439 has the higher figure. The estimate in *UK Memorial I*, p. 60 is 2,000.

43 For the change in the property ownership in the oasis see also Kelly, *Eastern*, p. 46. See also below, pages 50ff.

44 Some of them are listed by Kelly in *Eastern*, p. 45, footnote 2; and in *UK Memorial I*, p. 60.

45 Shaikh Sulṭān bin Surūr al Dhāhiri had been the representative of

Shaikh Shakhbūṭ and Shaikh Zāyid in the Jabal al Dhannah area from 1962; he became chairman of the National Assembly of Abu Dhabi in 1971 until 1990.

46 For details see below, pages 116f.

47 "Five thousand Jirābs of dates worth $1 per Jirāb, rendered as tribute by the Dhawāhir of the Buraimi Oasis ($5,000). Lucerne supplied by the same Dhawāhir for 100 tribal horses maintained by the Shaikh in the Baraimi Oasis ($3,000)." Lorimer, *Geogr.*, p. 409. A *jirāb* is a measure of weight used for purposes of taxation. In the 1950s a Līwā *jirāb* was about 180lb; a Buraimi *jirāb* was less than half because the production of dates was so much easier there.

48 Thesiger, Wilfred, *Arabian Sands*, London, 1959, p. 53f and map p. 55. Wilkinson, *Water*, describes in some detail on pp. 195–7 how the ʿAwāmir came to Oman, became assimilated and in some cases settled. He sums up: "So it can be seen that the history of the ʿAwāmir migration into Oman covers roughly half a millennium, and it is for this reason that its sub-groups are widely dispersed and range from one of the wildest bedu groups who inhabit the outer sand desert of the Dhāhira but have as yet not established an exclusive *dār* there, to the *falaj* experts who inhabit the collection of villages between the Jawf and Sharqīya called the Buldān ʿAwāmir" (p. 196).

49 Lorimer, *Geogr.*, pp. 186–8, and Thesiger, "Desert Borderlands of Oman" in *Geographical Journal*, CXVI, December 1950, pp. 137–71.

50 See below, page 42, and footnote 57; see also *UK Memorial I*, p. 22, and *Bombay Selections*, vol. XXIV, pp. 16–17, reprinted in *UK Memorial II*, Annex C, no. 5, p. 128. He gained the impression that Bani Yās, Manāṣīr, and ʿAwāmir were sub-sections of one tribe.

51 See below, pages 302ff, and Kelly, *Eastern*, p. 44ff, and *UK Memorial I*, p. 59, and *II*, p. 319ff.

52 See Lorimer, *Geogr.*, p. 187. Thesiger used an ʿAfār guide because unlike the ʿAwāmir, the ʿAfār were accepted as guides through Durūʿ territory. See Thesiger, *Arabian Sands*, p. 137.

53 See ibid.

54 *Arabian Sands*, p. 54. This tribal name is not to be confused with the Rawāshid, a subtribe of the Bani Yās. See Kelly, *Eastern*, p. 37 footnote.

55 See the anthropological study of this tribe by Donald Powell Cole, *Nomads of the Nomads: The Al Murrah Beduin of the Empty Quarter*, AHM Publishing Corporation, Arlington, 1975. Another tribe who frequented Abu Dhabi territory are the Aḥbāb from Najd. A group of about 60 families eventually stayed for good early this century and made their home in the foothills of Jabal Ḥafīt, recognising the Ruler of Abu Dhabi's authority. During the 1968 census 319 Aḥbāb were counted. The Najādāt were originally part of the Naʿīm, they live in some of the villages of the Buraimi oasis and in the nearby plain of al Jau;

some live in Fujairah. In the 1968 census 662 Najādāt were counted as living in the state of Abu Dhabi.

56 Lorimer, *Geogr.*, p. 1932.

57 "The Beniyas are . . . divided into three branches: one called Beniyas, another Manasir, and a third Owaimir ('Awāmir)." Report by the British Assistant Political Agent in Turkish Arabia in 1818, in *Bombay Selections*, XXIV, p. 16, reprinted in *UK Memorial II*, p. 128.

58 See e.g. Miles, *Countries*, p. 438 and *UK Memorial I*, p. 21f for references to the early history of the Bani Yās.

59 See also Heard-Bey, Frauke, "Development anomalies in the Beduin Oases of Al-Liwa" in *Asian Affairs*, vol. 61, Oct. 1974, pp. 272–86.

60 See *Kashf al Ghumma*, translated by E.C. Ross (Political Agent at Muscat) and printed under the title "Annals of 'Omān from early times to the year 1728 AD" (from an Arabic manuscript by Sheykh Sirhan-bin-Said-bin-Sirhan-bin Muhammad of the Benu Ali tribe of Oman) in *Journal of the Asiatic Society of Bengal* (Calcutta 1874), vol. 43. pt I, p. 162; also in *UK Memorial II*, Annex C, no. 2, p. 125.

61 A work attributed to the Omani historian Ḥumaid bin Muḥammad bin Ruzaiq and translated by G.P. Badger, entitled *History of the Imāms and Sayyids of 'Omān* (London 1871) also mentions the Bani Yās in Dhafrah at that time: "On learning this, Nasir retired into the fort of Ezh-Zhafrah, where he was joined by the Bani Yas, and then sent one of his followers to Muhammed-bin-Saif soliciting peace . . .". Also quoted in *UK Memorial I*, p. 21.

62 *Bombay Selections*, vol. XXIV, pp. 462–3, compiled in 1856 from material collected during preceding decades by officials of the Government of Bombay. Used in *UK Memorial II*, Annex C, no. 1, p. 123.

63 As the name, which means "stomach" or "inside", suggests, this village is on the leeward side of the island; the other beach facing the deep water is open to the full force of the northern wind called *shamāl*.

64 See above, page 42.

65 See e.g. *UK Memorial I*, pp. 56–8 (items 25–36) where many examples for the period from 1828 to 1947 are given of the Manāṣīr fighting alongside the Bani Yās, with and for the Bani Yās, and vice versa. See also the historical references quoted by J.B. Kelly, *Eastern*, on the Manāṣīr's loyalty to the Āl Bū Falāḥ and their co-operation with the Bani Yās in war and in peace time; and see also Lorimer, *Histor.*, pp. 819ff on the role of the Manāṣīr during the wars between Abu Dhabi and Qatar.

66 See also below, pages 123f.

67 *Bombay Selections*, vol. XXIV, pp. 462–3, reprinted in *UK Memorial II*, Annex C, no. 1, p. 123.

68 See above footnote 50.

69 It was also often referred to as Sirr; see e.g. Wilkinson, *Water*, p. 14. Sirr is not identical with Sīr, which is the coastal plain around Ra's al Khaimah, nor the Jiri plain to the east of the latter.

70 Kashf al Ghumma, *Journal of the Asiatic Society of Bengal*, vol. 43, pt I, 1874, p. 162, in *UK Memorial II*, Annex C, no. 2, p. 125 and *I*, p. 31.

71 Shaikh Khalīfah bin Shakhbūṭ to the Political Resident, Persian Gulf, August 1839, in: *UK Memorial II*, Annex B, no. 5, p. 46 (*Bahrain Archives Book*, no. 117, pp. 26–8).

72 See Kelly, *Eastern*, pp. 51ff. for details of the Saudi military occupation of Buraimi in the first half of the 19th century and Miles, *Countries*, p. 302.

73 See Lorimer, *Histor.*, pp. 764–72 and *UK Memorial I*, p. 33.

74 ". . . and a caravan of 50 people bringing dates from Baraimi to Abu Dhabi was intercepted by the enemy (Qawasim)" is reported in the Gazetteer for 1833; Lorimer, *Histor.*, p. 693.

75 See *UK Memorial I*, p. 33.

76 See footnote 71 and Kelly, *Eastern*, p. 65.

77 The wider background of this visit, i.e. British support for local resistance against joint Wahhābi-Egyptian advances on the British protected areas, is given by Kelly, *Eastern*, pp. 64–6.

78 See *UK Memorial II*, Annex B, no. 8, p. 49.

79 Kelly, *Eastern*, p. 66f.

80 See Lorimer, *Histor.*, p. 771 and Kelly, *Eastern*, p. 96. The position of the Naʿīm soon after the expulsion of the Wahhābis is described by Colonel S.B. Miles, British Political Agent in Muscat, who visited the oasis in 1875: "They occupy el-Bereymi proper and Suʿareh (Ṣaʿarah) and their possession of the fort enables them to overawe the whole of the settlement. Since the time of Seyyid ʿAzan they have been practically uninterfered with by the Muscat Government, but of course owe allegiance to the present Sultan. The Naʿim are at feud with the Beni Yas who occupy part of el-Bereymi and their hostility is interrupted only by occasional truces; collisions frequently occurring between them. Of the two sections of the Naʿim one inhabits more particularly el-Jow and Bereymi, the other el-Dhahireh." Miles, "On the Route between Sohar and el-Bereymi in Oman", *Journal of the Asiatic Society of Bengal* (1877), p. 52, repr. Kelly, *Eastern*, pp. 95f.

81 See footnote 47. For details on the administration under successive *wālis* see below, page 109f.

82 See below, pages 59ff and Lorimer, *Geogr.*, pp. 1301ff, for the divisions and distribution of the Naʿīm; see also Kelly, *Eastern*, p. 100ff for their relationship with the Sultan.

83 This situation becomes obvious in a collection of letters which Aḥmad bin Hilāl received from Zāyid and other shaikhs. The collection was found in 1955 and translated on behalf of the British Foreign Office, which acted as a custodian; in 1976 the laminated originals were brought back to Abu Dhabi and deposited in the Centre for Documentation and Research; quoted henceforth consistent with Kelly as "Dhawāhir Collection"; see also Kelly, *Eastern*, pp. 97ff.

84 Both quotations from the *Dhawāhir Collection.* The people of Ḥajarain in the Wādi Ḥattā were usually at enmity with those of Masfūṭ, and looked to Dubai for protection. It became a dependency of Dubai at the beginning of this century, and is now called Ḥattā after the *wādi* it is in. See also below, page 66.

85 See Sir Percy Cox, "Some Excursions in Oman" *Geographical Journal*, 1925, LXVI, p. 207. A lot of details concerning the economy of the oasis, its water supply etc. are given by this perceptive traveller, who was the Political Resident in the Gulf from 1904 to 1913 and before that Political Agent in Muscat from 1899 to 1904.

86 Lorimer, *Histor.*, p. 753 and below, page 66.

87 In this context it is interesting that Cox travelled in December 1905 as far as ʿIbri under the protection of the Ruler of Abu Dhabi.

88 It involved the British Government as the authority responsible for the conduct of foreign affairs of the Trucial Ruler, the Saudi Government, the Sultan of Muscat and Oman, the oil companies which had concessionary agreements, i.e. the subsidiary of the Iraq Petroleum Company, Petroleum Development Trucial Coast (PD(TC)) and the Arabian American Oil Company (ARAMCO); see also below pages 302ff.

89 See Lorimer, *Geogr.*, p. 1425ff, footnote.

90 Prepared by the Saudi Government in accordance with the agreement of 30 July 1954 and submitted in September 1955 to the other party. For a detailed analysis of its content see Kelly, *Eastern*, pp. 209ff. The full title is: *Memorial of the Government of Saudi Arabia: Arbitration for the Settlement of the Territorial Dispute between Muscat and Abu Dhabi on the one side and Saudi Arabia on the other*, AH 1374/AD 1955. See also footnote 19.

91 Lorimer, *Geogr.*, p. 264 and p. 1368 for statement that Buraimi is "independent" and about the extent of "Independent Oman".

92 According to Lorimer, *Geogr.*, p. 1302 there were about 10,500 non-nomadic Naʿīm in the area—excluding those who went to Qatar and Bahrain several generations ago. 4,500 lived in the Sultanate of Oman, 3,500 in shaikhdoms of the Trucial Coast and 2,500 lived in this district of "Independent Oman". Beside there were about 2,500 beduin Naʿīm.

93 See *UK Memorial I*, p. 61 and footnote 7; see also Kelly, *Eastern*, p. 48.

94 See *UK Memorial I*, p. 62 and *II*, Annex B, no. 9, p. 53 and no. 12, p. 58.

95 *UK Memorial I*, p. 62.

96 Ṣaqr's representative in Dhank was during the 1950s a slave *wāli* by the name of Sālim bin Samsūn.

97 Already in the preceding years the contact between Muscat and the various factions of the Naʿīm had improved, and many of the minor shaikhs had visited the Sultan and received presents; and Sayyid Ṭāriq, the half brother of the Sultan, had in return visited Buraimi in 1945; see *UK Memorial I*, p. 62f.

98 See Kelly, *Eastern*, p. 152ff.

99 As was common among some beduin tribes of Oman, he ruled in conjunction with other, usually related, shaikhs; in this case they were his cousins Mānī' and Ḥamad bin 'Ali bin Raḥmah.

100 Their origin is discussed by Wilkinson, *Water*, p. 207. For a brief summary on the Balūsh see also Lorimer, *Geogr.*, p. 258 and pp. 1409f.

101 See for the following Lorimer, *Histor.*, p. 753 and Kelly, *Eastern*, p. 98f.

102 Letter to Aḥmad bin Hilāl of April 1906 in *Dhawāhir Collection*.

103 See Kelly, *Eastern*, p. 231, who quotes the example of Sa'īd bin Rāshid, the son of the shaikh of the Balūch at 'Arāqi; he visited Saudi Arabia several times and eventually became the most active supporter of the Saudis in that area.

104 See Lorimer, *Geogr.*, pp. 962ff for Bani Ka'ab.

105 See Lorimer, *Geogr.*, pp. 1558ff.

106 The enṭire Wādi Ḥattā had once been under the authority of the Sultan of Muscat and a small section is still today Omani territory. See for the following Lorimer, *Histor.*, pp. 752–5.

107 For details of such agreements see below, pages 294ff.

108 See Landen, R.G. *Oman Since 1856: Disruptive Modernization in a Traditional Arab Society*, Princeton, 1967, pp. 414–22.

109 See Lorimer, *Histor.*, p. 178ff and *Geogr.*, pp. 1547f and Miles, *Countries*, p. 430 and elsewhere, and Hawley, Donald, *The Trucial States*, London, 1970, pp. 90ff. See also Lorimer, *Histor.*, pp. 630–786 for the external relations of the Qawāsim during the 18th and 19th centuries.

110 After a peace with the Bani Ma'īn of Hormuz in 1763 the Qawāsim obtained one third of the revenues of Qishim. See also Warden, Francis, "Historical Sketch of the Joasmee Tribe of Arabs", *Bombay Selections*, pp. 301ff; he had observed the growing share of the Qawāsim in the trade of the Gulf of India and noted ". . . in a very few years (they) carried on a most profitable concern"; see also Hawley, *Trucial*, p. 92f.

111 The implication of the role of the Qawāsim rulers in this wider context is discussed below, pages 279ff.

112 This is even true for the extensive authority which Shaikh Zāyid bin Khalīfah attained towards the end of his long rule, which included many Omani tribes in Dhāhirah and beyond. The agreement of 1906 between all the Trucial Rulers in Dubai according to which he obtained authority over the people of Ru'ūs al Jibāl and the Sharqiyīn was a declaration and was never exercised in practice.

113 See Lorimer, *Geogr.*, pp. 1425ff. Material used for the relevant articles in this Gazetteer has been for the most part specially collected during the years 1904 to 1907, and was revised several times by officials and others who had lived in or extensively visited the area.

114 The following tribes of the Trucial Coast were either entirely nomadic or, as was more often the case, had beduin sections: Bani Yās (about 2,000 beduin), Bani Qitab (about 2,100 beduin but some lived in the

territory of the Sultan of Muscat and Oman), Manāṣīr (about 1,300 beduin), ʿAwāmir (uncertain), Ghafalah (about 500 beduin), Āl Bū Mahair (about 100 beduin), Marar (about 350 beduin), Qawaid (part of the Mazārīʿ, about 250 beduin), Naʿīm (about 1,200 beduin in Trucial Oman), and Bani Kaʿab (an uncertain number of beduin there) and a few other small groups of partly Omani tribes; see Lorimer, *Geogr.*, pp. 1432ff.

115 For definition see e.g. Stiefel, Matthias "Der Nomadismus als sozioökonomisches und politisches Entwicklungsproblem, eine allgemeine Einführung" in *Seminar über das Nomadentum in Zentralasien*, Nov. 1975, Schlussbericht, Nationale Schweizerische UNESCO-Kommission, Bern, 1976, pp. 5–25.

116 See Trucial States Council, Development Office, Census 1968, Table (d) mimeograph.

117 For Shamailīyah see Lorimer, *Geogr.*, pp. 1694–9; on Sharqiyīn see ibid, p. 1769.

118 See also about the politics of Fujairah in the Kalba affair below pages 93f.

119 This is not so in the shaikhdom of ʿAjmān, where the ruling family is from a section of the Naʿīm who were a minority of about 25 houses among 80 houses of the Āl Bū Mahair, 12 of the Sūdān, 14 of the Āl Bū Kalbi and others.

120 See Lorimer, *Geogr.*, p. 62, and for the following pp. 1936, 1858f and 1361 for articles on the Zaʿab, Ṭanaij and Naqbiyīn.

121 See below, Chapter Three, pages 91ff.

122 Lorimer, *Geogr.*, p. 572.

123 At times large numbers of beduin Manāṣīr, Naʿīm, ʿAwāmir, and even Bani Yās appeared in the northern territories and played a role in local politics there, but sooner or later they always went back to the sands or the Buraimi area.

124 The minor tribes not mentioned so far but listed in both Lorimer, *Geogr.*, pp. 1391–411 or 1432–6 as well as in the 1968 census, are the Bidūwāt of Ḥajarain and Masfūṭ, the Dahāminah of Wādi Qūr in Ra's al Khaimah. the Ḏabābiḥah in Shārjah territory, the Omani tribe Bani Jābir, which has a few families in the UAE, the Maḥārizah of Masāfi, the Masāfarah (or Mashāfirah) of Shārjah town with a beduin section east of the Jiri plain and the Shahā'irah of Ra's al Khaimah territory.

The tribes mentioned in Lorimer as belonging to Trucial Oman which do not figure in the 1968 census are the ʿAbādilah of Shārjah town and Fujairah territory, the already then practically extinct ʿAwānāt, the Bahārinah in Dubai and Abu Dhabi town, the Bani Ḥamad living in the *wādis* behind Khaur Fakkān, the Jalājilah of Shamailīyah and Wādi Qūr, now forming part of the Sharqiyīn, the Maḥārah who may have merged with the Zaʿāb, the Maṭārīsh of Shārjah town, the Bani Shamaili who became part of the Shiḥūḥ, the Shāqūsh of ʿAjmān, a section of the Bani Maʿīn of Qishim Island, and the Zaḥūm of Wādi Ḥām, also now part of the Sharqiyīn.

Others such as the Āl Bū Amīn, Daḥailāt, Ḥalālmah and Thamairāt are now counted as subsections of the Bani Yās (see above, footnote 21). Two tribes which are mentioned in table (d) of the census of the six northern Trucial States as well as in the table for Abu Dhabi but do not figure in the *Gazetteer* are the Aḥbāb and the Najādāt (see above, footnote 55).

125 Dostal, Walter "The Shiḥūḥ of Northern Oman: A contribution to cultural Ecology" in *Geographical Journal*, vol. 138, Pt I, March 1972, pp. 1–8. Bertram Thomas, Financial Adviser to the Sultan in Muscat from 1925 to 1931, dedicated much time and effort to the study of the tribes of south-eastern Arabia, not least of the Shiḥūḥ; see e.g. Thomas, Bertram "The Kumzari dialect of the Shihuh tribe of Arabia, and a vocabulary" *Journal of the Royal Asiatic Society*, 1930 p. 785–854; and "The Musandam Peninsula and its people—the Shihuh" in *Journal of the Bombay Central Asiatic Society*, 1929. The Ph.D. thesis by Wolfgang Zimmermann provides the most comprehensive research of the living conditions of the Shiḥūḥ to date: *Tradition und Integration mobiler Lebensformgruppen. Eine empirische Studie über Beduinen und Fischer in Mūsāndam/Sultanat Oman*, Göttingen 1981.

The differences in behaviour, language, and to some degree the practice of religion are obvious enough to be widely reported among the other tribal population of eastern Arabia; the erroneous belief is widespread that the Shiḥūḥ are descendants of the Portuguese.

126 See Caskel, Werner, *Ǧamharat an-Nasab, Das genealogishce Werk des Hišām Muhammad al-Kalbī* 2 vols, I, p. 41, Leiden, 1966.

127 Lorimer, *Geogr.*, pp. 1805–10. His estimate of 7,000 nomad Shiḥūḥ belonging to the interior is being put forward with doubt, and, indeed, some of the people who move up to the mountains only in the winter may have been counted twice.

128 According to Dostal the former settlement is called *bulaidah* and the larger one *ḥārah*.

129 In the vicinity of Dibah and elsewhere on the east coast such *muṣaif* are often folded together and left as a compact tent-like shape which can withstand storms much better than the ordinary *barasti* when empty for several months.

130 Dostal (p. 5) recounts that out of twenty-eight men in one particular settlement only five did not marry their *bint ʿamm*, that is the daughter of the paternal uncle.

131 During the 1968 census 6,030 Shiḥūḥ, Ḥabūs and Dhahūriyīn were counted, 5,845 of whom lived in Ra's al Khaimah territory.

132 See below, pages 273ff.

133 Lorimer, *Histor.*, p. 623, Annexure no. 3: History of Ru'ūs Al-Jibāl.

CHAPTER THREE

1 The territorial extent of a *wāli's* area of responsibility was nowhere well defined, and therefore the related term *wilāyah* was not current. Such an administrative assignment was specified only by referring to the place in which the *wāli* resided.

2 The first car was imported to the coast by the Residency Agent, 'Īsa bin 'Abdul Laṭīf in 1928. He brought it in through Ra's al Khaimah, where he used it between his summer house on the mainland and the town. He imported a Ford into Shārjah in 1929 which could be used for the journey to Dubai on the *sabkhah* but had to be left outside the town because the streets there were too narrow. Muḥammad bin Aḥmad bin Dalmūk, a prominent merchant in Dubai, brought a car from Bombay in 1930 and gave it to Shaikh Sa'īd, the Ruler of Dubai, who a year later imported a Ford himself from Bahrain.

3 The population centres and enclaves which were considered to be part of the territory of a certain shaikhdom were called "dependencies" in the correspondence of British officials.

4 Dubai has the one dependency, Ḥattā, where a *wāli* was maintained at times; 'Ajmān's main inland dependency is Masfūṭ, also in the Wādi Ḥattā. Umm al Qaiwain has no enclave at all; the inland oasis, Falaj al Mu'allā, is part and parcel of Umm al Qaiwain territory, and because most of the gardens there were always the private property of the ruling family, the small oasis was administered like an estate, not like a dependency; a slave of the household was usually in charge there.

5 See above pages 68ff for a description of this tribe and a statement regarding the Qawāsim in Lorimer, *Geogr.*, pp. 1547f.

6 See Lorimer, *Geogr.*, p. 1759f.

7 Ṣāliḥ was the son of a slave wife of Ṣaqr bin Rāshid (1777–1803). See Lorimer, *Histor.*, p. 765 and for the following pp. 756ff.

8 See letter no. 79 of 26 Sep. 1900 by the Residency Agent in Shārjah to the Political Resident in Bushire; India Office Records (IOR) Persian Gulf Political Residency and Agency Archives, Series R/15/1, Collection 244: "Correspondence regarding succession of Chief of Ras al Khaimah 1900–1928". For a guide to this group of archival material see Tuson, Penelope, *The Records of the British Residency and Agencies in the Persian Gulf*, IOR R/15, India Office Records, Guides to Archive Groups, HMSO, London, 1979.

9 He applied several times through the Residency Agent for a set of the treaties; if this had been supplied to him, this would have been as good as a formal recognition. One of the main reasons why Sālim bin Sulṭān was not formally recognised was his connection with Abū Mūsa and his entitlement to income from the island's oxide mines, for which a German

company had obtained the concession. Britain protested the validity of this concession; see e.g. the confidential letter of 4 Aug. 1912 from the Political Resident in Bushire, Sir Percy Cox, to the Secretary to the Governor of India in the Foreign Department, IOR R/15/1/244. See also Plass, J.B., *England zwischen Deutschland und Russland*, 1899–1907, Hamburg, 1966, pp. 410ff.

10 They jointly owned over 15,000 date trees and about 130 camels, 175 donkeys, 150 cattle and about 800 goats and 20 horses; See Lorimer, *Geogr.*, p. 1008.

11 Khojah is the name applied to Muslims whose ancestors were Hindus from Sind or Kach, and who were converted in the 15th century to the Ismāʿīli sect of Shīʿah Islam. Wherever they were settled in the Trucial States or Oman they had their families with them. See also pages 133f.

12 The town was permanently guarded by armed retainers and in an emergency there were several hundred rifles in private possession of the local inhabitants.

13 See Lorimer, *Histor.*, p. 1547. Some members of the family, such as Nāṣir bin Sulṭān, who was the *wāli* for a brief period early in this century and who had lived in Ra's al Khaimah for most of his life, had acquired private property either by inheritance or through business enterprises in pearling. Nevertheless, Ḥumaid bin ʿAbdullah gave an allowance to his uncle Nāṣir as to all the other members of the family, and according to a note written by the Residency Agent on 16th January 1927 to the Political Resident in Bushire this practice of maintaining both male and female members of the family continued by all *wālis* and Rulers of Ra's al Khaimah; see IOR R/15/1/244.

14 Lorimer, *Geogr.*, p. 1761.

15 See IOR R/15/1/244. The Residency Agent stated in a letter of the 26th September 1900 to the Resident in Bushire that Sālim bin Sulṭān obtained M.T. Dollars 400 per year from the Shaikh of Shārjah as compensation and M.T. Dollars 250 from the red oxide mines of Abū Mūsa, yet his income was said to be inadequate for him and his family.

16 Other Shiḥūḥ communities in the Qāsimi area were: Ghalīlah 50 houses one mile south of the Shaʿam, Khaur Khuwair 30 houses, half way between there and Rams, and al Ḥail in Ṣīr. In all there were about 2,000 souls. Some of the settled tribes in the Qāsimi Shamailīyah district on the east coast were closely connected with the Shiḥūḥ. The sections of the Shiḥūḥ who lived under the Sultan of Muscat's authority were of course very much in evidence in the Qāsimi areas, and clashes with the local population were so frequent that the Political Resident in Bushire at the time, Lt. Col. Prideaux, seriously worked at a plan in November 1926 suggesting to the Trucial Shaikhs and the Sultan of Muscat and Oman an exchange of territory. It would have meant removing all the

Shiḥūḥ of the west coast (he states Rams but must have meant other places further north as well) and giving them the Shamailīyah including Kalba in exchange. The opinion of Bertram Thomas. Adviser in Muscat, was sought and the latter prepared a sketch map of the tribal distribution in the Musandam promontory. See exchange of telegrams between the Resident in Bushire and the Political Agency in Muscat in November 1926 in IOR R/15/1/278. "Punishment of the Shaikh of Fujairah 1925–34."

17 The other part of the settled section lived at D̲aid while there are also Ṭanaij beduin who use the port of Rams and are at times in evidence in the village.

18 See e.g. the account of a dispute in 1921 between the Ruler of Ra's al Khaimah and the leading families of Rams assisted by the Shiḥūḥ in Bai'ah; see IOR R/15/1/275 "Fight between Shaikh of Ras al Khaimah and Shihuh tribe at the instigation of the Headman of Rams."

19 See footnote 8.

20 The ʿAwānāt ceased to be a separate tribe by about the end of the 19th century, having become virtual dependents of the Qawāsim.

21 But during the later years of Sālim bin Sulṭān's rule in Shārjah, Aḥmad bin Sulṭān seems to have often acted as deputy for his brother, leaving Dibah for long periods.

22 After this event, when the affairs between the usurper Sulṭān bin Ṣaqr and the family of the deposed Khālid bin Aḥmad were sorted out, Rāshid bin Aḥmad, the former fief of Dibah, resided for some time with the Ruler of Umm al Qaiwain, but later stayed in Dubai "as a dependent of the Shaikh of Dubai and married a woman of the Āl Bū Falāsah". See letter by the Residency Agent to the Resident in Bushire of 25 July 1925, in IOR R/15/1/276: "Deposition of the Shaikh of Sharjah 1924–32". See for the following IOR, R/15/1/284: "Correspondence regarding the Shaikh of Dibbah 1933–1938".

23 Letter no. 124 from the Residency Agent in Shārjah to the Political Resident in Bushire dated 24 March 1926 in IOR, R/15/1/276. The Residency Agent was, together with other people, of the opinion that this move was "done at the insistence of his father"; ibid. Immediately upon receiving this news the Ruler of Umm al Qaiwain, who by affording protection to the deposed Khālid bin Aḥmad and his relatives had taken on a considerable financial and political burden, claimed that the income from Dibah should be allocated to his protégé Khālid.

24 He describes this in a very self-possessed way in a letter to the Residency Agent of February 1926. Enclosed in letter no. 124 from the Residency Agent to the Political Resident in Bushire dated 24 March 1926; IOR R/15/1/276.

25 Though the latter seems to have had problems preventing some Shiḥūḥ from stopping repair work on the tower of Dibah fort. In November/

December 1921 Khālid, then Ruler of Shārjah, asked the permission of the British Government to have it repaired; the real reason for this request was that he wanted the British Government to influence the overlord of the Shiḥūḥ, the Sultan of Muscat and Oman; see IOR R/15/1/239: "Trucial Coast Affairs 1920–22".

26 The Sultan of Muscat, on a visit to the Musandam Peninsula in November 1932, "called together the leaders of the Kumzarah and Shihuh tribes and by a majority of votes given there appointed Zaid bin Sinan, Sheikh of Dibah"; in IOR L/P&S/12/3731 "Arab States News Summary 1931–33", November 1932.

27 Badr bin Sa'ūd was not, as most previous *wālis* at Khaṣab, a Shiḥḥi but a member of the ruling Āl Bū Sa'īd family.

28 Translation of the letter of 19 April 1934 in IOR R/15/1/284. On 10 September 1936 Rashīd bin Aḥmad contacted the Residency Agent in Shārjah, requesting for himself and on behalf of his subjects protection by the British Government, ibid., p. 48.

29 In exchange for the Ruler of Shārjah's assistance in the matter of landing facilities for aircraft, see e.g. aide memoire at Residency in Bushire of 12 September 1934 in IOR R/15/1/284.

30 The Shamailīyah includes the Gulf of Oman coast from just south of Dibah to Khaur Kalba in the south and the *wādis* of the Ḥajar range emptying onto that coast; it even extends to the vicinity of Khatt in Ra's al Khaimah, west of the watershed.

31 Lorimer, *Histor.*, p. 778; see for the earlier history of Shamailīyah ibid. pp. 776–84.

32 "Including 150 skins of dates, 12 cwt. of wheat and $10 in cash." Lorimer, *Histor.*, p. 782.

33 Sa'īd bin Ḥamad's wife was the sister of Sulṭān bin Sālim of Ra's al Khaimah.

34 In his attempt to obtain Kalba for himself, Sulṭān bin Sālim of Ra's al Khaimah tried to win over the influential Naqbiyīn shaikh by offering him the position as *amīr* of Khaur Fakkān and Kalba. See cable from Residency Agent in Shārjah to Political Agent, Bahrain of 8 May 1937 in IOR R/15/1/287, "Succession to the Sheikhdom of Kalba and Kalba Affairs, May 1937 to October 1937".

35 This choice was as good as unanimous, and in July even the Naqbiyīn promised to pay allegiance to him. He is called "Waḷi of Kalba" by the Political Agent in Muscat in a cable to the Resident in Bushire on 21 June 1937, and he called himself "Wali of Kalba and guardian and representative of Shaikh Hamad bin Sa'id al Qasimi" in a letter to the Political Resident at Bushire dated 22 June 1937 in IOR R/15/1/287.

36 The Sharqiyīn of Shamailīyah and other locations in Ra's al Khaimah and Shārjah territories numbered about 7,000 people which made them the second largest tribe, after the Bani Yās, of the whole Trucial States;

see Lorimer, *Geogr.*, pp. 1698 and 1769.

37 This may not have been so during the later part of the 19th century, for whenever an attempt at secession by the headmen of Fujairah was successfully foiled by Qawāsim Rulers, the resulting agreement included terms of tribute paid by the Sharqiyīn to the Ruler of Shārjah.

38 See e.g. the following passage in Lorimer, *Histor.*, p. 780: "In the spring of 1879 the people of Fujairah rose against and expelled one Sarūr, who had been set in authority over them by the Shaikh of Shārjah, and replaced him by a certain Marzūq . . . Shaikh Sālim sent a land force against the fort of Fujairah, which was recaptured and garrisoned with Balūch, and even transported some prisoners to the island of Bū Mūsa."

39 In a letter to the Political Resident at Bushire on 20 February 1927 the Ruler of Ra's al Khaimah stated "Fujairah used to be ruled by the Qawāsim tribe. The Headmen of Fujairah by help of certain men had acquired independence . . .", IOR R/15/1/278.

40 For a brief account of the earlier attempts at independence see Hawley, *Trucial States*, p. 349; see also Lorimer, *Histor.*, pp. 777ff. ("Internal Affairs of Trucial Oman", Annexure no. 6). Succession of headmen in Fujairah: ʿAbdullah bin Khamīs, (around 1866 mentioned), Ḥamad bin ʿAbdullah, (1879 till early 1930s) Saif bin Ḥamad, (possibly as deputy then until 1939), Muḥammad bin Ḥamad, (was recognised as Trucial Ruler in 1952, died 1975), Ḥamad bin Muḥammad, Ruler since 1975.

41 Ḥamad bin ʿAbdullah of Fujairah had a daughter of Saʿīd bin Ḥamad as his wife; her sister was married to Khālid bin Aḥmad, ex-Ruler of Shārjah.

42 In 1925/26 the bone of contention was whether Kalba should be allowed to erect a tower on the outskirts of the town but near a path customarily used by the Sharqiyīn. This time the ensuing series of disputes drew the attention of most of the relatives and neighbours of the two sides into the conflict, including the Sultan of Muscat and his *wāli* at Ṣūḥār. The settlement, which was reached on 20 to 23 May 1926, was attended or signed by "half a dozen shaikhs of the Trucial Coast" including Sulṭān bin Sālim (Ra's al Khaimah), Aḥmad bin Ibrāhīm (Umm al Qaiwain), Ṣāliḥ bin Muḥammad (Shiḥūḥ part of Dibah—Baiʿah), ʿAbdul Raḥman bin Saif (Ḥamrīyah), Muḥammad bin Sulṭān (Buraimi), Sālim bin Dayīn (Bani Kaʿab); see a letter written by Bertram Thomas (Muscat) to the Political Resident in Bushire, Col. Prideaux, of 24 June 1926 in IOR R/15/1/278.

43 Lorimer, *Geogr.*, p. 435; see for the following ibid., pp. 433ff.

44 In recent years Shaikh Zāyid of Abu Dhabi acquired an extensive date garden in this climatically and scenically pleasant oasis.

45 See letter no. 277 from the Residency Agent at Shārjah to the Political Resident in Bushire dated 30 June 1927 and enclosures in IOR R/15/1/276.

46 The Ruler of Umm al Qaiwain was not willing to risk antagonising the beduin of that region for his neighbour's sake.

47 See letter no. 232 from Residency Agent to the Political Resident dated 16 May 1928 and enclosures in IOR R/15/1/276.

48 Letter no. 388 by the Residency Agent to the Political Resident in Bushire dated 23 July 1928; ". . . the village has at last surrendered to Shaikh Khalid bin Ahmad who sent a man on his behalf of Dhaid to collect the tax (*zakat*) on date trees. I have also heard from a reliable source that the Shaikh himself is proceeding within a few days (i.e. to Dhaid) in order to arrange for his guards for it and to do some work of cleaning of the spring . . .", IOR R/15/1/276.

49 See Lorimer, *Histor.*, pp. 760ff.

50 See translation of the document granting independence from Shārjah in the presence of the Residency Agent on 9 August 1923 in IOR R/15/1/293: "Headman of Hemriyah desires Independence from Shargah, 1922–1932". The letter (no. 405) of 17 September 1929 from the Residency Agent to the Political Resident in Bushire cited all the agreements—verbal and written—between the headman of Ḥamrīyah and the Ruler of Shārjah and described the attitude the former had taken to the British Government; this plea seems to have contributed to the British intention of recognising Ḥamrīyah as independent. Letter no. 1109 dated 29 May 1931 from the Political Resident to the Foreign Secretary proves that the Resident had considered recommending the recognition but was cut short in executing this intention by the sudden death of the headman ʿAbdul Raḥman bin Saif; both in IOR R/15/1/293.

51 The account of this attempt which was given in detail in letter no. 115 dated 14 April 1932 from the Residency Agent to the Political Resident reads like a bad script for a crime film, with boats creeping up to the town at night, a hired murderer proving to be a faithful slave to his master and with one of the intruders being left behind in the confusion, who then had to hide in the cupboard of the intended victim's *majlis*; see IOR R/15/1/293.

52 The agreement made aboard *Lawrence* was cited verbatim in a letter from the Deputy Political Resident in Bushire reminding Muḥammad bin ʿUbaid of his undertaking. A similar letter was sent to the Ruler of Shārjah; nos. 306 and 305 both dated 15 June 1920 in IOR R/15/1/239.

53 The incident which brought the pot to the boil in 1920 was an attack on 30 June by some Manāṣīr and Āl Bū Shāmis beduin who plundered a house in Dubai jurisdiction where some women from Khān were harvesting their dates; the beduin "carried off the women's jewellery as well as their provisions, rice dates, coffee and their copper cooking pots. The Headman of Khān came to Shaikh Khaled ben Ahmad but could not get any help." Letter no. 600 from the Residency Agent to Political Resident dated 31 July 1920 in IOR R/15/1/239.

54 Letter from Muḥammad bin ʿUbaid to the Deputy Political Resident dated 1 August 1920. In this letter he claims "I used to go to him every day but I never saw him with good countenance", in IOR R/15/1/239.

55 Letter no. 611 from the Residency Agent to the Deputy Political Resident dated 4 August 1920 in IOR R/15/1/239.

56 See IOR R/15/1/236, "Arab States Monthly Summary 1929–1931", September 1931.

57 See below pages 214ff and Chapter Eight, footnote 41.

58 An extreme example was the case of ʿAbdullah bin Khamīs, who was styled *amīr* of Daqta, belonging to Ra's al Khaimah and near to the town. But he was from the Naqbiyīn tribe, most of whom resided in and near Kalba and he was therefore considered a subject of the Qāsimi shaikh of Kalba. He was killed near Masāfi in 1928 by Sharqiyīn, subjects of the Ruler of Fujairah; thus the aftermath of this murder involved Sulṭān bin Sālim of Ra's al Khaimah and Saʿīd bin Ḥamad of Kalba as well as Ḥamad bin ʿAbdullah of Fujairah; see IOR R/15/1/278.

59 See *UK Memorial II*, Annex E, nos 4 and 5, pp. 246ff. Much of the information used in this paragraph which does not appear in the Memorial was obtained from talking to elderly people of Abu Dhabi and to employees of the oil companies.

60 Wells drilled were Bāb no. 1 (January 1953 to October 1954), Gezira no. 1 (January 1955 to March 1956) and Shuwaihat no. 1 (November 1956 to November 1957). The first seismic survey was made in 1949/50 on Abu Dhabi island, then at Mirfa (1951), Jebel Baraka east of the Subkhat Matti (1953/4), Subkhat Matti (1954/5), Bainūnah (1955), Sila (1955) and Udaid (1956), Murban (1957); from the end of 1954 to early 1956 seismic marine surveys were also made in the shallow waters of Rās Sadr, Rās Mushairib, Udaid, West Murban, Ruwais Shuwaihat and Sila (spelling according to oil company usage).

61 Some names of head guards mentioned were Bandūq, ʿAbdullah bin Ṣāliḥ, Māniʿ bin ʿAbdullah al Muhairi and Ghaiṣ Muḥanna al Qubaisi.

62 The most prominent case was the strike of spring 1963 at the camp of the Santa Fe drilling company soon after the oil company had started to use contractors for drilling, construction and various other activities, and marked differences in the conditions of work and pay became apparent. On this occasion Shaikh Zāyid, the Ruler's representative in al ʿAin, was sent to Ṭarīf and he succeeded in persuading the excited tribesmen to return to work. Because all major issues concerning the local labour force were in those days discussed with Shaikh Shakhbūṭ, company representatives informed him in September 1961 of the intention to terminate the employment of most of the local labour force, who would, however, all be re-employed immediately under the same conditions by the various contractors. Shaikh Shakhbūṭ did not object to this in principle but was adamant that it was ultimately the

responsibility of the company to ensure that the local labour force always got a fair deal. The company subsequently laid down standard conditions of service with which all contractors were obliged to comply.

63 During the latter half of 1967 a local labour force of 110 men, which had been assembled for the construction of the Bū Ḥaṣā degassing station, were laid off and Aḥmad bin Ḥasan ensured that their interests were safeguarded.

64 He has also been the *ʿarīf* in one of the villages of the Buraimi area and later became the chairman of the National Assembly of Abu Dhabi when it was created in 1971.

65 See also for the following, above, pages 50ff.

66 See also *UK Memorial II*, Annex G, no. 1, pp. 273ff.

67 See below, page 217.

68 This was why Buṭi bin Muḥammad bin Khalfān, a Mazrūʿi who was married to the Ruler's Qubaisi aunt Wudīmah, was sometimes called *wāli* of Dalmā although he did not even always reside in his house on the island.

69 The examples for the various manifestations of actual authority exercised by a Ruler over a tribal society are drawn mostly from Abu Dhabi because for this part of the Trucial States there exists the most comprehensive documentation especially for the early 1950s in form of material collected for and used in the *UK Memorial*. This material has also been used and quoted extensively in J.B. Kelly, *Eastern Arabian Frontiers*.

70 The growth of the trade may be seen by comparing the earliest and the last of the years for which statistics of the value of the pearl exports are given in the *Gazetteer*: In 1873/74 the Trucial States exported about 1,180,000 Rupees-worth to India; in 1905/6 it was 8,000,000 Rupees, a more than sixfold increase in just over three decades. See Lorimer, *Histor.*, p. 2252.

71 "The first chief to levy dues is believed to have been the Shaikh of Bahrain, who is said to have instituted, about the beginning of the 19th century under the name of Nōb, a tax which was devoted (at least in theory) to the maintenance of four armed vessels on the banks for the protection of the Bahrain pearl fleet." Lorimer, *Histor.*, p. 2241.

72 After Wilson, A.T. "Some Early Travellers in Persia and the Persian Gulf", in *Journal of the Royal Central Asian Society*, vol. 12, pp. 68–82, 1925.

73 See also for the following Lorimer, *Histor.*, pp. 2240ff and Annexure no. 6, pp. 2284ff., with a table of the taxes levied annually by local authorities.

74 One bag of rice was then worth about 14 Rupees.

75 Other taxes mentioned for this period in Lorimer, *Histor.*, pp. 2284–9 were *mabāʿiyah*, a royalty on the sale of pearls by captains,

nawākhidah; *raḍaf* was an emergency tax levied when war was apprehended; *khānjīyah* was originally a tax by houses; *riyāl al sūr*, or the "town wall dollar", was originally taken to defray the cost of repairs to fortifications; *naub al naṣāra*, "the Christain nōb", relates to an incident about twenty years earlier when an Aden *sanbūk* was plundered by ʿAjmān pearl fishers in the Red Sea; payment of compensation having been ordered by the British Political Resident, the Shaikh of ʿAjmān imposed a special fine on the pearl-fishing community and maintained it for some time for his own benefit under this title.

76 Memorandum prepared by the Residency Agent, Shārjah, no. 141D, dated 4 September, 1906, reproduced in *UK Memorial II*, Annex G, no. 2, p. 275.

77 According to one source five of the islands east of Abu Dhabi were inhabited during the 1950s and had together about 33 houses; 13 islands west of Abu Dhabi were inhabited and had about 75 houses; about half of those were occupied the year round while others were only used for fishing in the winter.

78 *UK Memorial II*, Annex G, no. 1, p. 274 and I, pp. 66f, and II, Annex G, no. 5, p. 282, for names of the people who were taxed *ḥāṣilah* on Dalmā in 1954.

79 See Lorimer, *Geogr.*, p. 409. The other income derived from that area was a cash subsidy of 3,000 M.T. Dollars paid to the Ruler of Abu Dhabi by the Sultan of Oman for maintaining peace among the beduin in the vicinity of the oasis and in the Dhāhirah.

80 See *UK Memorial I*, pp. 68 and 70.

81 See Lorimer, *Geogr.*, p. 434.

82 See *UK Memorial I*, p. 70.

83 A Saudi ʿ*amīl* collected such *zakāh* in 1926 only from some ʿAwāmir, Durūʿ and beduin Āl Bū Shāmis; in 1927 the repetition was not opposed by the Āl Bū Falāḥ Ruler, Ṣaqr bin Zāyid, because he hoped that such favour would discourage the governor of al Ḥasā from assisting the sons of Sulṭān bin Zāyid to avenge the murder of their father; see Kelly, *Eastern*, pp. 119ff and 238f.

84 A definition of *zakāh* is given by J. Schacht in the *Encyclopaedia of Islam*, reproduced in the *Shorter Encyclopaedia of Islam*, edited by H.A.R. Gibb and J.H. Kramers, reprint, Brill and Luzac, Leiden and London, 1961, pp. 654ff. The usage and understanding of the expression in Eastern Arabia during the 20th century are discussed by J.B. Kelly, *Eastern*, particularly on pp. 239ff and in Appendix B, pp. 293–304.

85 Thomas, Bertram S., *Alarms and Excursions in Arabia*, London, 1931, p. 175.

86 For the 1940s and 1950s see the already mentioned statement by the *amīr*, ʿAli bin Shaibān, in *UK Memorial II*, Annex G, no. 1, p. 274, and also I, p. 67ff.

87 On customs in Dubai see below, page 249.
88 See letters no. 86 and 92 dated 8 and 16 July 1899 from the Residency Agent in Lingah to the Resident in Bushire; reprinted in *UK Memorial II*, Annex B, no. 44, p. 120. For further details on this German trading company see Plass, Jens B., *England* pp. 395ff.
89 See also below, page 174.
90 During the rule of Shaikh Sulṭān bin Zāyid in Abu Dhabi a monopoly for the purchase of dried sharks and turtles from fishermen operating on the coast between Ra's Ghanādhah and Yāsāt was given for 290 Rupees to a Persian and his brother; see *UK Memorial II*, Annex G, no. 7, p. 284. The trade in oyster shells was the beginning of the trading activities of Robert Woenckhaus & Co. in the Gulf. During the last years of the 19th century this German firm had agents in Dubai and Shārjah who also visited Dalmā during the pearling season to buy shells. For this trade they paid an export fee of M.T. Dollars 13 for a hundred sacks. The company tried—unsuccessfully because of British intervention—to secure mining rights for red oxide on Abū Mūsa, for which the Ruler of Shārjah collected royalties. Concessions for mining red oxide were also given at different times to different concessionnaires for the Tunbs, Ṣīr Bū Na'īr, Dalmā and Sīr Bani Yās; see Plass, *England*, pp. 410ff.
91 This practice continued during the 1920s and after; see Kelly, *Eastern*, p. 133 and *UK Memorial II*, Annex J, no. 1, p. 320.
92 After the death of Zāyid bin Khalīfah politics in Abu Dhabi depended very much on the relationship of the Āl Bū Falāḥ Ruler of the time with the Manāṣīr.
93 See e.g. the assessment of Sa'īd bin Taimūr's rule by Townsend, John, Oman. *The Making of a Modern State*, London, 1977.
94 See also below, pages 156ff.
95 People often talk about a certain person by adding that "his father was a good man, he was a *muṭawwa'*."
96 In one such case a woman of the Hawāmil subsection of the Bani Yās claimed possession of some jewellery, a rifle and a date garden as inheritance from her late husband; her claim was confirmed.
97 See for examples of some such cases *UK Memorial I*, p. 69.
98 See *UK Memorial I*, pp. 69–71 and a selection of examples of such cases in II, Annex F, pp. 249ff; they are mostly taken from the *Dhawāhir Collection* of letters from or to Aḥmad bin Muḥammad bin Hilāl, *wālı* for the Āl Bū Falāḥ in the Buraimi area for 40 years.
99 See Heard-Bey, *Asian Affairs*, 1974, p. 278.

CHAPTER FOUR

1 In this chapter the name al Bahrayn is used as it is by Arab geographers such as Yāqūt and Abū al Fidā'; see also above, Chapter Two note 13.

2 Connections between the Arabian Gulf Coast and the Sabaeans and Himyarites are indicated by the find of a tombstone with Himyaritic inscriptions and of a typically South Arabian alabaster vessel in Milaiḥah in Shārjah territory. More systematic archaeological research will, no doubt, produce more such evidence.

3 See Miles, *Countries*, pp. 23ff. See also for the following the research drawn from Arabic and other sources by Fiey, J.-M., "Diocèses Syriens Orientaux du Golfe Persique" in: *Mémorial Mgr Gabriel Khouri-Sarkis* (1898–1968), Louvain, Belgique 1969, pp. 177–219, about "Le Bét Qatrāyé", an entity of a number of dioceses reaching from al Baḥrayn and Yamāmah to the islands of the Gulf and to Oman.

4 The bishop's seat was founded in AD 410, and the first bishop was called Paul.

5 See Fiey, *Diocèses*, pp. 210ff; The last mention of a Christian community in al Baḥrayn which he could find was when under the Catholicos Yuwanis III (AD 893–9), the (Carmathian) rebel Abū Sa'īd al Jannaibi, who took possession of al Baḥrayn, was alleged to have treated Christians with consideration.

6 See Miles, *Countries*, pp. 30ff.

7 According to many Arab historians similar messages were sent to other Arab and non-Arab Rulers.

8 The Prophet's messenger, 'Amru, on his way which took him through Buraimi (then called Tu'ām), first went to the Persian governor Moksan in the Bāṭinah; but his message was refused out of hand.

9 Miles, *Countries*, p. 36.

10 ibid, p. 37.

11 It was significant for the spread of Islam as an easily accepted religion in this area, that it did not appear as political domination by outsiders; initially not even the otherwise customary tax was to be remitted to Medina—the Prophet himself had ordered that in the case of Oman the annually collected *zakāh* was to be distributed among the poor of that country.

12 Miles, *Countries*, p. 32.

13 In about the year AH 30, Jaifar died and was succeeded by his nephew 'Abbād bin 'Abd. Miles, *Countries*, p. 46f.

14 See also the remarks by Miles: "With Islam, however, Oman awoke, like the rest of the peninsula from its trance; a new spirit of religious fervour, of literature, of warlike enterprise was quickly engendered; the population began to increase, industrial occupations were eagerly learnt and followed; many of the youths took service in the imperial wars; every family sent some member to push his fortunes as a merchant, sailor, or adventurer; internal feuds and quarrels passed into at least temporary oblivion . . . flourishing towns and villages grew up everywhere; cultivated land increased, and in an astonishingly short

time the order and regularity, conveniences and benefits of civilized life permeated the inhabitants of a country which a short time before was sunk in the rank and stagnant mire of paganism." *Countries*. p. 46.

15 In AD 752 (AH 135) the Caliph Abū al'Abbās sent Khāzim bin Khuzaimah to Oman to avenge a defeat suffered at the hands of the Ibāḍis (whose elected Imām was al Julandā' bin Mas'ūd) two years previously, and to punish the Umayyads who had escaped from Iraq three years earlier and found refuge with the Ibāḍis; this was already the fifth invasion of Oman by a Muslim army since 'Abd and Jaifar had accepted Islam in the year AD 630 (AH 9).

16 See Miles, *Countries* p. 52. Yet another example was the devastating defeat which the *amīr* of Eastern Arabia in al Baḥrayn, Muḥammad bin Nūr, effected by invitation of the mostly Sunni Nizār faction of Oman in AD 893 (AH 280) and from which the entire country did not recover for centuries (because many *aflāj* were destroyed and the country depopulated). This campaign also began in Trucial Oman territory: ". . . altogether an army of about 25,000 men, including 3,500 cavalry in chain armour, raised principally from the warlike tribes of Maaddic stock, assembled under the white banner of the imperial general. This large and well equipped expedition appears to have been divided into two divisions, one of which set sail from Busra with the impedimenta and stores in a flotilla of transports and disembarked at Julfar, while the other, comprising the main body under Mohammad bin Noor, marched by land from Lahsa (al Ḥasā) and crossing the Sabkheh reached Abu Thubi, from whence, engaging on the way with the tribes of Al-Sirr in skirmishes and desultory warfare, after the fashion of Arabia, he moved on to Al-Beraimi in Al-Jow or Towwam, as it was then called, where he arrived on the 24th Moharram, 280 AH (AD 893)." p. 81.

17 A yearly sum, was paid to the Caliph by the provinces in lieu of poll tax and tithes. If records could be found of such a remittance having been paid for all of al Gharbīyah province of Oman, this might shed some light on the administrative links between the Gulf coast and Oman proper.

18 For instance the Caliph's *amīr*, Yūsuf bin Wajīh, who had taken Oman from the Carmathians, collected a large flotilla and material at Julfār to pursue the Persian adventurer al Baridi in AD 942 (AH 331); see Miles, *Countries*, p. 105.

19 For the origin of the division of the tribes into Hināwi and Ghāfiri factions, see below, pages 273ff.

20 Sunnis were predominant in the districts of Rud-hillah, Shībkūh, Lingah, Bastak, Biyābān and Jāshk, in the town of Bandar 'Abbās and on the islands of Qishim, Hanjām and Lārak; in all they were estimated at about 100,000 souls; see Lorimer, *Histor.*, p. 2350. The Balūchis who settled among the Arabs of Trucial Oman were also mostly Sunnis.

21 Some of the moral points which were emphasised by the puritan *Muṭawwa'* movement within the Ibāḍi movement during the 19th century did have a deep influence on the attitudes of the tribal people who had close links with the people of Inner Oman. This movement was particularly concerned with reforming public morals and wanted to see the veiling of women more rigidly enforced; see Lorimer, *Histor.*, pp. 2374f.

22 For more details on the Khojahs, see Lorimer, *Histor.*, pp. 2377ff.

23 ibid. p. 2379.

24 ibid. p. 2383ff.

25 ibid. p. 2397. For a history of the western Christian missions in the area see ibid, Appendix I, pp. 2386–99.

26 See below, pages 212ff and 291ff.

27 See Alfred Bonné, *State and Economics in the Middle East: A Society in Transition*, 2nd rev. edn Westport, 1973 (Greenwood Press); quotation p. 333.

28 A term used extensively for instance by Edwin E. Calverley, "The Fundamental Structure of Islām" in *Asian Affairs*, 1939, vol. XXVI, pp. 280–302.

29 The simplest of all mosques is a rectangle staked out with palm fronds or stones and indicating the *qiblah*; such makeshift mosques were made if a large group of people was encamped somewhere in the desert or mountains for any length of time.

30 From aerial photographs taken of Abu Dhabi in the early 1960s some 20 mosques can be identified for the town, which then housed an estimated 30,000 people.

31 See below pages 244f.

32 According to one source the Friday mosque of Dubai used to have a women's gallery during the 1950s.

33 See Thesiger, *Arabian* p. 111.

34 Hence the official support for the establishment of the Roman Catholic St. Joseph's church in 1966 in Abu Dhabi and St. Mary's in 1967 in Dubai; Anglican churches followed in both towns in 1967 and 1970, and there is an Evangelical Church in al 'Ain.

35 When asked why they built their houses at a distance from the cool and shade of their date gardens rather than inside, many people said that there were evil spirits in the gardens—possibly a notion which arose out of a long experience of malarial cases among the people who slept regularly in *falaj*-irrigated gardens.

36 Boys were usually circumcised at the age of about nine or ten. Every community had a man who did the operation and who was very often also a *muṭawwa'*. Girls were sometimes circumcised soon after birth by the midwife of the community.

37 In this respect there was a recognisable difference between the tribal

population on the Trucial Coast and some of the tribes of Dhufār, whose customs and practices were described most extensively by Bertram Thomas, for instance in *Arabia Felix*, 2nd edn. 1936, pp. 41ff.

38 As elsewhere on the peninsula, poetry was often sung to the accompaniment of a *rabābah* (a simple stringed instrument).

39 If someone did not have the necessary means of subsistence or could not guarantee those means for his family during his absence, or if the journey was too dangerous, he was not obliged to go.

40 According to the *Enclyclopaedia of Islam*, *ḥarīm* is "a term applied to those parts of the house to which access is forbidden, and hence more particularly to the women's quarters": *The Encyclopaedia of Islam*, new edition, Brill and Luzac, Leiden and London, 1971, vol. III, p. 209. The word *ḥarīm* is derived from the root ḥ r m, meaning to be forbidden, unlawful, unpermitted. Other words using this root are e.g. *ḥaram* (forbidden; offence; taboo; sacred or sacrosanct; accursed; illegitimate) and *ḥurmah*, pl. *ḥuram* (woman, lady, wife.). The term *ḥarīm* is to some extent interchangeable with *ḥarām*, according to Hans Wehr it denotes a "sacred inviolable place, sanctum, sanctuary, sacred precinct"; the singular may also be used to mean "wife" as well as collectively "female members of the family"; see Wehr, Hans, *A Dictionary of Modern Written Arabic* ed. by J.M. Cowan, Wiesbaden, 1971, pp. 171f.

41 In the more elaborate houses of the merchant families of the coastal towns and in some villages of the Buraimi area there was sometimes a second summer *majlis* on the upper floor of a mudbrick building, and the stairs to it as well as the areas for washing were reserved for male guests.

42 If a child is breast-fed by a woman of another family because his mother has no milk, the baby of this wet-nurse fed at the same time becomes a brother or sister in the full sense of the meaning and marriage between the two children would be considered incestuous, while marriage with a foster-sister's sister is possible.

43 The status of male servants in the house, particularly since they were rarely of Arab tribal origin, was partly that of a close member of the family in that they had access to most areas of the compound when they were expected to serve coffee, to clean, or to do other duties; but the women nevertheless pulled their veils over their faces on the approach of any but the oldest and most trusted servant, and they rarely had a long conversation with a servant.

44 Traditionally the marriage contract did not have to be written out nor sanctioned by a *qāḍi*. If both sides agreed on all the details and communicated this agreement to a trusted witness, the latter was expected to remember those details even after many years; this was important in view of the fact that the wife could take back with her an agreed part of the bride price if the husband divorced her.

45 The use of rock salt as a disinfectant and astringent after giving birth was universal. But because the salt had been stored and handled unhygenically the risk of infections was augmented; the salt also hardened the tissue, making every subsequent birth more difficult.

46 For some details on these fratricides and an abridged genealogical chart see Anthony, John Duke, *Arab States of the Lower Gulf; People, Politics, Petroleum*, Washington, 1975, pp. 128f.

47 The strong reaction of most local women against second marriages of their husbands underlines the fact that among the average families in the Trucial States polygamy was quite exceptional. Only in recent years a greater number of men have used their vastly increased financial resources to set up houses for a second or a third wife, and some even brought new brides from other countries such as India and Egypt. The reaction of some of the local first wives was simply to leave husband—and if necessary children—and to go back to their fathers; see also below, pages 149ff and 233ff.

48 Labourers in the date gardens were not in every case domestic servants but often people who had their own households and were paid for their work in kind; see also below, pages 224f. There were few people of African origin resident with any of the Līwā-based tribal families.

49 Everywhere in Arab countries the function of slaves was primarily that of domestic servants, unlike in ancient Greece and Rome or in America. The moral outcry against this institution was in the case of the Arab countries of the Gulf only justified with regard to the way in which these people used to be captured in their native countries, the mode of their transportation in overcrowded boats and the transactions until someone was established with his master. They did not normally change hands after that and there was no place for the regular sale of slaves in the coastal towns after the First World War. See also below, pages 231ff and 288ff.

50 See the article on 'ABD in the *Encyclopaedia of Islam*, 1960, pp. 24–40.

51 The issue of interference by the British Government in transactions in and possession of slaves caused a great deal of ill feeling, particularly in Dubai, where during the 1930s several of the pearl merchants and owners of boats which were chiefly manned by their slaves, saw their business threatened. See below, pages 251f.

52 Although many families were quite glad to liberate their slaves to rid themselves of these additional mouths to feed, there was on the other hand a marked increase in abductions of people into slavery on the Trucial Coast during the 1940s and 1950s. This was yet another reflection on the desperate economic situation in the area at the time; money could no longer be made easily in any respectable business or by selling the camels one had reared. But there was still a ready market for slaves in al Ḥasā in Saudi Arabia. Therefore some daring bands of

tribesmen and of impoverished town dwellers snatched people from their homes or elsewhere and took them to Ḥamāsah village, from where they were sold into slavery. They usually picked on Balūchis, but also black people and slaves who were not yet freed were taken; there were some incidents where even tribal people were the unfortunate victims. See also Thesiger, *Arabian Sands*, pp. 263ff.

53 Dibah, Kalba, and Falaj al ʿAli were all governed at some period in recent history by slaves.

54 In the more remote communities it was not uncommon to use the shoulder blade of dead domestic animals to write on.

55 The *kuttābs* were still used for the girls when early this century the al Aḥmadīyah School was opened in Dubai; this school survived all economic problems of the following decades and had in 1935 about 250 boys. When the girls graduated from their Koran course they would go together with their mothers and the teacher round the town chanting and calling on merchants and homes collecting funds; the celebration was called *tamīmah*. For details of the beginnings of more formal education see, Abdullah, Muhammad Morsy, *The United Arab Emirates. A Modern History*, London, 1978, pp. 107ff.

56 Such purpose-built *kuttābs* were quite common throughout Oman; they were usually simple buildings with a few low windows and one of the short walls was partly or completely open to admit enough light. There is one such *kuttāb* in the seasonally inhabited capital of the Jannabah at ʿIzz.

57 *Shorter Encyclopaedia of Islam*, 1961, "Shariʿa", p. 525 (pp. 524–9). Compare also the useful definitions of Islam and *sharīʿah* in Bernard Lewis *The Arabs in History*, 4th edn., 1968, pp. 133f.

58 The *sunnah* comprise the Prophet Muḥammad's deeds, utterances, judgements and implied approvals which were recorded and help to make God's law intelligible—and therefore obligatory—for man.

59 See also above, 122ff.

60 The first *qadhi* who was officially appointed by Shaikh Saʿīd bin Maktūm some time before 1911 was Shaikh Muḥammad bin ʿAbdul Salām from Morocco. After his death in the 1940s he was succeeded by Shaikh ʿAbdul Raḥman bin Hāfidh, an Arab from Lingah, and Shaikh Mubārak bin ʿAli bin Bashīt, a native of Dubai. They were succeeded by Shaikh Aḥmad bin Ḥasan from Bukha in Ru'ūs al Jibāl, who was trained in a Sunni *madrasah* for religious studies on Qishim Island. Shaikh Saif Muḥammad Shanghīti was brought from Morocco as a second *qāḍi*. In Abu Dhabi one of the *qāḍis* appointed by Shaikh Shakhbūṭ, Shaikh Badr bin Yūsuf, was a Bahraini; earlier, during the first decade of the 20th century a man from Tunis, Muḥammad bin ʿAli Buzainah had been *qāḍi* in Abu Dhabi. At that same time the *qudāh* of R'as al Khaimah and Shārjah both came from Najd, the former was

Aḥmad bin Ḥumaid al Raghbāni, the latter was ʿAbdulraḥman bin ʿAbdullah bin Fāris.

61 See above pages 121ff.

62 See above page 123.

63 IOR R/15/1/236, "Arab States Monthly Summary, 1929–31", March 1931.

64 See ibid, December 1931.

65 The division of jurisdiction in the Trucial States after the Second World War (and in particular after 1947) will be dealt with below, pages 314ff.

66 See the detailed study of the recent changes in law and jurisdiction in the UAE, particularly in Abu Dhabi, by Professor Fitz Steppat, "Bemerkungen zur Rechtsentwicklung in Abu Dhabi und den Vereinigten Arabischen Emiraten" (Notes on the legal development in Abu Dhabi and the UAE), *Zeitschrift der Deutschen Morgenländischen Gesellschaft*, Supplement III, 1, 1977, pp. 617–24.

67 See also above, page 117 on *zakāh* as the tax on camels.

68 For details on the general understanding of *zakāh*, see the article in the *Shorter Encyclopaedia of Islam*, 1961, pp. 654ff.

69 See above pages 112ff, on taxation in general.

CHAPTER FIVE

1 Lorimer, *Geogr.*, p. 1437.

2 See e.g. Thesiger, *Arabian Sands*, p. 249: "The Wahiba in the interior of Oman own a famous breed, the *Banat Farha*, or 'The Daughters of Joy', and the Duru own the equally famous *Banat al Hamra*, or 'The Daughters of the Red One'."

3 Many nomadic families of eastern Arabia do not have proper woven tents but carry a few pieces of cloth which are made into some sort of shelter with a few sticks or hung from an acacia bush.

4 Places such as Muqshin, inland and north of Dhufār, are rare in the Arabian Peninsula. Mugshin is described by Bertram Thomas: "Wadi Mugshin, surely the Prince of Wadis in all South-east Arabia. . . . At its eastern extremity (altitude about 400 feet) drinkable water comes to the surface at ʿAin or ʿAinain. A considerable date grove growing wild and unattended lines the banks of a marshy bed, and to the eastward is a trough-like pond a few hundred yards long and some fifteen wide." *Arabia Felix*, p. 139.

5 See Thesiger, *Arabian Sands*, p. 141, and the information given by Al ʿAuf, his Rashīdi guide, pp. 112–14.

6 Goatskins and goat-hair were more widely used among the nomads as material for making articles for daily use.

7 For details, see Heard-Bey, *Asian Affairs*, 1974.

8 See Thesiger, *Arabian Sands*, p. 256, where he reports having shot some on his way between al ʿAin and Shārjah.

9 According to Lorimer, *Geogr.*, p. 263, there were, for instance, about a hundred horses belonging to the Ruler of Abu Dhabi, usually kept in the Buraimi Oasis, and some fifty horses belonging to other people.

10 A specimen of a wooden plough is kept in the museum at al ʿAin.

11 *Gazella gazella arabica*. See David L. Harrison, *Mammals of Arabia*, vol. 2, p. 350ff. Within this species the local population distinguish several subspecies by the colouring of their coats; *dhabi* is light brown to white; *damāni* is reddish brown; *rīm* is another name also applied to the whitish gazelle.

12 According to Philby, H. St J.B., *The Empty Quarter*, London 1933, p. 78. Some oryx (*oryx leucoryx pallas*, Harrison, *Mammals*, vol. 2, pp. 344ff) were then reported to still be on the borders of the Rubʿ al Khāli. In the 1980s oryx were released into the wild in Oman.

13 See Harrison, *Mammals*, vol. 2, pp. 334ff.

14 The local methods of hunting wild birds of prey are described in detail in Abū ʿĀḏara, Saʿīd Salmān, *Al Ṣukūr* (Falcons), Amman, 1977. See also Zaid Bin Sultan Al Nahayan, *Falconry as a Sport. Our Arab Heritage*, Abū Dhabi, 1976, published in English and Arabic for the occasion of a conference on falconry and the conservation of wildlife, in December 1976 in Abu Dhabi. The content of the book is taken largely from interviews with H.H. The President of the UAE, Shaikh Zāyid bin Sulṭān, about traditional falconry. An enthusiastic description of a month of hunting with *shāhīn* and *salūqi* in Dhafrah is given by Thesiger, *Arabian Sands*, pp. 271–5.

15 Harrison, *Mammals*, vol. 2, pp. 337ff (picture on p. 340).

16 See FAO Technical Advisory Mission, *Agricultural Development in the United Arab Emirates*: report on the present position, prospects and priorities, Cairo, 1973, p. 135. In 1969 the Trucial States Council's estimate of annual production was only 7,000 tons. For an enumeration of species see White, A.W. and Barwani, M.A., *Common Sea Fishes of the Arabian Gulf and Gulf of Oman*. Trucial States Council, vol. I, Dubai, 1971.

17 Trucial States Council, *Report 1969*, p. 17. In the northern emirates and Dubai, 11,257 people were counted as working in agriculture and fisheries during the 1968 census; 5,635 of these stated that they were self-employed. From this, K. Fenelon, *The Trucial States*, estimated that there were about 7,000 people who could be called fishermen in all the Trucial States including Abu Dhabi. In the report on fisheries of 1972, 6,445 nationals were listed as fishermen for the UAE excluding Abu Dhabi (1,545 living in Fujairah, 1,404 in Ra's al Khaimah). See White, A.W. and Barwani, M.A., *A Survey of the United Arab Emirates Fisheries Resources 1969–71*, Dubai, 1972.

18 This area was previously let for 300 Rupees per year to someone called

Aḥmad bin ʿAbdullah bin Ghumailāt (Rumaithi), and from 1936 to 1940 for 350 Rupees to ʿAbdullah bin Murshid, brother of the late head of the Rumaithāt and an influential businessman in Abu Dhabi. See *UK Memorial II*, Annex G, no. 6, p. 283, where further examples are listed.

19 Dugong are a species threatened by extinction. The community which lived on Umm al Nār five thousand years ago left many bones of the dugong, and there is reason to believe that they were once so numerous in the Gulf as to form a staple diet for the fishermen. Currently there are about sixty to seventy dugong a year brought into the fish-market in Abu Dhabi. They are usually caught alive in the net, and it is now hoped that a preservation order will be issued, as has been the case with gazelle.

20 See Dowson, V.H.W., "The Date Cultivation and Date Cultivators in Basrah" in *Journal of the Royal Central Asian Society*, vol. 26, 1939, pp. 247–60.

21 For construction with mudbrick and coral stones, imported *chandel* wood from Malabar or East Africa was preferred.

22 For a description of such houses in the Līwā, see Heard-Bey, *Asian Affairs*, 1974, p. 275.

23 For the method of pollinating see Heard-Bey, op. cit., pp. 276 and 278ff.

24 See Lorimer, *Histor.*, p. 2296.

25 The most detailed studies of the *aflāj* in Eastern Arabia were made by J.C. Wilkinson, *Water*. For details of the characteristics of a covered *falaj* see pp. 76ff. Two interesting accounts of how such underground water channels are constructed are given by Noel, E., "Qanats", in *Journal of the Royal Central Asian Society*, vol. 31, 1944, pp. 191–202, and Beckett, P., "Qanats round Kirman", ibid., vol. 40, 1953, pp. 47–58. An excellent graphic description of the anatomy of a small *falaj* can be found in Birks, J.S. and Letts, S.E., "Diqal and Muqayda: Dying Oases in Arabia", in *Tijdschrift voor economische en sociale geografie* (TESG: *Journal of Economic and Social Geography*), 68, 1977, no. 3, pp. 145–51.

26 The settled ʿAwāmir of Adam are now almost the only people who repair and extend old *aflāj*, and who would be able to build new ones; see Birks, J.S. and Letts, S.E., "The ʿAwāmr: Specialist Well- and Falaj-Diggers in Northern Interior Oman", in *Journal of Oman Studies*, vol. 2, 1976. See also Wilkinson, *Water*, pp. 195ff; he states that there is no record of the ʿAwāmir constructing a major new *falaj*. Wilkinson concludes from a variety of written and physical evidence that the *aflāj* of Oman are a heritage from the periods of Persian occupation.

27 See Gibb, Sir Alexander, & Partners, *Water Resources Survey, Final Report*, December 1970, p. 22. The Interim Report to the Government of Abu Dhabi of April 1970 provides data on the availability of water, its flow, the rock formations, and the productivity of certain crops and of

the agricultural methods used in the oasis. See also Stevens, J.H., "Changing Agricultural Practice in an Arabian Oasis" in *Geographical Journal*, vol. 136, Part 3, September 1970, pp. 410–18.

28 See Wilkinson, *Water*, pp. 74ff, with a graph of the *ghayl aflāj* in Bithnah in the Wādi Ḥām, on p. 75.

29 On average, a garden in the Buraimi Oasis would be irrigated every 12 to 15 days in the winter and about every three weeks in the summer. But gardens participating in the water from Mu 'tiriḍ *falaj* had intervals of 20 and 30 days respectively; see Stevens, *Geographical Journal* 1970, p. 415. See also *UK Memorial I*, p. 70. For other payments in connection with *aflāj* see above, pages 115ff and 179f.

30 The position of *'arīf* at Mu'tiriḍ was held for some time by the paramount shaikh of the Dhawāhir, Shaikh Sulṭān bin Surūr, before he became Shaikh Shakhbūṭ's representative in Jabal al Dhannah in 1962.

31 For a description of the traditional agriculture in the Buraimi Oasis see Lorimer, *Geogr.*, p. 263. There were about 60,000 date trees in the oasis at that time. See also Cox, Sir Percy, "Some Excursions in Oman", in *The Geographical Journal*, vol. LXVI, no. 3, September 1925, pp. 193–227, particularly p. 207.

32 See Lorimer, *Histor.*, p. 2220.

33 See India Office Records, R/15/1/236 "Arab States Monthly Summary 1929–1931".

34 Bahrain had a total number of 917 boats, and Kuwait had 461 boats at that time. See Lorimer, *Geogr.*, p. 1438, and *Histor.*, pp. 2256 and 2220.

35 See *Encyclopaedia Britannica*, 1973, vol. 17, pp. 504ff.

36 See Lorimer, *Histor.*, pp. 2262–80 for a description of the pearl banks on the Arab and the Persian sides. 184 such banks are named and located by latitudinal and longitudinal co-ordinates for the bay from Ra's Tannūrah to Dubai alone. A chart which was supplied in December 1906 by the naval authorities of the Foreign Department of the Government of India for this bay is provided in Part III of the Historical volume of the Gazetteer. A map of the pearl banks was made by Shaikh Māni' bin Rāshid, a cousin of the Ruler of Dubai in 1940.

37 For information about Arab sailing boats and for a photograph of a pearling *sanbuk* and an interesting description of life aboard an Arab *dhow* (in this case a trading and passenger vessel) see Villier, A., *The Sons of Sindbad*, Scribner's Sons, New York, 1940.

38 There are quite extraordinary claims of people spending five or even ten minutes under water; these must be considered erroneous due to the lack of proper methods of timing. Ibn Baṭūṭah claims that they may even stay one to two hours; see *Voyages d'Ibn Batoutah* translated into French by C. Defrémery et B.R. Sanguinetti, Paris, 1912 etc., vol. II, pp. 24ff.

39 The Muslim year has 12 months of 29 or 30 days; since it is only 354 days

long its beginning—first of Muḥarram—and all other events in the Muslim calendar occur 11 days earlier each solar year.

40 See Lorimer, *Histor.*, pp. 2244ff and below, page 293. Similar approaches, often by the same firms, were made to the authorities on the Persian side, and in some cases concessions were actually granted by the Government in Teheran, but they brought nothing except loss to the operators.

41 See Lorimer, *Histor.*, p. 2248.

42 See Lorimer, *Histor.*, p. 2247.

43 Information which was obtained by interviewing members of the pearling community especially in Dubai is supplemented by the chapter on the trade in pearls in the Gazetteer, Lorimer, *Histor.*, pp. 2235ff.

44 The biggest pearls in this category passed through the *ra's* (head) with an 0.18 of an inch wide holes, but not through the *baṭn* (inside, stomach); the smallest pearls were less than 0.11 of an inch in diameter and therefore fell through the sieves called *ḥadrīyah al d̲ail* (lower tail).

45 See also below, page 209ff.

46 See Lorimer, *Geogr.*, p. 411.

47 Rice as a staple food of the population of the Trucial States seems to have assumed its present dominant position only during the 20th century; it proved its worth particularly as a satisfying, cheap, easy to store and to cook main dish for the evening meals of the pearling crews.

48 See Lorimer, *Geogr.*, p. 1440. For information about the types of boats which were traditionally used in the Gulf see Lorimer, *Histor.*, p. 2319ff.

49 See Lorimer, *Geogr.*, p. 1760.

50 See Lorimer, *Histor.*, p. 2568 the general Appendix on the Arms and Ammunition Traffic in the Gulf, and pp. 2587ff for a table of yearly imports into Trucial Oman and a copy of the 1902 Arms Agreement. At that time Ra's al Khaimah and Fujairah were part of Shārjah.

51 See above, page 176; and also the very detailed studies of the date palms made by Dowson, V.H.W., particularly his lecture entitled "The Date and the Arab", in: *Journal of the Royal Central Asian Society*, 36, 1949, pp. 34–53. See also for the following, Heard-Bey, *Asian Affairs*, Oct., 1974.

52 In July 1971 the author saw a caravan of 17 camels carrying nothing but water containers made in Bahlah for sale in Maṭraḥ. Bahlah pots were taken in the same fashion to the *sūq* in Buraimi.

53 The same model is still now in use in some households in the United Arab Emirates.

54 The undecorated brass coffee-pots with a belly, which are now being sold in the *sūq* both old and new, began to come into use in the Trucial States only about twenty years ago. They are made in al Ḥasā.

55 Drawings of some such silver jewelry are given by Dostal, *Beduinen*, S.56ff. See also Hawley, Ruth, *Omani Silver*, London, 1978.

56 Dyeing cotton and wool is still an industry in which at least two families are involved in Firq near Nizwā in Oman; in 1975 the author saw one shop in the *sūq* in ʿIbri where woven cloth was being dyed indigo.
57 A typical weaving frame from Buraimi is exhibited in the museum of al ʿAin. An identical one was seen by the author in 1971 being used by the weaver in Firq who made lengths of material for the unsewn *lungi* or *wizār* which men wear under their shirt (*kandūrah*).
58 See also for the following, Dostal, *Beduinen*, especially the photograph of a saddle on Abb. 2 and 3 Dostal proposes the theory that only after this type of saddle had been developed was full camel nomadism possible.
59 The fish oil which was used to rub the bottom of the boats at frequent intervals for impregnation could also be burnt, but it was not used for cooking because of the amount of smoke it developed; the same applied to animal fat.
60 Even nowadays charcoal is not always available in a market such as ʿIbri, for it is brought in on certain mornings by the beduin who still manufacture it.
61 Lorimer, *Geogr.*, p. 1440.

CHAPTER SIX

1 Examples of these types of social differentiation are to be found within the context of the age-old confrontation of the desert and the sown in the Middle East. See e.g. Nieuwenhuijze, C.A.O. Van, *Sociology of the Middle East* Leiden 1971, Wilkinson, J.C., 1972 in Hopwood, ed. and in some of the articles collected and edited by Louise E. Sweet, *Peoples and Cultures of the Middle East*, 2 vols, New York 1970, particularly vol. I, part III; Rural Peoples of the Middle East; Nomadic Pastoralists.
2 Many settled Dhawāhir in the villages of the Buraimi oasis did not own the date gardens they tended. Similarly, when an increasing number of people were needed to man the many pearling boats sailing from the Trucial Coast, beduin such as the Ṭanaij and the Bani Qitab participated just for the season without really becoming members of the social structure of the pearling communities.
3 There was the example of agriculture in Oman, which according to some theories declined dramatically after the importation of slaves was forbidden in 1845 and became increasingly risky.
4 Baḥārinah is a term which became practically a synonym for a Shīʿah Muslim whose mother tongue was Arabic; they had no coherent tribal organisation, but some of the leading families were distinguished by names such as Al Mājid and Al Raḥmah. See Lorimer, *Geogr.*, pp. 207f.
5 See Lorimer, *Geogr.*, p. 411.

6 The term "urbanisation" is used here to indicate the change in certain customs, particularly the tendency of more and more tribal people to winter in Abu Dhabi town rather than in the desert.

7 The number of inhabited settlements varied and sources therefore give different figures; see e.g. Kelly, *Eastern*, p. 32.

8 See ibid and *UK Memorial*, Annex E, pp. 239–43; the comparative table shows the compositions of the Līwā settlements from west to east. The figures which were obtained from three sources for the *Memorial* date from 1952 to 1955.

9 See also above, page 115ff.

10 A list of Abu Dhabi subjects who own pearling boats on the coast and palms in the Līwā is given in the *UK Memorial II*, Annex E, no. 2, p. 244. The names do not always correspond with those given by other sources. See also the list of the names of places of residence of the people from whom pearling tax was collected in 1950 by the Ruler's representative on Dalmā island, Hilāl Abū al Ghāfiri al Falāhi, ibid., Annex G, no. 5, p. 282.

11 In the 1930s a sack of rice weighing 18 man (72kg) was worth 6 Riyal, a live goat cost 3/4 Riyal, 1 man of sugar cost half a Riyal, which increased to 25 during the Second World War.

12 See also above, page 120f.

13 Examples: An expedition in winter 1936/7 in the W. and S.W. of Abu Dhabi and to Khaur al 'Udaid on which occasion Shaikh Zāyid bin Sulṭān and sixteen retainers accompanied two PD (TC) geologists and a British interpreter, Ḥajji 'Abdullah Williamson. Also a party visited the western area of the Abu Dhabi shaikhdom in April 1949 to investigate a report of ARAMCO activities in that area. The party was made up of the Political Officer Trucial Coast, H.M. Jackson of PD(TC), two Agency guards, five drivers, one cook and seven guards who accompanied Shaikh Hazzā' bin Sulṭān. Also two members of the Locust Research team based in Shārjah journeyed by camel from al 'Ain to the Līwā in January 1952. Shaikh Mubārak bin Muḥammed was detailed by Shaikh Zāyid to accompany them and the large group of camel men.

14 This was done, for instance, by the person in charge of the Ruler's post at al Māriyah in the Līwā.

15 As reported after a visit to Līwā in 1955 by an oil company official.

16 In Dubai the two types were taxed differently. See Lorimer, *Histor.* pp. 2286f.

17 The following description of the system of financing the pearling industry is based on the author's enquiries as well as on Lorimer, *Histor.*, p. 2227ff, on an early draft of an article on Bahrain published by Charles Belgrave in the *Times* in June 1934 (IOR L/P&S/12/3762 "Publicity in the Gulf 1932–47") and on a passage about the economic interdependence of the members of the pearling community in the

doctoral theses by Broer, Hans-Joachim, *Wirtschaftliche Entwicklung in Kuwait, Ein Beispiel für die Rolle der Mentalität in einem Entwicklungsland*. Diss. Köln (Wiso-Fak) 1965.

18 For more details see pages 288ff. and Thomas Bertram, *Alarms and Excursions in Arabia*, London, 1931, pp. 236ff.

19 Even during the 1960s many a head of a household claimed the wages which his servant earned as an oil company employee.

20 See also, pages 291f.

21 See Lorimer, *Histor.*, p. 2243. That this agreement was still honoured is born out by the way in which a dispute between ʿAjmān and Shārjah (on behalf of its dependency of Ḥīrah) was settled in the presence of the Ruler of Dubai and the Residency Agent who reported on 30 January 1934, in Dispatch no. 33, that the claims between the Rulers were settled "according to the agreement registered in the Book of Pacts on 3rd of Rajab 1297 (24 June 1879) (sic!) and the Shaikh of Ajman accepted the settlement." IOR R/15/1/268 "Ajman Affairs 1922–30" (including 1934).

22 See ibid. and IOR R/15/1/267 "Ajman Affairs 1910–21".

23 They had a common grandfather, Muḥammad Dhanji; see IOR R/15/1/267 "Ajman Affairs 1910–21", p. 82. They were related by marriage to the Residency Agent ʿAbdul Laṭīf, who in 1890 married one of their cousins; his son ʿĪsa, married another of their cousins in 1910.

24 In letters dated 2 January and 16 February 1912 from the Ruler of Dubai, Buṭi bin Suhail, to the Residency Agent, Khān Bahadur ʿAbul Laṭīf, the Bin Lūtāh are alleged to have made plans to kill the Residency Agent; see ibid. pp. 55f and 96f; Buṭi bin Suhail also indicated that if the British Government did not step in, the Residency Agent and Government would lose credibility.

25 Translation of the Arabic letter written on 24 February 1912 by the Political Resident on board R.I.M.S. *Lawrence* off ʿAjmān. Another 5,000 Rupees had to be deposited for one year as a security for future good conduct; on three pages the shortcomings of the Bin Lūtāh over two years are described in detail. IOR R/15/1/267, pp. 89ff.

26 See ibid., letter no. 146 from the Residency Agent to the Political Resident of 11 May 1913, p. 139.

27 They are named as Jumaʿh bin Muḥammad and Ḥumaid bin Saif; they owed Shaikh Dalmūk of Dubai 6,000 Rupees. See ibid., letter from Buṭi bin Suhail to the Residency Agent of 21st November 1911.

28 See extracts 7 and 8 from letter of proceedings no. 52 dated 22 April 1924 from the Senior Naval Officer in IOR R/15/1/268, p. 62. Ḥumaid bin ʿAbdul ʿAzīz sent there and then a letter to Saʿīd bin Maktūm, Ruler of Dubai, asking him to send back the divers, which he did; see ibid. p. 78.

29 See IOR R/15/1/267, letter no. 32 from the Residency Agent in Shārjah to the Political Resident in Bushire dated 12 January 1921, p. 248. Other foreigners who resided at Ḥīrah, for instance Persian traders and

their families, were said to number about 100. ʿAbdul Raḥman bin Muḥammad's claim, stated in his letter of June 1920 to the Residency Agent (IOR R/15/1/267, p. 174), is substantiated in a chronology of events of the late 18th century concerning the relationship between the shaikhs of ʿAjmān and Buraimi (ibid. pp. 218f, with letter no. 762 from the Residency Agent to the Political Resident dated 28 October 1920). A detailed account of events in ʿAjmān in June 1920 is given in letter no. 505 from the Residency Agent to the Political Resident dated 29 June 1920, pp. 169ff in IOR R/15/1/267.

30 The Residency Agent provided a list "showing the claims of British and foreign subjects against Abdur Rahman on account of diving" in letter no. 648 to the Political Resident dated 11 September 1920, pp. 212ff in IOR R/15/1/267.

31 While he was there, men of the Ruler of Shārjah unsuccessfully attacked the house. Therefore in a letter to Khālid bin Aḥmad, the Political Resident warned that he expected the Ruler of Shārjah to respect the pledge of safe conduct; however, he conceded that "in view of the chance of disturbances and reprisals etc. I think it is not an infringement of your guarantee to prohibit their residing in your territory for a time, so I agree to this." Letter of 26 July 1920, ibid., pp. 190f in IOR R/15/1/267.

32 Letter no. 509 from the Political Resident, Lt. Col. A.P. Trevor, to Ḥumaid bin ʿAbdul ʿAzīz, written on 21 October 1920 in IOR R/15/1/267, p. 214.

33 See letter no. 999 from the Residency Agent to the Political Agent dated 28 December 1920, p. 221 in IOR R/15/1/267.

34 ibid. p. 226, telegram no. 0700 from Senior Naval Officer, Captain Pearson, on *Triad* to Political Resident Bushire, 5 January 1921.

35 See ibid. p. 232f, telegram no. 0645 from Senior Naval Officer to Political Resident, 8 January 1921; see also the full report dated 13 January 1921 on pp. 235f, a translation of the treaty and a report by the Residency Agent in letter no. 30 to the Political Resident, dated 12 January 1921, pp. 242ff in IOR R/15/1/267.

36 Letter no. 65 dated 10 January 1921 in IOR R/15/1/267, p. 250. The refusal of the Ruler of ʿAjmān to join the gathering on *Triad* hastened the change of his image from one who had been wronged in June 1920 by ʿAbdul Raḥman's unjustifiable occupation of the fort of ʿAjmān to one who, in the eyes of the British officials, threatened the business and life of ʿAbdul Raḥman, whose creditors might then have to wait that much longer for their money.

37 See also above, footnote 23. The incident when the cousin of the Residency Agent was killed and its consequences are again referred to below, page 216.

38 In one such petition, written on 10 February 1927, some Persian subjects complained about the state of lawlessness, plunder and robberies gong

on in Shārjah at the time, which were alleged to be the responsibility of some *fidāwis* of the Ruler. This petition is similar to one written by 9 Banians and Hyderabadis in Shārjah on 12 February, see ibid. pp. 220ff.

39 See letter no. 33 from the Residency Agent to the Political Resident, dated 19 January 1927 in IOR R/15/1/279 "Attempted Murder of Residency Agent, Sharjah, II, 1926–29", p. 213ff and enclosed translation of a letter by Sulṭān bin Ṣaqr.

40 Because of the decline of the pearling industry and the Second World War such problems were put off and only became acute again when substantial numbers of people from other Muslim and some non-Muslim countries came to work in the Trucial States. The question of jurisdiction over these immigrants was therefore only tackled in the 1950s. See below, pages 314ff.

41 This development is described in greater detail in Chapter Seven.

42 In the days of Zāyid the Great a Rumaithi was appointed to the *sālifah al ghauṣ*; he was followed by Yūsuf bin Aḥmad, assisted by Muḥammad bin ʿAbdulghani al Khamīri, who held the post for twenty years; the last one was Khalfān bin Maṭar bin Jubārah. See also *UK Memorial I*, p. 67.

43 He, like many other local pearl merchants during the 1930s, was no longer able to dispose of the pearls for cash at the end of the season, but had to give them to an Indian merchant on credit and had to wait until that person had sold the pearls in Bombay. See letter no. 1109 from the Political Resident in Bushire to the Foreign Secretary in Simla, dated 29 May 1931, explaining this case, in IOR R/15/1/293, p. 40ff.

44 ibid. Saif bin ʿAbdullah himself did not remain headman of Ḥamrīyah for long because ʿAbdul Raḥman bin Saif's son Ḥumaid, who had been a roaming outcast since he had himself attempted to overthrow his father in 1922 and had later lived in Dubai, obtained the leadership in Ḥamrīyah some months later.

45 See letter no. 221 from the Residency Agent to the Political Resident, dated 9 June 1927 in IOR, R/15/1/276 pp. 130ff.

46 See translation of a letter of 12 April 1924 from the bin Lūtāh to the Residency Agent in IOR, R/15/1/268 pp. 75ff, in which they complain bitterly about the Ruler of ʿAjmān, his greed and ill treatment of them as British subjects.

47 See letter no. 147 from the Residency Agent to Political Resident, dated 25 April 1924, ibid p. 72f.

48 See IOR, R/15/1/236 "Arab States Monthly Summary 1929–1931", July 1929.

49 ibid. March 1930.

50 ibid. September 1930.

51 ibid. November 1930.

52 See extract from the Summary of News from the Arab States for the

Month of November 1932, no. 11, in IOR, L/P & S/12/3718 *Pearling 1929–48*.

53 For this and the following see the report to the Department of Overseas Trade, "Economic Conditions in the Persian Gulf", of October 1934, p. 19 of the printed version in IOR, L/P & S/12/3797 "Trade of the Gulf 1930–1948"; the quotation is on p. 20 of this report. The third point in the quotation was one which local pearl merchants seemed to consider as particularly important. See also Extract from Bahrain Intelligence no. 20, 15 November 1935, where it is reported that Māni' bin Rāshid said that he would be glad if a closed season were introduced in the Gulf and the pearling were cut down to a couple of months each year; IOR, L/P & S/12/3718.

54 See ibid., a memorandum prepared for the British Consulate General in New York in 1948, and a letter by a leading New York pearl dealer, Mr René Bloch. In the memorandum it was pointed out that principal pearl buyers who visited the Gulf or Bombay in previous years such as Mr L. Rosenthal were by 1948 dealing entirely in cultured pearls. Others, mostly French Jews from firms such as Pack, Bienenfeld and Murray bought directly from Arab pearl merchants in Bahrain. "Since Europeans ceased to come the market has shifted to Bombay and Bahrain dealers have to take their goods to India for selling." Letter from C.D. Belgrave, Adviser to the Government of Bahrain, dated 10 December, 1945, ibid. IOR, L/P & S/12/3718.

55 "This is due to the absence of rice and the difficulty of cooking wheat and baking bread in small overcrowded sailing vessels." Extract from Intelligence Summary of the Political Agency Bahrain for period of 1 to 15 May 1944 in IOR, L/P & S/12/3718.

56 See e.g. letter no. 702—J.S. By the Finance Department, Government of India, 3 August 1943 to the Financial Department, India Office, Whitehall in IOR, L/P & S/12/3718.

57 See Public Notices no. 813 issued by the Deputy Chief Controller of Imports and Exports on 21 November 1947, and the correspondence between the Residency in Bahrain and various departments in London in IOR, L/P & S/12/3718.

58 See, for instance, the assessments by American pearl importers such as Mr René Bloch of 610 Fifth Avenue, New York, in reply to enquiries made by the Commercial Secretary of the British Embassy in Washington in 1947–8; in IOR, L/P & S/12/3718 and footnote 53.

59 Extract from Bahrain Intelligence Summary for the period of 1 to 15 January 1948. The Ruler of Dubai was reported to have published a similar ban. See IOR, L/P & S/12/3718.

60 See extract from Confidential Report no. 81 from the Persian Gulf Residency, Bahrain, dated 8 June 1948, in IOR, L/P & S/12/3718.

61 In Bahrain the high and steady wages which could be obtained for work

in the refinery which was completed there in 1937 drew thousands of hands out of the declining pearling industry.

62 It is extremely difficult to identify such groups and therefore to verify this status within village communities in the Trucial States. Material concerning the origin, name and status of the *bayāsirah* has been compiled and evaluated by J.C. Wilkinson in an article in *Arabian Studies*, vol. 1, 1974 entitled "Bayāsirah and Bayādīr", pp. 75–85.

63 See Lorimer, *Geogr.*, p. 453.

64 Most of the information which the author could obtain so far on the position of a *bīdār* in the Trucial States oases corresponds with an account of his duties, payment etc. in Oman, which are described by Wilkinson, "Bayāsirah", pp. 80ff.

65 Khalīfah bin Zāyid bought for instance a garden called "al khris" from a certain Sālim bin ʿAli in 1940 for 150 Rupees. This garden was situated in Masʿūdi, and must therefore have become Sālim's property originally as a gift from that same shaikh, because it was he who established Masʿūdi in the first place. See Lorimer, *Geogr.*, p. 264 and *UK Memorial II*, Annex F, no. 5, p. 256.

66 According to the documents reproduced in the *UK Memorial II*, Annex F, no. 5, pp. 256f, he paid in four transactions recorded for the years 1946 and 1949 between 530 Rupees and 1,700 Rupees for such gardens; the sale always included the mud-brick boundary walls and a stated share of the *falaj* water (one sixth in the case of the garden in Hīli, one quarter in the case of one in Muʿtiriḍ).

67 The population table given in the *UK Memorial II*, Annex F, no. 1, p. 251 for the Buraimi oasis during the 1950s, shows that in the villages of Buraimi and Ḥamāsah 94 out of 369 houses were occupied by people who belonged to neither of the local tribes of the oasis and were either shop-keepers in the *sūq* of Buraimi village or farm labourers in the open fields, work which was looked down upon by tribal people.

68 As did for instance many Bani Yās, ʿAwāmir and Manāṣīr in the Buraimi oasis; see villages with asterisks in table in *UK Memorial II*, Annex F, no. 1, p. 251.

69 This does not apply to the members of the tribe called Balūsh, which has been in Dhāhirah for a very long time and is accepted as if it were an Arab tribe.

70 See Lorimer, *Geogr.*, p. 1938f. The Zaṭūṭ rendered services which the tribal Arab would not perform; many were goldsmiths, blacksmiths, armourers, carpenters and pedlars.

71 They are discussed on pages 281ff.

72 For details of these American and French ships see Lorimer, *Histor.*, p. 654. The incidents of piracy in the Gulf since 1778 are described in Lorimer, *Histor.*, pp. 633ff.

73 It was estimated at 1816 to consist of some 60 large boats carrying 80 to

300 people each and about 40 smaller ones; see Lorimer, *Histor.*, p. 656.

74 One such example of 1835 was described by Lorimer as: "an expiring flicker of the old piratical spirit, which this time flamed up, not among the subjects of the Qāsimi Shaikh, but in the formerly well-behaved and law-abiding tribe of the Bani Yās." *Histor.*, p. 682.

75 See IOR, R/15/1/236.

76 Ibid., April 1931.

77 Ibid., April 1931.

78 See Thesiger, *Arabian Sands*, p. 263 and 265. The high prices which were current during the 1920s were reached again in the late 1940s, i.e. between 1,000 and 1,500 Rupees for a negro. But because it was very much more difficult to sell free Arabs they fetched a very much lower price (400 Rupees in the 1920s; only 230 Rupees were paid for two *sayyids* from the Hadhramaut who were to be sold by a Shaikh in Ḥamāsah to ʿAli al Murri). See for the early reference letter no. 539 from the Residency Agent to the Political Resident of 11 July 1920 in IOR, R/15/1/239. "Miscellaneous Dec. 1904–Nov. 1922."

79 One such instance would be if someone's camel had earlier in the year strayed into and damaged someone's date garden and the owner of the camel was sentenced to pay the owner of the garden so many *man* of his dates at harvest time.

CHAPTER SEVEN

1 In 1969 Dubai's production was half a million tons, while Abu Dhabi exported 28.9 million long tons; by 1974 Dubai had reached 13 million but Abu Dhabi had increased to 68 million. The income from oil was estimated at 3,000 million U.S. Dollars in Dubai in 1980 as compared to 15,000 million Dollars for Abu Dhabi.

2 "Notwithstanding the separate signature on behalf of its chief Hazzaʿ-bin-Zaʿal, then a minor, of the General Treaty of Peace in 1820, Dibai appears to have existed . . . as a dependency of the Abu Dhabi Shaikhdom." (Lorimer, *Histor.*, p. 772). See also for the following, ibid. pp. 772–5, Annexure no. 3: "International History of the Dibai Principality".

3 This incident is described by Lorimer, *Histor.*, p. 765 as follows: "This violence on the part of Shaikh Khalīfah (of Abu Dhabi) was highly prejudicial to his own interests, for it led to the secession from Abu Dhabi to Dibai, during the pearl fishery, of a large number of Bani Yās of the Al Bū Falāsah section. Dibai . . . seems to have been readily surrendered by the individual who then governed it . . . to the seceders; and they, in the following autumn, were joined there by the bulk of their relatives, returning from the pearl banks. The secession was permanent,

almost the entire body of the Al Bū Falāsah being to the present day domiciled at Dibai."

4 Shaikh Maktūm bin Buṭi was followed in 1852 by his brother Sa'īd bin Buṭi, who died in 1859 of smallpox. From 1859 to 1886 Ḥashar bin Maktūm was the Ruler, followed by his brother Rāshid bin Maktūm (1886–94). The latter's nephew Maktūm bin Ḥashar was Ruler from 1894–1906. An uncle, Buṭi bin Suhail, ruled from 1906–12 when Sa'īd bin Maktūm, who was a minor at the time of the death of his father Maktūm bin Ḥashar, took over and ruled until his death in 1958. Shaikh Rāshid bin Sa'īd was the Ruler until his death in October 1990.

5 According to Lorimer, there were 67 Hindus and 23 Khojahs, including women and children, settled in Dubai at the time of the last count before the Gazetteer was printed; Lorimer, *Geogr.*, p. 455.

6 See Lorimer, *Geogr.*, p. 1121f and p. 1204.

7 Lorimer, *Histor.*, p. 2256.

8 See Lorimer, *Histor.*, pp. 2286f and above, pages 113ff.

9 For example Ḥumaid bin 'Abdul Raḥman bin Saif Āl Bū Shāmis, who had unsuccessfully tried to oust his father from the headmanship of Ḥamrīyah in 1922, settled in Dubai after his cousins had murdered his father in 1931; he succeeded in expelling them from Ḥamrīyah and became headman. See above, page 98.

10 On Bastak see Lorimer, *Geogr.*, p. 279f.

11 Khamīr, on the coast of the Bastak district, about 12 miles WNW of Lāft on Qishim Island, was an example of the close relationship between the populations on the opposite coasts of the Gulf; Lorimer described the port: "Khamīr contains about 350 houses, and the total population may be 1,800 souls. The people, except a very few, are Sunnis and belong to various Arab tribes: they are chiefly engaged in navigation, fishing, date-growing, wood-cutting and lime-burning." (*Geogr.*, p. 1016).

12 See the detailed study on the construction and use of a house in the Bastakīyah by Anne Coles and Peter Jackson, entitled: *A Windtower House in Dubai.* Art and Archaeology Research Papers, June 1975 (102 St Paul's Road, London N.1.).

13 *See Trucial States Census Figures 1968*, published in mimeograph by the Development Office of the Trucial States Council. Of the 12,193 households of Dubai, 6,189 were then accommodated in stone and mud-brick houses.

14 The word *barasti* is not Arabic and is predominantly used by English-speaking foreigners. The local word for a palm-frond house is *'arīsh* or *khaimah* (pl. *khiyām*). Handhal speculates that the word is of Spanish origin, See Handhal, Fāliḥ, *Mu'ajam al Alfadh al 'Āmīyah* (*The Dictionary of the local dialect of the UAE*), published by the UAE Ministry of Information and Culture, Abu Dhabi, (about 1979).

15 The piece of land on which they built their houses was either bought or

was granted by the Ruler; but whether someone settled in the densely built-up areas near the *sūq* or further outside, the Ruler's consent always had to be obtained either personally or through the original contact, the headman of the tribe or quarter.

16 Maktūm bin Ḥashar (1894–1906) lived in the fort near Shindaghah and used to come almost every morning to Dairah to talk to the merchants and settle their disputes and problems. Buṭi bin Suhail (1906–12) resided in an ordinary house near the creek in Dairah and visited Dubai and Shindaghah frequently for the same purpose.

17 For many years during the rule of Shaikh Sa'īd bin Maktūm there was one officially appointed *qāḍi*; after he died two *qāḍis* were appointed. See also above, pages 159f.

18 Gray Mackenzie and Co. opened an office in Basra in the middle of the 19th century to handle steamers of the British Indian Steam Navigation Co., See Griffiths, Sir Percival, *A History of the Inchcape Group*, London, 1977, Inchcape & Co., Chapter Five, "The Gulf".

19 Outside port limits the Persian Gulf Lighting Service maintained a lightship and serviced all lights and buoys; nowadays this service is performed by the Middle East Navigation Aid Service based in Bahrain. Each ship pays a fee for this service, which is collected at the first port of call.

20 See proclamation by the Ruler of Dubai issued on 21 July 1955: "In pursuance of the general reorganisation of the Departments of our State, we have decided that in future all customs duty shall be paid direct to the Official Customs banking account, we have opened with the British Bank of the Middle East, and to this end we have decreed that in future no institution, whether Shipping Agents, Airline representatives or Post Officer, functioning in our territory may issue a Delivery Order or deliver goods, to the consignee(s) or his (their) order unless the Bill of Lading, or document tendered in place thereof, is supported by the Customs Receipt of the British Bank of the Middle East, Dubai, evidencing that Customs Duty has been received by them for the credit of our official Dubai Customs Account."

21 See below, pages 255ff.

22 See also pages 152f, 231ff and 288ff.

23 A civil air agreement to provide night-stop facilities for Imperial Airways was signed on 23 July 1937.

24 As in the agreement with other Trucial Rulers and the Sultan of Oman, the royalty was fixed at 3 Rupees per ton once oil exports started. (Longrigg, St H. *Oil in the Middle East*, 3rd edn., London, 1968, p. 116). The annual rent was some 50,000 Rupees.

25 See above, page 219 and footnote 48 of Chapter Six, see also IOR, R/15/1/236 "Arab States Monthly Summary 1929–31", July 1929.

26 The following quotation from a Report for the Department of Overseas

Trade by F.H. Gamble, Acting British Vice-Consul in Bushire, on the Economic Conditions in the Persian Gulf of October 1934, (HMSO, no. 601) underlines some of the problems: "Very different trade conditions prevailed on the Arab and Persian sides of the Gulf. On the Arab side, customs duties ranged from 4 per cent to 15 per cent but there were no restrictions on the quantities of merchandise imported and exported and the statistics for the year (1 April 1933 to 31 March 1934) show that the total volume of trade though still far below the level of five or six years ago, increased slightly in comparison with that of the previous year. . . . On the Persian side, . . . it is doubtful if there will be an increase owing to the numerous regulations which remained in force . . . In addition to the difficulties of a quota system and the payment of customs duties and road tax, merchants importing into Persia were faced with the necessity of procuring certificates of export before they could obtain certificates of import and when importing certain classes of goods . . . and of first purchasing foreign exchange from the Government at unfavourable rates. The monopolies of opium, sugar and matches contributes still further to their difficulties . . . with the result that money became generally scarce." (p. 5) in IOR, L/P & S/12/3797 "Trade of the Gulf 1930–1948".

27 All these items are mentioned regularly in the "Extracts from the Diary of the British Residency and Consulate General Bushire", which are collected in the file entitled "Smuggling in the Gulf 1928–38", IOR L/P & S/12/3766. The procedure is for instance explained in paragraph 86 of the Extract from the Diary of the British Resident in Bushire for June 1935: "The (Persian) gun boat *Chahrokh* succeeded in catching 2 smugglers' dhows in June. One of them had the following goods on board: 20 bags sugar, 10 boxes tea, 5 bales cotton fabrics and the other a sum of Rials 170,000 of Iranian silver which smugglers had sent out to buy Rupees with. It is reported that smugglers can buy Rupees at Fao and in other Arab ports at the rate of Rials 290 per hundred while the rate of exchange for Rupees in Bushire is Rials 600 to 620 a hundred. The smuggling of silver coins is reported to be vigorous in the Gulf ports."

28 See IOR L/P & S/12/3766 (P.Z. 7888/34) Extract for November 1934.

29 Had this been the case, the British Government of India might have been obliged to step in, but as it was it could—not without lengthy internal consultations—adopt the view that smuggling was a Persian problem and that the Indian Navy would not police the Gulf on behalf of the Persian Government for nothing and even risk being driven out of Persian ports. See in particular correspondence during 1929 between the British Ambassador in Teheran, the Foreign Office, the Admiralty and the Political Resident in IOR L/P & S/12/3766.

30 See for instance, extract from Teheran despatch no. 89 dated 16

February 1929, repeated in a letter from the SNO then at Bombay, to the Political Resident in Bushire, revising his earlier statement, L/P & S/12/3766.

31 See for a description of the various circumstances in which these many clashes took place from 1929, a collection of the IOR R/15/1/285 "Unrest at Dubai and Trucial Coast Policy 1934–36".

32 See for the following Rosemarie J. Said, "The 1938 Reform Movement in Dubai" in: *Al-Abhath*, A Quarterly Journal for Arab Studies Published by the American University, Beirut, vol. XXIII, nos. 1–4, Dec. 1970, pp. 247–318. Many details of the plans, achievements and frustrations of the "Majlis" are given in the correspondence which was conducted between the leaders of the reform movement, the Ruler and the Residency Agent in Shārjah. This material was deposited with the Political Agent in Bahrain and is now in the IOR under R/15/2/1882. The entire collection was transcribed by R. Said and forms the documentary part of her paper on the movement (pp. 264–318).

33 See for the following Rosemarie Said, *Al-Abhath*, p. 258. This idea is voiced in a letter by Ḥashar to Saʿīd (p. 308 of Appendix) in which he tries to convince the Ruler that the income from oil concessions and the air facilities should be added to the state funds so that the well-being of the state could be promoted. This is an important letter because it gives in six points the principles of the ideas of the *Majlis* on "constitutional rule" in Dubai.

34 The first school, called al Aḥmadīyah, was opened on 10 Shawal (3 December 1938). As soon as it opened 200 students were enrolled; three teachers and a servant were appointed to it. Al Saʿada school opened with two teachers for 60 students and only days later al Falāḥ (Falāsah?) school was opened with three teachers in Dubai; see letter from Māniʿ to Saʿīd of 15 December 1938 in Said, *Al-Abhath*, Appendix p. 283.

35 The first well on the Trucial Coast was spudded at Ra's al Ṣadr in Abu Dhabi territory in February 1950. After 13 months' drilling the well was abandoned and the rig was moved to Jabal ʿAli, a hill to the west of Dubai, which according to a recent delimitation made by the Political Resident was inside the shaikhdom of Dubai (see Longrigg, *Oil*, p. 233).

36 A sum of money was given to the Ruler of Shārjah, Shaikh Ṣaqr bin Sulṭān, by the Ruler of Qatar to improve the creek, but it was never used for that purpose.

37 The dredging provided about 7 feet of water at low tide and 12 feet at high tide over the shallowest part at the entrance to the creek. The spoil from dredging also proved very welcome to protect Shindaghah, where the beach was eroding away.

38 By 1966 two steel-piled, fendered wharfs, each with 60-feet-wide heavy duty pavements were completed. The East Wharf had 270,000 square

feet of open storage and 39,000 square feet of warehouse storage. Seven mobile cranes and three forklift trucks were available for both wharfs.

39 The power station came into operation in July 1961 on the Dairah side; the capacity was then 6,400 Kw. In the following years essential services, such as water and telephones, and the operation of Port Rāshid were also all organised on a commercial basis. Dubai Port Services, which was given a charter by the Ruler and is directly answerable to him, is expected to earn a reasonable return but does not have to recover the original capital cost of the harbour.

40 Examples were Dubai Airport Services, Dubai Post Office and Dubai Port Services, a subsidiary of Gray Mackenzie & Co. of Dubai.

41 One of the reasons for going ahead with building this airstrip and a small administration building was that the Ruler of Shārjah, Shaikh Ṣaqr bin Sulṭān, had tried to put a tax on the gold which came into Shārjah by air but was bound for Dubai.

42 The cost of reclaiming was sometimes as little as one thousandth of the value of the land obtained after dredging was completed.

43 The step from land management and town planning to formal building licences issued and supervised by the Municipality was an obvious one. Previously the Ruler had to be consulted if someone wanted to put up a new building, but as for the actual construction of the building and the observation of safety or fire precautions, the owner was largely free to handle this in any way he chose.

44 The exact figure of the census taken in Spring 1968 was 58,971 inhabitants. In December 1980 it was 278,440.

45 When India gained independence in 1947 it took several years for the British government to re-assess the British policy towards the Trucial States. It was decided to adopt some responsibility for their internal security and to give financial and practical assistance for development projects. See also, below, pages 319ff and Hawley, *Trucial States*, pp. 243ff.

46 In 1962 £100,000 Sterling capital for hospital improvement and £40,000 Sterling for recurrent expenditure were given by the British Government. See also, below page 325.

47 Members of this committee included all the seven Rulers, Mr ʿĪsa Gurg (longstanding Dubai employee of the British Bank of the Middle East), Mr W.R. Duff (Director of the Customs Department), Mr Kendall (Director of the Trucial States Development Office), Dr Ross (Maktum Hospital) and the British Political Agent in Dubai. The committee was disbanded in 1970.

48 There was an outbreak of smallpox in Dubai in 1967; vaccinations were carried out by the Trucial States Council's medical services, the Maktūm Hospital, and the Political Agency's medical services, under the co-ordination of the Council's Health Adviser, Dr ʿĀṣim Jamāli.

49 With the exception of an extra Dh 100 a day for a private room, all treatment, medicine and hospitalisation have always been free for everyone there. It opened in April 1973.

50 In the mid 1970s there were about 40 doctors in private practice in Dubai, mostly of Indian and Pakistani nationality.

51 By the school year 1967–8 when 38 schools existed already in the Trucial States, 28 of them were financed and run by the Kuwaiti government. See also below, pages 332.

52 The intake for 1960/61 was a total of 30 students; see also for the following, Trucial States Council *Report, 1969*, p. 7.

53 Subjects taught were Arabic and English language, Arabic and English typing, mathematics and accountancy, business administration, office practice and procedure, commercial law and commercial geography. The annual intake was 15 and the course lasted for 3 years.

54 Major P. Lorimer, who was the first commander, was succeeded by Major J. Briggs, who had already served in several Arab countries including Bahrain and Qatar. He remained in charge until 1975 after which he was retained as an adviser.

55 Most Indian, Iranian, British, American, French, German and Dutch children are educated in schools built by their own community and do not contribute to the numbers of pupils in Dubai state schools. The number of expatriate Arab children had reached 80 per cent in some of the higher classes in secondary schools of the government by 1981.

56 The manpower needed to operate the huge workshops, where every component of a super tanker could be replaced, puts this project into the category of a large factory; it may not be described as a service industry.

CHAPTER EIGHT

1 See Danvers, F.C., *The Portuguese in India*, 2 vols (1st edn, 1894) repr. 1966, and Arnold Wilson, *The Persian Gulf*, London, 3rd repr., 1959, pp. 92ff. For the whole period of Portuguese domination of the Indian Ocean and the Gulf see also Serjeant, R.B., *The Portuguese off the South Arabian Coast*, 1974.

2 See Albuquerque, Alfonso de, *The Commentaries of the Great Affonso Dalboquerque*. 4 vols Hakluyt Society, 1875, p. 93; see also Miles, *Countries*, pp. 137ff, and Hawley, *Trucial States*, p. 71f.

3 See e.g. Miles, *Countries*, pp. 191, 195 and 198, on role of Khaṣab.

4 The Turks were repeatedly locked in battle with the Portuguese and later the Persians, and there had been unsuccessful or shortlived attempts by the Turks in 1550 and 1581 to capture Muscat. Midhat Pasha, the Turkish Wālī in Baghdad (1868–72) succeeded in bringing al Ḥasā and Qatar under Ottoman control. There was a small Turkish

garrison at Doha, but there was never a Turkish presence anywhere on the Trucial Coast.

5 See above, pages 68ff.

6 "The subjects of the Qāsimi, to whatever tribe they might belong, were generally spoken of as Qawāsim; and it seems possible that, abroad, the name was applied to almost all Arabs hailing from the western coast of the 'Oman promontory. It was the decline of Persian influence in the Gulf after the death of Nadir Shah that in the end brought the Qawāsim upon the general scene". (Lorimer, *Histor.*, p. 631). See also above, page 68 and footnote 109 of Chapter Two.

7 See above pages 21f, and see also for the following Kelly, *Britain*, p. 4 and 8ff, Miles, *Countries*, pp. 238ff and Landen, R.G. *Oman*, Princeton, 1967, pp. 34f.

8 For a detailed description of the course of the Civil War see Lorimer, *Histor.*, pp. 403ff.

9 The chronology of events leading to the end of the Civil War is a subject of disagreement among the various sources for this period. See for different dates Kelly, *Britain*, p. 9 footnote 3 and p. 10.

10 When Sa'īd bin Aḥmad's grandson Ḥamad became virtual Ruler of Oman during his father's lifetime, he did not attempt to become the *Imām* but he adopted the title of *Sayyid*, meaning Lord; during the second half of the 19th century the title of *Sultan* took its place; see for this development Kelly, *Britain*, pp. 11ff.

11 One such exception are the Bani Ghāfir themselves, whose Dhāhirah-based section changed to become Hināwi after they once felt badly let down by the Ghāfirīyah, who did not assist them when they were attacked.

12 The principal sources are the enumerations in Miles, *Countries*, pp. 422ff, and Lorimer, *Geogr.*, pp. 1391–1411 and p. 1437.

13 They were subordinate to the Qawāsim; it may also have something to do with the Hināwi connections that Shaikh Zāyid bin Sulṭān offered them the right of residence in Abu Dhabi, when a large number of them fell out with the Ruler of Ra's al Khaimah and emigrated from Jazīrah al Za'āb in 1969.

14 The word "Wahhābi" derives from the name of the founder but is not used by those who adhere to this strict form of Islamic observance. They call themselves either simply Muslim or Muwaḥḥidūn (Unitarians). See for a description of the movement e.g. Kelly, *Britain*, pp. 45ff with a guide to further material on the subject in English.

15 Burckhardt, J.L., *Notes on the Beduins and Wahābys, collected during his Travels in the East,* 2 vols, London, 1831, p. 286.

16 The history of repeated Wahhābi incursions into Oman during the 19th century may be followed in detail in Kelly, *Britain*, pp. 102ff and elsewhere.

17 In 1839/40 Sa'ad bin Muṭlaq, a former Wahhābi *wāli* in Buraimi, came to Shārjah hoping to re-occupy Buraimi in the name of the new Wahhābi Ruler, Khālid bin Sa'ūd, but it was feared that he was acting on behalf of the Egyptian general Khurshid Pasha; see Kelly, *Britain*, pp. 313f and 328ff.

18 Incorporated in London by Queen Elizabeth I on 31 December 1600 as the "Governor and Company of Merchants of London trading into the East Indies"; 217 merchants subscribed at the time; see Lorimer, *Histor.*, p. 10.

19 Factories, whether located in Europe or in the colonies, were organisations which ran warehouses and could sell the commodities which were consigned to them on account of their principals; they guaranteed the credit of purchases and could make cash advances to their principals before the actual sale of the goods. The warehouse-cum-office compound was often fortified.

20 For an account of the siege by the combined forces and the distribution of the spoil afterwards, see Lorimer, *Histor.*, pp. 23ff.

21 The Gulf is no exception to the rule that wherever there was profitable trade conveyed across a sea whose shores offered refuge for the local population in their bid to intercept the merchant vessels, piracy was likely to flare up time and again. For such outbreaks of piracy in the Gulf before the arrival of the Portuguese see Hawley, *Trucial States*, p. 90f; Wilson, *Persian Gulf*, 1959, p. 192f, footnote 2. See also J.R. Perry, "Mīr Muhannā and the Dutch: Patterns of Piracy in the Persian Gulf" in *Studia Iranica* 2 (1973), pp. 79–95.

22 These cases were all minutely reported in the records of the East India Company which formed part of the material from which Lorimer's Gazetteer was compiled; see Lorimer, *Histor.*, pp. 633ff and elsewhere.

23 Description of such incidents are numerous in all the accounts of the Portuguese conquest and rule. See Alfonso de Albuquerque, *Commentaries*, and Danvers, *Portuguese*, in particular vol. 1, pp. 158ff on the capture of Quriyāt, Muscat and Khaur Fakkān.

24 Printed in Aitchison, *A collection of Treaties, Engagements and Sanads relating to India and neighbouring Countries*, vol. XI, Delhi, 1933, pp. 287ff.

25 For a description of the various encounters between British and Qāsimi vessels, leading up to the expeditions of 1809 and 1819/20 and the first British treaty with the Qawāsim in 1806, see Lorimer, *Histor.*, pp. 636ff; Kelly, *Britain*, pp. 99ff; and Moyse-Bartlett, H. *The Pirates of Trucial Oman*, London 1966, pp. 32ff and pp. 237ff. The Ruler of Shārjah, Dr. Sulṭān bin Muḥammad Āl Qāsimi is the author of a book which refutes the claims that such encounters can be termed acts of piracy: *The Myth of Arab Piracy in the Gulf*, 2nd ed. London, 1988. At the end of 1809 a joint British-Omani operation took the Qawāsim-held fort at Shināṣ on the Shamailīyah coast; Kelly, Britain, 118ff.

26 See Kelly, *Britain*, pp. 139ff.

27 After the tribal leaders of Shārjah, Abu Dhabi, Dubai, ʻAjmān and Umm al Qaiwain had signed preliminary treaties of truce in the weeks following the surrender of Ḥasan bin Raḥmah of Jazīrah al Hamrā' on 9 December 1819, Keir ordered a squadron to search every port on the coast between Ra's al Khaimah and Dubai for warlike vessels, strong fortifications, and British Indian prisoners. Several dozens of vessels, worth about 300,000 Rupees, were destroyed or impounded and handed over to the Omanis. See Kelly, *Britain*, pp. 154ff.

28 Sulṭān bin Ṣaqr's authority as shaikh of all the Qawāsim was reduced firstly by the emergence of a rival, Ḥasan bin Raḥmah, who threatened British shipping from Bandar ʻAbbās against Sulṭān bin Ṣaqr's will, even after a treaty had been signed between the Qawāsim and the British in February 1806, secondly by the Wahhābis, who allowed him only to rule over Ra's al Khaimah and then took him into custody in 1809 in their capital Daraʻiyah while Ḥasan bin Raḥmah ruled in Ra's al Khaimah. Sulṭān bin Ṣaqr escaped eventually and assumed his authority as Ruler of Shārjah before the major confrontation with the British in 1819/20. He had tried to co-operate with the British authorities by making them appreciate that the Qawāsim deserved to have their share in the Gulf trade restored to them, and he was the first Ruler to tender his unconditional surrender in January 1820. The British were eager to see him reinstated as the Ruler over all the Qawāsim of the Arab coast.

29 Since no instructions had arrived from the Presidency in Bombay by the time the British fleet had to leave the coast of Ra's al Khaimah for reasons of safety in the approaching season of strong north winds, Keir himself had to take the decision of how to turn the military success of early December into a political one. Most of the text of the treaty which he presented to the Rulers was, in fact, drafted by his interpreter, Captain T. Perronet Thompson. The latter had struck up friendships with many of the shaikhs and the people of Ra's al Khaimah. See Moyse-Bartlett, *Pirates*, pp. 99ff, with the text of the "General Treaty with the Arab Tribes of the Persian Gulf" on pp. 239–41. A photographic reproduction of the signed and sealed Arabic version of this treaty is held by the Centre for Documentation and Research in Abu Dhabi.

30 ". . . an arrangement for this purpose shall take place between the friendly Arabs and the British at the time when such plunder and piracy shall occur." (Moyse-Bartlett, *Pirates*, Appendix, p. 240). For full details of the signators of the 1820 treaty, see Lorimer, *Histor.*, p. 671, and Kelly, *Britain*, p. 156ff.

31 The clause about slavery was written into the agreement at the personal insistence of translator, Captain T. Perronet Thompson, who in later years often pointed out as an MP and publicist, that this was the first

instance when the disapproval of this trade had assumed the character of an official agreement.

32 Qishim was a base only for two years and was eventually superseded by Bāsīdu. See Kelly, *Britain*, pp. 167ff, Lorimer, *Histor.*, p. 676. The force consisted in 1823 of four cruisers patrolling the Gulf and one cruiser employed for supplies and communications.

33 Earlier, some pearl merchants of Shārjah had actually offered payment to the British Government if the safety of their boats at sea could be guaranteed. See Lorimer, *Histor.*, p. 695, and for the texts of the ten-year "Maritime Peace" and the "Perpetual Treaty of Peace of 1853" see Aitchison, *Treaties*, 1933 edn pp. 250 and 252.

34 For a brief summary of the stages leading to this point see e.g. Wilson, *Persian Gulf*, pp. 213ff and Eldon Rutter, "Slavery in Arabia", *Journal of the Royal Central Asian Society*, vol. XX, 1933, pp. 315–32.

35 Aitchison, *Treaties*, 1933 edn p. 289f. The fact that slavery became a somewhat overrated issue in the relationship between the Government of India and the Arab principalities, particularly Oman, cannot be sufficiently explained through the incidence and the nature of slavery in that part of the world. It rather reflects the fixation which many British politicians developed as a result of a sense of "national conscience" over the very active part played by some Englishmen in this trade, which flourished most of all in the New World of both Americas. The overreaction in the Arab context can almost be compared to the bending over backwards of the new German Government to demands of the Israeli Government after the Second World War. The general sense of guilt spurred the authorities into enormous efforts in order to wipe out or make redress for what happened in the past.

36 For details of further agreements with Oman see Wilson, *Persian Gulf*, pp. 216ff and Lorimer, *Histor.*, p. 2475 to 2516.

37 See Lorimer, *Histor.*, p. 725.

38 The Native Agent was in fact never during the 19th century a person of tribal origin from the Arab coast of the Gulf, but usually an Arabic-speaking Muslim from the Indian subcontinent or the Persian coast. For a list of the names of people holding this post between 1829 and 1890 see Lorimer, *Histor.*, p. 2678; see for further names until this appointment was abolished in 1949, Hawley, *Trucial States*, p. 328 and Said-Zahlan, *Origins*, pp. 248ff.

39 This was not the first instance when the British Government assumed the right to collect a fine if certain conditions were not met by the shaikhs. The treaty which was concluded between the East India Company and the Qawāsim on February 1806 laid down a fine of 30,000 M.T. Dollars to be paid by Sulṭān bin Ṣaqr if the Qawāsim did infringe on the conditions of the treaty. See Aitchison, *Treaties*, vol. XI, 1933 edn pp. 239ff. A fine of 25,000 M.T. Dollars was imposed on the Ruler of Abu

Dhabi, Zāyid bin Khalīfah in September 1868 for an attack on the Qatari coast. See Aitchison, *Treaties*, vol. XI, 1933 edn pp. 254f. In the latter case, the rest was remitted after the first instalment was paid.

40 Text of the agreement printed in Lorimer, *Histor.*, pp. 784f.

41 This matter became a preoccupation of the Residency Agent and the Resident to the extent of taking at times priority over fair judgement, as for instance in the case when 'Abdul Raḥman bin Muḥammad al Shāmisi of Ḥīrah occupied without obvious justification the fort of the Ruler of 'Ajmān in June 1920. The first reaction of the Resident was to severely punish 'Abdul Raḥman, who had substantial interests in the pearling industry. Later on, however, the Resident adopted the Residency Agent's view, arguing that the considerable claims which British and foreign, in particular Persian, subjects had on 'Abdul Raḥman could never be met by the latter, if he were deprived of the means to earn enough money to pay back these debts. If he were to seek refuge with a tribe of the hinterland, the British subjects would also lose their chance of recovering the money. Thus, upon the news of 'Abdul Raḥman returning to Ḥīrah and of the approach of a joint Shārjah/'Ajmān force appearing at Ḥīrah, the Resident ordered a man-of-war to pass by, and on 8 January 1921 Captain Pearson on HMS *Triad* effected an agreement between 'Abdul Raḥman and the Shaikh of Shārjah. The former was allowed to reside unmolested in Ḥīrah. See IOR, R/15/1/268 *'Ajman Affairs 1922–1930*.

42 Bahrain, Kuwait and Qatar, were in similar treaty relationship with Britain, while the Sultan of Muscat and Oman had for economic, political and strategic advantages to either side become very much more dependent on the consent of the British Government of India even for day-to-day matters such as the levy of export taxes.

43 For details see Wilson, *Persian Gulf*, pp. 237ff.

44 In 1891 two Frenchmen visited the coast who were suspected of wanting to negotiate some privileges, possibly the lease of land for an agency; see Lorimer, *Histor.*, p. 738. They had some shortlived success in Umm al Qaiwain.

45 Aitchison, *Treaties*, vol. XI, 1933 edn and Lorimer, *Histor.*, pp. 738ff, with the text of the agreement on p. 786.

46 Identical or similar agreements were concluded with Oman, Bahrain and Kuwait and also with the states on the south western coast of Arabia (the so-called Protectorate Treaties of 1888 and after) and with a number of tribal states along the North West Frontier of India.

47 The proposal to make Oman (or at least Muscat) and the shaikhdoms proper protectorates, was repeatedly discussed in Parliament in London during 1902; it was eventually abandoned because it was convincingly argued that this would imply an unnecessary effort to control the hinterland. Instead, the Trucial States, Kuwait, Bahrain, Oman, Qatar

and the principalities of south western Arabia were also in the 20th century made to conclude specific treaties for specific issues which touched on British interests. When and where the need arose, agreements were made concerning trade, customs, monopolies, legal protection for British Indian subjects, subsidies for health measures, telegraph lines, postal stations, navigational demarcation, etc.

48 At the request of the Persian Government as much as for the sake of securing the peace in the area, Britain tried to suppress the large-scale arms traffic which had developed during and after the Afghan War of 1879–80. The Trucial Rulers signed an agreement in 1902 to prohibit the import and export of arms and ammunition for sale. See Lorimer, *Histor.*, Appendix N, pp. 2556–93, with the text of the 1902 agreement on pp. 1588f.

49 A similar undertaking was given by the Shaikh of Kuwait; see Aitchison, *Treaties*, vol. XI, 1933 edn p. 263.

50 This was demonstrated by the many cases in which British, Indian and other nationalities were prevented from participating in the pearling industry in order not to disturb this prime source of income for the Arab littoral population.

51 An undertaking to this effect was given in a letter by Shaikh Khālid bin Aḥmad, Ruler of Shārjah, written on 17 February 1922; a similar letter was written by the Ruler of Ra's al Khaimah on 22 February. The Rulers of Abu Dhabi, 'Ajmān and Umm al Qaiwain gave, on 3, 4 and 8 May 1922 respectively, written promises similar to the one given by the Ruler of Dubai on 2 May 1922 which had stated: "Let it not be hidden from you that we agree, if oil is expected to be found in our territory, not to grant any concession in this connection to any one except to the person appointed by the High British Government." Aitchison, *Treaties*, vol. XI, 1933 edn p. 261.

52 See Longrigg, *Oil*, 1961, pp. 12ff and pp. 27ff.

53 The New Zealander, Major Holmes, had obtained in 1924 an exploration agreement from the Ruler of Bahrain. The investment required for exploration anywhere in Eastern Arabia was considered too high by British oil companies, and Holmes could only dispose of his concession to an American firm, which had to be made to "look British" to fulfil the terms of the 1914 undertaking, by incorporating it in Canada in 1930 as Bahrain Petroleum Company (BAPCO), a subsidiary of Standard Oil Co. of California.

54 The shareholding in the IPC at the time was as follows: 23.75 per cent each to BP, Shell, Compagnie Française des Pétroles, and Near East Development Corporation (half Mobil and half Standard Oil Co. of New Jersey) and 5 per cent to Participations and Explorations (Gulbenkian).

55 An agreement between the Standard Oil Co. of California and King 'Abdul 'Azīz was concluded in July 1933; this was conducive to the

sudden interest of IPC in the remaining areas of Eastern Arabia. "It was therefore rather in prudent self-defence than in spirit of self-aggrandizement that the IPC looked abroad in 1933 and thereafter," Longrigg, *Oil*, p. 113.

56 In the shaikhdoms other than Abu Dhabi various people were involved. The name of the company interested in oil concessions here was changed in 1935 to Anglo-Iranian Oil Co. According to Mann these options were obtained thanks to Ḥajji Williamson, an English adventurer and then an employee of the IPC. See Mann, Clarence *Abu Dhabi: Birth of an Oil Sheikhdom*, Beirut 1964, pp. 84f; and Stanton-Hope, W.E. *Arabian Adventurer: The Story of Haji Williamson*, London, 1951, pp. 310ff.

57 The Ruler of Ra's al Khaimah wanted all the Trucial Shaikhs to conduct the negotiations jointly with PD (TC).

58 When the Ruler of Kalba died in April 1937, Sulṭān bin Sālim tried to establish his sovereignty over this former Qāsimi province. Despite warnings by the Political Residency he proceeded to Kalba with a force of armed men and was eventually punished for his action by being forcibly taken to Bahrain. See also above pages 91ff.

59 In 1864 a station was established on an island in the Elphinstone Inlet at the tip of the Musandam Peninsula; the island was then claimed by the Ruler of Shārjah. But in the 1920s the then Ruler of Shārjah could not uphold this claim to Shiḥūḥ territory and thus could no longer guarantee the safety of the station. The telephone line through this station was abandoned in favour of the line running along the Persian coast.

60 The Shaikh of Dubai refused in 1906 to agree to the establishment of a post office which would have served primarily the Indian merchants on the coast and was seen by the population of Dubai as yet another sign of imminent annexation of their territory by the British Government.

61 See above pages 214f and footnote 41 of this chapter.

62 This was built on the seashore of Shārjah in the shape of a local fort. It provided rooms and messing for about 15 people. When it was no longer used by Imperial Airways the building became the Seaface Hotel before it was turned into a police station in 1973.

63 Thus the British authorities became involved in the protracted disputes over the succession to rule in Kalba after Shaikh Saʿīd's death in April 1937. See also above, pages 91ff.

64 Geologists of Petroleum Concessions Ltd. (later PD (TC)) explored some *wādis* of Ra's al Khaimah territory in 1935 and again in 1936. On both occasions they encountered stiff opposition from the Shiḥūḥ and the Khawāṭir, who claimed that the party had entered their territory. Similar incidents happened near Jabal Fāyah, for which the Ruler of

Shārjah had given permission for a visit by PCL geologists in 1937; in this case the Bani Qitab claimed the area as their *dār*.

65 For continuation of the narrative on oil exploration see below pages 306f.

66 Qaṣr al Ṣubbārah, built in spring 1800 and used for 18 years as a base for forays into Oman. A Wahhābi force was in possession of Buraimi again from 1833 to 1839, from 1845 to 1850, and from 1853 to 1869 the oasis was occupied by the Amīr Faiṣal bin Turki's strong troops while he was a dependent of the Ottoman Porte. See also above, pages 278f.

67 See for the following particularly Kelly, *Britain*, pp. 290ff.

68 Quoted in Kelly, *Eastern*, p. 122; see also for the following, ibid. pp. 123ff.

69 A record of the seven plenary (not the five informal) sessions is given in the *UK Memorial II*, Annex D, no. 36, pp. 211ff.

70 See *UK Memorial I*, pp. 104ff.

71 For the main provisions in the agreement see Kelly, *Eastern*, p. 163.

72 Reprinted as Appendix A in Kelly, *Eastern*, pp. 281–92.

73 Both parties had prepared Memorials to put their cases before the tribunal; these were the often quoted UK Memorial and the Saudi Memorial. Both are now published by Archive Editions.

74 See Kelly, *Eastern*, p. 174; for details of the proceedings in Geneva see ibid., pp. 199–206 and *Keesing's Contemporary Archives*, vol. X (1955–6), p. 14445A.

75 See below, pages 311ff.

76 See Hansard, Parliamentary Debates, 5th series, House of Commons, vol. 545 (1955–6) and *Keesing's*, vol. X (1955–6), p. 14534Af.

77 The frontier declared by the British Government in October 1955 differed from the Riyadh Line in that it did not start at Dauḥah al Salwā (the south-western coast of Qatar), but at a point several kilometres west of Khaur al 'Udaid; the 1955 line deviated some kilometres east from the Riyadh Line, to touch the Ṣufūk wells. In the south-eastern part it deviated again, turning north-west to reach Umm al Zumūl, the final point of the common border between Abu Dhabi and the Sultanate of Oman. See map in Kelly, *Eastern*.

78 See below, page 368.

79 Because the oil company which held the concessions in the Trucial States, PC (TC) was a consortium of British, Dutch, American, French and other interests. On shareholding of the IPC see above, footnote 54 of this chapter, and for more details of oil exploration in this period see above pages 105ff. ADMA was $66\frac{2}{3}$ per cent BP and $33\frac{1}{3}$ per cent CFP.

80 The number of people, who were connected during the 1950s with either of the oil companies or their service companies, was boosted firstly by the insistence of the Rulers that, while drilling went on in their territory,

labourers from their tribes had to be employed, and secondly because local people tended to work for short periods only, and new recruits took their places.

81 From 1943/44 the British Government sponsored the search for the main breeding grounds of the desert locust and the campaign to eradicate these pests in Arabia as well as Africa and the Indian subcontinent. The first European to travel to the Līwā, Wilfred Thesiger, was attached to the Middle East Anti-Locust Unit, which had already been in operation throughout Saudi Arabia, the Trucial Coast and parts of Oman under its field officer Desmond Vesey-FitzGerald in the late 1940s. In the early 1950s the Trucial States were visited by several locust swarms, and almost the entire crop of the Līwā oases was destroyed in 1951. In 1960 a locust field officer was appointed by the British Government for liaison duties from the Trucial States with the Pakistan Locust Mission which had been set up in 1957 by the FAO. His presence was no longer required in 1965.

82 This post witnessed a rapid turnover of officers: During the decade in which this arrangement lasted, eight different people were Political Officers in Shārjah: Capt. J.B. Howes (1937–40), Capt. R.D. Metcalfe (1940–1). C.J. Pelly (1941–43), Capt. M.B. O'C. Tandy (1943–4), Capt. R.E.R. Bird (1944–5)—later an employee of PCL, respectively IPC, Capt. R.C. Murphy (1945–6), Capt. J.E.H. Hudson (1946–7), G.N. Jackson (1947–8); see Hawley, *Trucial States*, p. 328.

83 He stayed in this post until 1951 and was succeeded by A.J. Wilton (1951) and M.S. Weir (1952).

84 Political Agents resident in Dubai and responsible for all the seven Trucial States were: C.M. Pirie Gordon (1954–5), J.P. Tripp (1955–8), D.F. Hawley (1958–61)—ex Sudan Civil Service. The Political Agents who were responsible for all the states with the exception of Abu Dhabi were: A.J.M. Craig (1961–4), H.M. Balfour-Paul (1965–6), D.A. Roberts (1966–8), J.L. Bullard (1968–71). After 1971 the post became that of a Consul General. Political Officers in Abu Dhabi, under the Political Agent in Dubai were: Hon. M. Buckmaster (1957–8), E.R. Worsnop (1958–9), E.F. Henderson (1959–61). In the decade when Abu Dhabi had a Political Agency, the post was filled by three officers: Col. Sir Hugh Boustead (1961–5)—ex Sudan Civil Service, A.T. Lamb (1965–8), C.J. Treadwell—also ex-Sudan Civil Service; Treadwell was Political Agent from 1968 to December 1971, when he became the first British Ambassador to serve in the newly created state of the UAE.

85 See below, pages 314ff.

86 See below, pages 311ff.

87 See below, pages 319ff.

88 The accounts of travellers in the area testify this—from Wellsted, Miles, Cox and Zwemer before the first world War to Thomas and Thesiger in the 1930s and late 1940s.

89 Some examples are quoted above, pages 230ff.

90 See also above, page 232 and Thesiger, *Arabian Sands*, pp. 263ff.

91 See Article 2 of the King's Regulations of 1951 (*Trucial States*). Apart from this regulation, which was allowed and signed by the Secretary of State for Foreign Affairs, at the time Ernest Bevin. "Rules of Discipline for the Trucial Oman Levies", published in the *Persian Gulf Gazette*, were drawn up by the Political Resident in Bahrain and approved by Bevin's successor, Herbert Morrison. This and all other regulations concerning the legal situation in the Gulf were published in *The Persian Gulf Gazette*, published by HM Political Resident in the Persian Gulf by authority (HMSO).

92 There were TOS camps at Shārjah, al Manāmah, Masāfi, Mirfā and Jāhili in the vicinity of al 'Ain, and the force had a small presence in other locations.

93 It was only fully recognised in hindsight that a considerable number of Dhufāris seem to have already been preparing for the rebellion against the Sultan of Oman which broke out in 1965. After receiving some training many Dhufāris went on leave, took their guns with them and never came back, a certain amount of material was probably also diverted and ended up in Dhufār.

94 A short account of the campaign is given in Hawley, *Trucial States*, p. 175. The assignment of the force had to be amended in March 1956 by a Queen's Regulation for this purpose. To Article 2 of the King's Regulation no. 1 of 1951 was added: "(2) The Political Resident shall have power to require members of the Force to proceed and serve outside the limits of the Trucial States Order, 1956."

95 The relevant legal basis for these powers were Articles 4 and 5 of the King's Regulation no. 1 of 1951. See above, footnote 91.

96 See also above, page 268f.

97 Certain changes were made over the years and other Trucial States Orders were issued in 1956 and 1959 (published as Statutory Instruments, 1956, no. 90 and 1959, no. 1039) before provisions were made in the 1960s for the transfer of jurisdiction to the local Rulers. When Fujairah was finally recognised as a Trucial State in July 1952, the Ruler was required to recognise in writing the Order in Council of 1950 (Statutory Instruments, 1952, no. 1420).

98 See the relevant Orders in Council of 1950, 1956 and 1959, Parts III.

99 Part III, Article 13 of the Orders in Council; in the 1959 version the Judges of the High Courts of Kenya and Cyprus were replaced by "Persons who hold or have held judicial office under the Crown."

100 The matter of jurisdiction is further elaborated on in Article 8, b) to e), regarding British property, ships, aircraft, and certain persons who were physically outside the limits of this order.

101 Regulations no. 7 of 1960, no. 1 of 1962 and no. 1 of 1963.

102 See also below, page 368.

103 Statutory Instruments, 1963, no. 2095, entitled "The Trucial States (Amendment) Order 1963"; it came into operation on 15th January 1964.

104 On 18 May 1952 the Ruler of Shārjah decreed the Shārjah Air Navigation Regulation which was then made to apply to all persons subject to the Trucial States Order in Council by the Queen's Regulation no. 3 of 1952. Other examples of such regulations which were adopted in the same manner by publishing the official translation in a schedule of the Queen's Regulations, are the "Abu Dhabi Income Tax Regulation of 1965", the "Northern Trucial States Pesticide (Control) Regulation 1965", the "Fujairah Income Tax Regulation 1967", the "Dubai Municipal Regulations 1958", the "Dubai Traffic Regulation 1960", the "Dubai Air Traffic Regulation 1966", the "Dubai Police Force Regulation 1966", and the "Dubai Traffic Regulation 1968".

105 The enactment dealt with various matters such as "Trade Licenses", "Officials Conduct Law", "Social Assistance Law" and the "Law for Control of Hunting"; see Queen's Regulation no. 10 of 1971 (June 1971).

106 Regulation no. 7 of 1971.

107 To regulate the investigation of a particular accident which took place on 3 August 1953 in Shārjah.

108 To protect the local pearling trade it became an offence to import, export or sell any cultured, tinted, or Venezuelan pearls, to manufacture them or sell bleached undrilled pearls.

109 Another example was the "Trucial States Insolvency Law Regulation", 1961, which abolished the use of the enactment of the Presidency of Bombay.

110 See below, pages 375ff and also Steppat, Fritz, "Bemerkungen zur Rechtsentwicklung in Abu Dhabi und den Vereinigten Arabischen Emiraten" in: *Zeitschrift der Deutschen Morgenländischen Gesellschaft*. Supplement III, 1 (XIX. Deutscher Orientalistentag 1975) pp. 617–24.

111 Since 1964 a legal adviser was employed by the Trucial States Council to draft laws for the five northern emirates and Dubai, while Abu Dhabi excepted itself. The adviser, Mr Aḥmad al Bīṭār from Jordan, drafted several ordinances for the Rulers; he also planned for three courts to be set up to cover these six Trucial States (a Court of the First Instance, a Criminal Assize Court and a Court of Appeal), and he drafted a Penal Code for the Trucial States Council. But none of these proposals were enacted before the Council ceased to exist in 1971.

112 See Trucial States Orders in Council, Part VIII.

113 Article 62, part (2) of the Order in Council of 1950.

114 See the examples given by Hawley, *Trucial States*, pp. 180f.

115 There is an eye-opening chapter on the manifestations of a craving for modern education which beset many families on the Trucial Coast in particular in Shārjah, Dubai and Ra's al Khaimah after the Second World War in Abdullah, M. Morsy. *The United Arab Emirates*, pp. 143ff.

116 Mr E.F. Henderson, then an employee of PD (TC), who had previously assisted in compiling evidence for the *UK Memorial*, was sent to Buraimi during the fighting which ousted the Saudi garrison from Ḥamāsah on 26 October 1955 to bring the tribes of the area to accept the new situation. During the course of his mission he noticed that about half of all date groves were dead or dying because during the preceding years of political instability the routine maintenance on the *aflāj* had not been carried out. He applied to the British Political Agent in Dubai for funds to implement a restoration project, which was thought out in conjunction with the Ruler's *wāli*, Shaikh Zāyid, and the *'urafā'* of Abu Dhabi's *aflāj*. Over a period of six months all seven *aflāj* (about 50 per cent of their combined length) were cleaned of debris and silt, working upstream from the outlet. Each section of a *falaj* was inspected by Mr Henderson, together with an *'arīf* and prospective local contractors, to ascertain the amount of repair work which needed to be done. The work was then auctioned in small lots of about 50 metres to 1,000 metres, and price, time scale and other conditions were verbally agreed between Mr Henderson and the citizen who, with members of his family and friends, carried out this work. The result of this work was a 50 per cent increase in the flow of water, which meant revitalising all the existing date gardens. The cost to the British Government amounted to £5,000 Sterling.

117 Members of this Deliberative Committee were officials or important merchants delegated by each Ruler. Abu Dhabi was not represented during the first years. The Committee met more frequently than the Trucial States Council (22 times between September 1964 and October 1968); it decided upon priorities for projects, discussed the annual budgets, and served in many other ways as a cabinet. It was superseded in December 1968 by the newly formed Executive Committee.

118 Trucial States Council, *Report 1969*, p. 48.

119 Kuwait and Saudi Arabia had already gone ahead with various educational and medical projects and established their own administration through which to channel their substantial aid. In 1963 the Kuwait State Office was opened in Dubai, which co-ordinated the educational and health projects and the construction of mosques. In 1968 Saudi Arabia opened an office in Dubai through which generous assistance was allocated. See also for the following, Hawley, *Trucial States*, pp. 227ff.

120 See "Analysis of Capital Expenditure by States", Appendix A to the *Newsletter of the Trucial States Council*, 15 September to 31 October 1970, issued by the Development Office, and "Analysis of Recurrent & Minor Capital Expenditure (1965–70)", ibid., Appendix C.

121 See *Newsletter*, 15 September to 31 October 1970, p. 4.

122 A very fundamental tool for further development planning was also provided by a population survey; see "First Population Census of the Trucial States, March/April 1968" and Fenelon, K.G. *The Trucial States—A Brief Economic Survey*, Beirut, 2nd edn, 1969, pp. 17f and 136.

123 Out of 237 expatriates; 195 of the 926 employees were Trucial States subjects or Omanis. These figures did not include daily paid labour.

124 In 1965 the following facilities were provided with British assistance: Al Maktūm Hospital opened 1950 (38 beds), Ra's al Khaimah Hospital opened 1962 (10 beds); Clinics: Shārjah and Umm al Qaiwain, opened 1959, Fujairah and Kalba, opened 1960, Ḥiṣn Dibah (Shārjah) opened 1961, Falaj al Muʿallā (Umm al Qaiwain), and Musfūṭ (ʿAjmān) opened 1963, Fāyah (Shārjah) and Ḥuwailāt (Ra's al Khaimah) opened 1964. The clinic at Shārjah was visited daily by a doctor. The other clinics were visited every other week on pre-arranged circuits of doctors touring from Dubai. See Trucial States Council, *Report 1969*, p. 12.

125 The Kuwait State Office opened a hospital in Dubai in 1963 and small hospitals and clinics in Shārjah, Ra's al Khaimah, ʿAjmān, Umm al Qaiwain, Khaur Fakkān and Fujairah. Iranian hospitals opened in ʿAjmān, Dubai and Fujairah, and the Arabian Mission financed by the Reformed Church in America had hospitals in Shārjah, Ra's al Khaimah, Fujairah and al ʿAin.

126 Trucial States Council, *Report 1969*, p. 14.

127 During 1970 the hospital cost a total of BD 446,030 in recurrent and minor capital expenditure; 276 staff were employed.

128 See also mention of this scheme in the FAO Report: *Agricultural Development in the United Arab Emirates. Report on present conditions, prospects and priorities*, Cairo 1973, p. 12.

129 See Trucial States Council, *Report 1969*, pp. 54ff, with a complete list of the reports and surveys submitted to the Development Office from 1965.

130 For instance a hydrological survey was made by the consultant engineers Sir Alexander Gibb and Partners in 1969/70; see also above, Chapter One, footnote 3.

131 This Beirut Office monitored and in some cases even initiated development work in the Trucial States. Its archive was the repository of a wealth of data which had been collected in Dubai and the northern states. During the Civil War in Lebanon most of this material was destroyed by Embassy staff in anticipation of the imminent need to

evacuate; only some very hastily selected documents could be transported to the British Embassy in Amman.

132 It comprised a total distance of 125 kilometres (75 kilometres from Khaur Kalba to Dibah and 50 kilometres through the mountains from Fujairah via Masāfi and Sīji to D̲aid).

133 Appendix to *Newsletter of the Trucial States Council*, 1 September to 15 September 1970, p. 4.

134 The initiative for building a trade school in Dubai in addition to the one which had been in existence in Shārjah since 1958 came from the Ruler of Dubai. He provided £17,500 for it; a contribution of £14,000 was received from the British Government and a further sum of £4,500 was granted by the Ruler for housing teachers. The school was the result of much enthusiastic effort on all sides, and part of the carpentry and other work was carried out by students of the Shārjah Trade School; see Trucial States Council *Report 1969*, p. 7.

135 For details regarding scholarships and levels of training received abroad see *Trucial States Council Report*, 1969, p. 10.

136 This does not mean that there were not also some people who pleaded for spending the available funds on institution building and training of cadres rather than on immediately visible social services. The Five Year Plan of 1955 demonstrated this division.

CHAPTER NINE

1 See the summary of the White Paper in *Keesing's*, vol. XVI (1967–8), p. 21954–9 and 22256–61; quotation from p. 21956.

2 See Harold Wilson, *The Labour Government 1964–70, A Personal Record*, 2nd edn, 1974, pp. 482ff.

3 Wilson, pp. 502 and 507f.

4 *Keesing's*, vol. XVI (1967–8), p. 22490.

5 See for text and interpretation of the agreement, Albaharna, Husain M., *The Arabian Gulf States. Their Legal and Political Status and Their International Problems*, 2nd revised edn, Beirut, 1975, pp. 40ff and pp. 330f. On 23 January 1899, Shaikh Mubārak, Ruler of Kuwait signed an "Exclusive Agreement" with Britain; see Lorimer, *Histor.*, pp. 1022ff.

6 The United Kingdom was bound by treaties dating back to 1861 to be responsible for Bahrain's defence and external affairs.

7 The UN Secretary-General, U Thant, announced on 28 March 1970 that he had agreed "to exercise his good offices in a matter concerning the status of Bahrain at the request of the Government of Persia, concurred by the Government of the United Kingdom", *Keesing's*, vol. XVI (1967–8), p. 23998 A.

8 *Keesing's*, vol. XVI (1967–8), p. 23999.
9 Discussed below, pages 364ff.
10 This policy evolved within a few months of the initial British decision to withdraw; it was spelled out in an interview which the Shah gave to Mr Winston S. Churchill published in *The Times* of 10 June 1969 (p. 11), where the Shah is quoted as saying: "We would be willing in conjunction with Saudi Arabia, to provide protection for the Gulf states. Our paratroops and armoured regiments at Shiraz can give them as much protection as the British forces in the area today."
11 Between 1959 and 1965 eighteen Arab states and shaikhdoms in the South Arabian Protectorate joined the South Arabian Federation, which then disintegrated during the period from August to October 1967 in a tide of nationalistic, anti-British feelings, which also turned against the traditional rulers of the member states. For a chronological record see *The Middle East and North Africa*, 1968–9, 5th edn, London 1968, pp. 599–619; and Kennedy Trevaskis, *Shades of Amber, A South Arabian Episode*, London, 1968.
12 See interview with *Al Ra'y al 'Amm* of Kuwait on 5 February 1968, reprinted in *Arab Report and Record*, issue 3, 1–15 February 1968.
13 See in ARR (Arab Report and Record), issue 4, 16–29 February 1968 and the complete text of the agreement, issue 5, 1–15 March 1968.
14 The Trucial States Council met about twice a year; the seven Rulers brought their relatives and advisers with them for these informal gatherings. The Council's status was not defined by a constitution and it had no executive power; it could merely advise on the best use of the funds which were at the disposal of the Trucial States Development Office. After the chairmanship had been relinquished in 1965 by the Political Agent in favour of rotation among the seven Rulers, the Council functioned in some ways like a small parliamentary body. See above, pages 319ff; and Hawley, *Trucial States*, p. 176ff.
15 In 1965 for the first time, a capital works programme allocating expenditure for various projects, mostly in the poorer states, was discussed and approved by the Council. After this the Rulers became increasingly involved in such development decisions as necessitated thinking about the area as a whole. This was further institutionalised by the establishment of a Deliberative Committee in 1964 to which all the States were invited to send representatives, who themselves discussed the issues at stake with their respective Rulers. This committee was superseded in 1968 by the Executive Committee, which had wider powers but again served as a link between the bodies which worked for the development of the entire Trucial States area and the individual Rulers.
16 A first draft was already prepared in January 1968 by Dr Ḥasan Kāmil, Adviser to the Government of Qatar, and submitted to the Ruler and the

Deputy Ruler of Qatar. An amended draft which was less specific and less detailed was prepared in Doha immediately before the meeting in Dubai.

17 The text of the draft of an "Agreement for the Establishment of the United Arab Coastal Emirate" is filed in a collection of resolutions, decisions, joint communiqués and documents concerning the Union of Arab Emirates compiled in the office of the Adviser to the Ruler of Qatar (henceforth quoted as *Resolutions*). This documentation also contains his draft of January 1968, running to 34 articles and the Government of Qatar's draft, which was used as the basis for the discussions in February. The latter was reduced to 26 articles.

18 The final agreement was cut down to 11 points, but the preamble of the actual agreement is more verbose than that of the draft, calling the first federation between Abu Dhabi and Dubai a stepping stone for this larger federation, but also stressing that this move was "in response to the desire of the people of the area to strengthen the means of stability in their countries". The text is printed in Albaharna, 1975, p. 380ff.

19 The President of this Supreme Council was also the President of the Union; he was to be elected annually from among the nine Rulers.

20 Albaharna, 1975, p. 381.

21 The Arabic name "*al Majlis al Ittiḥ*ādi" was in other instances translated as the "Union Council".

22 While the draft provided that the Union Council should perform its functions ". . . in accordance with the higher policy adopted by the Supreme Council . . .", the agreement itself reads: "The decisions of the Federal Council shall not be final until approved by the Supreme Council." Albaharna, 1975, p. 382.

23 In the original draft of January a maximum of four representatives from each Emirate was envisaged.

24 Albaharna, 1975, p. 382.

25 The author of the draft also wanted to create an official gazette for the publication of this agreement and subsequent federal laws, but the relevant passage in the draft was not adopted in the agreement.

26 The Dubai agreement was signed by: Shaikh ʿĪsa bin Salmān Āl Khalīfah, Ruler of Bahrain; Shaikh Zāyid bin Sulṭān Āl Nahyān, Ruler of Abu Dhabi; Shaikh Rāshid bin Saʿīd Āl Maktūm, Ruler of Dubai; Shaikh Ṣaqr bin Muḥammad Āl Qāsimi, Ruler of Ra's al Khaimah; Shaikh Khālid bin Muḥammad Āl Qāsimi, Ruler of Shārjah; Shaikh Aḥmad bin Rāshid Āl Muʿallā, Ruler of Umm al Qaiwain; Shaikh Rāshid bin Ḥumaid Āl Naʿaimi, Ruler of ʿAjmān; and Shaikh Muḥammad bin Ḥamad Āl Sharqi, Ruler of Fujairah.

27 But as was the case in most European states, even many Arab governments had at that time precious little knowledge of that part of the Arab World; according to a report of 15 March 1968 in Beirut's *Daily*

Star, the Lebanese Ministry of Foreign Affairs had instructed their missions to collect "whatever information they may come across" about the Emirates and their Federation.

28 ARR, issue 7, 1–15 April 1968.

29 Participants in this meeting were national advisers and foreign Arab legal experts working for the governments: On behalf of Abu Dhabi two advisers, Dr Maḥmūd Ḥasan Juma'h and Ṣāliḥ Faraḥ, took part; on behalf of Qatar, Dr Ḥasan Kāmil, 'Ali al Anṣāri, and 'Abdul Wahhab al Nīdāni; on behalf of Dubai, Aḥmad bin Sulṭān bin Sulayyim, Mahdi al Tājir, and legal adviser to Shaikh Rāshid, Aḥmad al Bīṭār; on behalf of Bahrain, Shaikh Muḥammad bin Mubārak Āl Khalifah, Yūsuf al Shīrāwi, Sayyid Maḥmūd al'Alawi, and legal adviser Waṣfi al Nimr; on behalf of Shārjah, Muḥammad bin Sulṭān Āl Qāsimi, Ibrāhīm al Midfa', 'Abdullah bin 'Ali al Maḥmūd, the legal adviser Mukhtār al Tūm, and Tariam' Umrān; on behalf of Umm al Qaiwain, Rāshid bin Ḥamad and the adviser Burhān Shams al Dīn; on behalf of Ra's al Khaimah, Shaikh Khālid bin Ṣaqr Āl Qāsimi; Fujairah authorised the delegation of Abu Dhabi to speak on its behalf; (see *Resolutions*).

30 This meeting of advisers made it already clear that the five small Emirates, particularly Ra's al Khaimah, felt uneasy about being relegated to a secondary role while the four larger Emirates seemed to be preparing to implement whatever they agreed between themselves.

31 See also for the following, "Why is the establishment of the Union of Arab Emirates being delayed" in *Al Jarīdah* of Beirut on 18 June 1969. (English translation in: *Resolutions*); see also ARR, issue 10, 16–31 May 1968 and ARR, issue 11, 1–15 June 1968 with a report from a Bahraini journalist who blamed Qatar for the breakdown of the talks because Qatar insisted that the issues of the presidency and the capital must be discussed.

32 Professor Charles Rousseau from Paris University and Dr Waḥīd Ra'fat, the Egyptian legal adviser to the Ruler of Kuwait.

33 For the text of the resolutions of this meeting see *Federation of Arab Emirates. A Report*, published by the Department of Information and Tourism, Research and Publication Section, Abu Dhabi, October 1970; and ARR, issue 13, 1–15 July 1968. It is interesting to note that physical communications between the member states themselves and also with other Gulf states were still rather rudimentary at that time. The first weekly air service between Kuwait and Bahrain only started on 1 January 1969 and the first telephone communication to Fujairah, by VHF radio telephone from Dubai, was established in January 1969.

34 It included Dr Ḥasan Kāmil, the Egyptian legal adviser to the Government of Qatar; Ṣāliḥ Faraḥ, a Sudanese judge in Abu Dhabi; Waṣfi al Nimr, legal adviser in Bahrain; and Aḥmad al Bīṭār, a

Palestinian legal adviser to the Ruler of Dubai and Secretary-General of the Trucial States Development Council.

35 The members and their aides were: for Abu Dhabi: Shaikh Aḥmad bin Ḥamad, Khalaf bin Aḥmad al Otaibah, Otaibah bin 'Abdullah al Otaibah, Muḥammad bin Khalīfah al Kindi; for Bahrain: Yūsuf al Shirāwi, Muḥammad Jābir al Anṣāri, Jāsim Bū' Alay, Ḥabīb Qāsim; for Qatar: Shaikh Khalifah bin Ḥamad (who later became Ruler), 'Ali al Anṣāri, 'Ali Jaidah, and later this delegation was joined by Mubārak bin 'Ali Abū Khātir; for Dubai: Shaikh Maktūm bin Rāshid, Aḥmad bin Sulayyim, and later also Juma'h al Mājid and Mājid al Futaim; for Umm al Qaiwain: Shaikh Sulṭān bin Aḥmad Āl Mu'allā and Rāshid bin Ḥamad Sulṭān; for Ra's al Khaimah: Shaikh Khālid bin Ṣaqr Āl Qāsimi, Aḥmad bin Sa'īd Ghabāsh, 'Abdullah bin Aḥmad Sirḥān, and Muḥammad 'Abdul Raḥmān Abū Qaṣīdah; for Shārjah: Shaikh Muḥammad bin Sulṭān al Qāsimi, Muḥammad bin 'Ubaid al Shāmisi, and Tariam 'Umrān; for Fujairah: Shaikh Ḥamad bin Saif, 'Abdullah 'Abdul Raḥman bin Faris; for 'Ajmān: Shaikh Ḥumaid bin Rāshid, Ḥamad bin Muḥammad bin Shihāb, Muḥammad Raḥmah al 'Āmiri, 'Abdullah 'Amīn; see Federation of Arab Emirates, Department of Information, Abu Dhabi, October 1970, p. 4f and ARR, issue 13, 1–15 July 1968.

36 See ARR, issue 17, 1–15 September 1968.

37 See ARR, issue 14, 16–31 July 1968.

38 The latter provision prompted the Ruler of Abu Dhabi to underline in an interview broadcast on the eve of his visit to Iran by Cairo Radio on 3 November 1968 that, the planned build-up of the Abu Dhabi Defence Force "represents support for the Federation and strength for the Arabian Gulf Amirates". See ARR, issue 21, 1–15 November 1968.

39 ibid.

40 After an initial hitch because Abu Dhabi had objected to the meeting being held again in Doha.

41 As mentioned above, one meeting was held in Shārjah on 26 to 28 November 1968; another one, due to be held in Dubai on 28 January 1969, was postponed until 4 March 1969; this meeting's time was mostly taken up in reviewing reports of the specialised committees; the third meeting was in 'Ajmān on 1 and 2 April 1969.

42 See ARR, issue 21, 1–15 November and issue 24, 16–31 December 1968.

43 Iran's attitude to Bahrain was indeed mellowing, and in an interview in Delhi on 4 January 1969 when the Shah was asked about the possibility of holding a referendum in Bahrain he said that anything which would serve to find out "the will of the people" would be welcome; see ARR, issue 1, 1–15 January 1969.

44 Ra's al Khaimah's Ruler had a grievance because the Za'āb tribe with whom he had quarrelled had emigrated to Abu Dhabi; he was

enigmatically told by the Ruler of Abu Dhabi: "the two countries are one". ARR, issue 4, 15–28 February 1969.

45 See ARR, issue 6, 16–31 March 1969.

46 The Temporary Union Council held its last session on 22/23 June 1969, at which it set up some more committees. It was to give way to the new cabinet which was, however, not yet nominated when the Temporary Union Council was disbanded on 7 July 1969.

47 See MEES (Middle East Economic Survey), vol. XII, no. 29, 16 May 1969 for a report on other points which were raised at this Supreme Council meeting.

48 Dr Turābi, Dean of the Faculty of Law at Khartoum University, was a member of the Sudanese Constituent Assembly and the President of the Islamic Charter Front, a political party formed on the basis of the ideas of the Muslim Brotherhood. See ARR, issue 19, 1–15 October 1968.

49 Shaikh Zāyid stayed away for nearly two months that summer, leaving Abu Dhabi on 1 June and visiting Jordan, Switzerland, Britain, Spain, Lebanon and Iraq.

50 Soon afterwards the British adviser to the Federation in military matters, Major-General Sir John Willoughby, finalised his recommendations for the organisation of the Federal Defence Force; he favoured the formation of a mobile infantry brigade equipped with light armour and with an initial strength of about 2,000 soldiers, to be increased to about 5,000 later on. See ARR, issue 19, 1–15 October 1969.

51 See MEES, vol. XIII, no. 1, 31 October 1969, translation from the Arabic version published in the Beirut daily *Al Jarīdah*.

52 At first it was suggested that a number of portfolios should be allocated to each state. There was a great deal of bargaining; Ra's al Khaimah for instance demanded Defence and Interior, but could be persuaded to settle for Agriculture and Public Works. But it was not clear whether a particular portfolio should remain with a particular Emirate or whether it should rotate.

53 Part of the text is reprinted in MEES, vol. XIII, no. 1, 31 October 1969, p. 9. See also for this period Khalīfah ʿAli Moḥammed, *The United Arab Emirates: Unity in Fragmentation*, London, 1979, pp. 32ff.

54 As claimed in the Beirut daily *Al Jarīdah* of 27 October; see MEES, vol. XIII, no. 1, 31 October 1969.

55 MEES, vol. XIII, no. 2, 7 November 1969. Statement of 25 October 1969.

56 Amid rumours that Iran and Saudi Arabia were dividing up the area into spheres of influence; see ARR, issue 22, 16–30 November 1969, p. 56.

57 ARR, issue 24, 16–31 December 1969. The population of Bahrain was then estimated at over 200,000; at the 1971 census 216,000 inhabitants were counted.

58 For a list of the names of members of Bahrain's Council of State see ARR, issue 2, 16–31 January 1970.

59 The Iranian daily *Kayhan International* of 11 March reiterated that Iran would not tolerate being ignored when the future of Bahrain was decided, and suggested that there should be a federation of the seven Trucial States, omitting Bahrain and Qatar. This came at a time of intensive secret consultations between Bahrain, Kuwait and Saudi Arabia, allegedly to arrange for a defence pact, and while Iran agreed to the UN commission to ascertain the views of the people of Bahrain. There had also been another spate of visits of Arab Gulf Rulers or their deputies and aides to Iran during the last months of 1969 and January 1970. The Rulers of Ra's al Khaimah and Shārjah went on official visits.

60 See above, pages 338f.

61 There were so many intra-Gulf visits by Rulers and members of the ruling families and Iranian officials that ARR had to give up its usual way of reporting on every move, and summarised only the most important contacts.

62 See also the "Memorandum Concerning the Membership of Qatar of the Union of Arab Emirates as provided by the Provisional Constitution of Qatar" in; *Resolutions*.

63 Law no. 5 of 1970, published in the *Official Gazette of the State of Qatar*.

64 See also for the following MEES, vol. XIII, no. 34, 19 June 1970.

65 The committee met on 28 June to study a draft prepared by a group of legal experts and officials from the nine emirates and to consider the draft prepared by Dr Waḥīd Ra'fat, who was himself present at this meeting; see MEED (Middle East Economic Digest), 10 July 1970, p. 815.

66 The establishment of Iranian schools, hospitals, regular air services and trade agreements was suggested and an arrangement was envisaged whereby Iranians no longer needed visas to visit the state of Shārjah; see ARR, issue 2, 16–31 January 1970.

67 E.g. a road linking Ra's al Khaimah with other Trucial States and an Islamic College similar to the one established in Dubai.

68 Statement made on 15 July 1970 in the National Assembly of Kuwait; see MEES, vol. XIII, no. 38, 17 July 1970.

69 See e.g. the interview given by Shaikh Rāshid bin Sa'īd, Ruler of Dubai to *The Times* in London, published on 14 July 1970.

70 See also above pages 340, 358 and footnote 79.

71 See the letter from the Ruler of Qatar in his capacity as Chairman of the Supreme Council to the Ruler of Abu Dhabi of 19 October 1970 urging the meeting to be convened soon, in *Resolutions*.

72 This committee was formed by a resolution of the Committee of Deputy Rulers in their meeting of 14 June 1970. It presented a draft which was based on the draft prepared by the first constitutional committee and on

the draft submitted by Dr Waḥīd Ra'fat. A combination of the two was then circulated and commented on.

73 'Aḥmad al Bīṭār (Dubai), Ḥasan Kāmil (Qatar), Ṣāliḥ Faraḥ (Abu Dhabi) and Ḥusain Albaharna (Bahrain).
The fact that the British Government concentrated at this point on obtaining a consensus of the four bigger states on outstanding issues aggravated the already voiced suspicion which the five smaller states had that they were being made to accept what the others agreed upon. At times the voting of the smaller states therefore reflects nothing more than the desire to make their presence felt.

74 See "Minutes of the Second Meeting of the Committee of Their Excellencies the Deputy Rulers to Prepare for the Second Meeting in the Fourth Session of the Supreme Council", and a list of the participants of each state's delegation in *Resolutions*.

75 See "Minutes of the Meeting of the Committee for the Revision of the Draft Provisional Constitution of the Union of Arab Emirates which was prepared by the Second Constitution Committee that was formed on the basis of Recommendations Adopted on 14 June 1970 by the Committee of Their Excellencies the Deputy Rulers" in *Resolutions*. The participants of this committee included Dr Adnān al Pachachi, Khalaf al Otaibah, Muḥammad Ḥabrūsh and Ṣāliḥ Faraḥ from Abu Dhabi.

76 Estimates of population figures for the nine states were in 1970:

Bahrain	over 200,000	(1971 census: 216,000)
Qatar	112,000	(1970 census not published)
Seven Trucial States	217,000	(1968 census: 180,000)*
Abu Dhabi	60,000	(1968 census: 46,400)
Dubai	70,000	(1968 census: 59,000)
Shārjah	40,000	(1968 census: 31,700)
Ra's al Khaimah	27,000	(1968 census: 24,400)
Umm al Qaiwain	4,000	(1968 census: 3,800)
'Ajmān	4,500	(1968 census: 4,200)
Fujairah	11,000	(1968 census: 9,700)

*with Trucial Oman Scouts

77 Qatar by then suggested that only once the Union had become a single (and possibly more centralistic than federal) state could the principle of representation of the people on the basis of the number of citizens in the constituencies be applied. See p. 53 of the minutes in *Resolutions*.

78 Quote from p. 76 of the Minutes in *Resolutions*. The meeting of Deputy Rulers continued by discussing the method of voting in the Supreme Council of Rulers; eight members rejected the stipulation that the two thirds majority should include Abu Dhabi, Bahrain, Dubai and Qatar. Another proposal requiring unanimity—which in case this could not be

obtained, allowing a two-thirds majority vote, taken at a subsequent meeting about the same subject, to be binding—was approved only by Shārjah, Fujairah and Abu Dhabi. Bahrain again reserved its opinion. The committee settled for unanimity to be the method of voting in the Supreme Council of Rulers (see p. 65 of the Minutes in *Resolutions*). The next point was the approval by eight members of the provision regarding the capital, i.e. that Abu Dhabi should be the temporary seat and that the permanent capital should be built on the border between Abu Dhabi and Dubai. Bahrain again abstained. A motion by Dubai requesting that the individual Emirates should be allowed to deal with all aviation matters which did not explicitly fall within the executive power of the Union was also approved by eight delegations while Bahrain abstained. The budget committee's recommendation, that each member emirate should contribute 10 per cent of its revenues from oil and that the budget for the first year should be 19 million Bahraini Dinars, was adopted while Bahrain again refused to discuss the matter (see p. 71–74 of the Minutes in *Resolutions*); the same pattern was repeated regarding the draft agenda for the Supreme Council meeting.

79 Sir William Luce, the special envoy of the new British Government, had from the outset of his mission tried to combine the re-appraisal of its Gulf policy with assisting the Federation members to sort out their constitutional disagreements. At this point he suggested in his informal talks with the legal advisers about the dispute over representation that a suitable compromise was the already familiar proposal to give six seats to some of the big Emirates and four and three seats respectively to the smaller ones. The five small Emirates resented the fact that Qatar, Dubai, Bahrain and Abu Dhabi agreed to this solution without consulting them and voted against it in the October meeting of Deputy Rulers. The same fate was met by the idea, discussed between Sir William Luce and the four, to give some form of veto to the big Emirates in certain decisions of the Supreme Council.

80 ARR, issue 24, 15–31 December 1970.

81 After 14 November 1970 a battalion of the Scots Guards prepared to leave Shārjah without being replaced.

82 *Daily Telegraph* of 16 December 1970.

83 Eventually relations between the neighbours cooled because of border disputes.

84 On 18 November 1970 the Ruler of Qatar sent a letter to the Ruler of Abu Dhabi who was the current President of the Supreme Council; he accused Bahrain of being disruptive by changing its mind on certain issues which had already been agreed. He asked Shaikh Zāyid "to prevail upon our sister, Bahrain, to change its attitude" and implied that he would work for a solution without Bahrain if need be; see *Resolutions*.

85 See memorandum by the Government of Qatar to the Saudi-Kuwaiti delegation dated 27 January 1971 in *Resolutions*.
86 See letter from the Foreign Minister of Kuwait to the Ruler of Qatar dated 14 April 1971, dealing with the seven proposals.
87 In March a Kuwaiti delegation had already sounded out the chances of reaching agreement; see ARR, issue 6, 16–31 March 1971.
88 In doing so Qatar wanted to eliminate the reasons for Abu Dhabi's objection to the stipulation which would have made it obligatory for that state to pay more because of its very large income and small population.
89 See ARR, issue 8, 15–21 April 1971.
90 See below, pages 367f.
91 *The Times* of 3 March 1971; see also an interview published by the *Daily Telegraph* on 29 March 1971.
92 The Iranian Foreign Minister celebrated the Conservative confirmation of Britain's withdrawal as a diplomatic victory for Iran.
93 On 12 May Shaikh Zāyid's close adviser, Aḥmad Khalīfah al Suwaidi, visited Bahrain; Sir William Luce returned from the Arab shore to Teheran on 22 May and went via Cairo back to London on 30 May. King Faiṣal of Saudi Arabia visited the Shah on 16 May; a Saudi Minister of State for Foreign Affairs visited Kuwait on 26 May, and the Ruler of Kuwait had talks with the Egyptian Foreign Minister on 31 May. King Faiṣal and President Sādāt of Egypt discussed the Gulf on 21 June; Shaikh Zāyid had a meeting with the British Foreign Secretary on 16 June, and the Iranian Ambassador to Britain visited the Foreign Secretary, Sir Alec Douglas-Home, on 21 June 1971.
94 According to the daily *Beirut* of 27 June, these were: 1. that Iran would lease the military base which was to be vacated by Britain, 2. that Bahrain should not follow Kuwait's invitation to form a federation of these two states if the bigger federation failed, 3. that Bahrain should not interfere with Iran's claim to the islands, and 4. that Iran should have favoured nation status in Bahrain. See ARR, issue 12, 16–31 June 1971.
95 See Heard-Bey, Frauke, "Katar" in *Handbuch der Dritten Welt*, Bd. 4, Hamburg, 1978, pp. 329–35.
96 The majority of the sixteen ministers were members of the ruling family who had already been in charge of departments in the previous government organisation.
97 Other such duties were: exchange controls, responsibility for civil aviation, control of the importation of weapons and ammunition and the licensing of alcohol for the consumption by non-Muslims. A detailed account of such responsibilities is given in the weekly *Abu Dhabi News* of Thursday, 15 July 1971.
98 See above, pages 319ff.

99 MEES, vol. XIV, no. 39, 23 July 1971.

100 The advisers of the Rulers met in August, Shaikh Rāshid visited Abu Dhabi in September, and in October five Emirates, excluding Abu Dhabi, reached agreement to co-ordinate immigration controls from Dubai.

101 In November a defence organisation was formed, headed by Colonel F. D. Butts, which was to take over control of the Trucial Oman Scouts on behalf of the Federation. This force was then 1,700 strong. But because the Federation had not been proclaimed and no federal decree had been issued yet, formal handover proved a last minute problem.

102 The island of Abū Mūsa lies some 35 miles off the Shārjah coast and about 43 miles off the opposite coast of Iran. In a memorandum sent by the Ruler of Shārjah to various Arab states on 23 August 1971 it is claimed that at that time around 800 persons were living on the island. There were then some 130 students taught in two schools provided by Shārjah, which also had a hospital and a police station on the island. See translation of this memorandum in MEES, vol. XV, no. 6, 3 December 1971, pp. 4–8.

103 See also Plass, Jens B., *England zwischen Russland und Deutschland. Der Persische Golf in der britischen Vorkriegspolitik, 1899–1907, dargestellt nach englischem Archivmaterial.* Hamburg, 1966, 410ff. See also Abdullah, Muḥammad M., *The United Arab Emirates*, pp. 233ff, for background on the Iranian claim.

104 See also above Chapter Three, footnote 9.

105 As mentioned above, page 339. See also for the following, ARR, issue 13, 16–30 June 1971 and the interview which the Shah gave to the *Guardian*, published on 28 September 1971, when he said "We need them (the islands); we shall have them; no power on earth shall stop us . . . If Abu Musa and the Tunbs fell into the wrong hands they could be of a great nuisance value . . . my country has no territorial ambitions. The islands are a different matter."

106 A complicating factor was a new territorial dispute between Shārjah and its neighbours over the boundaries of offshore oil concession areas which had been granted recently. On 10 September 1969 the Ruler of Shārjah, in line with the governments of Kuwait, Saudi Arabia and Iran, extended the territorial waters of the emirate from 3 to 12 miles. This decree did not become generally known until March 1970. On 19 November 1969 the American company Occidental obtained the offshore concession for Umm al Qaiwain and on 2 February for ʿAjmān. On 29 December 1969 another American consortium, Buttes Gas and Oil Company and Clayco Petroleum Consortium, obtained the concession for Shārjah's offshore areas, including all of Shārjah's islands and their territorial waters. The same consortium also obtained a concession onshore and offshore in Dubai's relinquished areas. After completing

some seismic work Occidental decided early in 1970 to drill on a location nine miles from Abū Mūsa in what it considered to be Umm al Qaiwain's territorial waters, but was soon made aware of Shārjah's twelve mile claim. On 15 May 1970 the British Government notified the parties concerned that the dispute should be referred to arbitration, but that meanwhile Occidental should be allowed to proceed with drilling plans. Five days later Iran for the first time officially notified the British Government of the renewal of its claim to Abū Mūsa and the two Tunbs, and implied that if drilling was not suspended Iran would take matters into its own hands. In order to avoid a showdown at such an inopportune moment Britain proposed a temporary three-month suspension of drilling, pending the outcome of arbitration. The proposal was enforced when a British minesweeper intercepted Occidental's offshore rig and ordered it to move out of the disputed area. See in particular MEES, vol. XIII, no. 27, 1 May 1970 and no. 32, 1 June 1970.

107 See also for the following MEES, vol. XV, no. 6, 3 December 1971.

108 This memorandum was sent to several Arab states on 23 August 1971. It was published by *Al Anwār* in Beirut on 30 November 1971; according to this paper the few states who actually replied to the memorandum all urged restraint upon Shārjah. Translation published by MEES, vol. XV, no. 6, 3 December 1971, pp. 4–8; quotation p. 8.

109 One reason for the improvement in the climate may have been that the main "hawk", Ardeshir Zahedi was in the meantime replaced as Foreign Minister by 'Abbās 'Ali Khalatbari.

110 As part of the agreement the Ruler of Shārjah announced that the consortium headed by Buttes Gas and Oil Company would "undertake exploration for oil on the island and its territorial waters." Since Iran as well as Shārjah recognised the twelve mile territorial limit this meant that Occidental had to withdraw. Text of the agreement in MEES, vol. XV, no. 6, 3 December 1971, p. 4.

111 See MEES, vol. XV, no. 7, 10 December 1971 and supplement to no. 8, 17 December with a translation of the text of the law establishing the new company.

112 A publication of the full text of the communiqué in MEES, vol. XV, no. 6, 3 December 1971, pp. 8ff.

113 For the names see MEES, vol XV, no. 8, 17 December 1971.

114 For the names see *Reuters Bulletin*, 7 February 1972.

115 Defence Minister Shaikh Muḥammad bin Rāshid Āl Maktūm was present for ceremonies at the headquarters and the various outposts in the mountains and the desert. The 1,700 strong force became known as the Union Defence Force, and was commanded by a Briton, Lt-Col. Watson. Thirty-three British officers and about forty NCOs were still attached to the force.

116 See also above, pages 317ff.

117 The Development Office was incorporated into several ministries.

118 See MEES, vol. XIV, no. 8, 18 December 1970.

119 See for instance the occasion in October 1969 when Ra's al Khaimah boycotted the last part of the Supreme Council meeting; see above, pages 343, 353 and footnote 79.

120 Gas was struck at 17,900 feet and high quality oil was found at 16,000 feet, according to *The Times*, 21 December 1971. See also for the following MEES, vol. XV, nos. 3 and 8, 12 November and 17 December 1971.

121 See *Reuters Bulletin*, 4 December 1971.

122 Although there was some speculation in 1979 that the new regime in Iran would return the islands as a gesture of goodwill this possibility seems to have faded quite soon.

123 A translation into English entitled *Provisional Constitution of the United Arab Emirates* was published as a booklet by the United Arab Emirates' Ministry of Information in 1972. This version was used for the study of the federal state's constitutional basis. An early analysis of the constitution was written by John Duke Anthony, "The Union of Arab Amirates", in *Middle East Journal*, vol. 26, no. 3, pp. 271–87.

124 A case in point is for instance the once hotly disputed issue of the individual Emirates' membership in organisations such as OPEC and OAPEC, which was permitted in Article 123 of the Provisional Constitution.

125 Note the similarity to *jumhūrīyah al ʿarabīya al muttaḥidah* (United Arab Republic) which was the name chosen for the federation of Egypt and Syria, when unification proceeded to the extent of having one President and a central government consisting of fourteen Egyptian and seven Syrian Ministers (1958–61).

126 *Al ittiḥād al jumhūrīyāt al ʿarabīyah* was the name of the much looser federation between Egypt, Libya and Syria which was agreed upon in 1971 and ceased to function in 1977, although the agreement has not yet been formally abrogated.

127 See also Heard-Bey, Frauke, "Der Prozess der Staatswerdung in arabischen Ölexportländern. Politischer und gesellschaftlicher Wandel in Bahrain, Qatar, den Vereinigten Arabischen Emiraten und Oman" in: *Vierteljahreshefte für Zeitgeschichte*, Heft 2, 1975, pp. 155–209, particularly pp. 178ff.

128 "The Union shall have exclusive legislative and executive jurisdiction in the following affairs: 1. Foreign Affairs; 2. Defence and the Union Armed Forces; 3. Protection of the Union's security against internal or external threat; 4. Matters pertaining to security, order and rule in the permanent capital of the Union; 5. Matters relating to Union officials and Union judiciary; 6. Union finance and Union taxes, duties and fees; 7. Union public loans; 8. Postal, telegraph, telephone and wireless

services; 9. Construction, maintenance and improvement of Union roads which the Supreme Council had determined to be trunk roads. The organisation of traffic on such roads; 10. Air Traffic Control and the issue of licences to aircraft and pilots; 11. Education; 12. Public health and medical services; 13. Currency board and coinage; 14. Measures, standards and weights; 15. Electricity services; 16. Union nationality, passports, residence and immigration; 17. Union properties and all matters relating thereto; 18. Census affairs and statistics relevant to Union purposes; 19. Union Information." (Article 120).

129 The Union has exclusive legislative authority in the following matters: "Labour relations and social security; real estate and expropriation in the public interest; extradition of criminals; banks; insurance of all kinds; protection of agricultural and animal wealth; major legislation relating to penal law, civil and commercial transactions and company law, procedures before the civil and criminal courts; protection of cultural, technical and industrial property and copyright; printing and publishing; import of arms and ammunitions except for use by the armed forces or the security forces belonging to any emirate; other aviation affairs which are not within the executive jurisdiction of the Union; delimitation of territorial waters and regulation of navigation on the high seas." (Article 121).

130 It is, however, not made entirely clear in the text of Article 47, paragraph 2, whether this means that absolutely all Union laws are subject to this procedure; the text in English is vague; "Sanction of various Union laws before their promulgation." In other parts of the constitution provision is made for retroactive approval of already promulgated laws if the Supreme Council cannot be summoned in time (Article 113).

131 The President of the Union calls the Council into session "according to the rules of procedure upon which the Council shall decide in its bye-laws. It is obligatory for him to convene the Council for session whenever one of its members so requests" (Article 54, paragraph 2).

132 See Articles 107, 108 and Article 54, paragraph 10.

133 Article 110, paragraph 3 part a, and paragraph 4.

134 The first published translation of the Provisional Constitution uses the term Union National Assembly for *al majlis al waṭani al ittiḥādi* but later the parliament became known in English as the Federal National Council (FNC).

135 Eight each from Abu Dhabi and Dubai, six each from Shārjah and Ra's al Khaimah, and four each from 'Ajmān, Umm al Qaiwain and Fujairah.

136 ". . . unless the Council of Ministers informs the Union National Assembly that such discussion is contrary to the highest interest of the Union." (Article 92).

137 See Articles 95 to 101.

138. See Article 103, Part Two.

139 See Article 102. The constitution envisages here and in other places some kind of extraterritorial status for the permanent capital, which was expected to be located on land to be donated by two Emirates on their common border, but which would then cease to belong to either of these Emirates. However, no progress has been made in the creation of this capital during the twenty five years of the Federation's existence.

140 See below pp. 407ff, 412.

CHAPTER TEN

1 The southern border of the emirate of Abu Dhabi was moved north a few miles, thus placing part of the Zarrārah oil field in Saudi Arabia. Also a corridor to the sea was ceded in the west between the UAE and Qatar.

2 The UAE only contributed money and equipment to the volunteers heading for South Lebanon in June 1982.

3 As exports from Iran and Iraq dwindled and prices soared, the UAE's revenue reached a peak of nearly US $ 20 billion in 1980, according to *Central Bank Bulletin,* vol. 2 December 1981, p. 163.

4 The platform was attacked a second time on 26 November 1986, leaving six dead and several wounded.

5 See the interview given by the President to the Kuwaiti newspaper *Al Ra'y al 'Amm* before departing for the Arab summit in Amman in November 1987 and *Emirates News,* 2 February and 7 November 1987.

6 One example of Gulf-wide co-operation was the Gulf Area Oil Companies Mutual Aid Organisation set up in 1972 by the National Oil Companies of Iraq, Saudi Arabia, Kuwait, Bahrain, Qatar, Abu Dhabi and Dubai. Iraq was expelled in November 1991. Another example is the Regional Organisation for Protection of Marine Environment, of which Iran is also a member.

7 In December 1977 in Libya, five Arab countries and the PLO formed the Arab Resistance and Confrontation Front; see *Keesing's*, 1978, p. 29163f.

8 In Arabic *"majlis al ta'āwun al khalīj al'arabī".*

9 The matter was addressed in a seminar of GCC officials, economists and scholars; see *Emirates News,* 16 June 1993.

10 See *Emirates News,* 27 May to 1 June 1990.

11 On 7 September 1990 US Secretary of State, James Baker held discussions with the President of the UAE and the two sides affirmed that "a solution of the current crisis in the region requires complete and unconditional withdrawal from Kuwait ...", see *Khaleej Times,* 8 September. During the days of highest tension before the 15 January deadline, James Baker conferred with the key figures in the Middle East and elsewhere, stopping in Ankara, Riyadh, Abu Dhabi, Cairo and Damascus; the editorial in a UAE newspaper to mark this visit encapsulated the

view prevailing in the country at the time: "Even those who traditionally see the US as an imperialist entity must perforce accept that the restraint, the sheer effort and candour of its role in this crisis has been salutary and reflective of a global point of view ..." see *Khaleej Times*, 11 January 1991.

12 See *The Military Balance, 1992–1993*, published by the International Institute for Strategic Studies, IISS, London 1992, p. 125.

13 At the time the UAE had an estimated 44,000 military personnel according to *The Military Balance 1990–1991*, p. 120; the IISS estimates for 1994/5 are 61,500; see p. 140. Military service is still not compulsory.

14 Egypt and Syria were compensated for their war efforts. Egypt was forgiven some of its US $ 7bn debt by the US; see *The Military Balance 1991–1992, p. 99.*

15 *Khaleej Times*, 13 March 1991.

16 See above pp. 364–366.

17 See *Emirates News,* 10 September 1992 on the GCC foreign ministers' meeting and *Gulf News,* 11 September on their meeting with Egyptian and Syrian ministers.

18 See *Emirates News,* 13 September 1992 on the meeting in Cairo, attended by UAE Minister of State, Shaikh Ḥamdān bin Zāyid.

19 Ra's al Khaimah reached 10,000 b/d, but production has declined to a very low level. In October 1993, Umm al Qaiwain invited tenders for new oil concessions.

20 In 1995 it was US$12.77 billion; see *Emirates News*, 13 January 1996 and also above footnote 3.

21 33 per cent belong to the oil related sector.

22 Increased services fees helped to reduce the deficit; see *Emirates News,* 31 January 1995.

23 Made by the Rulers of Abu Dhabi and Dubai on 13 March 1980.

24 The estimate for 1970 was 217,000, see above footnote 76, p. 492.

25 See *MEED*, 20 August 1993.

26 Ministry of Education 32,777, and 12,306 Ministry of Health; see *Emirates News,* 4 October 1995.

27 For pre-1970s see above p. 332 and K.G. Fenelon, *The United Arab Emirates, An Economic and Social Survey,* London 1973, pp. 93ff.

28 In the school year 1991/2, 261,692 students attended government schools, 137, 057 were in private schools; see *UAE Ministry of Planning, Annual Statistical Abstract,* 17th (and latest) edn. 1992, table 195, p. 326ff. By June 1995 291,000 students were in public education.

29 In 1991 the Ministry of Health operated 29 hospitals with 4,306 beds. Four hospitals with 1,144 beds in Dubai are run by the emirate's authorities, others, such as a 157-bed hospital in Dubai and a small one in Fujairah are still run by the Iranian government; the Oasis Hospital in Al 'Ain is funded by charities in America. The military and Abu Dhabi

Police have hospitals; see *Statistical Abstract* 1992, pp. 359ff. In all there are 44 hospitals in the UAE. Infant mortality rate is 10.6 per thousand births; see *Emirates News,* 5 February 1993.

30 These projects were implemented by the Federal Ministry of Public Works, Housing and Town Planning. The road between Abu Dhabi and Dubai was financed by these two emirates. Abu Dhabi finances the construction of highways throughout that emirate.

31 The Social Services and Commercial Buildings Committee, known as 'Khalīfah Committee', provides loans at low interest rates and supervises construction and letting of commercial buildings.

32 See Ghanim, S.M. "Jebel Ali Free Zone: Environmental and Social Aspects" in: *Economic Horizon, A Quarterly Journal of the Federation of UAE Chambers of Commerce,* 14th Year, January 1993.

33 ibid, p. 182. See also by the same author *Industrialisation in the United Arab Emirates,* Aldershot, 1992, Ashgate Publishing.

34 The municipalities of Abu Dhabi and Al 'Ain , have responsibility for outlying towns, villages and desert areas, the latter covering the countryside around Al 'Ain as far as the southern border at Umm Zumūl, the former covering the rest of the emirate to beyond Jabal al Dhannah. Separate municipalities of Fujairah and Shārjah exist in Dibah, of 'Ajmān in Masfūṭ near Ḥattā, and of Shārjah in Khaur Fakkān and Kalba.

35 Much can be learnt about the finances of Abu Dhabi and the UAE in the 1970s from the account by John Butter, *Uncivil Servant,* Edinburgh, 1989, Pentland Press; see here pp. 131ff.

36 Abu Dhabi investors held a majority interest in the Bank of Credit and Commerce International; it was closed in July 1991. On 13 June 1994 eleven Pakistani former key employees and the bank's absent founder, Hassan Abedi, were sentenced by the Abu Dhabi Court of First Instance to a joint total of 61 years imprisonment and payment of US$9.13 billion.

37 See *Emirates News,* 8 January 1996.

38 The official estimate for 1970, when the federation of nine emirates was still being discussed, was 217,000 for the Trucial States; see above footnote 76 on p. 492. The figure of 2.5 million is given by Robert Edwards of Dryland Consultants, Dubai; see MEED, 1 April 1994.

39 See below p. 407f.

40 By the end of 1985 nearly 40,000 "peoples' houses" had been built; some 52,500 houses were built by nationals for their own use, 26,000 villas and 102,000 flats for rent; *Statistical Abstract,* 1991 pp. 200f.

41 The Abu Dhabi Housing Loans Authority was set up in 1990, and by 1993 had approved loans worth Dh. 380 million to 889 citizens in Abu Dhabi town and Al 'Ain , see *Emirates News,* 10 March 1993.

42 See above footnote 31.

43 These issues were dealt with comprehensively in a PhD thesis at Durham University by the late Ann Fyfe.

44 Translation of the main points of the memorandum in *Emirates News,* 22 March 1979.
45 See the cables sent by students of the University on 21 March to the President, or the account of a demonstration by women of Kalba and Fujairah. On 25 March the President called for an end to marches and demonstrations, see *Emirates News,* 22 to 26 March 1979.
46 For this text and the reply by the FNC to the Dubai statement, see *Emirates News,* 31 March 1979.
47 Shaikh Khālid bin Muḥammad of Shārjah was killed in January 1972 by the ex-Ruler Ṣaqr bin Sulṭān, deposed in 1965. He was replaced by Shaikh Sulṭān bin Muḥammad. In 1975 Shaikh Ḥamad bin Muḥammad succeeded his father as Ruler of Fujairah. In 1981 the Rulers of 'Ajmān and Umm al Qaiwain were succeeded by their sons, Shaikhs Ḥumaid bin Rāshid and Rāshid bin Aḥmad respectively.
48 The petrol stations in Dubai and the other emirates were still operated by foreign companies, charging market prices. Stations in Abu Dhabi were supplied from ADNOC. In January 1981 the subsidised Emirates General Petroleum Corporation began distribution in the northern emirates; see *Emirates News,* 4 January 1981.
49 It last met in June 1990; the speaker, Shaikh Sultan bin Surūr al Dhāhiri died in August 1990. The next meeting was in November 1994, the new Speaker being 'Abdullah Masūd.
50 The members are heads of the Abu Dhabi government departments; some are members of the ruling family. They hold weekly meetings under the chairmanship of the Crown Prince, Shaikh Khalīfah bin Zāyid.
51 See John E. Peterson, *The Arab Gulf States. Steps towards Political Participation,* New York, 1988, CSIS, p. 101.
52 The council's term expired in 1982; see *Khaleej Times, Special Report,* 14 September 1985. No new council has been appointed.
53 New names are in *Emirates News,* 9 May 1994.
54 See *Emirates News,* 12 May 1993.
55 See *Gulf News,* 20 March 1993.
56 Shaikh Rāshid's health began to fail in 1982; he remained Prime Minister, when a new cabinet was announced on 8 July 1983. Due to the absence of some key ministers its effectiveness was reduced. Shaikh Sultān bin Zāyid is Chairman of the Abu Dhabi Public Works Department, a member of the Consultative Council and is often entrusted by his father to head special committees and delegations.
57 See also above pp. 314–319, p. 368 and pp. 372–378.
58 The number of students of *shari'ah* and law fell from 543 in 1987/8 to 147 in 1991/2; see *Statistical Abstract,* 1992, p. 353. Some of the first national faculty members are specialised in constitutional law; such expertise is essential to revitalise the quest for a revised constitutional framework of the federation.

Bibliography

I UNPUBLISHED MATERIAL, GOVERNMENT PUBLICATIONS, ETC.

CURRENCY BOARD, see *Bulletin*.

DHAWĀHIR COLLECTION, correspondence containing some 200 letters of the *wāli* of Shaikh Zāyid bin Khalīfah, Aḥmad bin Hilāl al Dhāhiri, 1890 to 1910, now deposited in the Centre for Documentation and Research, Abu Dhabi.

COLES, ANNE and JACKSON, PETER, *A Windtower House in Dubai*, Art and Archaeology Research Papers, London, 1975.

GIBB, SIR ALEXANDER AND PARTNERS, see Government of Abu Dhabi.

GOVERNMENT OF ABU DHABI, DIRECTORATE-GENERAL OF PLANNING & CO-ORDINATION, *Statistical Abstract*, vol. I, July 1969.

GOVERNMENT OF ABU DHABI, DEPARTMENT OF INFORMATION & TOURISM, *Federation of Arab Emirates*. A Report, Abu Dhabi, 1970.

GOVERNMENT OF ABU DHABI, DEPARTMENT OF DEVELOPMENT & PUBLIC WORKS, *Water Resources Survey*, Interim Report by Sir A. Gibb & Partners, April, 1969.

GOVERNMENT OF ABU DHABI, DEPARTMENT OF DEVELOPMENT & PUBLIC WORKS, *Water Resources Survey*, Final Report by Sir A. Gibb & Partners, December 1970.

GOVERNMENT OF ABU DHABI, GENERAL SECRETARIAT OF THE COUNCIL OF MINISTERS (LATER THE EXECUTIVE COUNCIL), *Al Jarīdah al Rasm*īyah, (the Official Gazette), Abu Dhabi, 1972ff.

GOVERNMENT OF BOMBAY, *Selections from the Records of the Bombay Government, Historical and Other Information connected with the Province of Oman, Muskat, Bahrain and Other Places in the Persian Gulf*, New Series no. XXIV, compiled and edited by R. Hughes Thomas, Bombay, 1856.

GOVERNMENT OF QATAR, *Al Jarīdah al Rasmīyah*, (the Official Gazette), Doha, 1970.

GOVERNMENT OF QATAR, OFFICE OF THE ADVISER TO THE RULER, compiled, *Union of Arab Emirates. Resolutions, decisions, joint communiqués and documents, (a collection of material concerning the formation of the Union of Arab Emirates)*, (mimeograph), Doha, 1968–71.

GOVERNMENT OF THE UNITED ARAB EMIRATES, MINISTER OF STATE FOR CABINET AFFAIRS, *Al Jarīdah al Rasmīyah*, (the Official Gazette), Abu Dhabi, 1971ff.

GOVERNMENT OF THE UNITED ARAB EMIRATES, MINISTRY OF INFORMATION, *Archaeology in the United Arab Emirates*, Introduction by Serge Cleuziou, Director of the French Archaeological Mission in the UAE, 1979.

GOVERNMENT OF THE UNITED ARAB EMIRATES, MINISTRY OF PLANNING, CENTRAL STATISTICAL DEPARTMENT, *Annual Statistical Abstract*, Abu Dhabi, 1978.

GOVERNMENT OF THE UNITED KINGDOM OF GREAT BRITAIN AND NORTHERN IRELAND, *Arbitration Concerning Buraimi and the Common Frontier between Abu Dhabi and Sa'ūdi Arabia*, (quoted as *UK Memorial*, vol. I or II), 1955.

HALCROW, see —TRUCIAL STATES COUNCIL.

HYDROLOGICAL YEARBOOK, see TRUCIAL STATES COUNCIL.

INDIA OFFICE RECORDS (FOREIGN AND COMMONWEALTH OFFICE, LONDON), (IOR)*. The following files of the Political Residency in Bushire were used in quotations:**

		Corresponding to the old number
R/15/1/236	Arab States Monthly Summary 1929–31	R/15/1/14/49
R/15/1/239	Renewed quarrel between the Shaikh of Sharjah and the Headman of Khan, June 1920–Nov. 1922, (part of Miscellaneous Dec. 1904–Nov. 1922)	R/15/1/14/7
R/15/1/244	Correspondence regarding succession of Chief of Ras al Khaimah 1900–28	R/15/1/14/6
R/15/1/267	Ajman Affairs 1910–21	R/15/1/14/29
R/15/1/268	Ajman Affairs 1922–30	R/15/1/14/30
R/15/1/275	Fight between Shaikh of Ras al Khaimah and Shihuh tribe at the instigation of the Headman of Rams 1934–6	R/15/1/14/36
R/15/1/276	Deposition of the Shaikh of Sharjah 1924–32.	R/15/1/14/37
R/15/1/278	Punishment of the Shaikh of Fujairah 1925–34.	R/15/1/14/39

* Unpublished Crown copyright material in the IOR reproduced in this book appears by permission of the Controller of Her Majesty's Stationery Office.

** These files were copied before the new numbering system was introduced: Compared to the lists provided in the book by Penelope Tuson. *The Records of the British Residency*, some differences exist, where titles and dates were altered to correspond with the contents of the file.

R/15/1/287	Succession to the Shaikhdom of Kalba and Kalba Affairs 1937.	R/15/1/14/45
R/15/1/293	Headman of Hemriyah desires independence from Sharjah 1922–32.	R/15/1/14/47

The following files from Departmental Records were used in quotations:

L/P&S/12/3718	Pearling 1929–48	L/P&S/12/30/8
L/P&S/12/3731	Arab States News Summary 1931–3.	L/P&S/12/30/20
L/P&S/12/3762	Publicity in the Gulf 1932–47.	L/P&S/12/30/48
L/P&S/12/3766	Smuggling in the Gulf 1928–38.	L/P&S/12/30/50
L/P&S/12/3797	Trade of the Gulf 1930–48.	L/P&S/12/30/80
R/15/1/279	Attempted Murder of Residency Agent, Sharjah, II, 1926–9.	R/15/1/14/40
R/15/1/284	Correspondence regarding the Shaikh of Dibbah 1933–8.	R/15/1/8/1
R/15/1/285	Unrest at Dubai and Trucial Coast Policy 1934–6.	R/15/1/14/43

JACKSON, PETER see COLES, ANNE

KLEIN, HEDWIG, *Kapitel XXXIII der anonymen arabischen Chronik Kašf al-Ǧumma al-Ǧāmi' li-Ahbār al-Umma, betitelt Aḫbār ahl 'Oman min auwạl Islāmihim ilā' Ḫtilāf Kalimatihim (Geschichte der Leute von 'Omān von ihrer Annahme des Islam bis zu ihrem Dissensus) auf Grund der Berliner Handschrift unter Heranziehung verwandter Werke herausgegeben*, PhD thesis, Hamburg, 1938.

Newsletter of the Trucial States Council and *Round-up of News*, irregularly issued by the Development Office, Dubai.

Persian Gulf Gazette, (Bahrain), published by Her Majesty's Political Resident in the Persian Gulf by authority, (quarterly from October 1953, more frequently during 1969–71) with a varying number of supplements, London (HMSO).

Statutory Instruments, published in loose leaf form, London (HMSO).

Trucial States, publication of King's (Queen's) Regulations with reference to the Trucial States Orders in Council, (published in loose leaf form), London (HMSO).

TRUCIAL STATES COUNCIL, Analysis of Capital Expenditure by States, (1965–70), Appendix 'A' to *Newsletter of the Trucial States Council*, September/October 1970.

TRUCIAL STATES COUNCIL, Analysis of Recurrent and Minor Capital Expenditure (1965–70), Appendix 'C' to *Newsletter of the Trucial States Council*, September/October 1970.

TRUCIAL STATES COUNCIL, *First Population Census of the Trucial States*, March/April 1968 (mimeograph).

TRUCIAL STATES COUNCIL, *Hydrological Yearbook 1967/68*, by Sir William Halcrow and Partners, Dubai, 1969.

TRUCIAL STATES COUNCIL, *Report*, Dubai, 1969.

TRUCIAL STATES COUNCIL, *Report on the water resources of the Trucial States*, to the Trucial States Council by Sir William Halcrow & Partners, 3 vols., Dubai, 1967–9.

UNITED ARAB EMIRATES, MINISTRY OF INFORMATION, *Provisional Constitution of the United Arab Emirates*, Abu Dhabi, 1972.

II BOOKS

ABDULLAH, MUHAMMAD MORSY, *United Arab Emirates. A Modern History*, Croom Helm and Barnes & Noble, London & New York, 1978.

ABU 'ĀḎARA, SA'ĪD SALMĀN, *Al Ṣukūr* [Falcons], Jordan Press Foundation, Amman, 1977.

ADMIRALTY, THE, HYDROGRAPHIC OFFICE, *The Persian Gulf Pilot. Comprising the Persian Gulf, the Gulf of Omān and the Makran Coast*, 6th edn, HMSO, London, 1915.

AITCHISON, C.U., *A collection of Treaties, Engagements and Sanads relating to India and neighbouring countries*, compiled by C.U. Aitchison, vol. XI containing the Treaties etc. Relating to Aden and the South Western Coast of Arabia, the Arab Principalities in the Persian Gulf, Muscat (Oman), Baluchistan and the North West Frontier Province, Government of India, Manager of Publications, Delhi, 1933.

ALBAHARNA, HUSAIN M., *The Arabian Gulf States. Their Legal and Political Status and Their International Problems*, 2nd rev. edn, Librairie du Liban, Beirut 1975.

ALBUQUERQUE, ALFONSO DE, *The Commentaries of the Great Affonso Dalboquerque*, 4 vols, Hakluyt Society, London, 1875.

ANTHONY, JOHN DUKE, *Arab States of the Lower Gulf; People, Politics, Petroleum*, The Middle East Institute, Washington, 1975.

BADGER, G.P., ED. AND TRANSL., *History of the Imāms and Sayyids of 'Omān* by Salīl-Ibn-Razīk from AD 661–1856, Hakluyt Series xliv, London, 1871 [being a translation of a manuscript in the University Library of Cambridge, entitled *al Fatḥ al Mubīn fī Sīrat al Sādāh Āl Bū Sa'īdīn* by Ḥumaid bin Muḥammad bin Ruzaiq al Ibāḍi, completed in AH 1275/AD 1858].

BARWANI, M.A. and WHITE, A.W., *Common Sea Fishes of the Arabian Gulf and Gulf of Oman*, Trucial States Council, vol. I, Dubai, 1971.

BARWANI, M.A. and WHITE A.W., *A Survey of the United Arab Emirates Fisheries Resources 1969/71*, Dubai, 1972.

BIBBY, GEOFFREY, *Looking for Dilmun*, Collins, London, 1970.

BONNÉ, ALFRED, *State and Economics in the Middle East. A Society in*

Transition, 2nd rev. edn, Routledge and Kegan Paul, London, 1955, repr. in 1973 by Greenwood Press, Westport.

BROER, HANS-JOACHIM, *Wirtschaftliche Entwicklung in Kuwait. Ein Beispiel für die Rolle der Mentalität in einem Entwicklungsland*, PhD thesis, 1965 Köln (Wiso-Fak).

BURCKHARDT, J.L., *Notes on the Beduins and Wahābys, collected during his Travels in the East*, 2 vols, Henry Colburn & Richard Bentley, London, 1831, repr. by Johnson Reprint Co. in 1967.

CASKEL, WERNER, *Ĝamharat an-Nasab. Das genealogische Werk des Hišām ibn Muḥammad al-Kalbī*, 2 vols, Brill, Leiden, 1966.

COLE, D.P., *Nomads of the Nomads. The Al Murrah Beduin of the Empty Quarter*, AHM Publishing Corporation, Arlington, 1975.

DANVERS, FREDERICK CHARLES, *The Portuguese in India. Being a History of the Rise and Decline of their Empire*, 2 vols, Allen & Co., London, 1894, repr. in 1966 by Frank Cass.

DOSTAL, WALTER, *Die Beduinen in Südarabien. Eine ethnologische Studie zur Entwicklung der Kamelhirtenkultur in Arabien*, Verlag Ferdinand Bergner, Wien, 1967.

The Encyclopaedia of Islam. New Edition, edited by H.A.R. Gibb and others under the patronage of the International Union of Academies, Leiden and London, 1960ff (Brill & Luzac).

FAO TECHNICAL ADVISORY MISSION, *Agricultural Development in the United Arab Emirates. Report on present position, prospects and priorities*, FAO Near East Regional Office, Cairo, 1973.

FENELON, KEVIN G., *The United Arab Emirates, An Economic and Social Survey*, Longman, London, 1973.

FENELON, KEVIN G., *The Trucial States, A Brief Economic Survey*, 2nd rev. edn, Khayats, Beirut, 1969.

FISHER, W.B., *The Middle East. A Physical, Social and Regional Geography*, 2nd edn, Methuen, London, 1952.

GRIFFITHS, SIR PERCIVAL, *A History of the Inchcape Group*, Inchcape & Co., London, 1977.

HANDHAL, FĀLIḤ, *Mu'a jam al Alfādh al Āmīyah*, (Dictionary of the local dialect of the United Arab Emirates), UAE Ministry of Information & Culture, Abu Dhabi, no date (about 1979).

HARRISON, DAVID L., *The Mammals of Arabia*, 2 vols, Ernest Benn, London, 1968.

HAWLEY, DONALD, *The Trucial States*, Allen & Unwin, London, 1970.

HAWLEY, RUTH, *Omani Silver*, Longman, London, 1978.

HOPWOOD, DEREK, ED., *The Arabian Peninsula: Society and Politics*, Allen & Unwin, London, 1972.

IBN BATUTA, *Voyages d'Ibn Batoutah*, texte Arabe accompagné d'une traduction par Defrémery C., et Sanguinetti, B.R., 4 vols, Imprimerie Nationale, Paris, 1912.

IBN RUZAIQ, see BADGER, G.P.

KELLY, J.B., *Britain and the Persian Gulf 1795–1880*, Clarendon Press, London, 1968.

KELLY, J.B., *Eastern Arabian Frontiers*, Faber & Faber, London, 1964.

KHALIFAH, ALI MOHAMMED, *The United Arab Emirates: Unity in Fragmentation*, Croom Helm, London, 1979.

LANDEN, R.G., *Oman Since 1856: Disruptive Modernization in a Traditional Arab Society*, Princeton University, New Jersey, 1967.

LEWIS, BERNARD, *The Arabs in History*, 4th edn, Hutchinson, London, 1968.

LONGRIGG, S.H., *Oil in the Middle East, Its Discovery and Development*, 3rd edn, Oxford University Press, London, 1968.

LORIMER, J.C., *Gazetteer of the Persian Gulf, 'Omān and Central Arabia*, Volume I—Historical, Volume II—Geographical and Statistical, Superintendent Government Printing, Calcutta, 1908–15.

MANN, CLARENCE, *Abu Dhabi, Birth of an Oil Sheikhdom*, Khayats, Beirut, 1964.

The Middle East and North Africa, 1968–69, 15th edn, Europa Publications, London, 1968.

MILES, S.B., *The Countries and Tribes of the Persian Gulf*, 2nd edn, Frank Cass, London, 1966.

MOYSE-BARTLETT, H., *The Pirates of Trucial Oman*, Macdonald, London, 1966.

NIEUWENHUIJZE, C.A.O. VAN, *Sociology of the Middle East. A Stocktaking and Interpretation*, Brill, Leiden, 1971.

PHILBY, H.ST.J.B., *The Empty Quarter. Being a description of the Great South Desert of Arabia known as Rub' al Khali*, Constable, London, 1933.

PLASS, JENS B., *England zwischen Russland und Deutschland. Der Persische Golf in der britischen Vorkriegspolitik, 1899–1907 dargestellt nach englischem Archivmaterial*, Institut für Auswärtige Politik, Hamburg, 1966.

SAID ZAHLAN, ROSEMARIE, *Origins of the United Arab Emirates. A Political and Social History of the Trucial States*, Macmillan, London, 1978.

SERJEANT, R.B., *The Portuguese off the South Arabian Coast. Ḥaḍramī Chronicles*, Oxford University Press, Oxford, 1963, repr. Librairie du Liban, Beirut, 1974.

Shorter Encyclopaedia of Islam, edited by H.A.R. Gibb and J.H. Kramers, repr. Brill and Luzac, Leiden and London, 1961.

SWEET, LOUISE E., *Peoples and Cultures of the Middle East*, 2 vols, The Natural History Press, New York, 1970.

THESIGER, WILFRED, *Arabian Sands*, Longman, London, 1959.

THOMAS, BERTRAM S., *Alarms and Excursions in Arabia*, Allen & Unwin, London, 1931.

THOMAS, BERTRAM S., *Arabia Felix*, Jonathan Cape, London, 1932.

TOWNSEND, JOHN, *Oman. The Making of a Modern State*, Croom Helm, London, 1977.

TREVASKIS, KENNEDY, *Shades of Amber. A South Arabian Episode*, Hutchinson, London, 1968.

TUSON, PENELOPE, *The Records of the British Residency and Agencies in the Persian Gulf. IOR R/15*, HMSO, London, 1979.

VILLIER, A., *The Sons of Sindbad*, Scribner's Sons, New York, 1940.

WEHR, HANS, *A Dictionary of Modern Written Arabic*, ed. by J.M. Cowan, Harrassowitz, Wiesbaden, 1971.

WHITE, A.W., see BARWANI, M.A.

WILKINSON, J.C., *Water and Tribal Settlement in South-East Arabia. A Study of the Aflāj of Oman*, Clarendon Press, Oxford, 1977.

WILSON, ARNOLD T., *The Persian Gulf. An Historical Sketch from the earliest Times to the Beginning of the Twentieth Century*, 3rd repr., 1st edn, 1928, Allen & Unwin, London, 1959.

WILSON, HAROLD, *The Labour Government 1964–70. A Personal Record*, 2nd edn, Penguin, London, 1974.

ZAID BIN SULTAN AL NAHAYAN, *Falconry as a Sport. Our Arab Heritage* compiled by Yahya Badr, Abu Dhabi, 1976.

III ARTICLES

ANTHONY, JOHN DUKE, "The Union of Arab Amirates", in *Middle East Journal*, vol. 26, no. 3, 1972, pp. 271–87.

BECKETT, P., "Qanats round Kirman", in *Journal of the Royal Central Asian Society*, vol. 40, 1953, pp. 47–58.

BIRKS, J.S. and LETTS, S.E., "The 'Awāmr: Specialist Well- and Falaj-Diggers in Northern Interior Oman", in *Journal of Oman Studies*, vol. 2, 1976, pp. 93–100.

BIRKS, J.S. and LETTS, S.E., "Diqal and Muqạyda: Dying Oases in Arabia", in *Tijdschrift voor economische en sociale geografie*, 68, no. 3, 1977, pp. 145–51.

BRUNSCHVIG, R., "'Abd", in *The Encyclopaedia of Islam*, New Edition, vol. I, Leiden and London, 1960 Brill and Luzac, pp. 24–40.

CALVERLEY, EDWIN E., "The Fundamental Structure of Islam", in *Journal of the Royal Central Asian Society*, vol. 26, 1939, pp. 280–302.

COX, SIR PERCY, "Some Excursions in Oman", in *Geographical Journal*, vol. 66, 1925, pp. 193–227.

DOSTAL, WALTER, "The Shiḥūḥ of Northern Oman: A contribution to Cultural Ecology", in *Geographical Journal*, vol. 138, pt I, 1972, pp. 1–8.

DOWSON, V.H.W., "The Date and the Arab", in *Journal of the Royal Central Asian Society*, vol. 36, 1949, pp. 34–41.

DOWSON, V.H.W., "The Date Cultivation and Date Cultivators in Basrah", in *Journal of the Royal Central Asian Society*, vol. 26, 1939, pp. 247–60.

THE ENCYCLOPAEDIA OF ISLAM, EDITORS, "Ḥarim", in *The Encyclopaedia of*

Islam, New Edition, Brill and Luzac, Leiden and London 1971, p. 209.

FIEY, J.M., "Diocèses Syriens Orientaux du Golfe Persique", in *Mémorial Mgr Gabriel Khouri-Sarkis* (1898–1968), Louvain, Belgique, 1969, pp. 177–219.

FRIFELT, KARIN, "Archaeological investigations in the Oman peninsula. A preliminary report", in *KUML* (Årbog for Jysk Arkaeologisk Selskab), 1968, pp. 170–75.

HEARD-BEY, FRAUKE, "Development Anomalies in the Beduin Oases of Al-Liwa", in *Asian Affairs*, vol. 61, 1974, pp. 272–86.

HEARD-BEY, FRAUKE, "Katar", in *Handbuch der Dritten Welt*, Bd. 4, Hoffmann und Campe, Hamburg, 1978, pp. 329–35.

HEARD-BEY, FRAUKE, "Der Prozess der Staatswerdung in arabischen Ölexportländern. Politischer und gesellschaftlicher Wandel in Bahrain, Qatar, den Vereinigten Arabischen Emiraten und Oman", in *Vierteljahreshefte für Zeitgeschichte*, Heft 2, Jg. 23, 1975, pp. 155–209.

HUNTER, FRASER F., "Reminiscences of the Map of Arabia and the Persian Gulf", in *Geographical Journal*, vol. 54, 1919, pp. 355–63.

KINSMAN, DAVID J.J., and ROBERT K. PARK, "Studies in Recent Sedimentology and Early Diagenesis, Trucial Coast, Arabian Gulf", paper for *Second Regional Technical Symposium, Society of Petroleum Engineering of AIME*, Dhahran, 1968, (mimeograph) 12 pages.

LETTS, S.E., see BIRKS, J.S.

LONGRIGG, S.H., "The Liquid Gold of Arabia", in *Journal of the Royal Central Asian Society*, vol. 36, 1949, pp. 20–33.

MILES, S.B., "On the Route between Soḥar and el-Bereymi in ʿOmān, with a note of the Zaṭuṭ, or gipsies in Arabia", in *Journal of the Asiatic Society of Bengal*, vol. XLVI, 1877, pp. 41–61.

NOEL, E., "Qanats", in *Journal of the Royal Central Asian Society*, vol. 31, 1944, pp. 191–202.

PARK, ROBERT K., see KINSMAN, DAVID.

PERRY, J.R., "Mīr Muhannā and the Dutch: Patterns of Piracy in the Persian Gulf", in *Studia Iranica*, vol. 2, 1973, pp. 79–95.

ROSS, E.C., "Annals of ʿOman from early times to the year 1728 AD (being a translation of Kashf al Ghumma)", in *Journal of the Asiatic Society of Bengal*, vol. 43, Calcutta, 1874, pp. 111ff.

RUTTER, ELDON, "Slavery in Arabia", in *Journal of the Royal Central Asian Society*, vol. 20, 1933, pp. 315–32.

SAID, ROSEMARIE J., "The 1938 Reform Movement in Dubai", in *Al-Abhath, A Quarterly Journal for Arab Studies, Published by the American University of Beirut*, vol. 23, 1970, pp. 247–318.

SCHACHT, J., "Sharīʿa", in *Shorter Encyclopaedia of Islam*, 1961, pp. 524–33.

SCHACHT, J., "Zakāt", in *Shorter Encyclopaedia of Islam*, 1961, pp. 654–6.

STEPPAT, FITZ, "Bemerkungen zur Rechtsentwicklung in Abu Dhabi und den Vereinigten Arabischen Emiraten", in *Zeitschrift der Deutschen Morgenländischen Gesellschaft*, 1977, Supplement III, 1, pp. 617–24.

STIEFEL, MATTHIAS, "Der Nomadismus als sozioökonomisches und politisches Entwicklungsproblem, eine allgemeine Einführung", in *Seminar über das Nomadentum in Zentralasian Nov. 1975*, Schlussbericht, Nationale Schweizerische UNESCO-Kommission, Bern 1976, pp. 5–25.

STEVENS, J.H., "Changing Agricultural Practice in an Arabian Oasis. A case study of the Al ʿAin Oasis, Abu Dhabi", in *Geographical Journal*, vol. 136, pt 3, 1970, pp. 410–18.

THESIGER, WILFRED, "Desert Borderlands of Oman", in *Geographical Journal*, vol. 116, 1950, pp. 137–71.

THOMAS, BERTRAM, "Anthropological Observations in Southern Arabia", in *Journal of the Royal Anthropological Institute*, vol. 62, 1932, pp. 83–103.

THOMAS, BERTRAM, "A Camel Journey across the Rub ʿal-Khāli", in *Geographical Journal*, vol. 78, 1931, pp. 209–42.

THOMAS, BERTRAM, "The Musandam Peninsula and its people—the Shihuh", in *Journal of the Central Asian Society*, vol. XVI, 1929, pp. 71–86.

THOMAS, BERTRAM, "The Kumzari dialect of the Shihuh tribe, Arabia, and a vocabulary", in *Journal of the Royal Asiatic Society*, 1930, pp. 785–854.

THOMAS, BERTRAM, Review of H.J.B. Philby's book *The Empty Quarter*, in *Journal of the Royal Central Asian Society*, vol. 20, 1933, pp. 438–44.

THOMAS, BERTRAM, "Ūrbār—The Atlantis of the Sands of Rub ʿal Khali", in *Journal of the Royal Central Asian Society*, vol. 20, 1933, pp. 259–65.

WELLSTED, J.R., "Narrative of a Journey into the Interior of Omān in 1835", in *Journal of the Royal Geographical Society of London*, vol. 7, 1837, pp. 102–13.

WILKINSON, J.C., "Arab-Persian Land Relationships in Late Sasānid Oman", in *Proceedings of the 6th Seminar for Arabian Studies held at the Institute of Archaeology, London, in September 1972*, 1973, pp. 40–51.

WILKINSON, J.C., "Bayāsirah and Bayādir", in *Arabic Studies*, vol. 1, 1974, pp. 75–85.

WILKINSON, J.C., "The Origins of the Omani State", in *The Arabian Peninsula. Society and Politics*, edited by Derek Hopwood, Allen & Unwin, London, 1972, pp. 67–88.

WILSON, ARNOLD T., "Some Early Travellers in Persia and the Persian Gulf", in *Journal of the Central Asian Society*, vol. 12, 1925, pp. 68–82.

IV PERIODICALS

Abu Dhabi News, weekly, Abu Dhabi, (May 1970—mid-September 1975, then till December 1975 weekly as *UAE News*; from 1976 as the daily *Emirates News*).

Al-Anwār, Arabic daily, Beirut.

Arab Report and Record (ARR), fortnightly, London.

Beirūt, Arabic daily, Beirut.

Bulletin, United Arab Emirates Currency Board, two issues per year since 1974, Abu Dhabi.

Daily Star, English language daily, Beirut.

Daily Telegraph, daily, London.

Emirates News, English language daily, Abu Dhabi.

Financial Times, daily, London.

The Guardian, daily, London.

Hansard, Parliamentary Debates, House of Commons, London.

Al Jarīdah, Arabic daily, Beirut.

Kayhan International, English language daily, Tehran.

Keesing's Contemporary Archives, Weekly Diary of World Events, established in 1931, London, vol. X (1955–6), vol. XVI (1967–8).

KUML, Årbog for Jysk Arkaeologisk Selskab, annually, Aarhus.

Middle East Economic Digest (MEED), weekly, since 1957, London.

Middle East Economic Survey, (MEES), weekly, Beirut, later Cyprus.

Al Ra'y al 'Amm, Arabic daily, Kuwait.

Reuters, Daily News Bulletin (received from Reuter service, London), 1970ff, Sharjah.

The Times, daily, London.

V SOME FURTHER READING

ABDULLAH, MUHAMMAD MORSY, "Changes in the Economy and Political Attitudes, and the Development of Culture on the Coast of Oman between 1900 and 1940" in *Arabian Studies*, vol. 2, 1975, pp. 167–78.

ABIR, MORDECHAI, *Oil, Power and Politics. Conflict in Arabia, the Red Sea and the Gulf*, Frank Cass, London, 1974.

ABU HAKIMA, AHMAD MUSTAFA, *History of Eastern Arabia 1750–1800: The Rise and Development of Bahrain and Kuwait*, Khayats, Beirut, 1965.

AMIN, ABDUL AMIR, *British Interests in the Persian Gulf*, Brill, Leiden, 1967.

Area Handbook for the Peripheral States of the Arabian Peninsula, prepared for the American University by Stanford Research Institute, US Government Printing Office, Washington, D.C., 1971.

BELGRAVE, SIR CHARLES, *Personal Column*, Librairie du Liban, Beirut 1972, repr.

BELGRAVE, SIR CHARLES, *The Pirate Coast*, Librairie du Liban, Beirut, 1960.

BERREBY, J.J., *Le Golfe Persique, Mer de Légende. Réservoir de Pétrole*, Payot, Paris, 1959.

BIRKS, J.S., "Development or Decline of Pastoralists. The Banī Qitab of the Sultanate of Oman", in *Arabian Studies* IV, 1977, pp. 7–19.

BOUSTEAD, HUGH, "Abu Dhabi, 1761–1963" in *Journal of the Royal Central Asian Society*, vol. 50, 1963, pp. 273–77.

BOUSTEAD, SIR HUGH, *The Wind of Morning. The Autobiography of Hugh Boustead*, Chatto & Windus, London, 1971.

BULLARD, SIR READER, *Britain and the Middle East. From earliest times to 1963*, 3rd edn, Hutchinson, London, 1964.

BURRELL, R.M., *The Persian Gulf*, (The Washington Papers, vol. I), Beverly Hills, Sage Publications, London, 1972.

BUSH, BRINTON COOPER, *Britain and the Persian Gulf, 1894–1914*, University of California Press, Berkeley and Los Angeles, 1967.

CHISHOLM, ARCHIBALD H.T., *The First Kuwait Oil Concession. A Record of the Negotiations, 1911–1934*, Frank Cass, London, 1975.

CORDES, RAINER and FRED SCHOLZ, *Beduins, Wealth and Change. A Study of Rural Development in the United Arab Emirates and the Sultanate of Oman*, The United Nations University, 1980.

CORNELIUS, P.F.S. AND OTHERS, "The Musandam Expedition 1971–72. Scientific Results", in *Geographical Journal*, vol. 139, 1973, pp. 400–421.

DICKSON, H.R.P., *The Arab of the Desert. A Glimpse into Bedawin Life in Kuwait and Sau'di Arabia*, Allen & Unwin, London, 1949.

DICKSON, H.R.P., *Kuwait and Her Neighbours*, Allen & Unwin, London, 1956.

DUBUISSON, PATRICIA, "Qāsimi Piracy and the General Treaty of Peace (1820)", in *Arabian Studies*, vol. 4, 1978, pp. 47–57.

FRIFELT, KARIN, "Jamdat Nasr graves in the Oman", in *KUML*, 1970, pp. 355–83.

GRAHAM, HELGA, *Arabian Time Machine. Self-Portrait of an Oil State*, Heinemann, London, 1978.

HAY, SIR RUPERT, "The Impact of the Oil Industry on the Persian Gulf Shaykhdoms", in *Middle East Journal*, vol. 9, 1955, pp. 361–72.

HAY, SIR RUPERT, "The Persian Gulf States and their Boundary Problems", in *Geographical Journal*, vol. 120, 1954, pp. 433–45.

HEARD-BEY, FRAUKE, "The Gulf States and Oman in Transition", in *Asian Affairs, Journal of the Royal Central Asian Society*, vol. 59, 1972, pp. 14–22.

HEARD-BEY, FRAUKE, "Social Changes in the Gulf States and Oman", in *Asian Affairs, Journal of the Royal Central Asian Society*, vol. 59, 1972, pp. 309–16.

HEARD-BEY, FRAUKE, "The Oil Industry in Abu Dhabi. A changing Role", in *Orient*, Jg, 17, March 1976, pp. 108–40.

HEUDE, W., *A Voyage up the Persian Gulf and a journey overland from India to England in 1817*, Longman, Hurst etc., London, 1819, repr. in 1970 by Gregg International.

JANZEN, JÖRG AND FRED SCHOLZ, "Die Weihrauchwirtschaft Dhofars (Sultanat Oman). Eine wirtschaftsgeographische Studie zur Frage nach der Bedeutung einfacher Wirtschaftsressourcen in einem erdölreichen Entwicklungsland", in *Innsbrucker Geographische Studien*, Bd, 5, no date, pp. 501–41.

JOHNSTONE, T.M., *Eastern Arabian Dialect Studies*, (London Oriental Series, vol. 17), Oxford University Press, London, 1967.

KAY, SHIRLEY, *The Bedouin*, Crane, Russak & Co., New York etc., 1978.

KELLY, J.B., *Arabia, the Gulf and the West. A critical view of the Arabs and their oil policy*, Weidenfeld & Nicolson, London, 1980.

KELLY, J.B., "The Buraimi Oasis Dispute", in *Journal of the British Institute of International Affairs*, vol. 32, 1956, pp. 318–26.

KELLY, J.B., "The Legal and Historical Basis of the British Position in the Persian Gulf", in *Middle Eastern Affairs*, 1958, pp. 119–40.

KELLY, J.B., "The Persian Claim to Bahrain", in *Journal of the British Institute of International Affairs*, vol. 33, 1957, pp. 51–70.

KHADDOURI, MAJID, "Iran's Claim to the Sovereignty of Bahrain", in *American Journal of International Law*, vol. 45, 1951, pp. 631–47.

KOSZINOWSKI, THOMAS, "Der Konflikt um Dhufar und die Aussichten auf seine Beilegung", in *Orient*, Heft 2, 1976, pp. 66–87.

KUMAR, RAVINDER, *India and the Persian Gulf Region 1858–1907. A Study in British Imperial Policy*, Asia Publishing House, Bombay, 1965.

LIEBESNY, HERBERT J., "Administration and Legal Development in Arabia. The Persian Gulf Principalities", in *Middle East Journal*, vol. 10 1956, pp. 33–42.

LIBESNY, HERBERT J., "British Jurisdiction in the States of the Persian Gulf", in *Middle East Journal*, vol. 3, 1949, pp. 330–2.

LIEBESNY, HERBERT J., "International Relations of Arabia", in *Middle East Journal*, vol. 1, 1947, pp. 148–68.

LIENHARDT, PETER, "The Authority of Shaykhs in the Gulf: an Essay in nineteenth-century history", in *Arabian Studies*, vol. 2, 1975, pp. 61–75.

LONG, DAVID E., *The Persian Gulf. An Introduction to Its Peoples, Politics and Economics*, revised edition, Westview Press, Boulder, Colorado, 1978.

MALLAKH, RAGAEI EL, "The Challenge of Affluence: Abu Dhabi", in *Middle East Journal*, vol. 24, 1970, pp. 135–46.

MARLOWE, JOHN, *The Persian Gulf in the Twentieth Century*, The Cresset Press, London, 1962.

MELAMID, ALEXANDER, "Oil and Evolution of Boundaries in Eastern Arabia", in *Geographical Review*, vol. 44, 1954, pp. 295–6.

MELAMID, ALEXANDER, "Political Geography of Trucial ʿOman and Qatar", in *Geographical Journal*, vol. 43, 1953, pp. 194–206.

MONROE, ELIZABETH, *The Changing Balance of Power in the Persian Gulf*, The Report of an International Seminar at the Centre for Mediterranean Studies, Rome, 26 June to 1 July 1972, American Universities Field Staff, New York, 1972.

MUGHISUDDIN, MOHAMMED, ED., *Conflict and Cooperation in the Persian Gulf*, Praeger, New York & London, 1977.

NIEBUHR, M. (CARSTEN), *Travels through Arabia and other Countries in the*

East, translated into English by Robert Heron, 2 vols, R. Morison, Edinburgh, 1972, reprinted by Librairie du Liban, Beirut.

OPPENHEIM, MAX FREIHERR VON, *Vom Mittelmeer zum Persischen Golf durch den Ḥaurān, die Syrische Wüste und Mesopotamien*, 2 vols, Dietrich Reimer, Berlin, 1899–1900.

AL-OTAIBA, MANA SAEED, *Petroleum and the Economy of the United Arab Emirates*, Croom Helm, London, 1977.

QUBAIN, FAHIM I., "Social Classes and Tensions in Bahrain", in *Middle East Journal*, vol. 9, 1955, pp. 269–80.

RUMAIHI, M.G., *Bahrain. Social and political change since the First World War*, Centre for Middle Eastern and Islamic Studies of the University of Durham, no. 5, Bowker, London and New York, 1976.

SADIK, MUHAMMAD T and WILLIAM P. SNAVELEY, *Bahrain, Qatar and the United Arab Emirates. Colonial Past, Present Problems and Future Prospects*, D.C. Heath & Co., Lexington, Mass., 1972.

SCHOLZ, FRED, "Die beduinischen Stämme im östlichen Inner-Oman und ihr Regional-Mobilitäts-Verhalten", in *Sociologus*, vol. 27, Heft 2, pp. 97–133.

SCHOLZ, FRED. "Entwicklungstendenzen im Beduinentum der kleinen Staaten am Persisch/Arabischen Golf—Oman als Beispiel", in *Mitteilungen der Österreichischen Geographischen Gesellschaft*, Bd. 118, I, 1976, pp. 70–108.

SCHOLZ, FRED, see also CORDES, RAINER.

SCHWARZ, P., "Hurmuz", in *Mitteilugen der Deutschen Morgenländischen Gesellschaft*, 1914, pp. 531–43.

SCHWEIZER, GÜNTHER, *Bandar ʿAbbas und Hormoz. Schicksal und Zukunft einer iranischen Hafenstadt am Persischen Golf.*, Beihefte zum Tübinger Atlas des Vorderen Orients, Ludwig Reichert Verlag, Wiesbaden 1972.

SERJEANT, R.B., "Historical Sketch of the Gulf in the Islamic Era from the Seventh to the Eighteenth Century, AD", in *Qatar Archaeological Report. Excavations 1973*, ed. by Beatrice de Cardi, published in 1978 for the Qatar National Museum by Oxford University Press.

SHEPHERD, ANTHONY, *Arabian Adventure*, Collins, London, 1961.

SOFFAN, LINDA USRA, *The Women of the United Arab Emirates*, Croom Helm and Barnes and Noble Books, London and New York, 1980.

STANTON-HOPE, W.E., *Arabian Adventurer. The Story of Haji Williamson*, Robert Hale, London, 1951.

STEVENS, J.H., "Man and Environment in Eastern Saudi Arabia", in *Arabian Studies*, vol. I, 1974, pp. 135–45.

STEVENS, J.H., "Some Effects of Irrigated Agriculture on Soil Characteristics in Ras al-Khaimah, Union of Arab Emirates", in *Arabian Studies*, vol. 2, 1975, pp. 148–66.

THESIGER, WILFRED, "Across the Empty Quarter", in *Geographical Journal*, vol. III, 1948, pp. 1–21.

THESIGER, WILFRED, "A Further Journey Across the Empty Quarter", in *Geographical Journal*, vol. 13, 1949, pp. 21–46.

THESIGER, WILFRED, "A New Journey in Southern Arabia", in *Geographical Journal*, vol. 108, 1946, pp. 130–45.

THOMAS, BERTRAM S., "Among some unknown tribes of South Arabia", in *Journal of the Royal Anthropological Institute*, vol. 59, 1929, pp. 97–111.

TOMKINSON, MICHAEL, *The United Arab Emirates. An Insight and a Guide*, Michael Tomkinson Publ., London, 1975.

VIDAL, F.S., "Date Culture in the Oasis of Al-Hasa", in *Middle East Journal*, vol. 8, 1954, pp. 417–28.

WELLSTED, J.R., *Travels to the City of the Caliphs along the shores of the Persian Gulf and the Mediterranean, including a voyage to the Coast of Arabia and a tour on the Island of Socotra*, 2 vols, Henry Colburn, London, 1840, reprinted by Gregg International in 1968.

WHITEHOUSE, D., "Sirāf: a medieval port on the Persian Gulf", in *World Archaeology*, vol. 2, no. 2, 1970, pp. 141–58.

WILKINSON, J.C., "A Sketch of the Historical Geography of the Trucial Oman down to the Beginning of the Sixteenth Century", in *Geographical Journal*, vol. 130, 1964, pp. 337–49.

WILLIAMSON, ANDREW, "Hormuz and the Trade of the Gulf in the 14th and 15th centuries AD", in *Proceedings of the Sixth Seminar for Arabian Studies held at the Institute of Archaeology, London, Sept. 1972*, 1973, pp. 52ff.

WILSON, D., "Memorandum respecting the pearl fisheries in the Persian Gulf", in *Journal of the Royal Geographical Society of London*, vol. 3, 1833, pp. 283–6.

ZWEMER, S.M., "Three Journeys in Northern Oman", in *Geographical Journal*, vol. 19, 1902, pp. 54–64.

VI SELECTED READING OF PUBLICATIONS SINCE 1982

Algosaibi, Ghazi A. *The Gulf Crisis. An Attempt to Understand*, Kegan Paul, London & New York 1993.

al-Alkim, Hassan Hamdan, *The Foreign Policy of the United Arab Emirates*, Saqi Books, London, 1989.

Ballantyne, W.M., *Commercial Law in the Arab Middle East: The Gulf States*. Lloyd's of London Press, London & New York, 1986.

Butter, John, *Uncivil Servant*, Pentland Press, Edinburgh, 1989.

Codrai, Ronald, *An Arabian Album. A collection of Mid-Twentieth Century Photographs*, Motivate Publishing, Dubai, 1992/93 (in three books entitled *Dubai*; *Abu Dhabi* and *Travels Through the Shaikhdoms*.)

Dyck, Gertrude, *The Oasis. Al Ain Memoirs of 'Doctora Latifa'*, Motivate Publishing, Dubai, 1995.

Frifelt, Karen, *The Island of Umm An-Nar*, 2 vols., Vol. 1: Third Millenium

Graves, Vol. 2: Third Millenium Settlement, Aarhus University Press, Aarhus, 1991/95.

Ghanem, Shihab M., *Industrialization in the United Arab Emirates.* Avebury, Aldershot & Brookfield USA, 1992.

Gabriel, Erhard F., ed. *The Dubai Handbook,* Institute for Applied Economic Geography, Ahrensburg, 1987.

Heard-Bey, Frauke, *Die arabischen Golfstaaten im Zeichen der islamischen Revolution. Innen-, aussen- und sicherheitspolitische Zusammenarbeit im Golf-Rat,* (Arbeitspapiere zur Internationalen Politik 25) Europa Verlag, Bonn 1983.

Henderson, Edward, *This Strange Eventful History. Memoirs of Earlier Days in the UAE and Oman,* Quartet Books, London & New York, 1988.

Kanafani, Aida S., *Aesthetics and Ritual in the United Arab Emirates. The Anthropology of Food and Personal Adornment among Arabian Women.* American University, Beirut, 1983.

Peterson, J.E. *The Arab Gulf States. Steps towards Political Participation* (Washington Papers 131), Praeger, New York etc., 1988.

Al-Qasimi, Sultan Muhammad, *The Myth of Arab Piracy in the Gulf,* Croom Helm, London, 1986.

Rumaihi, Muhammad, *Beyond Oil, Unity and Development in the Gulf,* Saqi Books, London, 1986.

Rush, A. de L., *Ruling Families of Arabia; United Arab Emirates,* 2 vols., Archive Editions, London, 1991 and other titles of this on-going series of selected archival material.

Slot, B.J., *The Arabs of the Gulf 1602–1784,* Leidschendam, 1993.

Taryam, A.O., *The Establishment of the United Arab Emirates 1950–85,* Croom Helm, London & New York, 1987.

United Arab Emirates, *Central Bank Bulletin,* (6-monthly since 1980).

Wilkinson, John C., *The Imamate tradition of Oman,* Cambridge University Press, Cambridge, London, etc., 1987.

Wilkinson, John C., *Arabia's Frontiers. The Story of Britain's Boundary Drawing in the Desert,* J. B. Tauris, London & New York, 1991.

Zimmermann, Wolfgang, *Tradition und Integration mobiler Lebensformgruppen. Eine empirische Studie über Beduinen und Fischer in Musandam.* PhD Dissertation, Göttingen, 1981.

Appendix
Distribution of Bani Yās subtribes
(see Map No. 4b)

Subsections of the Bani Yās were predominant in:

Abu Dhabi Town and in some cases also in Baṭīn
Āl Bū Amīn (L)
Āl Bū Falāh (L) (M) including Āl Nahyān)
Āl Bū Falāsah (M)
Āl Bū Ḥamīr (L)
Āl Bū Mahair (L) (M)
Āl Mishāghīn (M)
Daḥailāt (L)
Ḥalālmah (L)
Hawāmil (L) (M)
Khamārah (L)
Maḥāribah (M)
Mazārī' (L) (M)
Qubaisāt (L) (M)
Qumzān (L) (M)
Rumaithāt (L) (M) also on the coast and inshore islands
Rawāshid (M)
Sūdān (L) (M)
Thamairāt (L)

Līwā
Āl Bū Falāḥ (L) (M)
Āl Bū Ḥamīr (L) and elsewhere in Dhafrah
Āl Falāḥ (L)
Āl Sulṭān (L)
Bani Shikir (L)
Hawāmil (L) (M)
Maḥāribah (M)
Marar (sometimes Āl Murur) (L) (M)
Mazārī' (L) (M)
Qanaiṣāt (L)
Qaṣal (L)
Qubaisāt (L) (M) and western coast of Dhafrah and at times at Khaur al 'Udaid

Dalmā and/or other Abu Dhabi islands
Āl Bū Falāsah (M)
Qubaisāt (L) (M)
Rawāshid (M)
Rumaithāt (M)
Sūdān (M)

Al Ain area
Āl Bū Falaḥ (L) (M)
Āl Bū Mahair (M)
Āl Mishāghīn (M) and in Khatam
Hawāmil (M)
Marar (M) (L)
Nuwāṣir (M)
Qumzān (M)
Rawāshid (M)
Sabā'is (Jubais) (M)
Sūdān (M)

Dubai
Āl Bū Falāsah (L) (M)
Āl Bū Mahair (L) (M)
Marar (M) (L)
Mazārī' (M)
Qumzān (M)
Sabā'is (L) (M)
Sūdān (L) (M)

Elsewhere
Āl Bū Falāsah in Bahrain, Qatar, Tārūt island (L) (M)
Āl Bū Mahair in Ra's al Khaimah, Shārjah, Khān, 'Ajmān (L) (M)
Marar in Shārjah (M) (L)
Qubaisāt in Wakrah in Qatar (L)
Sūdān in Shārjah (L) (M), 'Ajmān (L) (M), Ra's al Khaimah (M), Umm al Qaiwain (M)
Abū Mūsa (L) (M), Qatar (L) (M), Sirri Island (L) (M) and Bahrain (L) (M)

(L) at the time of the compilation of Lorimer
(M) at the time of the compilation of the U.K. Memorial

Glossary

Note. Where a word appears frequently only a few examples have been entered.

'abā'ah (pl. *'abā'āt* also *abāyah*): cloak 145, 195, 233
'abrah (pl. *'abrāt*): type of boat 247, 248–9
adab (pl. *ādāb*): good manners 156
aflāj see falaj
ahl al kitāb: belonging to "the book" (i.e. Jews and Christians) 128
'ā'ilah (pl. *'ā'ilāt*): family 151–2
'ālim (pl. *'ulamā'*): scholar 131, 275
'āmil (pl. *'āmilāt*); mode of operating a pearling boat 208, 445n
amīr (pl. *umarā'*): representative 103, 110–12, 124, 131, 206 *and passim*
'āmlah: type of boat 173
'aqāl (pl. *'uqul*): headrope 140
'arīf (pl. *'urafā'*): falaj warden 121, 124–5, 179–80, 483n
'arīsh or *'arīshah*: house built of palm fronds 466n
'askar (pl. *'asākir*): guard 102, 104, 118
aṣl (pl. *uṣūl*): root, origin, descent 224
'azīmah: type of duty (tax) 115

baghlah: type of boat 85, 183, 191
baluch: immigrants from the Persian coast 225, 226
baqarah: type of boat 184
barasti: house built of palm fronds 137, 248, 405
barr: open country 196
batīl: type of boat 184
bāṭin: undisclosed wealth 161
baṭn: interior 457n
bayāsirah (singl. *baisar* or *baisari*): agricultural labourers 224, 464n
bīdār (or: *baidār*) (pl. *bayādīr*): gardener 224, 226
bin (correct: *ibn*) (pl. *abnā'*): son of *passim*
bint (correct: *ibnah*) (pl. *banāt*): daughter of *passim*
bint 'amm: paternal cousin 79, 145
bisht: cloak 233
bulaidah: small settlement 436n
būm: type of boat 254
burqa': face mask 145, 150, 235

chandel (Indian origin): a type of wood 246, 455n
chau (pl. *achwah*): a measure of Indian origin 189

dallal: trader in pearls 188–9
damāni: type of gazelle 454n
dār: tribal grazing area 23, 42, 56 *and passim*
darwīsh: religious man 139
dawlah al imārāt al 'arabīyah al muttaḥidah (pronounced: dawlat al . . .): United Arab Emirates 372
dhabb: type of lizard 170
dhabi: type of gazelle 171, 454n
dhow: type of boat (the word is probably of Indian origin and is hardly ever used by Arabs) 254
diyyīn: pearling basket 185
dūri: camel guard (in Līwā) 124

falaj (pl. *aflāj*): underground water channel 13–14, 177–80, 449n, 455–6n; control of 224; dues collected for (*naub*) 116, 117; introduction of mechanical pumps 226
farīḍah: money allowance 50
faṭām: noseplug for divers 185
fidāwi (pl. *fidāwīyah* or *fidā'īyah*): guard 118, 124, 304
fiqh (*al fiqh*): Islamic jurisprudence 158, 160
firmān (or *farmān*): decree 280

gargūr (dialect) *see qarqūr*: type of fishtrap
ghāf (singl. *ghāfah*): type of tree 196
ghaiṣ (pl. *ghāṣah*): diver 184
ghauṣ al bārid: cold diving season 185
ghauṣ al kabīr: main diving season 185, 199
ghayl: type of water channel 179, *see also falaj*
ghazū: raid 229–30, 287
ghutrah: headcloth 140

ḥadrīyah al ḏail: a measure in the pearling trade 457n
ḥajj: pilgrimage 141–3
ḥākim (pl. *ḥukkām*): wise man, ruler 158, 257
hammām: bath house 121, 223
ḥārah: hamlet 436n
ḥarām (pl. *ḥurum*): forbidden 450n
ḥarīm (pl. *ḥurum*): women's quarters 143–5, 405, 418; word derivation 450n
ḥāris (pl. *ḥaras*): guard 124
harm: type of desert vegetation 167
ḥāṣilah: type of tax 115
ḥaṭab ghāf: wood of a tree 196
ḥaṭab samar: wood of a tree 196
hawlāni: camel saddle 195
ḥubāra: bustard (lat. *otididae*) 171
ḥukum: rule 83
ḥukūmah: government 100, 124
ḥurmah (pl. *ḥuram*): woman 146, 155, 449n
ḥuwaif: type of tree 196

idfārah: method of fishing 175
ikhluwi: mode of operating a pearling boat 208
imām: title 137–8, 156
iskār: method of fishing 175
al ittiḥād al imārāt al 'arabīyah: Union of Arab Emirates 372
al ittiḥād al yumhūrīyāt al 'arabīyah: Union of Arab Republics (formed by Egypt, Libya, Syria in 1971) 497n

jalibūt or *jālbūt*: type of boat (Persian origin) 254
jinn: demon 139–40
jirāb: a measure 95, 116–17, 204, 430n
al jumhūrīyah al 'arabīyah al muttaḥidah: United Arab Republic 497n
jumruk: customs post 249
junīyah: type of duty 115
juwāri: type of crop 180

kandūrah (pl. *kandurāt*): dress 419, 458n
khaimah (pl. *khiyām*): tent (also type of house) 192, 466n
khānjīyah (of Persian origin): type of tax 445n
khanjar (pl. *khanājir*): dagger 194
khuṭbah: address in the mosque 138
kīs: a measure 191
kuttāb: Koran – school 156, 201, 452n

lungi (Anglo-Indian word used for *wizār*): type of garment 458n

mabā'iyah: type of tax 444n
maḏhab (pl. *maḏāhib*): school of law in Islam 132–3
madrasah (pl. *madāris*): school 156, 452n
majhūlah (pl. *majhūlāt*): type of pearl 189
majlis: meeting and meeting place 122, 139, 141, 143–4, 155, 405, 413, 416, 450n
makhīḍ: a milk product 170
mākhir: pole used for fishing 175
man: a measure of weight 459n
marbūb: method of operating a pearling boat 208
māshā: type of tax 179–80
maskar (pl. *masākir*): type of fishing net 175
maulid: celebration of the birthday of the Prophet Muhammad 140
mawāli: dependent 224

muʾaḏḏīn: person who calls to prayer 137
mufliqah: knife used to open oysters 185
mujannah: part of the pearling season 185
mullah (correct: *mullā*): religious official 133
muqaddām: tribal leader 78
muṣaif: summer dwelling 78, 436n
musaqqam (pl. *musaqqamīn*): financier in pearling industry 209–11
muṭārzi (pl. *muṭārzīyah*): attendant, guard, bodyguard 85, 120
muṭawwaʿ: wise and religious man 122, 123, 132, 138, 146, 161, 262, 446n, 449n; as doctor 266; as judge 46; on pearling boats 184; Persian Arabs as 201; and schools 155–6
muzakki: tax collector 111, 124

nāʾib: representative, caretaker 112, 124
naub: tax 113, 114, 117
naub al naṣārā: type of tax 445n
nisab: a measure 116, 117
nūkhaḏā (pl. *nawākhiḏah*): captain (Persian origin) 184–5, 188, 203, 208–11, 217, 236; share of catch 198

qāḍi (pl. *quḍāh*): 122–3, 132, 155–60, 161; and law 157–8; nature of disputes settled 217–18, (marriage and divorce) 248; origin and places of training 201; appointments (from 1911) 452–53n; and schools 155–6
qalṭah: diver-hauler pair 114, 115
qanāt (pl. *qanawāt*): watercourse 21
qarqūr: fish trap 175
qiblah: central niche in the mosque 137, 449n
quffāl: part of the pearling season

rabābah: a string instrument 236, 450n
raḍaf: type of pearling tax 445n
rāʾib: a milk product 170
rajul (pl. *rijāl*): man 155
raʾs: head, headland 457n
rīm: type of gazelle 454n
riyāl al sūr: type of tax 445n

sabkhah: salt/mud flat 12, 129, 247, 260, 424n
saib (pl. *siyūb*): diver 113, 115, 184, 198
ṣalāt: prayer 138, 155
sālifah al ghauṣ (pronounced: *sālifat al ghauṣ*): diving court 86, 111, 158, 209, 210, 217, 251
sāliyah: method of fishing 175
salūqi: breed of hunting dog 171
sanbūk: type of boat 85, 88, 184, 456n
ṣaqr (pl. *ṣuqūr*) (lat. *Falco cherrug*): falcon, hawk 171
sarūj: kind of building material 246
shafiyah: type of tax 120
shāhīn (lat. *Falco peregrinus*): peregrine falcon 171
shailah: lady's garment (veil) 138, 145
shamāl: north (and local word for north wind) 431n
sharīʿah: Islamic law 122, 135, 156–60, 318
shāshah: type of boat 173, 176, 193
shūʿai: type of boat 184
shūfah: type of tax 50, 113–14
sufrah: type of headgarment 140
sunnah: sayings of the Prophet Muḥammad 157, 452n
sūq (pl. *aswāq*): market 85, 106, 118, 125, 244 *and passim*
ṣūrah: part of the Koran

taḥwīl: seasonal move 78
tājir (pl. *tujjār*): merchant 188–90, 209
tamīmah: paramount shaikh 39, 40, 51, 52, 163, 274 *and passim*
tamr: dates (esp. processed) 234
ṭarāz: type of tax 113, 114, 120
ṭawwāsh (pl. *ṭawāwīsh*): trader in pearls 188–90, 207
tūmān: a measure 115

ʿūd: incense 193
ʿulamāʾ (singl. *ʿālim*): wise men, well versed in religious matters 131, 275
ʿurafāʾ see *ʿarīf*
ʿurf: customary or tribal law 125, 157, 158

waʿal (lat. *hemitragus yayakari*): mountain goat 172
wādi: valley 16, 179, 328, 330 *and*

passim
wāli: governor 81–100, 124 *and passim*
waqf (pl. *auqāf*): endowment 136, 137, 156
wasm: brand mark (on animals) 166
wazīr (pl. *wuzarā'*): minister 84
wilāyah: governorate 437n
wizār: a garment 458n

yal: method of fishing 175

zakāh: alms-tax 117–18, 127, 130, 161, 442n, 445n, 447n
zarūqah: type of boat 184

Index of Tribal Names

Page numbers in bold refer to maps. *00* indicates the end paper.

Index

Page numbers in bold refer to maps.

Index

Index

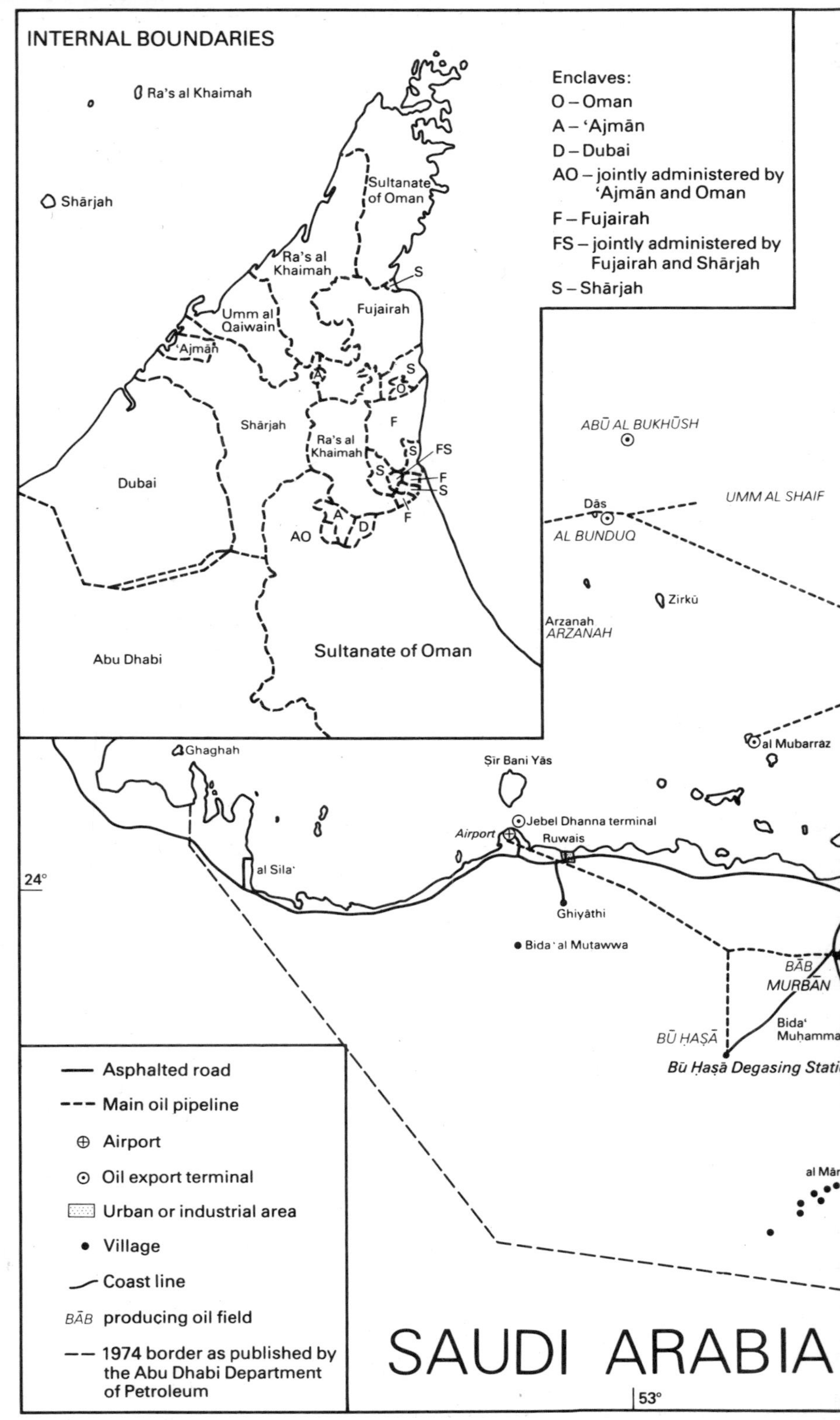
INTERNAL BOUNDARIES
Ra's al Khaimah
Shārjah
Sultanate of Oman
Ra's al Khaimah
Umm al Qaiwain
'Ajmān
Fujairah
S
A
O
F
Shārjah
Ra's al Khaimah
FS
Dubai
AO
D
Abu Dhabi
Sultanate of Oman
Enclaves:
O – Oman
A – 'Ajmān
D – Dubai
AO – jointly administered by 'Ajmān and Oman
F – Fujairah
FS – jointly administered by Fujairah and Shārjah
S – Shārjah
ABŪ AL BUKHŪSH
Dās
UMM AL SHAIF
AL BUNDUQ
Zirkū
Arzanah
ARZANAH
Ghaghah
Ṣīr Bani Yās
al Mubarraz
Jebel Dhanna terminal
Airport
Ruwais
al Sila'
24°
Ghiyāthi
Bida' al Mutawwa
BĀB
MURBĀN
Bida' Muḥammad
BŪ ḤAṢĀ
Bū Ḥaṣā Degasing Station
al Māriy
Asphalted road
Main oil pipeline
Airport
Oil export terminal
Urban or industrial area
Village
Coast line
BĀB producing oil field
1974 border as published by the Abu Dhabi Department of Petroleum
SAUDI ARABIA
53°